Law and Economics
Volume I

The International Library of Essays in Law and Legal Theory
Series Editor: Tom D. Campbell

Schools

Natural Law, Vols I & II *John Finnis*
Justice *Thomas Morawetz*
Law and Economics, Vols I & II *Jules Coleman and Jeffrey Lange*
Critical Legal Studies *James Boyle*
Marxian Legal Theory *Csaba Varga*
Legal Reasoning, Vols I & II *Aulis Aarnio and Neil MacCormick*
Legal Positivism *Mario Jori*
American Legal Theory *Robert Summers*
Law and Language *Fred Schauer*
Sociological Theories of Law *Kahei Rokumoto*
Rights *Carlos Nino*
Law and Psychology *Martin Levine*
Feminist Legal Theory *Frances Olsen*

Areas

Criminal Law *Thomas Morawetz*
Tort Law *Ernest Weinrib*
Contract Law, Vols I & II *Larry Alexander*
Anti-Discrimination Law *Christopher McCrudden*
Consumer Law *Iain Ramsay*
International Law *Martti Koskenniemi*
Property Law *Elizabeth Mensch and Alan Freeman*
Constitutional Law *Mark Tushnet*
Procedure *Denis Galligan*
Evidence and Proof *William Twining and Alex Stein*
Administrative Law *Denis Galligan*
Child Law *Harry Krause*
Family Law, Vols I & II *Harry Krause*
Welfare Law *Peter Robson*
Medicine and the Law *Bernard Dickens*
Commercial Law *Ross Cranston*
Communications Law *David Goldberg*
Environmental Law *Michael Blumm*
Conflict of Laws *Richard Fentiman*
Law and Religion *Wojciech Sadurski*
Human Rights Law *Philip Alston*
European Community Law *Francis Snyder*

Legal Cultures

Comparative Legal Cultures *Csaba Varga*
Law and Anthropology *Peter Sack*
Hindu Law and Legal Theory *Ved Nanda*
Islamic Law and Legal Theory *Ian Edge*
Chinese Law and Legal Theory *Michael Palmer*
Socialist Law and Legal Theory *W. Butler*
Japanese Law and Legal Theory *Kiochiro Fujikura*
Law and Development *Anthony Carty*
Jewish Law and Legal Theory *Martin Golding*
Legal Education *Martin Levine*

Future Volumes

Labour Law, Common Law and Legal Theory, Civil Law and Legal Theory, Law and Society, African Law and Legal Theory, Legal Ethics and Cumulative index.

Law and Economics
Volume I

Edited by

Jules Coleman

John A. Garver Professor of Jurisprudence & Philosophy
Yale Law School

and

Jeffrey Lange

Assistant Professor of Law
University of Pennsylvania School of Law

NEW YORK UNIVERSITY PRESS
REFERENCE COLLECTION

First published in the U.S.A. in 1992 by
NEW YORK UNIVERSITY PRESS
Washington Square
New York NY 10003

Library of Congress Cataloging-in-Publication Data
Law and economics / edited [by] Jules Coleman and Jeffrey Lange.
p. cm. — (The International library of essays in law and legal theory)
Essays originally published in various journals from 1960 to 1988.
"New York University Press reference collection."
Includes bibliographical references and index.
ISBN 0-8147-1464-1 (set) — ISBN 0-8147-1462-5 (v. 1)
— ISBN 0-8147-1463-3 (v. 2)
1. Law. 2. Economics. I. Coleman, Jules L. II. Lange, Jeffrey.
III. Series.
K487.E3L378 1992
340—dc20 91-25108
CIP

Contents

PART IV ECONOMIC ANALYSIS OF PROPERTY LAW

PART V ECONOMIC ANALYSIS OF CRIME

Acknowledgements

The editor and publishers wish to thank the following for permission to use copyright material.

American Economic Association for the essay: Harold Demsetz (1967), 'Toward a Theory of Property Rights', *American Economic Association*, **57**, No. 2, pp. 347–59. Copyright © American Economic Association.

Columbia Law Review Association for essays: R. Cooter (1984), 'Prices and Sanctions', *Columbia Law Review*, **84**, pp. 1523–60. Copyright © 1984 by the Directors of the Columbia Law Review Association, Inc. All Rights Reserved. This article originally appeared at 84 Colum. L. Rev. 1435 (1984). Reprinted by permission; Susan Rose-Ackerman (1985), 'Inalienability and the Theory of Property Rights', *Columbia Law Review*, **85**, pp. 931–69. Copyright © 1985 by the Directors of the Columbia Law Review Association, Inc. All Rights Reserved. This article originally appeared at 85 Colum. L. Rev. 931 (1985). Reprinted by permission, and Steven Shavell (1985), 'Criminal Law and the Optimal Use of Nonmonetary Sanctions as a Deterrent, *Columbia Law Review*, **85**, pp. 1232–62. Copyright © 1985 by the Directors of the Columbia Law Review Association, Inc. All Rights Reserved. This article originally appeared at 85 Colum. L. Rev. 1232 (1985). Reprinted by permission.

Robert C. Ellickson (1986), 'Of Coase and Cattle: Dispute Resolution Among Neighbors in Shasta County', *Stanford Law Review*, **38**, pp. 623–87. Copyright © Robert C. Ellickson.

Harvard Law Review for the essay: Guido Calabresi and A. Douglas Melamed (1972), 'Property Rules, Liability Rules, and Inalienability: One View of the Cathedral', *Harvard Law Review*, **85**, pp. 1089–128. Copyright © 1972 by the Harvard Law Review Association.

Nomos XXVII for the essay: Alvin K. Klevorick (1985), 'On the Economic Theory of Crime, in *Criminal Justice: Nomos XXVII*.

Fred B. Rothman & Co. and the Virginia Law Review Association for the essay: John E. Calfee and Richard Craswell (1984), 'Some Effects of Uncertainty on Compliance with Legal Standards', *Virginia Law Review*, **70**, pp. 965–1003.

The University of Chicago Press for essays: R.H. Coase (1960), 'The Problem of Social Cost', *The Journal of Law and Economics*, **III**, pp. 1–44; Oliver E. Williamson (1979), 'Transaction-Cost Economics: The Governance of Contractual Relations', *The Journal of Law and Economics*, **22**, pp. 233–61; John Prather Brown (1973), 'Toward an Economic Theory of Liability', *The Journal of Legal Studies*, **2**, pp. 323–49 and A. Mitchell Polinsky (1983), 'Risk Sharing Through Breach of Contract Remedies', *The Journal of Legal Studies*, **117**, pp. 427–44. Copyright © The University of Chicago Press.

The Yale Law Journal for essays: Guido Calabresi and Jon T. Hirschoff (1972), 'Toward a Test for Strict Liability in Torts', *The Yale Law Journal*, **81**, pp. 1055–85. Reprinted by permission of The Yale Law Journal Company and Fred B. Rothman & Company from The Yale Law Journal, Vol. **81**, pp. 1055–85, and Charles J. Goetz and Robert E. Scott (1980), 'Enforcing Promises: An Examination of the Basis of Contract', *The Yale Law Journal*, **89**, pp. 1261–1322. Reprinted by permission of The Yale Law Journal Company and Fred B. Rothman & Company from The Yale Law Journal, Vol. **89**, pp. 1261–322.

Every effort has been made to trace all the copyright holders, but if any have been inadvertently overlooked the publishers will be pleased to make the necessary arrangement at the first opportunity.

Series Preface

The International Library of Law and Legal Theory is designed to provide important research materials in an accessible form. Each volume contains essays of central theoretical importance in its subject area. The series as a whole makes available an extensive range of valuable material which will be of considerable interest to those involved in the research, teaching and study of law.

The series has been divided into three sections. The Schools section is intended to represent the main distinctive approaches and topics of special concern to groups of scholars. The Areas section takes in the main branches of law with an emphasis on essays which present analytical and theoretical insights of broad application. The section on Legal Cultures makes available the distinctive legal theories of different level traditions and takes up topics of general comparative and developmental concern.

I have been delighted and impressed by the way in which the editors of the individual volumes have set about the difficult task of selecting, ordering and presenting essays from the immense quantity of academic legal writing published in journals throughout the world. Editors were asked to pick out those essays from law, philosophy and social science journals which they consider to be fundamental for the understanding of law, as seen from the perspective of a particular approach or sphere of legal interest. This is not an easy task and many difficult decisions have had to be made in order to ensure that a representative sample of the best journal essays available takes account of the scope of each topic or school.

I should like to express my thanks to all the volume editors for their willing participation and scholarly judgement. The interest and enthusiasm which the project has generated is well illustrated by the fact that an original projection of 12 volumes drawn up in 1989 has now become a list of some 60 volumes. I must also acknowledge the vision, persistence and constant cheerfulness of John Irwin and the marvellous work done by Mrs Margaret O'Reilly and Mrs Sonia Bridgman.

TOM D. CAMPBELL
Series Editor
The Faculty of Law
The Australian National University

Introduction

In these two volumes, we have assembled, first, many of the now classic papers in law and economics. These essays should give the newcomer to the field both a less technical introduction to the fundamental concepts of the economic approach to the law and, by consulting publication dates, a rough sense of the discipline's intellectual history.[1] The expert should find this portion of the collection useful either for reference or perhaps for instruction.[2]

Second, we have included shorter, more technical papers, which tend to be of more recent vintage. These contributions reflect the trend towards formal, mathematical treatment of discrete legal rules and institutions. They are intended to illustrate the methodology of the economic approach to law which, naturally, comprises the core of economics – the theories of price and social welfare, rational choice and public choice. Largely empirical studies using the tools of statistical measurement (econometrics) have been deliberately excluded from the volumes primarily due to space constraints, though it is fair to say that most scholarship in law and economics remains theoretical rather than empirical.

We have organized the volumes principally by subject area, but in some instances have grouped papers by methodology. Volume I begins with three essays which set out some of the basic principles of law and economics. The remainder of Volume I spans the traditional common law subjects – torts, contracts, property – and closes with a section on crime. In Volume II, we have chosen a more eclectic set of papers arranged under the following headings: the efficiency of the common law, corporations, public choice theory, game theory and the law, and philosophical foundations.

Law and economics literature has grown tremendously over the last ten years. Although in 1980, it might have been possible to summarize in a few pages the major achievements in the field, this is certainly not possible today. The reader should therefore keep in mind that the selections included in these volumes constitute only a small sample of the literature, with some bias towards the older, less technical papers. In the overview to follow, and that of Volume II, we try to identify other sources which readers may find helpful.

Part I Fundamental Concepts in Law and Economics

Consider the pollution of the water or air, the blaring of a neighbour's stereo, the filing of lawsuits or the production of a documentary film on a videocassette. These seemingly dissimilar activities have one important thing in common – each activity creates either an external cost or an external benefit. Generally speaking, when someone engages in an activity but does not bear the full cost or receive the full benefit from that activity, what economists call an 'externality' occurs. Water pollution is an example of a *negative* externality. The battery factory which dumps acid and lead into a river does not bear the cost that this dumping imposes on those who fish nearby. Because of this, the firm produces too many batteries and pollutes too much. A film company which makes a videotape but cannot prevent it from being copied does not receive the full benefits from its production. Those who pirate the tape receive an external benefit. Due to this *positive* externality, too few tapes will be produced – at least in the absence of some type of legal intervention. These externalities are one cause of what economists call 'market failure'. When markets fail, resources are not used in ways which maximize their value (such as the production of too many batteries and too few films). The dominant theme throughout the law and economics literature, apparent in the essays in this volume, is the repair of market failure, primarily by structuring the law to reduce, or 'internalize', externalities.

In Chapter 1, Ronald Coase's 1960 essay, 'The Problem of Social Cost', addresses the problem of externalities or 'social' cost. This stands as the most influential paper in law and economics for its indirect statement of the following theorem: If (1) property rights are well defined and (2) marketable, and (3) if bargaining among individuals is costless and not hampered by great disparities in wealth, then any assignment of legal rights will result in resources being put to their most-valued uses. When these conditions hold, legal intervention cannot improve upon nor harm the welfare of individuals because costless bargaining will take place until no individual can be made better off without making someone else worse off (economists term this a Pareto efficient state of affairs).[3]

The publication of Coase's Theorem was of great significance for two reasons. First, it overthrew the orthodox view that the problem of external costs should be solved through government taxation of the activity creating the external cost. Coase showed that the orthodox view, originating with the economist Pigou, was not the best solution as long as transaction costs do not impede bargaining.[4] If the level of the activity creating the externality is not efficient because external costs exceed the benefits from the activity, then those subject to the costs will simply bribe the cost-imposer to refrain from the activity. In costless bargaining, a deal will be struck: the cost-imposer will accept a bribe equal to the benefits he receives from imposing the cost. This deal will always be forthcoming exactly when imposition is inefficient, or when the costs of the activity exceed the benefits.

Second, the publication of the Coase Theorem has had a profound influence on the focus of subsequent law and economics scholarship, though understanding its influence is not easy. The Coase Theorem assumes away 'transaction costs' even though real markets are replete with them. It may be true that in a world without friction we would not need tractors, but in the real world surfaces are not frictionless, just as markets are not without 'friction'. The Coase Theorem would appear to have limited significance for real-life markets. This view of Coase, however, is incorrect. The real significance of the theorem lies not in its conclusion that in some (rare) instances, legal intervention is not justified on efficiency grounds, but rather because it focuses attention on what type of intervention is justified in the face of (nearly) ubiquitous transaction costs. The Coase Theorem is illustrative of Milton Friedman's well-known remark about the inverse relationship between descriptive accuracy and explanatory power. Coase's 'zero-transaction' costs assumption is descriptively inaccurate of most markets, yet it identifies transaction costs as a primary justification for different means of legal intervention into markets. The Coase Theorem suggests that law should be structured (1) to reduce the costs of private bargaining and (2) to minimize the social costs which may result when private bargaining is likely to fail.[5]

This is the point of departure for Calabresi and Melamed in Chapter 2 who show that in a world of high transaction costs, two forms of legal intervention or decisions can be distinguished. The first-order decision determines how legal entitlements (such as the right to be free of a neighbour's pollution) are assigned; the second-order decision specifies how entitlements, once assigned, should be protected (for example, must the neighbour pay for the right to pollute *before* doing so or should he instead be subject to a lawsuit *after* doing so?)

Using the criterion of Pareto efficiency, Calabresi and Melamed argue that the optimal first-order assignment of entitlements in the presence of positive transaction costs would locate entitlements with individuals who can most 'cheaply' minimize external costs, or failing that, with those individuals who can most cheaply engage in market transactions which lead to cost minimization.[6] The heart of the essay, however, analyses the optimal second-order decision: whether these entitlements, once assigned, should be protected by (1) property, (2) liability or (3) inalienability rules.

If an entitlement is protected by a property rule, the consent of the holder is required before it can be transferred. The Coase Theorem shows that such a rule is optimal only if obtaining the holder's consent *ex ante* is not too costly, i.e., if transaction costs are minimal. When transaction costs are not *de minimis*, a Pareto inferior allocation may persist under a property rule simply because transaction costs are too high.

But why are transaction costs likely to be high? There are two components to transaction costs; these may be termed the costs of surplus creation and surplus division.[7] Every desirable transaction creates a surplus, the sum total of net benefits to the parties of the transaction. The costs of surplus creation, however, may prevent such a transaction: for example, the buyers and sellers may be geographically dispersed, or there may be so many buyers that agreement cannot readily be reached as to how much each buyer should contribute towards the purchase price (the 'free rider' problem). The costs of surplus division are those associated with the incentive each party has to maximize his share of the transactional surplus at the expense of the other parties. The end result of an individual 'holding out' for most or all of the surplus may be that no agreement is reached.[8] Thus, Calabresi and Melamed conclude that when the costs of surplus creation and division are likely to be high, the optimal second-order decision is for entitlements to be protected by a liability rule, which would allow the transfer of an entitlement without *ex ante* consent (which entails costly bargaining), but would afford the 'seller' legal compensation after the transfer.

Finally, Calabresi and Melamed analyse the third, less common form of entitlement protection known as inalienability. An inalienability rule protects an entitlement by flatly prohibiting its transfer.[9] The main efficiency justification for inalienability rules is that external costs imposed on many individuals may not be adequately 'internalized' under a liability rule: perhaps no single individual has an incentive to sue (or even remain in a class action against) a polluter. In the case where the costs of pollution greatly exceed the benefits of the activity producing it, and where those affected are unlikely to avail themselves of the protections of a liability rule, it may be more efficient to ban pollution altogether; in other words, to prohibit the transfer of the right to be free of pollution. That is, inalienability may be the optimal entitlement protection where there are obstacles to transacting around property rules and where the cost of implementing liability rules is prohibitively high.

However, a very large part of the law – certainly most of the law of torts and crimes – falls into the middle area of legal intervention which Calabresi and Melamed have called liability rules. In his elegant paper entitled 'Prices and Sanctions' (Chapter 3), Bob Cooter gives more content to this type of legal intervention into markets by distinguishing the two ways in which liability rules function: they may either (1) exact prices or (2) impose sanctions on those imposing external costs onto others. Legal intervention in the form of a sanction is a detriment imposed when an individual behaves in violation of some legally defined standard, while a price exacts a payment for behaviour which is permitted.

This distinction is important. It shows how the economist's model of legal rules as prices and the jurisprudential model of legal rules as sanctions can be integrated. It also provides lawmakers with some norms for intervention into markets. Cooter explains that when it is difficult to determine what standard should govern behaviour – what standard is efficient – then lawmakers should set prices on behaviour, as long as prices more or less equal to the cost of the behaviour can be fixed. An example of legal pricing is strict products liability. Lawmakers and courts are likely to be bad at determining the efficient standard for manufacturer quality control, but quite good at calculating the harms caused by defective products. In this circumstance, the law should eschew a standard and instead fix prices equal in value to the harm caused. Thus, in strict products liability, a manufacturer must pay a price equal to the harm caused by a defective product regardless of whether the manufacturer has violated some legal standard of care.

By contrast, if lawmakers are good at determining what the efficient level of activity is, but relatively bad at calculating the exact costs of such activity, then sanctions, rather than prices, should be applied. An example of such a sanction is the law of negligence in tort which imposes a detriment only when behaviour violates a legal standard. The analysis of prices and sanctions applies in other areas of the law as well and will be revisited shortly in introducing the essays on torts.

Part II Economic Analysis of Tort Law

The first paper in Part II, by Calabresi and Hirschoff, focuses on a single aspect of tort law, but one which has probably received more attention in the law and economics literature than any other: when (if ever) should a party be held strictly liable for the harm he causes regardless of fault or negligence?[10] Bob Cooter's general theory of prices and sanctions, when applied to the law of torts, generated a specific test which we have already discussed. Calabresi and Hirschoff examine the subject in more detail and in less formal terms. They conclude, as did Cooter, that strict liability should govern when courts are relatively bad, but individuals relatively good, at determining the efficient level of care. When courts have good information about the efficient level of care, they should impose liability on the 'cheapest cost avoider' – the negligent party. When courts have bad information, they should impose liability on the 'cheapest cost calculator' – the party held strictly liable.

Chapter 5, John Prather Brown's 'Toward An Economic Theory of Liability' is a classic formal analysis of tort liability rules. It is also, in part, an attack on the utility of the 'cheapest cost avoider' concept. The basic intuition driving Brown's model is that the behaviour of the two parties to an accident, the injurer and victim, each supplies precaution 'inputs' in the production of accidents – the 'outputs'. The various tort rules are analysed to determine whether they induce efficient accident production (which in Brown's model means marshalling inputs which minimize the costs of precaution and accidents). Because each party to the accident is in control of her own precaution input, the production of accidents is different from a firm producing, say, widgets from two inputs such as capital and labour. This non-cooperative nature of accident production shows why the 'cheapest cost avoider' idea fails to identify who should be liable. In the case where both the injurer and the victim supply inputs to the production of an accident, both parties contribute to 'cheapest cost avoidance'. Similarly, where production of a widget requires both capital and labour, the injunction to a manufacturer to use the 'cheapest cost input' will not make much sense – both inputs must be used to minimize production costs. Brown shows that efficient tort rules are those which induce each party unilaterally to pick levels of precaution so that the total social costs of accidents are minimized.[11]

The final paper in Part II addresses the important question of legal uncertainty. In 'Some Effects of Uncertainty on Compliance with Legal Standards', Calfee and Craswell depart from the traditional assumption (made by Brown in the preceding paper) that parties subject to a legal standard always know exactly the standard of care that is legally required.[12] The authors focus on negligence, though their analysis applies to other areas of the law as well. We have already seen that legal standards (such as negligence) which carry sanctions for their violation may not be optimal if lawmakers have bad information about where to set such standards. Calfee and Craswell tackle the additional problem of legal uncertainty. Legal standards, whether set efficiently or not, will be uncertain in application due to (1) legal error by courts, (2) evidentiary problems and (3) variability in enforcement.

Because of these three main sources of legal uncertainty (and there may be others), parties subject to a negligence standard cannot be sure that they will not be held liable either if they comply or if they do not comply. As a consequence of this legal uncertainty, individuals subject to the standard will have an incentive to either over-comply or under-comply with it. For example, over-compliance occurs because increased precaution not only reduces the expected costs of accidents which a party faces, but in an uncertain legal system it also reduces the probability that the party will be held liable at all. The combined effect is an over-investment in precaution relative to the investment a party would make in a legal system free from uncertainty.

Part III Economic Analysis of Contract Law

The economic analysis of contract law comprises a vast and complex body of literature.[13] The process of contracting can be analytically divided into (1) formation (offer and acceptance), (2) performance (the terms of the contract) and (3) breach (remedies). Economic analysis has focused very little on the first subject, significantly more on the second, and very much on the third.[14] The reason for this uneven attention is no doubt because the common law of contract contains a variety of interesting remedial doctrines. In most cases, for example, a promisor who breaches a contract must pay the promisee an amount equal to the latter's 'expectation' – the net value of the promise to the promisee.[15] But in other cases, such as those involving non-reciprocal promises, a promisor may be compelled to pay an amount of money corresponding to whatever loss a promisee has incurred by relying on the promise. In a small body of other cases, a party 'unjustly enriched' by the breaking of a promise must disgorge promissory benefits to the promisee. Finally, in a still smaller class of cases, the promisee may be entitled to compel the promisor to do exactly what the contract specified, rather than pay a monetary equivalent (specific performance).[16]

In Chapter 7, 'Enforcing Promises: An Examination of the Basis of Contract', Goetz and Scott analyse the foundations of a contract – the making of a promise – and investigate how the law should be structured to maximize the net social benefits of promise-making. The authors distinguish between two types of contracts: those based on non-reciprocal or unilateral promises and those based on reciprocal promises. Again, the problem of externalities guides the analysis.

If A, for a price, promises B that he will do something, A's unilateral promise can impose an external cost on B because B will take certain actions in reliance upon A's word in order to take full advantage of A's performance. The external cost of A's promise is clear: after B has relied upon A's word, A may not perform after all, in which case B will have lost the amount of money spent in preparing to take full advantage of A's anticipated performance.

A's promise, however, also can provide B with an external benefit. B will be much better off having incurred costs in reliance than not having done so should A perform. Goetz and Scott show that efficient rules of contract, like efficient tort rules, require externalities to be internalized. The promisor must be brought to consider the external benefits and the external costs which his promise creates for the promisee. On this logic, an optimal damage measure would be the difference between the expected external costs and the expected external benefits of reliance ('expected', because there is discounting for the probability of breach and performance respectively). Damages which exceed this amount would lead the promisee to over-rely, whereas lower damages would not give the promisor sufficient incentive to invest in precautions to guarantee performance.[17]

Goetz and Scott then show that the same optimal damage measure applies for reciprocal promises – those in which both parties may adjust the quality and quantity of their promise-making. Consider the case of reciprocal promises in a competitive market where two or more promises may exist to which the promisee attaches roughly the same value (the promises are good 'substitutes'). If a promisor does not perform, the promisee's next-best alternative is not much worse than the value he would have obtained had the promisor performed. By relying on the broken promise, he merely loses the value which he attached to it, which is normally called his 'expectation' interest. Since good substitute promises exist, the extra benefits that a promisee can obtain by relying on the *promisor's* promise will be small; in fact, the external benefit conferred by the promisor's promise will be close to zero. The upshot is that for competitive, reciprocal promise-making, the Goetz and Scott formula reduces to the familiar contract damage measure of expectation damages.

This result is consistent with the parallel concept in the economic analysis of contract of 'efficient breach'. If damages for breach of reciprocal promises are set at the lost value or expectation of the promisee, then the promisor will only breach the contract when the benefits of breach exceed the damages that must be paid to the promisee. Breach in this instance will be efficient, in that the promisee will be indifferent between breach and performance after collecting his expectation damages, and the promisor will be better off after payment of damages.

Which contractual damage measure is efficient, however, depends not only on the structure of promise-making (reciprocal versus non-reciprocal), but also upon whether the parties to a contract are risk averse. The latter is the subject of Chapter 8, Polinsky's 'Risk Sharing through Breach of Contract Remedies'. Polinsky analyses five different contract damage measures where either the buyer, the seller, or both may be risk averse. The key insight is that where one or both parties to a contract are risk averse, contract damage rules serve an insurance function.

By insuring against accidents, risk-averse individuals are willing to pay an amount (a premium) to avoid a contingent loss. Polinsky analyses one type of contract where the relevant contingency is not a loss but a gain. Where a buyer contracts to make a purchase from a seller, there is a chance that a second buyer will later emerge who is willing to pay more than the first buyer. Resale to the potential second buyer presents a contingent gain. Polinsky shows which contractual damage measure efficiently allocates this contingent gain.

Consider the case where the first buyer is risk averse and the seller is risk neutral. Optimal risk-bearing in this case requires that the seller bear risk rather than the buyer. The buyer bears no risk if damages are set equal to the buyer's expectation interest: whether the second buyer materializes or not, the first buyer receives the value of the seller's performance. The seller in this case is willing to offer the first buyer a lower contract price in return for receiving the entire gain should the second buyer appear. Alternatively, the lower contract price can be viewed as the seller purchasing a lottery ticket from the buyer in the amount of the price discount, or the risk-averse buyer accepting a certain payment in return for foregoing a contingent gain. Polinsky also concludes that the only damage rule that is optimal when *both* the buyer and seller are risk averse is the liquidated damages remedy – the amount of damages which the parties themselves stipulate should be paid in the event of breach. Polinsky's results reinforce the point already evident from this brief discussion of contract damages: no single damage rule is optimal for all types of contracts and all contracting parties.

The final essay in Part III on contract law is an example of the 'new institutional economics' which in the words of its author, Oliver Williamson, is 'preoccupied with the origins, incidence and ramifications of transaction costs'.[18] The point of departure for transaction cost analysis is the Coase Theorem: if transaction costs are *de minimis*, then the form of legal intervention or structuring of economic activity is irrelevant (for efficiency) since costless contracting will always yield a Pareto efficient allocation.

Institutional economic analysis uses 'transaction costs' (where they exist) in order to explain the ways in which transactions are structured and governed. In Chapter 9, Williamson develops a taxonomy of transaction types and correlates these types to the institution which is apt to economize on transaction costs. The following characteristics identify the 'type' of transaction: (1) the specificity of investment (is it in nuclear power plants or ball bearings?), (2) the frequency of the transaction (is it recurrent or occasional?) and (3) uncertainty.

Williamson places these transaction types within three traditions of contract law. The first tradition is 'classical' contract law, which covers contracting parties and investment characteristics that are fungible, contractual terms that are specifiable, and remedies that are clear and prescribed. Such a contract corresponds to the ideal market transaction in microeconomic theory and is well suited for market governance.

The second tradition is 'neoclassical' contract law, which encompasses the rules applicable to contracts in which performance ranges over a longer term, is more uncertain, involves more specific assets (whose uses have much lower value outside the transaction), and is relatively infrequent. These transaction characteristics require a governance structure more specialized than that of the 'fungible' market. Third-party supervision or 'trilateral governance' (such as arbitration) of such contracts is the norm. Such a governance structure economizes on the costs of neoclassical contracting.

To complete the taxonomy, the last contracting tradition is called 'relational'. Relational contracts are investment specific, long-term, uncertain and recurrent. Investment in more specialized governance structures is cost-justified because of the frequency of the transactions, which in other respects resemble neoclassical-type contracts. Vertical integration of buyer and seller ('unified governance'), in which each party to the contract becomes part of a single firm, thereby removing the transaction from the market entirely, is a common governance structure for such contracts.

Williamson's paper reinforces the theme of this section: contracts are heterogeneous. No uniform set of legal rules or single institution is adequate to guarantee optimal transactions. Different damage remedies may be appropriate for different contractual settings; transactions may also arise in many different institutional settings including markets, within firms or under the supervision of regulatory bodies.

Part IV Economic Analysis of Property Law

So far, we have considered one explanation of legal rules – that they function to reduce externalities. We have also seen that if transaction costs are negligible, the mere existence of well-defined and marketable property rights will ensure that all externalities are internalized. But what explains the existence, or emergence, of property rights themselves? This is the question addressed by Demsetz in his well-known essay, 'Toward a Theory of Property Rights' (Chapter 10). The answer, again, is the control of external costs or, in Demsetz's words, 'guiding incentives to achieve a greater internalization of externalities'.[19]

New externalities are created, according to Demsetz, by changes in technology. Consider the effect of a discrete technological change, such as the invention of the radio. As more broadcasters claim portions of the electronic spectrum, radio signals will interfere with each other. Where previously no need existed for property rights in frequency bands, a new technology, with its new externalities, justifies the creation of new property rights. The creation occurs precisely when the benefits of creating these new rights exceed the costs of doing so. Private property rights in hunting, for example, will not emerge until over-hunting has significantly depleted the game; in other words, when the costs of over-hunting exceed the costs of limiting access to the hunting grounds. In addition to reducing externalities, private property rights also facilitate less costly negotiating. If remaining externalities exist, clearly-defined legal property rights should reduce transaction costs sufficiently so that individuals can bargain over external costs and benefits.

This last proposition has been investigated empirically by Robert Ellickson in Chapter 11, 'Of Coase and Cattle: Dispute Resolution Among Neighbors in Shasta County'. Ellickson conducted field research among cattle ranchers in Northern California to determine how cattle trespass costs were 'internalized' among neighbouring ranchers. The Coase Theorem would predict that as long as bargaining costs among neighbours were low, any differences in cattle trespass law would not affect the allocation of resources among residents. In fact, Ellickson found that differences in cattle trespass law – what are called changes in the 'assignment' of legal 'entitlements' in discussions of the Coase Theorem – had little effect on the behaviour of residents. The reason for this, however, was not due to low transaction costs, but to *high* transaction costs.

Ellickson found that very few of the Shasta County residents, including local lawyers and insurance adjusters, knew the relevant rules governing cattle trespasses. Knowledge of the law of trespass is costly, as is resorting to formal means of enforcing formal legal rights. Thus, although cooperative behaviour among the Shasta ranchers emerged, formal legal rules governing trespass did not mark their initial bargaining positions or 'threat points'.[20] Rather, informal norms of dispute-resolution guided 'bargaining' in Shasta County irrespective of any differences in formal trespass rules (which distinguished primarily between land zoned as 'closed' or 'open' range).

Thus, Ellickson found that the 'Coasean Parable' met mixed results in Shasta County. While the specific content of law did not change the way in which the residents cooperated with each other to solve the problem of externalities, low transaction costs were not responsible for this state of affairs. Rather, the high cost of finding out about the specific content of law and the costs of enforcing formal legal rights led the Shasta residents to pursue less costly means of controlling externalities, such as ignoring *de minimis* trespass, keeping informal accounts of damage and, in extreme cases, besmirching the reputation of recidivist trespassing ranchers. That resource allocation remains efficient under different legal rules even when transaction costs are high is, according to Ellickson, 'at odds' with the Coasean paradigm. Coase showed that law does not matter for efficiency because people will bargain over their legal rights. Ellickson discovered, instead, that law does not matter for efficiency because people do not know what their legal rights are. It is therefore important to emphasize that bargaining around formal legal rights when transaction costs are low may be sufficient (but not necessary) for allocative efficiency to remain unaffected by legal rules.

Of course, formal legal rights will matter for resource allocation if the law prohibits those rights from being transferred. In Chapter 12, entitled 'Inalienability and the Theory of Property Rights', Susan Rose-Ackerman examines 'inalienability', a type of legal rule discussed briefly in the Calabresi and Melamed paper. Rose-Ackerman addresses three dimensions of inalienability: restrictions on (1) who may hold an entitlement, (2) what a holder can do while in possession, and (3) transfers of the entitlement. The essay focuses on nine representative and important cases of inalienability.

Rose-Ackerman advances claims based on both efficiency and distributive justice in favour of inalienability restrictions in these nine cases. Only the efficiency-based argument will be surveyed here. Like other legal rules, inalienability restrictions are aimed at coping with market failures which, as we have seen, are sometimes caused by externalities. In some cases transaction costs are so high that the only way to control externalities is through restrictions on alienability. If some easily identifiable class of person is prone to imposing external costs while engaging in an activity, the most efficient means of controlling these costs may be to prevent that class of person from engaging in the activity altogether, such as prohibiting blind people from driving cars and convicted felons from owning firearms.

Externalities, however, are not the only cause of market failure. Sometimes markets fail because of informational asymmetries, the market for tort claims being a good example. While victims of an accident will generally have reliable private information about the extent of their injuries, lawyers are usually better informed regarding the merits of the victim's tort claim. A free market in tort claims would generally not be competitive because tort victims would not know the value of what they had to sell. Moreover, informing the victim or having a governmental body price tort claims would be very costly. Restricting transfer of tort claims and allowing only the victim to pursue her claim is one way in which the law has remedied this information gap.

Problems of collective action are another form of market failure which may warrant restrictions on alienability. The homesteading restrictions of the last century, as Rose-Ackerman notes, are good examples of this. A collective action problem arises when individual and collective interests do not coincide. For example, a prospective frontier settler would choose not to be an early pioneer, with its attendant hardships, and yet all settlers preferred to chance the frontier rather than remain poor and landless in the East. If individuals chose not to be the first to settle, the obvious result would be no settlement. In this classic 'Prisoner's Dilemma' scenario, inalienability restrictions provided one possible solution. The Homesteading Acts required settlers to farm their land for five years in order to become owners; during this probationary period, transfers were prohibited. These restrictions kept speculators out of the frontier market, thus furthering economic development.

Part V Economic Analysis of Crime

The starting point for the economic analysis of crime is to view criminal behaviour as yet another type of external cost. In the abstract, crimes resemble both torts and governmental takings of property in that an individual suffers harm to either property or person without his consent. (In fact, in historical terms, the distinction between crime and tort has been a recent development in Anglo-Saxon law.) As for torts and takings, one way to internalize external costs caused by criminal behaviour is to award damages to the victim. Yet modern criminal law generally does not provide any mechanism for making the criminal pay the victim compensation for harm caused. Instead, criminals are compelled to pay fines to the government, serve prison terms, or both. These alternative means of making the costs of criminal behaviour 'internal' to those engaged in criminal activity (but without compensation to victims) have therefore been a natural focal point for economic analysis.[21]

In his paper 'Criminal Law and the Optimal Use of Nonmonetary Sanctions as a Deterrent' (Chapter 13), Steven Shavell investigates when the criminal law should impose prison terms rather than fines in order to minimize the costs of criminal behaviour. Any model of criminal law, including Shavell's, must consider three relevant actors: the criminal, the victim and the official who enforces the law. But Shavell's model is specifically one of deterrence: the goal is to explain why and how criminal law imposes sanctions on criminal behaviour in order to minimize the costs of crime.

Consider law enforcement. One of the earliest insights in the economic analysis of crime is that, unlike accidents or contract breaches, criminal activity is likely to go undetected, and hence unpunished. Imposing a fine equal to the expected harm that a criminal may cause will not completely internalize the costs of crime to the criminal, because the criminal discounts his expected fine by the probability that his crime will be detected and the law enforced against him. A 'kicker' must therefore be added to expected harm in order to make the criminal indifferent between the increased fine and engaging in criminal activity (and a larger 'kicker' if we want the criminal strictly to prefer compliance).[22] Next consider the criminal himself.

Shavell notes that monetary sanctions may not be sufficient to control the external costs of crime when the assets of criminals are limited, or when criminals stand to reap very large private gains from criminal activity. In these circumstances, imprisonment may be necessary to deter criminal activity. Finally, consider the harm done to the victim. When the magnitude of harm is likely to be large and the probability of harm great, a very large deterrent, such as imprisonment, may be called for.

These five factors isolated by Shavell – a criminal's assets, the probability of punishment, private gains from crime, the probability of harm and the magnitude of harm – have considerable power in explaining both the domain of non-monetary sanctions as well as other features of the criminal law. One such feature is the requirement that certain harmful acts be done with intent in order to be considered criminal. Shavell relates the intent requirement to his model as follows. First, when a harmful act is done with intent, the probability of harm is likely to be greater. Second, the magnitude of the harm also tends to be greater when parties intend to do harm. Third, persons who intend harmful acts derive large private gains from the harm imposed. Finally, those who intend harm are more likely to succeed in avoiding arrest and punishment. The model therefore explains why intent should be isolated by the law for both criminal liability and high sanctions, such as imprisonment.

Concluding Part V is Alvin Klevorick's essay 'On the Economic Theory of Crime', which provides an overview of the economic models of criminal law and a discussion of their inherent limitations.[23] Klevorick discerns three distinct strands in the voluminous economic literature on crime. The first is the application of individual utility maximization – typically applied to consumers or firms in price theory – to the decision process of criminals. The translation from consumer to criminal is straightforward enough. For example, criminals respond to increases in criminal sanctions by committing less crime just as consumers react to an increase in prices by buying fewer goods. Or, criminals will substitute legitimate activities for illegitimate ones, just as consumers may substitute one good for another in response to changes in relative prices. Elasticity of criminal behaviour in response to changes in sanctions is also an important line of inquiry in the first strand of the literature Klevorick identifies.

The second theme of the literature on crime is concerned with the costs and benefits of criminal behaviour at the social level. (Roughly speaking, it bears the same relation to the first strand as welfare economics bears to the theory of individual utility maximization.) The object of the analysis is to specify a social cost (or welfare) function which captures the significant costs and benefits of criminal activity, including the costs of criminal acts, enforcement, punishment and private gains to criminals. Analysis proceeds by minimizing the net costs of crime – the difference between the harm to society and the aggregate value of crime to offenders.

Finally, a third concern of the economic literature on crime addresses a question logically prior to determining the optimal mix of enforcement, punishment and criminal behaviour; namely, why the law should contain a criminal category at all. Klevorick's review uncovers a common theme: a distinct criminal category is required in order to preserve the integrity of markets. Criminal laws punish those who flout property rules which prescribe that transfers of entitlements be voluntary. Without criminal laws, all transactions could be converted, at the criminal's will, into involuntary ones. Without a special legal category of criminal behaviour, property rules would collapse into liability rules.

Klevorick's essay also notes some important limitations of the economic models of the criminal law (which may be true of economic analysis in other areas of the law as well). First, as the three separate themes of the literature suggest, most economic analyses are only partial. A full and powerful model of the criminal law would yield both an optimal designation of those activities which should be crimes *and* the optimal levels of sanction, enforcement and criminal behaviour. The second major limitation is that any model of criminal law necessarily presupposes a certain kind of political structure. Reconsider, for example, the justification that criminal rules are needed to preserve the integrity of market transactions, to prevent property rules from being converted into liability rules. One can imagine a political structure (and name actual societies) in which it is a crime to sell goods to the highest bidder, instead of to the government, at a previously fixed price. Under such a structure, it would be a crime, Klevorick notes, for *liability rules to be converted into property rules*. At a minimum, then, any economic theory of criminal law must take as 'exogenous' to analysis whatever political presuppositions exist concerning the value of voluntary market exchanges.

Notes

1 The classic text in law and economics is Posner, R. (3d ed. 1986), *The Economic Analysis of Law*, Boston, Little, Brown & Co. A good introductory treatment is Polinsky, A.M. (2d ed. 1989), *An Introduction to Law and Economics*, Boston, Little, Brown & Co. For a comprehensive and interactive text, see Cooter, R. & Ulen, T. (1988), *Law and Economics*, Glenview, Scott, Foresman and Co.

2 This is why we have opted not to edit the essays but instead include them in their original form. For a useful collection of edited essays on a wide range of topics, see Ogus, A.I. & Veljanovski, C.G. (1984), *Readings in the Economics of Law and Regulation*, Oxford, Clarendon Press.

3 For further discussion of economic efficiency, see the essays in Part V , 'Philosophical Foundations', in Volume II of this collection.

4 The relationship between the solutions to the externality problem proposed by Pigou and Coase is analysed in J.L. Coleman (1988), 'Efficiency, Auction and Exchange' in *Markets, Morals and the Law*, Cambridge, Cambridge University Press.

5 These two important implications of the Coase Theorem are discussed in R. Cooter (1982), 'The Cost of Coase', *Journal of Legal Studies*, **11**(1), January.

6 The idea of locating entitlements with those who can most cheaply minimize external costs was first published in G. Calabresi (1970), *The Costs of Accidents: A Legal and Economic Analysis*, New Haven, Yale University Press.

7 Avery Katz has recently termed these two components to transaction costs the 'costs of implementation' and the 'costs of strategic behavior'. See A. Katz (1990), 'The Strategic Structure of Offer and Acceptance: Game Theory and the Law of Contract Formation', *Michigan Law Review*, **89**(2), November.

8 For further discussion of strategic behaviour in bargaining, see essays in Part IV, 'Game Theory and the Law', in Volume II of this collection.

9 Inalienability is discussed further by Susan Rose-Ackerman in Chapter 12.

10 For recent comprehensive treatments of tort law with discussions of strict liability, see S. Shavell (1987), *The Economic Analysis of Accidents*, Cambridge, Harvard University Press; W. Landes and R. Posner (1987), *The Economic Structure of Tort Law*, Cambridge, Harvard University Press.

11 Some technical corrections to Brown's reasoning, but not to (most of) his conclusions, may be found in G. Assaf (1984), 'The Shape of Reaction Functions and the Efficiency of Liability Rules: A Correction', *Journal of Legal Studies*, **13**(1), January.

12 The results of this paper are presented with a technical exposition in R. Craswell and J. Calfee (1986), 'Deterrence and Uncertain Legal Standards', *Journal of Law, Economics, and Organization*, **2**(2), Fall.

13 For a wide-ranging edited collection on the economics of contract law, see V. Goldberg (1989), *Readings in the Economics of Contract Law*, Cambridge, Cambridge University Press; see also, A. Kronman and R. Posner (1979), *The Economics of Contract Law*, Boston, Little, Brown & Co.

14 For a recent example of the literature on formation, see Avery Katz's article, *supra* note 7. The economic literature on contractual terms centres around the analysis of optimal contract 'default rules' – those provisions of contract law which contracting parties would, in most cases, choose for themselves were the costs of creating a completely specified contract negligible. If the law can supply a favoured contract term, the parties to contracts save transaction costs. For a recent analysis of contract default rules, see Ayres and Gertner (1989), 'Filling Gaps in Incomplete Contracts: An Economic Theory of Default Rules', *Yale Law Journal*, **99**(1), October.

15 A recent article by Alan Schwartz shows that in both market and bargain settings, promisees are willing to pay for damage remedies not in excess of their contractual expectations. This explains why the awarding of punitive damages in contract (damages in excess of expectation) is not (and should not be) a common phenomenon. See A. Schwartz (1990), 'The Myth That Promisees Prefer Supracompensatory Remedies: An Analysis of Contracting for Damage Measures', *Yale Law Journal*, **100**(2), November.

16 For an economic analysis in favour of the rule that specific performance should be infrequently awarded, see A. Kronman (1978), 'Specific Performance', *University of Chicago Law Review*, **45**(2), Winter. For the opposite position, see A. Schwartz (1979), 'The Case For Specific Performance', *Yale Law Journal*, **89**(2), December.

17 For a unified treatment of tort, property and contract emphasizing reliance and precaution, see R. Cooter (1985), 'Unity in Tort, Contract, and Property: The Model of Precaution', *California Law Review*, **73**(1), January.

18 See O. Williamson (1985), *The Economic Institutions of Capitalism*, New York, Free Press; O. Williamson (1985), 'Assessing Contract', *Journal of Law, Economics, and Organization*, **1**(1), Spring.

19 For an older collection of edited essays on the economics of property law, see B. Ackerman (1975), *Economic Foundations of Property Law*, Boston, Little, Brown & Co. For a recent philosophical account of property with an emphasis on distributive issues, see S. Munzer (1990), *A Theory of Property*, New York, Cambridge University Press.

20 Some experimental tests confirm the results predicted by the Coase Theorem and underline the importance of clearly-defined legal rights for successful bargaining. See, for instance, E. Hoffman and M. Spitzer (1982), 'The Coase Theorem: Some Experimental Tests', *Journal of Law and Economics*, **25**(1), April.

21 The seminal paper in the economic analysis of crime is G. Becker (1968), 'Crime and Punishment: An Economic Approach', *Journal of Political Economy*, **76**(2), March/April. For an edited collection of essays, see G. Becker and W. Landes (1974), *Essays in the Economics of Crime and Punishment*, New York, National Bureau of Economic Research.

22 For a fuller treatment of 'kickers' and other issues, see J.L. Coleman (1988), 'Crimes, Kickers and Transaction Structures', in *Markets, Morals and the Law*, Cambridge, Cambridge University Press.

23 A companion essay in which Klevorick elaborates on the limitations of the economic analysis of the criminal law is A. Klevorick (1985), 'Legal Theory and the Economic Analysis of Law', *Columbia Law Review*, **85**(5), June.

Part I
Fundamental Concepts in Law and Economics

[1]

The Journal of

LAW & ECONOMICS

VOLUME III OCTOBER 1960

THE PROBLEM OF SOCIAL COST

R. H. COASE
University of Virginia

I. The Problem To Be Examined[1]

This paper is concerned with those actions of business firms which have harmful effects on others. The standard example is that of a factory the smoke from which has harmful effects on those occupying neighbouring properties. The economic analysis of such a situation has usually proceeded in terms of a divergence between the private and social product of the factory, in which economists have largely followed the treatment of Pigou in *The Economics of Welfare*. The conclusions to which this kind of analysis seems to have led most economists is that it would be desirable to make the owner of the factory liable for the damage caused to those injured by the smoke, or alternatively, to place a tax on the factory owner varying with the amount of smoke produced and equivalent in money terms to the damage it would cause, or finally, to exclude the factory from residential districts (and presumably from other

[1] This article, although concerned with a technical problem of economic analysis, arose out of the study of the Political Economy of Broadcasting which I am now conducting. The argument of the present article was implicit in a previous article dealing with the problem of allocating radio and television frequencies (The Federal Communications Commission, 2 J. Law & Econ. [1959]) but comments which I have received seemed to suggest that it would be desirable to deal with the question in a more explicit way and without reference to the original problem for the solution of which the analysis was developed.

areas in which the emission of smoke would have harmful effects on others). It is my contention that the suggested courses of action are inappropriate, in that they lead to results which are not necessarily, or even usually, desirable.

II. The Reciprocal Nature of the Problem

The traditional approach has tended to obscure the nature of the choice that has to be made. The question is commonly thought of as one in which A inflicts harm on B and what has to be decided is: how should we restrain A? But this is wrong. We are dealing with a problem of a reciprocal nature. To avoid the harm to B would inflict harm on A. The real question that has to be decided is: should A be allowed to harm B or should B be allowed to harm A? The problem is to avoid the more serious harm. I instanced in my previous article[2] the case of a confectioner the noise and vibrations from whose machinery disturbed a doctor in his work. To avoid harming the doctor would inflict harm on the confectioner. The problem posed by this case was essentially whether it was worth while, as a result of restricting the methods of production which could be used by the confectioner, to secure more doctoring at the cost of a reduced supply of confectionery products. Another example is afforded by the problem of straying cattle which destroy crops on neighbouring land. If it is inevitable that some cattle will stray, an increase in the supply of meat can only be obtained at the expense of a decrease in the supply of crops. The nature of the choice is clear: meat or crops. What answer should be given is, of course, not clear unless we know the value of what is obtained as well as the value of what is sacrificed to obtain it. To give another example, Professor George J. Stigler instances the contamination of a stream.[3] If we assume that the harmful effect of the pollution is that it kills the fish, the question to be decided is: is the value of the fish lost greater or less than the value of the product which the contamination of the stream makes possible. It goes almost without saying that this problem has to be looked at in total *and* at the margin.

III. The Pricing System with Liability for Damage

I propose to start my analysis by examining a case in which most economists would presumably agree that the problem would be solved in a completely satisfactory manner: when the damaging business has to pay for all damage caused *and* the pricing system works smoothly (strictly this means that the operation of a pricing system is without cost).

A good example of the problem under discussion is afforded by the case of straying cattle which destroy crops growing on neighbouring land. Let us suppose that a farmer and a cattle-raiser are operating on neighbouring proper-

[2] Coase, The Federal Communications Commission, 2 J. Law & Econ. 26–27 (1959).

[3] G. J. Stigler, The Theory of Price 105 (1952).

ties. Let us further suppose that, without any fencing between the properties, an increase in the size of the cattle-raiser's herd increases the total damage to the farmer's crops. What happens to the marginal damage as the size of the herd increases is another matter. This depends on whether the cattle tend to follow one another or to roam side by side, on whether they tend to be more or less restless as the size of the herd increases and on other similar factors. For my immediate purpose, it is immaterial what assumption is made about marginal damage as the size of the herd increases.

To simplify the argument, I propose to use an arithmetical example. I shall assume that the annual cost of fencing the farmer's property is $9 and that the price of the crop is $1 per ton. Also, I assume that the relation between the number of cattle in the herd and the annual crop loss is as follows:

Number in Herd (Steers)	Annual Crop Loss (Tons)	Crop Loss per Additional Steer (Tons)
1	1	1
2	3	2
3	6	3
4	10	4

Given that the cattle-raiser is liable for the damage caused, the additional annual cost imposed on the cattle-raiser if he increased his herd from, say, 2 to 3 steers is $3 and in deciding on the size of the herd, he will take this into account along with his other costs. That is, he will not increase the size of the herd unless the value of the additional meat produced (assuming that the cattle-raiser slaughters the cattle), is greater than the additional costs that this will entail, including the value of the additional crops destroyed. Of course, if, by the employment of dogs, herdsmen, aeroplanes, mobile radio and other means, the amount of damage can be reduced, these means will be adopted when their cost is less than the value of the crop which they prevent being lost. Given that the annual cost of fencing is $9. the cattle-raiser who wished to have a herd with 4 steers or more would pay for fencing to be erected and maintained, assuming that other means of attaining the same end would not do so more cheaply. When the fence is erected, the marginal cost due to the liability for damage becomes zero, except to the extent that an increase in the size of the herd necessitates a stronger and therefore more expensive fence because more steers are liable to lean against it at the same time. But, of course, it may be cheaper for the cattle-raiser not to fence and to pay for the damaged crops, as in my arithmetical example, with 3 or fewer steers.

It might be thought that the fact that the cattle-raiser would pay for all crops damaged would lead the farmer to increase his planting if a cattle-raiser came to occupy the neighbouring property. But this is not so. If the crop was previously sold in conditions of perfect competition, marginal cost was equal to price for the amount of planting undertaken and any expansion would have reduced the profits of the farmer. In the new situation, the existence of crop damage would mean that the farmer would sell less on the open market but his receipts for a given production would remain the same, since the cattle-raiser would pay the market price for any crop damaged. Of course, if cattle-raising commonly involved the destruction of crops, the coming into existence of a cattle-raising industry might raise the price of the crops involved and farmers would then extend their planting. But I wish to confine my attention to the individual farmer.

I have said that the occupation of a neighbouring property by a cattle-raiser would not cause the amount of production, or perhaps more exactly the amount of planting, by the farmer to increase. In fact, if the cattle-raising has any effect, it will be to decrease the amount of planting. The reason for this is that, for any given tract of land, if the value of the crop damaged is so great that the receipts from the sale of the undamaged crop are less than the total costs of cultivating that tract of land, it will be profitable for the farmer and the cattle-raiser to make a bargain whereby that tract of land is left uncultivated. This can be made clear by means of an arithmetical example. Assume initially that the value of the crop obtained from cultivating a given tract of land is $12 and that the cost incurred in cultivating this tract of land is $10, the net gain from cultivating the land being $2. I assume for purposes of simplicity that the farmer owns the land. Now assume that the cattle-raiser starts operations on the neighbouring property and that the value of the crops damaged is $1. In this case $11 is obtained by the farmer from sale on the market and $1 is obtained from the cattle-raiser for damage suffered and the net gain remains $2. Now suppose that the cattle-raiser finds it profitable to increase the size of his herd, even though the amount of damage rises to $3; which means that the value of the additional meat production is greater than the additional costs, including the additional $2 payment for damage. But the total payment for damage is now $3. The net gain to the farmer from cultivating the land is still $2. The cattle-raiser would be better off if the farmer would agree not to cultivate his land for any payment less than $3. The farmer would be agreeable to not cultivating the land for any payment greater than $2. There is clearly room for a mutually satisfactory bargain which would lead to the abandonment of cultivation.[4] But the same argument applies not only to the whole tract cultivated by the farmer but also to any

[4] The argument in the text has proceeded on the assumption that the alternative to cultivation of the crop is abandonment of cultivation altogether. But this need not be so. There may be crops which are less liable to damage by cattle but which would not be as profitable as the crop grown in the absence of damage. Thus, if the cultivation of a new crop would yield a return to the farmer of $1 instead of $2, and the size of the herd which would cause $3 damage with the old crop would cause $1 damage with the new crop, it would be profitable to the cattle-raiser to pay any sum less than $2 to induce the farmer

subdivision of it. Suppose, for example, that the cattle have a well-defined route, say, to a brook or to a shady area. In these circumstances, the amount of damage to the crop along the route may well be great and if so, it could be that the farmer and the cattle-raiser would find it profitable to make a bargain whereby the farmer would agree not to cultivate this strip of land.

But this raises a further possibility. Suppose that there is such a well-defined route. Suppose further that the value of the crop that would be obtained by cultivating this strip of land is $10 but that the cost of cultivation is $11. In the absence of the cattle-raiser, the land would not be cultivated. However, given the presence of the cattle-raiser, it could well be that if the strip was cultivated, the whole crop would be destroyed by the cattle. In which case, the cattle-raiser would be forced to pay $10 to the farmer. It is true that the farmer would lose $1. But the cattle-raiser would lose $10. Clearly this is a situation which is not likely to last indefinitely since neither party would want this to happen. The aim of the farmer would be to induce the cattle-raiser to make a payment in return for an agreement to leave this land uncultivated. The farmer would not be able to obtain a payment greater than the cost of fencing off this piece of land nor so high as to lead the cattle-raiser to abandon the use of the neighbouring property. What payment would in fact be made would depend on the shrewdness of the farmer and the cattle-raiser as bargainers. But as the payment would not be so high as to cause the cattle-raiser to abandon this location and as it would not vary with the size of the herd, such an agreement would not affect the allocation of resources but would merely alter the distribution of income and wealth as between the cattle-raiser and the farmer.

I think it is clear that if the cattle-raiser is liable for damage caused and the pricing system works smoothly, the reduction in the value of production elsewhere will be taken into account in computing the additional cost involved in increasing the size of the herd. This cost will be weighed against the value of the additional meat production and, given perfect competition in the cattle industry, the allocation of resources in cattle-raising will be optimal. What needs to be emphasized is that the fall in the value of production elsewhere which would be taken into account in the costs of the cattle-raiser may well be less than the damage which the cattle would cause to the crops in the ordinary course of events. This is because it is possible, as a result of market transactions, to discontinue cultivation of the land. This is desirable in all

to change his crop (since this would reduce damage liability from $3 to $1) and it would be profitable for the farmer to do so if the amount received was more than $1 (the reduction in his return caused by switching crops). In fact, there would be room for a mutually satisfactory bargain in all cases in which a change of crop would reduce the amount of damage by more than it reduces the value of the crop (excluding damage)—in all cases, that is, in which a change in the crop cultivated would lead to an increase in the value of production.

cases in which the damage that the cattle would cause, and for which the cattle-raiser would be willing to pay, exceeds the amount which the farmer would pay for use of the land. In conditions of perfect competition, the amount which the farmer would pay for the use of the land is equal to the difference between the value of the total production when the factors are employed on this land and the value of the additional product yielded in their next best use (which would be what the farmer would have to pay for the factors). If damage exceeds the amount the farmer would pay for the use of the land, the value of the additional product of the factors employed elsewhere would exceed the value of the total product in this use after damage is taken into account. It follows that it would be desirable to abandon cultivation of the land and to release the factors employed for production elsewhere. A procedure which merely provided for payment for damage to the crop caused by the cattle but which did not allow for the possibility of cultivation being discontinued would result in too small an employment of factors of production in cattle-raising and too large an employment of factors in cultivation of the crop. But given the possibility of market transactions, a situation in which damage to crops exceeded the rent of the land would not endure. Whether the cattle-raiser pays the farmer to leave the land uncultivated or himself rents the land by paying the land-owner an amount slightly greater than the farmer would pay (if the farmer was himself renting the land), the final result would be the same and would maximise the value of production. Even when the farmer is induced to plant crops which it would not be profitable to cultivate for sale on the market, this will be a purely short-term phenomenon and may be expected to lead to an agreement under which the planting will cease. The cattle-raiser will remain in that location and the marginal cost of meat production will be the same as before, thus having no long-run effect on the allocation of resources.

IV. The Pricing System with No Liability for Damage

I now turn to the case in which, although the pricing system is assumed to work smoothly (that is, costlessly), the damaging business is not liable for any of the damage which it causes. This business does not have to make a payment to those damaged by its actions. I propose to show that the allocation of resources will be the same in this case as it was when the damaging business was liable for damage caused. As I showed in the previous case that the allocation of resources was optimal, it will not be necessary to repeat this part of the argument.

I return to the case of the farmer and the cattle-raiser. The farmer would suffer increased damage to his crop as the size of the herd increased. Suppose that the size of the cattle-raiser's herd is 3 steers (and that this is the size of the herd that would be maintained if crop damage was not taken into account). Then the farmer would be willing to pay up to $3 if the cattle-raiser would reduce his herd to 2 steers, up to $5 if the herd were reduced to 1 steer and would pay up to $6 if cattle-raising was abandoned. The cattle-raiser would therefore receive $3 from the farmer if he kept 2 steers instead of 3. This $3 foregone is therefore part of the cost incurred in keeping the third steer. Whether the $3 is a payment which the cattle-raiser has to make if he adds the third steer to his herd (which it would be if the cattle-raiser was liable to the farmer for damage caused to the crop) or whether it is a sum of money which he would have received if he did not keep a third steer (which it would be if the cattle-raiser was not liable to the farmer for damage caused to the crop) does not affect the final result. In both cases $3 is part of the cost of adding a third steer, to be included along with the other costs. If the increase in the value of production in cattle-raising through increasing the size of the herd from 2 to 3 is greater than the additional costs that have to be incurred (including the $3 damage to crops), the size of the herd will be increased. Otherwise, it will not. The size of the herd will be the same whether the cattle-raiser is liable for damage caused to the crop or not.

It may be argued that the assumed starting point—a herd of 3 steers—was arbitrary. And this is true. But the farmer would not wish to pay to avoid crop damage which the cattle-raiser would not be able to cause. For example, the maximum annual payment which the farmer could be induced to pay could not exceed $9, the annual cost of fencing. And the farmer would only be willing to pay this sum if it did not reduce his earnings to a level that would cause him to abandon cultivation of this particular tract of land. Furthermore, the farmer would only be willing to pay this amount if he believed that, in the absence of any payment by him, the size of the herd maintained by the cattle raiser would be 4 or more steers. Let us assume that this is the case. Then the farmer would be willing to pay up to $3 if the cattle raiser would reduce his herd to 3 steers, up to $6 if the herd were reduced to 2 steers, up to $8 if one steer only were kept and up to $9 if cattle-raising were abandoned. It will be noticed that the change in the starting point has not altered the amount which would accrue to the cattle-raiser if he reduced the size of his herd by any given amount. It is still true that the cattle-raiser could receive an additional $3 from the farmer if he agreed to reduce his herd from 3 steers to 2 and that the $3 represents the value of the crop that would be destroyed by adding the third steer to the herd. Although a different belief on the part of the farmer (whether justified or not) about the size of the herd that the cattle-raiser would maintain in the absence of payments from him may affect the total payment he can be induced to pay, it is not true that this different belief would have any effect on the size of the herd that the cattle-raiser will actually keep. This will be the same as it would be if the cattle-raiser had to pay for damage caused by his cattle, since a receipt foregone of a given amount is the equivalent of a payment of the same amount.

It might be thought that it would pay the cattle-raiser to increase his herd above the size that he would wish to maintain once a bargain had been made, in order to induce the farmer to make a larger total payment. And this may be true. It is similar in nature to the action of the farmer (when the cattle-raiser was liable for damage) in cultivating land on which, as a result of an agreement with the cattle-raiser, planting would subsequently be abandoned (including land which would not be cultivated at all in the absence of cattle-raising). But such manoeuvres are preliminaries to an agreement and do not affect the long-run equilibrium position, which is the same whether or not the cattle-raiser is held responsible for the crop damage brought about by his cattle.

It is necessary to know whether the damaging business is liable or not for damage caused since without the establishment of this initial delimitation of rights there can be no market transactions to transfer and recombine them. But the ultimate result (which maximises the value of production) is independent of the legal position if the pricing system is assumed to work without cost.

V. The Problem Illustrated Anew

The harmful effects of the activities of a business can assume a wide variety of forms. An early English case concerned a building which, by obstructing currents of air, hindered the operation of a windmill.[5] A recent case in Florida concerned a building which cast a shadow on the cabana, swimming pool and sunbathing areas of a neighbouring hotel.[6] The problem of straying cattle and the damaging of crops which was the subject of detailed examination in the two preceding sections, although it may have appeared to be rather a special case, is in fact but one example of a problem which arises in many different guises. To clarify the nature of my argument and to demonstrate its general applicability, I propose to illustrate it anew by reference to four actual cases.

Let us first reconsider the case of *Sturges v. Bridgman*[7] which I used as an illustration of the general problem in my article on "The Federal Communications Commission." In this case, a confectioner (in Wigmore Street) used two mortars and pestles in connection with his business (one had been in operation in the same position for more than 60 years and the other for more than 26 years). A doctor then came to occupy neighbouring premises (in Wimpole Street). The confectioner's machinery caused the doctor no harm until, eight years after he had first occupied the premises, he built a consulting room at the end of his garden right against the confectioner's kitchen. It was then found that the noise and vibration caused by the confectioner's machin-

[5] See Gale on Easements 237–39 (13th ed. M. Bowles 1959).

[6] See Fontainebleu Hotel Corp. v. Forty-Five Twenty-Five, Inc., 114 So. 2d 357 (1959).

[7] 11 Ch. D. 852 (1879).

ery made it difficult for the doctor to use his new consulting room. "In particular . . . the noise prevented him from examining his patients by auscultation[8] for diseases of the chest. He also found it impossible to engage with effect in any occupation which required thought and attention." The doctor therefore brought a legal action to force the confectioner to stop using his machinery. The courts had little difficulty in granting the doctor the injunction he sought. "Individual cases of hardship may occur in the strict carrying out of the principle upon which we found our judgment, but the negation of the principle would lead even more to individual hardship, and would at the same time produce a prejudicial effect upon the development of land for residential purposes."

The court's decision established that the doctor had the right to prevent the confectioner from using his machinery. But, of course, it would have been possible to modify the arrangements envisaged in the legal ruling by means of a bargain between the parties. The doctor would have been willing to waive his right and allow the machinery to continue in operation if the confectioner would have paid him a sum of money which was greater than the loss of income which he would suffer from having to move to a more costly or less convenient location or from having to curtail his activities at this location or, as was suggested as a possibility, from having to build a separate wall which would deaden the noise and vibration. The confectioner would have been willing to do this if the amount he would have to pay the doctor was less than the fall in income he would suffer if he had to change his mode of operation at this location, abandon his operation or move his confectionery business to some other location. The solution of the problem depends essentially on whether the continued use of the machinery adds more to the confectioner's income than it subtracts from the doctor's.[9] But now consider the situation if the confectioner had won the case. The confectioner would then have had the right to continue operating his noise and vibration-generating machinery without having to pay anything to the doctor. The boot would have been on the other foot: the doctor would have had to pay the confectioner to induce him to stop using the machinery. If the doctor's income would have fallen more through continuance of the use of this machinery than it added to the income of the confectioner, there would clearly be room for a bargain whereby the doctor paid the confectioner to stop using the machinery. That is to say, the circumstances in which it would not pay the confectioner to continue to use the machinery and to compensate the doctor for the losses that this would bring (if the doctor had the right to prevent the confectioner's using his

[8] Auscultation is the act of listening by ear or stethoscope in order to judge by sound the condition of the body.

[9] Note that what is taken into account is the change in income after allowing for alterations in methods of production, location, character of product, etc.

machinery) would be those in which it would be in the interest of the doctor to make a payment to the confectioner which would induce him to discontinue the use of the machinery (if the confectioner had the right to operate the machinery). The basic conditions are exactly the same in this case as they were in the example of the cattle which destroyed crops. With costless market transactions, the decision of the courts concerning liability for damage would be without effect on the allocation of resources. It was of course the view of the judges that they were affecting the working of the economic system—and in a desirable direction. Any other decision would have had "a prejudicial effect upon the development of land for residential purposes," an argument which was elaborated by examining the example of a forge operating on a barren moor, which was later developed for residual purposes. The judges' view that they were settling how the land was to be used would be true only in the case in which the costs of carrying out the necessary market transactions exceeded the gain which might be achieved by any rearrangement of rights. And it would be desirable to preserve the areas (Wimpole Street or the moor) for residential or professional use (by giving non-industrial users the right to stop the noise, vibration, smoke, etc., by injunction) only if the value of the additional residential facilities obtained was greater than the value of cakes or iron lost. But of this the judges seem to have been unaware.

Another example of the same problem is furnished by the case of *Cooke v. Forbes*.[10] One process in the weaving of cocoa nut fibre matting was to immerse it in bleaching liquids after which it was hung out to dry. Fumes from a manufacturer of sulphate of ammonia had the effect of turning the matting from a bright to a dull and blackish colour. The reason for this was that the bleaching liquid contained chloride of tin, which, when affected by sulphuretted hydrogen, is turned to a darker colour. An injunction was sought to stop the manufacturer from emitting the fumes. The lawyers for the defendant argued that if the plaintiff "were not to use . . . a particular bleaching liquid, their fibre would not be affected; that their process is unusual, not according to the custom of the trade, and even damaging to their own fabrics." The judge commented: ". . . it appears to me quite plain that a person has a right to carry on upon his own property a manufacturing process in which he uses chloride of tin, or any sort of metallic dye, and that his neighbour is not at liberty to pour in gas which will interfere with his manufacture. If it can be traced to the neighbour, then, I apprehend, clearly he will have a right to come here and ask for relief." But in view of the fact that the damage was accidental and occasional, that careful precautions were taken and that there was no exceptional risk, an injunction was refused, leaving the plaintiff to bring an action for damages if he wished. What the subsequent developments

[10] L. R. 5 Eq. 166 (1867–1868).

were I do not know. But it is clear that the situation is essentially the same as that found in *Sturges v. Bridgman*, except that the cocoa-nut fibre matting manufacturer could not secure an injunction but would have to seek damages from the sulphate of ammonia manufacturer. The economic analysis of the situation is exactly the same as with the cattle which destroyed crops. To avoid the damage, the sulphate of ammonia manufacturer could increase his precautions or move to another location. Either course would presumably increase his costs. Alternatively he could pay for the damage. This he would do if the payments for damage were less than the additional costs that would have to be incurred to avoid the damage. The payments for damage would then become part of the cost of production of sulphate of ammonia. Of course, if, as was suggested in the legal proceedings, the amount of damage could be eliminated by changing the bleaching agent (which would presumably increase the costs of the matting manufacturer) and if the additional cost was less than the damage that would otherwise occur, it should be possible for the two manufacturers to make a mutually satisfactory bargain whereby the new bleaching agent was used. Had the court decided against the matting manufacturer, as a consequence of which he would have had to suffer the damage without compensation, the allocation of resources would not have been affected. It would pay the matting manufacturer to change his bleaching agent if the additional cost involved was less than the reduction in damage. And since the matting manufacturer would be willing to pay the sulphate of ammonia manufacturer an amount up to his loss of income (the increase in costs or the damage suffered) if he would cease his activities, this loss of income would remain a cost of production for the manufacturer of sulphate of ammonia. This case is indeed analytically exactly the same as the cattle example.

Bryant v. Lefever[11] raised the problem of the smoke nuisance in a novel form. The plaintiff and the defendants were occupiers of adjoining houses, which were of about the same height.

> Before 1876 the plaintiff was able to light a fire in any room of his house without the chimneys smoking; the two houses had remained in the same condition some thirty or forty years. In 1876 the defendants took down their house, and began to rebuild it. They carried up a wall by the side of the plaintiff's chimneys much beyond its original height, and stacked timber on the roof of their house, and thereby caused the plaintiff's chimneys to smoke whenever he lighted fires.

The reason, of course, why the chimneys smoked was that the erection of the wall and the stacking of the timber prevented the free circulation of air. In a trial before a jury, the plaintiff was awarded damages of £40. The case then went to the Court of Appeals where the judgment was reversed. Bramwell, L.J., argued:

[11] 4 C.P.D. 172 (1878-1879).

. . . it is said, and the jury have found, that the defendants have done that which caused a nuisance to the plaintiff's house. We think there is no evidence of this. No doubt there is a nuisance, but it is not of the defendant's causing. They have done nothing in causing the nuisance. Their house and their timber are harmless enough. It is the plaintiff who causes the nuisance by lighting a coal fire in a place the chimney of which is placed so near the defendants' wall, that the smoke does not escape, but comes into the house. Let the plaintiff cease to light his fire, let him move his chimney, let him carry it higher, and there would be no nuisance. Who then, causes it? It would be very clear that the plaintiff did, if he had built his house or chimney after the defendants had put up the timber on theirs, and it is really the same though he did so before the timber was there. But (what is in truth the same answer), if the defendants cause the nuisance, they have a right to do so. If the plaintiff has not the right to the passage of air, except subject to the defendants' right to build or put timber on their house, then his right is subject to their right, and though a nuisance follows from the exercise of their right, they are not liable.

And Cotton, L.J., said:

Here it is found that the erection of the defendants' wall has sensibly and materially interfered with the comfort of human existence in the plaintiff's house, and it is said this is a nuisance for which the defendants are liable. Ordinarily this is so, but the defendants have done so, not by sending on to the plaintiff's property any smoke or noxious vapour, but by interrupting the egress of smoke from the plaintiff's house in a way to which . . . the plaintiff has no legal right. The plaintiff creates the smoke, which interferes with his comfort. Unless he has . . . a right to get rid of this in a particular way which has been interfered with by the defendants, he cannot sue the defendants, because the smoke made by himself, for which he has not provided any effectual means of escape, causes him annoyance. It is as if a man tried to get rid of liquid filth arising on his own land by a drain into his neighbour's land. Until a right had been acquired by user, the neighbour might stop the drain without incurring liability by so doing. No doubt great inconvenience would be caused to the owner of the property on which the liquid filth arises. But the act of his neighbour would be a lawful act, and he would not be liable for the consequences attributable to the fact that the man had accumulated filth without providing any effectual means of getting rid of it.

I do not propose to show that any subsequent modification of the situation, as a result of bargains between the parties (conditioned by the cost of stacking the timber elsewhere, the cost of extending the chimney higher, etc.), would have exactly the same result whatever decision the courts had come to since this point has already been adequately dealt with in the discussion of the cattle example and the two previous cases. What I shall discuss is the argument of the judges in the Court of Appeals that the smoke nuisance was not caused by the man who erected the wall but by the man who lit the fires. The novelty of the situation is that the smoke nuisance was suffered by the man who lit the fires and not by some third person. The question is not a trivial one since it lies at the heart of the problem under discussion. Who caused the smoke nuisance? The answer seems fairly clear. The smoke nuisance was caused both by the man who built the wall *and* by the man who lit the fires. Given the fires, there would have been no smoke nuisance without the wall; given the wall, there would have been no smoke nuisance without the fires. Eliminate the wall *or* the fires and the smoke nuisance would disappear. On the marginal principle it is clear that *both* were responsible and *both* should be forced to include the loss of amenity due to the smoke as a cost in deciding whether to continue the activity which gives rise to the smoke. And given the possibility of market transactions, this is what would in fact happen. Although the wall-builder was not liable legally for the nuisance, as the man with the smoking chimneys would presumably be willing to pay a sum equal to the monetary worth to him of eliminating the smoke, this sum would therefore become for the wall-builder, a cost of continuing to have the high wall with the timber stacked on the roof.

The judges' contention that it was the man who lit the fires who alone caused the smoke nuisance is true only if we assume that the wall is the given factor. This is what the judges did by deciding that the man who erected the higher wall had a legal right to do so. The case would have been even more interesting if the smoke from the chimneys had injured the timber. Then it would have been the wall-builder who suffered the damage. The case would then have closely paralleled *Sturges v. Bridgman* and there can be little doubt that the man who lit the fires would have been liable for the ensuing damage to the timber, in spite of the fact that no damage had occurred until the high wall was built by the man who owned the timber.

Judges have to decide on legal liability but this should not confuse economists about the nature of the economic problem involved. In the case of the cattle and the crops, it is true that there would be no crop damage without the cattle. It is equally true that there would be no crop damage without the crops. The doctor's work would not have been disturbed if the confectioner had not worked his machinery; but the machinery would have disturbed no one if the doctor had not set up his consulting room in that particular place. The matting was blackened by the fumes from the sulphate of ammonia manufacturer; but no damage would have occurred if the matting manufacturer had not chosen to hang out his matting in a particular place and to use a particular bleaching agent. If we are to discuss the problem in terms of causation, both parties cause the damage. If we are to attain an optimum allocation of resources, it is therefore desirable that both parties should take the harmful effect (the nuisance) into account in deciding on their course of action. It is one of the beauties of a smoothly operating pricing system that, as has already been explained, the fall in the value of production due to the harmful effect would be a cost for both parties.

Bass v. Gregory[12] will serve as an excellent final illustration of the problem. The plaintiffs were the owners and tenant of a public house called the Jolly Anglers. The defendant was the owner of some cottages and a yard adjoining the Jolly Anglers. Under the public house was a cellar excavated in the rock. From the cellar, a hole or shaft had been cut into an old well situated in the defendant's yard. The well therefore became the ventilating shaft for the cellar. The cellar "had been used for a particular purpose in the process of brewing, which, without ventilation, could not be carried on." The cause of the action was that the defendant removed a grating from the mouth of the well, "so as to stop or prevent the free passage of air from [the] cellar upwards through the well. . . ." What caused the defendant to take this step is not clear from the report of the case. Perhaps "the air . . . impregnated by the brewing operations" which "passed up the well and out into the open air" was offensive to him. At any rate, he preferred to have the well in his yard stopped up. The court had first to determine whether the owners of the public house could have a legal right to a current of air. If they were to have such a right, this case would have to be distinguished from *Bryant v. Lefever* (already considered). This, however, presented no difficulty. In this case, the current of air was confined to "a strictly defined channel." In the case of *Bryant v. Lefever,* what was involved was "the general current of air common to all mankind." The judge therefore held that the owners of the public house could have the right to a current of air whereas the owner of the private house in *Bryant v. Lefever* could not. An economist might be tempted to add "but the air moved all the same." However, all that had been decided at this stage of the argument was that there could be a legal right, not that the owners of the public house possessed it. But evidence showed that the shaft from the cellar to the well had existed for over forty years and that the use of the well as a ventilating shaft must have been known to the owners of the yard since the air, when it emerged, smelt of the brewing operations. The judge therefore held that the public house had such a right by the "doctrine of lost grant." This doctrine states "that if a legal right is proved to have existed and been exercised for a number of years the law ought to presume that it had a legal origin."[13] So the owner of the cottages and yard had to unstop the well and endure the smell.

[12] 25 Q.B.D. 481 (1890).

[13] It may be asked why a lost grant could not also be presumed in the case of the confectioner who had operated one mortar for more than 60 years. The answer is that until the doctor built the consulting room at the end of his garden there was no nuisance. So the nuisance had not continued for many years. It is true that the confectioner in his affidavit referred to "an invalid lady who occupied the house upon one occasion, about thirty years before" who "requested him if possible to discontinue the use of the mortars before eight o'clock in the morning" and that there was some evidence that the garden wall had been subjected to vibration. But the court had little difficulty in disposing of this line of argument: ". . . this vibration, even if it existed at all, was so slight, and the com-

The reasoning employed by the courts in determining legal rights will often seem strange to an economist because many of the factors on which the decision turns are, to an economist, irrelevant. Because of this, situations which are, from an economic point of view, identical will be treated quite differently by the courts. The economic problem in all cases of harmful effects is how to maximise the value of production. In the case of *Bass v. Gregory* fresh air was drawn in through the well which facilitated the production of beer but foul air was expelled through the well which made life in the adjoining houses less pleasant. The economic problem was to decide which to choose: a lower cost of beer and worsened amenities in adjoining houses or a higher cost of beer and improved amenities. In deciding this question, the "doctrine of lost grant" is about as relevant as the colour of the judge's eyes. But it has to be remembered that the immediate question faced by the courts is ***not*** what shall be done by whom ***but*** who has the legal right to do what. It is always possible to modify by transactions on the market the initial legal delimitation of rights. And, of course, if such market transactions are costless, such a rearrangement of rights will always take place if it would lead to an increase in the value of production.

VI. The Cost of Market Transactions Taken into Account

The argument has proceeded up to this point on the assumption (explicit in Sections III and IV and tacit in Section V) that there were no costs involved in carrying out market transactions. This is, of course, a very unrealistic assumption. In order to carry out a market transaction it is necessary to discover who it is that one wishes to deal with, to inform people that one wishes to deal and on what terms, to conduct negotiations leading up to a bargain, to draw up the contract, to undertake the inspection needed to make sure that the terms of the contract are being observed, and so on. These operations are often extremely costly, sufficiently costly at any rate to prevent many transactions that would be carried out in a world in which the pricing system worked without cost.

In earlier sections, when dealing with the problem of the rearrangement of legal rights through the market, it was argued that such a rearrangement would be made through the market whenever this would lead to an increase in the value of production. But this assumed costless market transactions. Once the costs of carrying out market transactions are taken into account it is clear that such a rearrangement of rights will only be undertaken when the increase in the value of production consequent upon the rearrangement

plaint, if it can be called a complaint, of the invalid lady . . . was of so trifling a character, that . . . the Defendant's acts would not have given rise to any proceeding either at law or in equity" (11 Ch.D. 863). That is, the confectioner had not committed a nuisance until the doctor built his consulting room.

is greater than the costs which would be involved in bringing it about. When it is less, the granting of an injunction (or the knowledge that it would be granted) or the liability to pay damages may result in an activity being discontinued (or may prevent its being started) which would be undertaken if market transactions were costless. In these conditions the initial delimitation of legal rights does have an effect on the efficiency with which the economic system operates. One arrangement of rights may bring about a greater value of production than any other. But unless this is the arrangement of rights established by the legal system, the costs of reaching the same result by altering and combining rights through the market may be so great that this optimal arrangement of rights, and the greater value of production which it would bring, may never be achieved. The part played by economic considerations in the process of delimiting legal rights will be discussed in the next section. In this section, I will take the initial delimitation of rights and the costs of carrying out market transactions as given.

It is clear that an alternative form of economic organisation which could achieve the same result at less cost than would be incurred by using the market would enable the value of production to be raised. As I explained many years ago, the firm represents such an alternative to organising production through market transactions.[14] Within the firm individual bargains between the various cooperating factors of production are eliminated and for a market transaction is substituted an administrative decision. The rearrangement of production then takes place without the need for bargains between the owners of the factors of production. A landowner who has control of a large tract of land may devote his land to various uses taking into account the effect that the interrelations of the various activities will have on the net return of the land, thus rendering unnecessary bargains between those undertaking the various activities. Owners of a large building or of several adjoining properties in a given area may act in much the same way. In effect, using our earlier terminology, the firm would acquire the legal rights of all the parties and the rearrangement of activities would not follow on a rearrangement of rights by contract, but as a result of an administrative decision as to how the rights should be used.

It does not, of course, follow that the administrative costs of organising a transaction through a firm are inevitably less than the costs of the market transactions which are superseded. But where contracts are peculiarly difficult to draw up and an attempt to describe what the parties have agreed to do or not to do (e.g. the amount and kind of a smell or noise that they may make or will not make) would necessitate a lengthy and highly involved document, and, where, as is probable, a long-term contract would be desir-

[14] See Coase, The Nature of the Firm, 4 Economica, New Series, 386 (1937). Reprinted in Readings in Price Theory, 331 (1952).

able;[15] it would be hardly surprising if the emergence of a firm or the extension of the activities of an existing firm was not the solution adopted on many occasions to deal with the problem of harmful effects. This solution would be adopted whenever the administrative costs of the firm were less than the costs of the market transactions that it supersedes and the gains which would result from the rearrangement of activities greater than the firm's costs of organising them. I do not need to examine in great detail the character of this solution since I have explained what is involved in my earlier article.

But the firm is not the only possible answer to this problem. The administrative costs of organising transactions within the firm may also be high, and particularly so when many diverse activities are brought within the control of a single organisation. In the standard case of a smoke nuisance, which may affect a vast number of people engaged in a wide variety of activities, the administrative costs might well be so high as to make any attempt to deal with the problem within the confines of a single firm impossible. An alternative solution is direct Government regulation. Instead of instituting a legal system of rights which can be modified by transactions on the market, the government may impose regulations which state what people must or must not do and which have to be obeyed. Thus, the government (by statute or perhaps more likely through an administrative agency) may, to deal with the problem of smoke nuisance, decree that certain methods of production should or should not be used (e.g. that smoke preventing devices should be installed or that coal or oil should not be burned) or may confine certain types of business to certain districts (zoning regulations).

The government is, in a sense, a super-firm (but of a very special kind) since it is able to influence the use of factors of production by administrative decision. But the ordinary firm is subject to checks in its operations because of the competition of other firms, which might administer the same activities at lower cost and also because there is always the alternative of market transactions as against organisation within the firm if the administrative costs become too great. The government is able, if it wishes, to avoid the market altogether, which a firm can never do. The firm has to make market agreements with the owners of the factors of production that it uses. Just as the government can conscript or seize property, so it can decree that factors of production should only be used in such-and-such a way. Such authoritarian methods save a lot of trouble (for those doing the organising). Furthermore, the government has at its disposal the police and the other law enforcement agencies to make sure that its regulations are carried out.

It is clear that the government has powers which might enable it to get some things done at a lower cost than could a private organisation (or at any

[15] For reasons explained in my earlier article, see Readings in Price Theory, n. 14 at 337.

rate one without special governmental powers). But the governmental administrative machine is not itself costless. It can, in fact, on occasion be extremely costly. Furthermore, there is no reason to suppose that the restrictive and zoning regulations, made by a fallible administration subject to political pressures and operating without any competitive check, will necessarily always be those which increase the efficiency with which the economic system operates. Furthermore, such general regulations which must apply to a wide variety of cases will be enforced in some cases in which they are clearly inappropriate. From these considerations it follows that direct governmental regulation will not necessarily give better results than leaving the problem to be solved by the market or the firm. But equally there is no reason why, on occasion, such governmental administrative regulation should not lead to an improvement in economic efficiency. This would seem particularly likely when, as is normally the case with the smoke nuisance, a large number of people are involved and in which therefore the costs of handling the problem through the market or the firm may be high.

There is, of course, a further alternative, which is to do nothing about the problem at all. And given that the costs involved in solving the problem by regulations issued by the governmental administrative machine will often be heavy (particularly if the costs are interpreted to include all the consequences which follow from the Government engaging in this kind of activity), it will no doubt be commonly the case that the gain which would come from regulating the actions which give rise to the harmful effects will be less than the costs involved in Government regulation.

The discussion of the problem of harmful effects in this section (when the costs of market transactions are taken into account) is extremely inadequate. But at least it has made clear that the problem is one of choosing the appropriate social arrangement for dealing with the harmful effects. All solutions have costs and there is no reason to suppose that government regulation is called for simply because the problem is not well handled by the market or the firm. Satisfactory views on policy can only come from a patient study of how, in practice, the market, firms and governments handle the problem of harmful effects. Economists need to study the work of the broker in bringing parties together, the effectiveness of restrictive covenants, the problems of the large-scale real-estate development company, the operation of Government zoning and other regulating activities. It is my belief that economists, and policy-makers generally, have tended to over-estimate the advantages which come from governmental regulation. But this belief, even if justified, does not do more than suggest that government regulation should be curtailed. It does not tell us where the boundary line should be drawn. This, it seems to me, has to come from a detailed investigation of the actual results of handling the problem in different ways. But it would be unfortunate if this investigation were undertaken with the aid of a faulty economic analysis. The aim of this article is to indicate what the economic approach to the problem should be.

VII. The Legal Delimitation of Rights and the Economic Problem

The discussion in Section V not only served to illustrate the argument but also afforded a glimpse at the legal approach to the problem of harmful effects. The cases considered were all English but a similar selection of American cases could easily be made and the character of the reasoning would have been the same. Of course, if market transactions were costless, all that matters (questions of equity apart) is that the rights of the various parties should be well-defined and the results of legal actions easy to forecast. But as we have seen, the situation is quite different when market transactions are so costly as to make it difficult to change the arrangement of rights established by the law. In such cases, the courts directly influence economic activity. It would therefore seem desirable that the courts should understand the economic consequences of their decisions and should, insofar as this is possible without creating too much uncertainty about the legal position itself, take these consequences into account when making their decisions. Even when it is possible to change the legal delimitation of rights through market transactions, it is obviously desirable to reduce the need for such transactions and thus reduce the employment of resources in carrying them out.

A thorough examination of the presuppositions of the courts in trying such cases would be of great interest but I have not been able to attempt it. Nevertheless it is clear from a cursory study that the courts have often recognized the economic implications of their decisions and are aware (as many economists are not) of the reciprocal nature of the problem. Furthermore, from time to time, they take these economic implications into account, along with other factors, in arriving at their decisions. The American writers on this subject refer to the question in a more explicit fashion than do the British. Thus, to quote Prosser on Torts, a person may

> make use of his own property or . . . conduct his own affairs at the expense of some harm to his neighbors. He may operate a factory whose noise and smoke cause some discomfort to others, so long as he keeps within reasonable bounds. It is only when his conduct is unreasonable, *in the light of its utility and the harm which results* [italics added], that it becomes a nuisance. . . . . As it was said in an ancient case in regard to candle-making in a town, "Le utility del chose excusera le noisomeness del stink."
>
> The world must have factories, smelters, oil refineries, noisy machinery and blasting, even at the expense of some inconvenience to those in the vicinity and the

plaintiff may be required to accept some not unreasonable discomfort for the general good.[16]

The standard British writers do not state as explicitly as this that a comparison between the utility and harm produced is an element in deciding whether a harmful effect should be considered a nuisance. But similar views, if less strongly expressed, are to be found.[17] The doctrine that the harmful effect must be substantial before the court will act is, no doubt, in part a reflection of the fact that there will almost always be some gain to offset the harm. And in the reports of individual cases, it is clear that the judges have had in mind what would be lost as well as what would be gained in deciding whether to grant an injunction or award damages. Thus, in refusing to prevent the destruction of a prospect by a new building, the judge stated:

> I know no general rule of common law, which . . . says, that building so as to stop another's prospect is a nuisance. Was that the case, there could be no great towns; and I must grant injunctions to all the new buildings in this town. . . .[18]

In *Webb v. Bird*[19] it was decided that it was not a nuisance to build a schoolhouse so near a windmill as to obstruct currents of air and hinder the working of the mill. An early case seems to have been decided in an opposite direction. Gale commented:

> In old maps of London a row of windmills appears on the heights to the north of London. Probably in the time of King James it was thought an alarming circumstance, as affecting the supply of food to the city, that anyone should build so near them as to take the wind out from their sails.[20]

In one of the cases discussed in section V, *Sturges v. Bridgman,* it seems clear that the judges were thinking of the economic consequences of alternative decisions. To the argument that if the principle that they seemed to be following

[16] See W. L. Prosser, The Law of Torts 398–99, 412 (2d ed. 1955). The quotation about the ancient case concerning candle-making is taken from Sir James Fitzjames Stephen, A General View of the Criminal Law of England 106 (1890). Sir James Stephen gives no reference. He perhaps had in mind *Rex. v. Ronkett,* included in Seavey, Keeton and Thurston, Cases on Torts 604 (1950). A similar view to that expressed by Prosser is to be found in F. V. Harper and F. James, The Law of Torts 67–74 (1956); Restatement, Torts §§826, 827 and 828.

[17] See Winfield on Torts 541–48 (6th ed. T. E. Lewis 1954); Salmond on the Law of Torts 181–90 (12th ed. R.F.V. Heuston 1957); H. Street, The Law of Torts 221–29 (1959).

[18] Attorney General v. Doughty, 2 Ves. Sen. 453, 28 Eng. Rep. 290 (Ch. 1752). Compare in this connection the statement of an American judge, quoted in Prosser, op. cit. supra n. 16 at 413 n. 54: "Without smoke, Pittsburgh would have remained a very pretty village," Musmanno, J., in Versailles Borough v. McKeesport Coal & Coke Co., 1935, 83 Pitts. Leg. J. 379, 385.

[19] 10 C.B. (N.S.) 268, 142 Eng. Rep. 445 (1861); 13 C.B. (N.S.) 841, 143 Eng. Rep. 332 (1863).

[20] See Gale on Easements 238, n. 6 (13th ed. M. Bowles 1959).

were carried out to its logical consequences, it would result in the most serious practical inconveniences, for a man might go—say into the midst of the tanneries of *Bermondsey*, or into any other locality devoted to any particular trade or manufacture of a noisy or unsavoury character, and by building a private residence upon a vacant piece of land put a stop to such trade or manufacture altogether,

the judges answered that

whether anything is a nuisance or not is a question to be determined, not merely by an abstract consideration of the thing itself, but in reference to its circumstances; What would be a nuisance in *Belgrave Square* would not necessarily be so in *Bermondsey;* and where a locality is devoted to a particular trade or manufacture carried on by the traders or manufacturers in a particular and established manner not constituting a public nuisance, Judges and juries would be justified in finding, and may be trusted to find, that the trade or manufacture so carried on in that locality is not a private or actionable wrong.[21]

That the character of the neighborhood is relevant in deciding whether something is, or is not, a nuisance, is definitely established.

He who dislikes the noise of traffic must not set up his abode in the heart of a great city. He who loves peace and quiet must not live in a locality devoted to the business of making boilers or steamships.[22]

What has emerged has been described as "planning and zoning by the judiciary."[23] Of course there are sometimes considerable difficulties in applying the criteria.[24]

An interesting example of the problem is found in *Adams v. Ursell*[25] in which a fried fish shop in a predominantly working-class district was set up near houses of "a much better character." England without fish-and-chips is a contradiction in terms and the case was clearly one of high importance. The judge commented:

It was urged that an injunction would cause great hardship to the defendant and to the poor people who get food at his shop. The answer to that is that it does not follow that the defendant cannot carry on his business in another more suitable place somewhere in the neighbourhood. It by no means follows that because a fried fish shop is a nuisance in one place it is a nuisance in another.

In fact, the injunction which restrained Mr. Ursell from running his shop did not even extend to the whole street. So he was presumably able to move to other premises near houses of "a much worse character," the inhabitants

[21] 11 Ch.D. 865 (1879).

[22] Salmond on the Law of Torts 182 (12th ed. R.F.V. Heuston 1957).

[23] C. M. Haar, Land-Use Planning, A Casebook on the Use, Misuse, and Re-use of Urban Land 95 (1959).

[24] See, for example, Rushmer v. Polsue and Alfieri, Ltd. [1906] 1 Ch. 234, which deals with the case of a house in a quiet situation in a noisy district.

[25] [1913] 1 Ch. 269.

of which would no doubt consider the availability of fish-and-chips to outweigh the pervading odour and "fog or mist" so graphically described by the plaintiff. Had there been no other "more suitable place in the neighbourhood," the case would have been more difficult and the decision might have been different. What would "the poor people" have had for food? No English judge would have said: "Let them eat cake."

The courts do not always refer very clearly to the economic problem posed by the cases brought before them but it seems probable that in the interpretation of words and phrases like "reasonable" or "common or ordinary use" there is some recognition, perhaps largely unconscious and certainly not very explicit, of the economic aspects of the questions at issue. A good example of this would seem to be the judgment in the Court of Appeals in *Andreae v. Selfridge and Company Ltd.*[26] In this case, a hotel (in Wigmore Street) was situated on part of an island site. The remainder of the site was acquired by Selfridges which demolished the existing buildings in order to erect another in their place. The hotel suffered a loss of custom in consequence of the noise and dust caused by the demolition. The owner of the hotel brought an action against Selfridges for damages. In the lower court, the hotel was awarded £4,500 damages. The case was then taken on appeal.

The judge who had found for the hotel proprietor in the lower court said:

> I cannot regard what the defendants did on the site of the first operation as having been commonly done in the ordinary use and occupation of land or houses. It is neither usual nor common, in this country, for people to excavate a site to a depth of 60 feet and then to erect upon that site a steel framework and fasten the steel frames together with rivets. . . . Nor is it, I think, a common or ordinary use of land, in this country, to act as the defendants did when they were dealing with the site of their second operation—namely, to demolish all the houses that they had to demolish, five or six of them I think, if not more, and to use for the purpose of demolishing them pneumatic hammers.

Sir Wilfred Greene, M.R., speaking for the Court of Appeals, first noted

> that when one is dealing with temporary operations, such as demolition and re-building, everybody has to put up with a certain amount of discomfort, because operations of that kind cannot be carried on at all without a certain amount of noise and a certain amount of dust. Therefore, the rule with regard to interference must be read subject to this qualification. . . .

He then referred to the previous judgment:

> With great respect to the learned judge, I take the view that he has not approached this matter from the correct angle. It seems to me that it is not possible to say . . . that the type of demolition, excavation and construction in which the defendant company was engaged in the course of these operations was of such an abnormal and unusual nature as to prevent the qualification to which I have referred coming

[26] [1938] 1 Ch. 1.

into operation. It seems to me that, when the rule speaks of the common or ordinary use of land, it does not mean that the methods of using land and building on it are in some way to be stabilised for ever. As time goes on new inventions or new methods enable land to be more profitably used, either by digging down into the earth or by mounting up into the skies. Whether, from other points of view, that is a matter which is desirable for humanity is neither here nor there; but it is part of the normal use of land, to make use upon your land, in the matter of construction, of what particular type and what particular depth of foundations and particular height of building may be reasonable, in the circumstances, and in view of the developments of the day. . . . Guests at hotels are very easily upset. People coming to this hotel, who were accustomed to a quiet outlook at the back, coming back and finding demolition and building going on, may very well have taken the view that the particular merit of this hotel no longer existed. That would be a misfortune for the plaintiff; but assuming that there was nothing wrong in the defendant company's works, assuming the defendant company was carrying on the demolition and its building, productive of noise though it might be, with all reasonable skill, and taking all reasonable precautions not to cause annoyance to its neighbors, then the planitiff might lose all her clients in the hotel because they have lost the amenities of an open and quiet place behind, but she would have no cause of complaint. . . . [But those] who say that their interference with the comfort of their neighbors is justified because their operations are normal and usual and conducted with proper care and skill are under a specific duty . . . to use that reasonable and proper care and skill. It is not a correct attitude to take to say: 'We will go on and do what we like until somebody complains!' . . . Their duty is to take proper precautions and to see that the nuisance is reduced to a minimum. It is no answer for them to say: 'But this would mean that we should have to do the work more slowly than we would like to do it, or it would involve putting us to some extra expense.' All these questions are matters of common sense and degree, and quite clearly it would be unreasonable to expect people to conduct their work so slowly or so expensively, for the purpose of preventing a transient inconvenience, that the cost and trouble would be prohibitive. . . . In this case, the defendant company's attitude seems to have been to go on until somebody complained, and, further, that its desire to hurry its work and conduct it according to its own ideas and its own convenience was to prevail if there was a real conflict between it and the comfort of its neighbors. That . . . is not carrying out the obligation of using reasonable care and skill. . . . The effect comes to this . . . the plaintiff suffered an actionable nuisance; . . . she is entitled, not to a nominal sum, but to a substantial sum, based upon those principles . . . but in arriving at the sum . . . I have discounted any loss of custom . . . which might be due to the general loss of amenities owing to what was going on at the back. . . .

The upshot was that the damages awarded were reduced from £4,500 to £1,000.

The discussion in this section has, up to this point, been concerned with court decisions arising out of the common law relating to nuisance. Delimitation of rights in this area also comes about because of statutory enactments. Most economists would appear to assume that the aim of governmental action in this field is to extend the scope of the law of nuisance by designating as nuisances activities which would not be recognized as such by the common law. And there can be no doubt that some statutes, for example, the Public Health Acts, have had this effect. But not all Government enactments are of this kind. The effect of much of the legislation in this area is to protect businesses from the claims of those they have harmed by their actions. There is a long list of legalized nuisances.

The position has been summarized in *Halsbury's Laws of England* as follows:

> Where the legislature directs that a thing shall in all events be done or authorises certain works at a particular place for a specific purposes or grants powers with the intention that they shall be exercised, although leaving some discretion as to the mode of exercise, no action will lie at common law for nuisance or damage which is the inevitable result of carrying out the statutory powers so conferred. This is so whether the act causing the damage is authorised for public purposes or private profit. Acts done under powers granted by persons to whom Parliament has delegated authority to grant such powers, for example, under provisional orders of the Board of Trade, are regarded as having been done under statutory authority. In the absence of negligence it seems that a body exercising statutory powers will not be liable to an action merely because it might, by acting in a different way, have minimised an injury.

Instances are next given of freedom from liability for acts authorized:

> An action has been held not to be against a body exercising its statutory powers without negligence in respect of the flooding of land by water escaping from watercourses, from water pipes, from drains, or from a canal; the escape of fumes from sewers; the escape of sewage: the subsidence of a road over a sewer; vibration or noise caused by a railway; fires caused by authorised acts; the pollution of a stream where statutory requirements to use the best known method of purifying before discharging the effluent have been satisfied; interference with a telephone or telegraph system by an elctric tramway; the insertion of poles for tramways in the subsoil; annoyance caused by things reasonably necessary for the excavation of authorised works; accidental damage caused by the placing of a grating in a roadway; the escape of tar acid; or interference with the access of a frontager by a street shelter or safety railings on the edge of a pavement.[27]

The legal position in the United States would seem to be essentially the same as in England, except that the power of the legislatures to authorize what would otherwise be nuisances under the common law, at least without giving compensation to the person harmed, is somewhat more limited, as it is subject to constitutional restrictions.[28] Nonetheless, the power is there and cases more or less identical with the English cases can be found. The

[27] See 30 Halsbury, Law of England 690–91 (3d ed. 1960), Article on Public Authorities and Public Officers.

[28] See Prosser, op. cit. supra n. 16 at 421; Harper and James, op. cit. supra n. 16 at 86–87.

question has arisen in an acute form in connection with airports and the operation of aeroplanes. The case of *Delta Air Corporation v. Kersey, Kersey v. City of Atlanta*[29] is a good example. Mr. Kersey bought land and built a house on it. Some years later the City of Atlanta constructed an airport on land immediately adjoining that of Mr. Kersey. It was explained that his property was "a quiet, peaceful and proper location for a home before the airport was built, but dust, noises and low flying of airplanes caused by the operation of the airport have rendered his property unsuitable as a home," a state of affairs which was described in the report of the case with a wealth of distressing detail. The judge first referred to an earlier case, *Thrasher v. City of Atlanta*[30] in which it was noted that the City of Atlanta had been expressly authorized to operate an airport.

> By this franchise aviation was recognised as a lawful business and also as an enterprise affected with a public interest . . . all persons using [the airport] in the manner contemplated by law are within the protection and immunity of the franchise granted by the municipality. An airport is not a nuisance per se, although it might become such from the manner of its construction or operation.

Since aviation was a lawful business affected with a public interest and the construction of the airport was authorized by statute, the judge next referred to *Georgia Railroad and Banking Co. v. Maddox*[31] in which it was said:

> Where a railroad terminal yard is located and its construction authorized, under statutory powers, if it be constructed and operated in a proper manner, it cannot be adjudged a nuisance. Accordingly, injuries and inconveniences to persons residing near such a yard, from noises of locomotives, rumbling of cars, vibrations produced thereby, and smoke, cinders, soot and the like, which result from the ordinary and necessary, therefore proper, use and operation of such a yard, are not nuisances, but are the necessary concomitants of the franchise granted.

In view of this, the judge decided that the noise and dust complained of by Mr. Kersey "may be deemed to be incidental to the proper operation of an airport, and as such they cannot be said to constitute a nuisance." But the complaint against low flying was different:

> . . . can it be said that flights . . . at such a low height [25 to 50 feet above Mr. Kersey's house] as to be imminently dangerous to . . . life and health . . . are a necessary concomitant of an airport? We do not think this question can be answered in the affirmative. No reason appears why the city could not obtain lands of an area [sufficiently large] . . . as not to require such low flights. . . . For the sake of public convenience adjoining-property owners must suffer such inconvenience from noise and dust as result from the usual and proper operation of an airport, but their private rights are entitled to preference in the eyes of the law where the inconvenience is not one demanded by a properly constructed and operated airport.

[29] Supreme Court of Georgia. 193 Ga. 862, 20 S.E. 2d 245 (1942).

[30] 178 Ga. 514, 173 S.E. 817 (1934).

[31] 116 Ga. 64, 42 S.E. 315 (1902).

Of course this assumed that the City of Atlanta could prevent the low flying and continue to operate the airport. The judge therefore added:

> From all that appears, the conditions causing the low flying may be remedied; but if on the trial it should appear that it is indispensable to the public interest that the airport should continue to be operated in its present condition, it may be said that the petitioner should be denied injunctive relief.

In the course of another aviation case, *Smith v. New England Aircraft Co.*,[32] the court surveyed the law in the United States regarding the legalizing of nuisances and it is apparent that, in the broad, it is very similar to that found in England:

> It is the proper function of the legislative department of government in the exercise of the police power to consider the problems and risks that arise from the use of new inventions and endeavor to adjust private rights and harmonize conflicting interests by comprehensive statutes for the public welfare. . . . There are . . . analogies where the invasion of the airspace over underlying land by noise, smoke, vibration, dust and disagreeable odors, having been authorized by the legislative department of government and not being in effect a condemnation of the property although in some measure depreciating its market value, must be borne by the landowner without compensation or remedy. Legislative sanction makes that lawful which otherwise might be a nuisance. Examples of this are damages to adjacent land arising from smoke, vibration and noise in the operation of a railroad . . . ; the noise of ringing factory bells . . . ; the abatement of nuisances . . . ; the erection of steam engines and furnaces . . . ; unpleasant odors connected with sewers, oil refining and storage of naphtha. . . .

Most economists seem to be unaware of all this. When they are prevented from sleeping at night by the roar of jet planes overhead (publicly authorized and perhaps publicly operated), are unable to think (or rest) in the day because of the noise and vibration from passing trains (publicly authorized and perhaps publicly operated), find it difficult to breathe because of the odour from a local sewage farm (publicly authorized and perhaps publicly operated) and are unable to escape because their driveways are blocked by a road obstruction (without any doubt, publicly devised), their nerves frayed and mental balance disturbed, they proceed to declaim about the disadvantages of private enterprise and the need for Government regulation.

While most economists seem to be under a misapprehension concerning the character of the situation with which they are dealing, it is also the case that the activities which they would like to see stopped or curtailed may well be socially justified. It is all a question of weighing up the gains that would accrue from eliminating these harmful effects against the gains that accrue from allowing them to continue. Of course, it is likely that an extension of Government economic activity will often lead to this protection against

[32] 270 Mass. 511, 523, 170 N.E. 385, 390 (1930).

action for nuisance being pushed further than is desirable. For one thing, the Government is likely to look with a benevolent eye on enterprises which it is itself promoting. For another, it is possible to describe the committing of a nuisance by public enterprise in a much more pleasant way than when the same thing is done by private enterprise. In the words of Lord Justice Sir Alfred Denning:

> . . . the significance of the social revolution of today is that, whereas in the past the balance was much too heavily in favor of the rights of property and freedom of contract, Parliament has repeatedly intervened so as to give the public good its proper place.[33]

There can be little doubt that the Welfare State is likely to bring an extension of that immunity from liability for damage, which economists have been in the habit of condemning (although they have tended to assume that this immunity was a sign of too little Government intervention in the economic system). For example, in Britain, the powers of local authorities are regarded as being either absolute or conditional. In the first category, the local authority has no discretion in exercising the power conferred on it. "The absolute power may be said to cover all the necessary consequences of its direct operation even if such consequences amount to nuisance." On the other hand, a conditional power may only be exercised in such a way that the consequences do not constitute a nuisance.

> It is the intention of the legislature which determines whether a power is absolute or conditional. . . . [As] there is the possibility that the social policy of the legislature may change from time to time, a power which in one era would be construed as being conditional, might in another era be interpreted as being absolute in order to further the policy of the Welfare State. This point is one which should be borne in mind when considering some of the older cases upon this aspect of the law of nuisance.[34]

It would seem desirable to summarize the burden of this long section. The problem which we face in dealing with actions which have harmful effects is not simply one of restraining those responsible for them. What has to be decided is whether the gain from preventing the harm is greater than the loss which would be suffered elsewhere as a result of stopping the action which produces the harm. In a world in which there are costs of rearranging the rights established by the legal system, the courts, in cases relating to nuisance, are, in effect, making a decision on the economic problem and determining how resources are to be employed. It was argued that the courts are conscious of this and that they often make, although not always in a very explicit fashion, a comparison between what would be gained and what lost by preventing

[33] See Sir Alfred Denning, Freedom Under the Law 71 (1949).

[34] M. B. Cairns, The Law of Tort in Local Government 28–32 (1954).

actions which have harmful effects. But the delimitation of rights is also the result of statutory enactments. Here we also find evidence of an appreciation of the reciprocal nature of the problem. While statutory enactments add to the list of nuisances, action is also taken to legalize what would otherwise be nuisances under the common law. The kind of situation which economists are prone to consider as requiring corrective Government action is, in fact, often the result of Government action. Such action is not necessarily unwise. But there is a real danger that extensive Government intervention in the economic system may lead to the protection of those responsible for harmful effects being carried too far.

VIII. Pigou's Treatment in "The Economics of Welfare"

The fountainhead for the modern economic analysis of the problem discussed in this article is Pigou's *Economics of Welfare* and, in particular, that section of Part II which deals with divergences between social and private net products which come about because

> one person A, in the course of rendering some service, for which payment is made, to a second person B, incidentally also renders services or disservices to other persons (not producers of like services), of such a sort that payment cannot be exacted from the benefited parties or compensation enforced on behalf of the injured parties.[35]

Pigou tells us that his aim in Part II of *The Economics of Welfare* is

> to ascertain how far the free play of self-interest, acting under the existing legal system, tends to distribute the country's resources in the way most favorable to the production of a large national dividend, and how far it is feasible for State action to improve upon 'natural' tendencies.[36]

To judge from the first part of this statement, Pigou's purpose is to discover whether any improvements could be made in the existing arrangements which determine the use of resources. Since Pigou's conclusion is that improvements could be made, one might have expected him to continue by saying that he proposed to set out the changes required to bring them about. Instead, Pigou adds a phrase which contrasts "natural" tendencies with State action, which seems in some sense to equate the present arrangements with "natural" tendencies and to imply that what is required to bring about these improvements is State action (if feasible). That this is more or less Pigou's position is evident from Chapter I of Part II.[37] Pigou starts by referring to "optimistic

[35] A. C. Pigou, The Economics of Welfare 183 (4th ed. 1932). My references will all be to the fourth edition but the argument and examples examined in this article remained substantially unchanged from the first edition in 1920 to the fourth in 1932. A large part (but not all) of this analysis had appeared previously in Wealth and Welfare (1912).

[36] *Id.* at xii.

[37] *Id.* at 127–30.

followers of the classical economists"[38] who have argued that the value of production would be maximised if the Government refrained from any interference in the economic system and the economic arrangements were those which came about "naturally." Pigou goes on to say that if self-interest does promote economic welfare, it is because human institutions have been devised to make it so. (This part of Pigou's argument, which he develops with the aid of a quotation from Cannan, seems to me to be essentially correct.) Pigou concludes:

> But even in the most advanced States there are failures and imperfections. . . . there are many obstacles that prevent a community's resources from being distributed . . . in the most efficient way. The study of these constitutes our present problem. . . . its purposes is essentially practical. It seeks to bring into clearer light some of the ways in which it now is, or eventually may become, feasible for governments to control the play of economic forces in such wise as to promote the economic welfare, and through that, the total welfare, of their citizens as a whole.[39]

Pigou's underlying thought would appear to be: Some have argued that no State action is needed. But the system has performed as well as it has because of State action. Nonetheless, there are still imperfections. What additional State action is required?

If this is a correct summary of Pigou's position, its inadequacy can be demonstrated by examining the first example he gives of a divergence between private and social products.

> It might happen . . . that costs are thrown upon people not directly concerned, through, say, uncompensated damage done to surrounding woods by sparks from railway engines. All such effects must be included—some of them will be positive, others negative elements—in reckoning up the social net product of the marginal increment of any volume of resources turned into any use or place.[40]

The example used by Pigou refers to a real situation. In Britain, a railway does not normally have to compensate those who suffer damage by fire caused by sparks from an engine. Taken in conjunction with what he says in Chapter 9 of Part II, I take Pigou's policy recommendations to be, first, that there should be State action to correct this "natural" situation and, second, that the railways should be forced to compensate those whose woods are burnt. If this is a correct interpretation of Pigou's position, I would argue that the first recommendation is based on a misapprehension of the facts and that the second is not necessarily desirable.

[38] In Wealth and Welfare, Pigou attributes the "optimism" to Adam Smith himself and not to his followers. He there refers to the "highly optimistic theory of Adam Smith that the national dividend, in given circumstances of demand and supply, tends 'naturally' to a maximum" (p. 104).

[39] Pigou, op. cit. supra n. 35 at 129–30.

[40] *Id.* at 134.

Let us consider the legal position. Under the heading "Sparks from engines." we find the following in Halsbury's Laws of England:

> If railway undertakers use steam engines on their railway without express statutory authority to do so, they are liable, irrespective of any negligence on their part, for fires caused by sparks from engines. Railway undertakers are, however, generally given statutory authority to use steam engines on their railway; accordingly, if an engine is constructed with the precautions which science suggests against fire and is used without negligence, they are not responsible at common law for any damage which may be done by sparks. . . . In the construction of an engine the undertaker is bound to use all the discoveries which science has put within its reach in order to avoid doing harm, provided they are such as it is reasonable to require the company to adopt, having proper regard to the likelihood of the damage and to the cost and convenience of the remedy; but it is not negligence on the part of an undertaker if it refuses to use an apparatus the efficiency of which is open to bona fide doubt.

To this general rule, there is a statutory exception arising from the Railway (Fires) Act, 1905, as amended in 1923. This concerns agricultural land or agricultural crops.

> In such a case the fact that the engine was used under statutory powers does not affect the liability of the company in an action for the damage. . . . These provisions, however, only apply where the claim for damage . . . does not exceed £ 200, [£ 100 in the 1905 Act] and where written notice of the occurrence of the fire and the intention to claim has been sent to the company within seven days of the occurrence of the damage and particulars of the damage in writing showing the amount of the claim in money not exceeding £ 200 have been sent to the company within twenty-one days.

Agricultural land does not include moorland or buildings and agricultural crops do not include those led away or stacked.[41] I have not made a close study of the parliamentary history of this statutory exception, but to judge from debates in the House of Commons in 1922 and 1923, this exception was probably designed to help the smallholder.[42]

Let us return to Pigou's example of uncompensated damage to surrounding woods caused by sparks from railway engines. This is presumably intended to show how it is possible "for State action to improve on 'natural' tendencies." If we treat Pigou's example as referring to the position before 1905, or as being an arbitrary example (in that he might just as well have written "surrounding buildings" instead of "surrounding woods"), then it is clear that the reason why compensation was not paid must have been that the railway had statutory authority to run steam engines (which relieved it of liability for fires caused by sparks). That this was the legal position was

[41] See 31 Halsbury, Laws of England 474–75 (3d ed. 1960), Article on Railways and Canals, from which this summary of the legal position, and all quotations, are taken.

[42] See 152 H.C. Deb. 2622–63 (1922); 161 H.C. Deb. 2935–55 (1923).

established in 1860, in a case, oddly enough, which concerned the burning of surrounding woods by a railway,[43] and the law on this point has not been changed (apart from the one exception) by a century of railway legislation, including nationalisation. If we treat Pigou's example of "uncompensated damage done to surrounding woods by sparks from railway engines" literally, and assume that it refers to the period after 1905, then it is clear that the reason why compensation was not paid must have been that the damage was more than £100 (in the first edition of *The Economics of Welfare*) or more than £200 (in later editions) or that the owner of the wood failed to notify the railway in writing within seven days of the fire or did not send particulars of the damage, in writing, within twenty-one days. In the real world, Pigou's example could only exist as a result of a deliberate choice of the legislature. It is not, of course, easy to imagine the construction of a railway in a state of nature. The nearest one can get to this is presumably a railway which uses steam engines "without express statutory authority." However, in this case the railway would be obliged to compensate those whose woods it burnt down. That is to say, compensation would be paid in the absence of Government action. The only circumstances in which compensation would not be paid would be those in which there had been Government action. It is strange that Pigou, who clearly thought it desirable that compensation should be paid, should have chosen this particular example to demonstrate how it is possible "for State action to improve on 'natural' tendencies."

Pigou seems to have had a faulty view of the facts of the situation. But it also seems likely that he was mistaken in his economic analysis. It is not necessarily desirable that the railway should be required to compensate those who suffer damage by fires caused by railway engines. I need not show here that, if the railway could make a bargain with everyone having property adjoining the railway line and there were no costs involved in making such bargains, it would not matter whether the railway was liable for damage caused by fires or not. This question has been treated at length in earlier sections. The problem is whether it would be desirable to make the railway liable in conditions in which it is too expensive for such bargains to be made. Pigou clearly thought it was desirable to force the railway to pay compensation and it is easy to see the kind of argument that would have led him to this conclusion. Suppose a railway is considering whether to run an additional train or to increase the speed of an existing train or to install spark-preventing devices on its engines. If the railway were not liable for fire damage, then, when making these decisions, it would not take into account as a cost the increase in damage resulting from the additional train or the faster train or the failure to install spark-preventing devices. This is the source of the di-

[43] Vaughan v. Taff Vale Railway Co., 3 H. and N. 743 (Ex. 1858) and 5 H. and N. 679 (Ex. 1860).

vergence between private and social net products. It results in the railway performing acts which will lower the value of total production—and which it would not do if it were liable for the damage. This can be shown by means of an arithmetical example.

Consider a railway, which is *not* liable for damage by fires caused by sparks from its engines, which runs two trains per day on a certain line. Suppose that running one train per day would enable the railway to perform services worth $150 per annum and running two trains a day would enable the railway to perform services worth $250 per annum. Suppose further that the cost of running one train is $50 per annum and two trains $100 per annum. Assuming perfect competition, the cost equals the fall in the value of production elsewhere due to the employment of additional factors of production by the railway. Clearly the railway would find it profitable to run two trains per day. But suppose that running one train per day would destroy by fire crops worth (on an average over the year) $60 and two trains a day would result in the destruction of crops worth $120. In these circumstances running one train per day would raise the value of total production but the running of a second train would reduce the value of total production. The second train would enable additional railway services worth $100 per annum to be performed. But the fall in the value of production elsewhere would be $110 per annum; $50 as a result of the employment of additional factors of production and $60 as a result of the destruction of crops. Since it would be better if the second train were not run and since it would not run if the railway were liable for damage caused to crops, the conclusion that the railway should be made liable for the damage seems irresistable. Undoubtedly it is this kind of reasoning which underlies the Pigovian position.

The conclusion that it would be better if the second train did not run is correct. The conclusion that it is desirable that the railway should be made liable for the damage it causes is wrong. Let us change our assumption concerning the rule of liability. Suppose that the railway is liable for damage from fires caused by sparks from the engine. A farmer on lands adjoining the railway is then in the position that, if his crop is destroyed by fires caused by the railway, he will receive the market price from the railway; but if his crop is not damaged, he will receive the market price by sale. It therefore becomes a matter of indifference to him whether his crop is damaged by fire or not. The position is very different when the railway is *not* liable. Any crop destruction through railway-caused fires would then reduce the receipts of the farmer. He would therefore take out of cultivation any land for which the damage is likely to be greater than the net return of the land (for reasons explained at length in Section III). A change from a regime in which the railway is *not* liable for damage to one in which it *is* liable is likely therefore to lead to an increase in the amount of cultivation on lands adjoining the railway. It will also, of course, lead to an increase in the amount of crop destruction due to railway-caused fires.

Let us return to our arithmetical example. Assume that, with the changed rule of liability, there is a doubling in the amount of crop destruction due to railway-caused fires. With one train per day, crops worth $120 would be destroyed each year and two trains per day would lead to the destruction of crops worth $240. We saw previously that it would not be profitable to run the second train if the railway had to pay $60 per annum as compensation for damage. With damage at $120 per annum the loss from running the second train would be $60 greater. But now let us consider the first train. The value of the transport services furnished by the first train is $150. The cost of running the train is $50. The amount that the railway would have to pay out as compensation for damage is $120. It follows that it would not be profitable to run any trains. With the figures in our example we reach the following result: if the railway is not liable for fire-damage, two trains per day would be run; if the railway is liable for fire-damage, it would cease operations altogether. Does this mean that it is better that there should be no railway? This question can be resolved by considering what would happen to the value of total production if it were decided to exempt the railway from liability for fire-damage, thus bringing it into operation (with two trains per day).

The operation of the railway would enable transport services worth $250 to be performed. It would also mean the employment of factors of production which would reduce the value of production elsewhere by $100. Furthermore it would mean the destruction of crops worth $120. The coming of the railway will also have led to the abandonment of cultivation of some land. Since we know that, had this land been cultivated, the value of the crops destroyed by fire would have been $120, and since it is unlikely that the total crop on this land would have been destroyed, it seems reasonable to suppose that the value of the crop yield on this land would have been higher than this. Assume it would have been $160. But the abandonment of cultivation would have released factors of production for employment elsewhere. All we know is that the amount by which the value of production elsewhere will increase will be less than $160. Suppose that it is $150. Then the gain from operating the railway would be $250 (the value of the transport services) minus $100 (the cost of the factors of production) minus $120 (the value of crops destroyed by fire) minus $160 (the fall in the value of crop production due to the abandonment of cultivation) plus $150 (the value of production elsewhere of the released factors of production). Overall, operating the railway will increase the value of total production by $20. With these figures it is clear that it is better that the railway should not be liable for the damage it causes, thus enabling it to operate profitably. Of course, by altering the figures, it could be shown that there are other cases in which it would be desirable that the railway should be liable for the damage it causes. It is enough for my purpose to show that, from an economic point of view, a situation in which there is "uncompensated damage done to surrounding woods by sparks from railway engines" is not necessarily undesirable. Whether it is desirable or not depends on the particular circumstances.

How is it that the Pigovian analysis seems to give the wrong answer? The reason is that Pigou does not seem to have noticed that his analysis is dealing with an entirely different question. The analysis as such is correct. But it is quite illegitimate for Pigou to draw the particular conclusion he does. The question at issue is not whether it is desirable to run an additional train or a faster train or to install smoke-preventing devices; the question at issue is whether it is desirable to have a system in which the railway has to compensate those who suffer damage from the fires which it causes or one in which the railway does not have to compensate them. When an economist is comparing alternative social arrangements, the proper procedure is to compare the total social product yielded by these different arrangements. The comparison of private and social products is neither here nor there. A simple example will demonstrate this. Imagine a town in which there are traffic lights. A motorist approaches an intersection and stops because the light is red. There are no cars approaching the intersection on the other street. If the motorist ignored the red signal, no accident would occur and the total product would increase because the motorist would arrive earlier at his destination. Why does he not do this? The reason is that if he ignored the light he would be fined. The private product from crossing the street is less than the social product. Should we conclude from this that the total product would be greater if there were no fines for failing to obey traffic signals? The Pigovian analysis shows us that it is possible to conceive of better worlds than the one in which we live. But the problem is to devise practical arrangements which will correct defects in one part of the system without causing more serious harm in other parts.

I have examined in considerable detail one example of a divergence between private and social products and I do not propose to make any further examination of Pigou's analytical system. But the main discussion of the problem considered in this article is to be found in that part of Chapter 9 in Part II which deals with Pigou's second class of divergence and it is of interest to see how Pigou develops his argument. Pigou's own description of this second class of divergence was quoted at the beginning of this section. Pigou distinguishes between the case in which a person renders services for which he receives no payment and the case in which a person renders disservices and compensation is not given to the injured parties. Our main attention has, of course, centred on this second case. It is therefore rather astonishing to find, as was pointed out to me by Professor Francesco Forte, that the problem of the smoking chimney—the "stock instance"[44] or "classroom example"[45] of the second case—is used by Pigou as an example of the first case (services rendered without payment) and is never mentioned, at any rate explicitly, in connection with the second case.[46] Pigou points out that factory owners who devote resources to preventing their chimneys from smoking render services for which they receive no payment. The implication, in the light of Pigou's discussion later in the chapter, is that a factory owner with a smokey chimney should be given a bounty to induce him to install smoke-preventing devices. Most modern economists would suggest that the owner of the factory with the smokey chimney should be taxed. It seems a pity that economists (apart from Professor Forte) do not seem to have noticed this feature of Pigou's treatment since a realisation that the problem could be tackled in either of these two ways would probably have led to an explicit recognition of its reciprocal nature.

In discussing the second case (disservices without compensation to those damaged), Pigou says that they are rendered "when the owner of a site in a residential quarter of a city builds a factory there and so destroys a great part of the amenities of neighbouring sites; or, in a less degree, when he uses his site in such a way as to spoil the lighting of the house opposite; or when he invests resources in erecting buildings in a crowded centre, which by contracting the air-space and the playing room of the neighbourhood, tend to injure the health and efficiency of the families living there."[47] Pigou is, of course, quite right to describe such actions as "uncharged disservices." But he is wrong when he describes these actions as "anti-social."[48] They may or may not be. It is necessary to weigh the harm against the good that will result. Nothing could be more "anti-social" than to oppose any action which causes any harm to anyone.

The example with which Pigou opens his discussion of "uncharged disservices" is not, as I have indicated, the case of the smokey chimney but the case of the overrunning rabbits: ". . . incidental uncharged disservices are rendered to third parties when the game-preserving activities of one occupier involve the overrunning of a neighbouring occupier's land by rabbits. . . ." This example is of extraordinary interest, not so much because the economic

[44] Sir Dennis Robertson, I Lectures on Economic Principles 162 (1957).

[45] E. J. Mishan, The Meaning of Efficiency in Economics, 139 The Bankers' Magazine 482 (June 1960).

[46] Pigou, op. cit. supra n. 35 at 184.

[47] *Id.* at 185–86.

[48] *Id.* at 186 n.1. For similar unqualified statements see Pigou's lecture "Some Aspects of the Housing Problem" in B. S. Rowntree and A. C. Pigou, Lectures on Housing, in 18 Manchester Univ. Lectures (1914).

analysis of the case is essentially any different from that of the other examples, but because of the peculiarities of the legal position and the light it throws on the part which economics can play in what is apparently the purely legal question of the delimitation of rights.

The problem of legal liability for the actions of rabbits is part of the general subject of liability for animals.[49] I will, although with reluctance, confine my discussion to rabbits. The early cases relating to rabbits concerned the relations between the lord of the manor and commoners, since, from the thirteenth century on, it became usual for the lord of the manor to stock the commons with conies (rabbits), both for the sake of the meat and the fur. But in 1597, in *Boulston*'s case, an action was brought by one landowner against a neighbouring landowner, alleging that the defendant had made coney-burrows and that the conies had increased and had destroyed the plaintiff's corn. The action failed for the reason that

> . . . so soon as the coneys come on his neighbor's land he may kill them, for they are ferae naturae, and he who makes the coney-boroughs has no property in them, and he shall not be punished for the damage which the coneys do in which he has no property, and which the other may lawfully kill.[50]

As *Boulston*'s case has been treated as binding—Bray, J., in 1919, said that he was not aware that *Boulston*'s case has ever been overruled or questioned[51]—Pigou's rabbit example undoubtedly represented the legal position at the time *The Economics of Welfare* was written.[52] And in this case, it is not far from the truth to say that the state of affairs which Pigou describes came about because of an absence of Government action (at any rate in the form of statutory enactments) and was the result of "natural" tendencies.

Nonetheless, *Boulston*'s case is something of a legal curiousity and Professor Williams makes no secret of his distaste for this decision:

[49] See G. L. Williams, Liability for Animals—An Account of the Development and Present Law of Tortious Liability for Animals, Distress Damage Feasant and the Duty to Fence, in Great Britain, Northern Ireland and the Common Law Dominions (1939). Part Four, "The Action of Nuisance, in Relation to Liability for Animals," 236–62, is especially relevant to our discussion. The problem of liability for rabbits is discussed in this part, 238–47. I do not know how far the common law in the United State regarding liability for animals has diverged from that in Britain. In some Western States of the United States, the English common law regarding the duty to fence has not been followed, in part because "the considerable amount of open, uncleared land made it a matter of public policy to allow cattle to run at large" (Williams, *op. cit. supra* 227). This affords a good example of how a different set of circumstances may make it economically desirable to change the legal rule regarding the delimitation of rights.

[50] 5 Coke (Vol. 3) 104 b. 77 Eng. Rep., 216, 217.

[51] See Stearn v. Prentice Bros. Ltd., (1919) 1 K.B., 395, 397.

[52] I have not looked into recent cases. The legal position has also been modified by statutory enactments.

The conception of liability in nuisance as being based upon ownership is the result, apparently, of a confusion with the action of cattle-trespass, and runs counter both to principle and to the medieval authorities on the escape of water, smoke and filth. . . . The prerequisite of any satisfactory treatment of the subject is the final abandonment of the pernicious doctrine in *Boulston*'s case. . . . Once *Boulston*'s case disappears, the way will be clear for a rational restatement of the whole subject, on lines that will harmonize with the principles prevailing in the rest of the law of nuisance.[53]

The judges in *Boulston*'s case were, of course, aware that their view of the matter depended on distinguishing this case from one involving nuisance:

This cause is not like to the cases put, on the other side, of erecting a lime-kiln, dye-house, or the like; for there the annoyance is by the act of the parties who make them; but it is not so here, for the conies of themselves went into the plaintiff's land, and he might take them when they came upon his land, and make profit of them.[54]

Professor Williams comments:

Once more the atavistic idea is emerging that the animals are guilty and not the landowner. It is not, of course, a satisfactory principle to introduce into a modern law of nuisance. If A. erects a house or plants a tree so that the rain runs or drips from it on to B.'s land, this is A.'s act for which he is liable; but if A. introduces rabbits into his land so that they escape from it into B.'s, this is the act of the rabbits for which A. is not liable—such is the specious distinction resulting from *Boulston*'s case.[55]

It has to be admitted that the decision in *Boulston*'s case seems a little odd. A man may be liable for damage caused by smoke or unpleasant smells, without it being necessary to determine whether he owns the smoke or the smell. And the rule in *Boulston*'s case has not always been followed in cases dealing with other animals. For example, in *Bland v. Yates*,[56] it was decided that an injunction could be granted to prevent someone from keeping an *unusual and excessive* collection of manure in which flies bred and which infested a neighbour's house. The question of who owned the flies was not raised. An economist would not wish to object because legal reasoning sometimes appears a little odd. But there is a sound economic reason for supporting Professor Williams' view that the problem of liability for animals (and particularly rabbits) should be brought within the ordinary law of nuisance. The reason is not that the man who harbours rabbits is solely responsible for the damage; the man whose crops are eaten is equally responsible. And given that the costs of market transactions make a rearrange-

[53] Williams, op. cit. supra n. 49 at 242, 258.

[54] Boulston v. Hardy, Cro. Eliz., 547, 548, 77 Eng. Rep. 216.

[55] Williams, op. cit. supra n. 49 at 243.

[56] 58 Sol.J. 612 (1913–1914).

ment of rights impossible, unless we know the particular circumstances, we cannot say whether it is desirable or not to make the man who harbours rabbits responsible for the damage committed by the rabbits on neighbouring properties. The objection to the rule in *Boulston*'s case is that, under it, the harbourer of rabbits can *never* be liable. It fixes the rule of liability at one pole: and this is as undesirable, from an economic point of view, as fixing the rule at the other pole and making the harbourer of rabbits always liable. But, as we saw in Section VII, the law of nuisance, as it is in fact handled by the courts, is flexible and allows for a comparison of the utility of an act with the harm it produces. As Professor Williams says: "The whole law of nuisance is an attempt to reconcile and compromise between conflicting interests. . . ."[57] To bring the problem of rabbits within the ordinary law of nuisance would not mean *inevitably* making the harbourer of rabbits liable for damage committed by the rabbits. This is not to say that the sole task of the courts in such cases is to make a comparison between the harm and the utility of an act. Nor is it to be expected that the courts will always decide correctly after making such a comparison. But unless the courts act very foolishly, the ordinary law of nuisance would seem likely to give economically more satisfactory results than adopting a rigid rule. Pigou's case of the overrunning rabbits affords an excellent example of how problems of law and economics are interrelated, even though the correct policy to follow would seem to be different from that envisioned by Pigou.

Pigou allows one exception to his conclusion that there is a divergence between private and social products in the rabbit example. He adds: ". . unless . . . the two occupiers stand in the relation of landlord and tenant, so that compensation is given in an adjustment of the rent."[58] This qualification is rather surprising since Pigou's first class of divergence is largely concerned with the difficulties of drawing up satisfactory contracts between landlords and tenants. In fact, all the recent cases on the problem of rabbits cited by Professor Williams involved disputes between landlords and tenants concerning sporting rights.[59] Pigou seems to make a distinction between the case in which no contract is possible (the second class) and that in which the contract is unsatisfactory (the first class). Thus he says that the second class of divergences between private and social net product

> cannot, like divergences due to tenancy laws, be mitigated by a modification of the contractual relation between any two contracting parties, because the divergence arises out of a service or disservice rendered to persons other than the contracting parties.[60]

[57] Williams, op. cit. supra n. 49 at 259.

[58] Pigou, op. cit. supra n. 35 at 185.

[59] Williams, op. cit. supra n. 49 at 244–47.

[60] Pigou, op. cit. supra n. 35 at 192.

But the reason why some activities are not the subject of contracts is exactly the same as the reason why some contracts are commonly unsatisfactory—it would cost too much to put the matter right. Indeed, the two cases are really the same since the contracts are unsatisfactory because they do not cover certain activities. The exact bearing of the discussion of the first class of divergence on Pigou's main argument is difficult to discover. He shows that in some circumstances contractual relations between landlord and tenant may result in a divergence between private and social products.[61] But he also goes on to show that Government-enforced compensation schemes and rent-controls will also produce divergences.[62] Furthermore, he shows that, when the Government is in a similar position to a private landlord, e.g. when granting a franchise to a public utility, exactly the same difficulties arise as when private individuals are involved.[63] The discussion is interesting but I have been unable to discover what general conclusions about economic policy, if any, Pigou expects us to draw from it.

Indeed, Pigou's treatment of the problems considered in this article is extremely elusive and the discussion of his views raises almost insuperable difficulties of interpretation. Consequently it is impossible to be sure that one has understood what Pigou really meant. Nevertheless, it is difficult to resist the conclusion, extroardinary though this may be in an economist of Pigou's stature, that the main source of this obscurity is that Pigou had not thought his position through.

IX. The Pigovian Tradition

It is strange that a doctrine as faulty as that developed by Pigou should have been so influential, although part of its success has probably been due to the lack of clarity in the exposition. Not being clear, it was never clearly wrong. Curiously enough, this obscurity in the source has not prevented the emergence of a fairly well-defined oral tradition. What economists think they learn from Pigou, and what they tell their students, which I term the Pigovian tradition, is reasonably clear. I propose to show the inadequacy of this Pigovian tradition by demonstrating that both the analysis and the policy conclusions which it supports are incorrect.

I do not propose to justify my view as to the prevailing opinion by copious references to the literature. I do this partly because the treatment in the literature is usually so fragmentary, often involving little more than a reference to Pigou plus some explanatory comment, that detailed examination would be inappropriate. But the main reason for this lack of reference is that the doctrine, although based on Pigou, must have been largely the product of an oral tradition. Certainly economists with whom I have discussed these problems have shown a unanimity of opinion which is quite

[61] *Id.* 174–75. [62] *Id.* 177–83. [63] *Id.* 175–77.

remarkable considering the meagre treatment accorded this subject in the literature. No doubt there are some economists who do not share the usual view but they must represent a small minority of the profession.

The approach to the problems under discussion is through an examination of the value of physical production. The private product is the value of the additional product resulting from a particular activity of a business. The social product equals the private product minus the fall in the value of production elsewhere for which no compensation is paid by the business. Thus, if 10 units of a factor (and no other factors) are used by a business to make a certain product with a value of $105; and the owner of this factor is not compensated for their use, which he is unable to prevent; and these 10 units of the factor would yield products in their best alternative use worth $100; then, the social product is $105 minus $100 or $5. If the business now pays for one unit of the factor and its price equals the value of its marginal product, then the social product rises to $15. If two units are paid for, the social product rises to $25 and so on until it reaches $105 when all units of the factor are paid for. It is not difficult to see why economists have so readily accepted this rather odd procedure. The analysis focusses on the individual business decision and since the use of certain resources is not allowed for in costs, receipts are reduced by the same amount. But, of course, this means that the value of the social product has no social significance whatsoever. It seems to me preferable to use the opportunity cost concept and to approach these problems by comparing the value of the product yielded by factors in alternative uses or by alternative arrangements. The main advantage of a pricing system is that it leads to the employment of factors in places where the value of the product yielded is greatest and does so at less cost than alternative systems (I leave aside that a pricing system also eases the problem of the redistribution of income). But if through some God-given natural harmony factors flowed to the places where the value of the product yielded was greatest without any use of the pricing system and consequently there was no compensation, I would find it a source of surprise rather than a cause for dismay.

The definition of the social product is queer but this does not mean that the conclusions for policy drawn from the analysis are necessarily wrong. However, there are bound to be dangers in an approach which diverts attention from the basic issues and there can be little doubt that it has been responsible for some of the errors in current doctrine. The belief that it is desirable that the business which causes harmful effects should be forced to compensate those who suffer damage (which was exhaustively discussed in section VIII in connection with Pigou's railway sparks example) is undoubtedly the result of not comparing the total product obtainable with alternative social arrangements.

The same fault is to be found in proposals for solving the problem of harmful effects by the use of taxes or bounties. Pigou lays considerable stress on this solution although he is, as usual, lacking in detail and qualified in his support.[64] Modern economists tend to think exclusively in terms of taxes and in a very precise way. The tax should be equal to the damage done and should therefore vary with the amount of the harmful effect. As it is not proposed that the proceeds of the tax should be paid to those suffering the damage, this solution is not the same as that which would force a business to pay compensation to those damaged by its actions, although economists generally do not seem to have noticed this and tend to treat the two solutions as being identical.

Assume that a factory which emits smoke is set up in a district previously free from smoke pollution, causing damage valued at $100 per annum. Assume that the taxation solution is adopted and that the factory owner is taxed $100 per annum as long as the factory emits the smoke. Assume further that a smoke-preventing device costing $90 per annum to run is available. In these circumstances, the smoke-preventing device would be installed. Damage of $100 would have been avoided at an expenditure of $90 and the factory-owner would be better off by $10 per annum. Yet the position achieved may not be optimal. Suppose that those who suffer the damage could avoid it by moving to other locations or by taking various precautions which would cost them, or be equivalent to a loss in income of, $40 per annum. Then there would be a gain in the value of production of $50 if the factory continued to emit its smoke and those now in the district moved elesewhere or made other adjustments to avoid the damage. If the factory owner is to be made to pay a tax equal to the damage caused, it would clearly be desirable to institute a double tax system and to make residents of the district pay an amount equal to the additional cost incurred by the factory owner (or the consumers of his products) in order to avoid the damage. In these conditions, people would not stay in the district or would take other measures to prevent the damage from occurring, when the costs of doing so were less than the costs that would be incurred by the producer to reduce the damage (the producer's object, of course, being not so much to reduce the damage as to reduce the tax payments). A tax system which was confined to a tax on the producer for damage caused would tend to lead to unduly high costs being incurred for the prevention of damage. Of course this could be avoided if it were possible to base the tax, not on the damage caused, but on the fall in the value of production (in its widest sense) resulting from the emission of smoke. But to do so would require a detailed knowledge of individual preferences and I am unable to imagine how the data needed for such a taxation system could be assembled. Indeed,

[64] *Id.* 192–4, 381 and Public Finance 94–100 (3d ed. 1947).

the proposal to solve the smoke-pollution and similar problems by the use of taxes bristles with difficulties: the problem of calculation, the difference between average and marginal damage, the interrelations between the damage suffered on different properties, etc. But it is unnecessary to examine these problems here. It is enough for my purpose to show that, even if the tax is exactly adjusted to equal the damage that would be done to neighboring properties as a result of the emission of each additional puff of smoke, the tax would not necessarily bring about optimal conditions. An increase in the number of people living or of business operating in the vicinity of the smoke-emitting factory will increase the amount of harm produced by a given emission of smoke. The tax that would be imposed would therefore increase with an increase in the number of those in the vicinity. This will tend to lead to a decrease in the value of production of the factors employed by the factory, either because a reduction in production due to the tax will result in factors being used elsewhere in ways which are less valuable, or because factors will be diverted to produce means for reducing the amount of smoke emitted. But people deciding to establish themselves in the vicinity of the factory will not take into account this fall in the value of production which results from their presence. This failure to take into account costs imposed on others is comparable to the action of a factory-owner in not taking into account the harm resulting from his emission of smoke. Without the tax, there may be too much smoke and too few people in the vicinity of the factory; but with the tax there may be too little smoke and too many people in the vicinity of the factory. There is no reason to suppose that one of these results is necessarily preferable.

I need not devote much space to discussing the similar error involved in the suggestion that smoke producing factories should, by means of zoning regulations, be removed from the districts in which the smoke causes harmful effects. When the change in the location of the factory results in a reduction in production, this obviously needs to be taken into account and weighed against the harm which would result from the factory remaining in that location. The aim of such regulation should not be to eliminate smoke pollution but rather to secure the optimum amount of smoke pollution, this being the amount which will maximise the value of production.

X. A Change of Approach

It is my belief that the failure of economists to reach correct conclusions about the treatment of harmful effects cannot be ascribed simply to a few slips in analysis. It stems from basic defects in the current approach to problems of welfare economics. What is needed is a change of approach.

Analysis in terms of divergencies between private and social products concentrates attention on particular deficiencies in the system and tends to nourish the belief that any measure which will remove the deficiency is necessarily desirable. It diverts attention from those other changes in the system which are inevitably associated with the corrective measure, changes which may well produce more harm than the original deficiency. In the preceding sections of this article, we have seen many examples of this. But it is not necessary to approach the problem in this way. Economists who study problems of the firm habitually use an opportunity cost approach and compare the receipts obtained from a given combination of factors with alternative business arrangements. It would seem desirable to use a similar approach when dealing with questions of economic policy and to compare the total product yielded by alternative social arrangements. In this article, the analysis has been confined, as is usual in this part of economics, to comparisons of the value of production, as measured by the market. But it is, of course, desirable that the choice between different social arrangements for the solution of economic problems should be carried out in broader terms than this and that the total effect of these arrangements in all spheres of life should be taken into account. As Frank H. Knight has so often emphasized, problems of welfare economics must ultimately dissolve into a study of aesthetics and morals.

A second feature of the usual treatment of the problems discussed in this article is that the analysis proceeds in terms of a comparison between a state of laissez faire and some kind of ideal world. This approach inevitably leads to a looseness of thought since the nature of the alternatives being compared is never clear. In a state of laissez faire, is there a monetary, a legal or a political system and if so, what are they? In an ideal world, would there be a monetary, a legal or a political system and if so, what would they be? The answers to all these questions are shrouded in mystery and every man is free to draw whatever conclusions he likes. Actually very little analysis is required to show that an ideal world is better than a state of laissez faire, unless the definitions of a state of laissez faire and an ideal world happen to be the same. But the whole discussion is largely irrelevant for questions of economic policy since whatever we may have in mind as our ideal world, it is clear that we have not yet discovered how to get to it from where we are. A better approach would seem to be to start our analysis with a situation approximating that which actually exists, to examine the effects of a proposed policy change and to attempt to decide whether the new situation would be, in total, better or worse than the original one. In this way, conclusions for policy would have some relevance to the actual situation.

A final reason for the failure to develop a theory adequate to handle the problem of harmful effects stems from a faulty concept of a factor of production. This is usually thought of as a physical entity which the businessman acquires and uses (an acre of land, a ton of fertiliser) instead of as a right to perform certain (physical) actions. We may speak of a person owning land and using it as a factor of production but what the land-owner in fact possesses is the right to carry out a circumscribed list of actions. The rights of a land-owner are not unlimited. It is not even always possible for him to remove the land to another place, for instance, by quarrying it. And although it may be possible for him to exclude some people from using "his" land, this may not be true of others. For example, some people may have the right to cross the land. Furthermore, it may or may not be possible to erect certain types of buildings or to grow certain crops or to use particular drainage systems on the land. This does not come about simply because of Government regulation. It would be equally true under the common law. In fact it would be true under any system of law. A system in which the rights of individuals were unlimited would be one in which there were no rights to acquire.

If factors of production are thought of as rights, it becomes easier to understand that the right to do something which has a harmful effect (such as the creation of smoke, noise, smells, etc.) is also a factor of production. Just as we may use a piece of land in such a way as to prevent someone else from crossing it, or parking his car, or building his house upon it, so we may use it in such a way as to deny him a view or quiet or unpolluted air. The cost of exercising a right (of using a factor of production) is always the loss which is suffered elsewhere in consequence of the exercise of that right—the inability to cross land, to park a car, to build a house, to enjoy a view, to have peace and quiet or to breathe clean air.

It would clearly be desirable if the only actions performed were those in which what was gained was worth more than what was lost. But in choosing between social arrangements within the context of which individual decisions are made, we have to bear in mind that a change in the existing system which will lead to an improvement in some decisions may well lead to a worsening of others. Furthermore we have to take into account the costs involved in operating the various social arrangements (whether it be the working of a market or of a government department), as well as the costs involved in moving to a new system. In devising and choosing between social arrangements we should have regard for the total effect. This, above all, is the change in approach which I am advocating.

[2]

VOLUME 85 APRIL 1972 NUMBER 6

HARVARD LAW REVIEW

PROPERTY RULES, LIABILITY RULES, AND INALIENABILITY: ONE VIEW OF THE CATHEDRAL

*Guido Calabresi * and A. Douglas Melamed ***

Professor Calabresi and Mr. Melamed develop a framework for legal analysis which they believe serves to integrate various legal relationships which are traditionally analyzed in separate subject areas such as Property and Torts. By using their model to suggest solutions to the pollution problem that have been overlooked by writers in the field, and by applying the model to the question of criminal sanctions, they demonstrate the utility of such an integrated approach.

I. INTRODUCTION

ONLY rarely are Property and Torts approached from a unified perspective. Recent writings by lawyers concerned with economics and by economists concerned with law suggest, however, that an attempt at integrating the various legal relationships treated by these subjects would be useful both for the beginning student and the sophisticated scholar.[1] By articulating a concept of "entitlements" which are protected by property, liability, or inalienability rules, we present one framework for such an approach.[2] We then analyze aspects of the pollution problem and of

* John Thomas Smith Professor of Law, Yale University. B.S. Yale, 1953; B.A. Oxford, 1955; LL.B. Yale, 1958; M.A. Oxford, 1959.

** Member of the District of Columbia Bar. B.A. Yale University, 1967; J.D. Harvard University, 1970.

[1] *See, e.g.*, Michelman, *Pollution as a Tort: A Non-Accidental Perspective on Calabresi's* COSTS, 80 YALE L.J. 647 (1971) (analysis of three alternative rules in pollution problems); Demsetz, *Toward a Theory of Property Rights*, 57 AM. ECON. REV. 347 (1967) (Vol. 2 — Papers and Proceedings) (analysis of property as a means of cost internalization which ignores liability rule alternatives).

[2] Since a fully integrated approach is probably impossible, it should be emphasized that this article concerns only one possible way of looking at and analyzing legal problems. Thus we shall not address ourselves to those fundamental legal questions which center on what institutions and what procedures are most suitable for making what decisions, except insofar as these relate directly to the problems of selecting the initial entitlements and the modes of protecting these entitlements. While we do not underrate the importance, indeed perhaps the primacy, of legal process considerations, *see* pp. 1116–17 *infra*, we are merely interested in the light

criminal sanctions in order to demonstrate how the model enables us to perceive relationships which have been ignored by writers in those fields.

The first issue which must be faced by any legal system is one we call the problem of "entitlement." Whenever a state is presented with the conflicting interests of two or more people, or two or more groups of people, it must decide which side to favor. Absent such a decision, access to goods, services, and life itself will be decided on the basis of "might makes right" — whoever is stronger or shrewder will win.[3] Hence the fundamental thing that law does is to decide which of the conflicting parties will be entitled to prevail. The entitlement to make noise versus the entitlement to have silence, the entitlement to pollute versus the entitlement to breathe clean air, the entitlement to have children versus the entitlement to forbid them — these are the first order of legal decisions.

Having made its initial choice, society must enforce that choice. Simply setting the entitlement does not avoid the problem of "might makes right"; a minimum of state intervention is always necessary.[4] Our conventional notions make this easy to compre-

---

that a rather different approach may shed on problems frequently looked at primarily from a legal process point of view.

As Professor Harry Wellington is fond of saying about many discussions of law, this article is meant to be only *one* of Monet's paintings of the Cathedral at Rouen. To understand the Cathedral one must see all of them. *See* G. HAMILTON, CLAUDE MONET'S PAINTINGS OF ROUEN CATHEDRAL 4–5, 19–20, 27 (1960).

[3] One could of course look at the state as simply a larger coalition of friends designed to enforce rules which merely accomplish the dominant coalition's desires. Rules of law would then be no more than "might makes right" writ large. Such a view does not strike us as plausible if for no other reason than that the state decides too many issues in response to too many different coalitions. This fact, by itself, would require a different form of analysis from that which would suffice to explain entitlements resulting from more direct and decentralized uses of "might makes right."

[4] For an excellent presentation of this general point by an economist, see Samuels, *Interrelations Between Legal and Economic Processes*, 14 J. LAW & ECON. 435 (1971).

We do not intend to imply that the state relies on force to enforce all or most entitlements. Nor do we imply that absent state intervention only force would win. The use by the state of feelings of obligation and rules of morality as means of enforcing most entitlements is not only crucial but terribly efficient. Conversely, absent the state, individuals would probably agree on rules of behavior which would govern entitlements in whole series of situations on the basis of criteria other than "might makes right." That these rules might themselves reflect the same types of considerations we will analyze as bases for legal entitlements is, of course, neither here nor there. What is important is that these "social compacts" would, no less than legal entitlements, give rise to what may be called obligations. These obligations in turn would cause people to behave in accordance with the compact in particular cases regardless of the existence of a predominant force. In this article

hend with respect to private property. If Taney owns a cabbage patch and Marshall, who is bigger, wants a cabbage, he will get it unless the state intervenes.[5] But it is not so obvious that the state must also intervene if it chooses the opposite entitlement, communal property. If large Marshall has grown some communal cabbages and chooses to deny them to small Taney, it will take state action to enforce Taney's entitlement to the communal cabbages. The same symmetry applies with respect to bodily integrity. Consider the plight of the unwilling ninety-eight-pound weakling in a state which nominally entitles him to bodily integrity but will not intervene to enforce the entitlement against a lustful Juno. Consider then the plight — absent state intervention — of the ninety-eight-pounder who desires an unwilling Juno in a state which nominally entitles everyone to use everyone else's body. The need for intervention applies in a slightly more complicated way to injuries. When a loss is left where it falls in an auto accident, it is not because God so ordained it. Rather it is because the state has granted the injurer an entitlement to be free of liability and will intervene to prevent the victim's friends, if they are stronger, from taking compensation from the injurer.[6] The loss is shifted in other cases because the state has granted an entitlement to compensation and will intervene to prevent the stronger injurer from rebuffing the victim's requests for compensation.

we are not concerned as much with the workings of such obligations as with the reasons which may explain the rules which themselves give rise to the obligations.

[5] "Bigger" obviously does not refer simply to size, but to the sum of an individual's resources. If Marshall's gang possesses superior brain and brawn to that of Taney, Marshall's gang will get the cabbages.

[6] Different cultures deal with the problem in different ways. Witness the following account:

> "Life Insurance" Fee is 4 Bulls and $1200. Port Moresby, New Guinea. Peter Howard proved that he values his life more than four bulls and $1200. But he wants $24 and one pig in change.
>
> Mr. Howard gave the money and livestock to members of the Jiga tribe, which had threatened to kill him because he killed a tribe member in an auto accident last October 29.
>
> The police approved the extortion agreement after telling the 38 year old Mr. Howard they could not protect him from the sworn vengeance of the tribe, which lives at Mt. Hagen, about 350 miles Northeast of Port Moresby.
>
> Mr. Howard, of Cambridge, England, was attacked and badly beaten by the tribesmen after the accident.
>
> They said he would be killed unless the payment of money and bulls was made according to the tribal traditions. It was the first time a white man in New Guinea had been forced to bow to tribal laws.
>
> After making the payment, Mr. Howard demanded to be compensated for the assault on him by the tribesmen. He said he wanted $24 and one pig. A Jiga spokesman told him the tribe would "think about it." New York Times, Feb. 16, 1972, at 17, col. 6.

The state not only has to decide whom to entitle, but it must also simultaneously make a series of equally difficult second order decisions. These decisions go to the manner in which entitlements are protected and to whether an individual is allowed to sell or trade the entitlement. In any given dispute, for example, the state must decide not only which side wins but also the kind of protection to grant. It is with the latter decisions, decisions which shape the subsequent relationship between the winner and the loser, that this article is primarily concerned. We shall consider three types of entitlements — entitlements protected by property rules, entitlements protected by liability rules, and inalienable entitlements. The categories are not, of course, absolutely distinct; but the categorization is useful since it reveals some of the reasons which lead us to protect certain entitlements in certain ways.

An entitlement is protected by a property rule to the extent that someone who wishes to remove the entitlement from its holder must buy it from him in a voluntary transaction in which the value of the entitlement is agreed upon by the seller. It is the form of entitlement which gives rise to the least amount of state intervention: once the original entitlement is decided upon, the state does not try to decide its value.[7] It lets each of the parties say how much the entitlement is worth to him, and gives the seller a veto if the buyer does not offer enough. Property rules involve a collective decision as to who is to be given an initial entitlement but not as to the value of the entitlement.

Whenever someone may destroy the initial entitlement if he is willing to pay an objectively determined value for it, an entitlement is protected by a liability rule. This value may be what it is thought the original holder of the entitlement would have sold it for. But the holder's complaint that he would have demanded more will not avail him once the objectively determined value is set. Obviously, liability rules involve an additional stage of state intervention: not only are entitlements protected, but their transfer or destruction is allowed on the basis of a value determined by some organ of the state rather than by the parties themselves.

An entitlement is inalienable to the extent that its transfer is not permitted between a willing buyer and a willing seller. The state intervenes not only to determine who is initially entitled and to determine the compensation that must be paid if the en-

[7] A property rule requires less state intervention only in the sense that intervention is needed to decide upon and enforce the initial entitlement but not for the separate problem of determining the value of the entitlement. Thus, if a particular property entitlement is especially difficult to enforce — for example, the right to personal security in urban areas — the actual amount of state intervention can be very high and could, perhaps, exceed that needed for some entitlements protected by easily administered liability rules.

titlement is taken or destroyed, but also to forbid its sale under some or all circumstances. Inalienability rules are thus quite different from property and liability rules. Unlike those rules, rules of inalienability not only "protect" the entitlement; they may also be viewed as limiting or regulating the grant of the entitlement itself.

It should be clear that most entitlements to most goods are mixed. Taney's house may be protected by a property rule in situations where Marshall wishes to purchase it, by a liability rule where the government decides to take it by eminent domain, and by a rule of inalienability in situations where Taney is drunk or incompetent. This article will explore two primary questions: (1) In what circumstances should we grant a particular entitlement? and (2) In what circumstances should we decide to protect that entitlement by using a property, liability, or inalienability rule?

II. The Setting of Entitlements

What are the reasons for deciding to entitle people to pollute or to entitle people to forbid pollution, to have children freely or to limit procreation, to own property or to share property? They can be grouped under three headings: economic efficiency, distributional preferences, and other justice considerations.[8]

A. Economic Efficiency

Perhaps the simplest reason for a particular entitlement is to minimize the administrative costs of enforcement. This was the reason Holmes gave for letting the costs lie where they fall in accidents unless some clear societal benefit is achieved by shifting them.[9] By itself this reason will never justify any result except that of letting the stronger win, for obviously that result minimizes enforcement costs. Nevertheless, administrative efficiency may be relevant to choosing entitlements when other reasons are taken into account. This may occur when the reasons accepted are indifferent between conflicting entitlements and one entitlement is cheaper to enforce than the others. It may also occur when the reasons are not indifferent but lead us only slightly to prefer one over another and the first is considerably more expensive to enforce than the second.

But administrative efficiency is just one aspect of the broader concept of economic efficiency. Economic efficiency asks that we

---

[8] *See generally* G. Calabresi, The Costs of Accidents 24–33 (1970) [hereinafter cited as Costs].

[9] *See* O.W. Holmes, Jr., The Common Law 76–77 (Howe ed. 1963). For a criticism of the justification as applied to accidents today, see Costs 261–63. *But cf.* Posner, *A Theory of Negligence*, 1 J. Legal Stud. 29 (1972).

choose the set of entitlements which would lead to that allocation of resources which could not be improved in the sense that a further change would not so improve the condition of those who gained by it that they could compensate those who lost from it and still be better off than before. This is often called Pareto optimality.[10] To give two examples, economic efficiency asks for that combination of entitlements to engage in risky activities and to be free from harm from risky activities which will most likely lead to the lowest sum of accident costs and of costs of avoiding accidents.[11] It asks for that form of property, private or communal, which leads to the highest product for the effort of producing.

Recently it has been argued that on certain assumptions, usually termed the absence of transaction costs, Pareto optimality or economic efficiency will occur regardless of the initial entitlement.[12] For this to hold, "no transaction costs" must be under-

---

[10] We are not here concerned with the many definitional variations which encircle the concept of Pareto optimality. Many of these variations stem from the fact that unless compensation actually occurs after a change (and this itself assumes a preexisting set of entitlements from which one makes a change to a Pareto optimal arrangement), the redistribution of wealth implicit in the change may well make a return to the prior position also seem Pareto optimal. There are any number of variations on this theme which economists have studied at length. Since in the world in which lawyers must live, anything close to Pareto efficiency, even if desirable, is not attainable, these refinements need not detain us even though they are crucial to a full understanding of the concept.

Most versions of Pareto optimality are based on the premise that individuals know best what is best for them. Hence they assume that to determine whether those who gain from a change could compensate those who lose, one must look to the values the individuals themselves give to the gains and losses. Economic efficiency may, however, present a broader notion which does not depend upon this individualistic premise. It may be that the state, for paternalistic reasons, *see* pp. 1113–14 *infra*, is better able to determine whether the total gain of the winners is greater than the total loss of the losers.

[11] The word "costs" is here used in a broad way to include all the disutilities resulting from an accident and its avoidance. As such it is not limited to monetary costs, or even to those which could in some sense be "monetizable," but rather includes disutilities or "costs" — for instance, the loss to an individual of his leg — the very expression of which in monetary terms would seem callous. One of the consequences of not being able to put monetary values on some disutilities or "costs" is that the market is of little use in gauging their worth, and this in turn gives rise to one of the reasons why liability, or inalienability rules, rather than property rules may be used.

[12] This proposition was first established in Coase's classic article, *The Problem of Social Cost*, 3 J. LAW & ECON. 1 (1960), and has been refined in subsequent literature. *See, e.g.*, Calabresi, *Transaction Costs, Resource Allocation and Liability Rules — A Comment*, 11 J. LAW & ECON. 67 (1968); Nutter, *The Coase Theorem on Social Cost: A Footnote*, 11 J. LAW & ECON. 503 (1968). *See also* G. STIGLER, THE THEORY OF PRICE 113 (3d ed. 1966); Mishan, *Pareto Optimality and the Law*, 19 OXFORD ECON. PAPERS 255 (1967).

stood extremely broadly as involving both perfect knowledge and the absence of any impediments or costs of negotiating. Negotiation costs include, for example, the cost of excluding would-be freeloaders from the fruits of market bargains.[13] In such a frictionless society, transactions would occur until no one could be made better off as a result of further transactions without making someone else worse off. This, we would suggest, is a necessary, indeed a tautological, result of the definitions of Pareto optimality and of transaction costs which we have given.

Such a result would not mean, however, that the *same* allocation of resources would exist regardless of the initial set of entitlements. Taney's willingness to pay for the right to make noise may depend on how rich he is; Marshall's willingness to pay for silence may depend on his wealth. In a society which entitles Taney to make noise and which forces Marshall to buy silence from Taney, Taney is wealthier and Marshall poorer than each would be in a society which had the converse set of entitlements. Depending on how Marshall's desire for silence and Taney's for noise vary with their wealth, an entitlement to noise will result in negotiations which will lead to a different quantum of noise than would an entitlement to silence.[14] This variation in the quantity

[13] The freeloader is the person who refuses to be inoculated against smallpox because, given the fact that almost everyone else is inoculated, the risk of smallpox to him is less than the risk of harm from the inoculation. He is the person who refuses to pay for a common park, though he wants it, because he believes that others will put in enough money to make the park available to him. *See* COSTS 137 n.4. The costs of excluding the freeloader from the benefits for which he refused to pay may well be considerable as the two above examples should suggest. This is especially so since these costs may include the inefficiency of pricing a good, like the park once it exists, above its marginal cost in order to force the freeloader to disclose his true desire to use it — thus enabling us to charge him part of the cost of establishing it initially.

It is the capacity of the market to induce disclosure of individual preferences which makes it theoretically possible for the market to bring about exchanges leading to Pareto optimality. But the freeloader situation is just one of many where no such disclosure is achieved by the market. If we assume perfect knowledge, defined more broadly than is normally done to include knowledge of individual preferences, then such situations pose no problem. This definition of perfect knowledge, though perhaps implicit in the concept of no transaction costs, would not only make reaching Pareto optimality easy through the market, it would make it equally easy to establish a similar result by collective fiat.

For a further discussion of what is implied by a broad definition of no transaction costs, see note 59 *infra*. For a discussion of other devices which may induce individuals to disclose their preferences, see note 38 *infra*.

[14] *See* Mishan, *Pareto Optimality and the Law*, 19 OXFORD ECON. PAPERS 255 (1967). Unless Taney's and Marshall's desires for noise and silence are totally unaffected by their wealth, that is, their desires are totally income inelastic, a change in their wealth will alter the value each places on noise and silence and hence will alter the outcome of their negotiations.

of noise and silence can be viewed as no more than an instance of the well accepted proposition that what is a Pareto optimal, or economically efficient, solution varies with the starting distribution of wealth. Pareto optimality is optimal *given* a distribution of wealth, but different distributions of wealth imply their own Pareto optimal allocation of resources.[15]

All this suggests why distributions of wealth may affect a society's choice of entitlements. It does not suggest why *economic efficiency* should affect the choice, if we assume an absence of any transaction costs. But no one makes an assumption of no transaction costs in practice. Like the physicist's assumption of no friction or Say's law in macro-economics, the assumption of no transaction costs may be a useful starting point, a device which helps us see how, as different elements which may be termed transaction costs become important, the goal of economic efficiency starts to prefer one allocation of entitlements over another.[16]

Since one of us has written at length on how in the presence of various types of transaction costs a society would go about deciding on a set of entitlements in the field of accident law,[17] it is enough to say here: (1) that economic efficiency standing alone would dictate that set of entitlements which favors knowledgeable choices between social benefits and the social costs of obtaining them, and between social costs and the social costs of avoiding them; (2) that this implies, in the absence of certainty as to whether a benefit is worth its costs to society, that the cost should be put on the party or activity best located to make such a cost-benefit analysis; (3) that in particular contexts like accidents or pollution this suggests putting costs on the party or activity which

---

[15] There should be no implication that a Pareto optimal solution is in some sense better than a non-Pareto optimal solution which results in a different wealth distribution. The implication is only that given the *same* wealth distribution Pareto optimal is in some meaningful sense preferable to non-Pareto optimal.

[16] *See* Demsetz, *When Does the Rule of Liability Matter?*, 1 J. LEGAL STUD. 13, 25–28 (1972); Stigler, *The Law and Economics of Public Policy: A Plea to the Scholars*, 1 J. LEGAL STUD. 1, 11–12 (1972).

The trouble with a term like "no transaction costs" is that it covers a multitude of market failures. The appropriate collective response, if the aim is to approach Pareto optimality, will vary depending on what the actual impediments to full bargaining are in any given cases. Occasionally the appropriate response may be to ignore the impediments. If the impediments are merely the administrative costs of establishing a market, it may be that doing nothing is preferable to attempting to correct for these costs because the administrative costs of collective action may be even greater. Similarly, if the impediments are due to a failure of the market to cause an accurate disclosure of freeloaders' preferences it may be that the collective can do no better.

[17] *See* COSTS 135–97.

can most cheaply avoid them; (4) that in the absence of certainty as to who that party or activity is, the costs should be put on the party or activity which can with the lowest transaction costs act in the market to correct an error in entitlements by inducing the party who can avoid social costs most cheaply to do so; [18] and (5) that since we are in an area where by hypothesis markets do not work perfectly — there are transaction costs — a decision will often have to be made on whether market transactions or collective fiat is most likely to bring us closer to the Pareto optimal result the "perfect" market would reach.[19]

Complex though this summary may suggest the entitlement choice to be, in practice the criteria it represents will frequently indicate which allocations of entitlements are most likely to lead to optimal market judgments between having an extra car or taking a train, getting an extra cabbage and spending less time working in the hot sun, and having more widgets and breathing the pollution that widget production implies. Economic efficiency is not, however, the sole reason which induces a society to select a

[18] In *The Costs of Accidents*, the criteria here summarized are discussed at length and broken down into subcriteria which deal with the avoidance of different types of externalization and with the finding of the "best briber." Such detailed analysis is necessary to the application of the criteria to any specific area of law. At the level of generality of this article it did not seem to us necessary.

[19] In accident law this election takes the form of a choice between general or market deterrence and specific deterrence, in which the permitted level and manner of accident causing activities is determined collectively. For example, society may decide to grant an entitlement to drive and an entitlement to be compensated for accidents resulting from driving, and allow decisions by individual parties to determine the level and manner of driving. But a greater degree of specific deterrence could be achieved by selecting a different set of initial entitlements in order to accord with a collective cost-benefit analysis — by, for example, prohibiting cars of more than a certain horsepower.

The primary disadvantage of specific deterrence, as compared with general deterrence, is that it requires the central decisionmaker not only to determine the costs of any given activity, but also to measure its benefits, in order to determine the optimum level of activity. It is exceedingly difficult and exceedingly costly for any centralized decisionmaker to be fully informed of the costs and benefits of a wide range of activities. The irony is that collective fiat functions best in a world of costless perfect information; yet in a world of costless transactions, including costless information, the optimum allocation would be reached by market transactions, and the need to consider the alternative of collective fiat would not arise. One could, however, view the irony conversely, and say that the market works best under assumptions of perfect knowledge where collective fiat would work perfectly, rendering the market unnecessary. The fact that both market and collective determinations face difficulties in achieving the Pareto optimal result which perfect knowledge and no transaction costs would permit does not mean that the same difficulties are always as great for the two approaches. Thus, there are many situations in which we can assume fairly confidently that the market will do better than a collective decider, and there are situations where we can assume the opposite to be true. *See* COSTS 103–13.

set of entitlements. Wealth distribution preferences are another, and thus it is to distributional grounds for different entitlements to which we must now turn.

B. *Distributional Goals*

There are, we would suggest, at least two types of distributional concerns which may affect the choice of entitlements. These involve distribution of wealth itself and distribution of certain specific goods, which have sometimes been called merit goods.

All societies have wealth distribution preferences. They are, nonetheless, harder to talk about than are efficiency goals. For efficiency goals can be discussed in terms of a general concept like Pareto optimality to which exceptions — like paternalism — can be noted.[20] Distributional preferences, on the other hand, cannot usefully be discussed in a single conceptual framework. There are some fairly broadly accepted preferences — caste preferences in one society, more rather than less equality in another society. There are also preferences which are linked to dynamic efficiency concepts — producers ought to be rewarded since they will cause everyone to be better off in the end. Finally, there are a myriad of highly individualized preferences as to who should be richer and who poorer which need not have anything to do with either equality or efficiency — silence lovers should be richer than noise lovers because they are worthier.[21]

Difficult as wealth distribution preferences are to analyze, it should be obvious that they play a crucial role in the setting of entitlements. For the placement of entitlements has a fundamental effect on a society's distribution of wealth. It is not enough, if a society wishes absolute equality, to start everyone off with the same amount of money. A financially egalitarian society which gives individuals the right to make noise immediately makes the would-be noisemaker richer than the silence

---

[20] For a discussion of paternalism, see pp. 1113–14 *infra*.

[21] The first group of preferences roughly coincides with those notions which writers like Fletcher, following Aristotle, term distributive justice. The second and third groups, instead, presumably deal with Fletcher's "corrective" justice — rewards based on what people do rather than what they are. *See* Fletcher, *Fairness and Utility in Tort Theory*, 85 HARV. L. REV. 537, 547 n.40 (1972).

Within the "corrective" justice category our second and third groupings distinguish those preferences which are transparently linked to efficiency notions from those whose roots are less obvious. If there were a generally accepted theory of desserts, one could speak in general terms about the role the third group plays just as one tends to speak about the role of either the first or second group. We do not believe that an adequate theory of desserts — even if possible — is currently available. *See also* pp. 1102–05 *infra*.

loving hermit.[22] Similarly, a society which entitles the person with brains to keep what his shrewdness gains him implies a different distribution of wealth from a society which demands from each according to his relative ability but gives to each according to his relative desire. One can go further and consider that a beautiful woman or handsome man is better off in a society which entitles individuals to bodily integrity than in one which gives everybody use of all the beauty available.

The consequence of this is that it is very difficult to imagine a society in which there is complete equality of wealth. Such a society either would have to consist of people who were all precisely the same, or it would have to compensate for differences in wealth caused by a given set of entitlements. The former is, of course, ridiculous, even granting cloning. And the latter would be very difficult; it would involve knowing what everyone's tastes were and taxing every holder of an entitlement at a rate sufficient to make up for the benefits the entitlement gave him. For example, it would involve taxing everyone with an entitlement to private use of his beauty or brains sufficiently to compensate those less favorably endowed but who nonetheless desired what beauty or brains could get.

If perfect equality is impossible, a society must choose what entitlements it wishes to have on the basis of criteria other than perfect equality. In doing this, a society often has a choice of methods, and the method chosen will have important distributional implications. Society can, for instance, give an entitlement away free and then, by paying the holders of the entitlement to limit their use of it, protect those who are injured by the free entitlement. Conversely, it can allow people to do a given thing only if they buy the right from the government. Thus a society can decide whether to entitle people to have children and then induce them to exercise control in procreating, or to require people to buy the right to have children in the first place. A society can also decide whether to entitle people to be free of military service and then induce them to join up, or to require all to serve but enable each to buy his way out. Which entitlement a society decides to sell, and which it decides to give away, will likely depend in part on which determination promotes the wealth distribution that society favors.[23]

---

[22] This assumes that there is not enough space for the noisemaker and the silence lover to coexist without intruding upon one another. In other words, this assumes that we are dealing with a problem of allocation of scarce resources; if we were not, there would be no need to set the initial entitlement. *See generally* Mishan, *supra* note 12.

[23] Any entitlement given away free implies a converse which must be paid for. For all those who like children, there are those who are disturbed by children:

If the choice of entitlements affects wealth distribution generally, it also affects the chances that people will obtain what have sometimes been called merit goods.[24] Whenever a society wishes to maximize the chances that individuals will have at least a minimum endowment of certain particular goods — education, clothes, bodily integrity — the society is likely to begin by giving the individuals an entitlement to them. If the society deems such an endowment to be essential regardless of individual desires, it will, of course, make the entitlement inalienable.[25] Why, however, would a society entitle individuals to specific goods rather than to money with which they can buy what they wish, unless it deems that it can decide better than the individuals what benefits them and society; unless, in other words, it wishes to make the entitlement inalienable?

We have seen that an entitlement to a good or to its converse is essentially inevitable.[26] We either are entitled to have silence or entitled to make noise in a given set of circumstances. We either have the right to our own property or body or the right to share others' property or bodies. We may buy or sell our-

for all those who detest armies, there are those who want what armies accomplish. Otherwise, we would have no scarce resource problem and hence no entitlement problem. Therefore, one cannot simply say that giving away an entitlement free is progressive while selling it is regressive. It is true that the more "free" goods there are the less inequality of wealth there is, if everything else has stayed the same. But if a free entitlement implies a costly converse, entitlements are *not* in this sense free goods. And the issue of their progressivity and regressivity must depend on the relative desire for the entitlement as against its converse on the part of the rich and the poor.

Strictly speaking, even this is true only if the money needed to finance the alternative plans, or made available to the government as a result of the plans, is raised and spent in a way that is precisely neutral with respect to wealth distribution. The point is simply this: even a highly regressive tax will aid wealth equality if the money it raises is all spent to benefit the poorest citizens. And even a system of outdoor relief for the idle rich aids wealth equality if the funds it requires are raised by taxing only the wealthiest of the wealthy. Thus whenever one speaks of a taxing program, spending program, or a system of entitlements as progressive or regressive, one must be assuming that the way the money is spent (if it is a tax) or the way it is raised (if it is a spending program) does not counter the distributive effect of the program itself.

[24] *Cf.* R. Musgrave, The Theory of Public Finance 13–14 (1959).

[25] The commonly given reasons why a society may choose to do this are discussed *infra* at pp. 1111–15. All of them are, of course, reasons which explain why such goods are often categorized as merit goods. When a society subsidizes a good it makes a similar decision based on similar grounds. Presumably, however, in such cases the grounds only justify making possession of the good less costly than would be the case without government intervention, rather than making possession of the good inevitable.

[26] This is true unless we are prepared to let the parties settle the matter on the basis of might makes right, which itself may also be viewed as a form of entitlement.

selves into the opposite position, but we must start somewhere. Under these circumstances, a society which prefers people to have silence, or own property, or have bodily integrity, but which does not hold the grounds for its preference to be sufficiently strong to justify overriding contrary preferences by individuals, will give such entitlements according to the collective preference, even though it will allow them to be sold thereafter.

Whenever transactions to sell or buy entitlements are very expensive, such an initial entitlement decision will be nearly as effective in assuring that individuals will have the merit good as would be making the entitlement inalienable. Since coercion is inherent because of the fact that a good cannot practically be bought or sold, a society can choose only whether to make an individual have the good, by giving it to him, or to prevent him from getting it by giving him money instead.[27] In such circumstances society will pick the entitlement it deems favorable to the general welfare and not worry about coercion or alienability; it has increased the chances that individuals will have a particular good without increasing the degree of coercion imposed on individuals.[28] A common example of this may occur where the good involved is the present certainty of being able to buy a future benefit and where a futures market in that good is too expensive to be feasible.[29]

---

[27] For a discussion of this inevitable, and therefore irrelevant degree of coercion in the accident context, see COSTS 50–55, 161–73.

[28] The situation is analogous to that which involves choosing between systems of allocation of accident costs which minimize rapid changes in wealth, through spreading, and those that do not. Indeed, if the avoidance of rapid changes in wealth is, itself, viewed as a merit good, the analogy is complete. In the accident field a great deal of attention has been devoted to the problem of rapid changes in wealth. *See, e.g.*, Morris & Paul, *The Financial Impact of Automobile Accidents*, 110 U. PA. L. REV. 913, 924 (1962). *But see* W. BLUM & H. KALVEN, PUBLIC LAW PERSPECTIVES ON A PRIVATE LAW PROBLEM — AUTO COMPENSATION PLANS (1965).

[29] A full discussion of this justification for the giving of goods in "kind" is well beyond the scope of this article. An indication of what is involved may be in order, however. One of the many reasons why the right to vote is given in kind instead of giving individuals that amount of money which would assure them, in a voteless society, of all the benefits which having the vote gives them, is that at any given time the price of those benefits in the future is totally uncertain and, therefore, virtually no amount of money would assure individuals of having those future benefits. This would not be the case if an entrepreneur could be counted on to guarantee those future benefits in exchange for a present money payment. That is what happens in a futures market for, say, sow's bellies. The degree of uncertainty in the cost of the future benefits of the vote is such, however, that a futures market is either not feasible, or, what is the same thing, much too costly to be worthwhile. In such circumstances the nonmarket alternative of giving of the good in kind seems more efficient. Many of the merit goods which are, in fact, given in kind in our society — for example, education — share this character-

C. Other Justice Reasons

The final reasons for a society's choice of initial entitlements we termed other justice reasons, and we may as well admit that it is hard to know what content can be poured into that term, at least given the very broad definitions of economic efficiency and distributional goals that we have used. Is there, in other words, a reason which would influence a society's choice of initial entitlements that cannot be comprehended in terms of efficiency and distribution? A couple of examples will indicate the problem.

Taney likes noise; Marshall likes silence. They are, let us assume, inevitably neighbors. Let us also assume there are no transaction costs which may impede negotiations between them. Let us assume finally that we do not know Taney's and Marshall's wealth or, indeed, anything else about them. Under these circumstances we know that Pareto optimality — economic efficiency — will be reached whether we choose an entitlement to make noise or to have silence. We also are indifferent, from a general wealth distribution point of view, as to what the initial entitlement is because we do not know whether it will lead to greater equality or inequality. This leaves us with only two reasons on which to base our choice of entitlement. The first is the relative worthiness of silence lovers and noise lovers. The second is the consistency of the choice, or its apparent consistency, with other entitlements in the society.

The first sounds appealing, and it sounds like justice. But it is hard to deal with. Why, unless our choice affects other people, should we prefer one to another?[30] To say that we wish, for

---

istic of involving present rights to future benefits in circumstances where a futures market does not exist and at first glance seems very difficult to organize cheaply. We do not suggest that this is the sole explanation for the way voting is handled in our society. For instance, it does not explain why the vote cannot be sold. (An explanation for that may be found in the fact that Taney's benefit from the vote may depend on Marshall's not having more of it than he.) It does, however, add another, not frequently given, explanation for the occasional allocation of goods rather than money to individuals.

[30] The usual answer is religious or transcendental reasons. But this answer presents problems. If it means that Chase, a third party, suffers if the noisemaker is preferred, because Chase's faith deems silence worthier than noise, then third parties *are* affected by the choice. Chase suffers; there is an external effect. But that possibility was excluded in our hypothetical. In practice such external effects, often called moralisms, are extremely common and greatly complicate the reaching of Pareto optimality. *See* pp. 1112–13 *infra*.

Religious or transcendental reasons may, however, be of another kind. Chase may prefer silence not because he himself cares, not because he suffers if noisemakers get the best of it when his faith deems silence lovers to be worthier, but because he believes God suffers if such a choice is made. No amount of compensation will help Chase in this situation since he suffers nothing which can be

instance, to make the silence lover relatively wealthier because we prefer silence is no answer, for that is simply a restatement of the question. Of course, if the choice does affect people other than Marshall and Taney, then we have a valid basis for decision. But the fact that such external effects are extremely common and greatly influence our choices does not help us much. It does suggest that the reaching of Pareto optimality is, in practice, a very complex matter precisely because of the existence of many external effects which markets find hard to deal with. And it also suggests that there often are general distributional considerations between Taney-Marshall and the rest of the world which affect the choice of entitlement. It in no way suggests, however, that there is more to the choice between Taney-Marshall than Pareto optimality and distributional concerns. In other words, if the assumptions of no transaction costs and indifference as to distributional considerations, made as between Taney and Marshall (where they are unlikely), could be made as to the world as a whole (where they are impossible), the fact that the choice between Taney's noise or Marshall's silence might affect other people would give us no guidance. Thus what sounds like a justice standard is simply a handy way of importing efficiency and distributional notions too diverse and general in their effect to be analyzed fully in the decision of a specific case.

The second sounds appealing in a different way since it sounds like "treating like cases alike." If the entitlement to make noise in other people's ears for one's pleasure is viewed by society as closely akin to the entitlement to beat up people for one's pleasure, and if good efficiency and distributional reasons exist for not allowing people to beat up others for sheer pleasure, then there may be a good reason for preferring an entitlement to silence rather than noise in the Taney-Marshall case. Because the two entitlements are apparently consistent, the entitlement to silence strengthens the entitlement to be free from gratuitous beatings which we assumed was based on good efficiency and distributional reasons.[31] It does so by lowering the enforcement costs of the entitlement to be free from gratuitous beatings; the entitlement to silence reiterates and reinforces the values protected by the entitlement to be free from gratuitous beatings and reduces the number of discriminations people must make between one activity and another, thus simplifying the task of obedience.

compensated, and compensating God for the wrong choice is not feasible. Such a reason for a choice is, we would suggest, a true nonefficiency, nondistribution reason. Whether it actually ever plays a role may well be another matter.

[31] The opposite would be true if noisemaking were thought to be akin to industry, and drive and silence to lethargy and laziness, and we had good efficiency or distributional reasons for preferring industry to lethargy.

The problem with this rationale for the choice is that it too comes down to efficiency and distributional reasons. We prefer the silence maker because *that* entitlement, even though it does not of itself affect the desired wealth distribution or lead us away from efficiency in the Taney-Marshall case, helps us to reach those goals in other situations where there are transaction costs or where we do have distributional preferences. It does this because people do not realize that the consistency is only apparent. If we could explain to them, both rationally and emotionally, the efficiency and distributional reasons why gratuitous beating up of people was inefficient or led to undesirable wealth distribution, and if we could also explain to them why an entitlement to noise rather than silence in the Taney-Marshall case would not lead to either inefficiency or maldistribution, then the secondary undermining of the entitlement to bodily integrity would not occur. It is only because it is expensive, even if feasible, to point out the difference between the two situations that the apparent similarity between them remains. And avoiding this kind of needless expense, while a very good reason for making choices, is clearly no more than a part of the economic efficiency goal.[32]

Still we should admit that explaining entitlements solely in terms of efficiency and distribution, in even their broadest terms, does not seem wholly satisfactory. The reasons for this are worth at least passing mention. The reason that we have so far explained entitlements simply in terms of efficiency and distribution is ultimately tautological. We defined distribution as covering *all* the reasons, other than efficiency, on the basis of which we might prefer to make Taney *wealthier* than Marshall. So defined, there obviously was no room for any other reasons. Distributional grounds covered broadly accepted ideas like "equality" or, in some societies, "caste preference," and highly specific ones like "favoring the silence lover." We used this definition because there is a utility in lumping together all those reasons for preferring Taney to Marshall which cannot be explained in terms of a desire to make everyone better off, and in contrasting them with efficiency reasons, whether Paretian or not, which can be so explained.

Lumping them together, however, has some analytical dis-

[32] We do not mean to underestimate the importance of apparent consistency as a ground for entitlements. Far from it, it is likely that a society often prefers an entitlement which even leads to mild inefficiencies or maldistribution of wealth between, say, Taney and Marshall, because that entitlement tends to support other entitlements which are crucial in terms of efficiency or wealth distribution in the society at large and because the cost of convincing people that the situations are, in fact, different is not worth the gain which would be obtained in the Taney-Marshall case.

advantages. It seems to assume that we cannot say any more about the reasons for some distributional preferences than about others. For instance, it seems to assume a similar universality of support for recognizing silence lovers as relatively worthier as there is for recognizing the relative desirability of equality. And that, surely, is a dangerous assumption. To avoid this danger the term "distribution" is often limited to relatively few broad reasons, like equality. And those preferences which cannot be easily explained in terms of these relatively few broadly accepted distributional preferences, or in terms of efficiency, are termed justice reasons. The difficulty with this locution is that it sometimes is taken to imply that the moral gloss of justice is reserved for these residual preferences and does not apply to the broader distributional preferences or to efficiency based preferences. And surely this is wrong, for many entitlements that properly are described as based on justice in our society can easily be explained in terms either of broad distributional preferences like equality or of efficiency or of both.

By using the term "*other* justice reasons" we hope to avoid this difficulty and emphasize that justice notions adhere to efficiency and broad distributional preferences as well as to other more idiosyncratic ones. To the extent that one is concerned with contrasting the difference between efficiency and other reasons for certain entitlements, the bipolar efficiency-distribution locution is all that is needed. To the extent that one wishes to delve either into reasons which, though possibly originally linked to efficiency, have now a life of their own, or into reasons which, though distributional, cannot be described in terms of broad principles like equality, then a locution which allows for "other justice reasons" seems more useful.[33]

III. Rules For Protecting and Regulating Entitlements

Whenever society chooses an initial entitlement it must also determine whether to protect the entitlement by property rules, by liability rules, or by rules of inalienability. In our framework, much of what is generally called private property can be viewed as an entitlement which is protected by a property rule. No one can take the entitlement to private property from the holder unless the holder sells it willingly and at the price at which he subjectively values the property. Yet a nuisance with sufficient public utility to avoid injunction has, in effect, the right to take property with compensation. In such a circumstance the entitlement to the property is protected only by what we call a liability rule:

[33] *But see* Fletcher, *supra* note 21, at 547 n.40.

an external, objective standard of value is used to facilitate the transfer of the entitlement from the holder to the nuisance.[34] Finally, in some instances we will not allow the sale of the property at all, that is, we will occasionally make the entitlement inalienable.

This section will consider the circumstances in which society will employ these three rules to solve situations of conflict. Because the property rule and the liability rule are closely related and depend for their application on the shortcomings of each other, we treat them together. We discuss inalienability separately.

A. Property and Liability Rules

Why cannot a society simply decide on the basis of the already mentioned criteria who should receive any given entitlement, and then let its transfer occur only through a voluntary negotiation? Why, in other words, cannot society limit itself to the property rule? To do this it would need only to protect and enforce the initial entitlements from all attacks, perhaps through criminal sanctions,[35] and to enforce voluntary contracts for their transfer. Why do we need liability rules at all?

In terms of economic efficiency the reason is easy enough to see. Often the cost of establishing the value of an initial entitlement by negotiation is so great that even though a transfer of the entitlement would benefit all concerned, such a transfer will not occur. If a collective determination of the value were available instead, the beneficial transfer would quickly come about.

Eminent domain is a good example. A park where Guidacres, a tract of land owned by 1,000 owners in 1,000 parcels, now sits would, let us assume, benefit a neighboring town enough so that the 100,000 citizens of the town would each be willing to pay an average of $100 to have it. The park is Pareto desirable if the owners of the tracts of land in Guidacres actually value their entitlements at less than $10,000,000 or an average of $10,000 a tract. Let us assume that in fact the parcels are all the same and all the owners value them at $8,000. On this assumption, the park is, in economic efficiency terms, desirable — in values foregone it costs $8,000,000 and is worth $10,000,000 to the buyers. And yet it may well not be established. If enough of the owners hold-out for more than $10,000 in order to get a share of the $2,000,000 that they guess the buyers are willing to pay over the

[34] *See, e.g.*, Boomer v. Atlantic Cement Co., 26 N.Y.2d 219, 309 N.Y.S.2d 312, 257 N.E.2d 870 (1970) (avoidance of injunction conditioned on payment of permanent damages to plaintiffs).

[35] The relationship between criminal sanctions and property entitlements will be examined *infra* pp. 1124–27.

value which the sellers in actuality attach, the price demanded will be more than $10,000,000 and no park will result. The sellers have an incentive to hide their true valuation and the market will not succeed in establishing it.

An equally valid example could be made on the buying side. Suppose the sellers of Guidacres have agreed to a sales price of $8,000,000 (they are all relatives and at a family banquet decided that trying to hold-out would leave them all losers). It does not follow that the buyers can raise that much even though each of 100,000 citizens *in fact* values the park at $100. Some citizens may try to free-load and say the park is only worth $50 or even nothing to them, hoping that enough others will admit to a higher desire and make up the $8,000,000 price. Again there is no reason to believe that a market, a decentralized system of valuing, will cause people to express their true valuations and hence yield results which all would *in fact* agree are desirable.

Whenever this is the case an argument can readily be made for moving from a property rule to a liability rule. If society can remove from the market the valuation of each tract of land, decide the value collectively, and impose it, then the holdout problem is gone. Similarly, if society can value collectively each individual citizen's desire to have a park and charge him a "benefits" tax based upon it, the freeloader problem is gone. If the sum of the taxes is greater than the sum of the compensation awards, the park will result.

Of course, one can conceive of situations where it might be cheap to exclude all the freeloaders from the park, or to ration the park's use in accordance with original willingness to pay. In such cases the incentive to free-load might be eliminated. But such exclusions, even if possible, are usually not cheap. And the same may be the case for market methods which might avoid the holdout problem on the seller side.

Moreover, even if holdout and freeloader problems can be met feasibly by the market, an argument may remain for employing a liability rule. Assume that in our hypothetical, freeloaders can be excluded at the cost of $1,000,000 and that all owners of tracts in Guidacres can be convinced, by the use of $500,000 worth of advertising and cocktail parties, that a sale will only occur if they reveal their true land valuations. Since $8,000,000 plus $1,500,000 is less than $10,000,000, the park will be established. But if collective valuation of the tracts and of the benefits of the prospective park would have cost less than $1,500,000, it would have been inefficient to establish the park through the market — a market which was not worth having would have been paid for.[36]

[36] It may be argued that, given imperfect knowledge, the market is preferable because it places a limit — the cost of establishing a market — on the size of the

Of course, the problems with liability rules are equally real. We cannot be at all sure that landowner Taney is lying or holding out when he says his land is worth $12,000 to him. The fact that several neighbors sold identical tracts for $10,000 does not help us very much; Taney may be sentimentally attached to his land. As a result, eminent domain may grossly undervalue what Taney would actually sell for, even if it sought to give him his true valuation of his tract. In practice, it is so hard to determine Taney's true valuation that eminent domain simply gives him what the land is worth "objectively," in the full knowledge that this may result in over or under compensation. The same is true on the buyer side. "Benefits" taxes rarely attempt, let alone succeed, in gauging the individual citizen's relative desire for the alleged benefit. They are justified because, even if they do not accurately measure each individual's desire for the benefit, the market alternative seems worse. For example, fifty different households may place different values on a new sidewalk that is to abut all the properties. Nevertheless, because it is too difficult, even if possible, to gauge each household's valuation, we usually tax each household an equal amount.

The example of eminent domain is simply one of numerous instances in which society uses liability rules. Accidents is another. If we were to give victims a property entitlement not to be accidentally injured we would have to require all who engage in activities that may injure individuals to negotiate with them before an accident, and to buy the right to knock off an arm or a leg.[37] Such pre-accident negotiations would be extremely ex-

possible loss, while the costs of coercion cannot be defined and may be infinite. This may be true in some situations but need not always be the case. If, for example, we know that the holdouts would sell for $500,000 more than is offered, because they recently offered the land at that higher price, coercing them to sell at an objectively determined price between the seller's offer and the purchaser's offer cannot result in more than $500,000 in harm. Thus, the costs of coercion would also not be infinite. Nor is it an answer to say that the man who would sell for a higher price but is coerced for a lower one suffers an indefinite nonmonetary cost in addition to the price differential simply because he is coerced and resents it. For while this may well be true, the same nonmonetary resentment may also exist in those who desire the park and do not get it because the market is unable to pay off those who are holding out for a greater than actual value. In other words, unascertainable resentment costs may exist as a result of either coercion or market failure.

[37] Even if it were possible, it should be clear that the good which would be sold would not be the same as the good actually taken. If Taney waives for $1,000 the right to recover for the loss of a leg, should he ever lose it, he is negotiating for a joint product which can be described as his "desire or aversion to gamble" and "his desire to have a leg." The product actually taken, however, is the leg. That the two goods are different can be seen from the fact that a man who demands $1,000 for a 1 in a 1,000 chance of losing a leg may well demand more

pensive, often prohibitively so.[38] To require them would thus preclude many activities that might, in fact, be worth having. And, after an accident, the loser of the arm or leg can always very plausibly deny that he would have sold it at the price the buyer would have offered. Indeed, where negotiations after an accident do occur — for instance pretrial settlements — it is largely because the alternative is the collective valuation of the damages.

It is not our object here to outline all the theoretical, let alone the practical, situations where markets may be too expensive or fail and where collective valuations seem more desirable. Economic literature has many times surrounded the issue if it has not

than $100,000 for a 1 in 10 chance of losing it, and more than $1,000,000 for the sale of his leg to someone who needs it for a transplant. *See generally* COSTS 88–94. This does not mean that the result of such transactions, if feasible, would *necessarily* be worse than the result of collective valuations. It simply means that the situation, even if feasible, is different from the one in which Taney sells his house for a given price.

[38] Such preaccident negotiations between potential injurers and victims are at times not too costly. Thus in a typical products liability situation the cost of negotiation over a potential injury need not be prohibitive. The seller of a rotary lawn mower may offer to sell at a reduced price if the buyer agrees not to sue should he be injured. Nevertheless, society often forbids such negotiations because it deems them undesirable. This may occur because of the reasons suggested in note 37 *supra*, or for any of the other reasons which cause us to make some entitlements wholly or partly inalienable, *see infra* pp. 1111–15.

Attempts have been made to deal with situations where ex ante negotiations are not feasible by fiscal devices designed to cause people to reveal their preferences. One of these contemplates requiring individuals to declare a value on their properties, or even limbs, and paying a tax on the self assessed value. That value would be the value of the good if it were taken in an accident or by eminent domain. *See generally* N. Tideman, Three Approaches to Improving Urban Land Use, ch. III (1969) (unpublished Ph.D. dissertation submitted to U. of Chicago Economics Department, on file in Yale Law Library). Of course, if the good is only taken as a result of an accident or eminent domain, the problem of gambling described in note 37 *supra* would remain. If, instead, the property or limb could be taken at will at the self assessed value, serious problems would arise from the fact that there are enormous nonmonetizable, as well as monetizable, costs involved in making people put money values on all their belongings and limbs.

An additional, though perhaps solvable, problem with self assessed taxes is the fact that the taking price would exclude any consumer surplus. This may have no significance in terms of economic efficiency, but if the existence of consumer surplus in many market transactions is thought to have, on the whole, a favorable wealth distribution effect, it might well be a reason why self assessed taxes are viewed with skepticism. *Cf.* Little, Self-Assessed Valuations: A Critique (1972) (unpublished paper, on file in Harvard Law School Library). The reader might reasonably wonder why many individuals who view self assessed taxes with skepticism show no similar concerns for what may be a very similar device, optional first party insurance covering pain and suffering damages in automobile injuries. *See, e.g.*, Calabresi, *The New York Plan: A Free Choice Modification*, 71 COLUM. L. REV. 267, 268 n.6 (1971).

always zeroed in on it in ways intelligible to lawyers.[39] It is enough for our purposes to note that a very common reason, perhaps the most common one, for employing a liability rule rather than a property rule to protect an entitlement is that market valuation of the entitlement is deemed inefficient, that is, it is either unavailable or too expensive compared to a collective valuation.

We should also recognize that efficiency is not the sole ground for employing liability rules rather than property rules. Just as the initial entitlement is often decided upon for distributional reasons, so too the choice of a liability rule is often made because it facilitates a combination of efficiency and distributive results which would be difficult to achieve under a property rule. As we shall see in the pollution context, use of a liability rule may allow us to accomplish a measure of redistribution that could only be attained at a prohibitive sacrifice of efficiency if we employed a corresponding property rule.

More often, once a liability rule is decided upon, perhaps for efficiency reasons, it is then employed to favor distributive goals as well. Again accidents and eminent domain are good examples. In both of these areas the compensation given has clearly varied with society's distributive goals, and cannot be readily explained in terms of giving the victim, as nearly as possible, an objectively determined equivalent of the price at which he would have sold what was taken from him.

It should not be surprising that this is often so, even if the original reason for a liability rule is an efficiency one. For distributional goals are expensive and difficult to achieve, and the collective valuation involved in liability rules readily lends itself to promoting distributional goals.[40] This does not mean that distributional goals are always well served in this way. Ad hoc decision-making is always troublesome, and the difficulties are especially acute when the settlement of conflicts between parties is used as a vehicle for the solution of more widespread distributional problems. Nevertheless, distributional objectives may be better attained in this way than otherwise.[41]

---

[39] For a good discussion of market failure which is intelligible to lawyers, see Bator, *The Anatomy of Market Failure*, 72 Q. J. ECON. 351 (1958).

[40] Collective valuation of costs also makes it easier to value the costs at what the society thinks they should be valued by the victim instead of at what the victim would value them in a free market if such a market were feasible. The former kind of valuation is, of course, paternalism. This does not mean it is undesirable; the danger is that paternalism which is not desirable will enter mindlessly into the cost valuation because the valuation is necessarily done collectively. *See* pp. 1113–14 *infra*.

[41] For suggestions that at times systematic distributional programs may cause

B. *Inalienable Entitlements*

Thus far we have focused on the questions of when society should protect an entitlement by property or liability rules. However, there remain many entitlements which involve a still greater degree of societal intervention: the law not only decides who is to own something and what price is to be paid for it if it is taken or destroyed, but also regulates its sale — by, for example, prescribing preconditions for a valid sale or forbidding a sale altogether. Although these rules of inalienability are substantially different from the property and liability rules, their use can be analyzed in terms of the same efficiency and distributional goals that underlie the use of the other two rules.

While at first glance efficiency objectives may seem undermined by limitations on the ability to engage in transactions, closer analysis suggests that there are instances, perhaps many, in which economic efficiency is more closely approximated by such limitations. This might occur when a transaction would create significant externalities — costs to third parties.

For instance, if Taney were allowed to sell his land to Chase, a polluter, he would injure his neighbor Marshall by lowering the value of Marshall's land. Conceivably, Marshall could pay Taney not to sell his land; but, because there are many injured Marshalls, freeloader and information costs make such transactions practically impossible. The state could protect the Marshalls and yet facilitate the sale of the land by giving the Marshalls an entitlement to prevent Taney's sale to Chase but only protecting the entitlement by a liability rule. It might, for instance, charge an excise tax on all sales of land to polluters equal to its estimate of the external cost to the Marshalls of the sale. But where there are so many injured Marshalls that the price required under the liability rule is likely to be high enough so that no one would be willing to pay it, then setting up the machinery for collective valuation will be wasteful. Barring the sale to polluters will be the most efficient result because it is clear that avoiding pollution is cheaper than paying its costs — including its costs to the Marshalls.

Another instance in which external costs may justify inalienability occurs when external costs do not lend themselves to collective measurement which is acceptably objective and nonarbitrary. This nonmonetizability is characteristic of one category of external costs which, as a practical matter, seems frequently to

greater misallocation of resources than ad hoc decisions, see Ackerman, *Regulating Slum Housing Markets on Behalf of the Poor: Of Housing Codes, Housing Subsidies and Income Redistribution Policy*, 80 YALE L.J. 1093, 1157–97 (1971); Calabresi, *supra* note 12.

lead us to rules of inalienability. Such external costs are often called moralisms.

If Taney is allowed to sell himself into slavery, or to take undue risks of becoming penniless, or to sell a kidney, Marshall may be harmed, simply because Marshall is a sensitive man who is made unhappy by seeing slaves, paupers, or persons who die because they have sold a kidney. Again Marshall could pay Taney not to sell his freedom to Chase the slaveowner; but again, because Marshall is not one but many individuals, freeloader and information costs make such transactions practically impossible. Again, it might seem that the state could intervene by objectively valuing the external cost to Marshall and requiring Chase to pay that cost. But since the external cost to Marshall does not lend itself to an acceptable objective measurement, such liability rules are not appropriate.

In the case of Taney selling land to Chase, the polluter, they were inappropriate because we *knew* that the costs to Taney and the Marshalls exceeded the benefits to Chase. Here, though we are not certain of how a cost-benefit analysis would come out, liability rules are inappropriate because any monetization is, by hypothesis, out of the question. The state must, therefore, either ignore the external costs to Marshall, or if it judges them great enough, forbid the transaction that gave rise to them by making Taney's freedom inalienable.[42]

Obviously we will not always value the external harm of a moralism enough to prohibit the sale.[43] And obviously also, external costs other than moralisms may be sufficiently hard to value to make rules of inalienability appropriate in certain circumstances; this reason for rules of inalienability, however, does seem most often germane in situations where moralisms are involved.[44]

[42] Granting Taney an inalienable right to be free is in many respects the same as granting most of the people a property entitlement to keep Taney free. The people may bargain and decide to surrender their entitlement, *i.e.*, to change the law, but there are limits on the feasibility of transactions of this sort which make the public's entitlements virtually inalienable.

[43] For example, I am allowed to buy and read whatever books I like, or to sell my house to whomever I choose, regardless of whether my doing so makes my neighbors unhappy. These entitlements could be a form of self paternalism on the part of the neighbors who fear a different rule would harm them more in the long run, or they could be selected because they strengthen seemingly similar entitlements. *See* pp. 1103–04 *supra*. But they may also reflect a judgment that the injury suffered by my neighbors results from a moralism shared by them but not so widespread as to make more efficient their being given an entitlement to prevent my transaction. In other words, people who are hurt by my transaction are the cheapest cost avoiders, *i.e.*, the cost to them of my being allowed to transact freely is less than the cost to me and others similarly situated of a converse entitlement.

[44] The fact that society may make an entitlement inalienable does not, of

There are two other efficiency reasons for forbidding the sale of entitlements under certain circumstances: self paternalism and true paternalism. Examples of the first are Ulysses tying himself to the mast or individuals passing a bill of rights so that they will be prevented from yielding to momentary temptations which they deem harmful to themselves. This type of limitation is not in any real sense paternalism. It is fully consistent with Pareto efficiency criteria, based on the notion that over the mass of cases no one knows better than the individual what is best for him or her. It merely allows the individual to choose what is best in the long run rather than in the short run, even though that choice entails giving up some short run freedom of choice. Self paternalism may cause us to require certain conditions to exist before we allow a sale of an entitlement; and it may help explain many situations of inalienability, like the invalidity of contracts entered into when drunk, or under undue influence or coercion. But it probably does not fully explain even these.[45]

True paternalism brings us a step further toward explaining such prohibitions and those of broader kinds — for example the prohibitions on a whole range of activities by minors. Paternalism is based on the notion that at least in some situations the Marshalls know better than Taney what will make Taney better off.[46] Here we are not talking about the offense to Marshall from Taney's choosing to read pornography, or selling himself into slavery, but rather the judgment that Taney was not in the position to choose best for himself when he made the choice for erotica or servitude.[47]

---

course, mean that there will be no compensation to the holder of the entitlement if it is taken from him. Thus even if a society forbids the sale of one's kidneys it will still probably compensate the person whose kidney is destroyed in an auto accident. The situations are distinct and the kidney is protected by different rules according to which situation we are speaking of.

[45] As a practical matter, since it is frequently impossible to limit the effect of an inalienable rule to those who desire it for self paternalistic reasons, self paternalism would lead to some restraints on those who would desire to sell their entitlements. This does not make self paternalism any less consistent with the premises of Pareto optimality; it is only another recognition that in an imperfect world, Pareto optimality can be approached more closely by systems which involve some coercion than by a system of totally free bargains.

[46] This locution leaves open the question whether Taney's future well-being will ultimately be decided by Taney himself or the many Marshalls. The latter implies a further departure from Paretian premises. The former, which may be typical of paternalism towards minors, implies simply that the minors do not know enough to exercise self paternalism.

[47] Sometimes the term paternalism is used to explain use of a rule of inalienability in situations where inalienability will not make the many Marshalls or the coerced Taney any better off. Inalienability is said to be imposed because the many Marshalls believe that making the entitlement inalienable is doing God's

The first concept we called a moralism and is a frequent and important ground for inalienability. But it is consistent with the premises of Pareto optimality. The second, paternalism, is also an important economic efficiency reason for inalienability, but it is not consistent with the premises of Pareto optimality: the most efficient pie is no longer that which costless bargains would achieve, because a person may be better off if he is prohibited from bargaining.

Finally, just as efficiency goals sometimes dictate the use of rules of inalienability, so, of course, do distributional goals. Whether an entitlement may be sold or not often affects directly who is richer and who is poorer. Prohibiting the sale of babies makes poorer those who can cheaply produce babies and richer those who through some nonmarket device get free an "unwanted" baby.[48] Prohibiting exculpatory clauses in product sales makes richer those who were injured by a product defect and poorer those who were not injured and who paid more for the product because the exulpatory clause was forbidden.[49] Favoring the specific group that has benefited may or may not have been the reason for the prohibition on bargaining. What is important is that, regardless of the reason for barring a contract, a group did gain from the prohibition.

This should suffice to put us on guard, for it suggests that direct distributional motives may lie behind asserted nondistributional grounds for inalienability, whether they be paternalism, self paternalism, or externalities.[50] This does not mean that giving

---

will, that is, that a sale or transfer of the entitlement would injure God. Assuming this situation exists in practice, we would not term it paternalism, because that word implies looking after the interests of the coerced party. *See* note 30 *supra*.

[48] This assumes that a prohibition on the sale of unwanted babies can be effectively enforced. If it can, then those unwanted babies which are produced are of no financial benefit to their natural parents and bring an increase in well-being to those who are allowed to adopt them free and as a result of a nonmarket allocation. Should the prohibition on sales of babies be only partially enforceable, the distributional result would be more complex. It would be unchanged for those who could obtain babies for adoption legally, *i.e.*, for those who received them without paying bribes, as it would for the natural parents who obeyed the law, since they would still receive no compensation. On the other hand, the illegal purchaser would probably pay, and the illegal seller receive, a higher price than if the sale of babies were legal. This would cause a greater distributive effect within the group of illegal sellers and buyers than would exist if such sales were permitted.

[49] *See* note 37 *supra*.

[50] As a practical matter, it is often impossible to tell whether an entitlement has been made partially inalienable for any of the several efficiency grounds mentioned or for distributional grounds. Do we bar people from selling their bodies for paternalistic, self paternalistic, or moralistic cost reasons? On what basis do we prohibit an individual from taking, for a high price, one chance in three of having

weight to distributional goals is undesirable. It clearly is desirable where on efficiency grounds society is indifferent between an alienable and an inalienable entitlement and distributional goals favor one approach or the other. It may well be desirable even when distributional goals are achieved at some efficiency costs. The danger may be, however, that what is justified on, for example, paternalism grounds is really a hidden way of accruing distributional benefits for a group whom we would not otherwise wish to benefit. For example, we may use certain types of zoning to preserve open spaces on the grounds that the poor will be happier, though they do not know it now. And open spaces may indeed make the poor happier in the long run. But the zoning that preserves open space also makes housing in the suburbs more expensive and it may be that the whole plan is aimed at securing distributional benefits to the suburban dweller regardless of the poor's happiness.[51]

IV. The Framework and Pollution Control Rules

Nuisance or pollution is one of the most interesting areas where the question of who will be given an entitlement, and how it will be protected, is in frequent issue.[52] Traditionally, and very ably in the recent article by Professor Michelman, the nuisance-pollution problem is viewed in terms of three rules.[53] First, Taney

to give his heart to a wealthy man who needs a transplant? Do we try to avoid a market in scarce medical resources for distributional or for some or all of the efficiency reasons discussed?

[51] There is another set of reasons which causes us to prohibit sales of some entitlements and which is sometimes termed distributional; this set of reasons causes us to prohibit sales of some entitlements because the underlying distribution of wealth seems to us undesirable. These reasons, we would suggest, are not true distributional grounds. They are, rather, efficiency grounds which become valid because of the original maldistribution. As such they can once again be categorized as due to externalities, self paternalism, and pure paternalism: (1) Marshall is offended because Taney, due to poverty, sells a kidney, and therefore Marshall votes to bar such sales (a moralism); (2) Taney, seeking to avoid temporary temptation due to his poverty, votes to bar such sales (self paternalism); and (3) the law prohibits Taney from the same sale because, regardless of what Taney believes, a majority thinks Taney will be better off later if he is barred from selling than if he is free to do so while influenced by his own poverty (pure paternalism). We do not mean to minimize these reasons by noting that they are not strictly distributional. We call them nondistributional simply to distinguish them from the more direct way in which distributional considerations affect the alienability of entitlements.

[52] It should be clear that the pollution problem we discuss here is really only a part of a broader problem, that of land use planning in general. Much of this analysis may therefore be relevant to other land use issues, for example exclusionary zoning, restrictive covenants, and ecological easements. *See* note 58 *infra*.

[53] Michelman, *supra* note 1, at 670. *See also* Restatement (Second) of Torts

may not pollute unless his neighbor (his only neighbor let us assume), Marshall, allows it (Marshall may enjoin Taney's nuisance).[54] Second, Taney may pollute but must compensate Marshall for damages caused (nuisance is found but the remedy is limited to damages).[55] Third, Taney may pollute at will and can only be stopped by Marshall if Marshall pays him off (Taney's pollution is not held to be a nuisance to Marshall).[56] In our terminology rules one and two (nuisance with injunction, and with damages only) are entitlements to Marshall. The first is an entitlement to be free from pollution and is protected by a property rule; the second is also an entitlement to be free from pollution but is protected only by a liability rule. Rule three (no nuisance) is instead an entitlement to Taney protected by a property rule, for only by buying Taney out at Taney's price can Marshall end the pollution.

The very statement of these rules in the context of our framework suggests that something is missing. Missing is a fourth rule representing an entitlement in Taney to pollute, but an entitlement which is protected only by a liability rule. The fourth rule, really a kind of partial eminent domain coupled with a benefits tax, can be stated as follows: Marshall may stop Taney from polluting, but if he does he must compensate Taney.

As a practical matter it will be easy to see why even legal writers as astute as Professor Michelman have ignored this rule. Unlike the first three it does not often lend itself to judicial imposition for a number of good legal process reasons. For example, even if Taney's injuries could practicably be measured, apportionment of the duty of compensation among many Marshalls would present problems for which courts are not well suited. If only those Marshalls who voluntarily asserted the right to enjoin Taney's pollution were required to pay the compensation, there would be insuperable freeloader problems. If, on the other

---

§§ 157–215 (1965). Michelman also discusses the possibility of inalienability. Michelman, *supra*, at 684. For a discussion of the use of rules of inalienability in the pollution context, see pp. 1123–24 *infra*.

[54] *See, e.g.*, Department of Health & Mental Hygiene v. Galaxy Chem. Co., 1 ENVIR. REP. 1660 (Md. Cir. Ct. 1970) (chemical smells enjoined); Ensign v. Walls, 323 Mich. 49, 34 N.W. 2d 549 (1948) (dog raising in residential neighborhood enjoined).

[55] *See, e.g.*, Boomer v. Atlantic Cement Co., 26 N.Y. 2d 219, 309 N.Y.S. 2d 312, 257 N.E.2d 870 (1970) (avoidance of injunction conditioned on payment of permanent damages to plaintiffs).

[56] *See, e.g.*, Francisco v. Department of Institutions & Agencies, 13 N.J. Misc. 663, 180 A. 843 (Ct. Ch. 1935) (plaintiffs not entitled to enjoin noise and odors of adjacent sanitarium); Rose v. Socony-Vacuum Corp., 54 R.I. 411, 173 A. 627 (1934) (pollution of percolating waters not enjoinable in absence of negligence).

hand, the liability rule entitled one of the Marshalls alone to enjoin the pollution and required all the benefited Marshalls to pay their share of the compensation, the courts would be faced with the immensely difficult task of determining who was benefited how much and imposing a benefits tax accordingly, all the while observing procedural limits within which courts are expected to function.[57]

The fourth rule is thus not part of the cases legal scholars read when they study nuisance law, and is therefore easily ignored by them. But it is available, and may sometimes make more sense than any of the three competing approaches. Indeed, in one form or another, it may well be the most frequent device employed.[58] To appreciate the utility of the fourth rule and to com-

[57] This task is much more difficult than that which arises under rule two, in which the many Marshalls would be compensated for their pollution injuries. Under rule two, each victim may act as an individual, either in seeking compensation in the first instance or in electing whether to be a part of a class seeking compensation. If he wishes to and is able to convince the court (by some accepted objective standard) that he has been injured, he may be compensated. Such individual action is expensive, and thus may be wasteful, but it presents no special problems in terms of the traditional workings of the courts. But where the class in question consists, not of those with a right to enjoin, but of those who must pay to enjoin, freeloader problems require the court to determine that an unwilling Marshall has been benefited and should be required to pay. The basic difficulty is that if we begin with the premise which usually underlies our notion of efficiency — namely, that individuals know what is best for them — we are faced with the anomaly of compelling compensation from one who denies he has incurred a benefit but whom we require to pay because *the court* thinks he has been benefited.

This problem is analogous to the difficulties presented by quasi-contracts. In terms of the theory of our economic efficiency goal, the case for requiring compensation for unbargained for (often accidental) benefits is similar to the argument for compensating tort victims. Yet courts as a general rule require compensation in quasi-contract only where there is both an indisputable benefit (usually of a pecuniary or economic nature) and some affirmative acknowledgment of subjective benefit (usually a subsequent promise to pay). *See* A. CORBIN, CONTRACTS §§ 231–34 (1963). This hesitancy suggests that courts lack confidence in their ability to distinguish real benefits from illusions. Perhaps even more importantly, it suggests that the courts recognize that what may clearly be an objective "benefit" may, to the putative beneficiary, not be a subjective benefit — if for no other reason than that unintended changes from the status quo often exact psychological costs. If that is the case, there has been no benefit at all in terms of our efficiency criterion.

[58] *See* A. KNEESE & B. BOWER, MANAGING WATER QUALITY: ECONOMICS, TECHNOLOGY, INSTITUTIONS 98–109 (1968); Krier, *The Pollution Problem and Legal Institutions: A Conceptual Overview*, 18 U.C.L.A.L. REV. 429, 467–75 (1971).

Virtually all eminent domain takings of a nonconforming use seem to be examples of this approach. Ecological easements may be another prime example. A local zoning ordinance may require a developer to contribute a portion of his land for purposes of parkland or school construction. In compensation for taking

pare it with the other three rules, we will examine why we might choose any of the given rules.

We would employ rule one (entitlement to be free from pollution protected by a property rule) from an economic efficiency point of view if we believed that the polluter, Taney, could avoid or reduce the costs of pollution more cheaply than the pollutee, Marshall. Or to put it another way, Taney would be enjoinable if he were in a better position to balance the costs of polluting against the costs of not polluting. We would employ rule three (entitlement to pollute protected by a property rule) again solely from an economic efficiency standpoint, if we made the converse judgment on who could best balance the harm of pollution against its avoidance costs. If we were wrong in our judgments and if transactions between Marshall and Taney were costless or even very cheap, the entitlement under rules one or three would be traded and an economically efficient result would occur in either case.[59] If we entitled Taney to pollute and Marshall valued clean air more than Taney valued the pollution, Marshall would pay Taney to stop polluting even though no nuisance was found. If we entitled Marshall to enjoin the pollution and the right to pollute was worth more to Taney than freedom from pollution was to Marshall, Taney would pay Marshall not to seek an injunction or would buy Marshall's land and sell it to someone who would agree not to seek an injunction. As we have assumed no one else was hurt by the pollution, Taney could now pollute even though the initial entitlement, based on a wrong guess of who was the cheapest avoider of the costs involved, allowed the pollution to be enjoined. Wherever transactions between Taney and Marshall are easy, and wherever economic efficiency is our goal, we could employ entitlements protected by property rules even though we would not be sure that the entitlement chosen was the right one. Transactions as described above would cure the error. While the entitlement might have important distributional effects, it would not substantially undercut economic efficiency.

the developer's entitlement, the locality will pay the developer "damages": it will allow him to increase the normal rate of density in his remaining property. The question of damage assessment involved in ecological easements raises similar problems to those raised in the benefit assessment involved in the question of quasi-contract. *See* note 57 *supra*.

[59] For a discussion of whether efficiency would be achieved in the long, as well as the short, run, see Coase, *supra* note 12; Calabresi, *supra* note 12 (pointing out that if "no transaction costs" means no impediments to bargaining in the short or long run, and if Pareto optimality means an allocation of resources which cannot be improved by bargains, assumptions of no transaction costs and rationality necessarily imply Pareto optimality); Nutter, *supra* note 12 (a technical demonstration of the applicability of the Coase theorem to long run problems). *See also* Demsetz, *supra* note 16, at 19–22.

The moment we assume, however, that transactions are not cheap, the situation changes dramatically. Assume we enjoin Taney and there are 10,000 injured Marshalls. Now *even if* the right to pollute is worth more to Taney than the right to be free from pollution is to the sum of the Marshalls, the injunction will probably stand. The cost of buying out all the Marshalls, given holdout problems, is likely to be too great, and an equivalent of eminent domain in Taney would be needed to alter the initial injunction. Conversely, if we denied a nuisance remedy, the 10,000 Marshalls could only with enormous difficulty, given freeloader problems, get together to buy out even one Taney and prevent the pollution. This would be so even if the pollution harm was greater than the value to Taney of the right to pollute.

If, however, transaction costs are not symmetrical, we may still be able to use the property rule. Assume that Taney can buy the Marshalls' entitlements easily because holdouts are for some reason absent, but that the Marshalls have great freeloader problems in buying out Taney. In this situation the entitlement should be granted to the Marshalls unless we are sure the Marshalls are the cheapest avoiders of pollution costs. Where we do not know the identity of the cheapest cost avoider it is better to entitle the Marshalls to be free of pollution because, even if we are wrong in our initial placement of the entitlement, that is, even if the Marshalls are the cheapest cost avoiders, Taney will buy out the Marshalls and economic efficiency will be achieved. Had we chosen the converse entitlement and been wrong, the Marshalls could not have bought out Taney. Unfortunately, transaction costs are often high on both sides and an initial entitlement, though incorrect in terms of economic efficiency, will not be altered in the market place.

Under these circumstances — and they are normal ones in the pollution area — we are likely to turn to liability rules whenever we are uncertain whether the polluter or the pollutees can most cheaply avoid the cost of pollution. We are only likely to use liability rules where we are uncertain because, if we are certain, the costs of liability rules — essentially the costs of collectively valuing the damages to all concerned plus the cost in coercion to those who would not sell at the collectively determined figure — are unnecessary. They are unnecessary because transaction costs and bargaining barriers become irrelevant when we are certain who is the cheapest cost avoider; economic efficiency will be attained without transactions by making the correct initial entitlement.

As a practical matter we often are uncertain who the cheapest cost avoider is. In such cases, traditional legal doctrine tends to

find a nuisance but imposes only damages on Taney payable to the Marshalls.[60] This way, if the amount of damages Taney is made to pay is close to the injury caused, economic efficiency will have had its due; if he cannot make a go of it, the nuisance was not worth its costs. The entitlement to the Marshalls to be free from pollution unless compensated, however, will have been given *not* because it was thought that polluting was probably worth less to Taney than freedom from pollution was worth to the Marshalls, nor even because on some distributional basis we preferred to charge the cost to Taney rather than to the Marshalls. It was so placed *simply because we did not know* whether Taney desired to pollute more than the Marshalls desired to be free from pollution, and the only way we thought we could test out the value of the pollution was by the only liability rule we thought we had. This was rule two, the imposition of nuisance damages on Taney. At least this would be the position of a court concerned with economic efficiency which believed itself limited to rules one, two, and three.

Rule four gives at least the possibility that the opposite entitlement may also lead to economic efficiency in a situation of uncertainty. Suppose for the moment that a mechanism exists for collectively assessing the damage resulting to Taney from being stopped from polluting by the Marshalls, and a mechanism also exists for collectively assessing the benefit to each of the Marshalls from such cessation. Then — assuming the same degree of accuracy in collective valuation as exists in rule two (the nuisance damage rule) — the Marshalls would stop the pollution if it harmed them more than it benefited Taney. If this is possible, then even if we thought it necessary to use a liability rule, we would still be free to give the entitlement to Taney or Marshall for whatever reasons, efficiency or distributional, we desired.

Actually, the issue is still somewhat more complicated. For just as transaction costs are not necessarily symmetrical under the two converse property rule entitlements, so also the liability rule equivalents of transaction costs — the cost of valuing collectively and of coercing compliance with that valuation — may not be symmetrical under the two converse liability rules. Nuisance damages may be very hard to value, and the costs of informing all the injured of their rights and getting them into court may be prohibitive. Instead, the assessment of the objective damage to Taney from foregoing his pollution may be cheap and so might the as-

[60] *See, e.g.*, City of Harrisonville v. W.S. Dickey Clay Mfg. Co., 289 U.S. 334 (1933) (damages appropriate remedy where injunction would prejudice important public interest); Madison v. Ducktown Sulphur, Copper & Iron Co., 113 Tenn. 331, 83 S.W. 658 (1904) (damages appropriate because of plaintiff's ten year delay in seeking to enjoin fumes).

sessment of the relative benefits to all Marshalls of such freedom from pollution. But the opposite may also be the case. As a result, just as the choice of which property entitlement may be based on the asymmetry of transaction costs and hence on the greater amenability of one property entitlement to market corrections, so might the choice between liability entitlements be based on the asymmetry of the costs of collective determination.

The introduction of distributional considerations makes the existence of the fourth possibility even more significant. One does not need to go into all the permutations of the possible tradeoffs between efficiency and distributional goals under the four rules to show this. A simple example should suffice. Assume a factory which, by using cheap coal, pollutes a very wealthy section of town and employs many low income workers to produce a product purchased primarily by the poor; assume also a distributional goal that favors equality of wealth. Rule one — enjoin the nuisance — would possibly have desirable economic efficiency results (if the pollution hurt the homeowners more than it saved the factory in coal costs), but it would have disastrous distribution effects. It would also have undesirable efficiency effects if the initial judgment on costs of avoidance had been wrong and transaction costs were high. Rule two — nuisance damages — would allow a testing of the economic efficiency of eliminating the pollution, even in the presence of high transaction costs, but would quite possibly put the factory out of business or diminish output and thus have the same income distribution effects as rule one. Rule three — no nuisance — would have favorable distributional effects since it might protect the income of the workers. But if the pollution harm was greater to the homeowners than the cost of avoiding it by using a better coal, and if transaction costs — holdout problems — were such that homeowners could not unite to pay the factory to use better coal, rule three would have unsatisfactory efficiency effects. Rule four — payment of damages to the factory after allowing the homeowners to compel it to use better coal, and assessment of the cost of these damages to the homeowners — would be the only one which would accomplish both the distributional and efficiency goals.[61]

An equally good hypothetical for any of the rules can be constructed. Moreover, the problems of coercion may as a

[61] Either of the liability rules may also be used in another manner to achieve distributional goals. For example, if victims of pollution were poor, and if society desired a more equal distribution of wealth, it might intentionally increase "objective" damage awards if rule two were used; conversely, it might decrease the compensation to the factory owners, without any regard for economic efficiency if rule four were chosen. There are obvious disadvantages to this ad hoc method of achieving distributional goals. *See* p. 1110 *supra*.

practical matter be extremely severe under rule four. How do the homeowners decide to stop the factory's use of low grade coal? How do we assess the damages and their proportional allocation in terms of benefits to the homeowners? But equivalent problems may often be as great for rule two. How do we value the damages to each of the many homeowners? How do we inform the homeowners of their rights to damages? How do we evaluate and limit the administrative expenses of the court actions this solution implies?

The seriousness of the problem depends under each of the liability rules on the number of people whose "benefits" or "damages" one is assessing and the expense and likelihood of error in such assessment. A judgment on these questions is necessary to an evaluation of the possible economic efficiency benefits of employing one rule rather than another. The relative ease of making such assessments through different institutions may explain why we often employ the courts for rule two and get to rule four — when we do get there — only through political bodies which may, for example, prohibit pollution, or "take" the entitlement to build a supersonic plane by a kind of eminent domain, paying compensation to those injured by these decisions.[62] But

[62] Of course, variants of the other rules may be administered through political institutions as well. Rule three, granting a property entitlement to a polluter, may be effectuated by tax credits or other incentives such as subsidization of nonpolluting fuels offered for voluntary pollution abatement. In such schemes, as with rule four, political institutions are used to effect comprehensive benefit assessment and overcome freeloader problems which would be encountered in a more decentralized market solution. However, this centralization — to the extent that it replaces voluntary payments by individual pollution victims with collective payments not unanimously agreed upon — is a hybrid solution. The polluter must assent to the sale of his entitlement, but the amount of pollution abatement sought and the price paid by each pollution victim is not subjectively determined and voluntarily assented to by each.

The relationship of hybrids like the above to the four basic rules can be stated more generally. The buyer of an entitlement, whether the entitlement is protected by property or liability rules, may be viewed as owning what is in effect a property right not to buy the entitlement. But when freeloader problems abound, that property right may instead be given to a class of potential buyers. This "class" may be a municipality, a sewer authority, or any other body which can decide to buy an entitlement and compel those benefited to pay an objective price. When this is done, the individuals within the class have themselves only an entitlement not to purchase the seller's entitlement protected by a liability rule.

As we have already seen, the holder of an entitlement may be permitted to sell it at his own price or be compelled to sell it at an objective price: he may have an entitlement protected by a property or liability rule. Since, therefore, in any transaction the buyer may have a property or liability entitlement not to buy and the seller may have a property or a liability entitlement not to sell, there are, in effect, four combinations of rules for each possible original location of the enall this does not, in any sense, diminish the importance of the fact that an awareness of the possibility of an entitlement to pollute, but one protected only by a liability rule, may in some instances allow us best to combine our distributional and efficiency goals.

We have said that we would say little about justice, and so we shall. But it should be clear that if rule four might enable us best to combine efficiency goals with distributional goals, it might also enable us best to combine those same efficiency goals with other goals that are often described in justice language. For example, assume that the factory in our hypothetical was using cheap coal *before* any of the wealthy houses were built. In these circumstances, rule four will not only achieve the desirable efficiency and distributional results mentioned above, but it will also accord with any "justice" significance which is attached to being there first. And this is so whether we view this justice significance as part of a distributional goal, as part of a long run efficiency goal based on protecting expectancies, or as part of an independent concept of justice.

Thus far in this section we have ignored the possibility of employing rules of inalienability to solve pollution problems. A general policy of barring pollution does seem unrealistic.[63] But rules of inalienability can appropriately be used to limit the levels of pollution and to control the levels of activities which cause pollution.[64]

One argument for inalienability may be the widespread exist-

---

titlement: voluntary seller and voluntary buyer; voluntary seller and compelled buyer; compelled seller and voluntary buyer; compelled seller and compelled buyer. Moreover, since the entitlement to that which is being bought or sold could have been originally given to the opposite party, there are, in effect, eight possible rules rather than four.

We do not mean by the above to suggest that political institutions are used only to allocate collectively held property rights. Quite the contrary, rule two, for instance, gives pollution victims an entitlement protected by a liability rule to be free from pollution. This rule could be administered by decentralized damage assessment as in litigation, or it could be effected by techniques like effluent fees charged to polluters. The latter type of collective intervention may be preferred where large numbers are involved and the costs of decentralized injury valuation are high. Still, under either system the "sale price" is collectively determined, so the basic character of the victims' entitlement is not changed.

[63] *See* Michelman, *supra* note 1, at 667.

[64] This is the exact analogue of specific deterrence of accident causing activities. *See* COSTS at 95–129.

Although it may seem fanciful to us, there is of course the possibility that a state might wish to grant a converse entitlement — an inalienable entitlement to pollute in some instances. This might happen where the state believed that in the long run everyone would be better off by allowing the polluting producers to make their products, regardless of whether the polluter thought it advantageous to accept compensation for stopping his pollution.

ence of moralisms against pollution. Thus it may hurt the Marshalls — gentleman farmers — to see Taney, a smoke-choked city dweller, sell his entitlement to be free of pollution. A different kind of externality or moralism may be even more important. The Marshalls may be hurt by the expectation that, while the present generation might withstand present pollution levels with no serious health dangers, future generations may well face a despoiled, hazardous environmental condition which they are powerless to reverse.[65] And this ground for inalienability might be strengthened if a similar conclusion were reached on grounds of self paternalism. Finally, society might restrict alienability on paternalistic grounds. The Marshalls might feel that although Taney himself does not know it, Taney will be better off if he really can see the stars at night, or if he can breathe smogless air.

Whatever the grounds for inalienability, we should reemphasize that distributional effects should be carefully evaluated in making the choice for or against inalienability. Thus the citizens of a town may be granted an entitlement to be free of water pollution caused by the waste discharges of a chemical factory; and the entitlement might be made inalienable on the grounds that the town's citizens really would be better off in the long run to have access to clean beaches. But the entitlement might also be made inalienable to assure the maintenance of a beautiful resort area for the very wealthy, at the same time putting the town's citizens out of work.[66]

V. The Framework and Criminal Sanctions

Obviously we cannot canvass the relevance of our approach through many areas of the law. But we do think it beneficial to examine one further area, that of crimes against property and bodily integrity. The application of the framework to the use of criminal sanctions in cases of theft or violations of bodily integrity is useful in that it may aid in understanding the previous material, especially as it helps us to distinguish different kinds of legal problems and to identify the different modes of resolving those problems.

Beginning students, when first acquainted with economic efficiency notions, sometimes ask why ought not a robber be simply charged with the value of the thing robbed. And the same question

[65] *See* Michelman, *supra* note 1, at 684.

[66] *Cf.* Frady, *The View from Hilton Head*, HARPER'S, May, 1970, at 103–112 (conflict over proposed establishment of chemical factory that would pollute the area's beaches in economically depressed South Carolina community; environmental groups that opposed factory backed by developers of wealthy resorts in the area, proponents of factory supported by representatives of unemployed town citizens).

is sometimes posed by legal philosophers.[67] If it is worth more to the robber than to the owner, is not economic efficiency served by such a penalty? Our answers to such a question tend to move quickly into very high sounding and undoubtedly relevant moral considerations. But these considerations are often not very helpful to the questioner because they depend on the existence of obligations on individuals not to rob for a fixed price and the original question was why we should impose such obligations at all.

One simple answer to the question would be that thieves do not get caught every time they rob and therefore the costs to the thief must at least take the unlikelihood of capture into account.[68] But that would not fully answer the problem, for even if thieves were caught every time, the penalty we would wish to impose would be greater than the objective damages to the person robbed.

A possible broader explanation lies in a consideration of the difference between property entitlements and liability entitlements. For us to charge the thief with a penalty equal to an objectively determined value of the property stolen would be to convert all property rule entitlements into liability rule entitlements.

The question remains, however, why *not* convert all property rules into liability rules? The answer is, of course, obvious. Liability rules represent only an approximation of the value of the object to its original owner and willingness to pay such an approximate value is no indication that it is worth more to the thief than to the owner. In other words, quite apart from the expense of arriving collectively at such an objective valuation, it is no guarantee of the economic efficiency of the transfer.[69] If this is so with property, it is all the more so with bodily integrity, and we would not presume collectively and objectively to value the cost of a rape to the victim against the benefit to the rapist even if economic efficiency is our sole motive. Indeed when we approach bodily integrity we are getting close to areas where we do not let the entitlement be sold at all and where economic efficiency enters

---

[67] One of the last articles by Professor Giorgio Del Vecchio came close to asking this question. *See* Del Vecchio, *Equality and Inequality in Relation to Justice*, 11 NAT. LAW FORUM 36, 43–45 (1966).

[68] *See, e.g.*, Becker, *Crime and Punishment: An Economic Approach*, 76 J. POL. ECON. 169 (1968).

[69] One might also point out that very often a thief will not have the money to meet the objectively determined price of the stolen object; indeed, his lack of resources is probably his main motivation for the theft. In such cases society, if it insists on a liability rule, will have to compensate the initial entitlement holder from the general societal coffers. When this happens the thief will not feel the impact of the liability rule and hence will not be sufficiently deterred from engaging in similar activity in the future. *Cf.* COSTS at 147–48.

in, if at all, in a more complex way. But even where the items taken or destroyed are things we do allow to be sold, we will not without special reasons impose an objective selling price on the vendor.

Once we reach the conclusion that we will not simply have liability rules, but that often, even just on economic efficiency grounds, property rules are desirable, an answer to the beginning student's question becomes clear. The thief not only harms the victim, he undermines rules and distinctions of significance beyond the specific case. Thus even if in a given case we can be sure that the value of the item stolen was no more than X dollars, and even if the thief has been caught and is prepared to compensate, we would not be content simply to charge the thief X dollars. Since in the majority of cases we cannot be sure of the economic efficiency of the transfer by theft, we must add to each case an undefinable kicker which represents society's need to keep all property rules from being changed at will into liability rules.[70] In other words, we impose criminal sanctions as a means of deterring future attempts to convert property rules into liability rules.[71]

The first year student might push on, however, and ask why we treat the thief or the rapist differently from the injurer in an auto

---

[70] If we were not interested in the integrity of property rules and hence we were not using an indefinable kicker, we would still presumably try to adjust the amount of damages charged to the thief in order to reflect the fact that only a percentage of thieves are caught; that is, we would fix a price-penalty which reflected the value of the good and the risk of capture.

[71] A problem related to criminal sanctions is that of punitive damages in intentional torts. If Taney sets a spring gun with the purpose of killing or maiming anyone who trespasses on his property, Taney has knowledge of what he is doing and of the risks involved which is more akin to the criminal than the negligent driver. But because Taney does not know precisely which one of many Marshalls will be the victim of his actions, ex ante negotiations seem difficult. How then do we justify the use of criminal sanctions and of more than compensatory damages? Probably the answer lies in the fact that we assume that the benefits of Taney's act are not worth the harm they entail if that harm were fully valued. Believing that this fact, in contrast with what is involved in a simple negligence case, should be, and in a sense can be, made known to the actor at the time he acts, we pile on extra damages. Our judgment is that most would act differently if a true cost-benefit burden could be placed. Given that judgment and given the impossibility of imposing a true cost-benefit burden by collective valuations — because of inadequate knowledge — we make sure that if we err we will err on the side of overestimating the cost.

There may be an additional dimension. Unlike fines or other criminal sanctions, punitive damages provide an extra compensation for the victim. This may not be pure windfall. Once the judgment is made that injuries classified as intentional torts are less desirable than nonintentional harms — either because they are expected to be less efficient or because there is less justification for the tortfeasor's not having purchased the entitlement in an ex ante bargain — then it may be that the actual, subjective injury to the victim from the tort is enhanced. One

accident or the polluter in a nuisance case. Why do we allow liability rules there? In a sense, we have already answered the question. The only level at which, before the accident, the driver can negotiate for the value of what he might take from his potential victim is one at which transactions are too costly. The thief or rapist, on the other hand, could have negotiated without undue expense (at least if the good was one which we allowed to be sold at all) because we assume he knew what he was going to do and to whom he would do it. The case of the accident is different because knowledge exists only at the level of deciding to drive or perhaps to drive fast, and at that level negotiations with potential victims are usually not feasible.

The case of nuisance seems different, however. There the polluter knows what he will do and, often, whom it will hurt. But as we have already pointed out, freeloader or holdout problems may often preclude any successful negotiations between the polluter and the victims of pollution; additionally, we are often uncertain who is the cheapest avoider of pollution costs. In these circumstances a liability rule, which at least allowed the economic efficiency of a proposed transfer of entitlements to be tested, seemed appropriate, even though it permitted the nonaccidental and unconsented taking of an entitlement. It should be emphasized, however, that where transaction costs do not bar negotiations between polluter and victim, or where we are sufficiently certain who the cheapest cost avoider is, there are no efficiency reasons for allowing intentional takings, and property rules, supported by injunctions or criminal sanctions, are appropriate.[72]

VI. Conclusion

This article has attempted to demonstrate how a wide variety of legal problems can usefully be approached in terms of a specific framework. Framework or model building has two shortcomings.

---

whose automobile is destroyed accidentally suffers from the loss of his car; one whose automobile is destroyed intentionally suffers from the loss of the car, and his injury is made greater by the knowledge that the loss was intentional, wilful, or otherwise avoidable.

[72] *Cf.* pp 1111–13.

We have not discussed distributional goals as they relate to criminal sanctions. In part this is because we have assumed the location of the initial entitlement — we have assumed the victim of a crime was entitled to the good stolen or to his bodily integrity. There is, however, another aspect of distributional goals which relates to the particular rule we choose to protect the initial entitlement. For example, one might raise the question of linking the severity of criminal sanctions to the wealth of the criminal or the victim. While this aspect of distributional goals would certainly be a fruitful area of discussion, it is beyond the scope of the present article.

The first is that models can be mistaken for the total view of phenomena, like legal relationships, which are too complex to be painted in any one picture. The second is that models generate boxes into which one then feels compelled to force situations which do not truly fit. There are, however, compensating advantages. Legal scholars, precisely because they have tended to eschew model building, have often proceeded in an ad hoc way, looking at cases and seeing what categories emerged. But this approach also affords only one view of the Cathedral. It may neglect some relationships among the problems involved in the cases which model building can perceive, precisely because it does generate boxes, or categories. The framework we have employed may be applied in many different areas of the law. We think its application facilitated perceiving and defining an additional resolution of the problem of pollution. As such we believe the painting to be well worth the oils.

[3]

PRICES AND SANCTIONS

*Robert Cooter**

Introduction

Scholars of jurisprudence traditionally view law as a set of obligations backed by sanctions, or commands backed by threats.[1] In contrast, economists tend to view law as a set of official prices.[2] Associated with each of these viewpoints is a characteristic blindness. The jurisprudential perspective blinds lawyers to the fact that officials cannot regulate the economy efficiently by giving orders.[3] Instead, they must rely upon legal instruments similar to prices. Conversely, the economic perspective is blind to the distinctively normative aspect of law, viewing a sanction for doing what is forbidden merely as the price of doing what is permitted. In brief, the economic analysis of law lacks a clear account of sanctions, and the jurisprudential tradition lacks a good account of prices. This Article attempts to bridge the two traditions by developing a theory about the difference between the effect of prices and sanctions upon behavior.

Part I of this Article offers working definitions of the two key concepts, defining a sanction as a detriment imposed for doing what is forbidden, and a price as money extracted for doing what is permitted. Officials should create prices to compel decisionmakers to take into account the external costs of their acts, whereas officials should impose sanctions to deter people from doing what is wrong. Part I then explains the difference in the way sanctions and prices typically control behavior. A sanction typically creates an abrupt jump in an individual's costs when he passes from the permitted zone into the forbidden zone where behavior is sanctioned. This abrupt

---

* Professor of Law, University of California, Berkeley. B.A. 1967, Swarthmore College; M.A. 1969, Oxford; Ph.D. 1975, Harvard University. I would like to thank Bruce Ackerman, Lucian Bebchuk, Alvin Klevorick, Mitch Polinsky, Joseph Raz, Dan Rubinfeld, Steve Shavell, Judy Thompson, and my colleagues on Berkeley's law faculty for helpful comments.

1. The view that law is the command of the sovereign or the obligations that the community imposes upon its members is so old that its origins cannot be established. John Austin stated the imperative theory with clarity in 1 Lectures on Jurisprudence (R. Campbell 5th rev. ed. 1911) and in The Province of Jurisprudence Determined (2d ed. 1861).

2. Two lawyers who have adopted the economic view that laws are prices have stated:

> [M]anagers do not have an ethical duty to obey economic regulatory laws just because the laws exist. They must determine the importance of these laws. The penalties Congress names for disobedience are a measure of how much it wants firms to sacrifice in order to adhere to the rules; the idea of optimal sanctions is based on the supposition that managers not only may but also should violate the rules when it is profitable to do so.

F. Easterbrook & D. Fischel, Antitrust Suits by Targets of Tender Offers, 80 Mich. L. Rev. 1155, 1177 n.57 (1982).

3. See C. Schultze, The Public Use of Private Interest (1977) and S. Breyer, Analyzing Regulatory Failure: Mismatches, Less Restrictive Alternatives, and Reform, 92 Harv. L. Rev. 549 (1979).

jump in costs disappears if the sanction is replaced by a price. Behavior is more elastic with respect to changes in prices than to changes in sanctions.

This fact is used in Part II to develop a prescription for guiding lawmakers' choice between prices and sanctions. Since behavior is relatively responsive to prices, an error in setting an official price will have a large effect upon behavior; since behavior is relatively unresponsive to the level of a sanction, modest errors in the level of sanctions will have little effect upon behavior. Finally, since most people will obey a reasonable legal standard backed by a reasonable sanction, an error in setting the legal standard will cause an error in most people's behavior.

These facts lead to a simple prescription. If lawmakers can identify socially desirable behavior, but are prone to error in assessing the cost of deviations from it, then sanctions are preferable to prices. However, if officials can accurately measure the external cost of behavior, but cannot accurately identify the socially desirable level of it, then prices are preferable to sanctions.

Part III develops a simple test for preliminary classification of laws according to whether they impose sanctions or create prices. Sanctions usually increase if the actor's offense is intentional or repeated, while prices do not.

In Part IV, this test is used to classify areas of tort, contract, criminal, and regulatory law. For example, strict liability imposes a price, whereas negligence imposes a sanction. Furthermore, the types of torts governed by strict liability and negligence conform to the prescription developed in Part II.

The Article is followed by an appendix in which the fundamental arguments are mathematically formulated as propositions and proved.

I. Contrasting Prices and Sanctions

A. *Definitions*

The mere existence of an obligation or issuance of a legal command[4] may provide insufficient motivation for obedience. In addition, a sanction or threat may be needed to induce conformity. A sanction is a detriment imposed for doing what is *forbidden*, such as failing to perform an obligation. For example, a defendant in a tort dispute may be ordered to pay compen-

4. A norm is a general name for rule-like guides to action, including rules, laws, and principles. See J. Raz, Practical Reason and Norms (1975); G.H. von Wright, Norm and Action (1963). This Article discusses norms that impose an obligation, such as "All citizens have a duty to vote," or "Working on the Sabbath is forbidden." A command is an act in which the speaker describes what he wants done with the intention that this description should cause the hearer to do it. See J. Searle, Speech Acts (1970). Although philosophers have dwelt upon the distinction between commands and norms, it is unimportant for my purposes so I shall limit my discussion to norms backed by sanctions, as opposed to commands backed by threats.

satory damages for an injury caused by his negligence, or a convicted criminal may be sentenced to jail.

In contrast, a price is payment of money which is required in order to do what is *permitted*. For example, a company may buy goods in the marketplace, but it must pay the seller's price. Similarly, individuals are permitted to earn income, but obliged to pay taxes on their earnings.

These definitions of sanction and price are not always consistent with ordinary speech. Tax evasion is forbidden, but in casual speech people often say a fine is the price of tax evasion, when by these definitions it is a sanction. Furthermore, these definitions are unlikely to satisfy philosophers in search of necessary and sufficient conditions for "sanction" and "price." To illustrate, paying an arsonist not to burn down a store is extortion, yet protection money fits the definition of a price—an exaction for doing what is permitted. Despite such shortcomings, these definitions lay the basis for the behavioral model developed in the next section.

B. *Incentive Effects of Prices and Sanctions*

Assume that someone engages in an activity that imposes costs upon others—external costs. The external cost might be the harm caused by an accident, the nuisance created by a polluter, or the injury that arises from breach of contract. External costs can usually be reduced by the injurer at some expense to himself—accident costs can be reduced by precaution, pollution can be reduced by abatement, and the probability of breach can be reduced by care in performance. This Article uses "precaution" as a generic term to refer to any costly activity that reduces external costs.

The relationship between precaution and external costs is summarized

FIGURE 1
SOCIAL COSTS

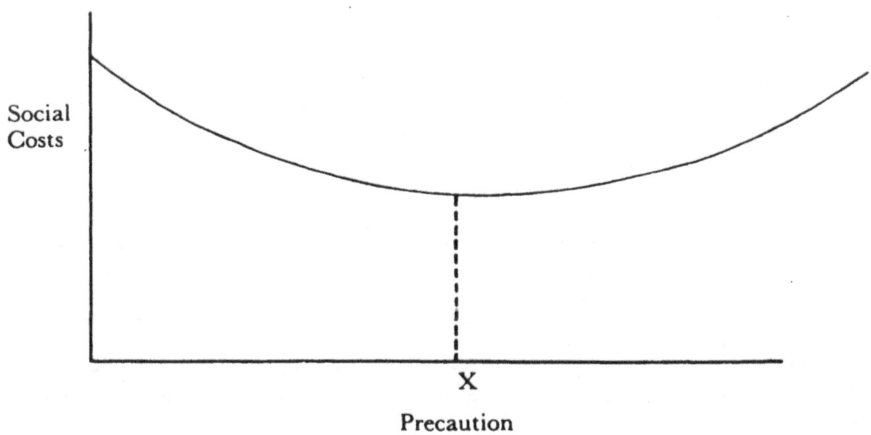

in Figure 1. Social costs, which refer to the sum of external costs and the cost of precaution, are shown on the vertical axis, and the actor's precaution is shown on the horizontal axis. This Article assumes that a small increase in precaution reduces external costs by a large amount when precaution is low, and a small increase in precaution reduces external costs by a small amount when precaution is high. Consequently, the graph of social costs is U-shaped and there is a level of precaution, denoted x', which minimizes social costs.[5]

1. *Incentives in the General Case.* — Now consider two rules for allocating the costs represented in Figure 1. Rule *A* partitions levels of precaution into a permitted zone and a forbidden zone. Specifically, Rule *A* creates a legal standard of precaution x^*, permitting the actor to take precaution as great or greater than the legal standard ($x \geq x^*$), and forbidding the actor to take less precaution than the legal standard ($x < x^*$). Furthermore, under certain conditions, Rule A exacts a sum of money as a sanction for being in the forbidden zone.

Figure 2 illustrates Rule *A*.[6] It shows precaution on the horizontal axis

FIGURE 2
RULE A

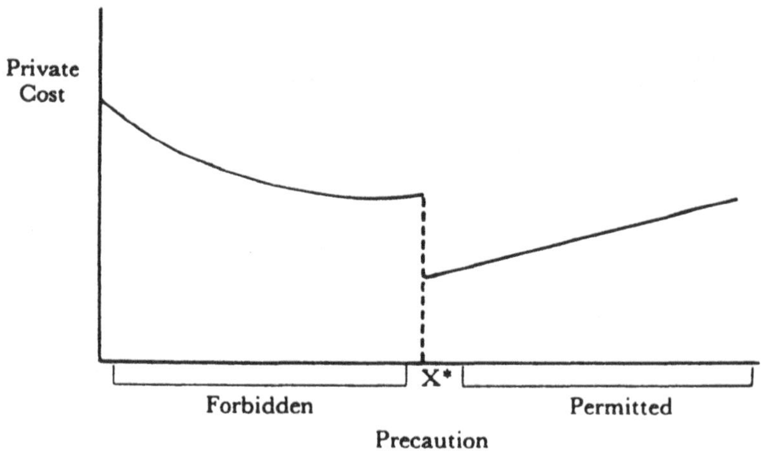

5. The social cost (SC) of accidents can be written $x+p(x)r$, where x is expenditure on precaution by the potential injurer, $p=p(x)$ is the probability of an accident, and r is the money value of the harm caused by an accident. Choosing x to minimize social costs yields the equation: $0 \geq 1+p'(x)r$. The solution of this equation for x yields x'. For a more general treatment, see infra Appendix, pp. 1554-61.

6. This figure first appeared in the law and economics literature in Brown, Toward an Economic Theory of Liability, 2 J. Legal Stud. 323, 341 (1973), but the discontinuity was not analyzed.

and the actor's private costs on the vertical axis. There are two components of the actor's private costs: precaution and sanctions. When precaution is below x^*, the actor bears the cost of his precaution and he must also pay the sanction; when the actor's precaution is above x^*, he pays only for his own precaution.[7]

To keep Figure 2 simple, this analysis assumes that the sanction equals the external cost of the act—the actor is liable for the full harm which he causes. Thus, the curve in figure 2 is identical to the curve in Figure 1 at those values of x below x^*. As precaution increases, there is a jump or discontinuity in the cost curve at the legal standard x^*, because that is the cutoff point for imposing the sanction. Above x^*, the sanction is not exacted, so the actor's private costs equal the cost of his precaution.[8]

A person who is rationally self-interested will choose his level of precaution to minimize his private costs. If he faces costs like those created by Rule *A*, he will search for the lowest point on the cost curve. This point occurs when his precaution equals the legal standard x^*. Thus, a self-interested person subject to Rule *A* will take just enough precaution to satisfy the legal standard and escape liability.[9]

It is not essential that the sanction equal the harm caused by the act to induce the self-interested actor to take precaution x^*. It is only essential that the sanction be large enough so that his private costs are minimized by conforming to the legal standard x^*. This point is illustrated in Figure 3, which shows the actor's private costs under four different assumptions about the sanction. The crucial feature of Figure 3 is that the lowest point in the graph is at x^*, regardless of whether the sanction corresponds to the high level *A*, the medium level *B*, or the low level *C*. Any one of these three sanctions will induce conformity with the legal standard x^*. However, if the sanction falls to the very low level indicated by *D*, then x^* is not the lowest point on the cost curve, so the actor will minimize his private costs by taking less precaution than the legal standard.

Another kind of rule achieves similar ends by different means.[10] In-

7. Using the same notation, see supra note 5, to the left of the discontinuity, the potential injurer's expected costs are $x+p(x)sr$, where sr stands for the injurer's expected liability in the event of an accident. To the right of the discontinuity, the potential injurer's costs are x.

8. See Cooter, Economic Analysis of Punitive Damages, 56 S. Cal. L. Rev. 79 (1982). This will hold true even if enforcement of the sanction is lax. Imperfect enforcement will reduce the size of the discontinuity in the cost curve, but this Article's analysis will be correct as long as the amount of enforcement is large enough to maintain some discontinuity.

9. Someone who acts from duty and obeys the law out of respect will also satisfy the legal standard, but not in order to minimize private costs.

10. This Article distinguishes two kinds of rules and identifies one of them with prices and the other with sanctions. Of course, it is possible to expand the definition of a price to cover sanctions by defining a sanction as a discontinuous price, or to expand the definition of a sanction to cover prices by defining a price as a continuous sanction. However, the important point is not to argue about names but to understand the differences in the behavior

stead of dividing precaution into permitted and forbidden zones, Rule *B* requires the actor to pay the external costs that his activity imposes upon others. Under Rule *B*, the private costs of the actor are equal to the social costs of his activity; thus the social cost is internalized. To illustrate Rule *B*, relabel the vertical axis in Figure 1 to read "private costs = social costs." Because the actor's private costs are lowest at x' when he is liable for the external cost of his acts, his private costs are minimized at the same level of precaution that minimizes social costs.

The incentives created by the two rules work in different ways. With Rule *B*, the actor balances the cost of additional precaution against the resulting reduction in the external costs for which he is responsible. His private costs are minimized when the benefits and costs of a small change in precaution offset each other.[11] By contrast, with Rule *A*, the benefits and costs of a small change in precaution are not offset, because the actor's private costs are much lower when he just satisfies the legal standard than they would be if he just failed to satisfy it.[12]

The incentive effects of prices and sanctions are different because benefits and costs are usually equipoised with prices but not with sanctions.[13]

FIGURE 3

RESPONSE TO DIFFERENT SANCTIONS

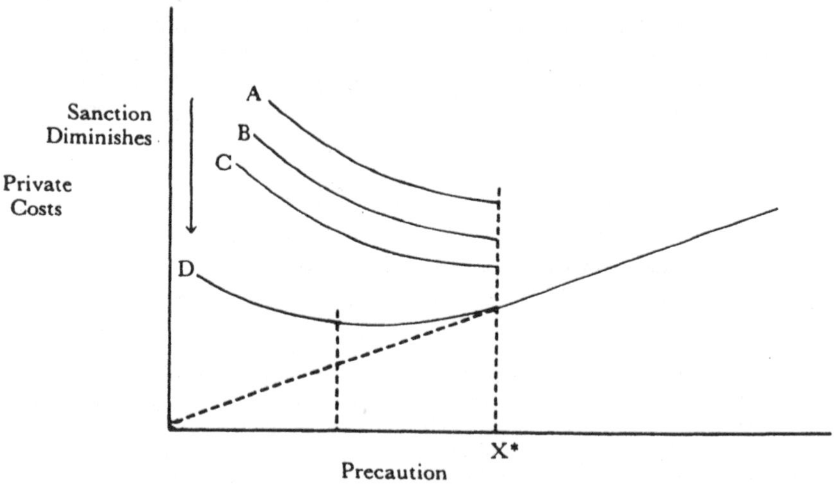

caused by Rule *A* and Rule *B*. In technical language, the actor under Rule *B* is at an interior solution where marginal private benefit equals marginal private cost. Thus, a tangent line to his cost curve in Figure 1 has zero slope at x'.

11. This assumes the actor is not on a flat portion of his cost curve. Flat portions of such curves are unusual but possible.

12. In technical language, the actor under Rule *A* is at a corner on the cost function where the cost of an incremental change exceeds the benefit.

13. I say "usually" because there are exceptional persons and special classes of rules that do not fit my model. Although many types of commands and obligations can be modeled by

When benefits and costs are equipoised, a small change in them causes a change in behavior. Thus, under Rule *B*, the actor's precaution is responsive to changes in the price. If the price equals a fraction of the external harm, then reducing the fraction will cause the level of precaution which minimizes private costs to be reduced. This fact is illustrated in Figure 4, where lowering the price causes the lowest point on the cost curve to shift to the left.[14] By contrast, when benefits and costs are not equipoised, moderate changes in them do not cause behavior to change. Thus, as was shown in Figure 3, the actor's precaution is unresponsive to modest changes in the sanction or the frequency of its application.[15]

The difference in responsiveness can be summarized in a sentence: *The amount of precaution an actor takes is more elastic with respect to changes in prices than*

FIGURE 4

CHANGES IN LIABILITY UNDER RULE B

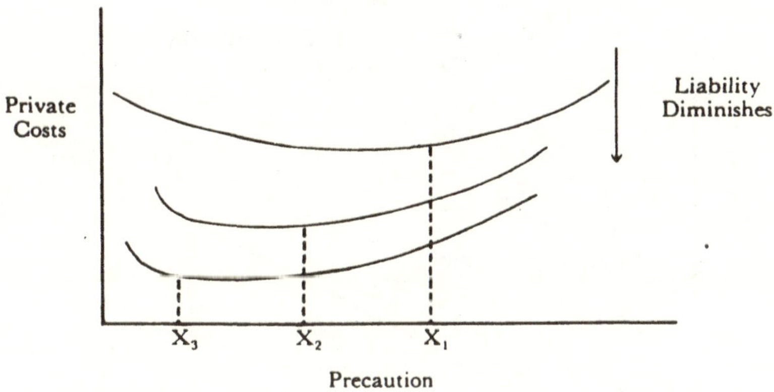

Rule *A*, and many types of prices can be modeled by Rule *B*, some behavior does not fit without altering the model. Exceptional persons are discussed in the next section of the Article. As for special rules, my graphs depict behavior as continuous and the optimum occurs when the actors engage in a positive amount of it. Some types of behavior, murder, for example, are discontinuous, and it is optimal not to do any of it. In the section on criminal law, I show how to adapt this model to such behavior. See infra notes 54-60 and accompanying text.

14. To prove this point, minimize $x+p(x)r$ with respect to x, then take the derivative of the cost-minimizing value of x with respect to r. By using the second order conditions, it is easy to see that the derivative is positive, proving that the cost minimizing value of x falls when liability r diminishes. See infra Appendix, pp. 1554-61.

15. In order for a change in the sanction to change the actor's behavior in Figure 3, the sanction would have to fall at least the full distance of the jump or discontinuity in the cost function at x^*, as occurred with sanction *D*.

to changes in levels of sanctions. On the other hand, an actor's precaution is responsive to a change in the obligation backed by a sanction, which corresponds to a change in the legal standard x^* under Rule *A*.

2. *Exceptional Actors.* — Figure 3 represents the typical decisionmaker facing a reasonable obligation backed by a reasonable sanction. In such a case, a fall in the sanction from *A* to *C* causes *no* change in the actor's precaution level. In reality, there are some atypical decisionmakers and some unreasonable laws which require modifying this behavioral theory.

Unlike the typical decisionmaker, some individuals will be in a situation where nonconformity with the legal standard is cheaper than conformity. To illustrate, consider someone whose compliance costs are extraordinarily high, as depicted in Figure 5.[16] The effect of exceptional compliance costs is to raise the straight-line portion of the graph, representing costs in the zone of compliance, relative to the curved-line portion of the graph, representing costs of noncompliance. Thus, when the penalty for noncompliance is modest in Figure 5, the lowest point on the graph is below

FIGURE 5

THE ACTOR WITH EXCEPTIONAL COMPLIANCE COSTS

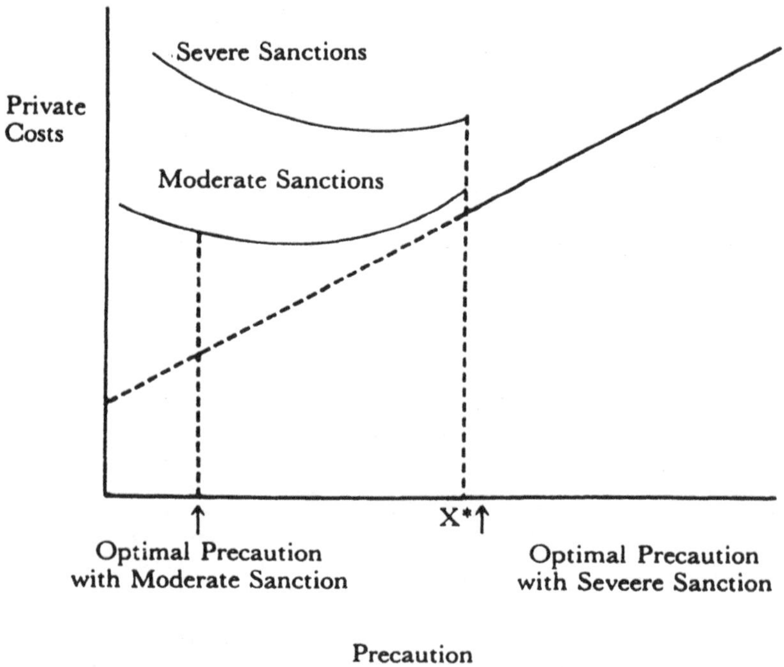

16. For example, drivers who ordinarily obey traffic laws may speed when they are in a big hurry. In this example, the cost of compliance, or the benefit from noncompliance, depends upon the value of the driver's time, which in turn depends upon his personal circumstances.

x^*, so that complying with the legal standard is more costly than not complying. Deterring an unusual person like the one depicted in Figure 5 requires a severe sanction.

In the usual case, where a reasonable obligation is backed by a reasonable sanction, most people will find conforming strongly advantageous, as described in Figure 3, and a few people will find nonconformity advantageous, as illustrated in Figure 5. Very few people will find themselves on the margin between compliance and noncompliance, where conforming to the legal standard costs the same as not conforming.[17] However, those on the margin are the only ones whose behavior changes when the sanction changes by a small amount. If the sanction is reduced or applied less frequently, then the people on the margin will tip in the direction of not conforming.[18]

Although few people tip, those who do will probably change their behavior a lot, rather than a little. The change in behavior will be substantial because the choice is between taking enough precaution to avoid the sanction entirely, or paying the sanction and taking little or no precaution. Cost minimizing behavior is either equal to the legal standard x^* or significantly short of x^*, but it is never a *little* short of x^*. Once it pays to fall short of the legal standard, it pays to fall significantly short of it.[19]

Thus, *a small change in a sanction usually causes a small number of people to change their behavior a lot.* In contrast, pricing the behavior causes most people to balance benefits and costs at the margin. Since many people would then be on the margin, *a small change in a price will cause many people to change their behavior a little.* In aggregate, then, behavior is more elastic with respect to prices than sanctions.[20]

---

17. I am assuming that a reasonable law is one for which the tipping point with respect to compliance is in the tail of the distribution where the density is low. It is possible that the tipping point for a law could be in the center of the distribution where it is dense, although many people would consider such a law unreasonable.

18. More technically, the response to a change in sanctions is on the extensive margin, not the intensive margin. In economic jargon, the margin for prices is *intensive*, involving many people, and the margin for sanctions is *extensive*, involving a few people.

19. This result is a consequence of the nonconvexity in the cost function. The fact that the change is substantial can be seen by examining Figure 3. When the sanction falls to the low level *D*, the cost minimizing level of behavior jumps substantially below x^*. In fact, the lowest point on any cost curve with a discontinuity at x^* will be located at some distance from x^*.

20. A similar argument applies when the obligation or sanction is unreasonable, in which case the law may be disobeyed by many people. Regardless of the extent of disobedience, it is likely that only a few people will be on the margin between obedience and disobedience, assuming that compliance costs are distributed smoothly, rather than bunched at the exact level where incentives are equipoised. See infra Appendix, pp. 1554-61. Only those people will respond to a modest change in the sanction. Thus, the conclusion about the elasticity of behavior with respect to a sanction is unchanged by the unreasonableness of the law.

II. A Normative Theory of Lawmaking

The difference in the incentive effects of prices and sanctions is important for lawmakers deciding whether to price or sanction behavior. If officials always possessed perfect information, socially desirable behavior could be induced by either prices or sanctions. Officials could either charge the price which exactly internalizes costs—which would induce individuals to choose the socially efficient level of behavior x'—or officials could create a legal standard—$x^* = x'$—and back that standard with a sanction strong enough to induce conformity. Regardless of the approach, individuals would respond by choosing the efficient level of precaution.

In reality, however, lawmakers and officials who administer the law often make mistakes because they lack information or the incentives to use information. The behavioral consequences of mistakes are different depending upon whether the law creates a sanction or a price. A normative theory for choosing between sanctions and prices can be based upon the propensity of lawmakers to make mistakes, which depends in part upon the cost of information to them.

Most people conform to a reasonable obligation backed by a reasonable sanction, even if the legal standard is inefficient or otherwise undesirable. Consequently, lawmakers who create an obligation backed by a sanction must be certain that the partition between permitted and forbidden zones is in the right place. On the other hand, mistakes in computing the level of the sanction or the frequency of its application are not crucial, because most people will conform in spite of these mistakes.[21]

In contrast, pricing behavior does not require dividing action into permitted and forbidden zones, so lawmakers need not compute the socially optimal behavior. Instead, the lawmakers must choose the price accurately. For efficiency, the price must fully reflect the external harm caused by the behavior. Since individuals are responsive to the magnitude of the price and the frequency of its collection, accuracy is crucial to induce behavior that is efficient or otherwise desirable.

This argument can be restated in algebraic terms. If lawmakers can identify the efficient precaution level, x', then the legal standard, x^*, can be equated with it. Errors in computing or assessing the sanction will not have a large influence on behavior. In contrast, if lawmakers can obtain accurate

21. Professor Wittman made a similar point, saying "[t]here would be low administrative costs if X [the decisionmaker] were charged only for acting inefficiently, a type of behavior rare in comparison to acting efficiently." Wittman, Liability for Harm or Restitution for Benefit, 13 J. Legal Stud. 57, 61 (1984). When private persons are uncertain about the legal standard or the evidence regarding their conformity that could be offered in court, the discontinuity in Figure 2 is smoothed. However, the cost-minimizing point will not be very different, nor will the decisionmakers' response to errors in enforcement or damages, after the curve is smooth. Smoothing the curve tends to result in overprecaution relative to the legal standard. In technical terms, uncertainty transforms the discontinuity into a nonconvexity. For a discussion of this point see Cooter, Note: Why Comparative Negligence is Efficient (1984) (unpublished manuscript, on file at the office of the Columbia Law Review).

information on external costs, then behavior can be priced at its external cost. However, behavior is more elastic with respect to prices than sanctions, so using prices to create efficient incentives requires accurate assessment of external costs.

These observations lead to a simple decisional rule for lawmakers: *If obtaining accurate information about external costs is cheaper for officials than obtaining accurate information about socially optimal behavior, then they should control the activity by pricing it; if the converse is true, then they should control the activity by sanctioning it.*[22]

It may seem paradoxical that lawmakers could have information about socially optimal behavior and not have information about external costs: isn't the latter needed to compute the former? This apparent paradox is resolved by the existence of community standards. A community standard represents a consensus among private individuals about socially optimal behavior. In many circumstances, government officials can observe the community standard, but not the costs and benefits which private individuals took into account when arriving at it. If the community's judgment is sound, then officials can achieve optimality by adopting the community standard as the legal standard and attaching a sanction to it, even though officials lack information about external costs.

To illustrate, suppose that everyone in a community is exposed to the risk of accidents of a certain type, and everyone can take precautions against them. Over time, the community may develop a negligence standard reflecting its judgment about the balancing of costs and benefits of precaution. If an accident occurs and the victim sues, then a court can accurately identify the community standard of negligence by hearing testimony from third parties. However, the victim may exaggerate the seriousness of his injury in order to increase his recovery, thus preventing the court from accurately assessing the cost.

The preceding example concerns a standard of the general public. Specialized communities may also have standards. For example, an accountant who plans to work in a town for many years will have a stronger incentive to maintain a good reputation by avoiding mistakes than an accountant whose aim is to turn a quick profit and leave town. This is an application of the well known result in game theory that cheating in one-shot games can be reduced or eliminated by replacing the one-shot game

22. This proposition is similar to the claim in the pollution literature that quantitative restrictions are preferable to pollution taxes when authorities know the optimal quantity of pollution but do not know the tax price which would achieve it. It has been suggested that this situation might occur when, for example, smog reaches an emergency level. Conversely, tax prices should be used when authorities know the external cost of pollution, but not the optimal quantity. See W. Baumol & W. Oates, The Theory of Environmental Policy (1975); see also Weitzman, Prices v. Quantities, 41 Rev. Econ. Stud. 477 (1974) (developing a model to determine the comparative advantages of indirect market control by prices versus direct regulation of quantities).

with a sequence of repeated games.[23] The practices of the accountant of good repute may be taken as evidence of the standards which the court should apply to all accountants. The importance of reputation may overcome market failures which would otherwise prevent accountants from adopting the most efficient standards. Thus, a community standard will be efficient in general when it is based on the long run need for its members to acquire the reputation for taking precautions whose costs are commensurate with the resulting reduction in accident costs.[24]

In the first example of a community standard, efficiency arises because of symmetry: each person could be either the victim or the injurer in an everyday accident. Symmetry facilitates a consensus regarding the appropriate level of care because each person must consider both the costs and benefits of precaution. In the second example, a specialized community achieves an efficient community standard because the importance of reputation overcomes a potential market failure. In either case, a court may be able to decide that the community standard is optimal by examining the institutional structure which gave rise to it.[25]

In some circumstances, however, lawmakers may be unable to observe

---

23. See, e.g., R. Radner, Collusion Behavior in Non-Cooperative Epsilon-Equilibria of Oligopolies with Long but Finite Lives (Mar. 1979) (Bell Tel. Laboratory Discussion Paper).

24. There are many different circumstances in which such a norm will reflect the balancing of benefits and costs. A full analysis of these circumstances would involve examining the conditions under which people act from motives other than self-interest. To be consistent with its economic foundations, this Article is limited to examining a mechanism by which rational self-interest will yield an efficient community standard.

Another illustration is provided by tests for glaucoma performed by ophthalmologists. Since glaucoma is common in old people and rare in young people, there is an age—say forty—before which the cost of routine testing exceeds the expected benefit. If these facts are known and appreciated by ophthalmologists and by informed members of the public, then an ophthalmologist who wanted to cultivate a good reputation would give the test routinely to patients whose age is over forty, and not give it routinely to patients under forty.

This example is drawn from the famous case of Helling v. Carey, 83 Wash. 2d 514, 519 P.2d 981 (1974). Curiously, the plaintiff accepted the defendant's claim that ophthalmologists in Washington at the time were not giving glaucoma tests routinely. A subsequent survey, however, revealed that more than half of ophthalmologists were doing so. See Wiley, The Impact of Judicial Decisions on Professional Conduct: An Empirical Study, 55 S. Cal. L. Rev. 345, 383 (1981). The community's balancing of costs and benefits suggested that the test should have been given routinely. Thus, it appears that the court could have awarded damages on negligence grounds, using the usual community standard, rather than resorting to a new standard of strict liability.

25. I have suggested two structural conditions which give rise to efficient community standards, specifically symmetry and repeated games. A complete analysis of the structural conditions for efficient community standards is beyond the scope of this Article, but an analogy may help the reader to appreciate the usefulness of community standards absent such a unified theory. It is well known that monopoly is inefficient, which is one reason why monopoly is prohibited. To guide the antitrust laws, economists have developed a detailed theory based upon the structure of the market, which bypasses questions concerning the conduct and performance of individual firms. Like the antitrust laws, courts can sometimes decide whether community standards are efficient by examining the structure which creates them, rather than directly evaluating their efficiency.

the community standard, or there may be a special interest standard instead of a community standard, or the problem may be so novel that no standard has arisen. Without a community standard to guide them, officials who attempt to control behavior through sanctions must assess the socially optimal level of behavior themselves. This assessment requires information about benefits and costs that may be difficult to obtain. If officials obtain the necessary information and create an optimal legal standard, then private persons will be required to obey the legal standard upon pain of suffering the sanction attached to it. Private persons will not need to assess the socially optimal behavior—the officials will have done that for them. An advantage of an obligation backed by a sanction, as opposed to a price, is that the computation is made once by officials rather than many times by individuals, thus reducing the costs of decisionmaking.

For example, suppose that scientists prove an ingredient widely used in cooking is carcinogenic. The legislature, using the scientists' results, balances benefits against costs and determines that the ingredient should never be consumed by humans. If the legislature outlaws use of the ingredient, private individuals will be required to obey the law and abstain from using the ingredient. If the ingredient were not banned, private individuals would have to decide whether to use it. To decide, they would have to collect information and replicate some aspects of the legislature's decision process. Thus, banning the ingredient by legislative fiat reduces the cost of decisionmaking for the community as a whole.

In reality, such decisions are difficult for officials to make, especially when the affected individuals are heterogeneous. To illustrate, if pollution has many sources and many victims, it will be excessive in the absence of government intervention.[26] If officials try to prescribe efficient pollution standards, they must know the abatement costs and the external harm for every source of pollution. It is impossible for officials to possess that much information, as the recent history of the Environmental Protection Agency has demonstrated. Obligations backed by sanctions will not succeed unless individual differences in compliance costs are comparatively small or receive no social weight.[27]

When individual differences in compliance costs are important, the amount of information officials need can be reduced by relying upon prices instead of sanctions. Assigning the correct price to an activity only requires officials to compute the external cost, as opposed to balancing the costs and benefits. For example, if government creates pollution rights and encourages their exchange in a market,[28] polluters will abate until the abatement

26. This assumes that the existence of many polluters and pollutees will prevent a solution through private negotiation.

27. The section on criminal law, see infra notes 54-60 and accompanying text, discusses illegitimate benefits or costs which receive no social weight. For example, the pleasure that some violent criminals apparently enjoy is not counted as a reason for allowing their crimes.

28. The Supreme Court recently held that the "bubble concept" definition of "source" was permissible under the Clean Air Act Amendments of 1977, Pub. L. No. 95-95, 91 Stat.

cost at the margin equals the price of pollution rights. Thus, the market in pollution rights will reveal the marginal abatement cost of polluters without officials having to know anything about the technology of abatement.

Once the market reveals marginal abatement costs, officials can compare these costs to their computation of the external harm from pollution and adjust the amount of pollution until it is efficient. If the external harm caused by pollution exceeds the marginal abatement cost, then efficiency requires further abatement, so government should buy back some pollution rights to reduce their number. If the relative magnitudes are reversed, government should create and distribute additional pollution rights.[29] These observations lead to the conventional conclusion that controlling pollution through prices requires less information than controlling it through obligations backed by sanctions.[30]

Table 1 summarizes the argument about information and policy making. If private persons are good observers of social costs and benefits, as indicated by the lower right cell of the table, then a community standard may arise reflecting a consensus about efficient behavior. Optimal incentives can be created by giving official sanction to such standards. If officials can observe benefits and costs more accurately than private persons, as indicated by the upper left cell of the table, then optimal incentives can be created by legislative fiat. In contrast, if private persons can assess the benefits from their own acts and officials can assess the external costs, as indicated by the lower left cell in the table, then optimal incentives can be created by pricing the externality.[31] Finally, turning to the upper right cell, if private persons can assess the costs of their own acts and officials can assess the external benefits, then optimal incentives can be created by official subsidies.

---

685. See Chevron U.S.A., Inc. v. Natural Resources Defense Council, Inc., 52 U.S.L.W. 4845 (U.S. June 25, 1984).

29. Pollution taxes, rather than a market in pollution rights, can achieve the same result while providing revenues to the government. Assuming transaction costs are minimal, the only difference between a pollution tax and a government auction of pollution rights is that the government chooses the price and the market chooses the quantity with taxes, while the opposite is true with an auction. See Cooter, The Cost of Coase, 11 J. Legal Stud. 1 (1982). Both approaches raise revenues for the government by correcting distortions in the allocation of resources rather than by creating such distortions. The revenues raised by nondistorting taxes can be substituted for the revenues raised by distorting taxes like the income tax, thus increasing efficiency. On the other hand, the government can allocate ownership of pollution rights to individuals, rather than operate a government auction, in which case the government will not derive revenues from pollution control.

30. This is the familiar Pigouvian tax solution to pollution. See W. Baumol & W. Oates, supra note 22.

31. As explained in the discussion of markets for pollution rights, supra notes 27-29 and accompanying text, private actors' responses to the first round of prices will establish the compliance costs and the government can accordingly reset the price to achieve the socially desired level of activity.

TABLE 1

Distribution of Information and the Optimal Policy
(Assuming Market Failure and External Costs)

		Best Observer of Social Costs	
		Officials	Private Persons
Best Observer of Social Benefits	Officials	legislative standard and sanction	official subsidy
	Private Persons	official price	community standard and sanction

III. DISTINGUISHING PRICES FROM SANCTIONS

The prescription for lawmakers developed in Part II can be tested to see whether it is being followed in various bodies of law. First, however, it is necessary to be able to distinguish prices from sanctions. Sometimes a rule clearly resembles Rule *A*, in which case it is an obligation backed by a sanction, and sometimes it clearly resembles Rule *B*, in which case it imposes a price. However, some rules appear opaque upon first examination, so it is useful to have a criterion for preliminary classification.

A criterion can be developed by recalling that sanctions attach to forbidden acts and prices attach to permitted acts. Since the purpose of a sanction is to deter people from wrongdoing,[32] the sanction will be adjusted to achieve this goal. Deterring actors whose fault is intentional, deliberate, or repeated requires a more severe sanction than deterring actors whose fault is unintentional, spontaneous, or committed for the first time. Therefore, sanctions increase with certain mental qualities of the act indicating more resistance to deterrence.

The efficient price depends upon the extent of external harm, not the actor's state of mind. If, contrary to fact, prices varied with the actor's state of mind—making the price higher if the act were done intentionally—then people would be deterred from doing the very acts that are permitted. Since a typical purpose of prices is to internalize costs, and since the external cost of an act is unrelated to the actor's state of mind, a price should not increase just because the activity is intentional, willful, or repeated.

These observations point to a simple test for deciding whether a law creates a sanction or a price: *Sanctions increase with the need for deterrence, as indicated by the actor's state of mind, whereas prices increase with the amount of exter-*

32. Deterrence is usually regarded as one motive for imposing a sanction. W. LaFave & A. Scott, Jr., Handbook on Criminal Law 23 (1972). Other motives, including punishment, are described in H.L.A. Hart, Punishment and Responsibility (1968).

nal harm caused by the act, which is invariant with respect to the actor's state of mind.[33]

IV. Relation to Various Areas of Law

Part II developed a prescription for lawmakers who must choose between prices and sanctions, and Part III developed a criterion for preliminary classification of laws as prices or sanctions. This Part distinguishes prices from sanctions in several bodies of law—specifically, tort, contract, criminal law, and regulation—to determine whether Part II's prescription is followed.

A. *Torts: Strict Liability v. Negligence*

Negligence and strict liablity rules in tort law present a stark contrast between sanctions and prices. For the sake of concreteness, imagine a manufacturing process in which some defective products inevitably slip through quality control and injure consumers. Precaution against these accidents is costly. To keep the example simple, assume that effective precaution is possible for the manufacturer and impossible for consumers. Social costs are the sum of the costs of the manufacturer's precaution and the cost of injuries caused by defective products. Thus Figure 1 can be interpreted as a graph relating the social cost of manufacturing defects to precaution against them. As explained earlier, social costs are minimized at the point x' in the graph, which is the efficient point.

1. *Incentives.* — A negligence rule partitions the world into permitted and forbidden zones, as illustrated in Figure 2, and the sanction for being in the forbidden zone is liability for the harm caused by accidents. If the manufacturer's precaution is below the legal standard x', then he is liable for accidents; if his precaution is at least as great as the legal standard x^*, then he is not liable. If the legal standard, x^*, equals the efficient level of precaution, x', a manufacturer whose precaution is inefficient is liable, and a manufacturer whose precaution is efficient is not liable. Thus, a negligence rule corresponds to Rule *A*—representation of an obligation backed by a sanction.

To understand the incentive effects of a negligence rule, consider the private costs of the manufacturer. If his precaution x is below the legal standard x^*, then he bears the cost of precaution and liability for accidents. If liability covers the full cost of the harm suffered by the victim, the injurer's private costs will equal the social cost in the zone of liability, as depicted in Figure 2. However, when the manufacturer's precaution satisfies

33. This proposition is not a statement of necessary or sufficient conditions. Other criteria could be mentioned, such as: Is shame attached to the activity? Can an injunction be obtained to prevent its recurrence? Is the cost deductible from the actor's tax liability? These ancillary criteria have some value, but this test proves especially useful in classifying laws.

the legal standard, he escapes liability under a negligence rule, so he only bears the cost of his own precaution in the zone of nonliability.

There is a jump, or discontinuity, in the manufacturer's costs at the legal standard of care because his liability plummets from one hundred percent to zero percent at the point where his precaution satisfies the legal standard.[34] The size of the jump is determined by the amount of damage caused by defective products when precaution exactly satisfies the legal standard.[35] As a consequence of the jump, it is far cheaper for the injurer to be nonnegligent than to be negligent.[36]

Since it is far cheaper to be nonnegligent than negligent, changes in the legal standard will induce equivalent changes in the manufacturer's precaution. The manufacturer will satisfy the legal standard, x^*, even if it is pegged at a level above or below the socially efficient level, x'. On the other hand, the manufacturer's precaution will not change if there is a moderate change in the sanction or the probability of its application.

The situation is quite different if a negligence rule is replaced by strict liability. If the manufacturer is strictly liable for the actual harm caused by defective products, he will bear the social cost of accidents. When social costs are borne by the manufacturer, minimizing his private costs is equivalent to minimizing social costs. Figure 1 can be interpreted as a graph of the manufacturer's private costs under strict liability, which are minimized at the efficient precaution level x'. Since there is no jump in the private cost function of the manufacturer under strict liability, the manufacturer minimizes private costs at a level of precaution where marginal benefit equals marginal cost.

Unlike negligence then, strict liability makes the manufacturer very responsive to imperfections in assessing and computing damages. If the courts sometimes allow a manufacturer to escape liability for harm caused by a defective product or award damages less than the harm caused by the

34. There will be a discontinuity in the cost curve whether a traditional negligence standard or a comparative negligence standard is applied. The curves will be identical when the plaintiff is entirely without fault. Where the plaintiff has been negligent, the size of the discontinuity in the cost curve will be reduced under comparative negligence but will still exist.

35. It is sometimes said that a person who is negligent is only liable for the harm that would have been avoided by nonnegligent care. This statement is misleading for many types of accidents, because nonnegligence just reduces the probability of an accident, rather than eliminating its possibility. To illustrate with a classic example, suppose that railroad trains emit sparks which sometimes set fire to farmers' fields. Nonnegligent operation of the train requires the use of spark arresters, which reduce, but do not eliminate, spark emissions. Under a negligence standard, a railroad using spark arresters would escape liability from fires caused by its trains, whereas a railroad failing to use spark arresters would be liable for fires caused by its trains. The point to notice is that failing to use spark arresters increases the probability of fires, but makes the railroad liable for all fires, including the fires which spark arresters would not have eliminated. This fact gives rise to the discontinuity in the railroad's cost function.

36. In economic jargon, the level of care which minimizes the manufacturer's private net costs is a corner solution where marginal private costs of a change far exceed marginal private benefits.

product, or if some consumers injured by defective products do not bring suit, then it will be profitable for the manufacturer to reduce his precaution below the efficient level. This conclusion is illustrated in Figure 4, where shifting the private cost curve below the social cost curve causes the cost minimizing level of precaution to fall.

2. *Prescription for Lawmakers.* — Since a negligence rule makes injurers responsive to the legal standard of care, and unresponsive to modest errors in computing damages or assigning liability, a court operating under a negligence rule must compute the legal standard with accuracy, but it can make modest errors in computing damages and assigning liability. In contrast, since a rule of strict liability makes injurers responsive to errors in computing damages or assigning liability, a court operating under strict liability must compute damages and assign liability with accuracy. Thus, a negligence rule should prevail when officials make relatively small errors in identifying the efficient level of care and relatively large errors in computing damages or assigning liability; and a rule of strict liability should prevail where officials make relatively large errors in identifying the efficient level of care and relatively small errors in computing damages or assigning liability.

To see whether this prescription is being followed, it is necessary to examine the frequency and magnitude of three types of court-made errors in tort disputes: (1) imperfections in setting the legal standard, (2) imperfections in determining liability, and (3) imperfections in setting damages.

a. *Imperfection in Setting the Legal Standard.* — To achieve efficiency by a negligence rule, a court must be able to determine the efficient level of precaution. If there is a community standard governing the activity, and the community has balanced incremental costs and benefits in arriving at the standard, then the court can achieve efficiency by enforcing the community standard. In many cases the community will have done so. The public experiences a broad class of everyday dangers such as household or automobile accidents. Since most people maintain a household and drive a car, the public has experience with the cost of precaution, as well as the harm caused by such accidents. Thus it has enough information to balance benefits and costs in deciding the appropriate standard of behavior required to be a safe driver or to properly maintain a house.

In court, testimony about the usual practice of community members with good reputations is accepted as evidence about the community standard.[37] A good reputation is acquired by proper behavior over a long period of time. Proper behavior may require giving similar weight to the cost of one's own precaution and to the resulting reduction in risk for others, as required for efficiency. It may also require taking the long run view of costs and benefits. To illustrate, recall the example of an accountant planning to

37. See W. Keeton, D. Dobbs, R. Keeton & D. Owen, Prosser and Keeton on The Law of Torts § 33 at 193-94 (5th ed. 1984).

work in a town for many years, who will have a stronger incentive to maintain a good reputation by avoiding mistakes than an accountant whose aim is to turn a quick profit and leave town. The practices of the accountant of good repute may be taken as evidence of the standards a court should apply to all accountants.

The community referred to in "community standard" is different for different activities. For example, in the case of driving, "community" refers to the general public; in the case of accounting, the term refers to a special group with its own private interests. The general public has extensive experience with driving and little experience with auditing. Naturally enough, the public is suspicious about whether specialized groups acting on their own will develop standards of precaution commensurate with the resulting savings in accident costs enjoyed by the public. In the specific case of defective products, concern with reputation may be insufficient to cause firms to internalize the full benefits of precaution, especially if consumers are unaware of the true risk of accidents. Thus the courts cannot automatically assume that the standard of care spontaneously adopted by specialized groups will be efficient.[38]

If the market failure prevents an efficient community standard from arising and the courts nonetheless decide to adopt a negligence rule, officials must compute the optimal standard directly or proceed by successive approximations. To proceed by approximation, the court can adopt the following rule: If the incremental benefits of precaution exceed the defendant's incremental costs, then precaution is held to be insufficient and the defendant is liable, whereas if the relative magnitudes are reversed, then the precaution is held to be sufficient and the defendant is not liable. A sequence of such determinations, each by courts with partial information, will eventually reveal the exact level of care that is efficient.[39] Proceeding by approximation requires less information than making the calculation directly, but the information requirements are high in either case. Reaching a satisfactory and consistent standard by this method is so difficult that lawmakers would usually do better to adopt a rule of strict liablity.

In reality, courts generally enforce community standards and are reluctant to impose novel obligations; where there is no satisfactory community standard, strict liability rules are often employed. This claim has been illustrated by contrasting tort liability for everyday accidents with tort liability for injuries to consumers. A reasonably efficient community standard spontaneously arises for everyday accidents and courts enforce it, thus conforming to the prescription outlined in Part II. If market failure prevents an efficient standard from arising for consumer products, then the adoption of a rule of strict liablity for consumer injuries conforms to the prescription.

38. The T.J. Hooper, 60 F.2d 737, 740 (2d Cir.) (L. Hand, J.) (refusing to adopt industry standard of care), cert. denied, 287 U.S. 662 (1932).

39. Judge Hand's ruling in *The T.J. Hooper* is thus regarded as an algorithm to search for the efficient negligence standard. See Cooter, Kornhauser & Lane, Liability Rules, Limited Information, and the Role of Precedent, 10 Bell J. Econ. 366 (1979).

b. *Imperfections in Determining Liability.* — A second source of error by officials is imperfections in determining liability. Rational accident victims will bring suit when the expected court award exceeds the plaintiff's cost of trial. A negligence rule imposes a difficult burden of proof upon the injured consumer. The injury has to be severe and the stakes large before the expected damage award exceeds the cost of a suit. The low probability of successfully proving negligence prevents many injured consumers from suing. Thus there is an imperfection in the enforcement of a negligence rule for defective products.

This imperfection is often cited as a reason for abandoning a negligence rule, but close inspection reveals some flaws in the conventional reasoning. Part I showed that precaution is inelastic with respect to the level of a sanction. It follows that imperfections in enforcing a negligence rule against manufacturers would probably not have much effect upon their behavior. Conforming to the legal standard would be cheaper than breaking it for most firms, in spite of imperfect enforcement. By contrast, mistakes in assigning liability would have a large effect upon the behavior of firms under a rule of strict liability. Fortunately, under strict liability the consumer's burden of proof is relatively light, so few injurers escape liability.

This theory suggests that traditional arguments about burden of proof confuse cause and effect. A correct statement is: that proof is hard under negligence does not cause suboptimal precaution; that proof is easy under strict liability is necessary for optimal precaution.

c. *Imperfections in Assessing Damages.* — A similar argument applies to the third source of error—imperfections in assessing damages. An injury often has aspects that are difficult to prove, as when property with sentimental value is destroyed or a business venture is disrupted before it becomes profitable. Proof is so difficult with subjective and speculative injuries that they are often excluded from damages, causing a bias toward undercompensation.

In recent years the courts have expanded the scope of compensable injury to include formerly excluded emotional and speculative losses. Insofar as this change has eliminated a bias towards undercompensation, it has eliminated a significant problem with a rule of strict liability, making such rules more efficient. By contrast, systematic undercompensation would not have much effect upon injurer's precaution under a negligence rule.

In summary, the prescription that negligence rules should be favored when courts can observe the socially desirable level of precaution more accurately than the external harm, enjoys limited success in explaining the contours of tort law. Community standards for everyday accidents represent legitimate judgments about the socially desirable level of precaution. Courts observe these standards and enforce them through negligence rules for tort liability. However, the standards of some industries are marred by market failures. For example, since courts cannot observe the socially desirable levels of precaution in manufacturing without difficulty, a strict liability standard is applied to consumer injuries. Thus, differences in the information available to courts and the errors to which courts are prone, provide part of the explanation for applying strict liability for consumer injuries, and negligence for everyday injuries.

3. *Punitive Damages in Tort.* — Economists sometimes think of sanctions as prices, which prevents them from understanding the normative character of the law. To illustrate this confusion in the area of tort law, suppose an individual believes that compensatory damages are the price of negligence. When accused of negligence, he might explain to the court that he deliberately took actions proscribed by the legal standard in order to avoid the high cost of compliance, and, in doing so, he was fully prepared to compensate anyone who was injured. The court might reply that the injurer has a duty to take reasonable care, not permission to be careless and pay compensatory damages. The court might add that deliberate violation of the legal standard, as admitted by the injurer, provides grounds for punitive damages. Finally, the court might suggest that punitive damages be set high enough to deter the injurer in the future.

This illustration suggests that punitive damages have the earmarks which distinguish a sanction from a price: (1) they are attached to a forbidden action; (2) they depend upon the actor's state of mind; and (3) their purpose is to deter. The law is murky, however, concerning standards for awarding punitive damages. This Article's behavioral theory can be used to clarify these standards.

According to this theory, most potential injurers will try to conform to standards of reasonable care. For them, nonconformity is accidental. For some exceptional injurers, however, compliance costs or the benefits from noncompliance are unusually high. For these injurers, violating the standard and paying compensatory damages is cheaper than conforming. When deterrence is appropriate, punititve damages can be used to deter such exceptional injurers.[40]

Intent distinguishes the usual injurer and the exceptional injurer, but intent is difficult to observe and prove. Intentional violation of the legal standard exposes the injurer to liability for compensatory and punitive damages. Consequently, his expected costs will jump when his precaution intentionally falls below the legal standard. As illustrated in Figure 5, exceptional injurers will choose a precaution level that is far short of the legal standard, not a little short of it. Thus their fault will be gross. Yet if puni-

40. Sometimes exceptional compliance costs or exceptional benefits from noncompliance are sound reasons for applying a different standard of care to the individual. In such cases it is appropriate to allow the actor to violate the usual legal standard. In other cases, the exceptional compliance costs or exceptional benefits from noncompliance are viewed as illegitimate, and deterrence by assessing punititve damages is appropriate. To illustrate the latter, a driver who loves to take risks may find complying with traffic laws subjectively difficult, yet he will be held to the same driving standards in court as someone who is instinctively cautious.

tive damages are sufficiently severe, even the exceptional injurer will minimize his expected costs by conforming to the legal standard.

According to many commentators, courts have appropriately assessed punitive damages when fault is gross, repeated, or willful and wanton.[41] This Article's behavioral theory explains the connection between gross fault and intent. Intentional fault is gross because once the injurer decides to disobey the legal standard it pays to fall far short of it.

B. *Contracts*

There is currently a dispute among theorists about whether breach of contract can be justified merely on the ground of economic efficiency. This Section argues that this dispute concerns whether damages for contract breach are sanctions or prices. Moreover, this section demonstrates that the analytical framework of Parts I and II can be used to resolve the dispute.

1. *The General Case.* — In America, the standard remedy for breach of contract is expectation damages.[42] The purpose of expectation damages is to put the victim of breach in as good a position as he would have been in if the promisor had performed.[43] Expectation damages which achieve this purpose can be called "perfect."[44]

If the promisor's nonperformance creates a benefit for him that exceeds perfect expectation damages for the promisee, then nonperformance is with compensation Pareto efficient—that is, it makes at least one person better off without making anyone worse off. Nonperformance under these circumstances creates a surplus equal to the amount by which the promisor's benefit from nonperformance exceeds perfect expectation damages.

The surplus can be divided between the parties in various ways. The promisor may offer to give the promisee a share of the surplus in exchange for a release from obligation. If the offer is accepted, the promisor will not have to breach the contract. Alternatively, the promisor can breach the contract and pay damages to the promisee. If the promisor breaches and pays perfect expectation damages and nothing more, then the promisee will get none of the surplus and the promisor will get all of it.

To illustrate, suppose that Farmer promises to sell 100 quarts of strawberries to Retailer for $.75 per quart, which Retailer will resell for $1.00 per quart, realizing a total profit of $25. Before Farmer delivers to Retailer, Buyer, who wants all 100 quarts, offers to pay Farmer $1.35 per

41. See Cooter, Economic Analysis of Punitive Damages, 56 S. Cal. L. Rev. 79 (1982); Ellis, Fairness and Efficiency in the Law of Punitive Damages, 56 S. Cal. L. Rev. 1 (1982); Landes & Posner, An Economic Theory of Intentional Torts, 1 Int'l Rev. L. & Econ. 127 (1981).

42. Unfortunately, the courts seem to have lost sight of this fact. See Cooter, supra note 8.

43. E. Farnsworth, Contracts § 12.1 (1982).

44. See R. Cooter & M. Eisenberg, Damages for Breach of Contract (Sept. 12, 1984) (unpublished manuscript, on file in the offices of the Columbia Law Review).

quart for immediate delivery. If Farmer diverts the strawberries to Buyer, instead of performing for Retailer, as promised, a surplus of $35 over the original plan will result. By diverting the strawberries to Buyer, Farmer can pay $25 in compensation to Retailer and still enjoy $35 in extra profits.

If negotiating a release from the contract is costly, then efficiency requires a promisor like Farmer to breach. However, it is often the case that a promisor like Farmer can negotiate a release from his contract at little cost. In such circumstances, it is equally efficient to negotiate a release or breach with compensation. If the two alternatives are indifferent from an efficiency viewpoint, should the law be indifferent between them? This is the subject of a dispute among theorists.[45] The proponents of the efficient breach hypothesis argue that Farmer can breach, rather than request release from his promise to Retailer. The opposite view holds that it would be wrong for Farmer not to perform unless he has a valid excuse.

A promisor who breaches whenever it is efficient weighs the benefits against the costs, just as a consumer weighs the benefits of a new overcoat against the price. No weight is given to the promise over and above the cost of perfect expectation damages. Thus, the promisor who breaches whenever it is efficient acts as if breach with compensation is permitted, which implies that damages are the price of breach.

On the other side of the dispute are theorists who maintain that a promisor should not breach *merely* because his benefits exceed his liability for expectation damages. According to this view, a stronger reason than efficiency is required to justify breach.[46] Efficiency is excluded because the promisor allegedly has an obligation to perform, not permission to breach with compensation. According to this view, the promise breaker does what is forbidden, even though he compensates his victim. Thus, the view that efficient breach is forbidden implies that damages for breach are a sanction.

The dispute over efficient breach can be described as a disagreement about whether damages are a sanction for wrongdoing or the price of breach. This Article suggests a simple criterion for a preliminary resolution of such disputes: Do damages vary with the state of mind of the injurer, or do they vary only with the extent of harm suffered by the victim? Facts about the promise breaker's state of mind do not usually influence the court's assessment of expectation damages. Thus, according to the preliminary criterion, damages for breach of contract are a price, not a sanction.

This conclusion is reinforced by considering punitive damages. The victim of breach cannot ordinarily increase the damage award simply by

45. For a recent article with citations, see Macneil, Efficient Breach of Contract: Circles in the Sky, 68 Va. L. Rev. 947 (1982).

46. Some justifications for breach are the traditional defenses, which enable the promise breaker to escape liability, such as impossibility, changed circumstances, or mutual mistake. Other circumstances may justify breach with compensation, such as a situation in which performance would impose extreme hardship on the promisor and produce only a small advantage to the promisee. The list is open ended, but the opponents of efficient breach insist that efficiency is excluded from it.

showing that the promise breaker's conduct was gross, repeated, or willful and wanton.[47] For punitive damages to be awarded, the contract must involve a special relationship, such as a fiduciary relationship.[48]

If expectation damages are perfect in the sense of compensating exactly for the lost expectation, then it can be shown by using economic analysis that the cost of breach is internalized, as required for efficiency.[49] If damages were increased over the expectation level, they would deter breach rather than internalize costs. Damages are rarely increased above the compensatory level, so they usually internalize the cost of breach, rather than deter it, which supports the conclusion that damages are the price of breach.

According to this Article's prescription, lawmakers ought to price an activity when it is easy for them to determine its external costs. In the case of contracts, the promisor makes a definite commitment—for example, to pay a certain sum of money on a particular date, to deliver a specific good, or to provide a specific service. Usually the performance has economic value which is much easier to quantify than, for example, the cost of a bodily injury in a tort suit, so it is relatively easy for the court to determine the harm caused by breach.

The prescription further suggests that lawmakers ought to sanction an activity when they can easily determine its optimal level. Because there are many legitimate circumstances which can interfere with the promisor's ability to perform, or increase the cost of performance, lawmakers would be hard-pressed to determine generally the optimal level of performance or the optimal level of precaution against breach.

To illustrate, suppose that a construction company fails to complete a project on time. The failure may be due to inclement weather, recalcitrant building inspectors, a wildcat strike by plumbers, or a shortage of materials. If damages were a sanction for wrongdoing, then the court would have to determine whether the construction company was at fault. It would be very difficult for the court to obtain information on all of the relevant facts and weigh them. Since it is much easier for courts to determine the external harm caused by breach of contract than to determine whether the promisor's behavior was faulty, the prescription leads to the conclusion that breach should be priced rather than sanctioned.

2. *The Exceptional Cases.* — While the broad contours of contract law correspond to the theory advocated here, there are details that pose difficul-

47. Insurance contracts are also an exception. See Sullivan, Punitive Damages in the Law of Contract: The Reality and the Illusion of Legal Change, 61 Minn. L. Rev. 207, 241–44 (1976–1977); Comment, Punitive Damages on Ordinary Contracts, 42 Mont. L. Rev. 93, 100 (1981). In these cases punitive damages are a sanction. Note also that compensation for partial performance under the quantum meruit principle may be blocked if the breach is willful. For a discussion of this point, see L. Fuller & M. Eisenberg, Basic Contract Law 316 (3rd ed. 1972).

48. E. Farnsworth, supra note 43, § 12.8 (1982).

49. See R. Cooter & M. Eisenberg, supra note 44.

ties. First, compensatory damages are the usual remedy for breach, but not the unique remedy.[50] Courts award damages which exceed the loss suffered by the victim of breach in cases involving unjust enrichment. For example, if an art dealer promises to sell a painting to the first buyer, and then sells the painting to the second buyer at a higher price, the art dealer may have to "disgorge" his profit by paying damages equal to the price differential. This is a situation in which a penalty is added to compensatory damages in order to offset the exceptional advantage gained by nonperformance. In cases involving unjust enrichment, the court imposes a sanction for wrongdoing in order to deter it.[51]

Another remedy for breach is specific performance. A leading theory holds that courts should order specific performance when breach involves a failure to deliver a unique good.[52] This theory is consistent with the prescription that courts should sanction an activity when they can determine the efficient social standard with more accuracy than they can determine the external harm. In cases where the good is unique, the courts cannot accurately assess its value to the victim of breach. The buyer of a unique good enjoys a surplus equal to the amount by which his willingness to pay for the good exceeds what he actually pays. The consumer's willingness to pay is impossible to assess for unique goods.[53] Since courts cannot observe the size of the surplus, the remedy for seller's breach is to order performance, backed by a sanction, rather than to award money damages.

Finally, standards similar to negligence are sometimes relevant in deciding whether or not a contract exists. Specifically, a person is liable for the careless use of the symbols by which contracts are formed. To illustrate, a person who raises his hand at an auction to point out an attractive light fixture on the ceiling may find that he has inadvertently made a purchase. If a person does not intend to make a promise, but uses the symbols of contracting in such a way that a reasonable person would believe a promise was made, then the courts may enforce it. Enforcing the contract is sometimes the sanction for careless use of the symbols of contracting.

---

50. There are also nonlegal remedies for breach. Business practice may correspond imperfectly to the law with regard to whether damages are a sanction or a price. In the usual case of breach, where compensatory damages are the remedy, the court proceeds as if breach were priced, rather than sanctioned. However, social custom may condemn a person whose breach is gross, repeated, or willful and wanton, even though courts do not pronounce on the question of fault. Such a loss of reputation can be costly to a businessman.

51. Deterrence is imperfect because disgorging profits eliminates the actual gain, but there is still an expected gain whenever there is a positive probability that the wrongdoing will go undetected. This is analogous to requiring a tax evader to pay the IRS what he owes, but attaching no additional fine to his liability.

52. See Kronman, Specific Performance, 45 U. Chi. L. Rev. 351 (1978).

53. This is an example of the well known problem of preference revelation, first identified with clarity by Professor Samuelson. See Samuelson, The Pure Theory of Public Expenditure, 36 Rev. Econ. & Stat. 387 (1954).

FIGURE 6

CRIME

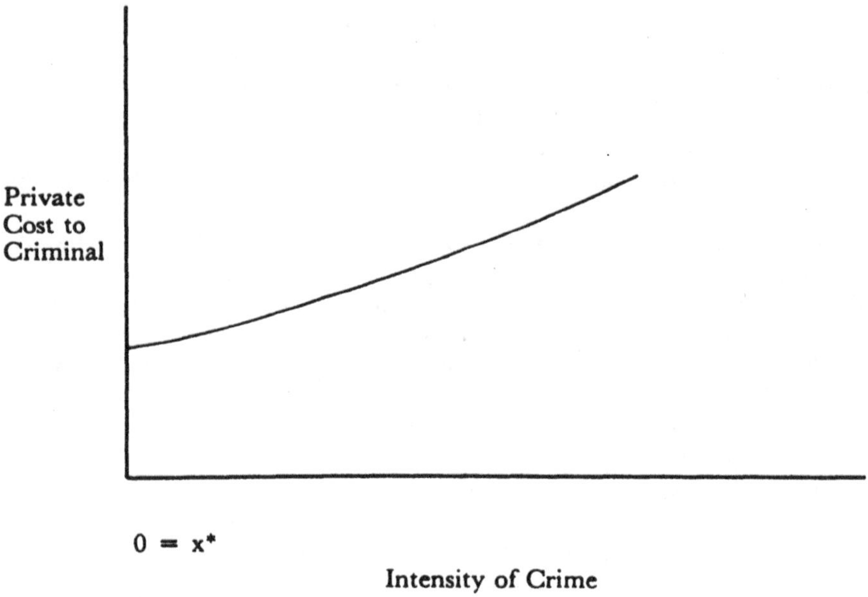

C. *Criminal Law*

The incentive effects of sanctions and prices, as represented by the contrast between Rules *A* and *B*, assume continuous behavior whose optimal amount is positive for some people. Some crimes fit this model. For example, vehicular manslaughter can be analyzed along the same lines as tortious negligence. However, other crimes cannot fit this model without being distorted. For example, premeditated murder is a discontinuous act whose optimal frequency is zero.[54] In this section the model is adapted to fit such behavior. The substantive question addressed is, "Why should crimes be punished rather than priced?"[55] This Article's prescription about when lawmakers should sanction behavior, rather than price it, provides an immediate answer to this question.

Figure 2 can be modified to represent behavior whose optimal amount is nil. As illustrated in Figure 6, the horizontal axis has been changed to indicate the seriousness of the crime and x^* has been moved to the origin to

54. A theorist determined to construe choice as continuous might argue that the probability of killing someone by a particular action is continuous, and it is optimal—whatever that means—for some people to be murdered. This line of argument strains the connection between my model and ordinary speech to the breaking point. Instead, I attempt a more immediate and natural modeling in terms of discontinuous choices with optima at corners.

55. This section does not consider the few cases of strict liability for crimes that have arisen in the business context. See, e.g., Morissette v. United States, 342 U.S. 246 (1952).

indicate that the legal standard requires that crimes not be committed. To take a concrete example, suppose that the crime in question is theft and that the seriousness of the theft is proportional to the amount of money stolen. The vertical axis shows the external costs of the crime, which include public and private expenditures on preventing, prosecuting, and punishing it, as well as the amount actually stolen and other consequential losses to the victims.[56] The legal standard, denoted x^*, is located at the origin of the graph, which indicates that stealing any positive amount of money, no matter how small, is prohibited.

A person who steals exposes himself to the risk of costly prosecution and loss of reputation, even if he steals very little.[57] Consequently, a person's private expected costs will often jump abruptly as soon as he steals a small amount. Thus, the private expected costs of the thief will have a discontinuity at the origin where he violates the legal standard, as shown in Figure 6. That the jump occurs at the origin in Figure 6, rather than at an internal point, does not change the conclusions reached in discussing Rule *A*. First, the theory of incentives shows that a typical person minimizes his private costs by conforming to a reasonable obligation backed by a reasonable sanction. Since most criminal laws are reasonable, most people will conform to them. Only an exceptional person finds crime advantageous when account is taken of its risks.

Second, according to the prescription, lawmakers should sanction activities when they have better information about community standards than about external costs. There are clear community standards with regard to many crimes such as robbery, murder, rape, burglary, or embezzlement—the standard being that no one should do them. Thus, the existence of community standards concerning many crimes solves one of the information problems lawmakers face.[58]

Community standards condemn many crimes unambiguously, but the

---

56. The reader who is troubled by the idea that victims can assign a dollar value to the cost of crime should bear in mind that many crimes are also torts, for which the jury must assign a dollar value for compensation. Thus, I am only assuming that a task already assigned to juries can actually be performed.

57. This fact is captured by the title of M. Feeley, The Process Is the Punishment (1979).

58. It is also the case that differences in compliance costs across individuals are unimportant in formulating many aspects of criminal law. Conforming to a legal standard can involve restraining an impulse. For example, a person who is *very* angry at someone may find it difficult not to batter him. Self-restraint is analogous to compliance costs. When the legal standard must be responsive to differences in compliance costs among individuals, the information requirements for sanctions are excessive, as illustrated by the discussion of pollution. See supra notes 25-29 and accompanying text. On the other hand, the legal standard for battery will not be adjusted according to the strength of the injurer's anger. Many psychological costs of compliance—anger, revenge, envy, or lust—receive little or no weight in court. The law treats restraint of an impulse to do wrong as an illegitimate compliance cost which receives no weight, so the information requirements for setting criminal standards are modest. In contrast, if criminal acts were priced, the actor would be permitted to give weight to these illegitimate costs.

public is often divided about the extent of punishment that should attach to crimes. Legal officials are left with the difficult task of constructing schedules of punishment. Fortunately, if the officials make a mistake and attach the wrong sanction to a crime—either too high or too low—the behavior of most people will not be affected by the error, because the cost of crime far exceeds the benefit. The social cost of moderate errors in calibrating punishments is low because behavior is relatively inelastic with respect to sanctions.[59]

Conversely, if crimes were priced, rather than sanctioned, people would be permitted to commit crimes provided that they paid the price. With prices, self-interested decisionmakers would balance the incremental benefit against the incremental cost of committing a crime. To internalize costs, the price would have to cover harm suffered by the victims and the enforcement activities of the state, adjusted by the probability of its collection. If benefits and costs are balanced at the margin, then the number of crimes would be relatively elastic with respect to the price, so errors in computing damages would affect the amount of crime. It is very difficult to compute the cost of crime to its victims, so large errors would occur. Thus the information requirements for pricing crimes are prohibitive, while the information requirements for sanctioning crimes are relatively low.[60]

D. *Regulation*

Most regulations consist of obligations backed by sanctions. Economists have consistently advocated replacing many regulations with prices. This section examines this policy problem using the analytical framework developed in Parts I and II.

1. *The Normative Issue.* — An example of the policy question is: Should pollution standards be replaced with pollution taxes? To compute the efficient tax, government officials must know the amount of external harm caused by the polluter and nothing more. By contrast, to discover the

59. This statement should not be interpreted to mean that deterrence is ineffective.

60. The usual reason economists offer for not pricing crime is different from the one offered here. According to the traditional argument, it is inefficient, if not impossible, to punish every crime, so potential criminals will discount the punishment by the probability of its application. If the punishment were the requirement of compensating the victim fully, then the discounted punishment would provide too little deterrence from an efficiency perspective, so there would be too much crime. See, e.g., Becker, Crime and Punishment: An Economic Approach, 76 J. Pol. Econ. 169 (1968). Furthermore, the cost of punishing the convicted offender must be taken into account. See Polinsky & Shavell, The Optimal Tradeoff between the Probability and Magnitude of Fines, 69 Am. Econ. Rev. 880 (1979). This argument, however, does not go to the root of the problem, because it does not explain what is wrong with pricing most crimes and punishing those who attempt to evade paying the price. There is a sense in which sanctions lie behind prices—the obligation to pay the price is itself sanctioned. Professors Calabresi and Melamed made this same point in somewhat different language when they explained the difference between property rights and liability rights. See Calabresi & Melamed, Property Rules, Liability Rules, and Inalienability One View of the Cathedral, 85 Harv. L. Rev. 1089 (1972).

efficient standard, officials must balance the external harm against the cost of abatement, which requires complete information on each polluter's abatement technology. Since knowledge of the technology of each polluter is difficult or impossible for officials to obtain, some economists recommend replacing regulations with taxes.

There is, however, a problem with prices that does not arise with standards. It is in the interest of most people to conform to standards backed by sanctions, even though violations often go unpunished. Specifically, if reasonable pollution standards are backed by reasonable sanctions, most polluters will comply, even though pollution sometimes goes undetected. By contrast, if a price sometimes goes uncollected, then most self-interested people will change their behavior. Polluters will respond to a decrease in the frequency of collection of pollution fees by increasing the amount of pollution. In general, a sanction requires lower enforcement costs than a price, even if the two are equal in magnitude, because precaution is elastic with respect to imperfections in collecting prices and inelastic with respect to imperfections in enforcing sanctions.[61]

Thus the choice between prices and sanctions in regulating pollution is a choice between the low enforcement costs of obligations backed by sanctions and the low information costs of prices.

2. *The Descriptive Issue.* — It is especially difficult with regulations to decide after the fact whether they create prices or sanctions. To illustrate, is a parking ticket a price or a sanction? What about a ticket for operating an overloaded truck, or a citation for a health violation in a restaurant? Officials often have discretion about whether to increase the penalty for intentional, repeated, or gross offenses. Whether or not they increase it is a good test of whether they regard it as a sanction or a price.

For example, there does not seem to be any additional penalty attached to repeated parking violations. Most judges are prepared to allow individuals to repeatedly break parking regulations provided that they pay the price. Perhaps lawmakers and judges allow individuals to balance the costs of compliance against the benefits of noncompliance because the legal officials do not have good information about these benefits. Apparently, judges treat parking tickets as if their purpose were to internalize the cost of parking congestion.

In contrast, most judges take a different attitude with respect to moving violations such as speeding or drunken driving. With these traffic regulations, the penalty increases with repetition of the offense, indicating that officials regard the fine as a sanction. Sanctions for moving violations probably make sense in light of the fact that obtaining information about community standards with regard to automobile safety is easier than determining the cost of automobile accidents.

---

61. This assumes that the distribution of compliance costs is such that the elasticity of precaution on the intensive margin, which is relevant for prices, is greater than the elasticity on the extensive margin, which is relevant for sanctions.

Conclusion

A sanction is a detriment imposed for doing what is forbidden, and a price is an amount of money exacted for doing what is permitted. An obligation partitions acts into permitted and forbidden zones, with the partition representing a social judgment about correct behavior. If a penalty is attached to forbidden activities, there is a jump or discontinuity in the private costs of the actor at the point of the partition. Consequently, the actor's behavior will be unresponsive to moderate changes in the penalty or the frequency of its application. By contrast, prices allow the individual to choose how he will behave, as long as he pays the price. The individual balances the cost of compliance against the benefit of noncompliance, so his behavior is responsive to moderate changes in price.

A prescriptive and a descriptive conclusion can be derived from this theory. If obtaining accurate information about external costs is cheaper than obtaining accurate information about efficient behavior, then price the activity. If the converse is true, then enact a standard backed by a sanction. The supply of an activity is more elastic when it is priced than when it is sanctioned, so the distortion from imposing the wrong price is greater than the distortion from imposing the wrong sanction. On the other hand, when an activity is sanctioned, the partition must be placed in the right place to avoid distortions. Typically, activities should be sanctioned when there is a clear community standard and unclear external costs, and should be priced when the opposite is true.

Sometimes it is difficult to determine whether a law prices or sanctions an activity. To classify such a law, it is useful to note that a price is invariant with respect to the actor's state of mind and variable with respect to the harm caused by his action, while a sanction is variable with respect to states of mind affecting the seriousness of the fault and the need for deterrence. A price only depends upon the extent of harm because its purpose is to internalize the cost of an activity and to allow individuals to decide whether to engage in it. By contrast, a sanction is often adjusted to the state of mind of the offender because its purpose may include deterrence and punishment as well as compensation.

Many lawyers are blind to the proper use of prices, which contributes to heavyhanded regulation. Conversely, many economists are blind to the distinctively normative element in law, which prevents them from understanding its essential nature. By supplying a unified theory of prices and sanctions, I hope to bring economics into contact with the tradition of jurisprudence and to advance our understanding of how law controls behavior.

MATHEMATICAL APPENDIX

A. *Variables and Functions*

Each of the individual decisionmakers (*DM*'s) control a nonnegative variable, x, indicating the intensity of an activity called precaution, that influences the probability, p, that others suffer external harm. The extent of the external harm is indicated by the variable h. Thus,

x = *DM*'s precaution, $x \geq 0$,
h = external harm,
p = probability density of external harm h occurring, $1 \geq p \geq 0$, where $p = p(h,x)$, $p_2 < 0$, and $p_{22} > 0$.

Precaution is costly to the *DM*. This cost increases with the amount of precaution. Furthermore, different *DM*'s may pay different prices for precaution. Let b denote a variable which differentiates *DM*'s according to the cost of precaution. Incorporating all elements into the cost function yields the following expression:

c = *DM*'s cost of precaution
= $c(b,x(b))$, where $c_2 > 0$, $c_{22} \geq 0$,
b = *DM*'s cost characteristic, and
$x(b)$ = precaution by a b-type *DM*.

B. *First Best Social Optimum*

Social costs *(SC)* created by a b-type *DM* consist of the expected value of the external harm which he imposes upon others and his own costs of precaution, as represented by Equation 1:

$$SC(b) = \int p(h,x(b))hdh + c(b,x(b)),$$

where *SC* is assumed to be a twice differentiable concave function of x(b) for all b.

The number of b-type *DM*'s is indicated by the density function f(b). Aggregate social costs are the integral of costs for each type of *DM*:

$$SC = \int SC(b)f(b)db.$$

Efficiency requires the *DM*'s to choose their precaution x(b) so as to minimize social costs *SC*:

$$\text{efficiency} = \min_{x(b)} SC \mid x(b) > 0,$$

with first order condition

$$SC = \int p_2 hdh + c_2 > 0 \text{ for all } b.$$

Figure 1 is a graph of Equation 1 for a value of b at which the solution is an equality.

C. *Prices and Sanctions*

If officials had perfect information and complete control over individuals, then officials could require each individual to choose his level of precaution to satisfy Equation 1. However, officials can only influence the choice of individual *DM*'s by changing their incentives. The two mechanisms for changing incentives considered here are prices and sanctions.

If the *DM*'s behavior imposes external harm h, which occurs with probability $p(h)$, then officials can attempt to impose a detriment upon the *DM*, where the detriment is denoted r. If officials impose the detriment r as a function of the amount of external harm, and no other variable influences the detriment, then the activity is *priced*: $r = r(h)$ = activity is priced.

Alternatively, the officials can control behavior by creating an obligation backed by a sanction. The *DM* is obligated to take precaution x which is at least as great as the legal standard of care, denoted x^*. The external harm the *DM* causes is said to be his *fault* whenever his precaution falls short of the legal standard, whereas the *DM* is not at fault whenever his precaution is at least as great as the legal standard:

$x < x^*$ = *DM* at fault
$x > x^*$ = *DM* not at fault

Officials are said to *sanction* behavior if fault is a necessary condition for the detriment to be positive and the detriment is an increasing function of the extent of the harm:

$$\begin{aligned} r &= r(h, x^* - x) \\ &= 0 \text{ if } x > x^* \\ &> 0 \text{ if } x < x^*, \text{ where } r1 > 0 \end{aligned} \quad = \text{activity is sanctioned}$$

Thus, fault is a necessary condition for the application of a sanction. Two levels of sanctions are distinguished in law. First, the sanction is said to consist of *compensatory damages* when the detriment equals the external harm: $r = h$ = compensatory damages. Second, whereas the detriment includes *punitive damages* to the extent that it exceeds the external harm: $r - h > 0$ = punitive damages.

D. *Minimizing Private Costs*

The individual *DM* minimizes his private expected costs that consist of the cost of precaution and the expected detriment imposed upon him. Prices and sanctions are particular forms of the detriment function $r = r(h, x^* - x)$. Regardless of whether the detriment is a price or a sanction, it is minimal in the event that he does not cause external harm. If he causes external harm in such a way that he owes a price or sanction, the debt may not be collected. It may not be collected because the injured party does not bring suit, the state does not prosecute, or the plaintiff cannot assemble enough evidence to win in court. Failure to collect an owed detriment constitutes an imperfection in enforcement. Let the imperfection be measured by the function $s(r)$, which indicates the probability that the detriment r, which is owed, is actually collected. The expected private costs of the individual *DM*, denoted *PC*, can be written as in Equation 2:

$$PC(b) = \int s(r) r(h, x^* - x)\, p(h, x)\, dh + c(b, x),$$

with the first order condition on precaution given by

$$\int [(s' rp + sp) r_2 + srp_2)] dh + c_2 > 0.$$

An activity is said to be *perfectly priced* for a *b*-type *DM* if the expected detriment equals the external harm:

$[\int rs(r)p(h,x)dh = \int hp(h,x)dh]$ = perfectly priced.

Perfect pricing results in the internalization of the externality by the *DM*. Thus, *when an externality is perfectly priced, first-best efficiency is achieved.*

1. *Proposition 1: When an externality is perfectly priced, first-best efficiency is achieved.* — To prove this proposition, simply observe that with perfect pricing the first order condition for minimizing private costs, which is given by Equation 3, reduces to Equation 4:

$\int p_2(h,x)hdh + c_2(b,x) > 0$, for all b.

Equation 4 is identical to Equation 1, so first-best efficiency is achieved.

2. *Proposition 2: If the official price does not exceed the external harm and enforcement is imperfect, or if enforcement is perfect and the official price is less than the external harm, then the amount of external harm will be excessive relative to first-best efficiency.* — To prove this proposition, assume that behavior is priced, $r=r(h)$, so private costs can be written

$$PC = \int sr(h)p(h,x)dh + c.$$

Let x'' denote the value of x which minimizes PC. Thus, the first order condition for an internal optimum can be written as in Equation 5:

$\int srp_2(h,x'')dh + c_2(b,x'') = 0.$

Proposition 2 assumes that either $s<1$ and $r=h$, or else $s=1$ and $r<h$. In either case, $sr(h)<h$. Replacing sr with h in Equation 5, and using the fact that $p_2<0$, yields

$$\int hp_2(h,x'')<dh + c_2(b,x'') < 0.$$

By Equation 1, first-best efficiency can be written

$SC' = \int hp_2(h,x')dh + c_2(b,x') = 0,$

where x' indicates the social optimum. By the second order condition, SC' is increasing in x at $x=x''$. Thus the two preceding expressions imply that $x''<x'$. Furthermore, the expected external harm is a decreasing function of x, so x'' results in too much external harm relative to first-best efficiency. This completes the proof.

Conversely, when an activity is sanctioned, the problem of cost minimization by any *DM* can be divided into three steps. First, compute the level of precaution which minimizes private costs subject to the constraint that the legal standard is satisfied:

$\min_x c(b,x) \mid x>x^*.$

Since c is an increasing function of x, the value of x which solves this problem is $x=x^*$.

Second, compute the level of precaution which minimizes private costs subject to the constraint that the legal standard is unsatisfied:

$\min \int s(r)r(h,x^*-x)p(h,x)dh + c(b,x) \mid x<x^*.$

Let the solution to this problem be denoted $PC(x@)$, where $x@$ denotes the optimal value of x.[62]

For the third and final step, compare the two costs to decide whether to conform with the legal standard:

$$[PC(x^*) - PC(x@)] \quad \begin{cases} < 0 & \Rightarrow \text{choose } x = x^*; \\ > 0 & \Rightarrow \text{choose } x = x@. \end{cases}$$

As explained, a sanction r stands behind a legal standard x^*. A legal standard will be described as perfect if it equals the first-best efficient precaution level for the *DM* to whom it is applied. Thus,

$$[x^*(b) + x'(b)] = \text{perfect legal standard for } b.$$

3. *Proposition 3: Assuming that a perfect legal standard* (x*(b)=x'(b)) *for decisionmaker* b *is backed by a perfectly compensatory sanction* (r=h) *which is perfectly enforced* (s=1), *then decisionmaker b's precaution will be first-best efficient.* — To prove this proposition, consider the three steps discussed above, that guide a *DM* faced with an obligation backed by a sanction. First, if the *DM* does not conform to the legal standard, his private cost are identical to social costs as a consequence of the asumptions in the proposition—that is, $PC=SC$ for $x<x^*$. Thus the *DM*'s private costs approach their lower bound at the first-best efficient level x', which equals x^* by assumption:

$$[\inf_{x<x^*} PC = \inf_{x<x^*} SC] \Rightarrow x=x^*.$$

Turning to the second step, if the *DM* does conform to the legal standard, then his private costs will be minimized by setting $x=x^*$. Thus, when the *DM* comes to the third step, he will choose $x=x^*$ in either case, so his precaution will be first-best efficient. This completes the proof.

Small imperfections in the price caused the *DM*'s precaution to fall below the first-best efficient level. Small imperfections in sanctions do not have this effect. To prove this, it is necessary to understand why a sanction results in a corner solution for the *DM*. It is often the case that $PC(x^*)-PC(x@) < 0$, in which case the *DM* is at a corner, as depicted in Figure 2. Specifically, assuming perfect enforcement, $s=1$, a perfect legal standard, $x^*=x'$, and a perfectly compensatory sanction, $r=h$, the discontinuity is given by

$$PC(x^*)-PC(x@) = - \int hpdh.$$

The existence of such a discontinuity leads to proposition 4.

4. *Proposition 4: Assuming that the legal standard is perfect,* (x*=x'), *and that the first-best efficient precaution for a* b*-type decision maker is strictly positive,* x'(b)>0, *then if there are imperfections in compensatory damages* (r=h-epsilon) *or in enforcement* (s=1−epsilon), *which are small relative to the perfect values of these variables* (sr=h), *precaution will still be first-best efficient.* — To prove this proposition small imperfections in sanctions and enforcement must be shown not to change the outcome of the *DM*'s decision rule. Let sr denote the ex-

62. If the constraint $x<x^*$ is not binding, then $x@<x^*$; if the constraint is binding, the x goes to x^* in the limit, $x@=x^*$, and 'inf' should be substituted for 'min'.

pected sanction, and $D(sr)$ denote a variation in the expected sanction. Similarly, let $D(PC)$ indicate the change in the DM's private costs PC caused by the variation $D(sr)$ in the expected sanction.

In the first step of the decision rule, the DM is assumed to conform to the legal standard, so his private costs are

$$PC(x^*) = c(b,x^*)$$

Since the DM is not liable, variations in the sanction and enforcement do not influence his costs. Thus, $D(PC(x^*)) = 0$. In the second step of the decision rule, assume the DM does not conform. His private costs are therefore

$$PC(x@) = \int s(r)r(x^*-x@,h)\ p(h,x@)dh + c(b,x@).$$

A first order approximation to the change in these private costs caused by a variation in the sanction or enforcement can be written

$$D(PC(x@)) = PC^7(x@)Dx + \int pD(sr)dh.$$

Assume that the sanction, enforcement of it, and the legal standard are all perfect in the initial situation, in which case $PC'(x@)=SC'(x^*) = 0$, as demonstrated in the proof to Proposition 3. Substituting this fact into the preceding equation yields

$$D(PC(x@)) = pD(sr)dh.$$

Now turning to the third and final step, the variation $D(sr)$ causes a change in the values of the DM's decision rule whose first order approximation is Equation 6:

$$\{PC(x^*)+D(PC(x^*)) - PC(x@) - D(PC(x@))\} = PC(x^*) - PC(x@) - \int pD(sr)dh \text{ evaluated at } x@ = x^*.$$

When $x^*=x@$, as is true in the initial situation, expansion of the expressions for PC gives $PC(x^*) - PC(x@) = -\int s\cdot rpdh$. Thus the change in the decision rule can be written

$$\{PC(x^*)+D(PC(x^*) - PC(x@)-D(PC(x@))\} = -\int p[(sr+D(sr)]dh.$$

As long as the variation $D(sr)$ is a fraction of the initial value of sr, then the right side of this equation is negative, which implies by the DM's decision rule that he should choose $x=x^*$, thus conforming to the legal standard. Obviously, this proposition will remain true if higher order effects are taken into account, so the proof is complete.

According to Proposition 2, small imperfections in a price will cause changes in precaution, and according to Proposition 4, small imperfections in a sanction will not cause changes in precaution. The elasticity of aggregate precaution is the proportional change in aggregate precaution caused by a proportional change in the expected sanction or price. These propositions lead to Proposition 5.

5. *Proposition 5: When measured at the first best optimum, precaution is relatively elastic with repsect to prices and inelastic with respect to sanctions.* — When an obligation is backed by a sanction, however, a small change in the legal standard will cause the DM to change his precaution. This leads to Proposition 6.

6. *Proposition 6: Assuming that the sanction is perfectly compensatory* (r=h) *and that enforcement is perfect* (s=1), *the* DM *will continue to satisfy the legal standard in spite of small imperfections in it* x*=x'+<−epsilon). — Since the proof of proposition 6 follows the same steps as the proof for Proposition 5, it can be abbreviated. Under the assumption in Proposition 6, the *DM*'s decision rule can be written

$[PC(x^*) - PC(x@) = -\int hpdh < 0 => [\text{choose } x=x^*]$.

Let x^* change by an amount Dx^*. A first order approximation to the change in the decision rule can be written

$PC(x^*) + D(PC(x^*)) - PC(x@) - D(PC(x@))$.

It is easy to see that $D(PC(x^*)) = c_2Dx^*$ and that $D(PC(x@)) = 0$. Hence, Equation 7 reads:

$\{PC(x^*) + D(PC(x^*) - PC(x@) - D(PC(x@))\} = [-\int hpdh] + [c_2Dx]$.

The first term in square brackets is the *total* external harm, and the second term in square brackets is the *marginal* cost of precaution, both measured as the social optimum $x=x'$. Obviously, the *total* harm exceeds the *marginal* cost of precation at the optimum: $\int hpdh >> c_2$.

Thus, the right side of Equation 7 is negative and the decision rule requires the *DM* to choose $x=x^*$. The proof is complete.

E. *Second Best Regulations*

In reality, most regulations are insensitive to individual differences. Thus a legal standard may require every *DM* to exercise the same precaution, even though their compliance costs are different. When regulations are insensitive to individual differences, they are not first-best efficient.

When a regulation imposes the same legal standard x^* on every *DM* aggregate precaution is affected. Assume that the individual cost parameter b has been scaled so that the cost of precaution increases with b: $c1(b,x(b))>0$. Under certain conditions, there will be a value of b, denoted b^*, which is the switching point between compliance and noncompliance. The effect of a change in the sanction or the frequency of enforcement will be to change the switching point. Thus, aggregate precaution will respond to changes in the sanction by adjustments on the extensive margin and a relatively small number of people will increase their precaution by a relatively large amount. This leads to Propostion 7.

1. *Proposition 7: Assuming that the individual cost parameter* b *can be scaled so that compliance costs,* PC(x*), *increase faster than noncompliance costs,* PC(x@(b), *an increase in the sanction* r *or the frequency of enforcement* s, *that causes the switching point* b* *to increase by* Db*, *will cause an increase in aggregate precaution whose first order approximation equals* [x*-x@(b*)]f(b*)Db*. — This proposition, which is little more than an application of definitions, can be proved as follows. Since compliance costs, $c(b,x^*)$, increase faster than noncompliance costs, $c(b,x@)$, there will be no more than one value of b at which $PC(x^*) - PC(x@) = 0$. This value is b^*, the switching point. According to

the decision rule, every *DM* for whom $b<b^*$ will conform to the legal standard, and every *DM* for whom $b>b^*$ will not conform. Thus, aggregate precaution equals

$\int b^* x^* f(b)db + b^* \int x@(b)f(b)db.$

Now the increase in the sanction or in the frequency of enforcement cause b^* to increase by Db^*. Thus, a first order approximation to the change in aggregate precaution is given by $[x^*-x@(b^*)]f(b^*)Db^*$. A relatively small number of people, indicated by $f(b^*)$, increase their precaution by a large amount, indicated by $x^*-x@(b^*)$. This completes the proof.

F. *Punitive Damages*

Detriments can be either compensatory of punitive. A detriment is punitive whenever it exceeds the actual harm—that is, $r-h > 0$. In law, the application of punitive damages is controlled by the *DM*'s attitutde. Specifically, noncompliance with a legal standard must be intentional or motivated by ill-will before punitive damages are awarded. This section develops this idea mathematically.

Besides controlling his own precaution, assume that the *DM* also controls some aspects of his attitude towards his own noncompliance. The law is especially concerned with the *DM*'s intentionality and ill-will. Noncompliance is conventionally graded according to degree of intent as suggested by the following legal categories: inadvertent < reckless < intentional < deliberate. Similarly, ill-will is conventionally graded according to the following categories: well-intentioned < indifferent < reckless < wanton < malicious. Let m denote a nonnegative variable indicating the *DM*'s attitude, where higher values of m represent a higher degree of intentionality or more ill-will.

$m(b)$ = attitude of a b-type *DM*.

In order to relate the *DM*'s mental attitude to his behavior and make sense of the idea of unintentional noncompliance, it is necessary to introduce a random element into the relationship between the *DM*'s action and the resulting precaution. Let t'' be a random variable, let x be the precaution actually achieved, and let y be the intended precaution, where $x = y + t''$. The decisionmaker chooses y, nature chooses t, and their sum determines x. The intentions of the *DM* are to be determined with reference to y, whereas the actual performance of the *DM* is measured by x. Thus, there are three possible conditions of a *DM* who causes external harm:

no fault	=	$x > x^*$,
intentional fault	=	$x < x^*$ and $y > x^*$,
unintentional fault	=	$x < x^*$ and $y < x^*$.

There is a connection between mental attitude m and the intended action y. A complete analysis of the *DM*'s behavior when faced with the random term t'', would be necessary to explain this connection fully. Such an analysis will not be undertaken here. The basic point of such an analysis, however, is that when private costs of compliance are heterogenous, and the legal standard does not take account of these individual differences, *DM*'s with high compliance costs will choose an intended precaution level y which is less than the legal standard x^*.

Part II
Economic Analysis of Tort Law

[4]

The Yale Law Journal
Volume 81, Number 6, May 1972

Toward a Test for Strict Liability in Torts

Guido Calabresi† and Jon T. Hirschoff‡

I. Introduction

The fifteen years since Fleming James addressed the question of whether manufacturers should be liable without negligence[1] have seen a remarkable expansion in the scope of strict liability in the law of torts, yet the very courts which have been the leaders in this trend have been consistently troubled by the question of how far strict liability should extend within the areas in which it is being applied.[2] While strict liability of the manufacturer for product defects, for example, has been announced in jurisdiction after jurisdiction,[3] in many jurisdictions this has simply led to a morass of questions regarding the *definition* of "defect" and how liability for a defect relates to (a) adequacy of warnings, (b) unexpected or improper use, (c) assumption of risk, and even (d) contributory negligence.[4] Nor is this at all surprising.

† John Thomas Smith Professor of Law, Yale Law School. B.S. 1953, LL.B. 1958, Yale University; M.A. 1959, Oxford University.
‡ Assistant Professor of Law, Indiana University School of Law. A.B. 1963, Stanford University; J.D. 1967, Yale University.

1. James, *General Products—Should Manufacturers Be Liable Without Negligence?*, 24 Tenn. L. Rev. 923, 924 (1957). *See also* James, *Products Liability*, 34 Texas L. Rev. 44, 192 (1955).

2. *See, e.g.*, Wasik v. Borg, 423 F.2d 44 (2d Cir. 1970); Lamendola v. Mizell, 115 N.J. Super. 514, 280 A.2d 241 (1971); Foster v. Preston Mill Co., 44 Wash.2d 440, 268 P.2d 645 (1954). *See also* James, *The Future of Negligence in Accident Law*, 53 Va. L. Rev. 911 (1967); Kalven, *Torts: The Quest for Appropriate Standards*, 53 Calif. L. Rev. 189 (1965); and Prosser, *The Fall of the Citadel—Strict Liability to the Consumer*, 50 Minn. L. Rev. 791 (1966).

Since writing this article, we have read Professor Franklin's excellent article analyzing the application of various theories of liability in cases of patient claims for hepatitis resulting from blood transfusions. Franklin, *Tort Liability for Hepatitis: An Analysis and a Proposal*, 24 Stan. L. Rev. 439 (1972). The test for strict liability which we suggest in this article looks to the same kinds of practical considerations, by and large, as those which Professor Franklin takes into account in concluding that hospitals and blood banks should be strictly liable for transfusion related hepatitis.

3. *See* L. Frumer & M. Friedman, Products Liability, § 16A[3], n.2 (1970).

4. *See, e.g.*, as to adequacy of warning, Alman Brothers Farms & Feed Mill, Inc. v. Diamond Laboratories, Inc., 437 F.2d 1295, 1303 (5th Cir. 1971); Davis v. Wyeth Laboratories, Inc., 399 F.2d 121 (9th Cir. 1968); Wright v. Carter Products, Inc., 244 F.2d 53, at 56-59 (2d Cir. 1957); as to unexpected or improper use, Hardy v. Hull Corporation, 446 F.2d 34 (9th Cir. 1971); Schemel v. General Motors Corporation, 384 F.2d 802 (7th Cir. 1967); Johnson v. Standard Brands Paint Co., 274 Cal. App. 2d 331, 79 Cal. Rptr. 194 (1969); as to assumption of risk, Greco v. Bucciconi Engineering Co., 407 F.2d 87 (3d Cir. 1969); Sperling v. Hatch, 10 Cal. App. 3d 54, 88 Cal. Rptr. 704 (1970); Bartkewich

The Yale Law Journal Vol. 81: 1055, 1972

Strict liability has never meant that the party held strictly liable is to be a general insurer for the victim no matter how or where the victim comes to grief. General insurance was not the rule in classical instances of strict liability, such as ultrahazardous activities, or in legislatively mandated instances, such as workmen's compensation, and it is not the rule in the recent instances of application such as products liability.[5] The questions which the courts now find themselves asking (and being asked) in the new areas of application, such as products liability, involve the same basic issue as did equally difficult questions faced in traditional areas of strict liability, which were couched in words such as "natural or unnatural use" and "arising out of and in the course of employment." The issue is just where strict liability should stop.

Despite the courts' recognition that strict liability must be limited, they have seldom been very confident in trying to describe the limits. Indeed, their efforts at answering the questions posed in strict liability cases seem in many cases to degenerate into either meaningless semantic disputes or attempts at balancing the costs of the accident against the costs of avoiding it;[6] yet the latter approach sounds devilishly like the very calculus of negligence, or Learned Hand's test for fault, which strict liability was meant to replace.

Strict liability's limits can, however, be defined in a meaningful way. The questions the courts have been asking are often highly relevant to those limits, and strict liability so limited is very different from the negligence calculus, or Learned Hand's test for fault. Analysis of strict liability's limits together with a suggested test for strict liability will, we believe, give insight into both the negligence calculus and its growing disfavor.

II. The Learned Hand Test Considered

Learned Hand's test for fault defines the defendant's duty of care as a function of three variables: (1) the probability that the accident will

v. Billinger, 432 Pa. 351, 247 A.2d 603 (1968); and as to contributory negligence, Friedman v. General Motors Corp., 411 F.2d 533 (3d Cir. 1969); Matthias v. Lehn & Fink Products Corp., 70 Wash.2d 541, 424 P.2d 284 (1967).

5. *See* as to ultrahazardous activities, W. Prosser, The Law of Torts 517 (4th ed. 1971); as to workmen's compensation, S. Harper, The Law of Workmen's Compensation 470 (2d ed. 1920); and as to products liability, *e.g.*, Suvada v. White Motor Co., 32 Ill.2d 612, 210 N.E.2d 182 (1965); Elliott v. Lachance, 109 N.H. 481, 256 A.2d 153, 156 (1969); Dippel v. Sciano, 37 Wis.2d 443, 451, 155 N.W.2d 55 (1967).

6. *See* Pike v. Frank G. Hough Co., 2 Cal.3d 465, 467 P.2d 229, 85 Cal. Rptr. 629 (1970); Christofferson v. Kaiser Foundation Hospitals, 15 Cal. App. 3d 75, 92 Cal. Rptr. 825 (1971); Dunham v. Vaughan & Bushnell Mfg. Co., 86 Ill. App. 2d 315, 327, 229 N.E.2d 684, 690 (1967); *cf.* Sanders v. Western Auto Supply Co., 183 S.E.2d 321 (S.Car. 1971). *See also* Wade, *Strict Tort Liability of Manufacturers*, 19 Sw. L.J. 5 (1965).

occur, (2) the gravity of the injury which will be suffered if the accident does occur, and (3) the burden of precautions adequate to prevent such accidents.[7] If the cost to the defendant of avoiding the accident would have been less than the cost of the accident, discounted by the probability of its occurrence, the defendant's failure to avoid the accident is termed negligence.[8]

For the purpose of the first parts of this discussion, we will assume that the traditional test for fault, as given expression in Learned Hand's formula, was designed to do what Professor Posner says it was designed to do,[9] namely to minimize the sum of accident costs and the costs of accident avoidance.[10] The Learned Hand test would seem to accomplish this objective in theory, because *if it were applied perfectly,* it would put the costs of the accident on the injurer when and only when it was cheaper for him to avoid the accident costs by appropriate safety measures than to pay those costs. *Assuming injurers had the requisite foresight,* this would cause potential injurers to avoid all accidents worth avoiding, *i.e.,* those where avoidance costs less than the accident, and to have only those accidents not worth avoiding.[11]

The application of the traditional rule of contributory negligence would make some difference, but not much. Using the rubric of the test, contributory negligence would exist when the victim, too, could have avoided the accident at a cost lower than the cost generated by the accident. Since under the traditional rule contributory negligence is a complete defense, the cost would remain on the victim despite the negligence of the injurer, *even if avoidance by the injurer would have*

7. Conway v. O'Brien, 111 F.2d 611, 612 (2d Cir. 1940), *rev'd on other grounds,* 312 U.S. 492; United States v. Carroll Towing Co., 159 F.2d 169 (2d Cir. 1947).

8. Perhaps anticipating what others would do in the name of his test, Judge Hand cautioned that "[the three elements of the test] are practically not susceptible of any quantitative estimate, and the second two are generally not so, even theoretically." Conway v. O'Brien, 111 F.2d 611, 612 (2d Cir. 1940). *See also* Moisan v. Loftus, 178 F.2d 148 (2d Cir. 1949).

9. Posner, *A Theory of Negligence,* 1 J. LEGAL STUD. 29 (1972) [hereinafter cited as Posner].

10. Our assumption, more precisely, is that the object is optimization of primary accident costs. *See* G. CALABRESI, THE COST OF ACCIDENTS 26-31 (1970) [hereinafter cited as COSTS]. But the statement in text is sufficiently accurate for purposes of this article.

11. The goal, strictly speaking, is accident cost avoidance rather than accident avoidance. It may be, for example, that minimization of the sum of automobile accident costs and avoidance costs would come about by measures designed to make automobiles "crashproof" rather than by measures directed at the avoidance of automobile accidents altogether.

In determining whether an accident cost is worth avoiding, the test would look not to the entire cost of the safety measure which would avoid it, but to the cost of that safety measure discounted appropriately to take account of all of the other accident costs that same measure would avoid. Thus the cost of avoiding a given accident is ten dollars if a 100 dollar safety device would also avoid nine other accidents of equal severity.

There are numerous other assumptions implicit in the application of any test of this kind, but this is not the place to discuss them. See COSTS, *supra* note 10, *passim.*

cost less than avoidance by the victim. Thus, even in the wonderful, let us freely admit, fantastic world of Professor Posner, in which none of the costs of an accident are borne by third parties other than the injurer and victim, and in which there is perfect foresight, the rule of contributory negligence would prevent the negligence calculus from optimizing primary accident cost reduction. The potential injurer who could avoid a $100 accident at a cost of $5, knowing that the victim could do so at a cost of $50, might well not undertake the $5 safety measure because of his knowledge that the victim will either avoid the accident or be held contributorily negligent. Given adequate foresight, one would expect the accident to be avoided, but at a cost $45 higher than necessary.[12]

A Learned Hand test for injurer liability with the defense of contributory negligence removed, however, would also fail to optimize accident costs, and for exactly the same reason. Under such a rule, there would be instances in which the victim who could avoid an accident more cheaply than could the injurer would fail to do so, because he would know that the injurer would nonetheless be held liable. Thus the *correct* optimizing rule, under the Learned Hand test, would be to have a doctrine of contributory negligence, but to apply it only where the cost of injurer avoidance exceeds the cost of victim avoidance.[13]

Whatever defects the Learned Hand test may have, given the existence of an absolute defense of contributory negligence, it can at least be said that if the test worked, all the accidents worth avoiding would be avoided. If they were occasionally avoided at somewhat greater expense than necessary, that would not be a matter of great consequence. At the same time, it must be recognized that all the costs of all the accidents not worth avoiding would fall on the victim, raising distributional or justice issues. We will, however, postpone consideration of those issues to a later section of this article, and limit our discussion here to primary accident cost reduction.[14]

If we make the assumptions under which the Learned Hand test would work adequately, the fascinating thing is that as good a result in terms of reducing primary accident costs could be achieved by a liability rule which is the exact reverse of the Learned Hand test. Un-

12. The $45 excess cost would be avoided only in the yet more wonderful world of Professor Coase, where transaction costs are nonexistent, and a pre-accident "bribe" of the injurer by the victim would result in the injurer taking the $5 safety measure. See Coase, *The Problem of Social Costs*, 3 J. LAW & ECON. 1 (1960), Calabresi, *Transaction Costs, Resource Allocation and Liability Rules—A Comment*, 11 J. LAW & ECON. 67 (1968), and COSTS, *supra* note 10, at 135-40.

13. Professor Posner realizes this, and adds that this refinement, though not explicit in the cases, may be implicit in them. Posner, *supra* note 9, at 33.

14. *See* part VI, *infra*.

der such a "reverse Learned Hand test," the costs of an accident would be borne by the *injurer* unless accident avoidance on the part of the victim would have cost less than the accident. If a reverse contributory negligence test were added, the victim would bear the accident costs only if the injurer could not also have avoided the accident at less cost than the accident entailed. A reverse Learned Hand test, in other words, which always made the injurer liable without fault unless the victim were negligent, and even then held the injurer liable if he also were negligent, would do for primary accident cost avoidance just what the actual Learned Hand test with contributory negligence is said to do. The only difference between the tests is distributional. Under the Learned Hand test, the costs of all accidents *not* worth avoiding are borne by victims, whereas under the reverse Learned Hand test they would be borne by injurers.[15]

In focusing on the reverse Learned Hand test, we are not simply playing with mirrors. The point is that a perfect world with perfect foresight is a prerequisite to optimization of primary accident cost reduction under *either* Learned Hand type test, and that given such a world, any number of other devices would also accomplish that goal.[16] To the extent that we are concerned with the practical minimization of accident costs, the choice among these devices will depend not on their *theoretical* ability to optimize accident costs given certain assumptions, but on the degree to which the particular assumptions required by each device actually do obtain.[17] We will suggest a test which we think is much more likely than either Learned Hand type test to accomplish a satisfactory job of primary accident cost optimization. We also think that application of the proposed test requires asking questions which are closely related to those questions courts have always asked in strict liability cases. That is why we believe the proposed test is an appropriate one for defining the limits of strict liability.

15. As our subsequent discussion indicates, the practical implications of the two tests are also very different. It may be, for example, that one test would result in more disputes over the shifting of losses than would the other, and thus in greater administrative costs. This practical consideration was, in Holmes' view, an overriding one. *See* O. Holmes, The Common Law (Howe ed. 1963) 76-77. *But cf.* Costs, *supra* note 10, at 261-62.

16. Consider, for example, a test pursuant to which an all-knowing accident prevention agency issues an accident avoidance order to the appropriate party whenever an accident is worth avoiding, with a sanction sufficiently severe to guarantee that the order will be followed. *Compare* Costs, *supra* note 10, at 111-13. *See* note 73 *infra*.

17. These assumptions relate, *inter alia*, to the cost of information to each party, the absence of psychological or other impediments to acting on the basis of available information, the administrative costs of shifting losses, and the extent to which parties actually bear the costs which the particular tests impose upon them. These are, in economists' terms, principally assumptions relating to transaction costs and externalization. *See generally* Costs, *supra* note 10, at 55-64, 143-50, 178-86, 244-50.

The Yale Law Journal Vol. 81: 1055, 1972

III. The Strict Liability Test Defined

When a case comes to judgment under either of the two Learned Hand type tests, a cost-benefit analysis is made by an outside governmental institution (a judge or a jury) as to the relative costs of the accident and of accident avoidance.[18] Liability would be placed on the party initially free of responsibility only if the *decider* found the benefits of avoidance (*i.e.*, not incurring the cost of the accident) to be greater than the costs of such avoidance to that party. The strict liability test we suggest does not require that a governmental institution make such a cost-benefit analysis. It requires of such an institution only a decision as to which of the parties to the accident *is in the best position to make the cost-benefit analysis between accident costs and accident avoidance costs and to act on that decision once it is made*. The question for the court reduces to a search for the cheapest cost avoider.[19]

So stated, the strict liability test sounds deceptively simple to apply. Instead of requiring a judgment as to whether an injurer *should* have avoided the accident costs because the costs of avoidance were less than the foreseeable accident costs as the Learned Hand test does, the strict liability test would simply require a decision as to whether the injurer or the victim was in the better position both to judge whether avoidance costs would exceed foreseeable accident costs and to act on that judgment.[20] The issue becomes not *whether* avoidance is worth it, but

18. The decision may also be made by the legislature, as it sometimes is through the application of the "negligence per se" concept. *See* 2 F. HARPER & F. JAMES, THE LAW OF TORTS, § 17.6 (1956). The history of the respective roles of judges and juries in the making of the analysis can be seen in cases such as Grand Trunk Ry. v. Ives, 144 U.S. 408 (1892); Baltimore & O.R.R. v. Goodman, 275 U.S. 66 (1927); Pokora v. Wabash Ry., 292 U.S. 98 (1934) (limiting *Goodman*); Lorenzo v. Wirth, 170 Mass. 596, 49 N.E. 1010 (1897); and Sylvester v. Shea, 280 Mass. 508, 182 N.E. 916 (1932). *See also* Nixon, *Changing Rules of Liability in Automobile Accident Litigation*, 3 LAW & CONTEMP. PROB. 476 (1936).

19. The cheapest cost avoider has been elsewhere defined as the party "an arbitrary initial bearer of accident costs would (in the absence of transaction and information costs) find it most worthwhile to 'bribe' in order to obtain that modification of behavior which would lessen accident costs most." COSTS, *supra* note 10, at 135. This definition, unlike the terminology we have been using in this article, includes the costs of accident avoidance within the term "accident costs." It should be clear upon reflection that the most "worthwhile" bribe would be one to the party who is in the best position both to determine what accident cost avoidance measures will result in the minimal sum of avoidance costs and accident costs (*i.e.*, to make the cost-benefit analysis) and to act upon that determination. We do not mean to suggest that the party in the best position to make the cost-benefit analysis is always in the best position to act upon it; where that is not the case, the decision requires weighing comparative advantages.

The imposition of accident costs on the cheapest cost avoider will, of course, have its own set of distributional consequences, and these may well differ from those resulting from applications of the Learned Hand or reverse Learned Hand tests.

20. We are assuming for purposes of the discussion in text that accident costs and avoidance costs are not only ascertainable but also fungible, so that the cost-benefit analysis involves only a comparison of relative costs. We would guess that in practice the judge or jury making the cost-benefit analysis under the Learned Hand test would

Toward a Test for Strict Liability in Torts

which of the parties is relatively more likely to find out whether avoidance is worth it. This judgment is by no means an easy one, but we would suggest that in practice it is usually easier to make correctly than is the judgment required under either the Learned Hand test or its reverse.[21] It also implies a lesser degree of governmental intervention than does either of the Hand type tests.[22]

As a first step toward seeing what is implied in such a strict liability test, we propose to examine how the issues raised by courts in various areas of strict liability relate to the proposed test. We will do this first in an oversimplified context, treating accidents as though they involved only the injurer and the victim. Subsequently, we will examine what is implied for the test in considering accidents as events involving whole categories of victims, injurers and affected third parties.

In strict products liability cases, the first question asked is, "was there a defect?" A defect may be defined to mean simply that something went wrong. All that in turn means, however, is that a safer product might have been designed, and this would mean that there is a defect whenever there is an accident. If, instead, existence of a defect is defined to mean a failure of a product to meet levels deemed customary in the trade, then strict liability would be even less successful in achieving optimal reduction of primary accident costs than is the Learned Hand test and would be far narrower than fault.[23] It is not surprising, therefore, that courts have tended to reject both of these extremes.[24]

be significantly affected by considerations other than the relative costs of accidents and accident avoidance, though this is expressly denied by Professor Posner. Posner, *supra* note 9, at 31-32, 33-34. These other considerations, involving the collectively determined worth of the parties or the activities they are engaged in, are in fact of crucial importance in determining the type and level of accident cost causing activities a society wishes to permit. The manner in which we would introduce them into the decision is discussed under the heading of "specific deterrence" in COSTS, *supra* note 10, at 95-129, 174-98. *See also* notes 72 & 73 *infra* and accompanying text.

21. It is an easier judgment because it looks to questions such as which party is better informed as to risks and alternatives instead of to questions requiring the weighing of accident costs and avoidance costs, both of which must be subjectively determined by the trier of fact.

22. *See* pp. 1074-75 *infra*.

23. The Learned Hand test asks whether an accident avoidance measure would cost less than it would save in accident costs, and this has very little to do with custom. *See* Posner, *supra* note 9, at 39. Custom has not generally been a defense under the fault system, although it may be admissible as relevant to what is proper conduct under the circumstances. 2 F. HARPER & F. JAMES, THE LAW OF TORTS § 17.3.

24. As to rejection of custom as an absolute defense in strict products liability cases, *see, e.g.*, Williams v. Brown Mfg. Co., 93 Ill. App. 2d 334, 236 N.E.2d 125, 138 (1968); Badorek v. General Motors Corp., 11 Cal. App. 3d 902, 935, 90 Cal. Rptr. 305, 328 (1970) (dictum), both citing Judge Hand's famous opinion in The T. J. Hooper, 60 F.2d 737 (2d Cir. 1932), *cert. denied sub nom.* Eastern Transportation Co. v. Northern Barge Co., 287 U.S. 662. Rejection of the other extreme is implicit in rejection of the notion that a manufacturer is liable without exception for accidents arising out of the use of his products. *See, e.g.*, the products liability cases cited in note 5 *supra*.

The courts have instead tended to determine whether a defect exists by asking a series of secondary questions relating to (a) the adequacy of warning and (b) the use to which the product was put. They have also noted that assumption of risk on the part of the victim might serve either to negate the existence of a defect or to be a defense to it.[25] In fact, the defense of assumption of risk may be viewed as broad enough to encompass adequacy of warning and appropriateness of product use, which are in turn appropriate ways of raising some of the questions implicit in the strict liability test we have offered.

Let us look first to adequacy of warning. Suppose that a product occasionally causes the user's leg to fall off. Failure to warn the potential user that this may happen in .0001 per cent of the cases will normally result in manufacturer liability.[26] But even such a warning is not likely to allow the user to make an intelligent cost-benefit analysis between accident and avoidance costs. Unless the user has reason to believe himself to be in the dangerous category and unless a close substitute exists which at some cost avoids the danger, the user is hardly in a position to evaluate the benefits of the product as against its costs. The producer may seem to be no better suited, but if we move from a static to a dynamic situation, this will not be the case. The producer is in a position to compare the existing accident costs with the costs of avoiding this type of accident by developing either a new product or a test which would serve to identify the risky .0001 per cent. The consumer, in practice, cannot make this comparison. Relatively, the producer is the cheapest cost avoider, the party best suited to make the cost-benefit analysis and to act upon it.

Should a patch test be developed which enables the consumer to identify himself as an especially risky user, the situation may well be changed. The existence of the patch test, sold together with the product and coupled with a warning, may be enough to make the consumer the party best able to avoid the costs of mishap.[27] This will depend in part, but only in part, on the nature of the warning and the adequacy (including ease of use) of the patch test. Even if the warning is unmistakably clear and the patch test 100 per cent accurate, however, the manufacturer may still be in the best position to make the cost-benefit analysis. For the analysis depends not only on the adequacy of the warning and the likelihood that a risky user will be able to identify him-

25. *See* note 4 *supra*.

26. *See, e.g.*, Davis v. Wyeth Laboratories, Inc., 399 F.2d 121 (9th Cir. 1968); Basko v. Sterling Drug, Inc., 416 F.2d 417, 430 (2d Cir. 1969).

27. *See, e.g.*, Matthis v. Lehn & Fink Products Corp., 70 Wash.2d 541, 424 P.2d 284 (1967).

self, but also on the availability of alternatives to the product.[28] If the product is a cosmetic with many reasonably close substitutes, identifying and clearly warning the risky group will very likely put the user in the best position to choose. If instead the product is a medicine, the use of which is the only way of saving the user's life, identifying and warning the risky users probably would not suffice to make the users the better choosers.[29] The manufacturer would in those circumstances be best suited to compare the cost of the occasional lost leg with the *cost of further research* designed to give rise to an adequate substitute entailing fewer risks, or equivalent risks but to another definable group.[30]

We do not mean to suggest that these examples resolve the issue, but they should serve to indicate why, when courts ask about adequacy of warning in attempting to determine whether a defect exists, they are often on the right track. The examples also demonstrate why mere clarity of warning or mere percentages of likelihood of harm may not by themselves resolve the issue. For these are only factors going to the basic question of who is in the best position to make the cost-benefit analysis and act upon it, and must be considered together with other factors such as availability of substitutes and the nature of the user's use of the product in order to determine liability.

The relevance of the use to which the product is put has seemed especially troublesome for the courts.[31] The fact that a lawn mower was not designed to protect its driver should he care to drive it on the throughway ought not to be viewed as a design defect making the man-

28. Alternatives include not only alternative products, but also non-use of the product.

29. This is because the cheapest cost avoider must be able to make the required analysis and act upon it, and the only meaningful action is one which would reduce the risk. Where the product is the only medicine which will save the user's life, it is meaningless to say that the user is in a position to act upon the basis of the analysis.

The cost of action by the manufacturer in such a situation (*i.e.*, research for alternative products) may have an undesirable effect in the long run. Charging the manufacturer may unduly reduce the number or output of drug companies. Whether the long run effect, if it exists, is sufficiently adverse to negate the short run effect depends on the relative ability of the users as against the manufacturers to avoid the accident costs in the long run, that is, on which is the cheapest cost avoider in the long run. In this example it is hard to see what the user could do in the long run. In other situations, however, the long run issue may turn on the relative merits of more output in different industries.

Undesirable long run effects may, of course, be dealt with through governmental subsidies funded by lump sum taxes on the long run cheapest cost avoider; this seems to us to be a better solution by and large than denying liability. For a more detailed treatment of the problems of long versus short run cost avoidance, *see* Calabresi, note 12 *supra*.

30. The discussion in text over-simplifies the alternatives. The manufacturer may, for example, decide to identify the high risk users and sell the product to them at a higher price. *See* COSTS, *supra* note 10, at 170-71. If he is allowed to do this, and if doing it is economically feasible, the long run consequences of imposing liability on him referred to in note 28, *supra*, may be avoided. *See id.* at 162, 168-72.

31. *See, e.g.*, Brown v. General Motors Corporation, 355 F.2d 814 (4th Cir. 1966); Helene Curtis Industries, Inc. v. Pruitt, 385 F.2d 841 (5th Cir. 1967).

ufacturer liable either to users or to rescuers. But neither should a warning that the lawn mower ought not to be used where there are rocks *preclude* manufacturer's liability to passers-by hit by rocks or even to the user himself. Again, the issue is who can best make a cost-benefit analysis and act on it, viewed in realistic terms. Many uses of a product, though forbidden by the producer, are actually not unexpected. Other uses, though not forbidden, are in fact so unusual as to make the user more suited to make the cost-benefit analysis than the manufacturer.

Moreover, the question whether the manufacturer could sufficiently anticipate the use[32] as to be in a good position to make the cost-benefit analysis has little to do with whether society deems the use worth its costs. In other words, it is logically distinct from the question of whether the user was contributorily negligent. Thus a user may have an excellent reason for driving down the throughway on a lawn mower (the benefits of the use outweigh the costs), in which case the collective decider in a negligence/contributory negligence regime ought not to deem his conduct to be contributorily negligent. Yet such a user would in all probability be a better evaluator than the manufacturer of the costs and benefits involved. As a consequence, his strict liability suit against the manufacturer for injuries resulting from such driving would fail.[33] Conversely, the fact that a use of the product is deemed contributorily negligent does not necessarily mean that the manufacturer is not in a better position than the user to evaluate the costs and benefits. To take an example from a different area of strict liability, a worker may negligently use a piece of equipment, but his employer may nonetheless be in a better position to evaluate the relevant costs and benefits. That is, he may know the propensity to negligent use and be better able to evaluate a substitute piece of equipment which cannot readily be negligently used. This explains why contributory negligence has not been an inevitable defense to an action based on strict liability.[34]

We hope that the foregoing discussion of adequacy of warning and appropriateness of use has caused the reader to think that what we have

32. *See, e.g.*, Higgins v. Paul Hardeman, Inc., 457 S.W.2d 943 (Mo. App., 1970); and Dunham v. Vaughan & Bushnell Mfg. Co., 86 Ill. App. 2d 315, 229 N.E.2d 684 (1967), holding that an abnormal use of a product relieves the defendant from liability only if such use is not reasonably foreseeable.

33. *See, e.g.*, Greeno v. Clark Equipment Co., 237 F. Supp. 427, 429 (D.Ind. 1965), where the court stated that although contributory negligence is not a defense to strict products liability, "misuse" is a defense.

34. *See, e.g.*, Bachner v. Pearson, 479 P.2d 319 (Alaska, 1970); Barth v. B.F. Goodrich Tire Co., 265 Cal. App. 2d 228, 71 Cal. Rptr. 306 (1968).

Toward a Test for Strict Liability in Torts

been talking about sounds strangely like assumption of risk, not in its secondary, and technically improper, sense of contributory negligence, but in its original sense.[35] The doctrine of assumption of risk—though grossly misapplied by courts which have not looked realistically to whether the plaintiff in practice had the requisite knowledge and possibility of choice the doctrine implied—is essential to an understanding of a non-fault world.[36] It is, and always has been, a kind of plaintiff's strict liability—the other side of the coin of defendant's strict liability. It may even go to negate defendant's negligence, by expressing a judgment that although the defendant's conduct was not worth its costs (*i.e.*, was negligent), the plaintiff was in a better position than the defendant to evaluate the costs and benefits involved (*i.e.*, the plaintiff assumed the risk). Just as the employer may be in the better position to evaluate the costs and benefits of a piece of equipment given the likelihood of occasional employee negligence (defendant's strict liability), so a spectator at a baseball game may be best suited to evaluate the desirability of sitting in an unscreened bleacher given the likelihood of occasional negligent wild throws by the players during the game which may result in the spectator's being hit on the head (plaintiff's strict liability, or assumption of risk).[37] In both these situations, the conclusion as to whether an accident cost should be shifted depends not on whether a party was negligent, but rather on a judgment as to which party was in a better position to make the cost-benefit analysis irrespective of the other's negligence.[38] In each situation, strict liability (whether defendant's or plaintiff's) is imposed regardless of whether the other party "ought" to have done what he did.

35. In its original, or "primary" sense, assumption of risk bars recovery by a plaintiff who voluntarily and reasonably chooses to encounter a known risk. *See* 2 F. HARPER & F. JAMES, THE LAW OF TORTS, § 21.1 (1956).

36. *Cf.* Kalven, *Torts: The Quest for Appropriate Standards,* 53 CALIF. L. REV. 189, 206 (1965), suggesting that there is a "haunting analogy" between Chief Justice Traynor's emphasis on the inability of the consumer to detect defects in the goods he buys (*i.e.*, to avoid the risks) and the distinction drawn in terms of assumption of risk between traffic accidents and "accidents" between adjoining landowners by Blackburn, J., in Fletcher v. Rylands, L.R. 1 Exch. 265, 287 (1866), *aff'd sub nom.* Rylands v. Fletcher L.R. 3 H.L. 330 (1868).

Another interesting analogy is that between Chief Justice Traynor's emphasis on distributional considerations (*see, e.g.*, Escola v. Coca Cola Bottling Co. of Fresno, 24 Cal.2d 453, 150 P.2d 436 (1944) (concurring opinion)) and Bohlen's suggestion that the judges who wrote the opinions in Fletcher v. Rylands sought to protect the landed gentry against the encroachments of industry. Bohlen, *The Rule in Rylands v. Fletcher,* 59 U. PA. L. REV. 298 (1911). *See generally* part VI, *infra.*

37. *Cf.* Kavafian v. Seattle Baseball Club Ass'n, 105 Wash. 215, 177 P. 776, 181 P. 679 (1919).

38. Thus strict liability cannot be explained as the "reverse" of negligence, or as a reverse Learned Hand test, for if it did it would have to take into account the negligence of the injurer, *i.e.*, reverse contributory negligence (*see* pp. 1058-59 *supra*) in determining whether to shift the cost from injurer to victim because of the victim's conduct.

The Yale Law Journal Vol. 81: 1055, 1972

The doctrine of assumption of risk, properly interpreted, not only encompasses the questions the courts are now asking about adequacy of warning and appropriateness of use, but also can be viewed as covering much of the traditional rubric by which the classical forms of strict liability were limited. These forms of liability, whether for animals, ultrahazardous activities, *Fletcher v. Rylands* situations[39] or even workmen's compensation, were limited in two general ways. The first limit was usually put in terms of whether the injury stemmed from the risk whose presence was the reason for making the activity strictly liable. Had a cow trespassed, or had it instead bitten a neighbor; had a tiger mangled somebody, or had it simply chewed grass; had a bomb exploded, or had it just rolled and crushed somebody's foot?[40] The second limit was usually put in terms of whether the victim had done something which, though not necessarily *negligent,* had especially exposed him to the risk. Had the victim engaged in an "unnatural" use of his land; had the victim, a zoologist, gone into the tiger's cage to study the family habits of large cats; had the victim gone where no blasting company could expect humans to be?[41] In setting out these limits, the courts were in effect expressing judgments as to whether the injurer or the victim could better decide the advantages of avoidance as against accident costs. Both limits suggest questions such as who has the greater knowledge of the risk involved and who is better able to choose to avoid that risk by altering behavior should the risk appear too great. In discussing both these limits, moreover, the courts seemed to consider irrelevant the question of whether a third-party decider would approve of the decision made or not, and concentrated instead on who could best make the decision. The issue was not, in other words, whether the owner of the land *ought* to build a reservoir or keep tigers as he did. Neither was it whether the victim acted "reasonably" in engaging in an unnatural use of *his* land or in entering the tiger's cage. Instead it was whether his situation made him better suited than the owner to compare the benefits and the costs of the risk he took.[42]

To say this, though, is to remain at much too simple a level. We have so far assumed simply an injurer and a victim, when in fact each be-

39. Fletcher v. Rylands, 3 H & C 774, 159 Eng. Rep. 737 (1865), *rev'd* Fletcher v. Rylands, L.R. 1 Exch. 265 (1866), *aff'd* Rylands v. Fletcher, L.R. 3 H.L. 330 (1868).

40. *See, e.g.,* Hartford v. Brady, 114 Mass. 466 (1874); Wiggins v. Industrial Accident Bd., 170 P. 9 (Mont., 1918); Scribner v. Kelley, 38 Barb. 14 (N.Y. 1862); Troth v. Wills, 8 Pa. Super. 1 (1897) (Wickham, J., dissenting).

41. *See, e.g.,* Rozewski v. Simpson, 9 Cal.2d 515, 71 P.2d 72 (1937); Oklahoma City v. Hudson, 405 P.2d 178 (Okla. 1965); Harder v. Maloney, 250 Wis. 233, 26 N.W.2d 830 (1947).

42. *See, e.g.,* Rozewski v. Simpson, 9 Cal. 2d 515, 71 P.2d 72 (1937).

longs to a category of blasters, factory owners, product users, workers, and so forth.[43] We have assumed that the costs of paying for accidents or avoiding them rest on the individual, and therefore that the cost-benefit decision under a strict liability rule is made at a totally decentralized level. Furthermore, we have ignored the problems which arise when the victim is neither the blaster nor the blastee, but a third party rescuer, neither the lawn mower manufacturer nor the user who rides it on the highway, but a pedestrian who is hit when it goes out of control. Such problems obviously cannot be ignored under either a fault or a strict liability standard.[44] Similarly, we have avoided the problem of who is to decide which category is in the best position to make the cost-benefit analysis and act on it, and how generalized this decision is to be. That is, we have ignored (a) who decides whether blasters are generally better suited than blastees to balance costs and benefits, (b) how many exceptions to this general notion will be permitted, and (c) who will be permitted to find that a given situation is an exception. These problems do not alter the test; they require, however, somewhat more sophistication in its application.

IV. The Strict Liability Test Refined

A. *Level and Generality of Application*

The greatest differences among areas of strict liability go precisely to the question of the level of generality at which a decision is made with respect to the category or party best suited to make the appropriate cost-benefit analysis. In blasting and ultrahazardous activities generally, the court-made decision that the blaster is best suited to make the cost-benefit analysis is at a high level of generality. In many jurisdictions the decision contemplates virtually no exceptions so long as the injury arises out of the risk which makes the activity ultrahazardous.[45] The likelihood of foolish behavior by the victim or the unusual sensitivity of some victims are deemed to be best considered by the blaster. Some courts, it is true, have raised the question of whether there would be liability if a blaster blasted in what seemed to be a totally deserted place.[46] The victim, these courts have in effect said, is better suited to gauge the costs of making his presence in such an

43. *See generally* Costs, *supra* note 10, *passim*.
44. *See* Sills v. Massey-Ferguson, Inc., 296 F. Supp. 776 (N.D. Ind. 1969), and cases there cited.
45. *See, e.g.*, Bedell v. Coulter, 199 Ore. 344, 261 P.2d 842 (1953).
46. *See, e.g.*, Houghton v. Loma Prieta Lumber Co., 152 Cal. 500, 93 P. 82 (1901); Kendall v. Johnson, 51 Wash. 477, 99 P. 310 (1909).

unusual place known as against the costs of taking whatever risks may be attendant on being in a place unexpectedly. But some judges have in effect reasoned that such an exception, precisely because it would require more individualized judgments, might not be worth making.[47] Perhaps an occasional victim would be better suited to make the cost-benefit analysis, but the administrative cost of dealing with such instances would not be worthwhile, given their presumed rarity.

In strict products liability, instead, the judgment, again court-made, that by and large producers are better suited than users to make the cost-benefit analysis is deemed much less generally applicable, and the manufacturer is allowed to try to show in each specific case that the user was in the best position to make the analysis. The questions asked as to the adequacy of warning and the appropriateness of use, and, in some jurisdictions, the availability of the defense of contributory negligence, suggest how far from certain courts are that the generalized premise that the producer is the cheapest cost avoider will apply to the individual case.[48] As a result, a combination of judge and jury is allowed to find that given the availability of substitutes, the adequacy of warning and the capacity of an individual user to identify himself as being especially risky or especially safe, the general assumption as to who is better suited to compare the risks and benefits will not apply. That such determinations must be made in ways which are much more realistic than were analogous decisions in old assumption of risk cases, is the lesson of cases like *Henningsen* and *Sills*.[49] But this in no way detracts from the judgment that in determining who is better suited to make a cost-benefit analysis in products liability cases, a fair degree of case by case analysis is worthwhile.

Workmen's compensation differs from both ultrahazardous activities and products liability in that the original decision was legislatively made. It also differs in that it tends to divide the decision of who is better suited to evaluate costs and benefits according to the *type of damage* rather than *type of accident*. We are not here concerned with

47. The administrative costs of making such individualized judgments would presumably be too great. *See, e.g.*, Whitman Hotel Corp. v. Elliott & Watrous Engineering Co., 137 Conn. 562, 79 A.2d 591 (1951) (Baldwin, J., concurring), noting that such limitations on strict liability for blasting "add a needless and confusing qualification or condition." 137 Conn. at 576, 79 A.2d at 598.

48. New Jersey is one jurisdiction where contributory negligence remains a defense to strict liability. Maiorino v. Weco Products Co., 45 N.J. 570, 214 A.2d 18 (1965). *Cf.* Cintrone v. Hertz Truck Leasing & Rental Service, 45 N.J. 434, 212 A.2d 769 (1965). This may be in part the result of the abandonment of the defense of assumption of risk in New Jersey. *See* note 55 *infra*. *See generally* Supp. to 2 F. HARPER & F. JAMES, THE LAW OF TORTS § 22.7 (1968).

49. Henningsen v. Bloomfield Motors, Inc., 32 N.J. 358, 161 A.2d 69 (1960); Sills v. Massey-Ferguson, Inc., *supra* note 44.

Toward a Test for Strict Liability in Torts

the fact that workmen's compensation schedules are hopelessly out of date,[50] but instead with the very fact that they deal with damages on a scheduled basis. The result of this is that the measure of damages for dignitary losses and even wage losses is that of the ordinary worker doing that job. If a great violinist mangles his hand in a steel mill, causing him extreme suffering and economic loss, that is his burden. One may contrast this with cases involving ultrahazardous activities where, except in very unusual situations, one takes one's victim as one finds him. On the other hand, the fact that a worker is warned that a machine is especially dangerous, or must be used in a given way, will not negate the employer's liability, short of extremes like wanton and wilful behavior by the victim.[51]

Without going into further detail, one can discern a certain rationality in these cases as to the appropriate level of generality of the original liability decision and the exceptions made to it. This does not mean we agree with all of the cases, by any means. But it is not unreasonable to suppose that a violinist is the best evaluator of the relative advantages and costs of working in a steel mill, with regard to the suffering he will feel if he loses his hand, while he is not as likely to be in that position with respect to blasting injuries. Similarly, a user of a product may be well suited to evaluate whether he wishes to use a given product in a given way despite a warning of danger, whereas an employee using that same product on the job would not be so suited. If we add to the foregoing considerations the administrative costs inherent in allowing an attempt to show an exception to the general rule, it is easy to understand the levels of generality which have in fact emerged.[52]

B. *Categories of Injurers and Victims*

So far we have discussed the problems involved in minimizing primary accident costs as if either the injurer or the victim actually bore the losses which occurred. As has been amply discussed elsewhere, that is clearly not the case.[53] The existence of insurance and of other ways in which a cost is removed from its initial bearer and borne ultimately by others need not be reexamined here. The effect of factors such as insurance on the choice of the party to hold liable under a strict liability test must, however, be made explicit.

50. *See* U.S. Dep't of Labor, Bureau of Labor Standards, Bull. No. 161 State Workmen's Compensation Laws (1969).

51. *See* 1A A. Larson, Workmen's Compensation Law § 31 (1967).

52. The administrative costs include, of course, the likelihood of error which may result from a particularized approach, as well as the costs of adjudicating particular disputes. *See* Costs, *supra* note 10, at 251, 255-59.

53. See the discussion of externalization in Costs, *supra* note 10, at 144-50, 244-50.

The Yale Law Journal Vol. 81: 1055, 1972

It does no good to leave the accident cost on the victim in a products liability case, on the ground that he is in a better position than the injurer to make a cost-benefit analysis, if the victim will not bear the loss in any event. The issue must be whether, given the fact of this "externalization," the *actual* bearer of the loss is better suited to make the analysis than is the injurer (assuming, of course, that the injurer would bear the loss if he were held liable). The point is a simple one and need not be gone into at length. The crucial decision on who is best suited to make the appropriate cost-benefit analysis must be made among the *categories* which actually bear a loss and not among the individuals who only do so initially.[54]

This point is, of course, equally valid for the two Learned Hand type tests. Sophisticated application of those tests would require that the collective judgment as to whether costs are worth avoiding be made at the level of categories which would end up paying, and not at the level of the single injurer and single victim. The fact that in practice this is almost impossible under existing fault rules is one of the weaknesses of the fault-insurance system as a device for reducing primary accident costs.[55] In theory, however, it should be admitted that one could apply a Learned Hand test at a category level. Whether the language of fault with the stigma it implies would also be appropriate to such a test at a non-individual level may be quite another matter.

C. *The Need for Realism in Applying the Test*

It should come as no surprise that considerations of knowledge, alternatives, and category levels are implicit in the search for the cheapest cost avoider. The very fact that these factors *are only implicit* in the test, however, requires us to be extremely practical in gauging their existence in specific situations.[56]

54. This does not mean that there should be one liability rule for insured persons and another for the uninsured. It means instead that in devising a rule appropriate to a particular category, the availability of insurance and other means of externalizing costs should be taken into account. The resulting liability rule would thus reflect the general extent of externalization from the individual to the entire category, though the rule might well be applied to all those within the category, whether insured or not. *See, e.g.*, Darling v. Charleston Community Memorial Hospital, 33 Ill. 2d 326, 336-38, 211 N.E.2d 253, 259-60 (1965), *cert. denied* 383 U.S. 946, abrogating the doctrine of charitable immunity in Illinois; *cf.* Gelbman v. Gelbman, 23 N.Y.2d 434, 297 N.Y.S.2d 529, 245 N.E.2d 192 (1969).

55. *See* COSTS, *supra* note 10, at 244-50. The current movement for reform in the treatment of automobile accidents can be explained in part by the tendency of the traditional system to incur considerable administrative costs as a result of focusing on specific accidents in allocating costs among the parties despite the fact that the costs allocated are externalized through liability insurance.

56. A recent opinion refusing to dismiss the complaint in an action seeking recovery from the entire blasting cap industry for injuries to children caused by blasting caps is a good example of the kind of approach which is required. Chance v. E.I. DuPont de Nemours & Co., 69 C-273 (E.D.N.Y., decided May 18, 1972).

Toward a Test for Strict Liability in Torts

In this regard, it is well to reemphasize the relational nature of the test. It does not matter that there is currently no way in which a manufacturer of a risky medicine can make it safer for users who have no realistic alternative to taking the medicine—even though the user can identify himself as an especially risky party. *Relatively,* the manufacturer is better suited to make the only cost-benefit analysis that matters, which is one between further research and current damages. The problem may be very different if the medicine has reasonably close substitutes which carry different risks for different groups of people. An example might be a birth control pill which carries some risks of thrombosis to a group which can readily identify itself (say, through a blood test), but which has substitutes—either another pill which avoids that risk but is slightly less than 100 per cent effective (and, therefore, carries a risk for another easily self-defining group, those who wish a baby under *no* circumstances and object to abortions even if legal), or other fully effective but cumbersome birth control devices. The existence of close substitutes in this case may make the user best able to conduct the appropriate cost-benefit analysis.

Similarly, the need to establish the relative ability to make a cost-benefit analysis requires us to look realistically at the ability of the parties to act upon a perception that they are in risky categories. If there are only two medicines available to combat a serious disease, one involving a .0001 per cent risk of losing a leg, and the other involving a .0001 per cent risk of losing an arm, it is not realistic to suggest that the user is well suited to act upon the findings of a cost-benefit analysis. True, violinists will tend to prefer one medicine and olympic runners the other, but for most people no meaningful choice is available, and the size of the risk involved is so small, that it seems likely that leaving the loss on the user will result in little incentive to research.[57] It seems to us preferable to make the producer liable and thereby create a situation where there is a meaningful incentive to research, even though this may somewhat increase pharmaceutical costs to people who value only their feet.[58]

Realism is especially necessary when third parties are involved. Then the question is not whether, for example, the category to which the seller belongs or the one to which the user belongs is in the best posi-

57. We are not suggesting that the basic purpose of strict liability necessarily is, or should be, the creation of additional incentives toward safety research. In the example in text, our proposed test imposes liability on the manufacturer because he is the party who can, by actions reasonably to be expected, reduce the risk. *See* note 29 *supra.*

58. It may be that the producer is not the cheapest cost avoider in the long run, and this needs to be kept in mind in deciding whether to impose liability. *See* note 29 *supra. Compare* Posner at 75-76, RESTATEMENT OF TORTS, SECOND, § 402A, Comment K, and McLeod v. W.S. Merrell Co., 174 So.2d 736, 739 (Fla. 1965).

tion to make the cost-benefit analysis; rather, it must be asked which category is in that position relative to the category to which the third-party victim belongs. Sometimes the third party's category is the cheapest cost avoider and then the problem is easy. At other times, however, things are not so simple. If both the manufacturer and the user are in a better position than the third party victim to make the cost-benefit analysis, the strict liability test would require, as a general rule, that the victim should recover, whether he sues the manufacturer or the user.[59] If the victim chose to sue the party other than the cheapest cost avoider, that defendant should be free to join the cheapest cost avoider as a defendant or to sue him subsequently for indemnity. In either case, the strict liability rule would make the cheapest cost avoider liable and optimization of primary accident costs would be achieved, at least if we ignore the administrative costs of joinder or of the indemnification suit. There may well be situations, however, in which the relative abilities of the manufacturer and the user to make the cost-benefit analysis are so clear, and the administrative costs of joinder or indemnification are so great, that we would deny liability if the victim made the "wrong" choice and sued a defendant other than the cheapest cost avoider. For in these cases the victim is in the best position to choose the optimal defendant and should be induced to do so. But courts may in some cases be misled into assuming that where the user is in a better position than the manufacturer to make the cost-benefit analysis, it follows that the manufacturer should not be liable to third parties.[60] This error may be compounded by a tendency to assume that in third party situations the user is in a better position merely because the manufacturer warned him.[61] Instead, the fact that a manufacturer has warned the user to avoid a particular use should serve to bar a third party victim from recovering from the manufacturer only if (a) the warning is so clearly adequate as to settle the issue between manufacturer and user and (b) this fact is sufficiently known to the victim after the accident as to put him in a good position to choose the proper

59. The trend is toward strict liability of the manufacturer for injuries to third-party bystanders. *See* Sills v. Massey-Ferguson, Inc., 296 F. Supp. 776 (N.D. Ind. 1969) and cases there cited.

60. *Compare* Sills v. Massey-Ferguson, Inc., 296 F. Supp. 776, 783 (N.D. Ind. 1969). An analogous assumption often made is that a drug manufacturer fulfills its duty to consumers ("third parties") by warning the medical profession ("the users") of possible side effects. *See, e.g.*, Basko v. Sterling Drug, Inc., 416 F.2d 417, 426 (2d Cir. 1969).

61. Thus in the drug cases it may be assumed that if a manufacturer warns the doctor of a slight risk associated with a valuable drug, the doctor is thereby placed in a better position than the manufacturer to make the cost-benefit analysis. *See, e.g.*, Davis v. Wyeth Laboratories, Inc., 399 F.2d 121, 130 (9th Cir. 1968). This will not necessarily be the case. *See* pp. 1062-63 *supra*.

Toward a Test for Strict Liability in Torts

defendant.[62] The point is not so much that the concepts are hard, but rather that they can quite easily be applied erroneously.

In this respect, the history of the doctrine of assumption of risk is instructive. The doctrine asked questions like whether the defendant had the "right" to impose the risk on the plaintiff, which frequently made it circular.[63] An emphasis instead on knowledge and appreciation of the risk and availability of alternatives, equally part of the doctrine, might easily have enabled it to serve to absolve defendants only in those situations where the plaintiff's category was the cheapest cost avoider—where, in other words, the cost-benefit analysis was better left to the plaintiff.[64] Instead, the doctrine came to be applied in cases where knowledge and appreciation of the risk and availability of alternatives were in no realistic sense present for the plaintiff.[65] This may well have been because goals other than primary cost reduction prevailed in those cases, and the circular elements in the language of assumption of risk were emphasized while non-existent knowledge and appreciation of risk were assumed in order to suit those goals.[66] Thus applied, the doctrine has been much attacked.[67] That it survived at all suggests that the

62. *Cf.* Eck v. E.I. DuPont de Nemours & Co., 393 F.2d 197 (7th Cir. 1968).

63. *See* F. Harper & F. James, The Law of Torts § 21.3 (1956).

64. There have been, of course, many assumption of risk cases where appreciation of the risk and the availability of alternatives have been emphasized. *See, e.g.*, Guerrero v. Westgate Lumber Co., 164 Cal. App. 2d 612, 331 P.2d 107 (1958); Ridgway v. Yenny, 223 Ind. 16, 57 N.E.2d 581 (1944); Rush v. Commercial Realty Co., 7 N.J. Misc. 337, 145 A. 476 (1929).

65. This was particularly true in industrial accident cases antedating the passage of workmen's compensation legislation. *See, e.g.*, Alabama G.S.R. Co. v. Carroll, 84 Fed. 772, 28 C.C.A. 207, 52 U.S. App. 442 (1898); Titus v. Bradford, B. & K. R.R. Co., 136 Pa. 618, 20 A. 517 (1890). *But see* Davidson v. Cornell, 132 N.Y. 234, 30 N.E. 573 (1892).

66. This suggestion is a familiar one. *See, e.g.*, Tiller v. Atlantic Coast Line R.R., 318 U.S. 54, 58-67 (1943).

Compare Posner's suggestion, Posner, *supra* note 9, at 45-46, that assumption of risk was "supported by economic logic," since it served to enable the risk preferring employee (a railroad brakeman employed on a train not equipped with standard safety appliances in Posner's example) to "market his taste for risk." Of course, the same objective could have been achieved without the assumption of risk doctrine by allowing the employer to "buy out" from liability. In theory, precisely the same wage differentials and safety precautions would result as are set forth in Posner's example. *See* Calabresi, *Fault, Accidents and the Wonderful World of Blum and Kalven*, 75 Yale L.J. 216, 225-28 (1965). In practice, however, the assumption of risk doctrine, by placing the risk on the employee in the first instance, may not have served adequately to inform the employee of the risk he was assuming, whereas a rule placing liability on the employer unless he could "buy out" (*i.e.*, persuade the employee to accept the risk) would presumably have served to inform the employee of the nature and magnitude of the risk. This assumes, of course, that during the period covered by Posner's study railroads were better informed about the hazards of operating without standard safety appliances than were brakemen.

67. *See, e.g.*, Bohlen, *Voluntary Assumption of Risk*, 20 Harv. L. Rev. 14, 91 (1906); James, *Assumption of Risk*, 61 Yale L.J. 141 (1952); James, *Assumption of Risk: Unhappy Reincarnation*, 78 Yale L.J. 185 (1968).

The doctrine has been abandoned in some jurisdictions, in part because of the confusion which has prevailed in its application. *See, e.g.*, McGrath v. American Cyanamid Co., 41 N.J. 272, 196 A.2d 238 (1963).

kernel of truth it contains is quite real, not that its application was often correct. Concepts like "the cheapest cost avoider" or "the category best suited to make the cost-benefit analysis" can be as easily misapplied as assumption of risk. This does not, however, mean they are useless. It only means that courts and legal scholars should be assiduous in scrutinizing their use, in criticizing misapplications and in pointing out when they are being employed to serve goals other than those of primary accident cost reduction.[68]

V. The Learned Hand Test Versus the Strict Liability Test

If the strict liability test is often difficult to apply correctly, and if Learned Hand type tests might, *in theory,* be just as capable of accomplishing optimal primary accident cost reduction, why have such fault-based tests fallen increasingly into disfavor?[69] It is not likely that the answer lies simply in the existence of distributional goals which are better served by the strict liability test. That such goals are relevant we have no doubt, and we shall discuss their relevance later. But their relevance must be limited, since the two Learned Hand tests themselves accomplish diametrically different distributional results.[70] Thus if the aim of the current trend away from the fault system were simply to favor victims as a category, this could be done as well—indeed better—by shifting from the Learned Hand test to the *reverse* Learned Hand test than by shifting to a strict liability standard. The suspicion must remain that the shift to strict liability is based in part on other grounds.

It has already been noted that the Learned Hand type tests are more "interventionistic," more collective, than is the strict liability test. Under either of the Hand tests, an organ of the state decides whether an action is worthwhile or not, and imposes the costs on the actor if it deems the action *not* worthwhile. It is not hard to see that this involves a greater degree of state involvement than that implied in the strict liability test. The latter implies state intervention only to decide which category can best determine whether an action is worthwhile, and this in turn implies less risk that traditional kinds of collective considerations will come into play.[71] But this difference between the tests, though politically significant, hardly accounts for the decline in popularity of the fault tests. After all, we have also seen an increase in recent

68. We do not mean to suggest that other goals are irrelevant to accident law, but that courts, legislatures and scholars should try to avoid confusing primary accident cost reduction with other goals. *See* part VI, *infra,* for a discussion of other goals.
69. *See* notes 1, 2 & 3 *supra.*
70. *See* p. 1059 *supra.*
71. *See* note 20 *supra.*

years in direct criminal prohibitions aimed at conduct in the accident area deemed not worthwhile.[72] Such prohibitions surely involve greater state intervention than do even the Learned Hand tests.[73] That political preference for laissez faire has spurred the move toward strict liability therefore seems as unlikely as the explanation that the move has been solely influenced by distributional goals. We suspect that the move to strict liability today, no less than similar moves to respondent superior, ultrahazardous activity liability and workmen's compensation in the past, are based at least in part on a desire to accomplish better primary accident cost reduction.

Earlier we noted that it seems unlikely that either Learned Hand test could effectively be applied in practice at the category level. We questioned whether at the level where it really mattered, that is at the level of who actually pays, the rubric of "fault" is likely to be congenial. And yet it is clear that if the Learned Hand tests *are* to accomplish optimal primary accident cost reduction they must be applied at that level, and not at the arbitrary level of parties to an accident who do not ultimately bear the costs and who are not therefore given any incentive to choose avoidance even where it is worthwhile. The appropriate avoidance decisions *must* be made at a category level, and at that level the Learned Hand tests may seem unjust. Furthermore, the categories which end up bearing the losses as a result of an application of negligence tests on a case by case basis are not likely to be those which would be selected were such tests applied at a category level, nor is this technique likely to be the most efficient way available for selecting the categories which *are* chosen. All this has been discussed at length elsewhere, and need not be gone into further,[74] but it is important to note that the reluctance to apply the Learned Hand test to categories may be a significant underlying explanation for the current disfavor of "negligence" calculus type tests.

There is, however, another set of reasons which may explain the move away from Learned Hand tests. Hard though the strict liability

72. The prohibitions which have received the most attention have been those relating to automobile safety. See the Traffic and Motor Vehicle Safety Act, 15 U.S.C.A. §§ 1381-1431 (Supp. 1972).

73. For example, under either Hand type test, a party burdened with the costs because the collective deciders have deemed avoidance to be worthwhile may, at least in some cases, choose to omit safety measures and pay compensatory damages instead. In contrast, a collective prohibition is generally meant to be obeyed. *See* Costs, *supra* note 10, at 68-69.

74. *See* Costs, *supra* note 10, at 255-59. To summarize that discussion briefly: case-by-case determination entails substantial administrative costs, tends to focus on unusual rather than recurring causes and on accident avoidance rather than accident cost avoidance, and is a misleading way of compiling those statistics which are meaningful at the category level.

test may be to apply correctly, it is nonetheless easier to apply than is the calculus of fault. We have seen that it may well be difficult to know whether the category to which a seller, user or third party belongs can best make a cost-benefit analysis of risks involved and act on that analysis. But it is more difficult still to decide correctly not only who can most cheaply act on a cost-benefit analysis, but also what the result of that cost-benefit analysis must be. Yet this is precisely what the Learned Hand-type tests require of the governmental deciders if they are to achieve optimal primary accident cost avoidance. None of the significant difficulties involved in the strict liability test are avoided, and to them is added the danger that the governmental deciders will resolve the cost-benefit analysis incorrectly.

One cannot answer, moreover, that the Learned Hand-type tests avoid some of the difficulties inherent in the strict liability test by deciding collectively whether or not avoidance is worthwhile, whereas the strict liability test leaves such judgments to the individual categories. This answer is not available because the negligence tests result in compensatory damages rather than prohibitions. Individual categories are, therefore, allowed to decide that avoidance is *not* worthwhile despite a contrary determination by the collectivity (or vice versa).[75]

This may serve to explain the concomitant, seemingly paradoxical rise of collective prohibitions together with the less interventionistic strict liability test, at the expense of negligence type tests. Where a collective determination that an action is *not* worthwhile can be made with a modicum of assurance, prohibitions enforced criminally or through uninsurable fines seem appropriate. Where, instead, there is serious doubt that such a collective determination of utility is likely to be correct, the best solution is an individualistic one. This implies a decision limited to selecting the best decider, the cheapest cost avoider, among the relevant categories, and not extending to which particular acts or forebearances are appropriate. Viewed in this light, the rise of criminally enforced prohibitions in some areas, and strict liability in others, rather than being paradoxical, can be viewed as a quite sensible reaction to the same stimulus—that is, to the desire to minimize the sum of accident costs and the costs of avoiding accidents.

VI. Relationship to Other Goals

We have seen that there are a variety of devices which could in theory be used to accomplish primary accident cost reduction. Concep-

75. *See* note 73 *supra*. Of course, a party may also decide to ignore a collective prohibition, but in considering the likelihood and magnitude of the penalty he must take into account the stigma involved, and this results in a very different kind of calculus.

tually, they range from: (a) those in which the decision-maker is highly centralized and makes criminally enforceable determinations of which actions are worthwhile and which are not through (b) those in which negligence type calculi are employed to make the same decisions at a more decentralized but nonetheless state agency level, enforcing those decisions through compensatory damages; to (c) those in which collective decisions are made only to identify who is the cheapest cost avoider —the category best suited to determine if avoidance of accidents is worth its costs—allowing the chosen category to make the cost-benefit decision itself. We have also seen that these devices in practice imply different likelihoods of success in accomplishing primary cost avoidance. Finally, we have seen that these approaches will each have a different distributional effect. Far from being insignificant, distributional differences may well determine the approach chosen. Some discussion of distributional effects and goals is thus essential to an understanding of the two Learned Hand type tests and the strict liability alternative.

In discussing the distributional aspects of liability rules there are two problems which it is well to separate. The first relates to the types of effects that are lumped together in the concept of distribution, and the proper role of each of these effects in the choice of liability rules. The second goes to the quite different question of the appropriate role of juries and courts, as against legislatures, in selecting among liability rules in order to accomplish distributional effects.

That both problems are crucial can be seen through an example. The present Learned Hand test tends to make injurers richer at the expense of victims. The reverse Learned Hand test would have precisely the opposite effect. In choosing between them a society will presumably be influenced not only by which of the two tests is more likely to accomplish optimal primary accident cost reduction, but also, if it has such a preference, by which category it wishes to make wealthier. This choice may be affected by factors such as the initial relative wealth of the categories, but relative wealth is only a part of the choice implied. For one category may be better able to spread losses than the other, or one category may in some sense be viewed as being worthier. Sorting out the relevant effects lumped under the term distribution, therefore, is a necessary task for society in choosing among liability rules. But when that is done another series of questions remains: Which, if any, of the distributional considerations are appropriate to judicial decisions among liability rules, which are appropriate to ad hoc jury determinations, and which can only be properly settled by legislatures?

It should be plain that a full treatment of these questions cannot be attempted in this article. Nevertheless, some indications of relevant distributional considerations and some reflections on the historical role of courts and juries with respect to these can be offered.

For the purposes of this article, we are lumping together as distributional all those effects of liability rules which do not relate to minimizing (a) the sum of accident costs and avoidance costs, and (b) the administrative costs entailed by that minimization. Thus under a society's distributional goals we are including preferences of quite varied types. These preferences may reflect a desire to distribute or fractionize losses, often called spreading. They may reflect a preference for moving toward a given distribution of wealth, such as greater wealth equality, better treatment for higher castes, or better treatment for castes which in the past have been poorly treated. They may instead reflect a desire to further what might be viewed as dynamic efficiency goals—as might occur by favoring the doers, the entrepreneurs in a society. Finally, they may reflect a society's notion, if it has one or if it has many, of rewarding individuals' merits—of recognizing their just deserts.

All of these preferences are in fact relevant in some way to the choice of liability rules. Indeed, all of them, together with the pure efficiency notion reflected in the aim of minimizing the sum of accident and accident avoidance costs, are part of what is at times called justice.[76] They are relevant because there is no a priori reason why a legislature might not choose a liability rule solely because it tends to redistribute income from, say, rich to poor. Whether a legislature would be wise to employ liability rules for this purpose is, of course, another matter. That depends on, among other things, the availability of alternative devices for accomplishing the desired income redistribution and on the effect which this use of a liability rule might have on the achievement of other goals whose effectuation is tied to the operation of such rules. But there is no logical reason why a legislature's desires with respect to income equality or caste preference cannot be well served through the choice of one liability rule as against another. Similarly, and in practice even more commonly, a legislature's preference as to spreading, desert and long run efficiency can effectively be furthered by choosing one liability rule rather than another.

Recently Professor Fletcher has argued instead that the only distributional considerations which should be considered in choosing among

76. *See* F. Harper, The Law of Torts §§ 1, 3 & 4 (1933). *See also* Bierman v. City of New York, 302 N.Y.S.2d 696, 60 Misc. 2d 497 (Civ. Ct. of the City of New York, 1969). *Cf.* Magrine v. Spector, 100 N.J. Super. 223, 238-41, 241 A.2d 637, 646-47 (Botter, J.S.C., dissenting).

liability rules are those which relate to an individual's just desert—those which decide who is to be richer or poorer on the basis of what people have done rather than what they are or where they start out.[77] Indeed the argument goes further, and suggests that such considerations should determine the choice of liability rules regardless of any "instrumentalist" goals like the reduction of the sum of accident costs and the costs of avoiding accidents.

In one sense, it is very easy to agree with Professor Fletcher. If a society has a sufficiently well-developed theory of deserts such that all the other considerations of efficiency and distributional equity we have mentioned are reflected in that theory, then "desert" tautologically will determine the appropriate liability rules for that society. Unfortunately, we do not find ourselves able to define, let alone find, such an all encompassing theory of deserts in our society.[78] Indeed, we often find that what pass for statements of desert, of who ought to be richer or poorer on the basis of merit, can quite readily be seen as judgments based on the desire to accomplish either efficient accident avoidance or some other of the distributional preferences mentioned previously.

Nor does Professor Fletcher's test for deserts help us very much. He argues that losses ought to lie where they fall unless the victim did not create a risk "reciprocal" to the one which resulted in his being injured. Examining examples of reciprocity and non-reciprocity, we are struck by three things. The first is that frequently reciprocity is simply an approximation of the result which would be required by that most instrumentalist of tests, the strict liability test described in this article.[79] The second observation is that when reciprocity and the test we propose seem to deviate, the strict liability result appears to be more desirable.[80]

77. Fletcher, *Fairness and Utility in Tort Theory,* 85 HARV. L. REV. 537, 547 n.40 (1972).

78. A recent book by Professor Rawls may be thought to be an attempt to formulate such a theory. J. RAWLS, A THEORY OF JUSTICE (1972). *But see* Hampshire, *A New Philosophy of the Just Society,* THE N.Y. REV. BOOKS, Feb. 24, 1972, at 34 (Vol. XVIII, No. 3) questioning whether the formulation of a complete theory of deserts is possible. *See also* Feinberg, Review, 81 YALE L.J. 1004 (1972).

79. The examples of liability set out by Fletcher, *supra* note 77, at 547-48, illustrate this point rather well. Liability for crop dusting as between neighbors is, we think, unrelated to whatever risks happen to be imposed upon the duster by those neighbors who breathe his dust. It is based instead on the relative ability of the duster to calculate the costs and benefits of dusting in the particular situation involved and act upon that calculation.

80. Returning to Fletcher's crop dusting example, suppose instead that the parties are a farmer who dusts his 500 acres of irrigated reclaimed desert and a homesteader who, with knowledge of the farmer's agricultural methods, chooses out of 500,000 acres of available (and equally beautiful, accessible and desirable, but undusted) desert one acre adjacent to the farmer's land for a homestead. Suppose also, to give reciprocity more than its due, that the homesteader in no way benefits from the farmer's presence, that is, he uses none of the farmer's produce. The homesteader imposes no risks on

The Yale Law Journal Vol. 81: 1055, 1972

The third observation is that when we do not approve (in terms of who is made richer and who is poorer) of a result dictated by the efficiency test, it is often in cases where reciprocity would lead to the same undesirable result.[81]

None of these observations should be especially surprising. Justice notions do attach to efficiency considerations such as those served by the strict liability test, and this is sufficient to explain why approximations of that test should seem just. They also attach to distributional preferences like "favor spreading," "further wealth equality," and "benefit a particular ethnic group," which go to what people are rather than what they do. This explains why that which is preferable, given a society's desire to further wealth equalization or a caste preference, may seem more desirable than the result which either a strict liability test or a reciprocity test would impose. Justice notions attach to other societal preferences which can only with difficulty be explained in terms of either efficiency or wealth distributional preferences designed to make some groups richer because of what they are. These other justice notions, which we are unable to describe in general terms, are, of course, crucial to the choice of liability rules.[82] Indeed, we have elsewhere left room for a veto of liability rules which violate such non-generalized justice imperatives,[83] because to date these imperatives have not been put together in a way which would enable us to talk about them other than as constraints within which other, more generalized goals can be seen to operate. Professor Fletcher instead offers reciprocity as a way of putting these imperatives together in the field of accidents.

It is with this in mind then, that one must examine reciprocity. Is there anything about reciprocity which should make it justify making someone richer or poorer apart from efficiency and apart from distributional preferences based on what people are? When the question is

the farmer, and reciprocity would therefore seem to require holding the farmer liable for the results of dust breathing by the homesteader, regardless of the availability and cost to the farmer of alternative methods of crop protection. The strict liability test, taking into account the relative abilities of the parties to compare the costs of dust breathing by the homesteader with the costs of avoidance, and to act on the basis of such a calculation, would not impose liability on the farmer. Professor Fletcher might respond that the homesteader "creates" the risk by moving, but that response would reduce the reciprocity test to a tautology. That is, reciprocity would give no guidance for decision, but would simply be a label attached to a result reached on other grounds.

81. If the farmers were a preferred group, such as disabled veterans, whose crop dusting was essential to their livelihood, we might disapprove of a liability rule (whether based on reciprocity or efficiency) which, in effect, prevented crop dusting.

82. *See* Calabresi & Melamed, *Property Rules, Liability Rules, and Inalienability: One View of the Cathedral*, 85 HARV. L. REV. 1089, 1104-05 (1972).

83. COSTS, *supra* note 10, at 24-26, 291-308.

Toward a Test for Strict Liability in Torts

thus posed, when reciprocity is viewed not as an approximation of efficiency but as an approximation of a generalized theory of desert, it turns out to be philosophically very meager.[84]

If income equality, dynamic efficiency, and spreading are all relevant to a society's choice of liability rules, it does not follow that all are equally suited to being considered by courts or juries. Obviously, those which are deemed suited to judicial considerations will depend on one's view of the nature of adjudication and the role of courts and juries in a legal process. We cannot possibly begin to resolve these issues in this article. We can, however, point out some solutions which are transparently too simple, both in themselves and in terms of what courts and juries have done historically.

One cannot write off distributional considerations based on ability to spread, or on wealth or caste, as Professor Fletcher has done, with a reference to Aristotle and a comment that taxation is for legislatures and not for courts.[85] When courts chose a Learned Hand test rather than a reverse Learned Hand test, they did not simply toss a coin, given that the tests were equally efficient in theory.[86] Distributive consequences may not have been the dominant or even a conscious motive for the decisions, but it is difficult to argue that historically these consequences were irrelevant to the choice.[87] Similarly, too many courts have explicitly considered the ability to spread losses in torts cases as a factor in choosing one liability rule instead of another to allow us to dismiss its relevance to judicial decisions out of hand.[88] One can, of

84. The examples discussed by Fletcher, *supra* note 77, at 547-48 seem to indicate that the reciprocity test is temporally bound. That is, the risk imposer who does not recover is usually the party who creates an "unusual" risk. An unusual risk may mean a risk which can be cheaply avoided, but that is the strict liability test. Fletcher seems to be looking instead to which risks are new. If this is what is meant, reciprocity, without more, is incapable of serving as a philosophical theory of desert. For it would amount basically to saying only that those who take new risks are less deserving than those who take customary risks.

85. *See* Fletcher, *supra* note 77, at 547, n.40.

86. Here we are assuming, with Professor Posner, that historically the courts did "choose" a Learned Hand test. Posner, *supra* note 9, *passim*. Certainly they did not choose the reverse.

If for some reason the tests in practice would not equally yield optimizing solutions, if, for example, victims in practice proved far less able to alter their behavior than injurers (notwithstanding that the value of their activity was less than the resultant accident costs), then the choice of the Learned Hand test rather than the reverse would imply a distributional effect *in spite of* efficiency considerations.

87. *Cf.* the explanation usually given for the development of the fellow servant rule. *See, e.g.*, W. Prosser, Torts 529 (4th ed. 1971). *Cf.* also note 66 *supra*.

88. These decisions in recent years have been an outgrowth of the concurring opinion of Justice Traynor in Escola v. Coca Cola Bottling Co., 24 Cal.2d 453, 461, 750 P.2d 436 (1944). *See* W. Prosser, Torts § 5 at 22 (4th ed. 1971).

course, question the wisdom of such decisions.[89] One might further suggest that courts should consider such distributive effects only when they reflect reasonably explicit societal goals. Alternatively, one might maintain that courts should be free to follow their own distributional preferences so long as they do not conflict with well defined societal goals (such as, perhaps, efficiency), provided that the legislature has the power to reverse the court's judgment. Finally, one might support the position that because of the way judges are picked, they are suited to balance other goals, like efficiency, with explicitly distributional ones in choosing liability rules for a society. All these are possible approaches worth considering. What one cannot do, we would suggest, is to act as if distributional considerations did not historically play a role in judicial choice of liability rules, and must not do so today regardless of the strength and clarity of a society's commitment to specific distributional preferences.[90]

Having said this, we do not here need to argue with Professor Posner over whether the particular choice of Learned Hand test made and applied between 1895 and 1905 was based, as many have said,[91] on distributional considerations or was, as he maintains, essentially an efficiency choice.[92] It is perfectly clear *at the very least* that that choice, both when made well before 1895 and as applied for many years, had distributional effects which are very different from those produced by alternative tests which were as, or more, likely to accomplish primary accident cost avoidance. That these different distributional goals seem to be in the ascendancy today may again help to explain the move away from the classical Learned Hand test. They do not, however, suffice to explain why the move has been to strict liability rather than to a reverse Learned Hand test, which would seem to serve the currently dominant distributional goals of spreading and distribution in favor of victims more fully than does the strict liability test.[93]

89. *See, e.g.*, the dissenting opinions of Chief Justice Taft in Lonzrick v. Republic Steel Corp., 6 Ohio St. 2d, 227, 218 N.E.2d 185 (1966), and of Judge Burke in Goldberg v. Kollsman Instrument Corp., 12 N.Y.2d 432, 191 N.E.2d 81 (1963). *See also* Wights v. Staff Jennings, Inc., 241 Ore. 301, 309, 405 P.2d 624, 628-29 (1965), where the court refused to adopt strict products liability based on a "risk spreading" rationale, stating that such a theory "proves too much."

90. Other institutions may do a better job of dealing with distributional considerations, but this need not mean that courts are compelled to ignore them.

91. *See, e.g.*, Horwitz, Did the Legal System Subsidize Economic Growth in Ante-Bellum America? (unpublished paper delivered at the annual meeting of the American Historical Association, Boston, 1970).

92. Posner, *supra* note 9, at 32.

93. There have been numerous suggestions that a strict liability test serves the goal of spreading; *see, e.g.*, James, *Accident Liability Reconsidered: The Impact of Liability Insurance*, 57 YALE L.J. 549 (1948).

It would require another article to go into all of the distributional ramifications of

Toward a Test for Strict Liability in Torts

One more consideration remains in discussing the relationship to the test chosen of goals other than efficiency. Not only does the choice of test have substantial distributive effects, but its application in specific or doubtful cases does also. Thus the issue is not simply whether a society opts for a direct prohibition, a Learned Hand test, a reverse Learned Hand test or a strict liability test. Whatever goals are sought will also be at the mercy of applications of the chosen test. It is here, of course, that Fletcher's caveat about the role of courts seems more directly in point, though even here we would not be as ready as he is dogmatically to exclude considerations of distributive justice from the purview of courts and juries. The issue is a nice one and reasonable men may differ as to whether distributive considerations should apply (1) at all, or (2) only in cases where primary cost avoidance considerations do not provide a clear outcome, or (3) whether they ought to dominate over efficiency considerations even when the latter would imply a clear result.

As a practical matter, we would suggest that in applications of the traditional Learned Hand test, distributive considerations have very frequently at least played the second role and not infrequently the third. Unlike Posner, we find some support for this point of view in his admirable collection of appellate decisions.[94] Many dubious and some clearly "inefficient" decisions can be thus explained.[95] Without doing a similar study in more recent times, we would suggest that the change in the application of the fault standard since 1905 which has seemed so obvious to so many writers, may well reflect a similar kind of interplay between new distributional goals and the efficiency implications of the traditional Learned Hand test.

This kind of interplay is unlikely to stop merely because a change is made to a strict liability test which combines better primary accident cost avoidance with distributional goals which seem more congenial to the current age. Even within a regime of strict liability, courts and juries deciding which category is the cheapest cost avoider will in unclear cases most likely continue to consider whether some distributional goals are not best served by one decision rather than the other.

the strict liability test. We believe that this test would tend to favor victims as a category, because in practice they are, *inter alia*, generally less well informed than injurers, but it would not do so to the same extent as a reverse Learned Hand test, which would put the cost of all accidents not worth avoiding on injurers.

94. Posner, *supra* note 9, at 52-96.

95. We find it difficult to agree, for example, that application of the principle of respondent superior to employers but not to families was based entirely on efficiency grounds. Posner, *supra* note 9, at 43. It seems more likely that distributional considerations were relevant to that determination.

Nor would we be surprised if distributional goals will fairly frequently lead to liability results under a strict liability test which are pretty clearly wrong if one considers primary cost avoidance alone. Sometimes this will be the effect of legislative determinations, but at other times it will be the result of decisions by judge and jury—as it has been in the past. To say that this is wrong would be to conclude that once a liability test is chosen the role of the courts is to give effect only to efficiency. It may well be that this conclusion is appropriate, given the nature of courts and the lack of consensus for particular distributional preferences like spreading, greater wealth equality, or compensation of maltreated castes. This conclusion is not, however, a necessary one. Indeed, many years ago, Professor Clarence Morris argued that courts were very well suited to make just this kind of distributional decision, though only when whole *classes* of cases were affected.[96] Similarly, the ability and suitability of the jury to do the same in *individual* cases has been frequently argued.[97]

As a practical matter, introducing such distributional considerations, whether at the legislative or the judicial level, does make application of the strict liability test easier, just as in the past it made application of the Learned Hand test easier. For often a hard issue of whether the victim's category or the injurer's category is best suited to make a cost-benefit analysis between avoidance and compensation becomes easy if one choice serves distributional goals while the other undercuts them. In practice it will also be as hard to tell just what the roles of efficiency and distribution were in making the choice as it is for Professor Posner and us to agree on what the roles of the two sets of goals were in his 1895-1905 cases. Analytical frameworks, and the distinctions made therein, serve to elucidate; they rarely tell us what judges and juries did in individual cases.

VII. Conclusion

We have tried, in this article, to describe a framework, a test, which might help to put into place the factors that seem to be central to defining the limits of strict liability in the areas of the law where it has come to dominate. We contrasted this test with the classical negligence calculus and its mirror image. We noted that this strict liability test seems more likely than either of the others to accomplish a minimization of the sum of accident costs and of accident avoidance costs. We

96. Morris, *Hazardous Enterprises and Risk Bearing Capacity*, 61 YALE L.J. 1172 (1952).
97. *See, e.g.*, F. JAMES, CIVIL PROCEDURE § 7.4 at 240 (1965).

then discussed why we believe the move toward such a test cannot be explained solely in terms of distributional goals, though we readily admitted that such goals might also be served by the move. Finally, we expressed the view that even though such a test is very well suited to accomplishing an optimal reduction of primary accident costs, we would expect that in its application goals other than efficiency will often predominate.

Because Fleming James, through his writing, teaching, and warm colleagueship, first guided and then sustained our earliest as well as our more recent work in this field, we gratefully dedicate this piece to him. May retirement for him, as it was for his teacher, Arthur Corbin, simply be an opportunity to push the quest further.

[5]

TOWARD AN ECONOMIC THEORY OF LIABILITY

*JOHN PRATHER BROWN**

RECENTLY there have appeared a number of important articles by both lawyers and economists analyzing the economic effects of liability rules.[1] This paper formalizes the analysis of these effects. When two parties, the injurer and the victim, can both take measures to reduce the likelihood of accidents, and the measures are costly for both, the standard theory of production with two inputs and one output yields the conditions for the socially optimal amount of each accident avoidance measure. The effects of decentralizing the problem and using only liability rules to solve it can then be analyzed in terms of a two-person noncooperative game. I first show that there is a complete symmetry within each of the following pairs of liability rules: no liability and strict liability; the negligence rule and strict liability with contributory negligence; and the negligence rule with contributory negligence and strict liability with what I call dual contributory negligence. An analysis of the legal standards for negligence follows. I show that there is an important ambiguity in the so-called "Learned Hand Rule" for determining the level of avoidance effort below which a party is adjudged negligent. Two of the formulations of the rule lead to inefficient results.

Next the main results of the paper are presented. First, given the negligence rule with contributory negligence and what I call the Incremental Standard of care, the social optimum is shown to be the unique equilibrium for the noncooperative game. A corollary is that the same results hold when the negligence standard is replaced by strict liability with contributory negligence. When the Incremental Standard is replaced by the Limited Information

* Assistant Professor of Economics, Brown University; Fellow in Law and Economics, University of Chicago Law School. The author would like to thank William Brock, Harry Kalven, Jr., J. Huston McCulloch, John L. Peterman, Lester Telser, John Ver Steeg, and the members of the Industrial Organization Workshop at the University of Chicago for helpful comments and criticism.

1 See Guido Calabresi, The Costs of Accidents: A Legal and Economic Analysis (1970), and (with Jon T. Hirschoff), Toward a Test for Strict Liability in Torts, 81 Yale L.J. 1055 (1972); R. H. Coase, The Problem of Social Cost, 3 J. Law & Econ. 1 (1960); Harold Demsetz, When Does the Rule of Liability Matter?, 1 J. Leg. Studies 13 (1972); Roland N. McKean, Products Liability: Trends and Implications, in Symposium on Products Liability, 38 U. Chi. L. Rev. 3 (1970); Richard A. Posner, A Theory of Negligence, 1 J. Leg. Studies 29 (1972), and Strict Liability: A Comment, 2 J. Leg. Studies 205 (1973).

Incremental Standard the identity between equilibrium and optimality is destroyed. In an appendix the Coase Theorem is restated in our framework and compared with our results.

I. The Model

Consider a small device, a black box, which is attached to some otherwise useful object such as a railway crossing, an airplane, or a sidewalk. The only function of the device is to emit a bill for a large amount of money from time to time, so we shall call it a liability generator. That large amount of money is fixed at A.

On the liability generator are two controls, X and Y. Each of these controls is continuously variable. Increasing either or both increases the probability that the accident will be avoided, but at a decreasing rate. The probability that an accident is avoided in a given time interval is denoted P(X, Y), so the probability that an accident occurs in that interval is 1 — P(X, Y).[2] Figure 1 shows the relationship between X, Y and P(X, Y). Examples of what will be meant here by controls are built-in safety devices and careful driving in the railway crossing case, defect-free radar and careful flying in the airplane case, and shoveling snow and careful walking in the sidewalk case.

By this description of accident avoidance we have constructed an almost exact analogue of the neoclassical production function, familiar to economists, where there are two inputs, X and Y, producing one output, P(X, Y), which in our case is the probability that an accident will be avoided.[3] Just as the inputs to production are costly and should be economized on, so the accident avoidance controls X and Y are costly. Let the cost per unit of X be W_x and the cost per unit of Y be W_y. The total cost for a given level of X and Y is then

[2] The time interval is chosen small enough that the probability of more than one accident in the interval is negligible.

[3] I say an almost exact analogue because we must take explicit account of the possibility that the accident can be completely avoided and further amounts of accident avoidance contribute nothing. Formally, we assume (1) that P(X, Y) is continuous and twice differentiable in X and Y, (2) that the marginal products of both inputs are non-negative, and (3) marginal products do not increase. The possibility of complete avoidance admits the possibility that marginal products and their rate of change are zero. Our final assumption about P(X, Y) is (4) that $P_{xy}(X, Y) \equiv \frac{\partial P^2(X, Y)}{\partial X \partial Y} < 0$. We shall discuss this assumption later in the analysis.

I have chosen to have two controls to concentrate on the necessity in most accident contexts of having more than one party take costly measures to avoid accidents. Formally, it is a trivial extension to have more than two parties, but the legal implications of explicitly recognizing that there are more than two parties with responsibilities to avoid accidents should be explored carefully. The occasional cases where only one party can avoid the accident are special cases of this analysis where the equiprobability curves of Figure 1 would be either horizontal or vertical straight lines.

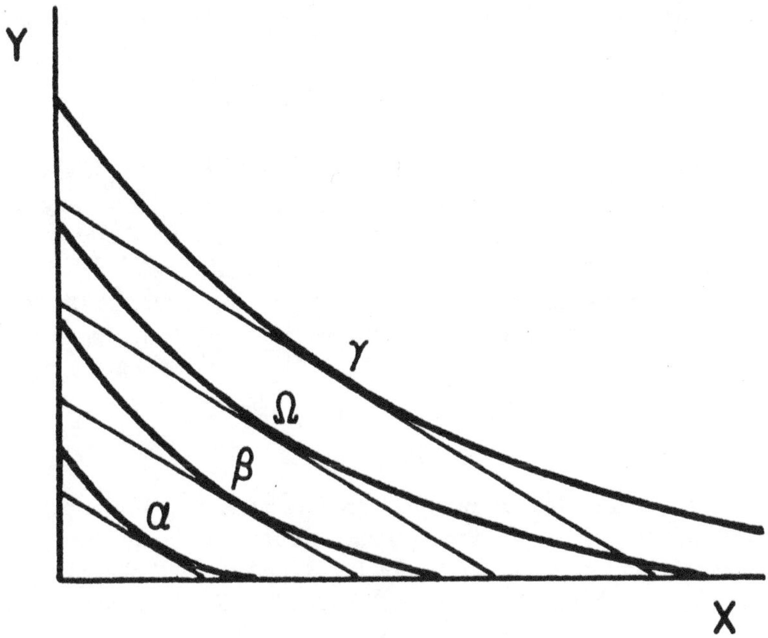

FIGURE 1

$W_xX + W_yY$. The straight lines in Figure 1 are all of the combinations of X and Y having the same total cost. This completes the transformation of the accident avoidance problem into the standard production theory format. To find the least cost combination to X and Y which will yield a given probability of accident avoidance one need only find the point on the equiprobability curve just tangent to a cost line. Examples are drawn in Figure 1 at α, β, γ and Ω.

Which combination of avoidance measures X and Y and the resulting probability of accident P(X, Y) is the most preferred? To answer that question we consider the case where both X and Y are under the control of the same party. In the simple case first before us, all quantities are measured in terms of money, so it makes no difference who makes the decision. The outcome we shall call the social optimum, and we shall use it to evaluate outcomes when X and Y are controlled by different people, which is of course the most interesting problem.

The social optimum we shall define as that combination of avoidance measures which minimizes the sum of the costs of the controls and the expected cost of the accident. With the apparatus that we have developed it is now a simple matter to write down the problem and to characterize the solution.

Formally, the socially optimal values of X and Y are those that minimize social cost, $C_S(X, Y)$. Thus

$$\min_{X,Y} C_S(X, Y) = W_x X + W_y Y + A[1 - P(X, Y)]. \tag{1}$$

The first two terms are the costs of the two controls, for example the costs of the crossing gates and of slower, more cautious driving in the railway crossing case. The last term is the expected cost of the accident and is the product of the cost of the accident and the probability that it will occur.

For the social cost to be at a minimum it must be true that the marginal cost of each input be equal to the expected value of its marginal product. That is

$$W_x = A\,P_x(X, Y) \qquad \text{and} \tag{2}$$

$$W_y = A\,P_y(X, Y) \tag{3}$$

where $P_x(X, Y)$ denotes the marginal product of X and $P_y(X, Y)$ denotes the marginal product of Y. The optimal solution can be found by solving equations (2) and (3) simultaneously for X and Y. Call the values which minimize social cost X_Ω and Y_Ω. Then it is true for all values of X and Y that

$$C_S(X_\Omega, Y_\Omega) \leqslant C_S(X, Y) \qquad \text{for all X and Y.} \tag{4}$$

The optimal values are those that would be chosen if both X and Y were under common control. The problem that interests us here is where X and Y are controlled by different people.

Before proceeding further it will be helpful to deal with two misleading concepts, one used by lawyers and the other used by economists. The first is the notion that liability ought to be placed on whoever caused the accident. In the scheme we have described, who caused the accident, the victim or the injurer? They both did. The problem is exactly analogous to the futile arguments among economists in the nineteenth century about whether capital or labor causes production. They both do. We must go on to further considerations to decide how the fruits of production should be divided; similarly we have to decide who should bear the liability for accidents when they are jointly caused. The only role for discussions of causation is to exonerate a party completely by proving that he is a stranger to the accident.

A similar issue arises with the notion of "least cost avoider." A number of writers, among them Calabresi and Demsetz, have recommended placing liability on the best cost avoider. For example, Demsetz states: "It is difficult to suggest any criterion for deciding liability other than placing it on the party able to avoid the costly interaction most easily."[4] Looking back at

[4] Harold Demsetz, *supra* note 1, at 28.

Figure 1, how can we identify the best cost avoider? One possible meaning would be to compare the cost of the victim's completely avoiding the accident (*i.e.*, setting $P(0, Y) = 0$, with the cost of the injurer's completely avoiding the accident $P(X, 0) = 0$). The party with the lowest cost would be the cheapest cost avoider. Another possible interpretation of the phrase "least cost avoider" is that it is a local notion depending on (X, Y), that is, on what the parties in fact chose to do. This leaves unanswered how liability should be assigned in order to induce the parties to take the optimal amount of avoidance action. The notion of least cost avoider is thus likely to confuse rather than to clarify matters.

II. Decentralization Using a Liability Rule

When the two avoidance mechanisms are in the hands of different people, for example the manufacturer and the driver when the liability generator is attached to an automobile, or the manufacturer and patient in the case of a drug, the question arises as to how the bill shall be paid when an accident takes place. The question is answered by the court. Since this paper is concerned with how injurer and victims can be expected to respond under different liability rules I have chosen to provide only the simplest abstraction of the court and its functioning. For our purposes the only function of the legal system is the impeccable administration of whatever liability rule is in force. In order to concentrate on what is our major concern, the parties' behavior, we ignore the distinction between judge and jury, the problems of proof and burden of proof, the uncertainty of the outcome, the mistakes that the court can make, and the expense of operating the legal system.

To fix ideas for the rest of the discussion, let X be controlled by Xavier the Injurer, and Y by Yvonne the Victim. The rule that determines which party must pay the bill emitted by the liability generator is called a liability rule. The liability rule will in general be a function of the level of avoidance chosen by each party and will be expressed as the fraction of the bill, A, owed by each party. Let $L_x(X, Y)$ and $L_y(X, Y)$ be the liabilities of Xavier and Yvonne, respectively. Then

$$L_x(X, Y) \geqslant 0, L_y(X, Y) \geqslant 0 \qquad \text{for all } X, Y \tag{5}$$

$$L_x(X, Y) + L_y(X, Y) = 1 \qquad \text{for all } X, Y. \tag{6}$$

The amount that must be paid by Xavier when an accident takes place is $A\,L_x(X, Y)$ and the amount to be paid by Yvonne is $A\,L_y(X, Y)$.

A number of different liability rules have been discussed in the recent literature.[5] They are simple to put into the framework we propose but for some

[5] See Calabresi, Calabresi and Hirschoff, and Posner works cited in note 1 *supra*.

of them we require one further notion, that of a legal standard of negligence. Let (X^*, Y^*) be the legal standard of negligence. If X is less than X^* then the injurer will be found legally negligent. Similarly, if Y is less than Y^*, the victim will be found negligent. Now we are ready to describe the liability rules.

1. *No liability*. The victim is liable under all circumstances.

$$L_x(X, Y) = 0 \qquad L_y(X, Y) = 1 \qquad \text{for all } X, Y. \tag{7}$$

2. *Strict liability*. The injurer is liable under all circumstances.

$$L_x(X, Y) = 1 \qquad L_y(X, Y) = 0 \qquad \text{for all } X, Y. \tag{8}$$

3. *The negligence rule*. The victim is liable unless the injurer is found negligent.

$$L_x(X, Y) = \begin{cases} 0 \\ 1 \end{cases} \quad L_y(X, Y) = \begin{cases} 1 & \text{if } X \geqslant X^* \\ 0 & \text{if } X < X^* \end{cases}. \tag{9}$$

4. *Strict liability with contributory negligence*. The injurer is liable unless the victim is found negligent.

$$L_x(X, Y) = \begin{cases} 1 \\ 0 \end{cases} \quad L_y(X, Y) = \begin{cases} 0 & \text{if } Y \geqslant Y^* \\ 1 & \text{if } Y < Y^* \end{cases}. \tag{10}$$

5. *The negligence rule with contributory negligence*. The injurer is liable if he is negligent *and* the victim is not. The victim is liable otherwise.

$$L_x(X, Y) = \begin{cases} 1 \\ 0 \end{cases} \quad L_y(X, Y) = \begin{cases} 0 & \text{if } X < X^* \text{ and } Y \geqslant Y^* \\ 1 & \text{otherwise} \end{cases} \tag{11}$$

The negligence rule with contributory negligence has been the dominant rule in tort law since *Brown v. Kendall*.[6] In that landmark case the defendant (the injurer) took up a stick to separate fighting dogs belonging to the plaintiff (the victim) and the defendant. In the course of beating the dogs the defendant accidentally hit the plaintiff in the eye, injuring him severely. Chief Justice Shaw laid down the rule: ". . . if both plaintiff and defendant at the time of the blow were using ordinary care, or if at that time the defendant was using ordinary care, and the plaintiff was not, or if at that time, both the defendant and the plaintiff were not using ordinary care, then the plaintiff could not recover."[7]

Notice that there is complete symmetry in our model between no liability and strict liability on the one hand and between the negligence rule on the

[6] 60 Mass. (6 Cush.) 292 (1850).

[7] *Id.* at 296.

one hand and strict liability with contributory negligence on the other. The strict liability rule that would be symmetrical to the negligence rule with contributory negligence has been mentioned only by Calabresi and Hirschoff in the recent literature. It might be called:

6. ***Strict liability with dual contributory negligence.*** The victim is liable if he is negligent *and* the injurer is not. The injurer is liable otherwise.

$$L_x(X, Y) = \begin{cases} 0 \\ 1 \end{cases} \quad L_y(X, Y = \begin{cases} 1 & \text{if } Y < Y^* \text{ and } X \geqslant X^* \\ 0 & \text{otherwise} \end{cases} \tag{12}$$

The six liability rules are displayed graphically in Figure 2.

There are two further liability rules that are somewhat outside the tradition encompassed in the six rules presented here in that the standard of care for one party is the level of care exercised by the other party. They are relative negligence and comparative negligence.

7. ***Relative negligence.*** The injurer is liable if the increment to accident avoidance per dollar of avoidance by him is greater than that per dollar of avoidance by the victim, *i.e.*, if a dollar spent by the injurer could have bought more avoidance than a dollar spent by the victim.

In our notation the liability rule for the injurer is

$$L_x(X, Y) = \begin{cases} 1 & \text{if } \dfrac{P_x(X, Y)}{W_x} > \dfrac{P_y(X, Y)}{W_y} \\ 0 & \text{otherwise} \end{cases} \tag{13}$$

$L_y(X, Y)$ is, as usual, the complement of $L_x(X, Y)$, that is,

$$L_y(X, Y) = 1 - L_x(X, Y) \tag{14}$$

Graphically, there is a very simple interpretation of the relative negligence rule. The slope of the equiprobability lines (isoquants) is $-\dfrac{P_x(X, Y)}{P_y(X, Y)}$ and the slope of the equal cost lines is $-\dfrac{W_x}{W_y}$. Therefore the injurer is negligent at (X, Y) if the equiprobability line is steeper than the equal cost line at (X, Y). Notice that at any (X, Y) either the injurer or the victim is relatively negligent. In case of ties we have arbitrarily assumed that the victim is liable. The negligence boundary is the locus of least cost combinations for different probabilities. See Figure 3.

8. ***Comparative negligence.*** The doctrine of comparative negligence apportions the liability according to the relative liability of the two parties. This doctrine is established in admiralty law, but otherwise it is not recognized

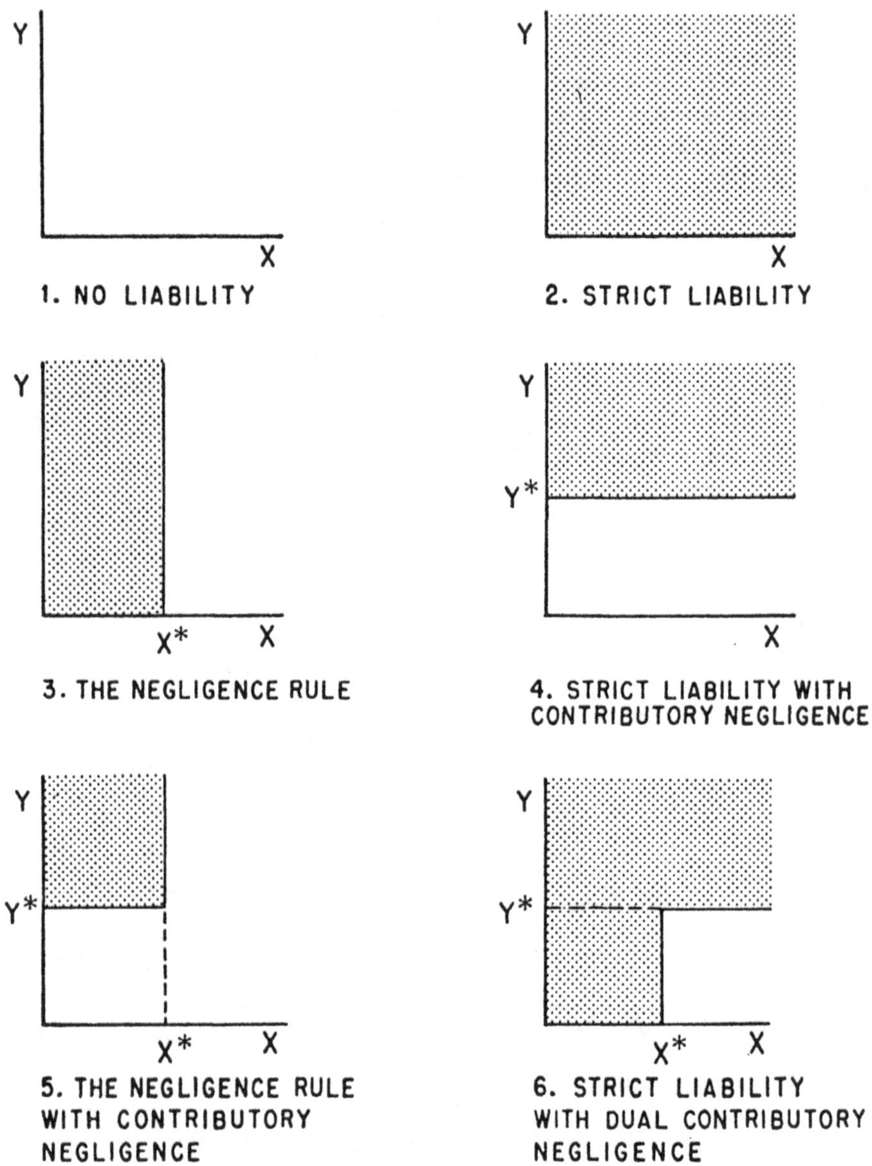

FIGURE 2 (INJURER LIABLE IN SHADED AREA)

in any state except where it is established by statute, *e.g.*, in Wisconsin, Georgia, and Mississippi.[8] It is not clear whether negligence is defined as a

[8] See Charles O. Gregory & Harry Kalven, Jr., Cases and Materials on Torts 250-54 (2d ed. 1969).

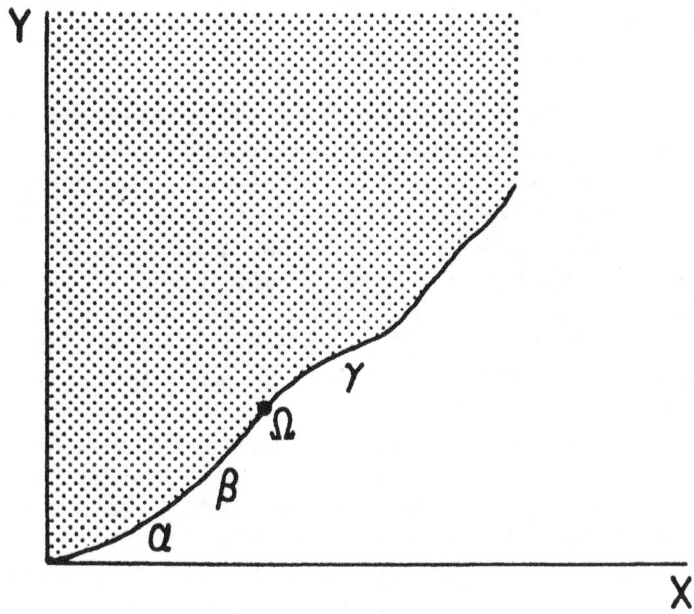

RELATIVE NEGLIGENCE

FIGURE 3 (INJURER LIABLE IN SHADED AREA)

marginal concept or an average one. If a marginal negligence concept is used, then, if n_x is the negligence of the injurer and n_y the negligence of the victim,

$$n_x = \frac{P_x(X, Y)}{W_x} \quad \text{and} \quad n_y = \frac{P_y(X, Y)}{W_y} \tag{15}$$

Negligence is the incremental reduction in accident probability per dollar spent, and the liability of the injurer is his negligence divided by the negligence of both parties:

$$L_x(X, Y) = \frac{n_x}{n_x + n_y} \tag{16}$$

The liability of the victim is $1 - L_x(X, Y)$.

III. THE LEGAL STANDARD OF NEGLIGENCE

We noted above that some of the liability rules require a legal determination of negligence by one party or the other. Call the legal standard of negligence for the injurer X* and for the victim Y*. In legal discussions this is often called the standard of care. If X is found to be less than X* then the injurer will be judged negligent. Similarly, if Y is found to be less than Y* the victim will be judged negligent.

The negligence standard most often cited in legal discussions of the problem is the so-called Learned Hand Rule,[9] which can be paraphrased as follows. The duty of a party is a function of three variables: (1) the probability of an accident; (2) the gravity of the accident; and (3) the burden of adequate precaution. Liability depends on whether the product of the first two is greater than the third. In our notation, the probability of an accident is $1 - P(X, Y)$, the gravity of the accident is A, and the burden of precaution is W_xX for the injurer and W_yY for the victim. Thus, the Learned Hand Rule compares $A(1 - P(X, Y))$ with W_xX for the injurer and with W_yY for the victim.

The Learned Hand Rule is ambiguous in important ways, as we shall show. In fact there are three closely related standards of negligence that can be derived from Judge Hand's formulation. The first we shall call the Literal Learned Hand Standard, or the Literal Standard for short. If we take literally the standard as given by Judge Hand, the injurer would be found negligent if

$$W_xX < A(1 - P(X, Y)) \qquad (17)$$

and the victim would be found negligent if

$$W_yY < A(1 - P(X, Y)). \qquad (18)$$

This standard compares the total cost to a party with the expected cost of the accident.

There is one question for which the Literal Standard unambiguously gives the correct answer, but it is typically the wrong question, and might well suggest the wrong answer to the right question. Consider Figure 4. As drawn, the expected benefits are greater than the costs to the injurer for every level of X. The question that the Literal Standard answers correctly is this: Is it better to provide complete protection, $X = T$, rather than no protection at all, $X = 0$? Then we need only compare the product of the probability of an accident and the gravity of the accident, TC, with the burden of adequate precaution, TB. In the case described in the figure, because TC is greater than TB, it is better to provide complete protection than no protection at all. Should it be the duty of the injurer to provide complete protection in this case? Clearly the answer is no. Although it is better to provide full protection than none at all, the optimal amount of protection from an overall point of view is Ω, where the marginal cost of protection is equal to the marginal expected benefit from the protection. By moving from

[9] United States v. Carroll Towing Co., 159 F.2d 169 (2d Cir. 1947)

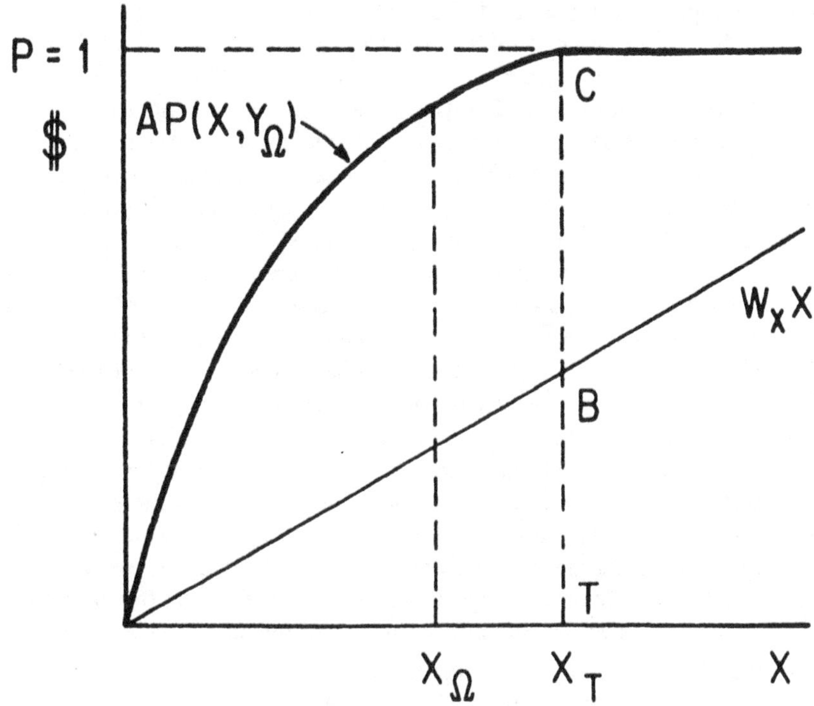

FIGURE 4

X_T to X_Ω costs would decrease more than benefits. Clearly, we need a better negligence standard.[10]

The second standard derivable from Judge Hand's formulation is the Incremental Standard. Here we assume that the judicial system can ferret out complete information about the underlying technology of accident prevention so that negligence for one party is determined on the *assumption that the other party is already acting in an optimal manner*. Thus the negligence standard for the injurer, X^*, is that value of X such that

$$W_x = A\,P_x(X^*, Y_\Omega) \tag{19}$$

and for the victim is Y^*, that value of Y such that

$$W_y = A\,P_y(X_\Omega, Y^*). \tag{20}$$

[10] Calabresi and Hirschoff seem to have been misled by a literal reading of the Learned Hand rule. They say, for example (*supra* note 1, at 1057), "If the cost to the defendant of avoiding the accident would have been less than the cost of the accident, discounted by the probability of its occurrence, the defendant's failure to avoid the accident is termed negligence." This is the Learned Hand Literal Standard, in our terminology.

Under the Incremental Standard the negligence standard is identical to the conditions for social cost minimization independently for both the injurer and the victim. Thus $X^* = X_\Omega$ and $Y^* = Y_\Omega$. Solving for the Incremental Standard is equivalent to identifying the social cost minimizing solution. The court uses the Incremental Standard to find the social optimum and defines any avoidance less than optimal as negligent. Below we shall investigate the effect of using the Incremental Standard with the various liability rules.

The third standard we shall call the Limited Information Incremental Standard. Rather than assuming that the court knows the entire technology of accident prevention as we did in the full information standard, we assume here that the court is able to investigate only the effects on the probability of an accident of small changes in the immediate neighborhood of the (X, Y) pair actually chosen by the two parties. In mathematical terms this means that the court is only able to determine the partial derivatives of $P(X, Y)$ at (X, Y). In effect, if the court uses the Limited Information Incremental Standard it is saying that an avoidance level is negligent if it is less than that which would be optimal *given what the other party has in fact done.* The injurer will be held negligent at some point (X, Y) if that X is less than would be required to minimize social cost, treating Y as fixed. Thus the lowest value of X for which the injurer will not be judged negligent is the minimum with respect to X of

$$C_S(X, Y) = W_xX + W_yY + A(1 - P(X, Y))$$

The necessary marginal conditions for a minimum imply that the injurer will be found negligent at (X, Y) if

$$W_x < A\,P_x(X, Y) \tag{21}$$

and the victim will be found negligent at (X, Y) if

$$W_y < A\,P_y(X, Y). \tag{22}$$

To emphasize that the level of X that just allows the injurer to avoid being found negligent, X^*, depends on the avoidance actions taken by the victim, we shall use the functional notation $X^*(Y)$. Similarly, since the level of Y that just allows the victim to avoid being found negligent depends on the actions taken by the injurer, we write $Y^*(X)$.

The Incremental Standards are a good approximation, I think, of the way that courts actually proceed. The attorney for the plaintiff will try to find some act which, if the defendant had taken it, would have significantly reduced the probability of the accident at low cost. But that is precisely the statement that the increment in the expected loss was greater than the cost of avoidance, which is the definition of the Incremental Standards of negligence. The defendant will try to respond that the expected benefits of the proposed act were, in fact, less than the costs of undertaking it. When the court is asked to decide between the two points of view it is being asked to compare the incremental expected benefits with the incremental costs. Thus it is not peculiar that the outcome of large, important cases often seems to turn on the value of small changes in the behavior of one party or the other.

IV. A Noncooperative Game Played According to Liability Rules

What are the equilibrium values of X and Y when they are chosen by different people independently? How will Xavier and Yvonne behave when their only communication with each other will be in court after an accident occurs? All other transactions are assumed to be so costly that they do not take place.

We shall assume that the goal of Xavier is to choose X to minimize his expected private costs, that is:

$$\min_{X} C_x(X, Y) = W_x X + A\,L_x(X, Y)(1 - P(X, Y)) \tag{23}$$

and Yvonne minimizes her private costs:

$$\min_{Y} C_y(X, Y) = W_y Y + A\,L_y(X, Y)(1 - P(X, Y)). \tag{24}$$

These are simply the sum of the cost of their own preventive efforts and their expected liability when an accident occurs.

Both parties are assumed to know A, W_x, W_y, and $P(X, Y)$ as well as the liability rule in force and that the other party is interested only in private costs. Our problem is to try to find equilibria for the games and determine whether they are unique. An equilibrium for a game is a pair of values (X, Y) chosen by the two players such that, given the choice by the opponent, neither party has an incentive to change his own choice.

Before analyzing the various rules it will be useful to describe two response functions for each party. They are called response functions because, like the response functions in Cournot's analysis of duopoly, they show what response a party would choose, given the choice of the opponent.

The first response function we call $X^f(Y)$. The superscript f denotes full cost. It is defined as the injurer's preferred value of X given Y, assuming that the injurer must pay in full for any damages. That is, $X^f(Y)$ is that X for which $W_x X + A(1 - P(X, Y))$ is at a minimum. Alternatively, $X^f(Y)$ is the value of X which minimizes social cost when Y is fixed, since the only difference between private and social costs is the constant $W_y Y$, since Y is considered fixed. It is a necessary condition of minimization that at each value of $X^f(Y)$

$$W_x = A\,P_x(X^f, Y). \tag{25}$$

We take the total differential of this condition

$$A\,P_{xx}\,dX^f + A\,P_{xy}\,dY = 0 \tag{26}$$

and solve it for $\frac{dX^f}{dY}$

$$\frac{dX^f}{dY} = -\frac{P_{xy}}{P_{xx}} \tag{27}$$

This gives us the change in the optimal X for a change in Y. Convexity implies that $P_{xx} < 0$. Therefore if $P_{xy} < 0$ as we assume, then

$$\frac{dX^f}{dY} < 0 \tag{28}$$

that is, a decrease in Y will call forth an increase in X.

Throughout the rest of our analysis we shall employ one slightly restrictive assumption about the technology of accident avoidance, namely that $P_{xy} < 0$. The technical effect of the assumption is to insure that the full cost response functions X^f and Y^f are both downward sloping. If they were upward sloping there could be a second intersection on one axis or the other and hence a second equilibrium. Assuming $P_{xy} < 0$ is equivalent to assuming that a decrease in accident avoidance by one party ought to call forth an increase in accident avoidance by the other. For example, if cars drive faster on one residential street than on another we would expect mothers to take greater care that their children do not stray onto the first street than onto the second, or as trains approach a crossing more rapidly we would expect cars to approach more slowly. Only in the bizarre case where the technology of accident prevention were such that the appropriate response to faster trains would be *less* caution on the part of drivers would the assumption of $P_{xy} < 0$ be inappropriate.

Correspondingly, there is, of course, the response function for the victim, $Y^f(X)$, which is the victim's preferred value of Y given X, assuming that the victim must pay in full for any damages. Therefore $Y^f(X)$ is the value of X which minimizes $W_yY + A[1 - P(X, Y)]$. Figure 5 shows $X^f(Y)$ and $Y^f(X)$.

The second response function we shall consider gives the party's preferred strategy, given the opponent's strategy, for the actual expected private costs, $C_x(X, Y)$ or $C_y(X, Y)$, which depend on the liability rule in force. This response function is denoted $X^e(Y)$ for the injurer and $Y^e(X)$ for the victim. The superscript e signifies equilibrium. $X^e(Y)$ is that value of X for each Y

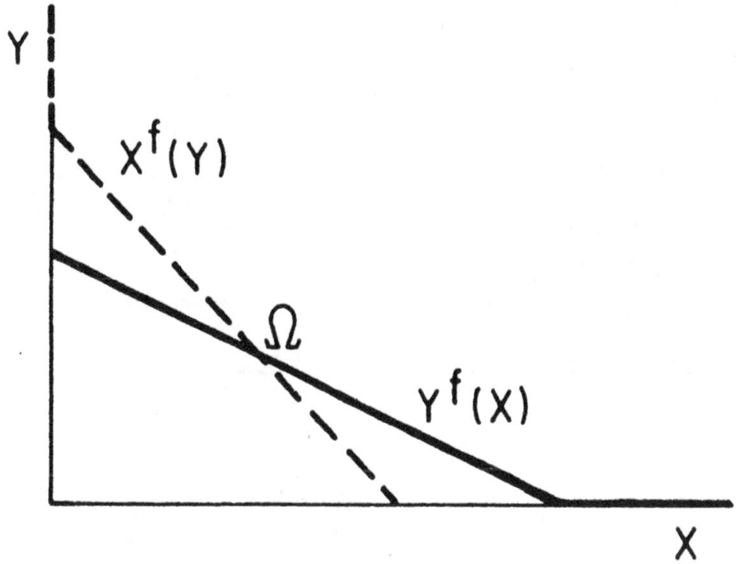

FIGURE 5

that minimizes $C_x(X, Y)$. For example, if the liability rule is the negligence rule with contributory negligence and the negligence standard is the Incremental Standard,

$$C_x(X, Y) = \begin{cases} W_xX + A[1 - P(X, Y)] & \text{if } X < X_\Omega \text{ and } Y \geqslant Y_\Omega \\ W_xX & \text{otherwise.} \end{cases} \quad (29)$$

In the same case $Y^e(X)$ is that value of Y which minimizes the victim's expected private costs, which are

$$C_y(X, Y) = \begin{cases} W_yY & \text{if } X < X_\Omega \text{ and } Y \geqslant Y_\Omega \\ W_yY + A[1 - P(X, Y)] & \text{otherwise.} \end{cases}$$

$X^e(Y)$ and $Y^e(X)$ are plotted in Figure 6. The shaded area is the area where the injurer is liable.

V. Equilibrium Under the Various Liability Rules

1. *No Liability*

First consider the rule of no liability. All bills emitted by the liability generator are to be paid by the victim, Yvonne, without regard to any measures either she or the injurer took. Then the costs paid by the injurer are only the costs of his own avoidance measures, so his problem is to

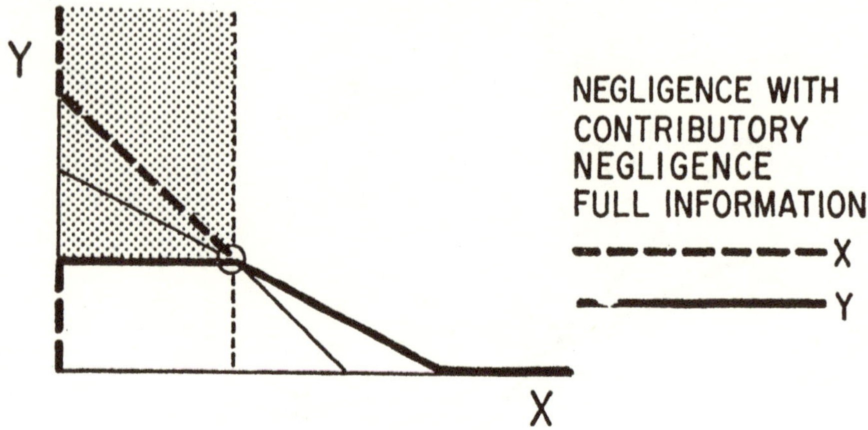

FIGURE 6

$$\min_{X} C_x(X, Y) = W_x X \tag{30}$$

It is obvious that he will choose $X = 0$; there are no benefits to him from avoiding accidents. In other words $x^e(Y) = 0$ for all Y.

For the victim the task is to

$$\min_{Y} C_y(0, Y) = W_y Y + A(1 - P(0, Y)) \tag{31}$$

that is, minimize the sum of his avoidance costs and expected losses given that the injurer will do nothing. This sum will be at a minimum when

$$W_y = A\, P_y(0, Y) \tag{32}$$

that is, at $Y^f(0)$. The equilibrium values of the game are $X = 0$ and $Y = Y^f(0)$, rather than the social optimum (X_Ω, Y_Ω). It is obvious that the equilibrium is unique. See Figure 7a.

2. *Strict Liability*

Next consider the rule of strict liability. The injurer is responsible for all accidents. The argument is identical to that for the rule of no liability except that the roles of injurer and victim, X and Y, are reversed. The victim will have no incentive to take any precautions: the injurer will choose the best level of precaution given that the victim takes none. The equilibrium is $(X^f(0), 0)$. Again, it is obvious that the equilibrium is unique. See Figure 7b.

The situation changes radically when we move on to liability rules that apply negligence standards to one or both parties.

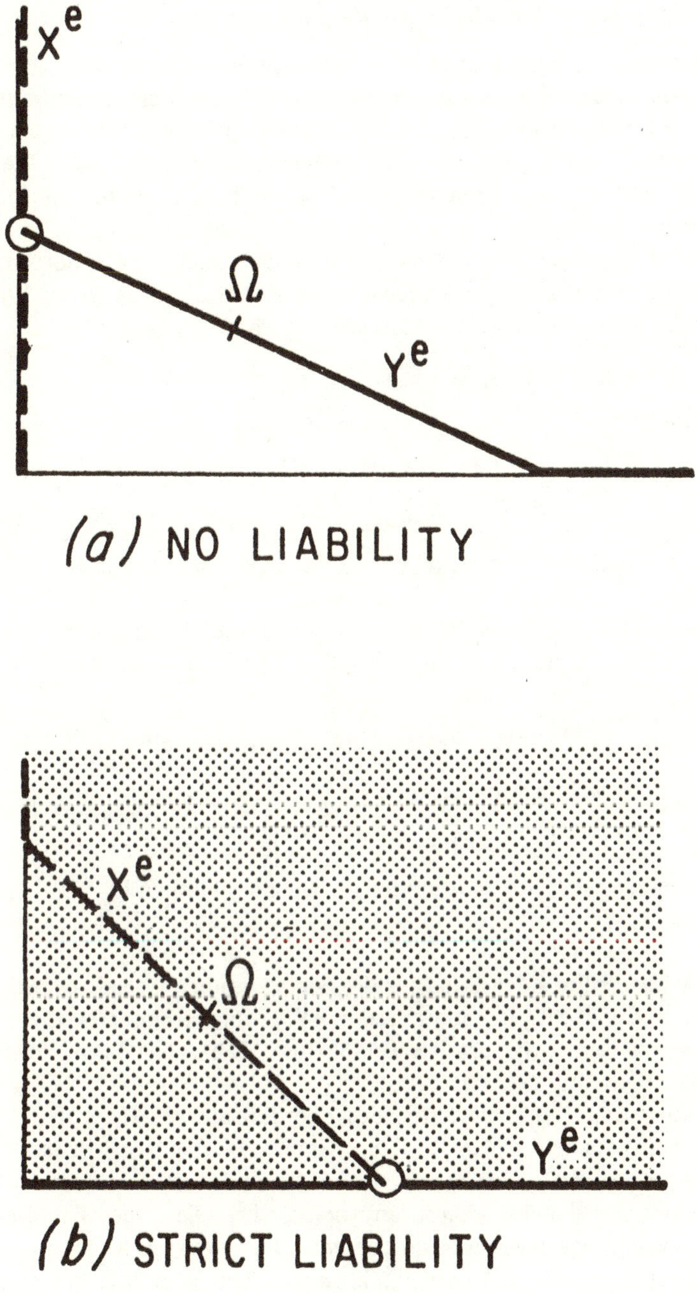

FIGURE 7

3. *Negligence Rule with Contributory Negligence, Incremental Standard*

We can now state the first of the major results of the paper.

Theorem 1: If the social optimum (X_Ω, Y_Ω) is a unique minimum of the social cost function $C_S(X, Y)$, the liability rule in force is the Negligence Rule with Contributory Negligence, the negligence standard is the Incremental Standard, and $P_{xy} < 0$, then the social optimum is a unique noncooperative equilibrium.

Proof of Theorem 1: First we show that (X_Ω, Y_Ω) is a non-cooperative equilibrium. For the injurer we have to show that his costs, given Y_Ω, are less at X_Ω than at any other value of X. That is, we have to show that

$$C_x(X_\Omega, Y_\Omega) \leqslant C_x(X, Y_\Omega) \qquad \text{for all X.} \tag{33}$$

Recall that

$$C_x(X, Y_\Omega) = \begin{cases} W_xX + A[1 - P(X, Y_\Omega)] & \text{if } X < X_\Omega \\ W_xX & \text{if } X \geqslant X_\Omega \end{cases} \tag{34}$$

This cost function is plotted in Figure 8a. It is clear that it is a minimum at X_Ω.

In analogous fashion we must show that given the injurer's choice of X_Ω, the victim can do no better than Y_Ω. See Figure 8b. That is, we must show that

$$C_y(X_\Omega, Y_\Omega) \leqslant C_y(X_\Omega, Y) \qquad \text{for all Y.} \tag{35}$$

This we do by writing out $C_y(X_\Omega, Y)$

$$C_y(X, Y) = W_yY + A[1 - P(X_\Omega, Y)] \tag{36}$$

and minimizing it. The condition for its being a minimum is

$$W_y = A\, P_y(X_\Omega, Y) \tag{37}$$

which is identically a condition for the minimization of social cost at (X_Ω, Y_Ω). Therefore $C_y(X_\Omega, Y)$ is minimized at Y_Ω, which completes the proof that (X_Ω, Y_Ω) is a noncooperative equilibrium. What has been shown is that $X^e(Y_\Omega) = X_\Omega$ and $Y^e(X_\Omega) = Y_\Omega$.

To show that (X_Ω, Y_Ω) is a unique equilibrium we show that X^e and Y^e intersect only once, at (X_Ω, Y_Ω). See Figure 9a. A party will never choose a point where he is liable other than on the full cost equilibrium, X^f or Y^f. Also a party will never choose any point where he is not liable other than the one which requires him to do the least. Therefore, each party's equilibrium will be either on the full cost equilibrium X^f or Y^f or the lowest cost point where he is not liable. Thus in the figure X^e crosses the shaded area on X^f and then drops to zero as soon as the injurer is not liable. Similarly, Y^e stays

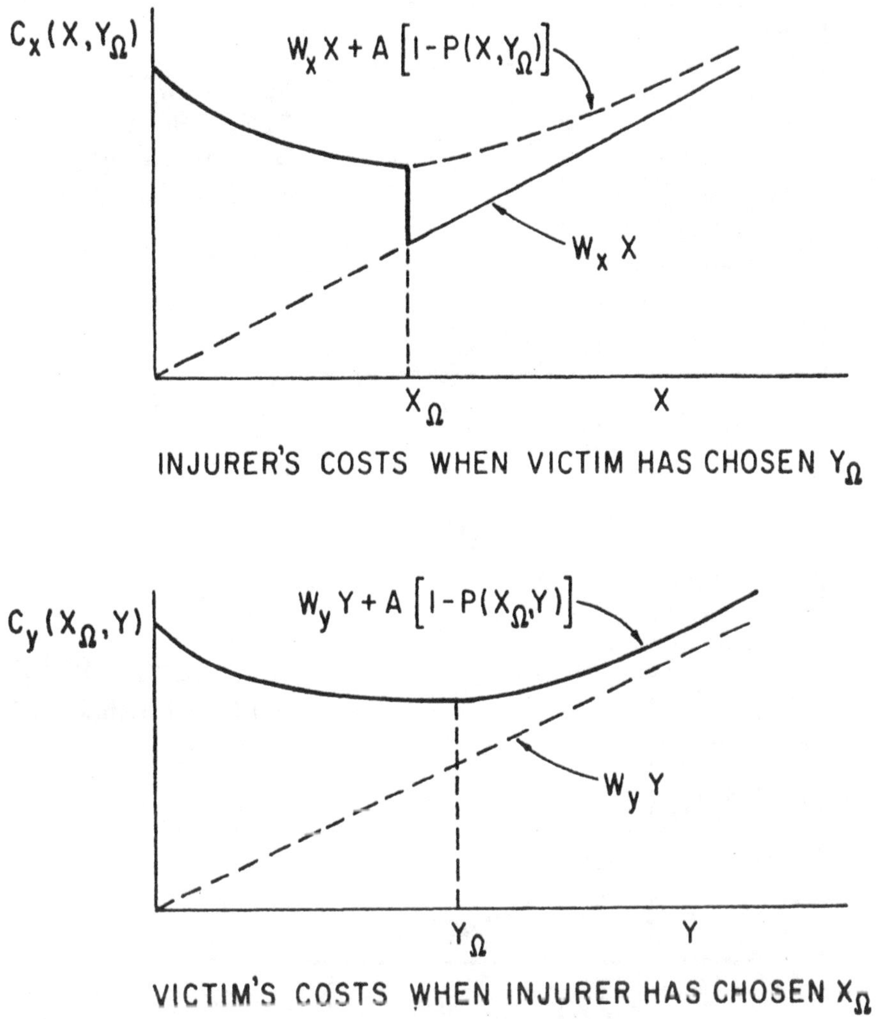

FIGURE 8

at the lowest part of the shaded area, where the victim is not liable, and then crosses the unshaded area, where she is liable, on Y^f. The only intersection of X^e and Y^o is at (X_Ω, Y_Ω); hence (X_Ω, Y_Ω) is a unique non-cooperative equilibrium, because both parties are in equilibrium there and only there.

4. *The Negligence Rule, Incremental Standard*

Corollary 1: The results of Theorem 1 hold if the liability rule is changed from the negligence rule with contributory negligence to the negligence rule.

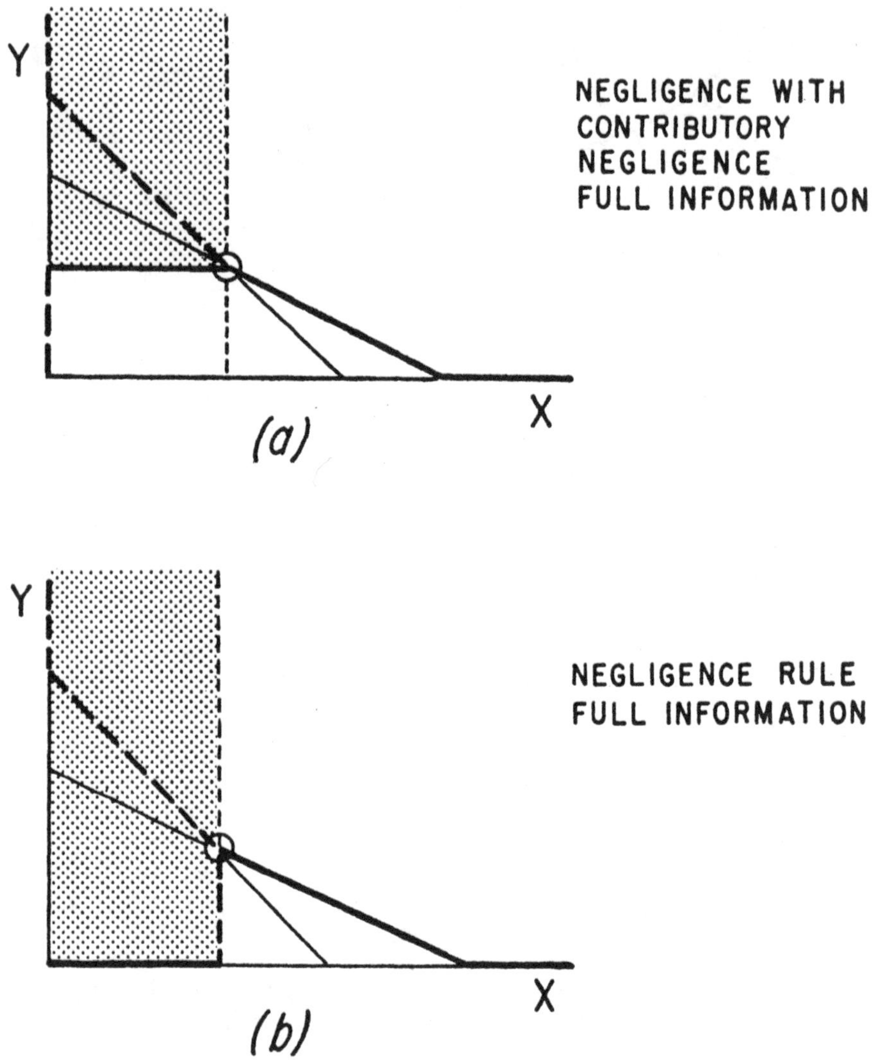

FIGURE 9

Proof: The equilibrium reaction functions $X^e(Y)$ and $Y^e(X)$ are plotted in Figure 9b for the case of the negligence rule and the Incremental Standard. The changes in the functions resulting from the change in liability rule are inconsequential from the point of view of the proof of the theorem. The reaction functions still only intersect at the social optimum, (X_Ω, Y_Ω).

5. *Strict Liability with Contributory Negligence and with Dual Contributory Negligence*

Corollary 2: The results of Theorem 1 hold if the liability rule is changed to either strict liability with contributory negligence or strict liability with dual contributory negligence.

Proof: To obtain the results for strict liability with contributory negligence we merely exchange the roles of X and Y in the proof of Corollary 1. To obtain the results for strict liability with dual contributory negligence we exchange X and Y in the argument of the theorem.

One can summarize the results on decentralized games with liability rules so far as follows: with either no liability or strict liability rules in effect the incentives on the party without liability are perverse so the resulting equilibrium will not be the optimal one. For all four remaining rules, which are based on negligence of one or both parties, given the Incremental Standard the game will have a unique equilibrium and that equilibrium is the social optimum. Within the framework of our analysis there is no preferred choice among any of the four rules.

Perhaps it would be useful to point out here what the analysis does not say. It does not say that there is no basis for choice among the four rules; only that the factors that we have chosen to analyze do not lead us to choose any one of the negligence rules. If the cost of using the courts to transfer liability is very high, then the negligence rule with contributory negligence becomes more attractive because it transfers liability least often. Within the scope of our analysis any of the negligence rules is preferable to either the no liability rule or strict liability. That preference could, of course, be overthrown by factors outside the analysis. One could construct an argument for no liability (as in the case of "no-fault" insurance schemes) by showing that the costs of administering the negligence system far outweigh the losses caused by the incorrect incentives which are inherent in no-fault schemes. Also our analysis assumes a completely informed court system that does not have difficulty in producing accurate evidence. There are no evidentiary problems and who has the burden of proof is irrelevant.

VI. The Limited Information Incremental Standard

Now we turn to the case where the court no longer knows what the social optimum is and only judges each party's behavior on the basis of small changes from where the parties actually were when the accident occurred. That is, we shall assume that the courts use the Limited Information Incremental Standard as the standard of care. The boundary between the injurer being negligent and not, $X^*(Y)$, is no longer a vertical line at X_Ω but rather is identical with $X^f(Y)$ passing through (X_Ω, X_Ω). Similarly, $Y^*(X) = Y^f(X)$.

1. *The Negligence Rule with Contributory Negligence*

Theorem 2: The results of Theorem 1 are destroyed when the Incremental Standard of negligence is replaced by the Limited Information Incremental Standard. The social optimum is not an equilibrium; in fact there is no equilibrium.

Proof: First we shall show that the social optimum, (X_Ω, Y_Ω), is not an equilibrium. To do so we need only consider the cost function of the injurer when the victim is at the social optimum $C_x(X, Y_\Omega)$.

$$C_x(X, Y_\Omega) = W_x X \tag{38}$$

That is, at no value of X is the injurer liable when $Y = Y_\Omega$; therefore the injurer will have no incentive to provide any accident avoidance measures at all. His costs will be at a minimum if $X = 0$. Therefore (X_Ω, Y_Ω) is not an equilibrium.

X^e and Y^e are plotted in Figure 10a for the case of the Limited Information Incremental Standard. The argument for the shape of the curves is the same as in Theorem I and does not need to be repeated. What appears to be an intersection at $(0, Y^f(0))$ is not. $X^e(Y^f(0))$ is not zero. (Only for $Y^f(0) - \epsilon$, where ϵ is arbitrarily small, is X^e zero.) Hence there is no equilibrium and the parties will cycle about as shown in Figure 10a.

Corollary 1: When the liability rule is changed from the negligence rule with contributory negligence to the negligence rule, the social optimum is again not an equilibrium.

Proof: Refer to Figure 10b. The logic of the proof is to confirm that X^e and Y^o are as drawn.

Corollary 2: Symmetrical results hold for strict liability with contributory negligence when the standard of care is the Limited Information Incremental Standard.

Proof: Merely exchange the roles of X and Y in Corollary 1.

Corollary 3: Symmetrical results hold for strict liability with dual contributory negligence when the standard of care is the Limited Information Incremental Standard.

Proof: Exchange the roles of X and Y in Theorem 2.

2. *Relative Negligence*

Theorem 3: If the liability rule in force is the relative negligence rule, then the social optimum is a unique noncooperative equilibrium.

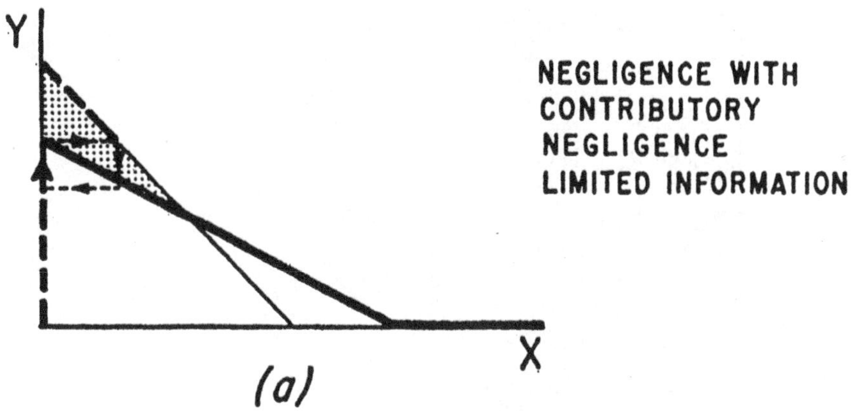

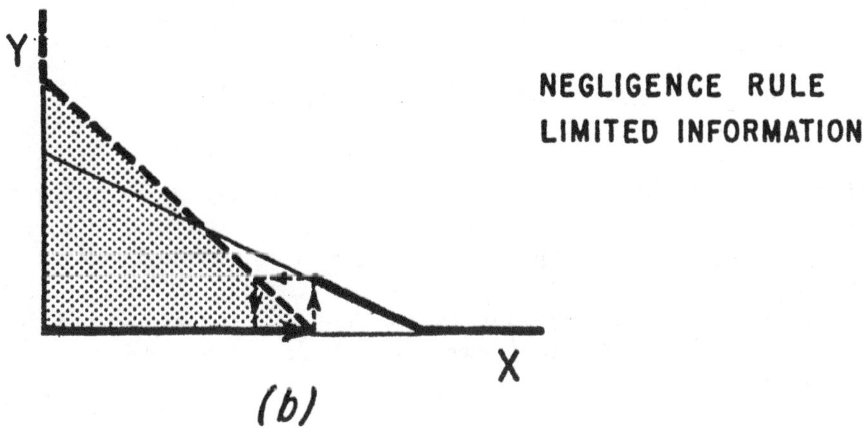

FIGURE 10

Proof: X^e and Y^e are plotted in Figure 11. The shaded area is the area where the injurer is liable. In the unshaded area, the victim is liable. As before, the injurer will choose the least costly place where he is not liable unless X^f lies to the left, *i.e.*, is less expensive. Then he will choose X^f. Similarly, the victim will choose a strategy of the least costly place where she is not liable unless Y^f lies below that point, in which case she will choose Y^f. X^e and Y^e intersect at (X_Ω, Y_Ω). The two equilibria are adjacent from zero to (X_Ω, Y_Ω). In that range the injurer's strategy will be to follow exactly the relative negligence boundary (the expansion path in conventional economic production theory parlance) because by our convention the victim is

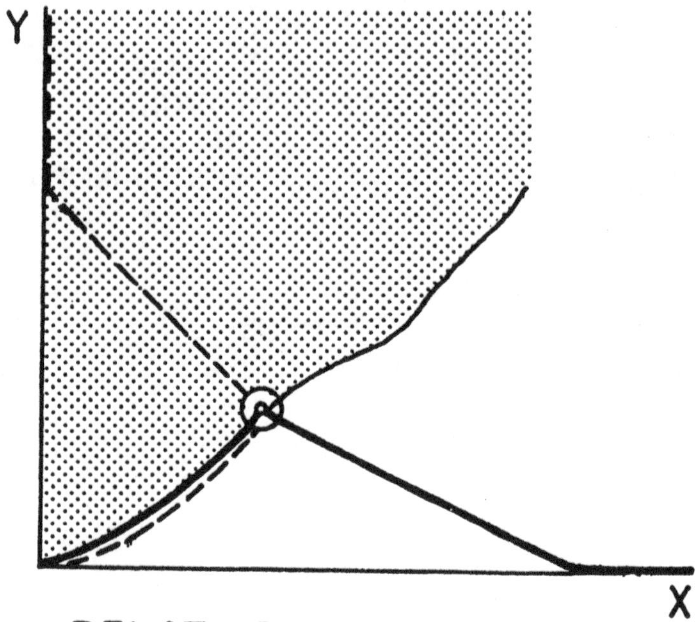

RELATIVE NEGLIGENCE

FIGURE 11

liable exactly on the boundary. The victim's strategy here is, in principle, undefined. There does not exist an optimal strategy in this area, only a limit to the strategy. What she wants to do is to get as close to the boundary as possible without touching it. For any given strategy not on the boundary one can in principle get closer to the boundary, *e.g.*, half as far, but this technical difficulty is not critical since (X_Ω, Y_Ω) is a well-defined equilibrium in any case.

3. *Comparative Negligence*

Rather than analyze completely the comparative negligence rule, I shall simply show that the social optimum is *not* an equilibrium under the comparative negligence rule. At (X_Ω, Y_Ω), $L_x(X, Y) = \frac{1}{2}$ since both parties are equally "negligent." Let Y be fixed at Y_Ω. The injurer will choose X_Ω only if his expected cost is at a minimum there. Now

$$C_x(X_\Omega, Y_\Omega) = W_x X + \frac{1}{2} A[1 - P(X, Y)] \tag{39}$$

which will be the minimum over X only if

$$W_x = \frac{1}{2} A\, P_x(X_\Omega, Y_\Omega). \tag{40}$$

But by the definition of (X_Ω, Y_Ω),

$$W_x = A\, P_x(X_\Omega, Y_\Omega) \tag{41}$$

so (X_Ω, Y_Ω) cannot be an equilibrium.[11]

CONCLUSIONS

In this paper economic analysis has been used to subject a variety of liability rules and standards of care to scrutiny in an abstract setting. It is my contention, which I hope the paper supports, that economic analysis is a useful method of organizing legal questions. It brings out similarities among apparently different legal doctrines, and it allows one to bring a large body of analysis to bear.

The paper first described accident avoidance by two parties in such a way that we could exploit the analogy with the economic theory of production. We used the model thus developed to characterize eight different liability rules discussed in the legal literature, and three variants of the Learned Hand formulation of the standard of care. The literal variant of Judge Hand's formulation we rejected immediately because it was not an incremental standard. Then we analyzed each of the liability rules, using (where appropriate) both of the remaining standards of care, the Incremental Standard and the Limited Information Incremental Standard. The analysis consisted of considering the victim and the injurer as noncommunicating parties in a game played according to liability rules. We identified the noncooperative equilibrium point as the solution for the game and in each case compared it with the social optimum.

To summarize the results, equilibrium for the simple no-liability rule as well as for the simple strict-liability rule did not coincide with the social optimum, nor did equilibrium for the comparative-negligence rule. When the standard of care was the Incremental Standard the social optimum was identical with the equilibrium for the relative-negligence rule, as well as with the equilibrium for all four of the common law negligence-based rules. The standard of care is critical, for, when it was changed to the Limited Information Incremental Standard, the identity between equilibrium and optimality was destroyed.

[11] This argument is not strictly true. We have left out the effect of changing X on the liability rule. It is possible, for particular values of the first and second derivatives, that the neglected effect will exactly cancel out the difference we point to in the text. Though it is possible, in general we cannot expect it to happen.

APPENDIX

The Case of Free Transactions: The Coase Theorem

In the body of the paper I analyzed the polar case where the only transactions that occurred between parties took place in court after an accident occurred. The parties played a game according to whatever liability rules were in force at the time. Here I explore briefly the opposite case, where transactions between parties may be freely arranged at any time. This problem has been examined by many authors since Ronald Coase's important article,[12] although Coase was not entirely or even primarily interested in the case of costless transactions. On the contrary, he was mainly interested in the costless-transaction case as a convenient expository device, a polar case. The Coase Theorem, a phrase coined and used by later writers, states roughly that regardless of the initial assignment of rights, if rights can be traded costlessly, the resulting allocation of rights will be efficient. Furthermore, if the income effects resulting from the transfer of rights can be neglected, the allocation of rights after bargaining will be independent of the initial assignment of those rights.

The questions that we shall ask here are, what transactions will take place between the parties, and what will the final amounts of X and Y be after all transactions have taken place? To set the stage let us define the initial property rights as follows: Xavier, the injurer, has complete control over the amount of X chosen as well as the liability for any bills that the liability rules assess him for. Similarly, Yvonne the victim has complete control over Y and responsibility for any bills that are assessed to her.

In the first situation we shall analyze, where the liability rule in force is no liability, all bills emitted by the liability generator must be paid by Yvonne. We have shown that the equilibrium amounts of X and Y in the absence of transactions will be $X = 0$ and $Y = Y^f(0)$. The expected cost to her is $C_y(0, Y^f(0))$, which is the same as the social cost since Xavier pays nothing.

Free bargaining assures that Yvonne will continue to pay Xavier to increase X until the marginal value of X to Xavier and to Yvonne are equal. The marginal value of X to Xavier is simply W_x; the marginal value to Yvonne is $A\,P_x(X, Y)$. This condition is exactly that in equation (3), and the cost-minimizing choice of Y by Yvonne assures us of (4). These two together are the conditions of the social optimum. The cost to Yvonne of attaining (X_Ω, Y_Ω) is

$$W_y Y_\Omega + A(1 - P(X_\Omega, Y_\Omega)) + \text{Payment to X}. \tag{A1}$$

The payment is undetermined except that it is bounded from below by $W_x X_\Omega$, the minimum amount that Xavier would accept in order to provide X_Ω, and from above by $C_S(0, Y^f(0)) - C_S(X_\Omega, Y_\Omega)$, the maximum that Yvonne would be willing to pay. If X is provided competitively, then the competitive price of X would be W_x and the payment to the injurer would be exactly $W_x X_\Omega$. In any event, the socially optimal amount of X and Y will be chosen and the net social cost will be $C_S(X_\Omega, Y_\Omega)$.

[12] R. H. Coase, *supra* note 1.

The result for the second liability rule, the rule of strict liability, is exactly the same, as is the argument leading to the result, except that the roles of the injurer and victim are reversed. The amount of X and Y chosen this time by Xavier will be X_Ω and Y_Ω, and the net social cost will be $C_S(X_\Omega, Y_\Omega)$. The only difference between the results of the first and second liability rules is a transfer of income. In the first case, when there is no liability, the victim, Yvonne, pays the whole social cost plus a net payment to Xavier. In the case of strict liability, Yvonne not only pays nothing but receives some net payment from Xavier which depends on relative bargaining strength, while Xavier must pay the whole social cost.

I turn now to the case of costless transactions when more complicated liability rules, such as the negligence rule, are in force. Consider the negligence rule. What transactions will take place when they are free?

In the absence of transactions X_Ω and Y_Ω will be chosen, as we have shown above. Thus the victim, Yvonne, can be assured that the injurer will set X at X_Ω without her having to pay a bribe. The benefit of having the injurer increase X above X_Ω would be less than the minimum cost of the increase, W_x. Similarly, Xavier would have no reason to bribe Yvonne to increase Y, because he is not liable. Therefore, under the negligence rule no transactions will take place and the level of avoidance measures chosen by the injurer and the victim will be X_Ω and Y_Ω. The cost to the injurer will be $W_x X_\Omega$, and the expected cost to the victim will be $W_y Y_\Omega + A\,(1 - P(X_\Omega, Y_\Omega))$. The results for the rest of the liability rules can easily be shown to be similar to those of the negligence rule.

[6]

SOME EFFECTS OF UNCERTAINTY ON COMPLIANCE WITH LEGAL STANDARDS

John E. Calfee and Richard Craswell***

WHEN analyzing legal standards, it is convenient to assume that the parties subject to a standard know exactly what behavior is required of them. In practice, however, such certainty is rarely present. This article analyzes some ways in which uncertainty about the application of legal standards can give parties economic incentives to "overcomply" or to "undercomply"—that is, to modify their behavior to a greater or lesser extent than a legal rule requires.

By introducing uncertainty about the legal standard, this article departs from the usual analysis of liability rules found in the law-and-economics literature. Those analyses almost always assume that parties subject to a negligence standard, for instance, know exactly what level of care is legally required.[1] When this assump-

---

* Economist, Federal Trade Commission.

** Assistant Professor, University of Southern California Law Center.

The views expressed are those of the authors and do not constitute an official position of the Federal Trade Commission. The authors are grateful for helpful comments and suggestions from a number of people, including Robert G. Bone, Roger Boner, Erwin Chemerinsky, Frank H. Easterbrook, Ronald R. Garet, Edward L. Golding, James Lacko, Martin L. Levine, Fred S. McChesney, Stephen J. Morse, Ivan P'ng, A. Mitchell Polinsky, Alan Schwartz, Steven Shavell, W. David Slawson, Matthew S. Spitzer, Christopher D. Stone, James F. Strnad, and participants in the faculty workshop at the University of Southern California and the Law and Economics Workshop at Stanford University.

[1] See, e.g., Brown, Toward an Economic Theory of Liability, 2 J. Legal Stud. 323 (1973); Diamond, Accident Law and Resource Allocation, 5 Bell J. Econ. & Mgmt. Sci. 366 (1974); Shavell, Strict Liability versus Negligence, 9 J. Legal Stud. 1 (1980). For an early exception, analyzing legal outcomes that are uncertain because of difficulties in knowing the defendant's level of care, see Diamond, Single Activity Accidents, 3 J. Legal Stud. 107, 123-40 (1974) [hereinafter cited as Diamond, Single Activity Accidents]. For more recent discussions closer to the spirit of this article, see C. Goetz, Cases and Materials on Law and Economics 299-303 (1984); Cooter, Economic Analysis of Punitive Damages, 56 S. Cal. L. Rev. 79, 100-01 (1982); Grady, Proximate Cause and the Law of Negligence, 69 Iowa L. Rev. 363, 403-09 (1984); E. Golding, Economic Efficiency of Liability Rules for Joint Torts with Uncertainty 2 (FTC Bureau of Econ. Working Paper No. 67, Oct. 1982) (copy on file with the Virginia Law Review Association); A. Polinsky, Optimal Liability When the Injurers' Information Is Imperfect (Mar. 1984) (unpublished manuscript) (copy on file with the Virginia Law Review Association). For some other economic analyses of uncertain legal outcomes, see

tion is abandoned, however, many traditional conclusions of the law-and-economics literature can no longer be defended on economic grounds.[2] For example, the proposition that negligence standards ought to be set at the cost-effective level of care becomes difficult to defend; efficiency often will be better served by setting a higher or lower standard. Another common recommendation of the economic literature on deterrence, that penalties should generally be increased when there is some chance of not being punished,[3] turns out to be valid only in a few special cases. All of these conclusions hold even when defendants are risk-neutral.

This article's analysis can be summarized as follows. If the legal standard is uncertain, even actors who behave "optimally" in terms of overall social welfare will face some chance of being held liable because of the unpredictability of the legal rule. More important, these actors can usually reduce that chance by "overcomplying," that is, modifying their behavior beyond the point that would be socially optimal. Potential defendants faced with an uncertain legal standard will consider three effects of taking extra precautions. First, overcompliance may raise a defendant's private costs because compliance is usually expensive. Second, overcompliance may reduce the damages the defendant's behavior causes to others, in turn reducing the amount that the defendant will have to pay if found liable. These costs and gains are social as well as private, however, and should roughly balance out at the optimal level of care (i.e., the level that equates the costs and benefits of further precautions). The third effect, however, is that extra care will increase the chance that the defendant will not be found liable at all, and thereby increase the likelihood that the social costs of the defendant's behavior will be borne by the victim rather than by the defendant. Because the private gain to the defendant is a loss to someone else, this is a pure externality, and not a true social gain

sources cited infra notes 10, 31, 74.

[2] Our analysis in this paper will be entirely economic, examining the effects of uncertainty on the economic incentives of parties subject to a legal rule. Obviously, uncertainty also implicates other issues such as fairness (giving citizens notice of the conduct for which they can be punished) or democratic theory (controlling the discretion of judges or enforcement agencies), but these are beyond the scope of this article.

[3] See infra note 31.

at all. This externality may induce potential defendants to take more than the optimal level of care.[4]

Section I of this article discusses some of the sources of uncertainty about the application of legal rules, and some methods of incorporating legal uncertainty into formal economic models. Section II analyzes the incentives of potential defendants to over- or undercomply when faced with a negligence standard whose application is uncertain. Section III explores the effects of uncertainty in other legal contexts, such as contributory negligence, inaccurate damage awards, and civil penalties or fines. Finally, Section IV discusses possible policy implications of our analysis of uncertain legal rules.

I. Thinking About Uncertainty

The primary focus of this paper is on parties who must choose some course of action from a more or less continuous range of choices. Thus, our analysis might apply to a motorist deciding how fast to drive, a factory owner deciding how much pollution to emit, a seller deciding how soon to deliver ordered merchandise, or a monopolist deciding how far to reduce prices to meet the threat of a new competitor. The article is less concerned with simple "either/or" situations where the actor has only two possible choices (e.g., to murder or not to murder).

Our focus is also limited to situations where there is some level of behavior that would be "optimal" from society's viewpoint, and where that optimal behavior does not lie at the extreme end of the available range of choices. Thus, we do not consider situations where society has no interest in the defendant's behavior, or where the social ideal would involve reducing the level of activity to zero. This last condition eliminates from our analysis activities such as murder or rape,[5] but virtually any activity whose desirability de-

[4] Factors that may lead to undercompliance rather than overcompliance will be discussed infra notes 30-36 and accompanying text.

[5] See, e.g., Stigler, The Optimum Enforcement of Laws, 78 J. Pol. Econ. 526, 527 (1970) (society brands murder, rape and arson as having no utility). Note, however, that even such apparently unmitigated evils as murder may not be undesirable in particular situations, as when there is at least a colorable claim of self-defense. Defining the amount of provocation required to justify killing in self-defense involves drawing a line at some point on a continuum, and there are costs to under- or overestimating that point.

In addition, the costs of enforcement may make it socially optimal to permit some amount of the evil activity, even for unmitigated evils. Societies rarely spend enough on police forces

pends on a balance among competing factors remains for consideration. We will speak most frequently of the balance between economic costs and benefits, but most of our conclusions would apply with only slight modifications[6] to a balance that included other social values.

In the most general terms, uncertainty occurs whenever people cannot be sure what legal consequences will attach to each of their possible courses of action. Such uncertainty arises from a number of sources. Perhaps the most common source (and the easiest to think about) is that people may not know in advance just where the legal standard will be set.[7] For example, it is difficult to predict where a negligence jury will draw the line between "reasonable" and "unreasonable" speeds, or how an antitrust court will distinguish between "predatory" and "competitive" price cuts.[8]

Although much of our analysis can be interpreted in terms of the difficulty in gauging the location of the legal standard, uncertainty may arise from other aspects of the legal process. For example, a fifty-five mile per hour speed limit is a clear legal standard known in advance, but potential defendants cannot be sure that they will be able to convince a court that they complied with that standard. Indeed, there is always some chance of error in the legal system, and at the time defendants must choose their behavior it will usually be hard to predict the kinds of evidence that will be available when they are brought to trial, the persuasiveness of the witnesses and advocates who will participate in that trial, or the temperament of the judge or jury at the time of their decision.[9] Defendants

---

to reduce the crime rate to zero. See, e.g., id. (suggesting that most criminals could be apprehended if society were willing to pay the price). This article assumes, however, that all enforcement expenditures (and the resulting uncertainty as to whether any given violation will be detected) are given exogenously.

[6] See infra note 48 and accompanying text.

[7] Uncertainty about the location of the legal standard would not be a factor under true strict liability, where defendants are liable regardless of their actual behavior. Nonetheless, other sources of uncertainty will still be present (such as uncertainty about being sued, or about the amount of damages that could be assessed). Moreover, many so-called "strict liability" rules (e.g., strict liability for defective products) incorporate an implicit threshold for liability (the product must be "defective"), and this threshold may also be uncertain.

[8] For a discussion of the inherent uncertainties of any legal rule or decision that stem from the difficulties of interpreting the language in which a rule is expressed, see Moore, The Semantics of Judging, 54 S. Cal. L. Rev. 151 (1981).

[9] The legal realists first emphasized these uncertainties. See, e.g., J. Frank, Law and the Modern Mind (1930). For an economic discussion of errors in the factfinding process, see

may also be uncertain whether a private plaintiff or a public prosecutor will bring them to trial at all.[10] Finally, defendants may be uncertain about the size of the damages or fine they might have to pay if found liable.[11]

These uncertainties, taken either singly or together, imply that defendants do not face a simple choice between actions certain to lead to liability and actions bearing no risk of liability at all. Instead, each possible action is accompanied by an associated probability that a defendant will be tried, found liable, and made to pay damages or a fine. There may be regions at either extreme where that probability approaches zero or one. For example, a polluter may know that if he puts out enough smoke to poison an entire city, he is sure to be liable, and that if he emits no smoke at all he is sure not to be liable.[12] But in the more interesting (and, usually, the more relevant) region, the defendant can only attempt to estimate the likelihood of liability at each level of pollution that he has the capacity to emit.

Posner, An Economic Approach to Legal Procedure and Judicial Administration, 2 J. Legal Stud. 399 (1973). Of course, legal errors may be undesirable because they reflect a failure to do justice in the case where the error is made, apart from the prospective effects of errors on incentives facing other potential defendants. Id. at 405. Our focus here, however, is entirely on the incentive effects.

[10] The likelihood that a private plaintiff will file suit should itself be a function of other uncertainties listed here, as plaintiffs' willingness to incur litigation costs partly depends on their chances of winning. These uncertainties may also affect the amount the plaintiff is willing to spend on attorney's fees and other litigation expenses, which should affect the chance that the suit will be successful. This article takes plaintiffs' litigation strategies as fixed—our focus is on the incentives facing defendants *given* the likelihood that they will be sued successfully. For an analysis of some ways in which defendants' compliance decisions may bear on plaintiffs' willingness to file suit, see Ordover, On the Consequences of Costly Litigation in the Model of Single Activity Accidents: Some New Results, 10 J. Legal Stud. 269, 282-88 (1981); Simon, Imperfect Information, Costly Litigation, and Product Quality, 12 Bell J. Econ. 171 (1981); I. P'ng, Private Enforcement of the Law—Incentives Under Asymmetric Information (Stanford Univ. Graduate School of Bus. Research Paper No. 711, Nov. 1983) (copy on file with the Virginia Law Review Association). Some relationships between defendants' compliance decisions and plaintiffs' litigation expenditures are discussed in Pashigian, Regulation, Preventive Law, and the Duties of Attorneys, *in* The Changing Role of the Corporate Attorney 3 (W. Carney ed. 1982).

[11] A. Polinsky, supra note 1, analyzes some effects of this form of uncertainty.

[12] In the terminology of H.L.A. Hart, the rule may have a "core" of certainty and a "penumbra" in which its application is uncertain. See Hart, Positivism and the Separation of Law and Morals, 71 Harv. L. Rev. 593, 606-08 (1958); see also Moore, supra note 8, at 281-92.

These estimates of the likelihood of liability attached to each course of action can be referred to as the defendant's "distribution of probabilities." To the extent that defendants are influenced by the fear of liability, their behavior will be influenced by this distribution of probabilities, rather than simply by the nominal legal standard.[13] Indeed, from the defendant's point of view the rule of law is that distribution of probabilities. Even if the legal system aspires to a more definite standard—such as a pollution standard of *X* parts per million or a negligence standard defined as the cost-effective level of care—liability-conscious defendants will consider the probability that they will or will not be held liable at a greater or lesser level of compliance.

Unfortunately, very little is known about the actual distribution of probabilities for any legal rule. It is plausible, however, to assume that the likelihood of liability increases as a defendant's behavior becomes more dangerous (that is, as its social costs increase).[14] The motorist who causes an accident while driving at eighty miles per hour should, at least, be more likely to be sued and found negligent than a motorist who causes a similar accident while travelling at forty miles per hour. Indeed, a positive (or, at least, non-negative) correlation between the likelihood of liability and the social costs of a defendant's behavior could be the definition of a minimally rational legal system.

---

[13] Potential defendants or their legal advisers may not make exact estimates of these probabilities. They are more likely to rely on a "horse sense" judgment as to how the risk of liability changes as they steer closer and closer to any given line, combined with an equally intuitive judgment as to what constitutes an "acceptable" risk of liability. Thus, the assumption made later in this article—that defendants know the exact distribution of probabilities and make their cost-benefit calculations accordingly—is not intended to describe how legal compliance decisions are actually made. Instead, we analyze the calculations that would be made by a hypothetical perfectly rational individual, and assume that the behavior predicted for the perfectly rational calculator will at least roughly correspond with the behavior of real actors.

Note that this analysis only applies to defendants who are at the margin: those who are influenced to at least some extent by the threat of liability. Defendants who are completely uninfluenced by the risk of liability (e.g., those who gain nothing by violating the standard, or those who would exercise the same care even if there were no standard or if the standard were never enforced) are beyond the scope of this or any other incentive-based analysis. Cf. infra note 85 (suggesting that some ideological behavior may be unresponsive to economic incentives).

[14] Thus, we assume not only that the defendant's behavior can vary along a continuous spectrum, but also that this spectrum can be ordered in terms of the social costs of each possible course of action.

To describe the distribution of probabilities for any legal rule in more detail, we must introduce some conventions and terminology from probability theory. Figure 1 displays three possible distributions of probabilities, known as probability density functions. In each case, the defendant's possible behavior, the amount of pollution he emits, for example, is measured along the horizontal axis, with social costs of the behavior increasing from left to right. The probability of liability at any point on the horizontal axis is represented by the total area under the curve to the left of that point.[16] Thus, each of the three graphs depicts a legal system in which manufacturers who emit little pollution (represented by points toward the left end of each horizontal axis) face a lower probability of liability than do manufacturers with larger emissions (represented by points farther to the right). The rate at which the likelihood of liability increases as defendants' behavior moves from left to right differs, however, under each of the three systems.

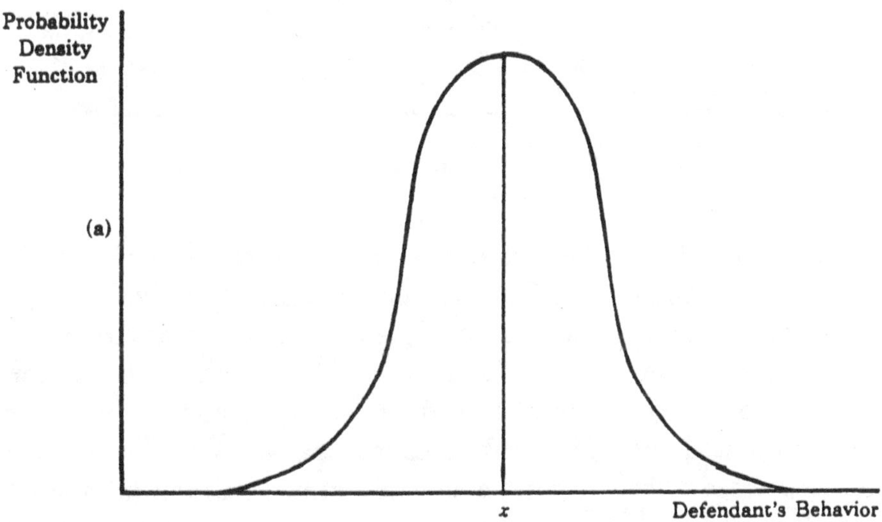

[16] The total area under the density function represents a probability of liability of one. Defendants whose behavior puts them at the midpoint of the curve will have only half of the area under the curve to their left, so the probability of these defendants being held liable will be exactly one-half. Defendants whose behavior puts them far to the right on the horizontal axis (with the entire curve to their left) will be held liable with a probability of one (absolute certainty).

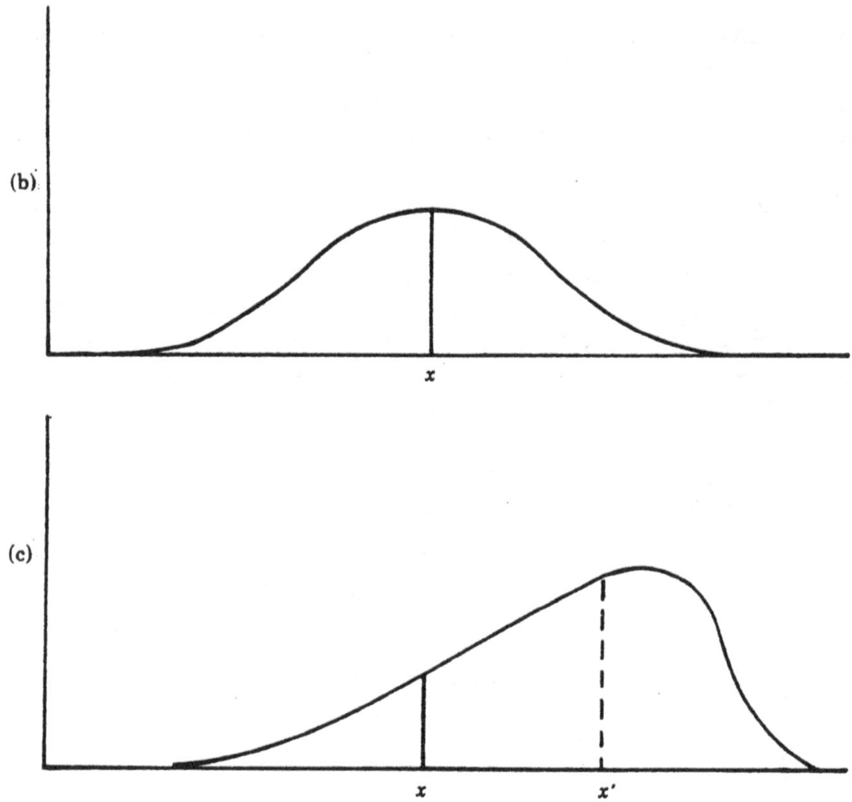

Figure 1

Figure 1 also illustrates two important characteristics of any distribution of probabilities. The first is the spread of the distribution, or its variance, which can be taken as a rough measure of the degree of uncertainty facing defendants. There is much less uncertainty surrounding the legal rule depicted by Graph (a) than the one represented by Graph (b), because the distribution in (a) is clustered more tightly around a central point. In Graph (a) a small reduction in pollution emissions below point x will eliminate any chance of being liable, but the same shift to the left in Graph (b) will still leave some positive risk of liability. A system with an easily measured and strictly enforced legal standard might produce a distribution of probabilities like that in Graph (a). An ambiguous standard ("no unreasonable pollution") or an unpredictable enforcement agency might produce probabilities more like Graph (b).

The second important characteristic of any distribution of probabilities is its mean, or weighted average. In this context, the mean can be characterized as the "average" legal standard, or the defendant's "best guess" about the point at which liability is most likely to attach.[16] Thus, Graphs (a) and (b) reflect different degrees of uncertainty, but each has the same mean, as each is perfectly symmetric about point x. By contrast, the distribution in graph (c) is not only nonsymmetric; it also has a mean to the right of x, at x'. Such a shift in the mean might be produced by any number of causes: a change in the substantive legal rule (e.g., from eight parts-per-million to twenty parts-per-million); a change in enforcement policy (e.g., deciding not to prosecute polluters who appear to be very close to the eight p.p.m. standard); or even a change in procedural or evidentiary rules that makes it harder to convict defendants at low levels of pollution.[17] Graph (c) can therefore be interpreted as reflecting a legal standard that is more permissive (at least in effect) than the standards depicted in Graphs (a) or (b).

This analysis lets us distinguish two possible causes of over- or undercompliance with legal standards. If x were the socially optimal level of pollution, but the distribution of probabilities had a mean to the right of x, defendants might well undercomply by emitting too much pollution. A mean well to the right of x would indicate that regulators had made the effective legal standard too permissive, thereby eliciting more than the optimal amount of pollution.[18] Decreasing the standard's uncertainty, by reducing the

---

[16] One could also refer to the median of the distribution as the defendant's "best guess" about the legal standard. The median is the point at which there is a 50-50 chance that the standard will be set higher or lower. In other words, there is a 50-50 possibility that the defendant will or will not be liable. The mean is a weighted average that weights each chance of a higher or lower standard by how much higher or lower that standard would be. For purposes of this paper, there is usually no need to choose between these two indices, because most references to the mean would be equally applicable to the median. Indeed, the median and mean coincide in the case of symmetric distributions like those depicted in Graphs (a) and (b).

[17] A change in the legal rule reducing the probability of conviction at all values of x (that is, for all defendants, regardless of the level of pollution they produce) would clearly shift the mean of the distribution. Of course, some legal changes might be more ambiguous: they might increase the likelihood of liability for some defendants while reducing it for others. See Posner, supra note 9, at 406 (noting "biased errors" in judicial procedure that affect certain parties more than others).

[18] Similarly, if the mean is to the left of x, defendants might emit less pollution than is

spread of the distribution but preserving the skewed mean, will not cure this cause of over- or undercompliance. Rather, in these cases the mean must be readjusted.[19]

A more interesting case is the distribution of probabilities that is already "correctly" centered—such as Graphs (a) or (b), where x is the optimal level of pollution. Such a distribution might arise if the location of the legal standard was uncertain (what is "reasonable" pollution?), and if the chance that the court would inadvertently set the standard too high was the same as the chance of inadvertently setting it too low. A correctly-centered distribution might also be generated if the legal standard had already been established exactly at the socially optimal level (e.g., a pollution standard of eight p.p.m.), but measuring any defendant's actual level of pollution was difficult, and trials were conducted under a simple "preponderance of the evidence" standard that made the chance of letting off a guilty defendant no greater or less than the chance of convicting an innocent one.[20]

The thesis of this paper is that even in this case most favorable to the legal system—when uncertainties have been centered around the socially optimal level of behavior—potential defendants will still have incentives to behave suboptimally. As the next section will demonstrate, the mere presence of uncertainty about legal outcomes can cause even risk-neutral defendants to over- or undercomply.

II. Uncertainty Under a Negligence Standard

The law attempts to control behavior through many different devices: negligence standards, rules of strict liability, fines or imprisonment, and even bounties and other affirmative incentives. To some extent, the uncertainties discussed in the last section will affect each of these approaches. The effects of uncertainty are more easily illustrated, however, in connection with a traditional negligence standard.

---

socially optimal, because the effective legal standard is too strict.

[19] Such an adjustment may be effected by a change in enforcement policy, evidentiary or procedural rules, or by changing the nominal legal standard until the effective legal standard centers around the optimal level. See supra text accompanying note 17.

[20] Cf. Kaye, The Laws of Probability and the Law of the Land, 47 U. Chi. L. Rev. 34, 36-41 (1979) (examining and rejecting criticisms of models that portray the "preponderance of evidence" standard of proof as permitting a 50% chance of erroneous decision).

Imagine an activity involving a risk of accidents, such as operating a railroad in an urban area with frequent automobile and pedestrian crossings. The railroad can reduce the number of accidents by posting guards at crossings, or by running its trains at slower speeds. Each of these steps is costly, and the railroad would prefer not to take them. Indeed, from a social point of view we would not want the railroad to take *all* possible precautions, because some of them (such as slowing trains to a speed of ten feet per hour) would cost far more than the accidents they would prevent.

A negligence standard establishes a legally required level of precautions, usually defined as "reasonable care." Defendants who violate this requirement are held liable for the costs of all resulting accidents, and defendants who satisfy the requirement are not held liable at all (even though some accidents may still take place after all "reasonable" precautions have been taken).[21] Such a rule is depicted by the heavy kinked line in Figure 2. If the straight line

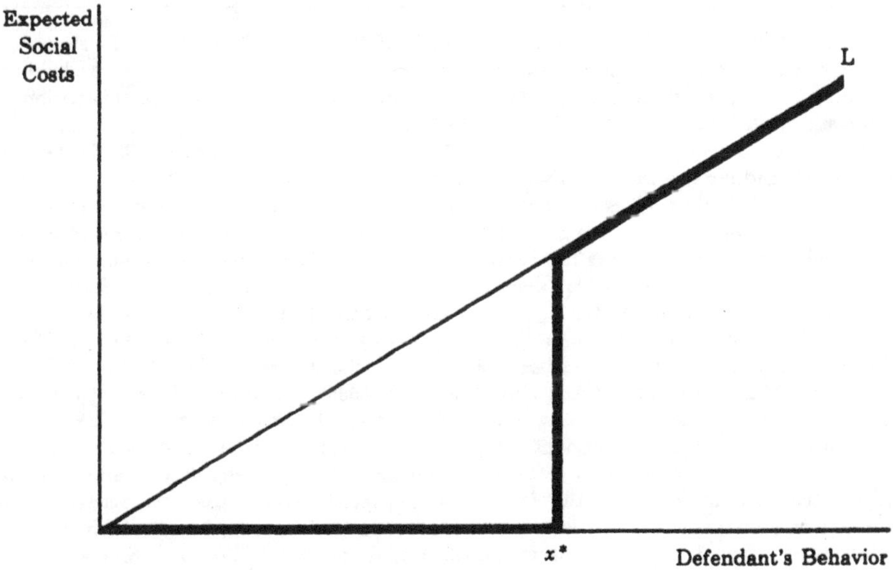

Figure 2

marked L gives the expected losses from accidents at each possible level of speed (to focus on just one precaution), and x^* is the speed

[21] We assume here that all accidents are deemed to have been caused by the defendant's negligence. See infra note 56.

that the legal system deems "reasonable," then railroads that operate at lower speeds will pay nothing in damages, and railroads who operate at higher speeds must pay for all resulting accidents.

When defendants know the exact location of the legal standard (x^*), the sudden jump in liability for damages at x^* gives them a powerful incentive to comply with that standard. Indeed, if x^* is set at the cost-effective level of care under the "Learned Hand Rule"[22] and defendants know this precise level of care, defendants' incentives will be to comply exactly with that standard and act at the socially optimal level.[23]

As discussed earlier, however, defendants will often be uncertain about the legal standard or its application. They may not know how the "reasonable care" standard will be interpreted, whether they will be able to convince a jury that they were actually driving at a lower speed, or whether they will be sued at all.[24] The result is that the railroad faces only a probability that it will have to pay

---

[22] United States v. Carroll Towing Co., 159 F.2d 169, 173 (2d Cir. 1947) (L. Hand, J.) (actor is negligent if the burden of taking adequate precautions is less than the probability of injury multiplied by its severity); see also Brown, supra note 1, at 332-34 (discussion of some ambiguities in the Learned Hand formulation).

[23] See, e.g., Brown, supra note 1, at 341-42; Shavell, supra note 1, at 11-12. "Cost-effective" is defined here as the level that minimizes the sum of accident plus prevention costs, given the level of all variables not included in that calculus. For a variety of what are essentially "second best" reasons, this may not be globally efficient. For example, if reductions in the number of miles driven are not considered as one method of reducing automobile accidents (i.e., if the "walk vs. drive" decision is not subject to a negligence standard), there may be too much driving, and a higher standard of care than would otherwise be efficient might still be called for in order to discourage driving. See Shavell, supra note 1, at 22-23. For a discussion of other "second best" issues, see Polinsky, Strict Liability Versus Negligence in a Market Setting, 70 Am. Econ. Rev. 363 (1980); Polinsky & Rogerson, Products Liability, Consumer Misperceptions, and Market Power, 14 Bell J. Econ. 581 (1983).

We also assume that all defendants are identical, to abstract from any difficulties caused by applying a uniform standard of care to defendants facing different costs and benefits. Alternatively, we could assume that in deciding negligence cases courts attempted to adjust the standard of care to find the level that was most cost-effective for each individual defendant. For a discussion of these issues, see Cooter, supra note 1; Diamond, Single Activity Accidents, supra note 1, at 149-60.

[24] Defendants also may not know how many accidents will actually result at any given speed, but this uncertainty is already reflected in Figure 2, because L represents the *expected* accident losses at each level of speed. If there is a 20% probability of an accident causing $10,000 in damages, and a 10% probability of one causing $50,000 in damages, the expected accident costs are (.20)(20,000) + (.10)(50,000) = $9000. We assume here that defendants accurately estimate these expected accident costs. For a discussion of the consequences of inaccurate expectations regarding damages (or of courts inaccurately measuring those damages), see infra notes 44-53 and accompanying text.

damages if it drives at speeds above x^*. Similarly, it also faces some probability that it might still have to pay damages even if it drives at speeds below x^*.

This situation is depicted in Figure 3, where the curve marked D represents the defendant's expected damage payments—the expected accident costs discounted by the chance that the defendant will not be found liable and therefore will not have to pay damages. Presumably, at very low speeds there is a very small chance that the railroad will be sued and found liable, so on the left side of the graph D is only a small fraction of L. Conversely, at very high speeds the probability of liability should become much higher, so on the right side of the graph D and L are closer together. If there is some outrageously high speed at which suit and liability are a virtual certainty, the D and L curves would then coincide.[25]

One effect of this uncertainty is to eliminate the abrupt jump in expected damage payments at x^*. More generally, the effect is to

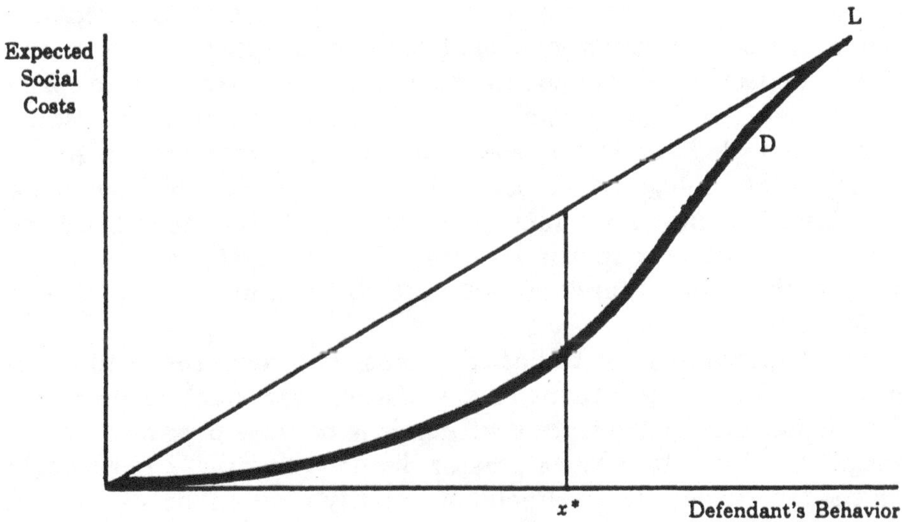

Figure 3

[25] This argument does not require the L function to be linear. It is drawn as a straight line in the graphs in the text purely for expositional convenience.

change the defendant's *marginal* incentives—that is, the marginal benefits the railroad can expect, in the form of lower expected damage payments, from reducing the speed of its trains. The social benefits from reductions in speed are given by the slope of the *L* curve: at this rate expected accident costs decline as speed is reduced. The socially optimal speed is the point at which the marginal benefits from reduced speed equal the marginal costs of reduced speed (e.g., slower delivery times, higher operating costs). This is also the speed the railroad would voluntarily choose if it knew that it would always have to pay the full accident costs (*L*), as it would under a true strict liability system. The railroad would compare the reduction in social costs (the slope of the *L* function) with the increase in its own costs, and choose the speed that minimized the sum of private and social costs.[26]

Under the system depicted in Figure 3, however, the defendant need not be concerned with the true social costs (*L*). Instead, a profit-maximizing railroad will look to the reduction in its expected damage payments (*D*) that would result from reducing the speed of its trains, and compare this to the private costs of reduced speed. If the *D* function is steeper than the *L* function, the reduction in expected damage payments from a given reduction in speed will exceed the reduction in expected social costs (i.e., the reduction in expected accident losses) from the same reduction in speed. That is, the change in expected damage payments will overstate the social benefits of a reduction in speed, and give the railroad too great an incentive to reduce its speed. In short, a *D* function that is steeper than the *L* function will give defendants an incentive to overcomply.

The important point to notice is that, as drawn, the *D* function in Figure 3 *is* steeper than the *L* function over much of its range. This is not due to arbitrary drafting; it is because over much of its range the *D* function has a greater distance to rise. It must begin on the left (where the likelihood of liability is small) as a tiny fraction of *L*, but must rise until it almost equals *L* on the right side of the graph (where the probability of conviction is high). Thus, its average slope over this range must be steeper than that of the *L* function. This does not mean that it will necessarily be steeper at

[26] See, e.g., Shavell, supra note 1, at 11 (arguing that strict liability is perfectly efficient where accidents are "unilateral" or not due to any fault of the victim).

every point,[27] but does mean that there will at least be a substantial range of points at which the legal system will overstate the benefits of increased care to defendants. Thus, even though the D function is always below the L function, indicating that defendants can expect to pay less than the true social costs of their activity, the steepness of the D function may give defendants an incentive to take more than the socially optimal level of care.[28]

This analysis has not assumed anything about the nature of the uncertainty giving rise to the D curve, except that the probability of being held liable increases as the speed of the train increases. The incentive toward overcompliance depicted in Figure 3 could arise even when the distribution of probabilities was perfectly symmetric and centered on the socially optimal speed of x^*. This result seems paradoxical. If the distribution of probabilities is such that the "average" legal standard (or the defendant's "best guess" about the legal standard) is x^*, why would defendants not choose x^* as the standard with which to comply?[29] Why would they ever have an incentive to overcomply, by reducing their speed further?

The answer turns on the balance between two conflicting tendencies.[30] First, even at a speed like x^*, there is still a positive probability that the railroad "won't get caught"—i.e., that it won't be sued, or that if it is sued it won't be found liable. This factor will lead the railroad to discount (or underestimate) the increased accident risks from excessive speeds. If this factor were the only

---

[27] As drawn in Figure 3, the D function is actually less steep than the L function at very small values of x, and only becomes steeper than the L function when x is larger. Thus, if the optimal value of x were extremely small, at that point the D function could *understate* the marginal value of care, and defendants would have an incentive to *undercomply*. See infra notes 35-36 and accompanying text.

[28] One might think that whenever the expected damage payments are less than the true social costs of the defendants' behavior (i.e., whenever D is less than L), the defendant would always undercomply. However, this intuition confuses the absolute levels of D and L with the marginal effect of changes in care on D and L—and it is the marginal effect that will govern defendants' behavior. A similar error was made in much of the economic literature on criminal deterrence, discussed infra notes 63-72 and accompanying text.

[29] For example, some writers have implicitly assumed that defendants would choose to comply with the "average" legal standard. See, e.g., R. Posner, Economic Analysis of Law 431-32 (2d ed. 1977) (arguing that judicial errors in setting legal standards will bias defendants' compliance decisions *only* when errors in one direction are more likely than errors in the other direction).

[30] For a similar exposition (developed independently), see C. Goetz, supra note 1, at 299-303 (1984).

one present, it would lead defendants to undercomply by taking too little care. For example, if the probability of not being held liable were fifty percent regardless of the speed at which the defendant drove, the *D* function in Figure 3 would always be exactly half of the *L* function, and would always have a flatter slope. Economists who have analyzed criminal deterrence note that the possibility of not getting caught reduces the deterrent effect of criminal penalties, and usually recommend that penalties be increased to compensate for that reduction.[31]

But these writers have almost universally ignored the second factor that is also present here. In most situations where the defendant can choose from a range of possible actions, the probability of being held liable varies with the egregiousness of the defendant's conduct.[32] A grossly negligent driver (or flagrant polluter) is surely more likely to be found liable than one driving at a speed that might have been reasonable (or one who is marginally polluting).[33] Whenever this is the case, the reduction in the likelihood of liability—e.g., the ability to reduce from fifty percent to thirty percent

[31] See, e.g., R. Posner, supra note 29, at 167-71; Becker, Crime and Punishment: An Economic Approach, 76 J. Pol. Econ. 169 (1968); Ehrlich, Participation in Illegitimate Activities: An Economic Analysis *in* Essays in the Economics of Crime and Punishment 68-134 (G. Becker & W. Landes eds. 1974); see also infra notes 64-72 and accompanying text.

The usual recommendation of this literature is that damages be made equal to the social costs of the activity divided by the probability of getting caught, so that if there is only a 50% chance of punishment the damage award should be doubled. If there are savings to be had by reducing the probability of punishment (e.g., by reducing expenditures on enforcement personnel), however, these models can imply that the optimal damage multiplier should be even greater. See A. Polinsky & S. Shavell, The Optimal Use of Fines and Imprisonment (Nat'l Bureau of Econ. Working Paper No. 932, July 1982) (copy on file with the Virginia Law Review Association). We ignore this potential for savings in administrative and enforcement costs, see supra note 5; our primary concern is with situations where the probability of punishment can be changed simply by raising or lowering the appropriate legal standard.

[32] Many models of criminal deterrence differ from our analysis by the assumption that the actor faces no chance of punishment if he behaves properly. The conclusions of the traditional deterrence models do not depend, however, on this assumption. In fact, if there is a chance that the innocent will be punished (as well as a chance that the guilty will go free) the traditional models imply that penalties must be made *even greater* to deter violations. See infra note 64-65.

[33] Stigler does note that the social resources devoted to pursuing criminal offenders, and therefore the likelihood of eventual punishment, will often vary with the seriousness of the crime. Stigler, supra note 5, at 529. He explicitly limits his analysis, however, to crimes like murder, where even the least egregious form is still socially undesirable, so that "overcompliance" need not be a concern.

the probability of having to pay any damages—provides the extra incentive to take additional care. In other words, additional care not only produces a marginal reduction in total accident costs, thereby reducing the amount the defendant can expect to pay *if* he is found liable, but also decreases the probability that he will have to pay for *any* of those accident costs.

Although the attractiveness of reducing the risk of exposure to any liability will vary from case to case, we can identify those factors that make the incentive to overcomply strongest. If a defendant is currently exercising the socially optimal level of care x^* and is deciding whether to exercise even more care, the attractiveness of reduced exposure to *any* liability will most obviously depend on the amount he would expect to pay if he is found liable. The defendant's incentive to overcomply will therefore be greatest in activities where the socially optimal level of care still involves a significant risk of costly accidents, and smallest in activities where the optimal level of care is one that reduces expected accident costs almost to zero. In the graph in Figure 2, the incentive to overcomply will tend to increase with the size of the vertical jump at x^*, or with the height of the L curve at that point.[34]

Conversely, the incentive to undercomply will be strongest when: (a) the amount the defendant can save in private costs by taking less care than the optimum is relatively large; and (b) the likelihood of not being found liable, or "not getting caught," is quite high even at levels of care slightly below the socially optimal level.[35] If the distribution of probabilities is symmetric around the optimal level of care x^*, the likelihood of escaping liability at lower levels of care will never be more than fifty percent, and the strength of the incentive to undercomply will be limited. If the private gains from engaging in less care are sufficiently large, however, and if the total expected accident costs at the efficient level of care are not very large (so that the incentive to overcomply is

[34] This incentive to overcomply is reflected in Figure 3: the D function is steeper at high values of x than at very low values. At the extreme left of Figure 3, at values of x where the likelihood of liability is small, the slope of the D function is less than the slope of the L function.

[35] For a mathematical proof of this result, and of the various conclusions stated in the following sections, see R. Craswell & J. Calfee, Incentives to Comply with Uncertain Legal Standards (unpublished manuscript, May 1984) (copy on file with the Virginia Law Review Association).

weak), the incentive to undercomply can still dominate.[36]

These possibilities are illustrated by the numerical examples in Table 1. These figures could represent the probabilities faced by a railroad deciding how fast to run its trains. In each case, the defendant's level of care, expressed in terms of the probability of an accident, is given in the first column, and the expected accident costs are given in the second column. The examples assume that all accidents cost $2,000. The third column gives the defendant's private costs (or profits foregone) required to achieve each level of care; the fourth lists the total social costs (the sum of columns two and three) and designates the efficient, cost-minimizing level of care with an asterisk. The defendant's *private* cost-minimizing level of care is that given in column seven, however, and will depend on the distribution of probabilities given in column five, and on the effect of these probabilities on his expected damage payments given in column six.

In the first example, a comparison of the starred figures in columns four and seven shows that the defendant has an incentive to overcomply, even though the distribution of probabilities in column five is perfectly symmetric and is centered at the optimal level of care. It is socially optimal for the railroad to slow its trains to the point where the probability of an accident is eight percent, because this level of care presents the lowest sum of private and social costs. The defendant, however, faces the lowest private costs when he slows his trains to the point where the chance of accident is seven percent, and thus has an incentive to overcomply. The second example is identical to the first, except that the optimal level of care now involves larger expected accident costs. Perhaps the train in example two runs through a more densely populated area

[36] Professor Grady has recently argued that defendants facing an uncertain negligence standard (who are made to pay the full accident costs if they are found negligent) will *always* overcomply as long as the uncertainty is symmetrical. Grady, supra note 1, at 405-06; see also Grady, A New Positive Economic Theory of Negligence, 92 Yale L.J. 799, 809-12 (1983). However, Grady compares the costs and benefits facing defendants who take too little care without taking into account that the benefits of too little care (reduced expenditures on care) accrue to the defendant with absolute certainty, whereas the costs of too little care (liability for tort damages) may not have to be paid if the defendant is fortuitously found not liable. In other words, Grady's analysis of uncertainty omits the effect of the chance that the defendant might not "get caught," which is precisely the factor that creates the incentive to undercomply.

Table 1

All accidents cost $2000

(1) Prob. of Accident	(2) Expected Accident Costs	(3) Total Prevention Costs	(4) Total Social Costs (2)+(3)	(5) Prob. of Liability	(6) Expected Liability Payments (5)x(2)	(7) Defendant's Expected Costs (3)+(6)
Example (1): Defendant has incentive to overcomply						
11%	$220	$150	$370	99%	$218	$368
10	200	156	356	80	160	316
9	180	165	345	62	112	277
8	160	180	340*	50	80	260
7	140	204	344	38	53	257**
6	120	240	360	20	24	264
5	100	291	391	1	1	292
Example (2): Defendant has greater incentive to overcomply						
15%	$300	$150	$450	99%	$297	$447
14	280	156	436	80	224	380
13	260	165	425	62	161	326
12	240	180	420*	50	120	300
11	220	204	424	38	84	288
10	200	240	440	20	40	280**
9	180	291	471	1	2	293
Example (3): Defendant has incentive to undercomply						
5%	$100	$141	$241	99%	$99	$240
4	80	150	230	80	64	214
3	60	162	222	62	37	197**
2	40	180	202*	50	20	200
1	20	207	227	38	8	215
0	0	246	246	20	0	246

*socially optimal level of care
**defendant's cost-minimizing level of care

than the train in example one. Because of higher expected accident costs, the benefit to the defendant of taking extra precautions is magnified, and the incentive to overcomply becomes stronger.

In the third example, the efficient level of care involves very low expected accident costs. The defendant's private prevention costs in column three also rise at a steeper rate, so that the private gains from exercising less care are now larger. The train may be running across unpopulated areas on long distance trips, and any decrease in speed may significantly raise the railroad's costs. In this situation, column seven indicates that the defendant will have an incentive to undercomply. Notice, though, that the optimal level of care in this example involved such a small risk of accidents (two percent) that the distribution of probabilities in column five had to be truncated, because the probability of an accident in column one can never fall below zero. In other words, the only way to induce undercompliance in this context is to make the optimal probability of an accident extremely low relative to the degree of uncertainty reflected in the legal system.[37]

As a final point, it should be noted that these results do not depend on the defendants being risk-averse, or having a particular aversion to uncertainty. The figures in Table 1 were calculated on the assumption that defendants were perfectly risk-neutral and cared only about the expected value of their liability payments. If defendants are risk-averse, the incentive to overcomply will generally be even stronger.[38]

III. Effects of Uncertainty in Other Legal Settings

A. *Contributory Negligence*

Thus far, we have assumed that only the defendant's conduct could affect expected accident costs. Often those costs can also be affected by victims (potential plaintiffs). As a result, the legal system often makes recovery conditional on the plaintiff's compliance with such legal rules as mitigation-of-damages, the "clean hands" doctrine, or traditional contributory negligence. Whenever there is any uncertainty involved in the application of these doctrines, as there generally is, one must then ask about the effect of uncertainty on plaintiffs' incentives to behave in a socially optimal way.[39]

---

[37] Of course, if the probability of accidents were literally zero, as in the last row of Example 3, then no accidents would ever occur, and the question of the defendant's negligence would never arise. However, all of the probabilities in column six are conditional probabilities—that is, the probability that a defendant would be found negligent *if* a court were ever called upon to decide that issue. Those who still find this troubling can reinterpret the bottom row of Example 3 as stating that there would still be a 20% chance the defendant would be found negligent, if an accident ever took place, even if his care was so great that it reduced the risk of accidents to a level arbitrarily close to zero.

[38] This intuition was expressed in Ellis, Fairness and Efficiency in the Law of Punitive Damages, 56 S. Cal. L. Rev. 1, 47-48 (1982) (risk aversion causes the deterrence of socially beneficial activities), and in Discussion, Symposium: Punitive Damages, 56 S. Cal. L. Rev. 155, 161 (1982). See R. Craswell & J. Calfee, supra note 35, at 41-42 (mathematical proof).

[39] E. Golding, supra note 1, analyzes the closely-related issue of the effect of uncertain legal outcomes on the compliance decisions of joint tortfeasors. The only difference is that a

For the most part, the effects on plaintiffs' incentives are similar to those just discussed for defendants. Increased care by the plaintiff will marginally reduce the expected accident losses that the plaintiff will be left to bear if recovery is denied because he is found contributorily negligent. More important, increased care will also reduce the likelihood of being deemed contributorily negligent, and therefore will reduce the possibility of the plaintiff having to bear any of the accident losses at all. If the expected accident losses at the efficient level of care are sufficiently large, the hope of reducing the risk of bearing those losses will lead potential victims to take more than the efficient level of care.[40]

Interestingly, only after uncertainty is admitted into the analysis can an economic rationale for contributory negligence be developed. If defendants face no uncertainty they will always exactly comply with the applicable negligence standard.[41] Victims, then, will always have to bear their own accident costs, and should therefore have every incentive to take cost effective precautions even without the threat of a contributory negligence defense. Thus, economic models that did not introduce uncertainty implied, although the point was rarely emphasized, that a contributory negligence defense is completely unnecessary in an otherwise efficient negligence system.[42]

This analysis changes once legal outcomes are admitted to be uncertain. Uncertainty about the application of the negligence standard creates some chance that defendants might be found liable, and thus, some chance that victims will not have to bear accident losses. This chance of not having to suffer the consequences of their carelessness gives victims too little incentive to take care, and creates an economic justification for some form of contribu-

contributory negligence rule applies when the plaintiff and the defendant can each influence accident costs, but joint tortfeasor rules apply when there are two defendants who can each influence accident costs.

[40] See R. Craswell & J. Calfee, supra note 35, at 9 (mathematical proof).

[41] See supra note 23 and accompanying text.

[42] See, e.g., Brown, supra note 1, at 340-42; Shavell, supra note 1, at 18 n.25. Contributory negligence is of course much more important if the defendant is otherwise strictly liable. In such a system the victim's incentives are exactly analogous to the defendant's incentives under a simple negligence standard; the victim will have to bear the accident costs if and only if his behavior fails to comply with some legal standard. The analysis in Section II of the defendant's incentive to overcomply therefore applies with equal force to potential victims under a strict liability system that provides a defense of contributory negligence.

tory negligence rule.[43]

B. Biased Damage Awards

In Section II we assumed that all damage awards (or at least, the defendant's estimate of the likely damage award) equalled the true social costs caused by the defendant's activity. This assumption may be inaccurate, but the effects of systematic biases in the calculation of damages can easily be incorporated into the framework developed here.[44]

If the expected damage awards are too high or too low by a constant amount, then the amount defendants expect to pay if found liable will actually be the true accident costs L, plus or minus some constant K. In Figure 2, the vertical jump at x^* would be raised (or lowered) by a fixed amount. As discussed in Section II, these changes will increase or decrease the defendant's incentives to take more care by increasing or decreasing private gains from reducing the probability of being held liable for any damages. Indeed, when the examples are reinterpreted as depicting increases and decreases in damages that will be assessed (column two) rather than changes in the socially optimal level of care (column one), the three examples in Table 1 illustrate this point perfectly. Excessive damage awards will not always produce overcompliance and insufficient awards will not always lead to undercompliance,[45] for, as already shown, uncertainty can produce incentives to over- or undercomply even when damages are calculated exactly. Nevertheless, excessive damage awards will tend to increase any incentives to overcomply, and inadequate damage awards should weaken those incentives or increase the incentives to undercomply.[46]

Again, this common sense conclusion could not be supported

---

[43] See R. Craswell & J. Calfee, supra note 35, at 15-16 (mathematical proof).

[44] Systematic bias means that defendant's estimates of the likely damage awards are known to be either too high or too low. A. Polinsky, supra note 1, analyzes what might be called unbiased error, where defendants form an incorrect estimate of the potential damage award but their estimate has an equal chance of being too high or too low.

[45] Posner makes the standard, but incorrect, argument that damages above or below the actual social losses will automatically lead to over- or underdeterrence. R. Posner, supra note 29, at 88-93, 142-43.

[46] Similar conclusions hold if damages are multiplied by a constant, rather than added to by a constant. Multiplication by constants greater than one will increase the incentives to overcomply, and multiplication by constants less than one will reduce these incentives. See R. Craswell & J. Calfee, supra note 35, at 12-14 (mathematical proof).

without admitting uncertainty into the analysis. If the legal standard were set at the optimal level of care, and defendants knew exactly what they had to do to comply with the standard, then their incentive would always be to comply exactly with that standard as long as the damages assessed were anywhere close to the true social costs.[47] Indeed, because in such a world defendants would never choose to be liable, the damages could be increased to infinity without inducing any overcompliance. Only when uncertainty has been introduced will excessive damage awards tend to increase, and inadequate awards tend to reduce, the incentives to overcomply.

Even these simple propositions should be treated with some care, moreover, for they rest on the assumption that damages were biased upward or downward by some constant. This assumption might be plausible if the error were due to the improper inclusion or exclusion of certain elements of the victim's damages, such as not allowing recovery for litigation costs or for unquantifiable harms, or if the defendant's conduct injured broader social values that were not counted in the damages awarded to individual plaintiffs.[48] An equally plausible assumption, though, is that damages tend to be much more sharply reduced, or less sharply increased, for careful defendants than for careless defendants. For example, juries may tend to be more sympathetic toward the former than the latter, and judges may be more inclined to award punitive damages[49] or to resolve ambiguities in measuring damages against defendants whose conduct seems more flagrant.[50] Indeed, the principles of comparative negligence or comparative fault could be regarded as attempts to make these differential damage awards more

[47] See Cooter, supra note 1, at 80-85 (under a negligence standard, actual liability must be far less than the actual costs of the injurer's behavior before the injurer will reduce his precautions below the legal standard of care).

[48] If the defendant's conduct produced some social benefits that were not deducted from his liability for damages, the damage awards would then systematically overstate the social costs of his behavior.

[49] See, e.g., Ellis, supra note 38, at 3-12 (discussing rationales for punitive damages).

[50] See, e.g., Restatement (Second) of Contracts § 352 comment a (1978) (doubts as to the amount of damages are "generally resolved against the party in breach"). Note that an intuitive causal connection may also run in the opposite direction. If the judge or jury believes that the defendant's conduct has caused great damage, they may be more likely to deem the defendant negligent or in breach of contract.

explicit.[51]

The effects of these "biases"[52] are very similar to the effects of the uncertainties already examined. Figure 4 shows what two such systems might look like. In each case the expected damage payments, given by D_1 or D_2, are far lower than the true social costs L for careful defendants. Careless defendants, however, face damage awards with an expected value much closer to L. In the case of D_2, which corresponds to punitive damages, the damage award actually exceeds L. In either case, the result is to increase the average slope of the expected damage curve, and to overstate the benefits to defendants of being more careful. Thus, even if damage awards are *always* underestimated, as in the case of D_1, when the degree of underestimation increases with the defendant's care the incentives

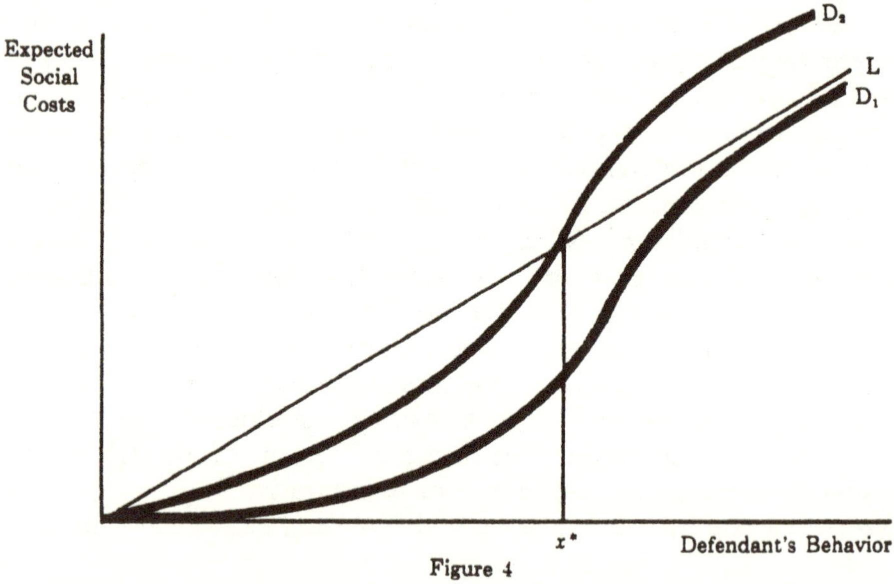

Figure 4

[51] The "more likely than not" causation rule can have a similar effect. Under this rule, if the defendant's negligence had so small an impact on the risk of an accident that other factors are more likely to be the cause, the defendant must pay nothing at all. If the defendant's negligence is more egregious, though, it is more likely to be deemed the cause of the accident, so such a defendant may have to pay for all resulting accident costs. For a detailed analysis of the circumstances under which this rule can induce overcompliance, see S. Shavell, Uncertainty over Causation and the Determination of Civil Liability (Harvard Inst. of Econ. Research Discussion Paper No. 997, Aug. 1983) (copy on file with the Virginia Law Review Association); see also Grady, supra note 1, at 410; Landes & Posner, Causation in Tort Law: An Economic Approach, 12 J. Legal Stud. 109, 123 (1983).

[52] Such awards are biased in the sense that they do not equal the true social costs of each defendant's behavior. See supra note 44.

to overcomply are increased.[53] A defendant performing at the optimal level (x^*) but faced with the expected damage curve D_1 can reduce his expected costs by overcomplying, even though expected damages are less than social losses at every level of compliance.

C. *Fines and Marginal Damage Rules*

The discussion to this point has focused on private liability rules, but much of what has been said can also be applied to fines imposed by the regulatory system. For example, if a railroad's speed were governed by a municipal ordinance or ICC regulation rather than by the negligence system, and if the fine for railroads caught exceeding the optimal speed just equalled the expected social costs at that speed, uncertainty about enforcement of the fine would have the same effect as uncertainty about application of the negligence standard. Similarly, if the fine were set at a level above or below the true social costs, the effect would be the same as the effect of excessive or inadequate damage awards. Of course, the contours of the uncertainty may be different. Administrative agencies may be more or less likely to make mistakes than courts, and discretionary enforcement by public administrators may be more or less predictable than discretionary lawsuits by private plaintiffs. Whatever the level of uncertainty, though, the qualitative effects of that uncertainty should be basically the same.

One type of liability system has not yet been addressed. It is not uncommon for fines to rise gradually from zero as the offender's behavior gets further from the legal limit—parking and library fines are two common examples. Even though there may be some social costs involved in just barely complying with the legal standard (e.g., occupying a parking space for the full two hours, or keeping a book out of circulation for the full two weeks), the defendant is, in effect, given a legal right to inflict those costs on society.[54] More important, if he transgresses the legal standard he does not then become liable for the full social costs, but only for

[53] See R. Craswell & J. Calfee, supra note 35, at 12-14 (mathematical proof).

[54] Of course, defendants will usually have paid for this "right" to inflict the social costs involved in barely complying with the legal standard, in the price that they paid for the parking space or the library card. Once that price is paid, however, it is usually a sunk cost for the defendant, and it will have no further effect on his incentive to comply with the legal standard. But see infra note 58 (discussing the effect of a defendant's conduct on future prices).

the marginal increase in social costs over and above those that he had a right to inflict.

Some contract damage rules fit this pattern. Late delivery of goods will often injure a buyer if the market is falling and the buyer was buying for resale, or if the buyer is delayed in putting the goods to productive use. Even delivery on the date specified in the contract imposes some "losses" on the buyer, in the sense that the buyer has lost the greater benefits he could have realized had the goods been delivered early. The seller who breaches by delivering late, however, is liable only for those losses attributable to the delay between the contract date and the date of actual delivery.[55] Although the seller in this example has acted wrongfully, he is not made to compensate the buyer for what was lost by not getting an even earlier delivery; the seller had a right to inflict this loss on the buyer. By contrast, a tort defendant deemed to have acted negligently is typically charged the full cost of all resulting accidents, even though he had a legal right, under the negligence standard, to inflict a "reasonable" risk of accidents on the rest of society.[56]

---

[55] See U.C.C. § 2-714 (1978) (damages for breach of warranty are the difference between the value of goods accepted and their value if they had conformed to the warranty).

[56] This distinction is partly an artifact of the legal concept of causation, as applied to probabilistic events. If a defendant negligently increases the risk of an accident from 10% to 30%, the legal system typically deems him to have "caused" all resulting accidents, just as if he had increased the risk from zero to 100%. An incremental damage rule applied to such accidents would charge the defendant not the full costs of those accidents, but only 20% of all accident costs, that is, the difference between the level of risks that he actually produced and the risks that he should have produced. For a discussion of such a rule in the context of the traditional assumption that there is no uncertainty about the legal system's application of that rule, see Landes & Posner, supra note 51, at 123-24; S. Shavell, supra note 51. Grady, supra note 1, presents a contrasting view of causation rules, but limits his analysis to cases where the court knows with certainty whether a given accident would have occurred if the defendant had not been negligent. See id. at 410 (discussing some effects of relaxing this assumption).

The probabilistic character of some losses can also affect the measure of damages under contract law. For example, if optimal precautions by a seller could reduce the chance of late delivery to 10%, but the seller has only promised "best efforts" or "workmanlike performance" to assure prompt delivery, the seller will not be liable at all unless he fails to take the optimal precautions. However, if he does fail to take optimal precautions, he will usually be held liable for the full difference between the value of late delivery and the value of timely delivery. The damages will not be measured by the difference between the value of late delivery and the value of a 90% chance of timely delivery, even though the latter is all that was actually promised under the "best efforts" clause. Thus, even in this context, courts appear to be applying a full damage rule rather than an incremental damage rule. We conjecture (although this topic could clearly benefit from further research) that incremental damage rules tend to be used primarily when courts know with certainty that the accident,

An incremental damage rule would correspond, if there were no uncertainty, to the heavy, bent line in Figure 5. The line L still

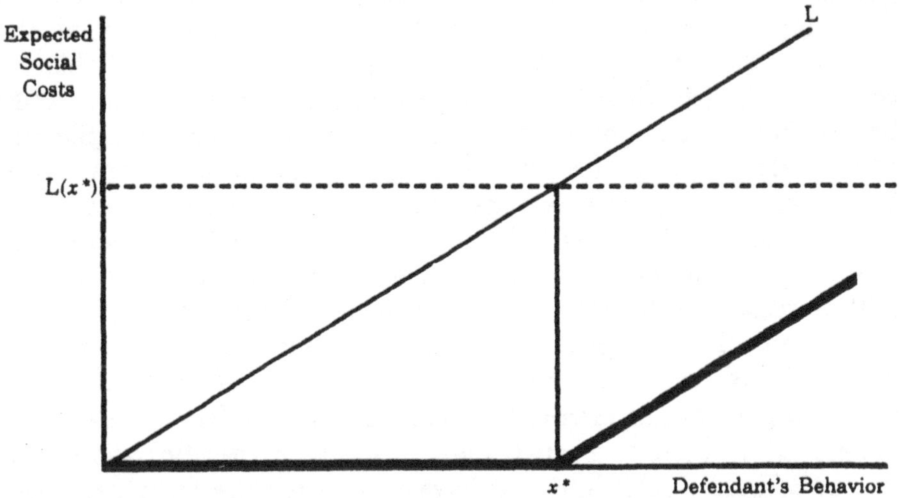

Figure 5

represents the total losses from increasingly careless behavior (e.g., later and later delivery). The defendant pays nothing at all if he complies with the applicable legal rule, so the heavy line is equal to zero everywhere to the left of x^*, just as under the negligence standard shown in Figure 2.[57] Unlike a negligence standard, however, if the defendant steps over the legal standard he pays only the *extra* losses inflicted by his transgression. Thus, to the right of x^* the heavy line measures only the incremental damages (i.e., the extent to which increased carelessness causes L to rise above $L(x^*)$). Under a full liability rule, then, the burden of the "inframarginal" accident costs (those that might have occurred even if due care had been exercised) is placed on negligent defendants. Under an incremental liability rule those losses are left on victims, notwithstanding the defendants' violation of the legal standard.[58]

---

late delivery, or other undesirable event would not have taken place if the defendant had acted optimally.

[57] See supra p. 974.

[58] In a contractual setting, these losses may eventually be passed back to the defendant, if noncompliance injures his reputation and reduces the prices he can charge in the future. If this reputation mechanism worked perfectly, however, the parties would not need to commit to binding delivery dates or to include any other binding terms in their contract. If reputa-

In this situation, uncertainty about application of the legal standard (unbiased uncertainty) can only create incentives to undercomply. As we discussed in Section II, the incentive to overcomply stems from the effect of increased care on reducing the chance of having to pay for any damages. The strength of this incentive will vary with the size of the damage payments that would be assessed for a slight violation of the legal rule (i.e., with the size of the vertical jump at x^* in Figure 2). Under the rule depicted in Figure 5, however, the damages charged to a defendant who just barely violates the legal rule approach zero, so the incentive to overcomply disappears. True, increased carelessness above x^* will still increase the defendant's risk of being held liable, but at worst he will only have to pay the marginal increase in damages caused by his carelessness. This risk will be more than offset by the marginal gains from not having to spend as much on care, because the defendant will get to keep these gains with certainty (whether or not he is held liable) and will have to pay for the marginal losses only if he is in fact found liable.[59]

It is interesting to note that this incentive would disappear if defendants, in addition to having to pay for any marginal increase in social costs caused by their carelessness, were also paid the value of any marginal *reduction* in social costs due to their exercising *more than* the legally required level of care. One could imagine a system under which citizens were paid bonuses for vacating parking spaces or returning library books before the required time, or

---

tions are perfect, then the market will provide all the appropriate incentives to perform without legally binding commitments. Recent theoretical work implies, however, that even when reputations are perfect there may still be costs to relying on reputations to enforce contractual performance. Thus, it may still be more efficient to rely on enforceable legal standards. See Farber, Reassessing the Economic Efficiency of Compensatory Damages for Breach of Contract, 66 Va. L. Rev. 1443, 1464-68 (1980) (information costs, free riders, and the indirect costs of conservative corporate policy make informal performance incentives socially inefficient). For more formal economic models, see Klein & Leffler, The Role of Market Forces in Assuring Contractual Performance, 89 J. Pol. Econ. 615, 628, 634-35 (1981) (establishing effective reputations may require firms to make otherwise unnecessary investments in nonsalvageable capital); C. Shapiro, Premiums for High Quality Products as Rents to Reputation 37-37A (FTC Bureau of Econ. Working Paper No. 43, Aug. 1980) (the resulting supramarginal prices may impose welfare losses that enforceable quality standards could reduce) (copy on file with the Virginia Law Review Association).

[59] See R. Craswell & J. Calfee, supra note 35, at 8-10 (mathematical proof). Grady reaches similar conclusions regarding an incremental damage rule (or what he terms a "P*-cutoff rule"). Grady, supra note 1, at 407.

where a seller who delivered goods earlier than required was entitled to bring an action in quantum meruit to recover any benefit conferred by him on the buyer.[60] Under such a system, the defendant who chose to exercise less care would benefit by not having to spend as much, but would lose by reducing his chance of being able to receive compensation, and at the margin these effects would exactly cancel out.[61]

[60] In some instances, parties are compensated for taking such extra measures. Some localities grant transferable development rights (TDRs) to land owners who do not fully exploit the potential development of an existing site that contains, for example, a landmark building. In return for preserving the socially desirable use of the site by utilizing only a fraction of the site's potential development, the land owner is permitted to transfer his unused rights to expand development on other sites. See J. Dukeminier & J. Krier, Property 1201-03 (1981), and sources cited therein. Similarly, under the "compliance bubble" policy of the Clean Air Act, a reduction in emissions from one smoke stack gives the emitter credit against emissions from other stacks in the same facility. See 48 Fed. Reg. 50,766-67 (1981).

[61] In graph form, such a rule would be represented by the heavy line in the Figure 6, where the portion of the line falling below zero indicates a payment from the plaintiff to the defendant rather than from the defendant to the plaintiff. For a mathematical analysis of the incentives created by such a rule, see R. Craswell & J. Calfee, supra note 35, at 19-21.

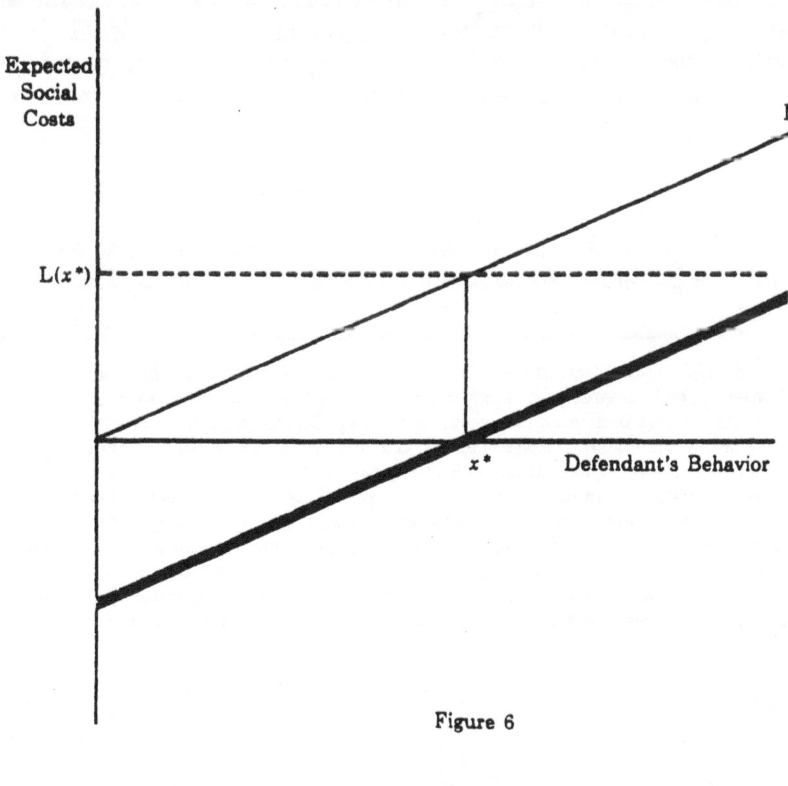

Figure 6

Of course, the administrative costs of such a system might by themselves be prohibitive, and could be objected to on distributional or other grounds.[88] A simpler correction would be to increase the level of damages so that the schedule of fines no longer increased marginally from zero. Increasing the level of damages up to the true social costs L could lead to the opposite problem, however, by creating an incentive to overcomply. In general, though, there will be some positive level of damages for marginal violations that will be just sufficient to give defendants proper incentives in the face of uncertainty. This may explain why many fine schedules do not literally rise marginally from zero, but instead start with an initial jump (a positive fine for even the slightest violation) and rise marginally thereafter.

IV. Policy Implications

As the preceding paragraphs suggest, it is theoretically possible to make adjustments in the legal system that would correct for any incentives to over- or undercomply. It is difficult to recommend such adjustments with confidence. As mentioned earlier, very little is known about the shape of the probability distribution for any actual legal rule, or about how various changes in the legal system would affect those distributions. Despite this cautionary note, though, we now examine some possible policy implications of our analysis.

A. *Damage Multipliers*

One possible adjustment for uncertainty, the idea that penalties should be increased by some multiple of the true social costs when-

[88] One might also object, at least in contractual settings, that if a seller wants to deliver earlier he ought to negotiate for a higher price, rather than attempting to collect that value through the courts in a quantum meruit action. Cf. R. Posner, supra note 29, at 39-40 (a trespasser may be ejected despite evidence that his use of the property is more economical than the owner's; this rule will force the trespasser to try to purchase the rights to use the property). This objection misses the point. If reputations are not perfect, see supra note 58, so that the parties prefer to write an enforceable performance standard into their contract, they may also prefer to add a clause compensating for overperformance, to eliminate any incentives to underperform that could otherwise result. The more telling objection to such a compensation clause is the administrative cost of making the compensatory payments. This suggests that parties would do better to look for some other method of correcting any incentives to underperform.

ever there is some chance that the offender will not get caught, has already gained wide acceptance in the economic literature on deterrence. Jeremy Bentham may have been the first to observe that the chance of not being punished will reduce the deterrent effect of any fine or punishment, and to conclude from this that "the more deficient in certainty a punishment is, the severer it should be."[63] Subsequent writers have developed formal economic models that seem to confirm this intuition.[64] As a result, this principle has been invoked not only to justify larger criminal penalties for difficult-to-detect offenses,[65] but also to support related concepts such as punitive damages for certain kinds of torts,[66] the treble damage rule of antitrust law,[67] and proposals to increase the damages available for breach of contract.[68]

This principle does not apply, however, to a number of important cases. Even when the probability of punishment is less than one, if that probability declines as defendants take more care, then defendants may tend to overcomply. In such a case, increasing the expected fine or damage award would only increase overdeterrence, exacerbating the problem rather than curing it.[69]

---

[63] J. Bentham, The Theory of Legislation 325 (1931).

[64] The seminal article is Becker, supra note 31. See also Stigler, supra note 5.

[65] See generally R. Posner, supra note 29, at 167-71 (combining probability of prosecution with severity of offense and costs of detection to determine the optimal level of punishment).

[66] See Ellis, supra note 38, at 52.

[67] Becker, supra note 31, at 199 n.55; cf. R. Posner, Antitrust Law: An Economic Perspective 223-27 (1976) (because many antitrust violations have probabilities of detection greater than one-third, treble damages may be inappropriate); Easterbrook, Predatory Strategies and Counterstrategies, 48 U. Chi. L. Rev. 263, 329-30 (1981) (arguing for a multiple of less than three for categories of offenses whose probability of conviction is higher than one-third).

[68] See, e.g., Farber, supra note 58, at 1462-64 (increasing awards reduces two inefficiencies of contract performance: cheating by the seller and detection costs to the buyer); I. P'ng, Damages for Breach of Contract in the Presence of Moral Hazard (October 1983) (unpublished manuscript) (copy on file with the Virginia Law Review Association). As P'ng proves mathematically, if there is both a probability that a "guilty" defendant will not be punished and a probability that an "innocent" defendant will be punished, the optimal multiplier should be one divided by the difference between these two probabilities. See also R. Posner, supra note 29, at 424-25 (if there is a probability that a guilty defendant will not be punished and a probability that an innocent defendant will be punished, the deterrent effect of the law will be reduced). This conclusion still depends crucially on the assumption that the defendant has only two discrete choices: to violate or not to violate the legal standard. See infra note 70 and accompanying text.

[69] A variable multiplier that multiplied each defendant's damages by one divided by that

The Benthamite argument that damages should always be increased to reflect the average probability of not being caught appears to be valid only in three types of situations: (1) when the conduct in question involves a pure either/or choice rather than a continuous range of choices with the optimum falling somewhere in the middle, so that overcompliance is meaningless;[70] (2) when the conduct can vary over a continuous range, but the probability of being sued and found liable is the same regardless of the conduct actually chosen by the defendant; or (3) when the conduct in question falls into one of the categories analyzed in this paper where undercompliance rather than overcompliance is more likely. As discussed in Section II, undercompliance may be more likely when the damages for even the slightest violation (that the plaintiff would like to avoid having to pay) are extremely small. Undercompliance would be particularly likely under any form of "incremental damage rule," under which the fines or damage awards increased gradually from zero, because in that case there would be *no* expected damages for slight departures from the optimal level of care.[71]

In any of these situations, then, some augmentation of damages may be economically justified. Yet many regulatory and private law subjects do not fit these special cases. Antitrust violations,

---

defendant's chance of being found liable would actually give defendants the correct incentives. See R. Craswell & J. Calfee, supra note 35, at 15-16 (mathematical proof). Nevertheless, this rule implies that the worst offenders (whose chances of being found liable are presumably quite high) should be given the smallest multipliers, while offenders who barely stepped over the legal line (and who therefore stood a much better chance of not being found liable) must have their damages multiplied by a much larger number. Perhaps because of this paradox, or because of the difficulty of calculating each defendant's individual multiplier, the multiplier principle is usually only invoked to support the idea of a constant multiplier, such as the treble-damage rule of antitrust.

[70] If there are only two choices, and the choice of committing the act has been prohibited by society, then the other choice must be the social optimum. Defendants can either exactly comply with the optimum by not committing the act, or undercomply by committing the undesirable act, but overcompliance is impossible. Overcompliance is also impossible where the conduct can vary over a continuum (e.g., thefts of greater and greater amount) but every point on that continuum is socially undesirable. The social optimum is still for the defendant not to commit the act at all. But cf. supra note 5 (indicating that the costs of enforcing a standard of zero may make the optimal attainable level of behavior greater than zero).

[71] Thus, when an incremental damage rule is used the recommendation of the deterrence literature (i.e., multiplying the marginal costs by one divided by the probability of punishment) will give defendants exactly the right incentives. See R. Craswell & J. Calfee, supra note 35, at 17-18 (mathematical proof).

speeding, pollution, and most negligent behavior, for example, all involve choices along a continuous spectrum, with an optimal level of behavior that is determined by a balancing of desirable and undesirable effects, so that overcompliance is both possible and socially costly. In these situations, arguments that penalties equal to the social costs of defendants' behavior will always lead to underdeterrence and therefore should be increased must be taken with a good deal of salt. A better rule in many cases might be to reduce the damage awards to compensate for what would otherwise be an incentive to overcomply. For example, the routine exclusion from damage awards of such items as attorney's fees or subjective losses may be less harmful than is often supposed, and could even be beneficial.

Such a recommendation cannot be unqualified, because it would be difficult, if not impossible, to calculate the size of the optimal adjustment. Moreover, the entire analysis of this article has been limited to cases where the nominal legal standard, or the mean of the distribution, was otherwise "correctly" centered.[72] If the legal standard were for some reason far below the optimal level of care, for instance, defendants could overcomply with respect to that standard without necessarily taking more than the optimal level of care. However, both of these difficulties—the difficulty of calculating the optimal adjustment and the possibility that the substantive legal standard may not have been set correctly—apply with equal force to the Benthamite proposal to increase damages. The suggestion that damages ought to be reduced instead thus rests on at least as strong a ground as the Benthamite position, and in many cases its support may be a good deal stronger.

B. Cost/Benefit Standards

Another position widely accepted in the law-and-economics literature is that liability standards (such as the level of "reasonable care" under a negligence system) ought to be set at the level that equates marginal costs and benefits. Of course, when uncertainty is recognized defendants will be faced not with a sharp line but with

[72] Recall also that even a reduction in damages will only be beneficial, in the sense of counteracting the tendency to overcomply, if it is reduced by a constant, or at least by some reduction that does not increase disproportionately with any increase in the defendant's care. See supra notes 48-53 and accompanying text.

a distribution of probabilities, and it becomes difficult even to speak in terms of "the" legal standard.[73] If all errors or variations in the application of the nominal standard are assumed to be unbiased, however, then the nominal legal standard will equal the mean of the resulting distribution. On this assumption, the recommendation that the nominal standard always be set at the cost-effective level of care can no longer be supported on economic grounds.

This conclusion follows directly from our earlier analysis. If defendants have an incentive to overcomply, setting the nominal standard at the optimal level of care will lead defendants to take more than optimal care, which by definition is undesirable. Society would be better off if juries were told to try for a standard somewhere below the cost-effective level of care, so that defendants who overcomplied relative to this standard would end up exercising the optimal amount of care. Of course, in those cases where the net incentives favored under- rather than overcompliance, the nominal standard would need to be set *above* the optimal level of care.

The difficulties with this recommendation are similar to those associated with trying to adjust damage awards: it would be very difficult to calculate the size of the optimal adjustment, and it is not clear that actual distributions of probabilities are centered at the nominal legal standard. Yet the same objections can be raised against the traditional argument for an exact cost-benefit standard. It is often difficult to calculate the cost-effective level of care,[74] and when courts or juries apply a cost-benefit standard there is no guarantee that the resulting distribution of probabilities will actually be centered at the cost-effective level.

This analysis would cast doubt on the idea that the common law

---

[73] Thus, in this model legal standards are more like the quarks and other basic particles studied in particle physics, which have no definite location and can only be expressed as a distribution of probabilities. See, e.g., S. Gasiorowicz, The Structure of Matter: A Survey of Modern Physics 177-83 (1979).

[74] See, e.g., Calabresi, Optimal Deterrence and Accidents, 84 Yale L.J. 656, 669-70 (1975) (suggesting that regulators probably overestimate costs of prevention); Rizzo, Law Amid Flux: The Economics of Negligence and Strict Liability in Tort, 9 J. Legal Stud. 291 (1980) (concluding that efficiency is an impossible goal in tort law; institutional certainty is a better goal). See also Epstein, The Social Consequences of Common Law Rules, 95 Harv. L. Rev. 1717, 1740-42 (1982) (negligence standards are not efficient, in part, because common law courts cannot award damages that account for the probability of the tortfeasor's apprehension or the costs to third parties).

is usually efficient[75] if common law courts have been trying to set the negligence standard at the cost-effective level of care. However, the evidence for this last proposition appears to consist of statements of judges such as Learned Hand, and the observations of Richard Posner and others, that negligence decisions vary in a way that at least reflects variations in costs and benefits.[76] The difficulty with this evidence is that courts would respond to changes in the costs and benefits of care even if they were not trying to set the standard exactly at the cost-effective level of care (i.e., exactly at x^*). A system where courts tried to set the standard slightly below the optimal level of care would reflect the same pattern of changes, so this evidence is consistent with either theory. Furthermore, because judges' statements of their grounds for decision are rarely given much weight when they seem to oppose various economic interpretations of legal rules,[77] it is dangerous to rely too heavily on them in this context as support for one theory or another.

Those who believe that the common law tends to be efficient should suspect that in some cases courts do aim for a standard of care below the cost-effective level and should thus begin to question judicial statements, such as Learned Hand's, to the contrary. Courts might be applying something closer to a gross negligence standard, or a simple negligence standard that includes some room for error, under which the reasonable man is only required to come "reasonably close" to the cost-effective level of care. Although either of these lower standards would lead to too little care in a world of absolute certainty, they may well be superior to a strict cost/benefit rule if there is any uncertainty about legal outcomes.

C. *Reducing Uncertainty*

Finally, there is a third approach to correcting the distortions caused by uncertainty: reducing the uncertainty itself. In legal terms, this could involve improving the fact-finding process to re-

---

[75] See, e.g., R. Posner, supra note 29, chs. 3-8.

[76] See Posner, A Theory of Negligence, 1 J. Legal Stud. 29 (1972) (negligence decisions impose a higher standard of care when the benefits of care are great and the costs of care are low, and a lower standard of care when the converse is true).

[77] See R. Posner, supra note 29, at 18 (legal opinions rarely refer to economics; true grounds of decisions are thus concealed by judicial rhetoric).

duce the chance of random error, promulgating enforcement guidelines to make enforcement decisions more predictable, or changing the substantive legal rule from a vague but flexible standard to a bright line test.[78] Reducing the uncertainty will not eliminate any incentives to overcomply, but it should reduce the extent of such overcompliance.

Reducing uncertainty is not costless, however. For example, administrative expenses would increase if special masters were hired to improve the fact-finding process. Reducing uncertainty may also impose other, more subtle costs. When increased certainty is obtained by adopting strict enforcement or bright line legal standards, these rules must be stated in terms of easily-observable factors that are usually only imperfect proxies for the variables that we would prefer to measure.[79] A fifty-five mile per hour per se negligence standard is certainly more predictable than a "reasonable speed" standard, but there will surely be some situations where that speed limit is far higher than the socially optimal speed, and others where it is too low.

As a result, there will often be a conflict between the goal of reducing the variance of the distribution of probabilities and the goal of keeping the mean of that distribution correctly centered.[80] A bright line standard may produce fewer distortions due to uncertainty, but more distortions due to imperfect location of the mean. Discovering which effect will be stronger in any given case presents a very difficult empirical question.

V. Conclusion

In some respects, our analysis of uncertainty is simply a more formal treatment of an issue that has often interested legal schol-

---

[78] See Diver, The Optimal Precision of Administrative Rules, 93 Yale L.J. 65 (1983) (analyzing three elements of regulatory precision—verbal clarity, ease of application, and ability to produce the desired behavior—that must be balanced to reach optimal precision).

[79] In addition, the greater detail of a precise rule often means that the rule must be changed more frequently as the socially optimal situation changes. This resulting uncertainty imposes additional social costs. See Ehrlich & Posner, Economic Analysis of Legal Rulemaking, 3 J. Legal Stud. 257, 278 (1974).

[80] Lawyers have long been aware of the potential conflict between the goals of legal certainty and legal accuracy. For example, a common defense of the principle of stare decisis is that "in most matters it is more important that the applicable rule of law be settled than that it be settled right." Burnet v. Coronado Oil & Gas Co., 285 U.S. 393, 406 (1931) (Brandeis, J., dissenting).

ars. Discussions of uncertainty frequently appear, for example, in debates over the choice between strict liability and negligence. Critics of the negligence standard have emphasized the difficulties facing courts attempting to determine the efficient level of care, and consequently, the small likelihood that the negligence system will induce efficient behavior.[81] Our analysis suggests that even an uncertain rule can be adjusted, in theory, to produce the optimal level of compliance by those subject to the rule. However, the information needed to calculate and implement the proper adjustment appears to be at least as complex as that required to calculate the cost-effective level of care. Thus, the need to account for uncertain legal outcomes makes an efficient negligence system even more difficult to implement than otherwise might have been supposed.

Legal debates have focused more particularly on the relationship between uncertainty and overcompliance. Not surprisingly, these concerns have been expressed most strongly in contexts where overcompliance by defendants is seen as particularly costly to society.[82] In a tautological sense, overcompliance is always costly because we have defined overcompliance to mean a level of care that is above the socially optimal level, but these costs may be greater in some contexts than in others.

Concerns about overcompliance have been particularly prominent in freedom of speech cases. The "chilling effect" and "void for vagueness" doctrines address precisely the concerns analyzed here—the danger that vague regulatory standards will lead some speakers to overcomply and refrain from making valuable political statements. Courts have struck down statutes whose prohibitions include constitutionally protected as well as unprotected speech on the grounds that forcing defendants to litigate the constitutional status of their speech on a case-by-case basis after the speech has already been made would expose would-be speakers to too much risk.[83] Similarly, a statute defining prohibited speech in vague

---

[81] See authorities cited supra note 74.

[82] See, e.g., R. Posner, supra note 29, at 425.

[83] See, e.g., Dombrowski v. Pfister, 380 U.S. 479, 487 (1965) (narrowly drawn statutes are required in the context of first amendment freedoms; otherwise "the contours of [constitutionally permissible] regulation would have to be hammered out case by case—and tested only by those hardy enough to risk criminal prosecution. . . ."). See generally L. Tribe, American Constitutional Law 710-22 (1978) (overbreadth doctrine is the Court's response to

terms may be struck down because it permits potential speakers to avoid the risk of punishment "only by restricting their conduct to that which is unquestionably safe."[84] Our analysis suggests that the fear that uncertainty may induce overcompliance may well have a solid economic basis.[85]

A similar concern has been prominent in the debate over the standard for judging predatory pricing under the antitrust laws. It has proven to be extremely difficult to define in advance the circumstances under which price cuts aimed at eliminating competitors will be deemed illegal,[86] and both courts and commentators have expressed concern that a vague standard may deter firms from making innocent, competitive price cuts.[87] Again, the obvious value to society of the conduct (lowered prices and political debate) that might be deterred adds sharpness to these concerns.

Other examples of concern with uncertainty and overcompliance can easily be found.[88] One purpose of this article is to demonstrate

---

the chilling effect of laws that deter both protected and unprotected speech).

[84] Baggett v. Bullitt, 377 U.S. 360, 372 (1964). See also Smith v. Goguen, 415 U.S. 566, 573 (1974) (void for vagueness doctrine "demands a greater degree of specificity" in statutes regulating expression sheltered by the first amendment).

[85] Of course, to the extent that political speech is motivated by ideological fervors unresponsive to changes in marginal costs and benefits, our analysis of defendants' economic incentives would be less relevant. Overcompliance may be more likely for advertising and other forms of "commercial speech" subject to uncertain regulatory standards; businessmen are usually thought to be more sensitive to marginal gains and risks. This conclusion may cast doubt on the Supreme Court's frequent assertions that commercial speech is less likely to be chilled than political speech. Note, however, that the assertion that commercial speech is less likely to be chilled is based on the Court's belief that the standard governing commercial speech is quite clear and certain. See, e.g., Bates v. State Bar, 433 U.S. 350, 381 (1977) (commercial speech is less vulnerable because advertisers are able to determine easily whether their speech is truthful, and hence protected); Virginia State Bd. of Pharmacy v. Virginia Citizens Consumer Council, 425 U.S. 748, 771-72 n.24 (1976) (an advertiser can verify the truth of his speech; therefore commercial speech is "more durable than other kinds" of speech).

[86] See, e.g., Easterbrook, supra note 67, at 333-34 (describing the difficulties of courts and juries in determining predation); Joskow & Klevorick, A Framework for Analyzing Predatory Pricing Policy, 89 Yale L.J. 213, 234-42 (1979) (probability of falsely identifying price cuts as predatory depends upon the prices set by the dominant firm, the strictness of the standard, and the ability of the courts to understand and apply the standard).

[87] Easterbrook notes that the concept of predation entails the "significant risk of condemning the outcome of hard competition." There is some weak evidence that overcompliance is not uncommon in antitrust contexts. Easterbrook, supra note 67, at 336. See Beckstein & Gabel, Antitrust Compliance: Results of a Survey of Legal Opinion, 51 Antitrust L.J. 459, 484 (1982).

[88] For example, the medical profession claims that vague malpractice standards cause

formally that uncertainty does indeed affect people's incentives to comply.[89] Propositions that seem intuitively obvious to writers accustomed to thinking in terms of simpler models—that liability standards should be set at the cost-effective level of care, that equal chances of error in either direction will have no net effect on the incentives of risk-neutral defendants, and that penalties should generally be increased by a factor reflecting the probability of not being punished—turn out to be of doubtful validity once legal uncertainty is admitted into the analysis. Other intuitive judgments concerning, for example, the effect of excessive damage awards, or the role of contributory negligence, begin to make sense only when uncertainty is introduced.

---

doctors to "overcomply" by engaging in too many costly defensive tests and procedures. See, e.g., Wiley, The Impact of Judicial Decisions on Professional Conduct: An Empirical Study, 55 S. Cal. L. Rev. 345 (1981); Project, The Medical Malpractice Threat: A Study of Defensive Medicine, 1971 Duke L.J. 939; Comment, The Price of Health Care Availability: The Economics of Medical Malpractice, 11 Sw. U.L. Rev. 1371, 1377-81 (1979).

[89] Some forms of uncertainty have been addressed in models of the evolution of the common law by postulating a probability greater than zero that a rule of law might be overturned on appeal. These models typically address only the decision to litigate or settle, however, and do not consider the effect of this uncertainty on parties' decision whether to comply with the underlying substantive rule. See, e.g., Priest, The Common Law Process and the Selection of Efficient Rules, 6 J. Legal Stud. 65 (1977); Priest, Selective Characteristics of Litigation, 9 J. Legal Stud. 399 (1980); Rubin, Why is the Common Law Efficient?, 6 J. Legal Stud. 51 (1977). Uncertainty and probability theory have also been introduced into formal models of statistical inference and the rules of evidence—but, again, without considering the effect of that uncertainty on compliance with the underlying substantive rules. See, e.g., Finkelstein & Farley, A Bayesian Approach to Identification Evidence, 83 Harv. L. Rev. 489 (1970); Kaye, supra note 20; Tribe, Trial by Mathematics: Precision and Ritual in the Legal Process, 84 Harv. L. Rev. 1329 (1970).

Part III
Economic Analysis of Contract Law

[7]

The Yale Law Journal

Volume 89, Number 7, June 1980

Enforcing Promises: An Examination of the Basis of Contract*

Charles J. Goetz† and Robert E. Scott‡

The obligation to keep promises is a commonly acknowledged moral duty.[1] Yet not all promises—however solemnly vowed—are enforceable at law.[2] Why are some promises legally binding and others not? Orthodox doctrinal categories provide only modest assistance in answering this persistent question. Conventional analysis, for example, has distinguished promises made in exchange for a return promise or performance from nonreciprocal promises.[3] Indeed, common law "bar-

* We would like to thank Michael Dooley, Stanley Henderson, Arthur Leff, Douglas Leslie, Alan Schwartz, Paul Stephan, and the participants in the University of Virginia Faculty Workshop and the University of Chicago Law and Economics Workshop for their helpful comments on earlier versions of this Article.

† Professor of Law, University of Virginia School of Law.

‡ Professor of Law, University of Virginia School of Law.

1. Pound, *Promise or Bargain?* 33 TUL. L. REV. 455, 455 (1959) ("From antiquity the moral obligation to keep a promise [has] been a cardinal tenet of ethical philosophers, publicists, and philosophical jurists.") [hereinafter cited as *Promise or Bargain?*]; *see id.* at 457-63. *See generally* Pound, *Individual Interests of Substance—Promised Advantages*, 59 HARV. L. REV. 1, 3-11 (1945). In terms of moral obligation, promises have been clearly distinguished from other representations or predictions. "A promise is not, therefore, merely an assurance one gives to help another, just as it is not merely an expression of a resolution to perform an action. It is, in addition, to *underwrite* any endeavor the other party to the transaction may choose to launch. . . ." A. MELDEN, RIGHTS AND PERSONS 46, 47-54 (1977). The peculiar status of promissory representations forms the basis of the law of contract.

2. The hint of this restraint is revealed in the common definition of contract as a promise that is legally enforceable. *See, e.g.*, 1 RESTATEMENT OF CONTRACTS § 1 (1932) [hereinafter cited without cross-reference as RESTATEMENT 1ST]. This definition of contract is retained in the *Second Restatement*. RESTATEMENT (SECOND) OF CONTRACTS § 1 (Tent. Draft Nos. 1-7, 1973) [hereinafter cited without cross-reference as RESTATEMENT 2D].

3. *See* RESTATEMENT 2D § 75. The traditional distinction between bargained-for and gratuitous promises suggests that only two categories can be identified. Actually the institutional environment is more accurately described as having three distinct contexts. Explicitly bargained-for promises are only a part of a larger exchange context in which the opportunity for interactive communication remains. We define nonreciprocal promises as being limited to those contexts in which the promisee has no realistic ability to obtain adjustments in promise-making through bargaining. *See* p. 1301 & note 38 *infra*.

gain theory" is classically simple: bargained-for promises are presumptively enforceable; nonreciprocal promises are presumptively unenforceable. But this disarmingly simple theory has never mirrored reality.[4] Contract law has ventured far beyond such narrow limitations, embracing reliance and unjust enrichment as additional principles of promissory obligation.[5]

Thus, a promise may be enforceable to the extent that the promisee has incurred substantial costs, or conferred benefits, in reasonable reliance on the promise.[6] Promissory estoppel under Section 90 of the *Restatement of Contracts* is the primary enforcement mechanism when action in reliance follows the promise.[7] If the change of position by the promisee precedes the promise, its nexus with the promise is more subtle. For example, a promise is enforceable when it follows a nondonative material benefit conferred by the promisee. Unjust enrichment principles are typically invoked to enforce such "past consideration" promises.[8] Despite this expansion of liability, "gratuitous" promises of gifts or unilateral pledges to confer benefits remain legally unenforceable.[9]

4. Professor Grant Gilmore has argued provocatively that a clearly defined "bargain theory" of contract never really existed in the first place. The "theory," he argues, was simply the creature of nineteenth-century formalism. *See* G. GILMORE, THE DEATH OF CONTRACT (1974).

5. The first breach in the armor of classical bargain theory is credited to Professor Corbin. *See id.* at 62-66. *See generally* 1 A. CORBIN, CONTRACTS §§ 109, 110 (1963). Subsequently, the pioneering scholarship of Lon Fuller and Stanley Henderson has demonstrated that the environment of promissory liability differs markedly from conventional assumptions. *See, e.g.*, Fuller & Perdue, *The Reliance Interest in Contract Damages* (pt. 1), 46 YALE L.J. 52 (1936); Henderson, *Promises Grounded in the Past: The Idea of Unjust Enrichment and the Law of Contracts*, 57 VA. L. REV. 1115 (1971) [hereinafter cited as *Unjust Enrichment*]; Henderson, *Promissory Estoppel and Traditional Contract Doctrine*, 78 YALE L.J. 343 (1969) [hereinafter cited as *Promissory Estoppel*].

In addition to Professor Gilmore's essay, the development of contract theory is thoughtfully explored by Lawrence Friedman, *see* L. FRIEDMAN, CONTRACT LAW IN AMERICA (1965), and by Patrick Atiyah, *see* P. ATIYAH, THE RISE AND FALL OF FREEDOM OF CONTRACT (1979).

6. *See* pp. 1345-54 *infra*. Under classical common law doctrine, a mere promise could be elevated to a legally binding contract only by the formality of a seal or a bargained-for exchange of consideration for the promise. L. FULLER & M. EISENBERG, BASIC CONTRACT LAW 124 (1972).

7. *See* note 106 *infra*. The inclusion of section 90 in the *Restatement 1st* is generally identified as the initial doctrinal recognition of the inadequacy of the simple bargain model in explaining the enforcement of promises. Professor Gilmore suggests that Corbin's "revolutionary" attack on bargain theory predates the *Restatement* by several decades. G. GILMORE, *supra* note 4, at 58. Following the adoption of the *Restatement*, scholarly attention turned to describing the emerging principle. *See* Boyer, *Promissory Estoppel: Principle From Precedents* (pts. 1 & 2), 50 MICH. L. REV. 639, 873 (1952); *Promissory Estoppel*, *supra* note 5; Shattuck, *Gratuitous Promises—A New Writ?* 35 MICH. L. REV. 908 (1937).

8. *See* pp. 1349-54 *infra*.

9. *See* pp. 1339-45 *infra*.

Enforcing Promises

These often overlapping, yet seemingly unconnected, principles of bargain, detrimental reliance, and unjust enrichment characterize all legally enforceable promises. They, in turn, are linked with corresponding sanctions that determine the level of enforcement for a given set of promises.[10] Contract damage rules embrace a variety of remedial choices. But the principles determining this choice of remedies are largely unarticulated. In most cases *A* can seek the value of what he expected from *B*'s promise. Such standard "compensatory" recovery puts *A* in the economic position he would have occupied had *B* fulfilled his obligation.[11] There are alternatives to the compensation rule, however. Thus, *A* may seek restitution of any benefit conferred on *B* as a result of *B*'s promise.[12] Alternatively, *A* may seek to recover identifiable costs incurred in reliance on *B*'s promise.[13] Recovering conferred benefits and reliance expenditures has the stated objective of returning the parties to the same economic position they occupied before the promise was made.

How can these interlocking doctrinal patterns be explained? Damage and liability rules have both redistributive and behavior-adaptive functions. In an earlier paper we commented on the apparently random—and arguably regressive—distributive effects of the basic contract remedial options.[14] The adaptive effects of contract rules seem to offer greater explanatory possibilities.[15] A liability or damage rule induces

10. *See* Farnsworth, *Legal Remedies for Breach of Contract*, 70 COLUM. L. REV. 1145 (1970); Fuller & Perdue, *supra* note 5; Goetz & Scott, *Liquidated Damages, Penalties and the Just Compensation Principle: Some Notes on an Enforcement Model and a Theory of Efficient Breach*, 77 COLUM. L. REV. 554, 558-62, 568-77 (1977); Shattuck, *supra* note 7.

11. *See* Goetz & Scott, *supra* note 10, at 558-59. Notwithstanding the universality with which the goal is articulated, scholars have long doubted the rigor of the law's commitment to compensation. We have previously suggested that "a strong argument can be made that the theory of damages is designed to err toward undercompensation." *Id.* at 558 n.19.

12. *See* p. 1337 *infra;* Childres & Garamella, *The Law of Restitution and the Reliance Interest in Contract*, 64 NW. U.L. REV. 433 (1969); Dawson, *Restitution or Damages?* 20 OHIO ST. L.J. 175 (1959).

13. *See* p. 1337 *infra*. The definitive work in this area remains Fuller & Perdue, *supra* note 5.

14. Goetz & Scott, *supra* note 10, at 566-68.

15. A wealth of theories has been advanced to explain the enforcement of promises. The "intuitionist" theory of the inherent moral force of promises formed the basis of obligation for the social contract theorists of the 17th and 18th centuries. Although the intuitionist perspective is appealing, it fails to explain the simple fact that no legal system attempts to enforce all promises. The 19th-century response to the morality of promising was the "will" theory of contract. The law of contract was conceived of as merely executing and protecting the will of the parties. The 19th-century formalists, typified by Langdell and Pollock, used the notion that the essence of contract is the agreement of wills—or the meeting of minds—to craft the classical bargain theory of consideration.

The obvious limitations of the will theory have produced a reaction among 20th-

contracting parties to adapt their behavior in ways that will affect social welfare. The rules of promissory liability can, therefore, be examined usefully in terms of these welfare effects. It is important to emphasize that the proper focus here is on prospective effects, that future promising is the behavior to be influenced by the rules summarized above. If only promises already made were considered, ease of measurement is a primary factor that might commend the compensation rule over any more complex damage measure.[16] With respect to past promises, choosing among reliance, compensatory, or punitive remedies involves primarily a distributional issue; the damage rule allocates the gains or losses from any particular broken promise between the promisor and promisee. But, considered prospectively, rules of promissory liability have efficiency consequences as well: they frequently alter the actual magnitude of the gains or losses to be divided between the parties. Whether a particular type of promise will be enforceable, and to what extent, are choices that may powerfully modify the nature and amount of future promising. We will evaluate these choices by separating the enforcement question into two parts:

First, which system of promissory enforcement yields the maximum net social benefits from promise making?

Second, does such an optimal enforcement scheme explain current doctrinal patterns?

Part I of this Article considers the first of these questions by developing an analytical model that examines both the function of promises and the impact of liability on the making of promises. Clarifying the function of promising is a necessary first step in deriving an optimal enforcement model. It is critically important to realize that a promise is conceptually distinct from the actual transfer that it announces. As advance information signaling a future transfer, a typical promise prospectively carries *both* benefit if kept and harm if broken. This entanglement of benefits and harms substantially complicates the en-

century contract scholars that leads toward an instrumentalist view of promissory liability: promises are enforceable because enforcement secures socially desirable ends. *See, e.g.*, Atiyah, *Contracts, Promises and the Law of Obligations*, 94 LAW Q. REV. 193, 197-98 (1978); Patterson, *An Apology for Consideration*, 58 COLUM. L. REV. 929, 941 (1958); *Promise or Bargain?*, *supra* note 1, at 463. Although evaluation of promises in terms of their welfare effects dominates current contract jurisprudence, alternative evaluations based on shared ethical norms or common moral intuitions continue to be asserted. *See* J. RAWLS, A THEORY OF JUSTICE 342-50 (1971); Havighurst, *Consideration, Ethics and Administration*, 42 COLUM. L. REV. 1, 9 (1942). Such claims have not proved very helpful, however, in explaining the observable limits that the law sets on enforcing the sanctity of promises. And if moral force is attached to promises merely because people rely upon them, the argument is subject to the claim that such reliance is dependent upon legal enforceability.

16. *See* Goetz & Scott, *supra* note 10, at 566-68.

forcement question. Thus, the enforcement of promises may have harmful consequences by deterring socially useful future promising. Alternatively, nonenforcement encourages more promises but also reduces the reliability of the announcement; the promisor's intent to perform is not tested against a potential penalty for its nonperformance. The value of social welfare is maximized by a system of legal rules that provides the optimal balance between the beneficial and the harmful effects of promising.

In Part II, we discuss the practical compromises necessary to implement efficient regulation of promises in a world of costly legal process and imperfect information. We examine common law rules of liability as proxies for theoretically optimal rules rendered impractical by the inherent difficulties of measuring the true social effects of promising. We conclude that a substantial congruence exists between traditional contract rules and optimal promissory enforcement. Indeed, this congruence offers a persuasive explanation for the peculiar patterns of promissory liability observed in actual practice.[17]

I. Optimal Enforcement of Promises

Attempts have been made to explain the overlapping patterns of promissory liability in terms of the economic implications of promise-making. Bargained-for promises support value-enhancing exchanges. Such promises are thus seen as fully enforceable under the compensation rule in order to protect and encourage value-maximizing resource allocation.[18] Measuring damages in terms of expectation rather than reliance is said to encourage more efficient breach decisions once the contract is made.[19] A nonreciprocal promise, on the other hand, is

17. A recent scholarly debate has centered on the hypothesis that the common law can be explained in terms of principles of economic efficiency. *See, e.g.*, R. POSNER, ECONOMIC ANALYSIS OF LAW 404-05, 439-41 (2d ed. 1977); Rubin, *Why is the Common Law Efficient?* 6 J. LEGAL STUD. 51 (1977); Priest, *The Common Law Process and the Selection of Efficient Rules*, 6 J. LEGAL STUD. 65 (1977); Michelman, *A Comment on* Some Uses and Abuses of Economics in Law, 46 U. CHI. L. REV. 307 (1979). We take no position on the extent to which economic efficiency is a dominant or merely subsidiary element in explaining the development of common law doctrine in general. Our intent is the more modest one of measuring a relatively narrow segment of legal doctrine against some underlying economic optimality considerations.

18. *See* RESTATEMENT 2D § 76, Comment b ("Bargains are widely believed to be beneficial to the community in the provision of opportunities for freedom of individual action and exercise of judgment and as a means by which productive energy and product are apportioned in the economy.") The assumption that enforcement of bargains promotes allocative efficiency is widespread. *See* Hays, *Formal Contracts and Consideration: A Legislative Program*, 41 COLUM. L. REV. 849, 852-53 (1941); Llewellyn, *What Price Contract?—An Essay in Perspective*, 40 YALE L.J. 704, 716-18 (1931); Patterson, *supra* note 15, at 945-48.

19. R. POSNER, *supra* note 17, at 88-93.

frequently labeled as a "sterile transaction," which does not facilitate the movement of resources to more valued uses.[20] On this basis, enforcement is justified only as a deterrent to the harm caused by any detrimental reliance on the promise.[21] In sum, these lines of analysis suggest that full enforcement of bargains consolidates benefits while protection of reliance-based promissory interests minimizes harms.

But existing explanations of the legal enforcement of promises are incomplete and perhaps misleading. A principal limitation has been the failure to consider the effects of various levels of legal enforcement on the making of promises. Inquiry has generally focused instead on the effects of legal sanctions on decisions to breach or perform, assuming that the promise has already been made.[22] Yet, a decision to enforce promises, and the subsequent choice of remedy, does not merely mold the performance behavior of contracting parties; it also shapes both the nature and amount of promise-making activity.

Appropriately calibrated enforcement rules can be used to achieve the optimal number and type of promises based on the degree and form of adaptation by promisor and promisee. Thus, the effects of legal enforcement on promise-making are critical factors in evaluating the seemingly disparate liability and damage rules of contract. In Part I we examine these effects by first describing the reactions of both the promisee and promisor to the risks inherent in promising. We then specify an enforcement model that encourages the socially optimal interaction between the promising parties.

A. *The Function of Promises: Adaptation by the Promisee*

In analyzing the promisee's reactions to a promise, it is critically important to bear in mind the conceptual distinction between the promise itself and the future benefit that it foretells. By communicating a

20. *See* C. Bufnoir, Propriété et Contrat 487 (2d ed. 1924); Fuller, *Consideration and Form*, 41 Colum. L. Rev. 799, 815 (1941); *cf.* R. Posner, *supra* note 17, at 69 (gratuitous, nonreciprocal promises not part of "process by which resources are moved").

21. *See* R. Posner, *supra* note 17, at 69-70; Fuller, *supra* note 20, at 811.

22. *See generally* Shavell, *Damage measures for breach of contract*, Bell J. Econ. (forthcoming 1980); W. Rogerson, Economic Efficiency and Damage Measures in Contract Law (unpublished paper on file with *Yale Law Journal*).

In order to increase its accessibility to a legal readership, this Article uses relatively nontechnical terms to present an underlying economic model that typically would be articulated by economists in highly formal mathematical terms. The formal model developed in the economic literature by Shavell and extended by Rogerson differs conceptually from ours in some important areas. For instance, we focus upon the influence of potential remedies on the quality and quantity of promises, rather than upon the optimal enforcement of a promise, the character of which is already determined. In addition, our definition of reliance damages differs because we incorporate the notion of "reasonableness." Hence, the implicit model underlying this Article is somewhat more complex conceptually than are those cited above.

promise, the promisor informs the promisee about the proposed future receipt of a benefit. The promise itself is merely the production of a piece of information about the future. Normally, advance knowledge of a future transfer will increase the benefit to the promisee because he can more perfectly adapt his consumption decisions to the impending change in wealth. For instance, a person informed of a $25,000 bequest to be made one year hence may revise some of the plans that he otherwise would have followed in the interim twelve months. Because of the revisions in plans, the individual can achieve a higher intertemporal level of satisfaction than if the wealth were transferred without any advance notice. Such adaptive gain from the information embodied in a promise may appropriately be termed "beneficial reliance." The problem occurs, however, when the transfer foretold by the promise is not actually performed. In this case, the information conveyed by the promise turns out to have been misleading and the promisee's induced adaptation in behavior makes him worse off than he would have been without the expectation of a future benefit. Losses incurred by ill-premised adaptive behavior are commonly termed "detrimental reliance." Because the role of promises as units of information is so fundamental to the entire analysis developed below, we will use an economic indifference curve model to give more rigorous content to such key legal concepts as reliance and the reasonableness of the promisee's adaptation process.

1. *Reliance Reactions of a Promisee*

Figure 1 will be used to develop a very simple intertemporal allocation model, one in which a person must allocate his income between two periods, present and future. *A*, the potential promisee, begins with $100, which he can divide between consumption now and consumption in the future. In Figure 1, his possible choices are represented by the straight line budget constraint indicating all combinations of present and future consumption that sum to $100. His preferences about alternative combinations of present and future consumption are summarized by the indifference curves, which define a kind of topographic map of the desirability of different present-future consumption patterns.[23] On these assumptions, the highest preference level consistent with the scarce resources is point e_1, where indifference curve I_1 is

23. Indifference curves may be thought of as a topographical map of a "preference mountain," on which higher "elevations" represent the greater preferences of outcomes. The points in any single indifference curve constitute equally preferred outcomes. An individual thus will be indifferent between any two points on an indifference curve. In the model represented by Figure 1, the higher an indifference curve lies to the northeast, the more utility the individual derives from the outcomes represented by the curves.

The Yale Law Journal Vol. 89: 1261, 1980

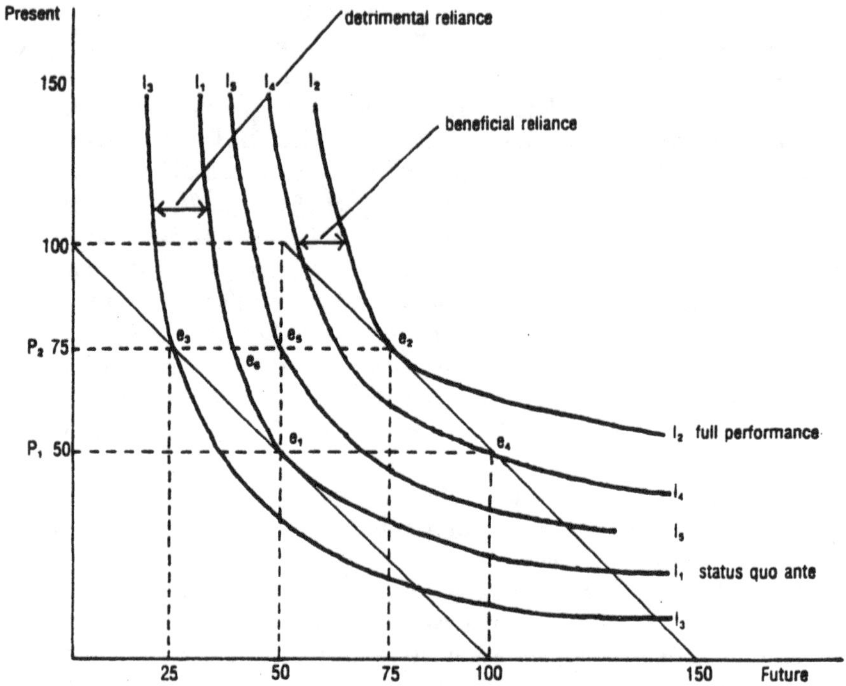

Figure 1

tangent to the budget constraint. This involves spending $50 now and a planned expenditure of $50 in the future.

Suppose now that *B* promises *A* a transfer of $50 to be made in the future period and that *A* believes the promise. Even neglecting the possibility of borrowing against his future wealth, *A*'s budget constraint will shift out to the dotted line in Figure 1.[24] The new constraint indicates that, although no more than $100 can be spent in the present, the two-period consumption levels may now total $150 rather than $100. Based on the new information, *A*'s best two-period plan would be point e_2. *A* is thus led to revise his current consumption upward to $75 and to project $75 worth of future consumption.[25] But what happens if

24. For simplicity, we assume that the interest rate on money is zero in order to produce a one-to-one tradeoff between present and future consumption. The introduction of interest is irrelevant to this analysis because it merely alters the rate of tradeoff, reflected in the slopes of the budget lines.

25. The promisee's consumption of all goods with nonzero income elasticities will be modified. His intertemporal consumption stream will be adjusted to the higher wealth level created by the gift.

the promise is broken when the second period actually arrives? *A* has already expended \$75 and has only \$25, rather than the prospective \$75, left to spend. In terms of Figure 1, breach of the promise pushes *A* leftward from his anticipated outcome of e_2 back to his original budget constraint at e_3. As indifference curve I_3 indicates, *A* is worse off at the post-breach result e_3 than he was at e_1, the pre-promise point on indifference curve I_1. In sum, *A* has been misled by the promise into making what is now recognizable as a mistake; the consequences of that detrimental reliance are captured in the difference between indifference curves I_1 and I_3.

Because detrimental reliance is widely regarded as a basis for damage computation, an advantage of the Figure 1 model is that it clearly illustrates why it is a mistake to use *A*'s observable action in reliance on a promise as the measure of his damages. Under the facts assumed, *A*'s observable reliance is the \$25 extra he spends in period 1. If, however, he were awarded this \$25 as damages for breach, his ultimate position would be at e_5 on indifference curve I_5. He would have spent \$75 in the first period and, including the \$25 damages, would have available \$50 for the final period. But since return to the status quo ante requires only that indifference curve I_1 be achieved, the true reliance damages are equal only to the lesser amount indicated by the horizontal distance between e_3 and e_6 in Figure 1. The common-sense explanation for this, of course, is that detrimental adaptation in behavior is usually only a partial rather than a total loss. In this case, *A* did get some benefit from the excessive \$25 consumption, even though not as much as he would have if the consumption had been postponed to the optimal time. Reliance is, simply, the opportunity cost of the broken promise. Thus, true damages are measured by the difference between the value of the stream of consumption choices not taken—indifference curve I_1—and those choices induced by the promise—indifference curve I_3. Because it is important to distinguish compensation based on observable reliance from true reliance damages, we shall refer to the former as "reimbursement damages" in the discussion below.

Even where the precise meaning is imperfectly captured, the notion of detrimental reliance tends to be better understood than that of beneficial reliance. This is unfortunate because the production of beneficial reliance is perhaps the principal social rationale of promising; the risk of detrimental reliance is merely the unavoidable concomitant cost. Figure 1 aptly illustrates the beneficial consequences of promising when the promise is performed. Assume, for instance, that the \$50 in our hypothetical is merely transferred to *A* in period two without any advance warning. Not knowing about the wealth increase, *A* will have committed himself to plan e_1. When period two arrives, *A* will unexpectedly find himself with $100 to spend. At this point, the best available choice is at e_4, which is on a lower indifference curve than e_2, the point that would have been achievable had *A* obtained advance knowledge of the transfer. In common-sense terms, the difference between I_2 and I_4 illustrates the benefits to *A* of being able to adjust, because of the promise, to revised expectations about the future.

2. *The "Self-Protection" Reaction to Uncertain Promises*

Conceptualizing beneficial and detrimental reliance in the context of a simple model such as Figure 1 does have one major limitation. We have assumed implicitly that the promisee places total credence in the promise. Against the background of the Figure 1 model, however, it is possible to consider at least heuristically the imperfect credibility situation. When the promisee does not completely believe a promise, the results illustrated in Figure 1 can be understood as extreme or limiting cases of reliance.

What happens if the promisee knows that the probability of the promisor's performance is less than certain? In this case, the beneficial results of any adaptive behavior when the promise is performed must be weighed against the detrimental results of the same adaptive behavior if the promise is breached. A prospective gain from an adaptive action is balanced against the risk of loss.[26] Whatever the reasons for the riskiness attached to the performance prospects of any promise, the promisee can protect himself against prospective losses from detrimental reliance by limiting his behavior adjustments. In practice, the attempt to do this is frequently manifested in intermediate courses of action taken by promisees who do not completely ignore the implications of a promise in their planning but do not react as fully as if performance were certain. The price for this self-protection against the risk of detrimental reliance is, therefore, the value of the prospective beneficial reliance that would accrue from full adaptation to the advance knowledge of a promissory performance.[27]

26. In formal statements of this balancing process, the promisee is usually regarded as weighting the alternative consequences by the probabilities of performance and nonperformance. It should be noted that the promisee's central concern is whether the preannounced transfer will take place, not whether the performance is a purely voluntary one as opposed to one motivated by legal or other sanctions. Thus, because legal sanctions presumably affect the expected performance probability of many promises, the extent of the reliance experienced can be modified by the legal treatment of promises.

27. An important observation with regard to the promisee's adjustments to uncertain

Enforcing Promises

The possibility of self-protection adjustments by promisees undermines the common assumption that detrimental reliance is the only behavior modified by the enforcement choice. This assumption often leads to characterizing certain "gratuitous" promises as incapable of inducing any reasonable reliance. Once the legal rule is announced, detrimental reliance on such announcements would, it is argued, not be reasonable. But the problem is quite simply that policies that reduce the reliability of promises are likely to reduce both beneficial and detrimental reliance. Thus, legal rules that encourage self-protective adaptation by the promisee achieve desired reductions in detrimental reliance only at the cost of concomitant reductions in beneficial reliance.

B. *Making Promises: Actions of the Promisor*

Understanding the behavior of the promisor is the next important step in our analytic model. How do promisors act and how do prospective sanctions modify their behavior? The initial phase of our analysis employs some strong simplifying assumptions. First, we assume that although future events may be uncertain, retrospective information is perfectly accurate. Second, we also posit that legal process costs are negligible, so that the theoretical gains from an otherwise beneficial regulatory rule are never counterbalanced by implementation costs. These assumptions are relaxed below when we discuss the practical compromises that may be dictated in a more realistic setting.

Potential promisees view promises as beneficial actions and as desirable economic goods. One can thus consider a promisor's willingness to make promises in much the same manner as his willingness to pursue any other economic goal. To predict the level of promise-making activity, the costs of promising must be examined.

1. *The Costs of Promising: The Regret Contingency*

Derivation of the promisor's cost of promising requires consideration of a number of potentially confusing factors. Therefore, we shall begin with the simplest possible environment. First we shall assume

prospects is that even very uncertain promises may produce substantial detrimental reliance if their prospective beneficial reliance is high. The mere improbability of performance does not destroy the informational significance of the promise. Recognition of this fact suggests that the legal concept of "reasonable" reliance is more complex than is sometimes realized. For example, it is perfectly reasonable and rational to rely detrimentally, to some extent, on many promises even though there is a substantial probability of nonperformance.

that the cost of communicating the promise is negligible.[28] Second, we assume that no legal mechanism exists to enforce promises. Absent a legal compulsion, the promisor remains free to refuse performance. If he does, the making of the promise will have generated costs in the amount of the detrimental reliance imposed on the promisee.

The option of nonperformance also imposes costs on the promisor in two situations. The first case is when the promisor exhibits some welfare interdependence with the promisee; that is, he is to some extent altruistic and cares about costs incurred by the promisee.[29] Then, the detrimental reliance costs imposed by nonperformance become, to some degree, costs to the promisor himself. Intrafamilial promises and promises between close friends are most likely to exemplify this phenomenon. In addition, and closely related, guilt may accompany the promisor's imposition of harmful results on others. In any event, this class of breach-related costs, which arise out of an altruistic or ethical sense, may be termed "self-sanctions."

The second extra-legal sanction arises when nonperformance would produce some post-breach reaction, either from the promisee or others, that is costly to the promisor. The resulting costs may range from hostile, retributive behavior to a mere loss of others' esteem to foreclosure of future beneficial dealings.

What are the effects of these extra-legal sanctions for breaking promises? To the extent that such sanctions are effective, their prospect acts as a "cost" of promising and deters promises that are worth less to the promisor than the prospective cost. Thus, extra-legal sanctions are a supplement to, or substitute for, legal sanctions.[30] Given the

28. On these facts, the cost of promising may be zero. One key question to ask, of course, is whether the act of promising has foreclosed any future opportunities to the promisor or made such opportunities more expensive.

29. The economic terminology for such relationship is "interdependent utility functions." The intrafamilial promise offers an obvious illustration of how such interdependency can increase the utility of any given transfer. *See* Posner, *Gratuitous Promises in Economics and Law*, 6 J. LEGAL STUD. 411, 412, 418-19 (1977).

30. Although the existence of extra-legal sanctions may properly affect the choice of legal measures, extra-legal sanctions have several disadvantages as mechanisms for inducing optimal promise-making. First, extra-legal penalties are highly circumstantial, are difficult to calibrate, and vary widely in their efficacy from individual to individual. Second, a sanction must constitute a cost to the person on whom it is imposed; it is not necessary, however, that no one benefit from the sanction. When damages or performance are extracted from a promisor, the resources are transferred to someone else who benefits thereby. Consequently, there may be no net social cost associated with the sanction; at least, the net loss is less than the gross loss imposed on the promisor. By contrast, many forms of extra-legal sanction represent a cost to one party without counterbalancing benefit to another. Prospects of retributive reaction or guilt, for example, tend to be inefficient sanctions in the sense that they could be replaced by resource transfers from promisor to promisee so that the promisee is made better off while the promisor is made no worse off than under the extra-legal sanction.

existence of extra-legal sanctions, under what circumstances might a promisor fail to perform his promise? When a promise is made in good faith, the promisor presumably believes that he is likely to perform. Still, many good-faith promisors would acknowledge the possibility that events may arise that cause them to regret having made the promise. Thereafter, if it were costless to do so, they would indeed breach the promise. Such contingencies may involve a wide range of factors, from changes in personal conditions to disappointment about external considerations that orginally made the promise seem desirable. The term "regret contingency" will be used to denote the future occurrence of a condition that would motivate breach if breach were a costless option for the promisor. Assuming any reliance, the occurrence of a regret contingency necessarily implies that either the promisor or promisee must bear a cost.

When a regret contingency arises, the promisor's options are either to bear the loss attributable to performance, which now costs more than it is worth, or to breach and accept the cost of any corresponding sanction. Presumably the promisor would adopt the cheaper of these regret costs. In any event, someone will suffer a net loss whenever a regret contingency arises, whether in the form of regret costs to the promisor, uncompensated detrimental reliance to the promisee, or both.[31]

2. *Adaptation by the Promisor: Precautions and Reassurance*

By what means does the promisor adapt to the prospective costs of promising?[32] The promisor can substantially influence the probability of a regret contingency, and thus its prospective costs, by adjusting his behavior ex ante. One means of mitigating potential costs is by altering the form of the promise. For instance, the promisor may condition performance on the proviso that certain circumstances—potential regret contingencies—not arise. Alterations in the form of the promise will generally entail a cost to the promisor either in terms of direct resource

31. The regret contingency is a key concept because much of the discussion below will involve either how society can adjust to an optimal volume of exposure to regret contingencies or how to achieve the objective that any given volume of such risk exposure be borne in a least-cost manner.

32. The prospective cost of promising is based on a two-step estimation process by the promisor. First, what is the probability that a regret contingency will arise? Second, if one does arise, what is the magnitude of the accompanying regret costs? The promisor uses the probability of the regrettable outcome to discount the costs of that outcome. Because the future consequences of promises are frequently uncertain, it should be emphasized that the adjective "prospective" is used in a particular sense. Specifically, it indicates that a set of alternative future consequences have been weighted by their probabilities, adjusted for any risk preference, and reduced to a single-valued equivalent.

cost—time and trouble—or in the possibility that the benefit of the promise-making to the promisor will be diminished. The second means of avoiding regret costs is simply to make fewer promises. The costs of this option are forgone benefits from unmade promises.

The costs that result from restrictions in the scope or number of one's promises can be termed "precautionary costs." It is useful to distinguish these further as either quality precautions or quantity precautions. Quality precautions involve adjustments restricting the scope of promises and impose a cost of decreased reliability. Quantity precautions, which consist of reductions in the number of promises made, result in a loss of benefits from promising. A rational promisor will pursue precautionary adjustments up to the point at which marginal precautionary costs are exactly balanced by marginal reductions in regret costs.

Precautionary adjustments by the promisor decrease the value of the promise. Conversely, when the promise is worth more to the promisor than its prospective cost, the promisor may engage in "reassurance." Reassurance includes such actions as the offer of guarantees, verbal persuasions, and the development of a reliable reputation, designed to convince the promisee that the promise is valuable. Reassurances increase the value of the promise to the promisee. Indeed, promisees may regard voluntary reassurance measures as substitutes for sanctions. Reassurance usually entails some cost to the promisor and, hence, will be pursued up to the point at which marginal reassurance costs are exactly balanced by increases in resulting benefits to the promisor.

Precautionary and reassurance reactions by promisors are triggered by variations in the cost of promising. It should be apparent, therefore, that an additional legal sanction will raise prospective costs, thereby precipitating adjustments of the scope and volume of promises. The net effects of these changes can be evaluated by combining the descriptive models of promisee and promisor reaction developed above.

C. *Optimizing Promisor-Promisee Interaction*

To what extent do legal sanctions optimize the interactions between promisor and promisee? In the present context, optimization is defined as maximizing the net social benefits of promissory activity—that is, the benefits of promises minus their costs.[33] This approach is equivalent

33. The adjective "prospective" should be applied to such costs and benefits, and this sense is intended below even when the term is not explicitly used. Strictly speaking, the maximization of prospective benefits need not produce results that, viewed retrospectively, will have truly maximized the net benefits ultimately realized. This is not a serious

Enforcing Promises

to the balancing of prospective costs and benefits under the widely accepted Learned Hand test for the required duty of care in potential tort-producing activities.[34] Indeed, there are strong theoretical parallels between the production of dangerous, but useful, products and the making of promises.[35]

The role of damages or sanctions in generating socially optimal behavior can be focused more sharply by observing the distinction between internal and external effects.[36] Because self-interested maximiz-

objection, however, because the prospective benefits criterion amounts to one under which people are induced to maximize benefits to the extent possible within the limits of the information at their disposal at the time the relevant decisions are made. There is no reason to believe that, as a practical matter, any other criterion can function as well.

34. Under the Hand definition, an actor is guilty of negligence if the loss caused by the accident multiplied by the probability of its occurrence exceeds the burden of taking adequate precautions. United States v. Carroll Towing Co., 159 F.2d 169, 173 (2d Cir. 1947).

35. The optimization process can be analyzed most clearly in terms of marginal effects—that is, the incremental variations in costs and benefits associated with a proposed change in legal treatment. If the marginal benefits attributable to a rule adjustment exceed the marginal costs, then the adjustment is beneficial, and vice versa. The system is optimized when no changes exist for which the marginal net benefits are positive. It is not necessary, therefore, to know the absolute levels of costs and benefits associated with alternative legal rules as long as the increases or decreases in the levels of costs and benefits can be estimated.

Social optimization implicitly presumes that the welfare of promisors and promisees is given equal weight ex ante. In the extreme, this assumption implies that even a promise with a high prospect of net cost to the promisee is optimal if the promisee's costs are outweighed by sufficient benefits to the promisor. In particular classes of cases, such results may be quite discomforting; their possibility constitutes one of the caveats applicable to any efficiency analysis of legal policy. In situations in which such cases arise, supplemental norms may be applied. One such case may be that of the bad-faith promisor who does not intend to perform, but who seeks nevertheless to benefit by making the promise. Here, standard intentional fraud analysis, providing for damages at least equalling the amount of detrimental reliance necessary to make the victimized promisee whole, would be appropriate. Indeed, it might be socially desirable to increase the sanction and extract any unjust gains from the bad-faith promisor.

The most commonly adopted measure of damages for fraud is the "benefit of the bargain" rule. Similar to the compensation principle, the rule puts the plaintiff in the same financial position as if the fraudulent representation had in fact been true. *See* Auffenberg v. Hafley, 457 S.W.2d 929, 938-39 (Mo. App. 1970); Lawson v. Citizens & S. Nat'l Bank, 255 S.C. 517, 180 S.E.2d 206 (1971).

Punitive damages are available when the defrauder has been guilty of morally reprehensible conduct. This generally requires more aggravated conduct than a mere intentional misrepresentation of fact or intentional lie; rather, the fraud must be gross, oppressive, or violative of a position of trust and confidence. *See, e.g.*, J. Truett Payne Co. v. Jackson, 281 Ala. 426, 203 So. 2d 443 (1967); Fowler v. Benton, 245 Md. 540, 552-53, 226 A.2d 556, 564, *cert. denied*, 389 U.S. 851 (1967).

When the plaintiff has transferred property or conferred benefits upon the defendant, he is entitled to a disgorgement of the property or its value. *See* Brooks v. Conston, 364 Pa. 256, 72 A.2d 75 (1950); RESTATEMENT OF RESTITUTION § 202 (1937).

36. Internal effects are those costs and benefits felt by the individual actor. External effects are those consequences of an act that are felt only by individuals other than the actor. Only if a party makes decisions as if he were experiencing all of the consequences of his behavior, external as well as internal, will his behavior be socially optimal.

ing behavior entails consideration of only internal costs and benefits, unfettered individual behavior is incompatible with social optimization in circumstances in which significant external costs or benefits are present. Individuals will oversupply activities with external costs and undersupply those with external benefits. By imposing costs and creating incentives, the law can cause individuals to consider external effects in their decisionmaking and thus "internalize" them.

Inducing optimal promise-making therefore requires that the promisor's costs of promising be adjusted to reflect any external effects on the promisee.[37] But this adjustment process is complex. Changes in the costs and benefits of promising are highly interactive in two senses. First, an individual's adjustments may substitute one category of his costs for another. Second, the actions of one party may produce reactions by the other and, in turn, feedback responses to the first party. The role of legal damages in optimizing this interaction depends upon whether a promise is reciprocal or nonreciprocal. Nonreciprocal or gratuitous promises, which are not conditioned upon performance of a return promise, do not typically enjoy the presumption of enforceability attached to reciprocal or bargained-for promises. As the analysis below reveals, the critical variable that distinguishes these categories of promises is whether the parties can interactively influence the nature and amount of promise-making through bargaining. It is the existence of effective impediments to interaction in the case of nonreciprocal promises that seems to explain why the law treats these two types of promises in such different fashions.[38]

1. *Nonreciprocal Promises*

Consider the case of a gratuitous promisor who has adjusted his promise-making to an arbitrarily assumed level of extra-legal sanction so that he cannot further improve his situation. In addition, assume that social considerations effectively prevent the promisee from influencing the promisor's calculations through bargaining. Under these conditions, when does the intervention of the law lead to optimal

37. As long as the effects of the announcement of the promise itself are carefully distinguished from those of any actual resource transfer, the value of the performance per se to the promisee can be ignored.

38. Barriers to effective interaction between parties to promises may arise from many different sources. Ordinary transaction-costs impediments may exist as a result of the time and trouble involved in negotiating. Alternatively, there may be something inherent in the very relationship of the parties that renders interaction impractical, such as a social taboo, a status relationship, or an institutional environment that obstructs meaningful communication. *See* Leff, *Injury, Ignorance and Spite—The Dynamics of Coercive Collection*, 80 YALE L.J. 1, 41 (1970).

results? We shall first discuss the conditions under which nonenforcement of such a nonreciprocal promise will produce suboptimal reassurance and precautionary adjustments. We then derive an optimal damage formula for those cases in which some level of enforcement is suggested.

a. *Legal Enforcement and Reassurance*

Legal enforcement of a particular class of nonreciprocal promises increases the reliability of the promises. This added reassurance increases social benefits in three situations. First, legal enforcement increases the net benefits of promissory reassurance if a legal sanction such as money damages displaces existing extra-legal penalties such as guilt or social pressure. If the total level of the sanction stays the same, the promisor's costs, benefits, and behavior all remain unchanged, while the promisee's benefits are increased by the receipt of the damages. The promisee's self-protection costs also fall. Because the consequences of a regret contingency are reduced by a prospect of legal compensation, the promisee can spend less on mitigating the risk of uncompensated detrimental reliance. In the event of breach, damage payments reduce the cost of nonperformance to the promisee. Thus, his beneficial reliance on the promise will increase. In essence, the substitution of one type of sanction for the other provides the promisee with the benefits of more reassurance against the regret contingency at no additional cost to the promisor. Hence, the imposition of legal sanctions may increase net reassurance benefits, if extra-legal sanctions are replaced by legal enforcement.[39]

Second, legal enforcement may increase net reassurance benefits regardless of the degree of substitutability of sanctions. Such an opportunity arises when a gratuitous promisor assesses the risk of a regret contingency at zero, because he is certain he will perform. In this case, if the law intervenes by raising the sanction for breach, the promisor's prospective regret and precautionary costs remain at zero. The prospect of sanctions is largely irrelevant to such a promisor. If the promisee knew that the risk of a regret contingency were in fact zero, he too would be unaffected by a stronger sanction. He would be perfectly assured already and, consequently, would incur no self-protection costs. Generally, however, a promisee's subjectively perceived risk of a regret contingency will be greater than the actual zero risk known to the

39. In the case of nonreciprocal promises, no basis appears for predicting when legal enforcement will successfully replace extra-legal sanctions. To the extent that sanctions are cumulative rather than substitutable, the net reassurance benefits of legal sanctions will be reduced.

promisor. Therefore, the increased sanction provides greater reassurance and permits a promisee who was originally engaging in excessive self-protection to decrease his self-protection costs.[40]

Third, even the gratuitous promisor who is not totally certain of future performance may prefer more enforcement. This will occur, for instance, when the promisor cares about the welfare or the reaction of the promisee. Then, the net benefit of promising to the promisor may be enhanced by the provision of additional reliability to the promisee through legal enforcement. Although enforcement puts such promisors at additional risk, the greater reassurance to the promisee may generate increased benefits to the promisor that outweigh any increased costs.[41]

Under what circumstances, then, will legally induced increases in the reliability of nonreciprocal promises be socially optimal? When the mutual interests of both parties are furthered by more assured promises, the promisor will voluntarily seek legal mechanisms for providing additional reassurance. However, often it will not be in the self-interest of the promisor to undertake voluntarily a more reliable promise. Even when some benefits to the promisor are produced by additional reassurance, the external benefits from performance may be inadequately communicated to the promisor by self-sanctions. As a general empirical premise, therefore, enforcement will be more likely to optimize promissory reassurance when extra-legal sanctions are relatively ineffective. The social desirability of enforcement, however, ultimately depends upon whether those gains are offset by corresponding costs. Before proposing a sanction for particular nonreciprocal cases, therefore, we must consider the societal effect of the promisors' precautionary adjustments triggered by legal liability.

b. *Legal Enforcement and Precautionary Action*

Although legal enforcement of nonreciprocal promises will initially increase the reliability of such promises, it may induce both qualitative and quantitative precautionary action by promisors. The net societal

40. As has been noted in different terms, the value of the transfer to the promisee is enhanced because the information content of the promise is improved and the beneficial reliance is increased. *See* Posner, *supra* note 29 (discussing the enforceability of gratuitous promises). The Posner analysis, though persuasive, is limited by its pristine premises.

41. Based on essentially this line of reasoning, Posner is critical of the abandonment of the formal promise under seal as a means of permitting a promisor to opt for legal enforcement of his gratuitous promise. *Id.* at 419-20. Reintroducing measurement costs may conceivably explain the abandonment of the seal. However, as a theoretical principle, an opportunity for the promisor voluntarily to adopt an enforceable form of promise does hold out the opportunity for gains to both parties.

effect of legal enforcement of a class of promises depends on the relative social value of these interacting adjustments.

Qualitative precautionary adjustments by promisors to increased sanctions may be thought of as merely the converse of reassurance. These precautionary moves entail a lessening of the scope of the promise and a shifting of the risk of potential regret contingencies to the promisee, while reassurance enhances the value of the promise and constitutes an assumption of risk by the promisor. These qualitative dimensions of a promise encompass two conceptually distinct effects: first, risk minimization by providing the promisee with better information on which to determine his degree of reliance; and, second, risk allocation by dividing the costs of regret contingencies between promisor and promisee. Analysis of these two factors suggests that legal sanctions can be used to induce risk-minimizing precautionary adjustments by both parties, but are much less successful in directing risk-bearing choices.

By providing the promisee with information concerning regret contingencies, precautionary adjustments by the gratuitous promisor improve the accuracy of the promisee's degree of reliance. Without a legal sanction, the benefits generated by the information effect of precautionary adjustments may not be maximized. The promisor is motivated to make precautionary adjustments only to the extent that his increased precautionary costs are outweighed by decreases in his regret costs. For instance, when only minimal extra-legal sanctions are imposed on breach, the savings in regret costs are relatively trivial, and precautionary moves by the promisor are not likely to be cost-effective. Under these circumstances, the promisee will be insufficiently forewarned about the risks of breach and will consequently overrely, failing to protect himself adequately against the prospect of breach.

Thus, where the external costs of a nonreciprocal promise are unlikely to be conveyed to the promisor, legal enforcement can induce the promisor to make optimal precautionary adjustments. Alternatively, the promisee must optimize self-protection and reliance in the light of the information he now possesses about the reliability of the promise. Paradoxically, if promises are unenforceable, the promisee has the correct incentives to protect himself to the optimal level against risks. Because the promisee bears all risks of breach, in this environment, he will rely on a promise only to the extent that the prospective cost of reliance is outweighed by prospective benefits. In contrast, if a promise is legally enforceable, and the regret costs shift to the promisor, the promisee may engage in a greater than optimal level of reliance. Because the reduction of regret costs becomes an external benefit of the promisee's actions, the promisee may ignore these costs in determining the extent of his reliance. In order to discourage the promisee from overrelying, the promisor must not be held liable for damages when the promisee knew or should have known that the marginal cost of self-protection was lower than the corresponding marginal reduction in prospective regret costs. This rule gives meaning to the concept of "reasonable reliance" and avoids not only an underinvestment in self-protection by the promisee, but also an overinvestment in precautionary adjustments by the promisor. It fills essentially the same function as does the rule of contributory negligence in tort.[42]

In addition to these risk minimization effects, legally induced qualitative precautionary moves reallocate the risk of regret to the promisee. What can be said of the risk allocation implications of these qualitative adjustments? The allocation of risk to a least-cost risk bearer by the manipulation of legal liability may have efficiency consequences that justify the costs of such adjustments. However, in the case of most nonreciprocal promises, the risk of a regret contingency ultimately will be borne by the promisee in spite of the promisor's risk-bearing advantages. Initially, the imposition of a legal sanction allocates some or all of the risk of a regret contingency to the promisor. But so long as the promisor is free to make qualitative adjustments, by conditioning his promise, he can shift that risk back to the promisee. In some cases, of course, the promisee may be the least-cost risk bearer. However, because it is the enforcement of the promise that removed the risk from the promisee initially, legally induced precautionary moves to shift it back again cannot be regarded as efficiency gains attributable to the liability rule. Thus, in terms of risk allocation, qualitative adjustments have only distributional consequences; their implementation costs may be regarded as net social losses.[43]

This analysis suggests that qualitative precautionary adjustments by

42. Imposition of a legal sanction equal to full detrimental reliance would, in the absence of a mitigation limitation, encourage overinvestment in reliance by promisees. Indeed, it has been suggested that enforcement of promises under a reliance scheme would create a moral hazard in terms of the promisee's adjustments. In other words, a promisee might be tempted to extend his reliance beyond any objectively reasonable point; if the promise is kept, he reaps the benefits, while if it is broken, the promisor bears the full costs under the liability rule. *See* Shavell, *supra* note 22. Optimal legal sanctions can respond to the problem of over-investment in reliance by structuring a compound liability rule under which the behavioral adaptations of both parties are scrutinized. Of course, the implementation costs of such a rule may be substantial. *See* pp. 1289-90 *infra*.

43. If promises are unenforceable, however, promisors may also engage in qualitative reassurance adjustments. This also entails social costs of implementation. These costs will be reduced under an enforcement rule.

the gratuitous promisor have mixed effects. Increasing these adjustments by legally enforcing nonreciprocal promises is optimal, therefore, only when gains in promisee reliance from improved information exceed the net implementation costs of reallocating the risk of regret to the promisee. This implies, as an empirical generalization, that enforcing nonreciprocal promises will improve outcomes when there exists a substantial prospect of beneficial information exchanges through qualitative adjustments. Conversely, in contexts in which self-sanctions are already effective and the prospects of improved information are poor, the social gains from enforcement are negligible and may be exceeded by implementation costs. Nonenforcement of such nonreciprocal promises is thus the optimal choice.

c. *An Optimal Damage Formula*

The effect of a decision to enforce legally any particular class of nonreciprocal promises depends upon the nature of the sanction imposed for breach. Promisors will respond to higher levels of sanction by increasing their qualitative and quantitative precautions, reducing both the reliability of a given volume of promises and the number of promises actually made.

A necessary starting point in determining an optimal damage rule is to specify the external effects of a nonreciprocal promise as the supply of such promises is increased by one marginal unit. The external effects are the prospective detrimental reliance incurred if the promise is broken and the prospective beneficial reliance enjoyed if the promise is performed. Proper reflection of external effects therefore requires not only that the promisor be charged for the harm expected from broken promises, but also that he be rewarded for the prospective benefits of performance. It is helpful to state this condition symbolically. Let p be the promisor's reasonable, subjective assessment of the probability that he will perform a promise under an existing legal rule calling for damages of D in the event of breach. For the damage rule to deter all promises with net social costs and encourage those with net benefits, the amount of damages awarded must satisfy the following equation:

$$(1-p)D = (1-p)R - pB$$

where R and B are the values of detrimental and beneficial reliances, respectively. Assuming that all broken promises are litigated, the left-hand side of the equation represents the expected value of the prospective legal sanction. Because only broken promises are affected by the law, the probability $(1 - p)$ of the promise being broken is used to "discount" the damages D. The values for R and B on the right-hand side of the equation should be understood as those resulting from optimal self-protection by the promisee. Thus, promisees will appropriately minimize the value of the right-hand term, which is the net social cost of the promise. In calculating this prospective net reliance, the magnitudes of the potential detrimental and beneficial reliances are each discounted by their probabilities. When the equation is satisfied through the imposition of optimal damages D, the promisor's internal cost-benefit calculus will reflect the external effects of his promise-making. If the external effects are thus accounted for, the promisor's maximization of his internal net benefits is consistent with supply of the socially optimal quantity and quality of promises. We call this damage rule the "prospective net reliance" formulation.

In some cases, the prospective beneficial reliance from a promise will exceed its prospective detrimental reliance. Because the net external effect of such a promise is beneficial, it would be optimal to reward the making of such promises. However, in the nonreciprocal setting no practical legal mechanism exists for rewarding promises. This limitation renders true optimization impossible; the situation is necessarily second-best. At minimum, promises with prospects of net beneficial reliance should not be the subject of damages if breached. Only promises with prospective net detrimental external effects should be enforceable.

The prospective net reliance formulation developed above can be used to analyze the optimal level of enforcement. By dividing both sides of the original equation by the probability of breach $(1 - p)$, the following damage rule emerges:

$$D = R - \left[\frac{p}{(1-p)}\right] B.$$

The optimal damage rule thus subtracts from the promisee's reliance cost a fraction of his potential beneficial reliance. This fraction is the ratio of the ex ante subjective probability of performance to that of nonperformance. It determines the extent to which the prospect of beneficial reliance when the promise was made is credited against the promisee's prospective detrimental reliance. Because this ratio may be thought of as an index of the promisor's good faith, we call it the "good-faith ratio." A damage offset based on the good-faith ratio and on the amount of potential beneficial reliance will encourage the optimal quantity and quality of promises by reflecting in the promisor's decision calculus both the harmful and beneficial effects of his promise-making. This optimal legal sanction is likely to be unattainable in an environment of costly legal process and imperfect information.[44] But specifying an optimal sanction permits more rigorous evaluation of the error produced by any practical adjustment attributable to process costs. In addition, the good-faith ratio and the damage offset suggest a possible explanation for the language of the *Restatement of Contracts*, which conditions both the enforceability and the magnitude of reliance-based sanctions upon the "requirements of justice."[45] This language may reflect the view that the prospective beneficial effects of a promise should be considered in effecting a remedy for nonperformance.

The rule suggested by the formula above will admittedly result in a large quantity of uncompensated damages from broken nonreciprocal promises. Although greater damages would deter many injurious transactions, a stricter standard also would deter beneficial transactions in even greater magnitudes. Viewing an already-broken promise, the affected promisee would always prefer the highest possible damage award. But from the ex ante standpoint, a promisee would not wish to discourage a promise that creates a prospect of gain outweighing the risk of uncompensated loss. Such promises are "good bets" for the promisee over the long run, even though some of the promises will result in uncompensated harm. The penalty formulation developed above awards damages both to protect promisees from "bad bet" promises and to avoid deterrence of promises that are "good bets."

Under this prospective net reliance damage formula, the gratuitous promisor also has an incentive to undertake cost-effective qualitative precautions to modify prospective reliance induced by any promise actually made. A properly calibrated legal sanction will induce the promisor to convey to the promisee socially beneficial information about the risk of regret contingencies. In essence, such a promisor is encouraged to make cost-effective adjustments in both the quality and the quantity of his promises because the legal rule converts social benefits into savings for him. If, in addition, the law recognizes only the amount of damages that constitutes a "reasonable"—*i.e.*, cost-effective—reliance by the promisee, then the promisee will also have an incentive to minimize net social costs. Thus, the rule penalizes each party for failing to take cost-effective steps to minimize the social costs of promising. Damages exceeding those described above will tend to induce the promisor to invest too much in precautionary adjustments. This phenomenon is analogous to the excessive level of prudence anticipated if tort victims were awarded a multiple of their true damages.

44. *See* pp. 1289-90 *infra*.
45. Restatement 1st § 90; Restatement 2d §§ 89B(2), 89D, 90(1), 217A(1).

2. *Reciprocal Promises*

Promising is reciprocal when the parties can adjust interactively to the nature and amount of promise-making. The prospective net reliance formulation is equally applicable to reciprocal as well as to nonreciprocal promises. But the net reliance damage rule seems in sharp conflict with accepted legal doctrine in the reciprocal promise context, in which damages for breach are typically based on the promisee's full-performance expectation rather than on his detrimental reliance. Upon analysis, the apparent conflict can be dissipated; moreover, reciprocal promises are easier than nonreciprocal promises for the law to address.

This conclusion is buttressed by two independent lines of argument. First, in the case of reciprocal promises, a plausible empirical generalization is that a promisee's acceptance of one promise frequently requires his foregoing a potential substitute promise. The forgone value of the best substitute promise available—the opportunity cost—is key in determining the promisee's detrimental reliance when an accepted promise is subsequently broken. In a well-organized market, alternative promises will be close, if not perfect, substitutes. In that case, detrimental reliance is equal to the full performance value of the breached promise.[46] Similarly, beneficial reliance will be small, because the promisor's pledge, even if performed, will not constitute a very substantial improvement over the potential beneficial reliance from substitute promises. This empirical generalization implies that, in the damage formula developed above, full performance expectation E can be substituted for detrimental reliance R because $E \approx R$. Furthermore, because $B \approx 0$, the term of $\left[\frac{1-p}{p}\right]$ B drops out. We are left with $D \approx E$; thus, expectation damages are a good proxy for the prospective net reliance damage formulation developed above.[47]

Second, a fundamental theoretical difference exists between reciprocal and nonreciprocal promises. In the case of a reciprocal promise,

46. The correlation between detrimental reliance and full performance expectation whenever there is a competitive market for the broken promise was first observed by Fuller and Perdue. *See* Fuller & Perdue, *supra* note 5, at 62-63.

47. Nothing in the logic of this argument limits its applicability to reciprocal promises. Although the argument's empirical premise tends to have greater validity with respect to bargained-for promises, classes of nonreciprocal promises may exist for which forgone substitute promises also yield a close convergence between reliance and expectation. The implications of using expectation as a proxy for reliance on reciprocal promises will become apparent when we introduce practical problems of measurement below. *See* pp. 1288-1321 *infra*.

the principal objective of a promisor is to obtain consideration in the form of a return promise. The value of the return promise elicited is the main element of the promisor's benefit. Therefore, changes in the qualitative aspects of the promise are reflected in commensurate shifts of benefits to the promisor; a higher quality promise motivates a more valuable return promise, and vice versa. In contrast to the case of nonreciprocal promises, qualitative adjustments are internalized in the promisor's cost-benefit calculus by generating a more or less valuable consideration for his promise. Hence, the bargaining process accomplishes an important part of the behavioral regulation that, for nonreciprocal promises, must be performed by the legal system.

Furthermore, the bargaining process, not available by definition in the nonreciprocal context, can facilitate the optimal allocation of risk for reciprocal promises. Precautionary action is subject to a test of the ability of the promisee to bribe the promisor to make an unconditioned promise. Within any scheme of enforcement, then, the parties can reallocate the risks of regretted promises by buying or selling protection through the terms of their agreement. The least-cost bearer of any risk will presumably agree to absorb that risk in exchange for an enhanced return promise.

For much the same reasons, the consequences of excessive damages for breaching reciprocal promises are also mitigated, as long as the rule providing for excessive damages is understood in advance. The parties can always bargain out from the rule, for instance by a limited damages agreement. Thus, when transactions costs are zero, the particular damage rule selected for reciprocal promises is irrelevant. Although the existence of transactions costs renders bargaining over damage rules costly in practice, the feedback adjustment of the return promise markedly reduces the potentially inefficient effects of legal rules. While in the nonreciprocal case, excessive damages overdeter the promisor from promissory activity, in the reciprocal relationship, the promisee will regard the excessive damages as a quality improvement and will offer an enhanced return promise. The enhanced return promise will tend to offset the deterrence effect of the damages. However, some inefficiencies remain. Legally mandated "overinsurance" induces a moral hazard because the promisee will not exercise optimal self-protection. Furthermore, there is a cheaper allocation of risk than the legally mandated level of reassurance provided to—and paid for by—the promisee.[48]

48. There is a close conceptual analogy between excessive contractual damages and specific guarantees or minimum quality requirements imposed by law on consumer

The result may be even more costly, however, when the law provides a suboptimal level of enforcement. The extreme case of a complete refusal to enforce reciprocal promises provides an instructive illustration.[49] The initial impact of the rule, which is to underdeter promisors, will be counterbalanced by reductions in the value of return promises. Promisors may then substitute extra-legal forms of reassurance for legal sanctions. Creating adequate extra-legal enforcement mechanisms is likely to be less efficient than legally sanctioned reassurance. If so, the inefficiency consequences of underenforcement may be more serious than those of overenforcement.

In sum, the theoretical damages principles developed in connection with nonreciprocal promises apply to reciprocal promises as well. The difference in their legal treatment may be due to a close empirical identity of reliance and expectation in reciprocal promises. However, modification of the return promise is a powerful additional adjustment mechanism, which exists, by definition, only for reciprocal promises. By internalizing many of the promissory interactions among contracting parties, the return promise reduces the stress placed on legal rules for optimally influencing the behavior of promisors and promisees.

D. *Summary and Implications*

The preceding analysis suggests that the function of promises can be observed more precisely by conceptually distinguishing the effects of the advance information from the actual transfer. Information from promises induces reliance whenever the promisee attaches a positive probability to performance. Reliance responses are beneficial when a promise is kept and detrimental when it is broken. The principal normative justification for permitting promises to be made freely is the belief that, on balance, promissory benefits exceed harms. Legally enforcing promises can sometimes increase this net social gain by encouraging cost-reducing behavior by both promisors and promisees.

The treatment of promises when performance or nonperformance is certain is simple: such promises can be fully enforced so as to maximize benefits or minimize costs respectively. In the sure performance case,

products. Because the product is required to be "better," it can command a higher price, which overcomes at least in part the reluctance of producers to supply a more expensive output. Nevertheless, a suboptimal result exists because consumers and producers could, if permitted, work out a mutually advantageous trade of less quality for less money.

49. In contrast to bargained-for limitations of standard damage measures, attempts to contract for supranormal remedies may run afoul of the rule against penalties. *See* Goetz & Scott, *supra* note 10, at 558-62.

enforcement, without deterring the promisor, increases the reliability of the promise to the promisee. In the certain nonperformance case, maximum deterrence of promises serves to prevent a bad-faith promisor from enriching himself at certain cost to the promisee.

The more important case of promises for which performance is potentially uncertain is more complex, because each promise carries both potential benefits and harms that must be balanced. Future contingencies may materialize rendering performance of such promises unattractive to the promisor. The risk of this regret contingency can be allocated several ways. On the one hand, nonenforcement of promises induces self-protective reductions in reliance by the promisee. These, in turn, may trigger reassurance reactions from the promisor. On the other hand, enforcement of promises increases promisee reliance, but also induces precautionary adjustments by the promisor. The social cost of the regret contingency is minimized when the optimal interactive adaptations are encouraged.

An examination of the function of legal rules in optimizing the interactions between the promisor and promisee explains the traditional distinction between nonreciprocal and reciprocal promises. In the case of reciprocal promises, the bargain mechanism provides a feedback of costs and benefits to the promisor and promisee. Thus, the liability rules for reciprocal promises do not directly influence promise-making; instead, they affect the costs of contracting between bargainers. For nonreciprocal promises, however, enforcement substantially shapes the adaptive responses of both parties.[50] For example, enforcement of nonreciprocal promises will optimize social benefits when extra-legal sanctions are minimal and the promisor can be encouraged to adapt the form of the promise to the risk of regret. Calibration of the optimal damages for such enforceable promises requires a consideration of both the beneficial and the detrimental reliance prospectively induced by the promise. Such a prospective net reliance formulation encourages promisors accurately to internalize social effects and thereby induces appropriate qualitative and quantitative adjustments.

But the practical implications of this ideal enforcement scheme must be considered. When nonenforcement is optimal, no measurement difficulties impede its implementation. When enforcement is indicated, implementation of the optimal rule is more difficult. A standard expectation-interest sanction may impose supra-optimal damages and deter socially valuable promise-making by inducing excessive precautionary behavior in promisors. The traditional reliance damage formulation—

50. *See* pp. 1307-08 *infra*.

return of the promisee to the status quo ante—most clearly approximates the optimal level of enforcement.[51] However, despite the language usually invoked, the status quo ante goal is rarely achieved by courts awarding so-called reliance damages. This systematic disparity between principle and practice isolates a central dilemma of promissory liability. True reliance damages, which include the value of opportunities forgone as well as the costs of actions taken, are extraordinarily difficult to measure accurately. Courts have generally responded to this largely unarticulated measurement conundrum by simply reimbursing the promisee for the gross value of any actions taken or actual expenditures incurred in reliance on the promise.[52] The recovery of such expenditures, which we have termed "reimbursement damages," should be distinguished from the theoretical objective of reliance damages.

We have developed the preceding model under an assumption of perfect measurement in order to evaluate the effects of legal rules on promissory behavior. Existing patterns of promissory liability often appear to produce substantial error costs in failing to regulate this conduct efficiently. Can this systematic error be explained? The complexity of the preceding analysis suggests that measurement of the true social cost of promising is likely to be itself a very costly activity. Enforcement costs increase the risk that the promisee's true reliance losses will not be fully recouped.[53] Moreover, process costs necessary to ascertain and implement the optimal level of enforcement may be so high that they exceed the error costs attributable to simpler rules of thumb such as no enforcement, full enforcement, or reimbursement. In Part II we relax the assumptions of perfect measurement and zero process costs to evaluate the efficiency of the rules of promissory obligation from a more practical standpoint.

II. Efficient Rules of Promissory Obligation

The second aspect of the promissory enforcement question asks whether the optimal enforcement model when adjusted for enforcement costs explains current patterns of promissory liability. We address this question first by describing the legal costs necessary to enforce promises and examining the relationship of these costs to different substantive rules. We then evaluate the rules of promissory liability by examining three basic categories of promises: fully bargained-for reciprocal prom-

51. *See* p. 1298 *infra*.
52. *See* pp. 1292-93 *infra*.
53. *See* Goetz & Scott, *supra* note 10, at 558 n.19; Schwartz, *The Case for Specific Performance*, 89 YALE L.J. 271, 274-78 (1979).

ises within the common law "consideration" model; nonreciprocal promises distinguishable by the parties' inability to adjust interactively the nature and amount of promising; and, finally, the intermediate category of unilateral promises in a reciprocal context, which, under the narrow common law standard, may be unenforceable despite the possibility of bargaining.

A. *Problems of Proof, Process, and Error Costs*

In Part I we developed damage rules that encourage the socially optimal production of beneficial reliance on future promises. Except when a nonenforcement rule is appropriate, imposition of such an optimal sanction necessitates that the detrimental reliance losses from the broken promise be ascertained. Unfortunately, promissory reliance is peculiarly impervious to accurate measurement and proof when it diverges from full performance expectation.[54] Because true reliance cost is equal to the opportunity cost of the promise, measurement of the loss requires a comparison of the promisee's behavior in response to the promise with his prospective conduct in the absence of the promise: the promisee's detrimental reliance cost is the difference in satisfaction between these two positions. This calculation entails identifying the value of alternative opportunities forgone because of the promise and the benefits retained from the actions taken in reliance. Generally, these values can be determined solely by evaluating the subjective claims of the promisee. Only when a competitive market generates prices indicating the value of foregone opportunities will there be reliable evidence of the position the promisee would have occupied had no promise been made.[55]

Furthermore, an optimal legal sanction may also include a discount for the effects of extra-legal factors—such as reputational losses or social restraints on breach—that independently reward the performing promisor for taking into account some of the social effects of promising.

54. The process costs of measuring reliance include both direct costs of litigation and the effects of "error," which are social costs that arise when the procedural mechanism fails to apply accurately the substantive rule. *See* Posner, *An Economic Approach to Legal Procedure and Judicial Administration*, 2 J. LEGAL STUD. 399, 400-02 (1973); Scott, *Constitutional Regulation of Provisional Creditor Remedies: The Cost of Procedural Due Process*, 61 VA. L. REV. 807, 810, 844-46 (1975).

Reliance expenditures are extraordinarily difficult to measure even in business contexts. Such expenditures often consist of overhead expenditures and joint costs not readily allocable to particular contracts. *See, e.g.*, Reiss & Weinsier, Inc. v. United States, 116 F. Supp. 562 (Ct. Cl. 1953); Houston Ready-Cut House Co. v. United States, 96 F. Supp. 629 (Ct. Cl. 1951).

55. Presumably, in a competitive market the prevailing market price reveals the opportunities forgone in reliance on the broken promise.

Thus, any theoretically precise reliance-based damage calculation may require an additional computation of the prospective beneficial effects that performance of the promise would have conveyed.[56] In addition to computing the magnitude of both detrimental and beneficial reliance, this "good-faith" calculation requires ascertaining the promisor's subjective probability of performance at the time the promise was made.

Adjustment of the damage formula may be necessary if measurement costs prohibit even the approximation of true reliance losses. The award of reliance-based reimbursement damages does not—despite its stated purposes of restoring the status quo ante—accurately measure true reliance.[57] In fact, there is no a priori reason to believe that a reimbursement award is preferable in any particular case to nonenforcement or full performance compensation.[58] In sum, the administrative and error costs of attempting to apply a theoretically optimal net reliance standard suggest that it may be worthwhile to adopt a surrogate measure that is cheaper to apply.

The ease of administration of rules regulating promising are in part a function of the clarity of the substantive rule. Clarity is enhanced by use of a substantive rule that reduces the number and complexity of facts to be determined. A clear rule, such as nonenforcement or full performance compensation, yields benefits of reduced litigation costs and increased procedural accuracy. The primary cost of a clear rule is that it regulates promissory conduct imprecisely.[59] Full performance compensation, for example, may deter some promises with positive expected benefits that an optimal rule would encourage. But a rule that better reflects true promissory reliance requires resolution of more

56. *See* p. 1283 *supra*.

57. In order to approximate the status quo ante position of the promisee, the damage rule must measure two additional variables: the cost of forgone opportunities and the gain to the promisee from the induced action. Mere recovery of the out-of-pocket costs of the induced action will overvalue the harm induced by actions taken and undervalue the hidden losses incurred from forbearance. Yet, only when there is a competitive market for such promises can either of these variables be measured confidently. *See* pp. 1296-97 *infra*.

58. When forbearance is significantly greater than out-of-pocket expenditures, a reimbursement award will be substantially lower than the value of true reliance. Alternatively, when the induced actions involve substantial expenditures that produce difficult-to-measure benefits to the promisee, a reimbursement award may substantially exceed the value of detrimental reliance.

59. A clearer enforcement/nonenforcement rule may be both overinclusive and underinclusive. For example, full performance enforcement may restrain some socially beneficial promises by imposing an excessive sanction. Alternatively, nonenforcement may fail to charge promisors for the social costs of nonperformance. *Cf.* Ehrlich & Posner, *An Economic Analysis of Legal Rulemaking*, 3 J. LEGAL STUD. 257, 267-71 (1974) (explaining how precision of legal rules generates costs of overinclusion and underinclusion).

factual issues and thereby reduces the rule's clarity. Thus, a particular rule is efficient when both substantive and procedural components are constructed so as to provide the cost-minimizing balance between accuracy and clarity.[60]

A theory of promissory liability that minimizes these costs remains elusive. The foundations for such a theory were established by Professor Lon Fuller over fifty years ago.[61] Fuller's claim for the preeminence of reliance, however, seems inconsistent with established bargain theory. For example, a gratuitous promise, unsupported by consideration, is commonly presumptively unenforceable. Yet that same promise, if a product of a bargained-for exchange, is fully enforceable without any evidence of reliance. Fuller explained this apparent anomaly by suggesting that gratuitous promises are unenforceable because reliance is lacking, while the bargained-for promise is fully enforceable in order to facilitate likely reliance.[62] Our analysis of the information function of promises confirms the inadequacy of these explanations. Gratuitous promises can induce reliance, whose costs are ignored under nonenforcement.[63] Furthermore, facilitation of likely reliance by awarding full compensation for executory bargains may deter the future production of socially useful promises.[64]

However, the rules of promissory liability can be reconciled with the reliance principle. The existing tension between bargain and reliance is a product of the failure to discriminate adequately between ideal and pragmatic objectives. For example, common law bargain theory and the doctrine of consideration, as well as the modern concept of promissory estoppel, can be examined best as cost-minimizing surrogates for true reliance. Introducing the complexities of measurement and proof indicates that the traditional choice between reliance damages and the alternatives of nonenforcement and full performance compensation should be recast as an attempt to select from potential contract rules the best achievable approximation of the optimal enforcement standard.

60. *See id.* at 262-71.

61. *See* Fuller & Perdue, *supra* note 5; Fuller, *supra* note 20. Three critical insights can be extracted from Fuller's exploration of the remedial and formal structures of contract: first, reliance is the organizing principle that supports all contractual obligation; second, typical contractual remedies—such as compensatory damages—serve as cost-reducing administrative surrogates for reliance; and third, a direct relationship can be identified—through the formal structure of promissory liability rules—between process considerations and the substantive rules of contract.

62. *See* Fuller, *supra* note 20, at 815-18.

63. *See* pp. 1267-70 *supra*.

64. *See* pp. 1285-86 *supra*.

B. *Reciprocal-Bargain Promises: The Consideration Model*

First, we examine reciprocal promises reached by bargaining, for which the common law developed the consideration doctrine.

1. *The Functions of Bargain*

Evaluating contract rules as cost-reducing surrogates for the theoretically optimal enforcement rule reemphasizes the importance of the distinction between reciprocal and nonreciprocal promises. Promises that satisfy the reciprocal exchange requirement of consideration are presumptively enforceable. Breach entitles the promisee to full performance compensation. The enforceability of reciprocal promises is supported by a rich normative literature emphasizing the social utility of bargains.[65] But more importantly, as suggested above, the bargain mechanism can reduce discrepancies between optimal and actual enforcement rules.

We have pointed out the identity between detrimental reliance and full-performance expectation whenever markets for promises are competitive.[66] Furthermore, bargaining tends to produce the optimal amount of promissory reliance even when the legal rule deviates from the optimal reliance principle. By modifying contractual terms, the parties can vary the standard liability rule in order to maximize net reliance benefits.[67]

What effects can be predicted from full enforcement of reciprocal bargain promises? As the model developed in Part I suggests, application of sanctions for breach imposes the risk of the regret contingency

65. *See, e.g.*, 1 A. SMITH, THE WEALTH OF NATIONS 12-15 (Everyman's Library ed. 1937); Patterson, *supra* note 15, at 945; *Promise or Bargain?*, *supra* note 1, at 463-65.

66. The competitive market offers one polar case in which the promisees' detrimental reliance is precisely equal to full performance expectation. *See* Goetz & Scott, *Measuring Sellers' Damages: The Lost Profits Puzzle*, 31 STAN. L. REV. 323, 333-35 (1979) (measuring damages in competitive markets). The other pole is represented by the classic bilateral exchange in which the promise made to one or both parties is singular or unique. An example drawn loosely from the facts of Hamer v. Sidway, 124 N.Y. 538, 27 N.E. 256 (1891), may illustrate this point. Suppose William II promises his Uncle William to refrain from smoking and drinking, while the uncle promises in return to pay his nephew $5000 for each year in which the youth remains an abstainer. Subsequently, Uncle William reneges on his promise. Because no alternative market existed in which William II could have obtained a promise of money in exchange for his own promise, he has not forgone any alternative promise and his "immediate reliance" is zero. Nonetheless, receipt of even a singular bargain promise does induce a "consequential reliance" of alterations in consumption, whose magnitude is unpredictable.

67. The bargaining context invites a promisee to obtain any promise with a positive expected value. Legal liability, like any other risk in an executory exchange, can be optimally allocated between the parties.

on the promisor. As the promisor's potential liability is increased, he is encouraged to take precautionary action to minimize the expected liability, by conditioning promises more carefully in negotiations. The promisee, in turn, may bargain for a less restricted promise by paying explicitly for the additional reassurance provided by a compensation award.

Alternatively, a rule denying enforcement of a bargained-for promise reduces precautionary costs incurred by promisors seeking to minimize the risks of regret, because it shifts that risk to the promisee. The promisee may adapt to this increased uncertainty by discounting the price he is willing to pay for the promise. If the promise is actually worth more than the promisee estimates, the promisor will incur costs up to the expected value of the promise in order to assure the promisee of the true worth of the promise. These additional reassurance costs induced by the promisee's adaptive behavior could include the voluntary assumption of legal liability through collateral guarantees or performance bonds.

Thus, because bargainers will attempt to allocate the risk of regret optimally themselves, the effects of enforcement rules depend on the transaction costs of risk allocation. Evaluation of these costs requires an analysis of how bargainers adapt to the risks of regret contingencies. If in certain transactions precautionary efforts by promisors would be more expensive than reassurance, nonenforcement enables the parties to shift the risk of regret more cheaply. Alternatively, when reassurance is more costly, fully enforcing promises induces cheaper precautionary conduct. If each type of transaction can be identified ex ante, specifying the cost-effective rule in advance produces the outcome that the parties would reach if they bargained over legal liability for breach.

2. *The Design of the Bargain Paradigm*

The classical bargain model can be examined on the basis of these assumed variations in precautionary and reassurance costs. Not all promises made in a bargaining context are presumptively enforceable. Indeed, the reciprocal bargain or consideration model is considerably more limited than the larger exchange context that it occupies. For example, promises made during preliminary negotiations[68] and prom-

68. In the words of the *Restatement 2d*: "A manifestation of willingness to enter into a bargain is not an offer if the person to whom it is addressed knows or has reason to know that the person making it does not intend to conclude a bargain until he has made a further manifestation of assent." RESTATEMENT 2D § 25; *see* 1 A. CORBIN, *supra* note 5, §§ 26-27, at 95-100.

ises to discharge contractual obligations[69] are traditionally unenforceable even though they are made in the context of a bargain. This failure to impose liability in certain exchange contexts can be contrasted with the wholly executory completed bargain, which is fully enforceable when supported by consideration. In each case, the liability rule can be explained by its impact on transactional efficiency.

Under traditional bargain theory, promises made during preliminary bargaining are not enforceable until the bargain is sealed by an agreed exchange. Complex rules of offer and acceptance have been developed in order to distinguish enforceable bargained-for promises from unenforceable preliminary negotiations. Suppose *A* promises to sell, and *B* to buy, 1000 widgets "at cost plus a nice profit." Subsequently, in a disagreement over the price, *A* refuses to deliver the widgets to *B*. Because the price term was not determined, the bargain remains incomplete. Hence *A*'s promise will probably be characterized as an unenforceable preliminary promise.[70] If, instead, a ten percent profit were negotiated, both promises would be fully enforceable. But assume that after the widgets have been delivered *A* promises *B*, "Your obligation will be cancelled. I will release my right to the $1000 that you owe me." As with the preliminary negotiation, this discharge promise is unenforceable. The rights that were created by the bargain cannot be extinguished by agreement without consideration.[71]

Freedom from liability upon entry and exit from bargaining, coupled with full enforcement of wholly executory promises once agreement has been achieved, is the basic design of the bargain model of traditional contract law.[72] This pattern typically has been explained in terms of differences in the magnitude of either actual or likely reliance. Neither explanation is persuasive. Disregarding the effect of the rule itself,

69. On promises to discharge contractual obligations, the *Restatement 2d* states the following: "A promise to discharge [a] duty must, like any other promise, be supported by consideration in order to be enforceable." RESTATEMENT 2D, Introductory Note, §§ 343-347, at 5 (Tent. Draft No. 13, 1978); *see* 5 A. CORBIN, *supra* note 5, § 1236; RESTATEMENT 1ST § 406.

70. *See* C.H. Leavell & Co. v. Grafe & Assocs., 90 Idaho 502, 414 P.2d 873 (1966); RESTATEMENT 2D § 32, Comment 7, Illustration e.

71. RESTATEMENT 2D § 343, Illustration 1 (Tent. Draft No. 13, 1978).

72. There are some imperfections in the symmetry of the common law design. The traditional preexisting-duty rule held that when a promisee agreed in exchange for a promised benefit to do what he was already legally obligated to do, the exchange lacked consideration and the return promise was unenforceable. *See* 1 A. CORBIN, *supra* note 5, §§ 171-192; Patterson, *supra* note 15, at 936-38. Because this rule was both overinclusive and underinclusive with respect to the coercive conduct it purported to attack, the modern view finds promises that modify a prior agreement presumptively enforceable absent unfair pressure or bad faith. *See* U.C.C. § 2-209(1), Comment 2; RESTATEMENT 2D §§ 76A, 89D, Comment b.

Enforcing Promises

there is no a priori reason to believe that reliance on either a preliminary or a termination promise will be less prevalent than reliance on the main promise itself. The enforcement choice, however, will affect the expected costs of bargaining between *A* and *B*. Enforcement of preliminary or termination promises will increase the cost of promising to promisors. Potential promisors will be willing to incur greater precautionary costs to avoid the risks of liability. Alternatively, a nonenforcement rule increases the cost of promises to promisees. Consequently, the amount of bargaining devoted to assurances of performance will be increased. The enforcement pattern could be explained if, during entry into, and exit from, bargaining, reassurance were cheaper than precaution. Then, the risk of a regret contingency could be allocated more cheaply by adjusting reliance once the promise is made rather than restricting the promise itself.

The design of the consideration model can be explained if the categories of bargaining risks are conceptually distinguished. Each bargainer, being both a promisor and promisee, faces two sets of parallel risks. As a promisor, the bargainer confronts the risk of liability should he fail to keep his promise. He also faces the risk of detrimental reliance should the promise made to him in return be broken. Based on the common empirical assumption that bargainers are generally risk-averse, the consideration model is justifiable in economic terms. Because the outcomes of negotiations are uncertain and gains and losses are indefinite, risk-averse parties will choose to forgo uncertain gains rather than incur equally uncertain losses of the same magnitude. In other words, risk-averse bargainers will prefer to bear uncertain risks as promisees rather than as promisors. Moreover, because a promisee can control reliance costs more easily than can a promisor, the risk of detrimental reliance is lower if borne by the promisee rather than the promisor. An enforcement rule would encourage excessive precautionary adjustments by risk-averse bargainers, because the uncertain consequences of nonperformance could not be controlled. Therefore, negotiations by such bargainers to reallocate risks through precautionary action would be more costly than the reallocation of identical risks through reassurance.[73]

73. The basic economic justification for such a scheme is that it saves most parties the costs of negotiating the preferred allocation of risks. Considerable flexibility to rearrange the risks of liability are retained by individual bargainers. Generally, the parties can elect to incur liability during preliminary exchanges by signaling their intention to be bound. *See* U.C.C. § 2-204(3) (requiring reasonably certain basis for granting remedy); RESTATEMENT 2D §§ 25, 32, Comment b (same). Alternatively, bargainers can choose a nonenforcement regime by indicating an intention not to be bound. *See* RESTATEMENT 2D § 21B, Comment b.

But bargainers prefer the risk of uncompensated reliance only on the periphery of bargaining. The crucial distinction between the periphery and the core of bargaining is the shift toward greater certainty of outcome. The impetus to bargain is the assumption that expected gains will exceed expected losses. Thus, when the transaction is finally negotiated, the expected value of gain outweighs the risk of liability upon breach.[74] Thus, after agreement, bargainers prefer to bear remaining risks as promisors rather than as promisees, thereby mutually enhancing the expected benefits to each. Consequently, expenditures required for reassurance under nonenforcement would exceed the investment in precaution required by full enforcement.[75]

The reluctance to enforce peripheral promises, on entry or exit, can also be explained on process grounds, even if the parties intend to be legally bound. The more incomplete and uncertain the details of an exchange, the greater the adjudicatory and error costs in resolving subsequent disputes. A greater allocation of resources to negotiation of the details of an agreement saves the parties expected litigation costs in case of subsequent dispute. If both litigation and negotiation costs were fully borne by bargainers, it would be efficient to permit them to negotiate to the point at which marginal expenditures in negotiations equalled marginal reductions in expected litigation costs. However, because litigation costs are partially subsidized by taxpayers, parties will engage in a suboptimal amount of negotiation and thereby generate an overinvestment in litigation. The refusal of the common law rules to enforce indefinite bargains can be seen as an attempt to compensate for this process distortion.[76]

In sum, the design of the consideration model can be explained persuasively by an analysis of efficient risk allocation. Manipulation of the liability rule shifts the risk of a regret contingency between prom-

74. Changed conditions producing regret will not necessarily induce the promisor to breach. Breach occurs only when the cost of performance exceeds liability for nonperformance. Breach is motivated, at least in part, by a belief that the promisee is better able to salvage or minimize the effects of the changed conditions than is the promisor. For example, a seller-promisee can generally resell unwanted goods more cheaply than a buyer-promisor who no longer wants to retain them. *See* Goetz & Scott, *supra* note 66, at 344 (optimal liability rule would make choice between performance and breach a matter of indifference).

75. Discharge negotiations seem characterized by less ambiguity and uncertainty than are preliminary negotiations. This intuition is confirmed by the fact that the nonenforcement rule has been applied much more hesitantly in the discharge context.

76. *See* 1 A. Corbin, *supra* note 5, §§ 95-97; Restatement 1st § 32; 1 S. Williston, Contracts §§ 37-48 (3d ed. 1957). Although the Uniform Commercial Code shifts the presumption in favor of party autonomy, it retains the injunction against enforcing indefinite bargains unless "there is a reasonably certain basis for giving an appropriate remedy." U.C.C. § 2-204(3).

isees and promisors. These varying liability patterns can induce interactive adaptations by the parties to allocate the social costs of promising efficiently. This cheapest-risk-allocation design is buttressed by process considerations that justify imposing promissory liability only if agreement upon the basic transaction has been reached.

3. *Remedies for Nonperformance of Bargained-for Promises*

The impact of any enforcement rule ultimately depends on the character of the remedy for nonperformance. Full enforcement compensation is the standard recovery for breach of reciprocal-bargain promises, whenever such an award can be determined accurately. The stated objective of this compensation rule is to place the promisee in the same economic position he would have occupied had the promise been performed.[77] As we have argued above, this rule, by imposing a sanction in excess of the social costs of breach, overdeters socially useful promising, except in competitive markets in which expectation is equivalent to reliance. The bargain context, however, enables the parties to vary, with low transactions costs, the legal rule by agreement and thereby mitigate the effects of any remedial distortion. Moreover, the disparity between compensatory recovery and optimal reliance damages is usually more than offset by gains in the clarity of the rule. Suppose *A* promises *B* $5,000 in exchange for *B*'s agreement to paint *A*'s portrait. After the painting is completed, *A* reneges. Because the market for similar promises is likely to be thin, the immediate reliance or opportunity cost of *A*'s promise may vary unpredictably from the $5,000 contract price. Furthermore, *A*'s promise and breach will have produced a detrimental adjustment in *B*'s pattern of consumption. The amount of such consequential reliance is even more difficult to measure. Full performance compensation in this example is precisely and objectively measured by the $5,000 face value of *A*'s promise. The administrative advantages of this clear rule outweigh the potential costs of distortion.

When the promisee's expectation includes the consequences of performance, the damage rule becomes more complicated. Suppose *A* promises to sell *B* the raw materials for manufacturing 1,000 widgets at the current market price of $5,000. *A*'s breach causes *B* to lose two weeks of production of widgets. The $5,000 contract price no longer approximates *B*'s expectations from performance. In this situation, *B* will not be entitled to recover his lost profits from *A* unless they were

77. 5 A. CORBIN, *supra* note 5, § 992.

foreseeable when the contract was made and can be proved with reasonable certainty.[78] If *B*'s expectation is unforeseeable or difficult to establish, reimbursement damages may be awarded rather than full performance compensation.

It is tempting to conclude that reimbursement recoveries are always preferable to full-performance damages as a more accurate approximation of the optimal reliance-based sanction. However, as suggested above, reimbursement recoveries are limited on practical grounds to the amount of the expenditures induced by the promise.[79] Courts have not even attempted to ascertain the value of forgone opportunities; expenditures have been reduced to their net value only when a salvage market exists. Thus, a reimbursement remedy is not necessarily a more accurate proxy for the optimal reliance-based sanction than full-performance compensation.

Following a total breach by the promisee, the value of a partial performance by the promisor can also be recouped through a reimbursement recovery.[80] The intricate patterns of recovery in partial performance cases can be explained by variations in magnitude of the costs of proof and valuation.[81] Courts usually award whichever recovery of reimbursement and compensation is readily measurable in monetary terms. In the more common cases in which neither compensation nor reimbursement is easily measured, the promisee may elect either compensation or reimbursement damages for partial performance so long as he is not made better off than his original expectation.[82]

Although objectively measurable recovery has the advantage of re-

78. *See* Farnsworth, *supra* note 10, at 1158-59 (also requiring effort to mitigate damages); Note, *Lost Profits as Contract Damages: Problems of Proof and Limitations on Recovery*, 65 YALE L.J. 992, 997-98 (1956) (relating causation to foreseeability and certainty).

79. *See* Royce Chem. Co. v. Sharples Corp., 285 F.2d 183 (2d Cir. 1960); L. Albert & Son v. Armstrong Rubber Co., 178 F.2d 182 (2d Cir. 1949); Gruber v. S-M News Co., 126 F. Supp. 442 (S.D.N.Y. 1954).

80. 5 A. CORBIN, *supra* note 5, § 1104; RESTATEMENT 1ST § 347.

81. The relation between process costs and the choice of remedies can be illustrated by returning to the example that was described above. Suppose *A* promises to sell *B* the raw materials for manufacturing 1,000 widgets at the current market price of $5,000. *A* reneges. If *B* has paid the agreed price, he is entitled to a $5,000 restitutionary reimbursement even though performance by *A* would have yielded a loss to *B*. *See* Bush v. Canfield, 2 Conn. 485, 488 (1818). Conversely, if *A* were to deliver the raw materials and *B* were to breach his promise to pay $5,000, reimbursement of expenditures would be denied to *A*; rather, *A* would be limited to his $5,000 expectancy even when the value of the raw materials delivered was significantly greater. *See* Oliver v. Campbell, 43 Cal. 2d 298, 306, 273 P.2d 15, 20 (1954).

82. A court will not "knowingly put the plaintiff in a better position than he would have occupied had the contract been fully performed." Fuller & Perdue, *supra* note 5, at 79; *see* Farnsworth, *supra* note 10, at 1178-79.

Enforcing Promises

ducing process costs, ease of measurement does not fully explain the selection of damage rules. In addition to the uncertainty of the loss, findings of remoteness and unforeseeability are used to limit consequential recoveries.[83] Courts appear unwilling to inflict socially harmful overdeterrence when the gains from awarding compensation are attenuated. Furthermore, the damage limitations of uncertainty and unforeseeability are not uniformly applied. The doctrines have been rigorously applied in cases in which liability appeared disproportionate to the gains the promisor anticipated from the contract, but have been rarely invoked when recoveries were of more limited magnitude.[84]

These limitations on consequential losses are consistent with the assumption of risk aversion discussed above. If a risk-averse promisor faces potential consequences of breach that are disproportionately large as well as unpredictable, he will increase his precautionary efforts. Limitation of the legal sanction divides the risk of regret between promisors and promisees. Promisors continue to bear the risk of the known and ascertainable consequences of concluded bargains, while promisees bear the risk of uncertain and unforeseeable consequences. A partial reallocation of the risk will reduce promisors' precautionary costs and increase their investment in reassurance. However, the expenditures on reassurance should be less than the investment in precaution under a fully compensatory scheme. First, risk-averse bargainers will choose to forgo gains rather than risk losses of equal magnitude. The cost to the promisee of forgoing profitable but unforeseeable actions in reliance on a promise will be lower than the cost to the promisor of bearing the risks that the promisee will engage in such action and that a regret contingency will arise. Thus, bargainers will prefer to bear the risk of uncertain and potentially severe consequences as promisees rather than as promisors. Second, because the consequences of breach are better known to the promisee, he is better able to select the optimal mix of promisor reassurance and self-protection through

83. *See* Fuller & Perdue, *supra* note 5, at 373-77 (analyzing other factors that limit recovery); *cf.* Note, *supra* note 78, at 997-1000 (criticizing rules limiting recoveries).

84. *See* Fuller & Perdue, *supra* note 5, at 375-76. *Compare* Dieffenbach v. McIntyre, 208 Okla. 163, 254 P.2d 346 (1952) (denying recovery for anticipated profits to plaintiff who received some damages) *with* Smith v. Onyx Oil & Chem. Co., 120 F. Supp. 674 (D. Del. 1954), *modified*, 218 F.2d 104 (3d Cir. 1955) (allowing recovery for anticipated profits to plaintiff who otherwise would recover nothing).

In addition to the disproportionate verdict problem, the bad faith or willfulness of the promisor's breach has been a relevant variable influencing the application of the uncertainty and foreseeability limitations. *See* Bauer, *The Degree of Moral Fault as Affecting Defendant's Liability*, 81 U. PA. L. REV. 586, 592 (1933); Fuller & Perdue, *supra* note 5, at 374-75. Imposition of full enforcement sanctions on the bad-faith promisor is consistent with the optimal enforcement model developed above. *See* note 35 *supra*.

limited reliance. In addition, the limitation on the award of damages for unascertainable consequences of breach induces the promisee to disclose to the promisor information that the promisor may not have concerning the consequences of breach. This information would not be disclosed to the promisor under a full-performance compensation rule and benefits from promise-making would not be maximized. Thus, the limitation on damages for unforeseeable consequences of breach increases the efficiency of promissory activity by stimulating the provision of information between bargainers.[85]

4. *The Implications of the Consideration Model*

Dissatisfaction with the mechanical rules of the common law has induced courts and commentators to offer more flexible alternatives.[86] For example, detrimental reliance has been urged as a basis for imposing discretionary liability for broken promises made in a bargaining context.[87] The current liability design of the consideration model appears to rest on crucial assumptions about bargainers' risk preferences and relative abilities to minimize risks. The indeterminacy of these empirical assumptions may explain the rigidity of the common law pattern. Liability based on future actions such as those in reliance increases bargaining uncertainty, the cost of which reduces the social value of the exchange. Whenever the outcome of private bargaining is unpredictable, liability rules that clearly specify the consequences of alternative actions will minimize uncertainty. By sharply distinguishing fully enforceable bargains from unenforceable promises, the formal rules of consideration permit bargainers to choose the outcome that minimizes expected bargaining costs.

The preceding analysis explains only the basic design of the consideration model. It does not help identify where to draw the line between enforcement and nonenforcement. At common law the category of enforceable bargained-for promises was rigidly narrow. The reluctance of common law courts to impose liability for a broader category of bargain promises perhaps can be explained by the frequent

85. Hadley v. Baxendale, 9 Exch. 341, 156 Eng. Rep. 145 (1854); *see* U.C.C. § 2-715(2)(a). Denial of lost profits as too uncertain or remote is generally accompanied by the recovery of reimbursement damages for expenditures incurred in pursuing the venture, on the presumption that the promisee would at least have covered his losses. *See, e.g.*, C.C. Hauff Hardware, Inc. v. Long Mfg. Co., 260 Iowa 30, 35, 148 N.W.2d 425, 428 (1967). In any event, the burden of reducing recovery below plaintiff's expenditures must lie on the defendant. *See, e.g.*, L. Albert & Son v. Armstrong Rubber Co., 178 F.2d 182, 189 (2d Cir. 1949).

86. *See, e.g.*, Knapp, *Enforcing the Contract to Bargain*, 44 N.Y.U. L. Rev. 673 (1969).

87. *See, e.g.*, Restatement 2d §§ 89B(2), 89C(c), 89D(c), 90.

Enforcing Promises

distortion between the standard compensation rule and the optimal reliance sanction. Because nonenforcement eliminates distortions in measurement, it may be the preferable treatment for bargain promises when full enforcement provides no compensating advantages. We suggest below, however, that the recent expansion of promissory liability is consistent with the judgment that, for certain types of bargain promises, a larger core of liability can be defined without causing a significant increase in enforcement costs. Our analysis of this development can be clarified by first examining promise-making outside the exchange model.

C. *Nonreciprocal Promises*

Promises that are not conditioned upon a return promise are, unlike bargained-for promises, generally unenforceable.[88] Although unbargained-for promises are frequently made in exchange contexts, we consider here only the case of promises made outside a bargain setting. Such nonreciprocal promises typically include promises of gifts, charitable subscriptions, and other unilateral pledges to confer benefits.

The substance rather than the form of bargain triggers the distinction between reciprocal and nonreciprocal promises.[89] For example, social engagements, domestic bargains, and sham exchanges may use the bargain form for an essentially gratuitous promise. Courts typically explain the nonenforceability of social promises with the tautology that no legal obligation was intended.[90] In the case of intraspousal bargains, this rationale is reinforced by an expressed deference to the marital relation. For sham exchanges, courts generally find "nominal consideration" insufficient to support the gift promise, whose enforceability depends on the reality, not the form, of bargain.[91] Enforcement of such purely formal bargains could entail high process costs, inasmuch as such frequently trivial promises would be relatively expensive to adjudicate. However, it is no less expensive to litigate most small contracts. Non-

88. "[A] mere promise, without more, lacks a consideration and is unenforceable," Stonestreet v. Southern Oil Co., 226 N.C. 261, 263, 37 S.E.2d 676, 677 (1946), though it "cannot be broken without a violation of moral duty," Mills v. Wyman, 20 Mass. (3 Pick.) 207, 210 (1825).

89. Obviously, any distinction between bargaining and nonreciprocating contexts is an arbitrary one. The test that we propose is whether the promisee has a realistic opportunity to affect the nature and supply of promising by altering the "price" of the promise. *See* note 38 *supra*.

90. 1 A. Corbin, *supra* note 5, § 34; Restatement 2d § 21B, Comment c & Illustration 5.

91. Lawhead v. Booth, 115 W. Va. 490, 177 S.E. 283 (1934); Restatement 2d § 76, Comment b & Illustration 5, Comment c.

enforcement of these promises can be more plausibly related to the same empirical assumptions that support the general unenforceability of nonreciprocal promises.

1. *The General Policy of Nonenforcement*

The hypothetical case of *Mortensen v. Central National Bank*[92] provides a convenient vehicle for evaluating the practical legal questions implicit in the treatment of nonreciprocal promises. Assume that on September 15, 1978, 72-year-old Mary Guillette wrote a letter to her nephew, James Mortensen, promising him a $10,000 Persian rug that he had long admired. The letter indicated that the rug would be shipped to Mortensen "sometime after I return from Florida in the spring, but no later than June 1." Guillette died in Florida on January 1, 1979, shortly after assuring Mortensen, "I'm looking forward to sending you the rug as soon as possible; you can count on it." Subsequently, Central National Bank, as the executor of Guillette's estate, refused to deliver the rug to Mortensen.

In practice, Mortensen's right to enforce his aunt's promise would depend crucially on whether the promise, which lacks the requisite bargained-for consideration, induced Mortensen to act visibly in detrimental reliance.[93] In fact, as shown above, detrimental reliance is likely to occur even if no visible evidence of it exists.[94] Between the date of the promise and that of the repudiation, Mortensen will have modified his consumption habits in adjustment to his suddenly increased expected wealth. If this expectation is disappointed, Mortensen's excessive consumption will have produced a permanent net loss in welfare; this loss is his reliance injury. Courts rarely acknowledge the existence of such uncompensated reliance when they refuse to enforce gratuitous promises.[95] The absence of bargained-for consideration triggers instead a presumption of nonenforcement.

The optimal enforcement model identified a series of interactive adaptations induced by legal enforcement of nonreciprocal promises. A legal sanction initially increases the reliability of a promise above the level the promisor voluntarily provided. But enforcement also triggers

92. The facts are drawn loosely from a case on which one of the authors consulted; it was ultimately resolved by settlement.

93. *But see* pp. 1305-07 *infra* (requirements for enforcement under § 90).

94. *See* pp. 1267-70 *supra*.

95. *See, e.g.*, Stonestreet v. Southern Oil Co., 226 N.C. 261, 263, 37 S.E.2d 676, 677 (1946) ("It is said that when one receives a naked promise and such promise is not kept, he is no worse off than he was before the promise was made. He gave nothing for it, loses nothing by it, and upon its breach he suffers no recoverable damage.")

Enforcing Promises

precautionary adjustments by promisors. Whether these interactions are optimal depends upon the promisor's certainty regarding performance, the effectiveness of extra-legal sanctions, and the capacity of qualitative adjustments to minimize the social costs of the regret contingency.

In this hypothetical case, Guillette intended to perform up until the time of her death. When the promisor is subjectively certain of performance, full enforcement offers the social benefits of increased beneficial reliance without countervailing precautionary costs. Even slightly uncertain promisors may obtain benefits through enforcement that exceed any increased precautionary or regret costs.[96] Thus, the certainty of performance seems critical in distinguishing the enforcement of sham bargains from the legal treatment of other nonreciprocal promises. At common law, the formal contract under seal provided a means for promisors to assure enforcement of gratuitous promises.[97] A sham bargain performs a similar function in encouraging deliberation, preserving evidence, and identifying the promisor's intention.[98] Although devices such as seals and sham bargains entail significant administrative costs, the voluntary use of these formal mechanisms suggests that the benefits to both parties of the additional reassurance from legal enforcement outweighs the transactions costs.[99]

The aggravated process costs of regulating social, rather than commercial, conduct seems to underlie nonenforcement even when the promisor is certain of performance. These additional costs may outweigh the gains in reliability under an enforcement rule. Enforcement of nonreciprocal promises in which formality suggests certainty requires

96. *See* pp. 1271-74 *supra*.

97. Dean Pound suggested that the seal fell victim to the "informality of pioneer America." *Promise or Bargain?*, *supra* note 1, at 468. The status of the seal is tenuous in many jurisdictions. *See* RESTATEMENT 2D, Introductory Note §§ 95-110. It is easy, however, to overlook alternative legal mechanisms that accomplish similar results. In particular, the decline of the seal has been paralleled by a corresponding increase in the use of *inter vivos* trusts and a relaxation in the delivery requirements for the validity of *inter vivos* gifts of personal property. Symbolic transfers, including informal writings, have been sustained when intent was clear and physical transfer was not easily accomplished. *E.g.*, Hawkins v. Union Trust Co., 187 A.D. 472, 473, 175 N.Y.S. 694, 695 (1919).

98. For the classic discussion of the rationale of legal formalities, see Fuller, *supra* note 20; *cf.* RESTATEMENT 2D § 76, Comment c. The sham bargain offers formal advantages that justify a distinction from the treatment accorded a simple donative promise. Although the evidentiary basis may not be any stronger, the fact that the promisor went to the trouble of constructing the sham exchange is substantial evidence of deliberation and intention.

99. One of the functions of legal formality, defined by Fuller as the cautionary function, is to deter inconsiderate action. Fuller, *supra* note 20, at 800. Professor Melvin Eisenberg argues that the information and process costs of ensuring a form adequate to guard against both improvidence and false claims are significant. *See* Eisenberg, *Donative Promises*, 47 U. CHI. L. REV. 1, 8-18 (1979).

additional procedural safeguards to protect against careless promise-making and false claims.[100] The problem of false claims is exacerbated by the context of many nonreciprocal promises. Many donative promises are oral[101] and the claims are often lodged against the promisor's estate.[102] The concern over resulting fraudulent claims is reflected by the more rigorous evidentiary rules governing the actual transfer of these property rights. Testamentary dispositions and *causa mortis* gifts require objective evidence of the transfer not required for *inter vivos* dispositions.[103]

If the gratuitous promisor is at all uncertain about future performance, nonenforcement can be explained by two empirical assumptions unrelated to process costs:

First, extra-legal sanctions against breach are effective in most nonreciprocal settings.

Second, even when extra-legal sanctions are not fully effective, the prospect of increasing the exchange of information through qualitative adjustments is small in most donative contexts.

Donative promises generally are more likely to be performed than are other promises and thus offer prospective benefits that outweigh prospective harms. Extra-legal sanctions are likely to be effective in the donative context because promisors generally care about the welfare of promisees. In contemplating a promise, the promisor may regard costs suffered by the promisee as equivalent to costs suffered by himself. Then, the promisor will have already taken into account the prospective detrimental reliance of the promisee. Thus, the need for a legal sanction to reflect the promisee's interests is obviated.

Furthermore, the supply of donative promises is likely to be very sensitive to the attachment of legal liability. Social considerations frequently will deter the qualitative precautionary option of attaching

100. *See, e.g.*, Haase v. Cardoza, 165 Cal. App. 2d 35, 38, 331 P.2d 419, 421 (1958) (informal promise not enforceable if utterly alone, without past consideration or reliance); Overlock v. Central Vt. Pub. Serv. Corp., 126 Vt. 549, 553, 237 A.2d 356, 358 (1967) (rigorous exactions required for enforceability because reliance unbargained-for and promise gratuitous).

101. *E.g.*, Haase v. Cardoza, 165 Cal. App. 2d 35, 331 P.2d 419 (1958); Dewein v. Estate of Dewein, 30 Ill. App. 2d 446, 174 N.E.2d 875 (1961).

102. *E.g.*, Dewein v. Estate of Dewein, 30 Ill. App. 2d 446, 174 N.E.2d 875 (1961).

103. Although *causa mortis* gifts do not require the same formality as testamentary dispositions, such transfers are policed more carefully than are *inter vivos* gifts. *See, e.g.*, Foster v. Reiss, 18 N.J. 41, 112 A.2d 553 (1955). On the other hand, when a gratuitous promise is in writing, courts have often manipulated the delivery requirements of the law of gifts in order to enforce the transfer. *See, e.g.*, Faith Lutheran Retirement Home v. Veis, 156 Mont. 38, 473 P.2d 503 (1970) (written promise is symbolic delivery executing gift); Hawkins v. Union Trust Co., 187 A.D. 472, 175 N.Y.S. 694 (1919) (delivery of letter evidencing gift sufficient to complete gift).

Enforcing Promises

explicit conditions to the promise. It seems implausible, for example, for Guillette to promise to "deliver the rug unless I decide to take a final Caribbean cruise." The only alternative to announcing a narrow promise may be forgoing any announcement at all. If donative promises are not enforced, promisees will adapt to the risk of a regret contingency by self-protective limitations on their beneficial reliance. These adjustments generally will be more precise and less costly in reduced reliance than the solely-quantitative precautionary adjustments available to promisors reluctant to impair the social relationship. Thus, the legal enforcement of donative promises may produce an excessively costly precautionary reduction in the quantity of future promising.

Although theoretically plausible, these two assumptions require empirical verification. The uncertainty surrounding the determination of the optimal legal sanction for nonreciprocal promises is reinforced by the parties' inability to bargain over legal liability. Without the bargain mechanism to reveal the value of a promise to the promisee, judicial efforts to approximate optimal enforcement are necessarily crude. In the next two sections, we evaluate whether these key empirical assumptions explain those circumstances in which courts have deviated from the general policy of nonenforcement for nonreciprocal promises.

2. *Change of Position in Reliance: Enforcement Under Section 90*

Although promissory estoppel is used most frequently in the context of bargained-for promises, the doctrine was first applied to nonreciprocal promises.[104] Conventional analysis has long assumed that promissory estoppel is a readily available means of enforcing relied-upon nonreciprocal promises.[105] Nevertheless, in the above hypothetical, Mortensen's prospects of obtaining enforcement are unlikely to improve under the provisions of section 90 of the *Restatement of Contracts*.[106] Thus, even if Mortensen could indicate specific actions in-

104. *See Promissory Estoppel, supra* note 5, at 346-54.

105. *See, e.g.*, Devecmon v. Shaw, 69 Md. 199, 14 A. 464 (1888); Ricketts v. Scothorn, 57 Neb. 51, 77 N.W. 365 (1898).

106. Section 90 is quoted below in a form that indicates the language of both the 1932 original *Restatement 1st* and its 1965 revision, the *Restatement 2d*. Bracketed words appear in the *Restatement 1st* but have been deleted in the current version. Italicized words are those added by the *Restatement 2d*.

> A promise which the promisor should reasonably expect to induce action or forbearance [of a definite and substantial character] on the part of the promisee *or a third person* and which does induce such action or forbearance is binding if injustice can be avoided only by enforcement of the promise. *The remedy granted for breach may be limited as justice requires.*

Most of the decided cases have used the language of the *Restatement 1st* in evaluating

duced in reliance on the promise, such as execution of a contract to sell the rug, the reliance would likely be found insufficiently "foreseeable" and "reasonable" to justify enforcement.

The existence, foreseeability, and reasonableness of claimed actions in reliance are difficult factual issues that the plaintiff must establish for the promise to be enforced under section 90.[107] Furthermore, under section 90 the plaintiff must demonstrate that "justice" requires the enforcement of the promise. Although in bargaining contexts courts have responded to this invitation to the exercise of judicial discretion with complex analysis, in nonreciprocal situations courts have followed clearer rules. Litigation to enforce nonreciprocal promises under section 90 has centered on charitable subscriptions, employee retirement benefits, and donative intrafamilial promises. An examination of recent decisions reveals distinct patterns of enforcement among each type of promise.

Courts generally refuse to enforce intrafamilial promises under section 90, even when the promisee claims he has incurred costs from tangible actions in reliance.[108] Indeed, in the only recent case in which

section 90 claims. But several courts have explicitly adopted the more flexible standard of the *Restatement 2d*. *See* Chapman v. Bomann, 381 A.2d 1123, 1127 (Me. 1978); Warder & Lee Elevator, Inc. v. Britten, 274 N.W.2d 339, 342-43 (Iowa 1979).

107. Under the terms of the *Restatement 1st*, the promisee would be obliged to establish the "definite and substantial character" of his reliance. Although this condition has been deleted in the *Restatement 2d*, a showing that the promise did actually induce reliance is still required. Courts have not been persuaded by the argument that changes in the promisee's consumption behavior create a presumptive case for the existence of detrimental reliance. For example, in Baggs v. Anderson, 528 P.2d 141 (Utah 1974), the court held that the requirement of substantial change in position because of reliance "is not satisfied by the mere fact that [the promisee] indulged in the pleasant and euphoric assumption that he would not have to meet his obligations and that he bought a more expensive car and moved to a more expensive apartment." *Id.* at 144.

In practice, a promisee will probably be required to indicate specific and identifiable instances of foreseeable reliance. *See, e.g.*, Corbit v. J.I. Case Co., 70 Wash. 2d 522, 539, 424 P.2d 290, 301 (1967). Thus, a plaintiff will tend to be disadvantaged if his behavioral adaptations in reliance on the promise were many, small, and diffuse rather than few, large, and identifiable. RESTATEMENT 2D § 90, Comment b. The specific-foreseeability requirement can be justified as a control on the "reliance shopping" behavior that might otherwise be anticipated. *Id.*

Finally, assume that facts reveal that the promisee knew that the gratuitous promise was not legally enforceable. Thus, it could be argued that reliance was unreasonable because the promisee knew that no legal rights were conveyed by the promise. From the perspective of true reliance this argument seems irrelevant. If a promise carries a substantial nominal value, considerable reliance would be expected even if the promisee were aware of the restrictive legal rules governing nonreciprocal promises. Hence, even assuming nonenforceability upon the death of the promisor, the value of the promise would merely be discounted by the probability of nonperformance. Nonetheless, such reliance is likely to be characterized as unreasonable and, therefore, unworthy of section 90 enforcement. *See, e.g.*, Union Tank Car Co. v. Wheat Bros., 15 Utah 2d 101, 387 P.2d 1000 (1964).

108. *E.g.*, Bush v. Bush, 278 Ala. 244, 246, 177 So. 2d 568, 570 (1964); Dewein v. Estate of Dewein, 30 Ill. App. 2d 446, 449-50, 174 N.E.2d 875, 877 (1961).

enforcement has been granted, specifically foreseeable action in reliance was used merely to buttress a promise grounded on formal evidence of an exchange after fifteen years of services rendered by the promisee.[109] In contrast, as provided by the second *Restatement*, courts tend to enforce fully charitable subscriptions regardless of reliance.[110] The frequent argument that the societal interest in eleemosynary activities explains the distinctive legal treatment of charitable promises is not convincing.[111] The social benefit from promise-making would be similarly impaired if enforcement led to restraints on future charitable promises.

Variations in legal process costs, including the risk of false claims, may explain the divergent enforcement patterns in these cases. Furthermore, the differing contexts of nonreciprocal promises suggest important differences in the ability of the parties to adjust the scope and volume of promises. Although charitable promises are formally nonreciprocal, they often are exchanged implicitly for recognition and esteem.[112] Hence, charitable promises are to some extent susceptible

109. *In re* Estate of Bucci, 488 P.2d 216 (Colo. App. 1971). In *Bucci*, after fifteen years of living with and being cared for by the plaintiff, the plaintiff's grandfather promised to give the plaintiff $17,000 to allow plaintiff to purchase a house, when the grandfather sold a certain tract of land or within three years, whichever came first. In reliance upon the promise, the plaintiff withdrew $2,000 of her savings and secured an option on the house. The grandfather died within three years without selling his land. The court held the promise enforceable on two grounds. First, "natural love and affection" constituted sufficient consideration to support the promise based on the 15 years of care and prior services performed. *Id.* at 218-19; *see* pp. 1310-12 *infra*. Second, the administratix of the estate was estopped from denying liability because of the promisee's detrimental reliance on the promise. The court concluded that the plaintiff would not have entered into the option contract without the assurance of completion provided by the promise. 488 P.2d at 219.

110. Restatement 2d § 90(2) ("A charitable subscription or a marriage settlement is binding under Subsection (1) without proof that the promise induced action or forbearance.")

Salsbury v. Northwestern Bell Tel. Co., 221 N.W.2d 609 (Iowa 1974), is illustrative of the cases that have supported a conclusive presumption of reliance. In *Salsbury*, the defendant telephone company promised to donate $15,000 to a newly formed college. The college failed and the defendant did not pay its pledge. The court held the promise enforceable without proof of detrimental reliance, on the basis of public policy. Requiring evidence of reliance, the court reasoned, may result in the enforcement of fewer charitable promises. *Id.* at 612-13; *cf.* Hirsch v. Hirsch, 32 Ohio App. 2d 200, 289 N.E.2d 386 (1972) (consideration for pledge to eleemosynary institution is accomplishment of purposes for which institution is organized).

Not all courts, however, have adopted the conclusive presumption of reliance. *See, e.g.*, Mount Sinai Hosp., Inc. v. Jordan, 290 So. 2d 484 (Fla. 1974). In *Mount Sinai*, the court refused to enforce the decedent's charitable pledge because the hospital did not "affirmatively show actual reliance of a substantial character." *Id.* at 487.

111. *See, e.g.*, Danby v. Osteopathic Hosp. Ass'n, 34 Del. Ch. 427, 434-35, 104 A.2d 903, 907 (1954); Restatement 2d § 90, Comment f.

112. The exchange model of charitable donations is not wholly explanatory. When the donation is purely altruistic, as in a gratuitous promise to make a charitable gift, the context may seem directly analogous to the intrafamilial donation. Enforcing such prom-

to bargaining.[113] Intrafamilial donations, on the other hand, are peculiarly resistant to interactive adjustment and epitomize the nonreciprocity of donative promises. When the nature and amount of promising can be adjusted, the choice of liability rule has less impact. As the importance of specifying the optimal enforcement choice is reduced, the value of a certain, clear rule increases.

The choice between the equally clear rules of full enforcement and nonenforcement, however, must rest upon other factors. First, self-sanctions are probably less effective in the charitable than in the intrafamilial setting, because extra-legal sanctions are often limited to the goodwill value of the promisor's word.[114] Second, in the extra-familial context, promisors are not as disabled by social considerations from making qualitative precautionary adjustments. Thus, in general, enforcement may induce cost-effective precautionary adjustments that increase the net beneficial reliance on charitable promises. Excessively costly self-protection by promisees may be reduced both because qualitative precautions improve the information concerning future regret contingencies and because legally imposed reassurance improves the promise's overall reliability.

Other types of nonreciprocal promises are more difficult to categorize. For example, promises relating to employee retirement benefits occur in a wide variety of promissory settings.[115] For purely gratuitous promises, enforcement efforts on grounds of either promissory estoppel or unjust enrichment have been largely unsuccessful.[116] However, when inferences of reciprocity can be drawn, pension promises have been enforced even though they are not strictly bargained-for.[117]

ises is partially explicable in process terms. The costs of identifying a narrow category of unenforceable promises would substantially increase process costs. A clear and certain rule is advantageous when the judgment whether to perform the promise is frequently made by risk-averse executors and administrators. But, more important, the enforcement choice may also be consistent with the judgment that self-sanctions are significantly reduced in these essentially arms-length transactions.

113. There are a number of mechanisms by which a promise can be solicited from a reluctant charitable donor by adjusting the cost of the subscription. For example, the common practice of commemorating the charitable donor by publicizing his name is one of the key strategies of charitable solicitation. *See, e.g.*, Allegheny College v. National Chautauqua County Bank, 246 N.Y. 369, 375, 159 N.E. 173, 175 (1927) (promisor imposed condition that "gift" be known as "Mary Yates Johnston Memorial Fund").

114. Of course, when a recurring pattern of similar promises exists, the loss of goodwill from nonperformance may be as substantial as other disincentives to breach. An interesting question for further empirical inquiry is whether the magnitude of reputational losses provides a reliable basis for distinguishing variations in the enforcement of promises made in commercial environments.

115. *See Unjust Enrichment, supra* note 5, at 1172-74; *Promissory Estoppel, supra* note 5, at 371.

116. *See, e.g.*, Pitts v. McGraw-Edison Co., 329 F.2d 412, 415-16 (6th Cir. 1964).

117. *E.g.*, Hurd v. Hutnik, 419 F. Supp. 630, 644-45 (D.N.J. 1976); Wickstrom v. Vern E. Alden Co., 99 Ill. App. 2d 254, 261-64, 240 N.E.2d 401, 405-07 (1968).

Enforcing Promises

The nonenforcement and full-enforcement options can be compared usefully with the intermediate scheme proposed by section 90(1) of the second *Restatement*.[118] This reformulation of section 90 eliminates the threshold requirement that action in reliance be definite and substantial and instead limits the degree of enforcement "as justice requires." The optimal damage formula proposed in Part I may explain the nature and role of this limited sanction. As we showed earlier, if the ex ante probability of a promisor performing a promise were high, the prospective beneficial reliance from the promise could exceed prospective detrimental reliance, in which case the overall ex ante prospects would represent a net social benefit. Section 90(1) can thus be read to authorize award of optimal damages based upon this calculation of the promisee's prospective net reliance. This may necessitate damages in amounts less than both full performance and full detrimental reliance.

The justification for abandoning the clearer alternatives of nonenforcement and full enforcement is the error cost of using remedies that do not accurately shape optimal promise-making. The advantage of an optimal net reliance rule is lost, however, if the rule cannot be applied accurately without substantial process costs. The problem in implementing a section 90(1) enforcement rule for nonreciprocal promises lies in the difficulty in determining true reliance on the basis of observable facts. Indeed, the intermediate sanction of reimbursement is as much an approximation of an optimal reliance rule as are the more extreme alternatives. Although relying upon crude liability options may be unsatisfying, incurring the costs necessary to apply more complex rules of recovery and to resolve more factual issues would not necessarily improve the outcomes.

The inclination of courts to ground legal rules in fact-specific contexts illustrates the risks of stipulating one rule for all actions for reliance-based recovery. Section 90 was drafted to address a variety of recurring circumstances in which promises outside the perimeters of traditional bargain theory have been enforced. Although within these specific factual contexts the effects of the enforcement choice could be more carefully observed, as a rule of general application, section 90 demands a degree of precision beyond current empirical understanding. Furthermore, a broad general rule blurs distinctions between bargaining and nonreciprocal environments that may legitimately influence judicial decisions.[119]

118. *See* note 106 *supra*.

119. Arguably, distributional goals explain the judicial discretion invited by the concern for the requirements of justice found in section 90. These goals are, perhaps, more effectively implemented by general statements of principle than by adherence to specific

3. *Moral Obligation: Promise for Benefit Received*

Conferral of benefits on the promisor by the promisee prior to a nonreciprocal promise may affect the decision whether to enforce the subsequent promise. Under the common law material benefit rule, a promise may be enforced if the benefits were conferred after either an express or an implied request of the promisor.[120] When the services were requested, the subsequent promise functions as a mechanism for valuing the implied preexisting bargain.[121] Alternatively, when unsolicited benefits create no quasi-contractual obligation, subsequent promises are ordinarily not enforced.[122] More recently, the material benefit rule was reformulated to reflect the broader instinct for enforcement suggested by case law development. Thus, section 89A of the second *Restatement* provides that a subsequent promise recognizing a prior benefit is enforceable unless "the promisee conferred the benefit as a gift or for other reasons the promisor has not been unjustly enriched."[123]

Discussion of the enforceability of the subsequent promise implies that the original conferral of benefits was not sufficient to support restitution for unjust enrichment. The subsequent promise may, however, fill the interstices between contract and quasi-contract by minimizing the prospect of reward for forcible imposition of "benefits." By removing these objections to a quasi-contractual liability, the subsequent promise justifies recovery of the conferred benefits.[124] But consider the effect of such an enforcement rule on future promising. When a promisor is uncertain about future performance, enforcement will deter socially beneficial promises, thus undermining the policy of

rules designed to regulate future conduct. But neither has a distributional principle that clarifies the enforcement choice under section 90 been identified nor have courts engaged in the kind of factual inquiry necessary to support principled redistributive outcomes. *See* pp. 1320-21 *infra*.

120. *See* 1 S. Williston, *supra* note 76, §§ 144-147. The material-benefit rule requires a finding that it is reasonable to suppose that the promisee expected to be compensated in some way for the conferred benefits, thereby creating a "moral obligation." Manwill v. Oyler, 11 Utah 2d 433, 436, 361 P.2d 177, 178-79 (1961). As Henderson has suggested, liability imposed under this formulation is haphazard and imprecise. *See Unjust Enrichment, supra* note 5, at 1120-26.

121. 1 S. Williston, *supra* note 76, § 146; *see* Jacobs v. Brock, 66 Wash. 2d 878, 883-86, 406 P.2d 17, 20-22 (1965).

122. *See* Perreault v. Hall, 94 N.H. 191, 193-94, 49 A.2d 812, 813-14 (1946); Pershall v. Elliott, 249 N.Y. 183, 187-88, 163 N.E. 554, 556 (1928).

123. Restatement 2d § 89A. As the Reporter conceded, this section "fairly bristles with unspecific concepts." Braucher, *Freedom of Contract and the Second Restatement*, 78 Yale L.J. 598, 605 (1969); *see Unjust Enrichment, supra* note 5 (charting case-law development underlying § 89A formulation).

124. *See* Restatement 2d § 89A, Comment b; *Unjust Enrichment, supra* note 5, at 1165-76.

Enforcing Promises

restoring a benefit unjustly retained.[125] A broader justification for enforcement can be identified. The emphasis on isolated cases involving the provision of emergency[126] or mistaken[127] services has blurred the true significance of the liability principle incorporated in section 89A. The concept of unjust enrichment can be examined most usefully as a symbol for the detrimental reliance resulting from an abortive exchange relationship.[128]

How do past events illuminate the detrimental reliance resulting from the broken promise? The application of section 89A sharpens the distinction between reciprocal and nonreciprocal settings. A subsequent promise is typically enforced when it recognizes a benefit conferred in the context of an exchange.[129] Alternatively, enforcement is denied if the benefits were donated or provided to satisfy existing contractual obligations.[130] Examination of the prior events that induced the promise may rebut the assumption of benevolence and instead suggest that the promise was made in a reciprocal context.

If the promise can be located in a bargaining context, the detrimental reliance on the promise can be approximately measured by the price paid in conferred benefits. Indeed, partial performance of this newly discovered bargain provides the strongest basis for the claim of unjust enrichment if the return promise is found enforceable.[131] Identification of the promise within an exchange also reduces the risk of false claims and process errors resulting from the absence of formality.[132] Furthermore, the assumption of reciprocity implies that the promisor can adjust to legal liability by attaching more explicit conditions to the promise. In general, when such qualitative precautionary adjustments

125. *See* p. 1275 *supra*. In the case of the certain promisor, for whom the probability of performance is either zero or one, use of the subsequent promise as a device for clarifying a prior unjust enrichment will have no deterrent effects on future promising. The bad-faith promise can be enforced fully under any circumstances. The more interesting question concerns the promisor who is certain that future performance will be forthcoming. When nonenforcement of such promises is justified on process grounds, the prior benefits may provide formal support for an otherwise gratuitous undertaking.

126. *E.g.*, Webb v. McGowin, 232 Ala. 374, 168 So. 199 (1936); Boothe v. Fitzpatrick, 36 Vt. 681 (1864); *see* RESTATEMENT 2D § 89A, Comment d.

127. *See* Drake v. Bell, 26 Misc. 237, 55 N.Y.S. 945, *aff'd on other grounds*, 46 A.D. 275, 61 N.Y.S. 657 (1899); RESTATEMENT 2D § 89A, Comment c.

128. *See Unjust Enrichment*, *supra* note 5, at 1158.

129. *See, e.g.*, Holland v. Martinson, 119 Kan. 43, 237 P. 902 (1925); Reece v. Reece, 239 Md. 649, 212 A.2d 468 (1965); Jacobs v. Brock, 66 Wash. 2d 878, 406 P.2d 17 (1965).

130. *See, e.g.*, Collord v. Cooley, 92 Idaho 789, 792, 451 P.2d 535, 538 (1969); Youngberg v. Holstrom, 252 Iowa 815, 819-21, 108 N.W.2d 498, 500-01 (1961); Jensen v. Anderson, 24 Utah 2d 191, 468 P.2d 300 (1970); RESTATEMENT 2D § 89A, Comments e & f.

131. *See* Fuller, *supra* note 20, at 812; Fuller & Perdue, *supra* note 5, at 53-57; *Unjust Enrichment*, *supra* note 5, at 1136-37, 1147-49, 1157-59, 1178-83.

132. *See Unjust Enrichment*, *supra* note 5, at 1159-65.

are feasible, the promisor has more accurate knowledge of future contingencies and, hence, can avoid risk more cheaply than can the promisee.[133]

The prior benefits principle of section 89A reflects an expanding enforcement of promises outside the consideration model even more clearly than does the promissory estoppel concept of section 90. Classic bargain theory delimited the borders of enforcement too narrowly to incorporate the full regulatory benefits of the exchange context. Courts are expanding liability under a variety of guises in order to reach the perimeters of exchange. Only when the effects of enforcement cannot be internalized by individual bargaining is the policy of nonenforcement clearly retained.

D. *Unilateral-Bargain Promises: The Expansion of Bargain Theory*

Reciprocal-bargain promises and nonreciprocal promises represent the polar extremes of promissory settings. The recent expansion in promissory liability has been concentrated in the intermediate contexts, in which bargaining and exchange remain a realistic, if not realized, prospect. Indeed, the main source of tension between traditional bargain theory and the optimal enforcement of promises lies in the incongruence between the narrowly drawn consideration model and

133. For promises judged enforceable under the prior benefits principle, section 89A invites a limitation of remedy when the face value of the promise is disproportionate to the benefit conferred. "A promise is not binding under Subsection (1) [of § 89A] . . . (b) to the extent that its value is disproportionate to the benefit." RESTATEMENT 2D § 89A. Framing the question of remedy in terms of disproportion may seem puzzling. A reimbursement recovery equal to the value of the conferred benefits is not necessarily an accurate approximation of the true reliance induced by the promise. The disproportion principle is more plausibly examined as a means of resolving the peculiar problem of mixed motivations. If limiting recovery to the reasonable value of the promisee's services successfully separates the hybrid elements of gift and bargain, the harmful consequences of overenforcement of nonreciprocal promises are reduced. Limiting enforcement to that portion of the promise that is subject to an exchange can be explained, therefore, as a further illustration of the distinction between nonreciprocal and reciprocal contexts.

Courts' traditional reluctance to assess the adequacy of consideration can be reconciled with the disproportion principle of section 89A by locating the promissory context on a continuum between the poles of benevolence and bargain. As promises approach the pure bargain, the uncertainty costs of judicial review of relative values increase. Even when both parties concede that a transaction is part bargain and part gift, common law consideration rules support full enforcement. *See, e.g.*, RESTATEMENT 2D § 81, Comment c; *id.* § 75, Comment c ("Even where both parties know that a transaction is in part a bargain and in part a gift, the element of bargain may nevertheless furnish consideration for the entire transaction.") The lesson of the expanding liability reflected in section 89A is that the exchange environment extends beyond the classic bargain model. In the prior benefits transaction, the elements of bargain are somewhat attenuated, as are the costs of judicial assessment of disproportion. Limiting recovery to the value of services exchanged is efficient when the resulting increase in uncertainty is outweighed by a reduction in the damaging effects of excessive enforcement on nonreciprocal transactions.

this broader exchange context. Courts have responded to this tension by using alternative theories of liability to enforce a much wider range of bargain promises, such as subsequent promises to renew an antecedent legal obligation barred by bankruptcy or the statute of limitations.[134] In addition, reliance-based theories have often been employed when rules of consideration deny enforcement.[135] We designate representations lacking any legally enforceable consideration as "unilateral-bargain" promises. Much of the uncertainty concerning the enforcement of such promises arises because the doctrinal support for enforcement has emerged from the gratuitous context. However, although the boundaries have been redefined, the distinction between the enforcement of nonreciprocal and reciprocal promises remains largely undisturbed.

Enforcement rules for unilateral-bargain promises may never be as precisely defined as the provisions regulating other promissory categories. Nevertheless, under recurring circumstances, patterns of enforcement emerge from which individual variables can be isolated. The examination of cases in which courts have recently expanded liability is necessary to isolate the key elements in the enforcement decision.

1. *Reduced Transactions Costs*

We have suggested that the classic consideration model can be explained by analysis of the transactions costs of exchange. When outcomes are uncertain, the risk of legal liability may be perceived as a greater threat than the risk of uncompensated reliance from a broken promise, because each actor can exercise greater control over his own detrimental reliance than over the potential losses of his promisee. Thus, all other things equal, forgoing an uncertain gain by reducing

134. *See* A. CORBIN, *supra* note 5, § 222 (observing this practice); G. GILMORE, *supra* note 4, at 55-65 (describing the historical use of alternative theories of obligation); 1 S. WILLISTON, *supra* note 76, § 158 (observing practice). The rhetoric of the cases typically explains enforcement of such promises on the basis of the moral obligation created by the original bargain. *See, e.g.*, Stanek v. White, 172 Minn. 390, 391, 215 N.W. 784, 784 (1927). The same pattern—enforcing subsequent promises arising out of a completed exchange—is found in those decisions renewing contractual obligations voidable by fraud or infancy. *See* 1 A. CORBIN, *supra* note 5, § 228 (fraud); S. WILLISTON, *supra* note 76, § 151 (infancy).

135. In addition to the obvious use of promissory estoppel to enforce promises inducing post-promise reliance, many of the enrichment cases enforcing promises following the conferral of benefits are usefully examined in terms of a presumption that such promises are most likely to induce post-promise reliance. *See Unjust Enrichment*, *supra* note 5, at 1181. Although the cases examined in this section are largely limited to promissory estoppel claims, many of the prior-benefit cases can be categorized on similar bases. Only a few courts have discussed the relationship of the reliance element. *E.g.*, General Bronze Corp. v. United States, 338 F.2d 117, 122-25 (Ct. Cl. 1964).

reliance will be preferred over suffering an equally uncertain loss of similar magnitude. This assumption helps explain both the offer and acceptance and discharge rules of consideration and the remedial limitations on liability.

Examining the disposition of promissory estoppel claims in bargain settings reveals patterns of enforcement that parallel the design of the consideration model. Promises made in either preliminary or termination negotiations are generally unenforceable under section 90.[136] Alternatively, reliance theories have been used successfully to enforce promises made in the context of an ongoing exchange transaction. Indeed, promises that modify an existing agreement have long been enforced, despite the common law preexisting duty rule, if there is evidence of reasonable reliance.[137] Although the decisions in such "waiver by estoppel" cases often focus doctrinally on equitable estoppel, the impact reliance has on the imposition of liability is clear.[138]

Similarly, courts have enforced a variety of collateral promises reinforcing completed but defective exchanges.[139] For example, in *Wheeler v. White*,[140] after an agreement had been signed, the promisor represented that funds for a projected shopping center would soon be available and convinced the promisee to demolish existing buildings. Although the original agreement was judged indefinite, the subsequent promises of performance were found enforceable under section 90.[141]

By enforcing such promises, the courts have not ventured far beyond the assumptions underlying the consideration model. The requirements for recovery under section 90 have been strictly construed whenever the outcome of bargaining is uncertain, but have been liberally interpreted when the essence of the bargain has been established. When agreements are unclear, risk-averse bargainers prefer to bear the risks

136. *See, e.g.*, Coley v. Lang, 339 So. 2d 70, 74 (Ala. App. 1976) (preliminary negotiations); Malaker Corp. Stockholders Protective Comm. v. First Jersey Nat'l Bank, 163 N.J. Super. 463, 473-74, 395 A.2d 222, 227 (App. Div. 1978) (same); McMath v. Ford Motor Co., 77 Mich. App. 721, 725-27, 259 N.W.2d 140, 142-43 (1977) (termination negotiations).

137. But for the preexisting-duty rule, which requires modifying promises to have a separate consideration, such promises would be fully enforceable at common law without the need to establish reliance. *See* note 72 *supra* (discussing evolution of rules).

138. *See, e.g.*, Albanese v. N.V. Nederl. Amerik Stoomv. Maats., 279 F. Supp. 635 (S.D.N.Y. 1967) (basing defendant's liability on plaintiff's reliance); Shell Oil Co. v. Kelinson, 158 N.W.2d 724, 729 (Iowa 1968) (same); *cf. Unjust Enrichment, supra* note 5, at 1173-74 (reliance theory grounded in notion of promissory estoppel has been "marginally successful").

139. *See, e.g.*, Travelers Indem. Co. v. Holman, 330 F.2d 142, 151 (5th Cir. 1964) (enforcing misleading promise that insurance policy covered specified damages); Alaska Airlines, Inc. v. Stephenson, 217 F.2d 295, 298 (9th Cir. 1954) (enforcing promise that business expenses ancillary to employment contract would be covered).

140. 398 S.W.2d 93 (Tex. 1965).

141. *Id.* at 95-97.

of regret contingencies as promisees, and the nonenforcement rule is optimally retained. When the bargain is clear but fails technically, however, parties may prefer pursuing gains to avoiding losses. Enforcement under section 90 allocates the risk of regret to promisors and thereby shifts resources to more efficient precautionary conduct.

These reflections of the assumptions underlying the consideration model also appear in the remedies provided under the doctrine of promissory estoppel. Generally, full-enforcement compensation has been awarded whenever such damages would have been available under the certainty and foreseeability limitations of bargain theory.[142] Reimbursement has been awarded when the harmful consequences of nonperformance were not reasonably foreseeable and the claim for greater damages was too speculative.[143] Although the rhetoric of some of these decisions suggests that reimbursement damages are the preferred recovery under promissory estoppel, the outcomes imply that courts are animated by the same concerns that have produced the design of the consideration model.

2. *Accuracy: Promises Made in Competitive Markets*

Traditional bargain theory does not distinguish between exchange transactions in established markets and exchanges of unique promises.[144] Because detrimental reliance and full expectancy are equivalent in competitive markets, however, when a promise made in a competitive market induces reasonable reliance, full enforcement is a more accurate approximation of the true detrimental reliance caused by the promise regardless of whether the promise was bargained for. Enforcement of competitive promises that reasonably induce reliance is efficient, however, only if marginal gains in accuracy exceed marginal increases in the process costs of enforcement. Thus, courts can be expected to expand liability when competitive markets are readily identifiable.

The expanding use of promissory estoppel to impose liability outside traditional boundaries is substantially explained by such net gains in the accuracy of the measurement of damages.[145] For example,

142. *See, e.g.*, Drennan v. Star Paving Co., 51 Cal. 2d 409, 414-17, 333 P.2d 757, 760-61 (1958) (subcontractors' bid); Southwest Water Servs., Inc. v. Cope, 531 S.W.2d 873 (Tex. Civ. App. 1975) (fixed water rates).

143. *See, e.g.*, Associated Tabulating Servs., Inc. v. Olympic Life Ins. Co., 414 F.2d 1306, 1311 (5th Cir. 1969) (new business profits); Goodman v. Dicker, 169 F.2d 684, 685 (D.C. Cir. 1948) (same).

144. *See* note 66 *supra* (discussing unique-bargain promises).

145. Similar inferences can be drawn from an examination of prior-benefits cases. *See, e.g.*, Husted v. Fuller, 361 F.2d 187 (7th Cir. 1966) (subsequent promise to refund forfeited

The Yale Law Journal Vol. 89: 1261, 1980

in a number of cases involving bids by subcontractors, courts have imposed liability for reasonable reliance on a firm offer even though the promise was not supported by bargained-for consideration.[146] The Uniform Commercial Code enforces similarly firm written offers by merchants,[147] and the second *Restatement* generalizes the rule to include all offers reasonably inducing reliance before acceptance, when "necessary to avoid injustice."[148] This discretionary provision can be interpreted as mandating enforcement only when enforcement is an accurate proxy for detrimental reliance. In each of these circumstances, the existence of a competitive market is the variable that best explains the enforceability of firm offers.

It is useful to examine the market for substitute promises in other reliance cases. Courts have generally circumvented the Statute of Frauds only in the presence of clear and substantial evidence of an "unconscionable injury" induced by detrimental reliance on an oral promise.[149]

earnest money enforced). The plaintiff in *Husted* was a businessman, and the promise could reasonably be inferred as having induced a forbearance on his part from alternative financing opportunities.

Because the theory of enforcement for prior-benefits promises focuses attention on prepromise facts, however, the cases rarely explore postpromise circumstances with sufficient detail to permit accurate judgment about the congruence between postpromise reliance and enforcement.

146. *See, e.g.*, Drennan v. Star Paving Co., 51 Cal. 2d 409, 333 P.2d 757 (1958). Since *Drennan*, promissory estoppel has been consistently employed to deny subcontractors the power to withdraw their bids after general contractors have relied on them by incorporating the bids into their prime bid for the construction job. *See, e.g.*, S.M. Wilson & Co. v. Prepakt Concrete Co., 23 Ill. App. 3d 137, 318 N.E.2d 722 (1974); Constructors Supply Co. v. Bostrom Sheet Metal Works, Inc., 291 Minn. 113, 190 N.W.2d 71 (1971). Traditionally, firm offers were not enforced unless they were supported by bargained-for consideration. *See, e.g.*, James Baird Co. v. Gimbel Bros., Inc., 64 F.2d 344 (2d Cir. 1933); Board of Control v. Burgess, 45 Mich. App. 183, 206 N.W.2d 256 (1973).

147. *See* U.C.C. § 2-205 (written offers by merchants, if announced as irrevocable, are binding without consideration for up to three months). The limited scope of § 2-205 increases the likelihood that the firm promises captured by its provisions will have been made in a competitive market.

148. *See* Restatement 2d § 89B(2) ("offer which the offeror should reasonably expect to induce action or forbearance of a substantial character on the part of the offeree before acceptance and which does induce such action or forbearance is binding as an option contract to the extent necessary to avoid injustice").

149. *See* Monarco v. Lo Greco, 35 Cal. 2d 621, 220 P.2d 737 (1950). *But see* FMC Fin. Corp. v. Reed, 592 F.2d 238, 243 (5th Cir. 1979) (following Mississippi law; holding that Statute of Frauds cannot be circumvented by doctrine of collateral estoppel).

The most familiar factual pattern of these estoppel cases involves oral promises of employment followed by acts of reliance by the promisee. But mere change in job or residence is generally held insufficient unless the forgone alternatives resulted in "unconscionable injury." Such injury has been found in cases in which the promisee relinquished pension benefits and sold a custom home, *see* Lucas v. Whittaker Corp., 470 F.2d 326 (10th Cir. 1972), or resigned from lifetime employment, *see* Ruinello v. Murray, 36 Cal. 2d 687, 227 P.2d 251 (1951). These examples suggest that the notion of unconscionable injury in these cases is usefully examined as a symbol of forgone substitute

Enforcing Promises

In the highly competitive commodities markets, however, oral promises by farmers to deliver their crops to grain elevators have been readily enforced.[150] Courts have also generally been reluctant to allow promissory estoppel to undermine the parol evidence rule.[151] However, in *Ehret Co. v. Eaton, Yale & Towne, Inc.*,[152] the promisee, a sales representative for a manufacturer, obtained enforcement of a promise of "extremely fair treatment" in sharing future commissions despite a fully integrated written agreement to the contrary.[153] The existence of a developed market for the promisee's services helps to explain the court's decision in *Ehret* to enforce the promise.[154]

Competition for the promisee's services explains the enforceability under section 90 of certain preliminary negotiations and indefinite agreements. Thus, detrimental reliance has been found an adequate basis for enforcing promises to lease business facilities,[155] to provide a construction job,[156] and to award a construction contract.[157] These cases are closely linked to decisions enforcing promises of insurance[158]

promises roughly equal in value to the oral one in question. In turn, these cases have provided the support for codifying the reliance principle as a means of enforcing oral promises within the Statute of Frauds. *See* RESTATEMENT 2D § 217A. Section 217A is complementary to section 90 and varies in its form only by identifying five specific "considerations" for determining whether justice can be avoided only by enforcement.

150. In the grain elevator cases, the operators typically use the farmers' oral promises in reselling their produce on the futures market. *See, e.g.*, Jamestown Terminal Elevator, Inc. v. Hieb, 246 N.W.2d 736 (N.D. 1976). *But see* Sacred Heart Farmers Coop. Elevator v. Johnson, 305 Minn. 324, 232 N.W.2d 921 (1975) (holding oral promisor not bound).

151. A number of courts have rejected the proposition that action in reliance might properly permit courts to avoid the application of the parol evidence rule. *See, e.g.*, Mack v. Jorgensen Co., 467 F.2d 1177 (7th Cir. 1972); Clark Oil & Ref. Corp. v. Leistikow, 69 Wis. 2d 226, 230 N.W.2d 736 (1975).

152. 523 F.2d 280 (7th Cir. 1975).

153. *Id.* at 282.

154. The plaintiff, Ehret Company, had an exclusive sales contract with the defendant and had invested up to 10 years of development work to adapt the defendant's products to its customers' needs. *See id.* at 281-83.

155. Mooney v. Craddock, 530 P.2d 1302 (Colo. App. 1974).

156. Hunter v. Hayes, 533 P.2d 952 (Colo. App. 1975).

157. Swinerton & Walberg Co. v. City of Inglewood-Los Angeles County Civic Center Auth., 40 Cal. App. 3d 98, 114 Cal. Rptr. 834 (1974).

158. Promises to procure insurance are the most common circumstances in which the amount of reliance greatly exceeds the face value of the promise. *See, e.g.*, Spiegel v. Metropolitan Life Ins. Co., 6 N.Y.2d 91, 160 N.E.2d 40, 188 N.Y.S.2d 486 (1959) (promise to pay life insurance premium of $39.75 causing reliance equal to $10,650, proceeds of policy). Consequently, some courts have been reluctant to use section 90 to enforce the full amount of the resulting loss. *See, e.g.*, Dillown v. Phalen, 106 Ohio App. 106, 153 N.E.2d 687 (1957). Nonetheless, a number of courts have explicitly used promissory estoppel to enforce a broken promise to insure. *See, e.g.*, Graddon v. Knight, 138 Cal. App. 2d 577, 292 P.2d 632 (1956); East Providence Credit Union v. Geremia, 103 R.I. 597, 239 A.2d 725 (1968). Furthermore, liability is often imposed on the additional basis of negligent failure to perform services gratuitously undertaken. *See, e.g.*, Colonial Sav. Ass'n v. Taylor, 544 S.W.2d 116 (Tex. 1976); RESTATEMENT (2D) OF TORTS § 323 (1965). The *Restatement of*

and gratuitous bailments,[159] for which a similar promise would have been available to the promisee.[160] In this case, the opportunity cost of acceptance of a promisor's representations that designated property would be insured or safeguarded is equal to the entire loss if the risk materializes after the promise is broken.[161]

At the other extreme are cases in which the exchange is negotiated between two unique bargainers. These disputes often materialize as breakdowns in preliminary negotiations,[162] indefinite agreements,[163] or franchise terminations.[164] Notwithstanding several celebrated decisions,[165] promissory estoppel has rarely been applied to enforce incomplete agreements reached by unique bargainers. Under this circumstance, full enforcement is not an accurate proxy for true reliance. Thus, when the exchange is isolated from a competitive market, enforcement is often denied in spite of the existence of credible evidence of detrimental reliance by the promisee.[166] Isolated decisions to enforce

Torts retains the distinction between nonfeasance and misfeasance and expresses no opinion as to whether the nonfeasance of a gratuitous promise is sufficient to establish liability under section 323. *Compare* Siegel v. Spear & Co., 234 N.Y. 479, 138 N.E. 414 (1923) (nonfeasance sufficient to establish liability) *with* Comfort v. McCorkel, 149 Misc. 826, 268 N.Y.S. 192 (Sup. Ct. 1933) (defendant guilty of nonfeasance not liable to plaintiffs).

159. *See, e.g.*, Abresch v. Northwestern Bell Tel. Co., 246 Minn. 408, 75 N.W.2d 206 (1956) (promise); Siegel v. Spear & Co., 234 N.Y. 479, 138 N.E. 414 (1923) (bailment); RESTATEMENT (2D) OF AGENCY § 378 (1958) (codifying enforceability of gratuitous bailments). The formulation of the reliance principle under section 378 is carefully tied to the availability of substitute promises on the market. This approach is consistent with the argument that enforcement is properly related to the existence of a competitive market for the promise in question.

160. *See, e.g.*, Lincolnland Properties, Inc. v. Butterworth Apartments, Inc., 65 Ill. App. 3d 907, 382 N.E.2d 1250 (1978) (promise to release mortgage enforced when competitive financing available); Homestead Supplies, Inc. v. Executive Life Ins. Co., 81 Cal. App. 3d 978, 147 Cal. Rptr. 22 (1978) (promise to offer insurance at quoted rates enforceable when competitive alternatives forgone).

161. *See* Industro Motive Corp. v. Morris Agency, Inc., 76 Mich. App. 390, 256 N.W.2d 607 (1977).

162. *See, e.g.*, Slater v. George B. Clarke & Sons, Inc., 186 F. Supp. 814 (D. Del. 1960); Hoffman v. Red Owl Stores, Inc., 26 Wis. 2d 683, 133 N.W.2d 267 (1965).

163. *See, e.g.*, Dovenmuehle, Inc. v. K-Way Assocs., 388 F.2d 940 (7th Cir. 1968); United Elec. Corp. v. All-Serv. Elec., Inc., 256 N.W.2d 92 (Minn. 1977); Silberman v. Roethe, 64 Wis. 2d 131, 218 N.W.2d 723 (1974).

164. *See, e.g.*, Chrysler Corp. v. Quimby, 144 A.2d 123 (Del. 1958). Other terminations subsequent to promises have been litigated. *See, e.g.*, McMath v. Ford Motor Co., 77 Mich. App. 721, 259 N.W.2d 140 (1977) (employment discharge); Aubrey v. Workman, 384 S.W.2d 389 (Tex. Civ. App. 1964) (release from secondary lien).

165. *See, e.g.*, Goodman v. Dicker, 169 F.2d 684 (1948); Wheeler v. White, 398 S.W.2d 93 (Tex. 1965); Hoffman v. Red Owl Stores, Inc., 26 Wis. 2d 683, 133 N.W.2d 267 (1965).

166. *See, e.g.*, Slater v. George B. Clarke & Sons, Inc., 186 F. Supp. 814 (D. Del. 1960); Baggs v. Anderson, 528 P.2d 141 (Utah 1974); Clark Oil & Ref. Corp. v. Leistikow, 69 Wis. 2d 226, 230 N.W.2d 736 (1975).

The unique promise made in a noncompetitive environment presents the best example of a reciprocal promise for which the original form of an optimal damages formula would be appropriate. Breach of such a promise would ideally entail damages in the

Enforcing Promises

such promises can be explained only by analyzing factors other than accuracy and transactional efficiency.

3. *The Probability of Nonperformance: Bad Faith*

When the behavior of the promisor at the time of promising clearly indicates that the probability of performance is zero, tort doctrines of fraud are adequate to protect the promisee fully.[167] However, in several celebrated cases, promissory enforcement seems to derive from more subtle inferences that the promisor did not intend to perform. In *Chrysler Corporation v. Quimby*,[168] the promisee was asked to buy out other interests in an automobile franchise as a condition for award of the franchise upon the death of the current operator. After the promisee acquired sole control, Chrysler terminated the promisee's franchise and awarded the dealership to another individual, as apparently had been contemplated from the outset.[169] Although the final terms of the agreement had not been resolved, the court awarded full performance damages to the plaintiff for detrimental reliance on Chrysler's promise.[170]

Although the deceit in *Quimby* is clear, the evidence of bad-faith conduct in *Hoffman v. Red Owl Stores, Inc.*[171] is less certain. In *Hoffman*, the promisee was awarded reimbursement damages following the breakdown of extensive negotiations for award of a grocery store franchise. During the negotiating period, the promisee performed several acts in clear preparation for receipt of the franchise, including sale of his bakery business and purchase and resale of a small grocery store. Negotiations were subsequently discontinued when the promisor suddenly increased the capital contribution required of the promisee.

difficult-to-measure middle range, between zero and expectation damages. But measurement costs may dictate a choice between the two extreme remedies.

The decision whether to grant zero or full damages may then be influenced by an empirical asymmetry in the costs to the parties of adjusting enforcement levels. Specifically, it may be cheaper for the parties to bargain out of an excessive enforcement scheme than to create additional enforcement mechanisms when inadequate ones existed. Hence, when some tentative initial allocation of legal rights must necessarily be avoided, erring on the side of excess enforcement has cost-minimization advantages over comparable errors on the side of inadequate enforcement. *See* p. 1286 *supra*.

167. *See* W. Prosser, Handbook of the Law of Torts 728-31 (4th ed. 1971). It has long been established that a promise carries an implied representation of present intention to perform. A promise made without a present intention to perform is a sufficient basis for a tort action of fraud. *See, e.g.*, Kauffman v. Bobo & Wood, 99 Cal. App. 2d 322, 221 P.2d 750 (1950); Sabo v. Delman, 3 N.Y.2d 155, 143 N.E.2d 906, 164 N.Y.S.2d 714 (1957).

168. 144 A.2d 123 (Del.), *modified and aff'd*, 144 A.2d 885 (1958).

169. *Id.* at 128.

170. *Id.* at 132-30.

171. 26 Wis. 2d 683, 133 N.W.2d 267 (1965).

The court expressly declined to enforce the promise on grounds of fraud, finding insufficient evidence to infer that the promisor "made any of the promises . . . in bad faith with [a] present intent that they would not be fulfilled."[172] Nonetheless, the sudden change in contract terms suggests that at some point in the negotiations Red Owl determined not to perform the promise. Although the mere failure promptly to withdraw a rash promise may not constitute fraud, it may help explain the court's use of promissory estoppel to enforce indefinite preliminary negotiations.

The historical nexus between promissory estoppel and equitable estoppel may blur the independent significance of bad-faith conduct, especially when the inferences of bad faith are based on post-promise factual representations concerning future performance. In *Goodman v. Dicker*,[173] for example, the promisor followed a promise to award a franchise with the representation that the promisee's application had been accepted. The court, without distinguishing promise from misrepresentation, held that the defendants were estopped by their statements from refusing to grant the franchise. Because doctrines of fraud and deceit are commonly invoked in equitable estoppel cases, their independent significance may not be clear when promissory reliance is at issue.[174] However, the "requirements of justice" language of section 90 offers courts opportunities to broaden the traditional scope of enforcement for bad-faith representation. When none of the enforcement alternatives carries either a presumption of accuracy or an obvious transactional advantage, the court's assessment of performance probabilities may often prove decisive.

4. *Certainty and Distributional Effects*

When considerations of accuracy, transactional efficiency, and bad faith are eliminated, a significant difference remains between the enforcement theories of bargain and reliance. Bargain rules are more certain; reliance rules invite greater flexibility and discretion. Because reliance-based enforcement requires evidence of future facts unknown at the time of bargaining, the availability of such enforcement doctrines increases bargainers' uncertainty as to the risks of legal liability. Un-

172. *Id.* at 695, 133 N.W.2d at 273.

173. 169 F.2d 684 (D.C. Cir. 1948).

174. The equitable roots of promissory estoppel explain, in part, the continuing confusion between equitable estoppel and promissory reliance that is evident in the case law. *See, e.g.*, Schmidt v. McKay, 555 F.2d 30 (2d Cir. 1977); C. & K. Eng'r Contractors v. Amber Steel Co., 23 Cal. 3d 1, 587 P.2d 1136, 151 Cal. Rptr. 323 (1978).

certainty imposes a social loss that reduces the value of exchange. The inefficiency of a discretionary rule of promissory estoppel may be worth incurring if it results in the achievement of socially desirable distributional goals.[175] However, examination of reliance cases does not yield discernible distributional policies.

Evidence of relative ability to sustain losses or of the reasons for breach is required before the losses, or gains, from the breach can be distributed according to any fairness norms. None of the litigated cases reveals careful exploration of the distributional consequences of alternative decisions. Furthermore, in most cases the redistributional effects of varying rules are difficult to predict. Absent a clear commitment to promissory redistribution, the uncertainty induced by broadly conceived discretionary rules is unjustified. Systematization of the expansion of the bargain model calls for developing clearly articulated liability rules paralleling those that have emerged from the rules of consideration. Such rules can be generally sketched from current patterns of enforcement.

Conclusion

Examination of the economic implications of promising reveals a tension between ideal and practical objectives. Because uncertainty cannot be eliminated, it may be tempting to resist systematization of expanding areas of liability.[176] The suggestion that the results in individual cases can safely be predicted by employing a handful of simple economic tools is misguided. Economic concepts are useful, however, in specifying the effects of legal objectives and in observing and isolating systemic patterns of enforcement. The indeterminacy of empirical parameters necessitates the use of assumptions that only crudely approximate the true theoretical objectives. Often the effects of using estimates are unclear, as undetermined factors affect the behavior under examination.[177] Nonetheless, systematic collection and observation of data increases understanding of the regulation of behavior by legal rules.

We have assumed that the economic objective of regulating promises is to maximize the net beneficial reliance derived from promise-making activity. In general, this objective is best achieved by a scheme of

175. For a discussion of the legitimacy of using contract law to achieve distributional ends, see Kronman, *Contract Law and Distributive Justice*, 89 YALE L.J. 472 (1980).

176. *See* G. GILMORE, *supra* note 4, at 102-03.

177. *See* Leff, *Law and*, 87 YALE L.J. 989, 1005-11 (1978).

promissory enforcement that induces adaptive behavior by the party better able to minimize the risk that future contingencies may materialize and cause the promisor to regret the announcement. Optimal adaptation requires a reduction in the prospective reliance on promising whenever this investment produces a greater decrease in expected harms from nonperformance. Both legal and extra-legal sanctions impose these social costs on the promising parties. Optimal legal sanctions are, therefore, a function of both the magnitude of these extra-legal factors and the parties' relative advantage in risk avoidance. The ideal liability choice ranges from zero enforcement to liability equal to the reasonable detrimental reliance caused by breach. However, because promissory reliance is peculiarly impervious to measurement, alternative rules are often applied as proxies for true reliance.

Promissory liability rules can be examined by classifying promises in three categories along principles of reciprocity and bargain. First, reciprocal promises are distinguishable from nonreciprocal promises on the basis of the ability of bargainers to adjust the volume and form of promising by varying the price of the promise. When such adjustments are not possible, promises are not enforced. Nonenforcement of gratuitous promises is justified because in the nonreciprocal setting, self-sanctions against breach are frequently effective, and promisees are often better able than promisors to adapt to the risks of regret. Second, the narrow consideration model defined by common law delineates a subdivision within the category of reciprocating promises. Enforcement is narrowly limited by assumptions that costs of promise-making are best reduced by precautions at the core of bargaining, and by reassurances on the periphery.

However, courts have used alternate theories of liability to expand enforcement appropriately beyond the confines of the consideration model. Promises have been enforced when increased accuracy, transactional efficiency, or bad faith justified the imposition of liability. These alternative bases of liability have been recently generalized into broad grants of judicial discretion. Although discretion permits the pursuit of distributional goals, it increases the uncertainty facing future bargainers. Absent careful articulation of distributional objectives, the social cost of uncertainty requires the development of clear rules for recoveries grounded on reliance.

[8]

RISK SHARING THROUGH BREACH OF CONTRACT REMEDIES

*A. MITCHELL POLINSKY**

WHENEVER parties enter into a contract they realize that circumstances might change and that one of them may want to breach the contract. For example, a seller may receive a higher offer from someone else or face higher production costs than he expected; or a buyer may no longer need the good for which he contracted. The remedy available against a breaching party will, of course, influence that party's decision whether to breach. The remedy will also affect each party's investment in "reliance"—expenditures made in anticipation of performance (for example, building a warehouse to store the goods to be delivered). These effects of contract remedies have been thoroughly examined by Shavell, Rogerson, and others.[1] In addition, the remedy for breach will allocate the risks among the parties due to changed circumstances. This effect, which has not been examined as systematically as the others, is the subject of this paper.[2]

* Stanford University and National Bureau of Economic Research. This is a substantially revised and expanded version of a paper with the same title circulated as Working Paper No. 714, National Bureau of Economic Research, July 1981. Work on this article was supported by a National Science Foundation grant (SOC 78-20159) to the Law and Economics Program of the NBER and by the Stanford Legal Research Fund, made possible by a bequest from the estate of Ira S. Lillick and by gifts from Roderick E. and Carla A. Hills and other friends of the Stanford Law School. Any opinions expressed are mine. I am grateful to Robert Cooter, Melvin Eisenberg, Thomas Jackson, Lewis Kornhauser, Jeffrey Perloff, Samuel Rea, Jr., William Rogerson, Steven Shavell, and Arthur Stinchcombe for helpful comments and to Raymond Squitieri for assistance in computing the numerical example.

[1] See, for example, Steven Shavell, Damage Measures for Breach of Contract, 11 Bell J. Econ. 466 (1980); and William P. Rogerson, Efficient Reliance and Contract Remedies (August 1980) (Social Science Working Paper No. 340, California Inst. Tech. Div. Humanities & Social Sciences).

[2] The studies that have emphasized the role of risk allocation in contract law have focused on the doctrines of excuse, impossibility, and foreseeability rather than, as here, the remedies for breach. See, for example, Richard A. Posner & Andrew M. Rosenfield, Impossibility and Related Doctrines in Contract Law: An Economic Analysis, 6 J. Legal Stud. 83 (1977); Paul L. Joskow, Commercial Impossibility, the Uranium Market and the Westinghouse Case, 6 J. Legal Stud. 119 (1977); Jeffrey M. Perloff, Breach of Contract and the

[*Journal of Legal Studies*, vol. XII (June 1983)]

The risk allocation effects of the choice of remedy for breach of contract are examined in two examples. The first example, on which the paper focuses, is described in Section I. It consists of a contract between a buyer and a seller of a good who both know that some third party who values the good more than the original buyer may come along before delivery and induce the seller to breach. Although both the buyer and the seller can potentially benefit from the higher third-party offer, the possibility of the offer creates uncertainty about their profits (the parties are assumed to be firms).

The damage payment that optimally allocates the uncertain benefit of a higher third-party offer between the buyer and the seller is derived in Section II. This payment depends, of course, on the relative risk aversion of the buyer and the seller. For example, suppose both parties are risk averse and therefore want to share the risk of the third-party offer. A damage payment that more than compensates the buyer for the breach, but that does not eliminate all of the seller's gain from selling to the third party, would accomplish this.

The results with respect to optimal risk sharing are compared in Section III to the risk allocation effects of five remedies for breach of contract: expectation damages, specific performance, reliance damages, restitution, and liquidated damages. It is shown in the third-party offer example that the expectation and specific performance remedies can optimally allocate the contract risk only if one of the parties is risk neutral, that neither the reliance nor the restitution remedies are ever ideal in terms of risk sharing, and that a liquidated damage remedy is always optimal in principle.

A numerical example is developed in Section IV to illustrate concretely how the optimal damage payment varies with the risk aversion of the parties. The numerical example is also used to measure the loss of welfare from employing the expectation remedy when it does not optimally allocate the contract risk. In the numerical example, the loss is as large as 20 percent of the value of the contract.

In Section V the optimal damage payment is derived in a second example in which the risk is due to uncertainty about the seller's production cost. The problem here is how to allocate a potential loss—due to a higher than normal production cost—rather than how to allocate a potential

---

Foreseeability Doctrine of *Hadley v. Baxendale*, 10 J. Legal Stud. 39 (1981); and Jeffrey M. Perloff, The Effects of Breaches of Forward Contracts Due to Unanticipated Price Changes, 10 J. Legal Stud. 221 (1981). Several studies have also considered the risk allocation effects of breach of contract remedies, although not as comprehensively as developed here. The ones which are most closely related to the present analysis are discussed in notes 7 & 15 *infra*. See also note 20 *infra*.

gain—such as a higher third-party offer. It is shown in this example that the expectation remedy can optimally allocate the contract risk only if the seller is risk neutral; that the specific performance, the reliance, and the restitution remedies are generally not ideal in terms of risk sharing; and that a liquidated damage remedy is always optimal in principle.

With respect to risk sharing, the discussion of both examples suggests that a liquidated damage remedy should be the normal remedy if, as seems reasonable, parties are usually risk averse at least to some extent. In practice, however, the expectation remedy is the normal remedy.[3] Reasons why the expectation remedy might still be preferred despite the generally superior risk sharing effects of a liquidated damage remedy are discussed briefly in Section VI.

I. Statement of the Problem

The first example is now described in more detail. A seller and a buyer enter into an agreement in which the seller promises to produce a good, which is not generally available in the market, for delivery to the buyer at some price paid in advance. In reliance on the contract, the buyer makes a fixed expenditure which has no value without the good. Both parties are assumed to know the probability that a third party will come along and the amount that he would offer. The third party, if he appears, is assumed to value the good more than the original buyer. In the event of breach, the seller must pay the buyer some amount of money.

The following notation will be used:

$U(.)$	utility of the seller ($U' > 0$, $U'' \leqq 0$)[4]
$V(.)$	utility of the buyer ($V' > 0$, $V'' \leqq 0$)
c	seller's production cost
r	buyer's reliance expenditure
y	buyer's benefit if contract completed ($y > c + r$)
k	contract price (paid in advance)
p	probability of third-party offer
z	amount of third-party offer ($z > y$)
δ	damage payment to buyer if breach occurs.

It is obvious (since $z > y$) that the first-best outcome is for the good to end up in the possession of the third party if the third-party offer materializes. This will occur for the following reason. The seller will breach in order to sell to the third party if the damage payment to the buyer is less

[3] See, for example, E. Allan Farnsworth, Contracts 40, 812–13, 839 (1982).

[4] Without loss of generality, it is assumed that $U(0) = 0$ and, when the seller is risk neutral, that $U(x) = x$. Analogous assumptions apply to the buyer.

than or, I will assume, equal to the third-party offer. It will be seen that the damage payment that optimally allocates the risk of the third-party offer satisfies this condition. Thus, since the breach decision is optimal and the reliance expenditure is fixed, the only issue here is one of risk allocation.

The buyer's expected utility EV is

$$EV = (1 - p)V(y - k - r) + pV(\delta - k - r). \tag{1}$$

The first term reflects the outcome if the third-party offer does not occur and the contract is completed, while the second term represents the outcome if the offer does occur and the seller breaches and pays damages. Similarly, the seller's expected utility EU is[5]

$$EU = (1 - p)U(k - c) + pU(z + k - c - \delta). \tag{2}$$

The optimal contract terms—the contract price and the damage payment—can be determined by maximizing the expected utility of the buyer subject to the constraint that the expected utility of the seller equals some constant:

$$\underset{k,\delta}{\text{Maximize}}\ EV \text{ subject to } EU = \bar{u}. \tag{3}$$

The constant $\bar{u}$ can be thought of as reflecting the relative bargaining strengths of the parties in the contract negotiations. The higher $\bar{u}$ is, the better bargainer the seller is relative to the buyer.

II. Optimal Risk Allocation

The problem described in the previous section can be easily solved to determine the optimal damage payment, δ^*, and the optimal contract price, k^*. The details of the solution are contained in accompanying footnotes.[6] Since the contract price is paid in advance, it does not directly

[5] Note that if the contract price, k, were paid on delivery rather than in advance, then k would not appear in the second term in both (1) and (2). However, nothing of substance would be affected since the damage payment, δ, could be reduced by k.

[6] The general solution can be derived by formulating (3) as a Lagrange multiplier problem. The first-order conditions (a unique interior maximum is assumed) with respect to k and δ are, respectively,

$$\begin{aligned} &-(1 - p)V'(y - k - r) - pV'(\delta - k - r) \\ &- \lambda[(1 - p)U'(k - c) + pU'(z + k - c - \delta)] = 0, \end{aligned} \tag{i}$$

$$pV'(\delta - k - r) + \lambda[pU'(z + k - c - \delta)] = 0, \tag{ii}$$

where λ is the Lagrange multiplier. Solving (ii) for λ and substituting this into (i) leads, after some simplification, to

$$\frac{V'(y - k - r)}{V'(\delta - k - r)} = \frac{U'(k - c)}{U'(z + k - c - \delta)}. \tag{iii}$$

TABLE 1
OPTIMAL DAMAGE PAYMENT, THIRD-PARTY OFFER EXAMPLE

		seller: risk neutral	seller: risk averse
buyer	risk neutral	indeterminate	$\delta^* = z$ (third-party offer)
buyer	risk averse	$\delta^* = y$ (buyer's benefit)	$y < \delta^* < z$

affect the allocation of risk. Thus, the focus of the discussion in this section is on the optimal damage payment.[7] (It will be assumed throughout this section that the constant $\bar{u}$ equals zero; this will simplify the discussion of the optimal contract price without affecting any of the statements regarding the optimal damage payment.)

The results regarding the optimal damage payment are summarized in Table 1. Obviously, if both parties are risk neutral, then every damage payment is equally desirable in terms of risk allocation.

This well-known condition for optimal risk sharing can be interpreted as requiring that the marginal rates of substitution between the "goods" of "income if performance occurs" and "income if breach occurs" be the same for both parties. The remaining first-order condition, with respect to λ, is of course the constraint that the seller's expected utility equals the constant

$$(1 - p)U(k - c) + pU(z + k - c - \delta) = \bar{u}. \qquad \text{(iv)}$$

Conditions (iii) and (iv) together determine the optimal damage payment, δ^*, and the optimal contract price, k^*.

[7] For related discussions of optimal risk allocation in breach of contract situations, see Lewis A. Kornhauser, Breach of Contract in the Presence of Risk Aversion, Reliance, and Reputation 12–19 (February 1980) (Working Papers in Economic Theory and Econometrics IP-284, Univ. California, Berkeley, Inst. Business & Economic Research, Center for Research in Management Science); and Steven Shavell, On the Design of Contracts and Remedies for Breach 8–9 (August 1981) (Working Paper No. 727, Nat. Bureau Econ. Research) (forthcoming Q. J. Econ.). See also Samuel A. Rea, Jr., Nonpecuniary Loss and Breach of Contract, 11 J. Legal Stud. 35 (1982).

If the buyer is risk averse and the seller is risk neutral, then the seller should bear all of the risk. This can be accomplished by making the seller pay the buyer in the event of breach an amount equal to the buyer's benefit: $\delta^* = y$.[8] Given this damage payment, the buyer's profit equals his benefit less the contract price and the reliance expenditure, $y - k - r$, regardless of whether the third-party offer materializes and the seller breaches. The seller's profit, however, does depend on whether the third-party offer occurs. If the offer does not occur, the seller's profit equals the contract price less his cost, $k - c$, whereas if it does occur, his profit is augmented by the offer less the damage payment, $k + z - c - y$.

When the buyer is risk averse and the seller is risk neutral, the optimal contract price equals the seller's production cost less his expected gain from the third-party offer: $k^* = c - p(z - y)$.[9] The seller is willing to accept a contract price below his production cost since, given the damage payment, he receives more than his production cost if the third-party offer materializes. To be precise, he is willing to accept a lower contract price to the extent of the expected gain from the third-party offer, $p(z - y)$.

Conversely, if the seller is risk averse and the buyer is risk neutral, all of the risk should be borne by the buyer. This can be achieved by a damage payment equal to the third-party offer: $\delta^* = z$.[10] The seller's profit then equals the contract price less his production cost, $k - c$, regardless of whether the contract is performed or breached. The buyer's profit equals his benefit less the contract price and reliance expenditure, $y - k - r$, if the contract is performed, or the third-party offer less the contract price and reliance expenditure, $z - k - r$, if the contract is breached. Thus, only the buyer's profit is uncertain.

In this case, the optimal contract price equals the seller's production cost: $k^* = c$.[11] The seller demands a contract price equal to his production cost since, given the damage payment, he receives none of the benefits of a third-party offer.

[8] This result follows from the general solution derived in note 6 *supra*. Since the seller is risk neutral, $U'(.) =$ constant. Thus, (iii) reduces to

$$V'(\delta - k - r) = V'(y - k - r). \qquad \text{(v)}$$

Since V' declines continuously, (v) implies that $\delta = y$.

[9] From note 4 *supra*, $U(x) = x$. The result then follows directly from (iv) and the assumption in this section that $\bar{\pi} = 0$.

[10] Since the buyer is risk neutral, (iii) becomes

$$U'(k - c) = U'(z + k - c - \delta), \qquad \text{(vi)}$$

which implies that $\delta = z$.

[11] Given $\delta = z$, the seller's expected utility is $U(k - c)$. From note 4 *supra*, $U(0) = 0$. The result then follows from the assumption in this section that $\bar{\pi} = 0$.

If both parties are risk averse, the risk should be shared between them in a way that reflects their relative aversion to risk. This can be accomplished by a damage payment between the two extremes discussed above: $y < \delta^* < z$.[12] To the extent that the damage payment is above the buyer's benefit, the buyer's profit reflects the uncertainty of a higher third-party offer; and to the extent that the damage payment is below the third-party offer, the seller's profit reflects this uncertainty. Thus, the more risk averse the buyer is relative to the seller, the lower the optimal damage payment.

In this case, the optimal contract price is between the contract prices in the previous two cases: $c - p(z - y) < k^* < c$.[13] The exact price depends, of course, on the optimal damage payment. The higher the damage payment, the higher the contract price demanded by the seller, since his expected gain from the third-party offer is less.[14]

III. Breach of Contract Remedies

The results of the previous section regarding optimal risk allocation can now be compared to the risk allocation effects of different remedies for breach of contract. As noted in the introduction, the expectation, specific performance, reliance, restitution, and liquidated damage remedies will be discussed.[15]

Under the *expectation remedy*, if the seller breaches, the buyer can recover from the seller an amount of money that puts the buyer in the same position he would have been in had the contract been completed.[16]

[12] This will be proved by contradiction. Suppose $\delta \leqq y$. Then, by the declining marginal utility of V and U, $V'(y - k - r)/V'(\delta - k - r) \leqq 1$ and $U'(k - c)/U'(z + k - c - \delta) > 1$. This contradicts (iii). Similarly, if $\delta \geqq z$, then $V'(y - k - r)/V'(\delta - k - r) > 1$ and $U'(k - c)/U'(z + k - c - \delta) \leqq 1$, again contradicting (iii). Thus, $y < \delta < z$.

[13] Since the seller is risk averse, his expected *profits* must be positive when, as assumed in this section, his expected utility is zero: $(1 - p)(k - c) + p(z + k - c - \delta) > 0$. The first inequality in the text follows directly from this condition. If $k \geqq c$, the seller's expected utility is positive, since $U(k - c) \geqq 0$ and $U(z + k - c - \delta) > 0$. The second inequality in the text follows from the fact that this would contradict the zero expected utility constraint.

[14] Totally differentiating (iv) with respect to δ shows that

$$\frac{dk}{d\delta} = \frac{pU'(z + k - c - \delta)}{(1 - p)U'(k - c) + pU'(z + k - c - \delta)} > 0.$$

[15] For other discussions of the risk allocation effects of these remedies, see Shavell, *supra* note 7, at 8–9, 27–28 (discussing the expectation, specific performance, reliance, and restitution remedies); Kornhauser, *supra* note 7, at 12–19 (discussing the expectation and liquidated damage remedies); and Samuel A. Rea, Jr., Efficiency Implications of Penalties and Liquidated Damages, 13 J. Legal Stud. (forthcoming January 1984).

[16] The definitions of the remedies discussed in this section are the standard ones. See, for example, Farnsworth, *supra* note 3, at 811–914; Lon L. Fuller & Melvin A. Eisenberg, Basic Contract Law 168–317 (4th ed. 1981); and Restatement (Second) of Contracts §§ 344–

In the third-party offer example, the position the buyer would have been in depends on whether the buyer would have been able to find (or be found by) the third party and to transact cheaply with him.

Suppose the buyer would not have been able to resell the good to the third party. Therefore, to put the buyer in the position he would have been in had the contract been completed, the buyer would have to receive from the seller an amount of money corresponding to his benefit, y. The buyer would then be indifferent between performance and breach, whereas the seller would be better off if the higher third-party offer materializes and breach occurs. Thus, based on the discussion in the previous section, the expectation remedy would optimally allocate the risk of a third-party offer only when the buyer is risk averse and the seller is risk neutral (see Table 1).[17]

Suppose now that the buyer would have had the same access to the third party as the seller. Then the buyer should be put in the position he would have been in had the third party come along and he, the buyer, had resold the good to the third party at the higher offer. To duplicate this position, the buyer would have to receive from the seller an amount of money equal to the third-party offer, z. Since the seller would then be indifferent between breach and performance and the buyer would be better off if breach occurs, the expectation remedy would optimally allocate the risk only if the seller is risk averse and the buyer is risk neutral.

In practice, if a court applying the expectation remedy were to set the level of damages on the basis of how likely the court thinks a resale from the buyer to the third party would have been, then the level chosen might be between the levels determined by the polar cases just discussed. The higher the probability of resale, then presumably the higher the damages awarded to the buyer. The important point to note is that this approach would not make sense in terms of optimal risk sharing. As the discussion in the previous section showed, the damage payment which optimally allocates the risk of a third-party offer depends on the relative risk aversion of the buyer and the seller, not on their relative abilities to sell to the third party.

Under the *specific performance remedy*, if the seller attempts to breach, the buyer can force the seller to deliver the good. The risk alloca-

---

77 (1981). There are, however, several qualifications and refinements regarding these remedies that are not germane to this paper (for example, having to do with the foreseeability of the injured party's loss).

[17] Although this result is well known—see, for example, Shavell, *supra* note 1, at 487–88—the dependence of the expectation measure of damages on the access of the buyer to the third-party offer has not to my knowledge been noted in the economic literature on breach of contract remedies. I am indebted to Thomas Jackson for first bringing this point to my attention.

tion effects of this remedy also depend on whether the buyer would be able to resell to the third party. Suppose he would be able to. Then if the third-party offer materializes, the buyer clearly will demand performance in order to resell to the third party. Since the seller would then make the same profit regardless of whether the third-party offer occurs and the buyer would be better off if it occurs, the specific performance remedy would optimally allocate the contract risk in these circumstances only if the seller is risk averse and the buyer is risk neutral. Note that when the buyer has access to the third party, the specific performance remedy is equivalent to the expectation remedy in terms of risk sharing since under the latter remedy the court presumably would award the buyer an amount of money equal to the third-party offer.

The risk allocation effects of the specific performance remedy are more complicated if the buyer is not in as good a position as the seller to sell to the third party. Suppose, for simplicity, that only the seller has access to the third party but that the buyer knows when a third-party offer has been made to the seller. Then if the seller attempts to breach in order to sell to the third party, it is in the buyer's interest to threaten to demand performance unless the seller pays the buyer some amount greater than the benefit the buyer attaches to the good, y. The seller could pay up to the level of the third-party offer, z, and still be better off. Assuming an agreement is reached, it will be somewhere between the buyer's benefit and the third-party offer. Since the allocation of the contract risk will depend on the parties' relative bargaining abilities rather than on their relative aversion to risk, the specific performance remedy generally will not be optimal in terms of risk sharing in these circumstances.

Under the *reliance remedy*, the buyer can recover from the seller an amount of money that puts the buyer in the same position he would have been in had he never entered into the contract with the seller. Assuming the buyer would have earned zero profit otherwise, the reliance measure of damages equals the buyer's reliance expenditure, r, plus the contract price, k, since the buyer paid the contract price in advance.[18]

It can easily be shown that the reliance remedy leads to a damage payment which is below the buyer's benefit, y. Since the buyer will earn zero profit if a breach occurs, he must be guaranteed a positive profit if the contract is performed—otherwise he would not have entered into the contract.[19] The buyer's profit if performance occurs equals his benefit net

[18] There is no loss of generality in assuming that the buyer would have earned zero profit otherwise. This assumption is maintained throughout the article.

[19] If the buyer earns zero profit when the contract is performed, he would be indifferent between entering and not entering into the contract. I assume for simplicity that he would not enter into the contract.

of the contract price and his reliance expenditure, $y - k - r$. Thus, for him to earn a positive profit, the sum of the contract price and the reliance expenditure must be less than his benefit: $k + r < y$. In other words, the damage payment under the reliance remedy is necessarily less than the buyer's benefit.

Recall from the previous section that, regardless of the parties' relative aversion to risk, the optimal damage payment in the third-party offer example is at least equal to the buyer's benefit. Thus, the reliance remedy never leads to the optimal allocation of the contract risk in this example. There is a simple intuitive explanation of this result. The effect of the reliance remedy is to accentuate the risk created by the possibility of a third-party offer. The more the damage payment falls below the buyer's benefit, the greater the variability of both the buyer's profit and the seller's profit.

Under the *restitution remedy*, the buyer can recover from the seller an amount of money corresponding to the benefit the buyer has conferred on the seller. Since, in the example, the only benefit the buyer has conferred has been that he paid the contract price in advance, the damage payment equals the contract price.

Given the restitution remedy, it is clear that the contract price must be less than the buyer's benefit, y. Otherwise the buyer would earn a negative profit regardless of whether the contract is performed or breached, and he would not have entered into the contract originally. Thus, the restitution remedy, like the reliance remedy, will never optimally allocate the contract risk because the damage payment will always be too low.

Under a *liquidated damage remedy*, if the seller breaches, the buyer can recover from the seller an amount of money to which the parties agree in advance. This remedy differs from the others in that it is arranged by the parties themselves before a breach occurs or is attempted. If their only concern is with the allocation of risk, as has been assumed throughout this paper, then of course they will choose a damage payment which allocates the risk according to their relative aversion to risk. In principle then, a liquidated damage remedy will always allocate the contract risk optimally because the liquidated damage payment will equal the optimal damage payment. In practice, however, courts do not enforce liquidated damage agreements unless the payment agreed on approximates the measure of damages under the expectation remedy. In terms of risk sharing, this practice clearly is undesirable since, as seen, the expectation remedy is optimal only if one of the parties is risk neutral.[20]

[20] Charles J. Goetz & Robert E. Scott, Liquidated Damages, Penalties and the Just Compensation Principle: Some Notes on an Enforcement Model and a Theory of Efficient

IV. A Numerical Example

This section describes a numerical version of the third-party offer example that will illustrate the results regarding optimal risk allocation and will show the welfare loss that can result from inappropriate risk sharing under the expectation remedy.

The utility functions of the seller and buyer are now assumed to be of the quadratic form

$$U(x) = x - sx^2,$$

$$V(x) = x - bx^2,$$

where $s \geqq 0$ and $b \geqq 0$ are risk aversion parameters. A zero value of the parameter corresponds to risk neutrality, and the higher the value, the more risk averse is the party.[21] The remaining data for the example are[22]

\$500	seller's production cost (c)
\$1,000	buyer's benefit if contract completed (y)
\$0	buyer's reliance expenditure (r)
.05	probability of third-party offer (p)
\$10,000	amount of third-party offer (z)[23]
0	seller's expected utility ($\bar{u}$).

The optimal damage payment, δ^*, and the optimal contract price, k^*, can now be computed using the general procedure described by (3), but with the quadratic utility functions and the specific values of the parameters assumed above. The results are shown in Table 2 for different degrees of risk aversion of the seller and the buyer. The values of the risk aversion parameters in the utility functions are chosen so that the certainty equivalent of a 50–50 chance of zero or \$10,000 is \$5,000, \$4,500, etc.[24] For the first column in Table 2, in which the buyer is risk averse and the seller is

Breach, 77 Colum. L. Rev. 554 (1977), also criticize the judicial treatment of the liquidated damage remedy. However, their primary concern is with protecting "idiosyncratic" and other losses that are difficult to measure, which is not an issue here.

[21] The values of s and b are limited to ranges such that $U'(x) = 1 - 2sx > 0$ and $V'(x) = 1 - 2bx > 0$. Although the quadratic utility function does not exhibit decreasing absolute risk aversion, this does not lead to peculiar results in the present application.

[22] These values guarantee that the seller will produce the good and enter into a contract with the buyer (rather than, for example, produce the good solely for the purpose of possibly selling it to the third party).

[23] The third-party offer is assumed to exceed the initial buyer's benefit by a relatively large amount in order to create an example in which the value of optimal risk sharing can be substantial.

[24] The values of b and s used (and the corresponding certainty equivalents) are 0 (\$5,000), .000016807 (\$4,500), .000029412 (\$4,000), .000039735 (\$3,500), and .000048780 (\$3,000).

TABLE 2
OPTIMAL DAMAGE PAYMENT AND CONTRACT PRICE

	certainty equivalent of 50-50 chance of 0 or $10,000	seller's risk aversion: $5,000 (risk neutral)	$4,500	$4,000	$3,500	$3,000 (most risk averse)
buyer's risk aversion	$5,000 (risk neutral)	indeterminate*	$10,000 / $500	$10,000 / $500	$10,000 / $500	$10,000 / $500
	$4,500	$1,000 / $50	$5,430 / $288	$6,662 / $349	$7,266 / $377	$7,641 / $395
	$4,000	$1,000 / $50	$4,159 / $235	$5,379 / $299	$6,054 / $332	$6,502 / $353
	$3,500	$1,000 / $50	$3,537 / $210	$4,669 / $273	$5,339 / $308	$5,801 / $331
	$3,000 (most risk averse)	$1,000 / $50	$3,152 / $195	$4,199 / $257	$4,845 / $293	$5,305 / $316

Key: damage payment / contract price

NOTE.—See text for details.
* Any $k > 0$ and δ satisfying $\delta = 20k$ is optimal.

risk neutral, $\delta^* = y = \$1{,}000$ and $k^* = c - p(z - y) = \$50$ (the expected gain to the seller of the third-party offer, $p(z - y)$, is \$450). For the first row, in which the buyer is risk neutral and the seller is risk averse, $\delta^* = z = \$10{,}000$ and $k^* = c = \$500$. For the remaining cases, in which both parties are risk averse, δ^* ranges between \$1,000 and \$10,000 (the low and high values are \$3,152 and \$7,641) and k^* ranges between \$50 and \$500 (the low and high values are \$195 and \$395). Note that, holding the buyer's risk aversion constant, both the damage payment and the contract price rise as the seller's risk aversion increases—thereby reducing the risk imposed on the seller. Conversely, holding the seller's risk aversion constant, the damage payment and contract price fall as the buyer's risk aversion increases.

To see the potential welfare loss from inappropriate risk sharing, the expectation remedy will be compared to the optimal damage payment or, equivalently, to the liquidated damage remedy. It is assumed that the buyer does not have access to the third-party offer, so the damage payment under the expectation remedy equals the buyer's benefit, y. Recall from Section III that the expectation remedy then leads to the optimal allocation of the contract risk only when the buyer is risk averse and the seller is risk neutral. In every other case, this remedy lowers at least one party's expected utility below what it otherwise could be. Since the seller's expected utility is held constant, this welfare loss can be calculated as the difference between the value to the buyer, w^*, of the optimal contract and the value to the buyer, w^e, of a contract with the expectation damage remedy, $\delta = y$, and the corresponding contract price, $k = c - p(z - y)$. In other words, the welfare loss is $w^* - w^e$, where w^* and w^e are defined implicitly by

$$V(w^*) = (1 - p)V(y - k^*) + pV(\delta^* - k^*),$$

$$V(w^e) = V(y - [c - p(z - y)]).$$

Table 3 shows the absolute welfare loss and the welfare loss as a percentage of the value of the optimal contract (w^*) from using the expectation remedy rather than the optimal damage payment or a liquidated damage remedy. In the case most favorable to the expectation remedy—when the buyer is most risk averse (certainty equivalent of \$3,000 in Table 3) and the seller is only slightly risk averse (certainty equivalent of \$4,500)—the welfare loss represents a 2 percent reduction in the value of the contract. In the case least favorable to the expectation remedy—when the buyer is risk neutral and the seller is most risk averse—the welfare loss corresponds to a 20 percent reduction in the value of the contract. Thus, the example suggests that in plausible circumstances the inappro-

TABLE 3
WELFARE LOSS FROM USING EXPECTATION DAMAGE REMEDY

buyer's risk aversion (rows) / seller's risk aversion (columns): certainty equivalent of 50-50 chance of 0 or $10,000	$5,000 (risk neutral)	$4,500	$4,000	$3,500	$3,000 (most risk averse)
$5,000 (risk neutral)	$0 / 0%	$65 / 7%	$114 / 12%	$154 / 16%	$189 / 20%
$4,500	$0 / 0%	$32 / 3%	$72 / 8%	$107 / 12%	$140 / 16%
$4,000	$0 / 0%	$23 / 3%	$55 / 6%	$87 / 10%	$116 / 13%
$3,500	$0 / 0%	$18 / 2%	$46 / 5%	$75 / 9%	$102 / 12%
$3,000 (most risk averse)	$0 / 0%	$16 / 2%	$40 / 5%	$66 / 8%	$91 / 11%

Key: welfare loss / percentage loss

NOTE.—See text for details.

priate allocation of contract risk under the expectation damage remedy can be of some importance.

V. Production Cost Uncertainty

This section briefly considers the allocation of contract risk resulting from uncertainty about the seller's production cost.[25] The basic structure of the third-party offer example can be used with two modifications. First, instead of the seller's production cost being known in advance, it may turn out to be "normal"—less than the benefit to the buyer of having the contract completed—or "extraordinary"—greater than the buyer's benefit. Both parties are assumed to know when they enter the contract what the probability is that the production cost will be extraordinary, and the seller is assumed to know just prior to production what his actual cost is (for example, he would know the prevailing wage rate). Second, in order to focus on production cost uncertainty, there is no possibility of a third-party offer.

The notation from the third-party offer example can be used with the following changes:

c	seller's normal production cost ($c < y$)
e	seller's extraordinary production cost ($e > y$)
p	probability that the seller's cost will be extraordinary.

The first-best solution is for the good to be produced if production cost is normal but not if it is extraordinary (since $c < y < e$).[26] The seller will produce when his cost is normal if the damage payment exceeds or, I assume, equals this cost, but he will not produce when his cost is extraordinary if the damage payment is less than or, I assume, equal to this cost. Since the damage payment that optimally allocates the risk of production cost uncertainty between the seller and the buyer is within these bounds, the production decision will be optimal. Thus, risk allocation is still the only issue of concern.

The buyer's expected utility is again described by (1). The seller's expected utility is now

$$EU = (1 - p)U(k - c) + pU(k - \delta). \tag{2'}$$

The only difference from before is that the second term omits the third-party offer and the seller's production cost. The optimal damage payment and contract price can again be determined by (3).

[25] See also the discussions referred to in note 15 *supra*.

[26] This statement presumes that it is optimal for the buyer to enter into a contract with the seller and, therefore, to incur the reliance expense.

TABLE 4
OPTIMAL DAMAGE PAYMENT, PRODUCTION COST EXAMPLE

		seller: risk neutral	seller: risk averse
buyer	risk neutral	indeterminate	$\delta^* = c$ (seller's normal production cost)
buyer	risk averse	$\delta^* = y$ (buyer's benefit)	$c < \delta^* < y$

The results concerning the optimal damage payment in the production cost example are summarized in Table 4. Since they closely parallel the corresponding results in the third-party offer example, the discussion here will be brief. (The results regarding the optimal contract price will not be mentioned at all.)

If the buyer is risk averse and the seller is risk neutral, then, as before, the optimal damage payment equals the buyer's benefit: $\delta^* = y$. Given this damage payment, the buyer's profit, $y - k - r$, does not depend on the seller's production cost, but the seller's profit does.

If the seller is risk averse and the buyer is risk neutral, the optimal damage payment equals the seller's normal production cost: $\delta^* = c$. The seller's profit then equals the contract price less his normal production cost, $k - c$, regardless of his actual production cost. The buyer's profit does depend on the seller's production cost. It equals his benefit less the contract price and his reliance expenditure, $y - k - r$, if the seller's production cost is normal and the contract is completed, or the damage payment less the contract price and reliance expenditure, $c - k - r$, if the seller's production cost is extraordinary and the contract is breached.

If both parties are risk averse, the optimal damage payment is between the two extremes: $c < \delta^* < y$. To the extent that the damage payment is below the buyer's benefit, the buyer bears the risk of an extraordinary production cost, and to the extent that the payment exceeds the seller's normal production cost, the seller bears this risk.

Observations about the risk allocation effects of the various breach of contract remedies differ somewhat from before. First of all, there is no longer any ambiguity about the computation of damages under the expectation remedy. In the production cost example, expectation damages clearly equal the buyer's benefit, y. Thus the expectation remedy will optimally allocate production cost uncertainty only when the buyer is risk averse and the seller is risk neutral.

The risk allocation effects of the specific performance remedy are somewhat indeterminate for the following reason: if the seller's production cost is extraordinary and the seller attempts to breach, the buyer can threaten to demand performance unless the seller pays the buyer some amount of money greater than the buyer's benefit from having the good, y. The seller can afford to pay up to the level of his extraordinary production cost, e, and still be better off than by producing. Assuming an agreement is reached, it will be between these values and will depend on the parties' relative bargaining abilities. The important point to note is that the specific performance remedy will never optimally allocate production cost uncertainty, since the optimal damage payment is always less than or equal to the buyer's benefit, y (see Table 4).

As in the third-party offer example, the damage payment under the reliance remedy equals the contract price plus the buyer's reliance expenditure, $k + r$; and the contract price must be such that the damage payment is less than the buyer's benefit, y, in order to induce the buyer to enter the contract.[27] Thus, it is now possible that the reliance remedy could lead to optimal risk allocation. However, this would only be coincidental since the contract price, and therefore the damage payment, is determined by the parties' relative bargaining strengths, not their relative risk aversion.[28]

Also as before, the damage payment under the restitution remedy equals the contract price. For reasons similar to those just discussed, the restitution remedy could optimally allocate the contract risk, but there is no reason to expect it to.

The observations about the liquidated damage remedy in the third-party offer example apply as well to the production cost example. The parties

[27] The reason is the same as before. See text accompanying notes 18–19 *supra*.

[28] Given the reliance remedy, with $\delta = k + r$, the contract price k is determined implicitly by $(1 - p)U(k - c) + pU(-r) = \bar{u}$, where, recall, $\bar{u}$ reflects the parties' relative bargaining strengths. The better the seller is at bargaining, the higher the contract price.

could select a liquidated damage payment which optimally allocates the production cost uncertainty, but the courts presumably would not enforce it unless it approximates the expectation measure of damages.

VI. Concluding Remarks

Assuming that parties to a contract are risk averse to some extent—even if only slightly—the analysis in this paper argues for use of a liquidated damage remedy. Why is it, then, that the normal remedy imposed by the courts is the expectation remedy? One possible answer is, of course, that optimal risk sharing is not the only goal of contract law. Other goals, such as inducing optimal breach behavior and optimal reliance expenditures, may favor other remedies. Another possible answer, even if optimal risk sharing were the only goal, has to do with the cost of implementing the various remedies. A liquidated damage remedy would require parties to negotiate over a damage payment every time a contract is entered into, whereas the cost of applying the other remedies would be incurred only when circumstances change and a breach occurs. When these additional considerations are taken into account, it is clear that no one remedy for breach of contract is best in every respect. It may be that, all things considered, the expectation remedy usually will come out on top, although one can imagine many situations in which the sharing of risk may be of primary importance and in which a liquidated damage remedy will be preferable.

[9]

TRANSACTION-COST ECONOMICS: THE GOVERNANCE OF CONTRACTUAL RELATIONS*

OLIVER E. WILLIAMSON
University of Pennsylvania

THE new institutional economics is preoccupied with the origins, incidence, and ramifications of transaction costs. Indeed, if transaction costs are negligible, the organization of economic activity is irrelevant, since any advantages one mode of organization appears to hold over another will simply be eliminated by costless contracting. But despite the growing realization that transaction costs are central to the study of economics,[1] skeptics remain. Stanley Fischer's complaint is typical: "Transaction costs have a well-deserved bad name as a theoretical device . . . [partly] because there is a suspicion that almost anything can be rationalized by invoking suitably specified transaction costs."[2] Put differently, there are too many degrees of freedom; the concept wants for definition.

* This paper has benefited from support from the Center for Advanced Study in the Behavioral Sciences, the Guggenheim Foundation, and the National Science Foundation. Helpful comments by Yoram Ben-Porath, Richard Nelson, Douglass North, Thomas Palay, Joseph Sax, David Teece, and Peter Temin and from the participants at seminars at the Yale Law School and the Institute for Advanced Study at Princeton are gratefully acknowledged. The paper was rewritten to advantage after reading Ben-Porath's discussion paper, the F-Connection: Family, Friends, and Firms and the Organization of Exchange, and Temin's discussion paper, Modes of Economic Behavior: Variations on Themes of J. R. Hicks and Herbert Simon.

[1] Ronald Coase has forcefully argued the importance of transaction costs at twenty-year intervals. See R. H. Coase, The Nature of the Firm, 4 Economica 386 (n.s. 1937), reprinted in Readings in Price Theory 331 (George J. Stigler & Kenneth E. Boulding eds. 1952) and R. H. Coase, The Problem of Social Cost, 3 J. Law & Econ. 1 (1960). Much of my own work has been "preoccupied" with transaction costs during the past decade. See especially Oliver E. Williamson, Markets and Hierarchies: Analysis and Antitrust Implications (1975). Other works in which transaction costs are featured include: Guido Calabresi, Transaction Costs, Resource Allocation, and Liability Rules: A Comment, 11 J. Law & Econ. 67 (1968); Victor P. Goldberg, Regulation and Administered Contracts, 7 Bell J. Econ. 426 (1976); Benjamin Klein, Robert G. Crawford, and Armen A. Alchian, Vertical Integration, Appropriable Rents, and the Competitive Contracting Process, 21 J. Law & Econ. 297 (1978); and Carl J. Dahlman, The Problem of Externality, 22 J. Law & Econ. 141 (1979). For an examination of Pigou in which transaction costs are featured, see Victor P. Goldberg, Pigou on Complex Contracts and Welfare Economics (1979) (unpublished manuscript).

[2] S. Fischer, Long-Term Contracting, Sticky Prices, and Monetary Policy: Comment, 3 J. Monetary Econ. 317, 322 n. 5 (1977).

Among the factors on which there appears to be developing a general consensus are: (1) opportunism is a central concept in the study of transaction costs;[3] (2) opportunism is especially important for economic activity that involves transaction-specific investments in human and physical capital;[4] (3) the efficient processing of information is an important and related concept;[5] and (4) the assessment of transaction costs is a comparative institutional undertaking.[6] Beyond these general propositions, a consensus on transaction costs is lacking.

Further progress in the study of transaction costs awaits the identification of the critical dimensions with respect to which transaction costs differ and an examination of the economizing properties of alternative institutional modes for organizing transactions. Only then can the matching of transactions with modes be accomplished with confidence. This paper affirms the proposition that transaction costs are central to the study of economics, identifies the critical dimensions for characterizing transactions, describes the main governance structures of transactions, and indicates how and why transactions can be matched with institutions in a discriminating way.

I am mainly concerned with intermediate-product market transactions. Whereas previously I have emphasized the incentives to remove transactions from the market and organize them internally (vertical integration),[7] the analysis here is symmetrical and deals with market, hierarchical, and intermediate modes of organization alike. The question of why there is so much vertical integration remains interesting, but no more so than the question of why there are so many market- (and quasi-market) mediated transactions. A discriminating analysis will explain which transactions are located where and give the reasons why. The overall object of the exercise essentially comes down to this: for each abstract description of a transaction, identify

[3] Opportunism is a variety of self-interest seeking but extends simple self-interest seeking to include self-interest seeking with guile. It is not necessary that all agents be regarded as opportunistic in identical degree. It suffices that those who are less opportunistic than others are difficult to ascertain ex ante and that, even among the less opportunistic, most have their price. For a more complete discussion of opportunism, see Oliver E. Williamson, *supra* note 1, at 7-10, 26-30. For a recent application see Benjamin Klein, Robert G. Crawford, & Armen A. Alchian, *supra* note 1.

[4] The joining of opportunism with transaction-specific investments (or what Klein, Crawford, and Alchian refer to as "appropriable quasi rents") is a leading factor in explaining decisions to vertically integrate. See Oliver E. Williamson, The Vertical Integration of Production: Market Failure Considerations, 61 Am. Econ. Rev. 112 (Papers & Proceedings, May 1971); Oliver E. Williamson, *supra* note 1, at 16-19, 91-101; and Benjamin Klein, Robert G. Crawford, & Armen A. Alchian, *supra* note 1.

[5] But for the limited ability of human agents to receive, store, retrieve, and process data, interesting economic problems vanish.

[6] See Carl J. Dahlman, *supra* note 1.

[7] See note 4 *supra*.

the most economical governance structure—where by governance structure I refer to the institutional framework within which the integrity of a transaction is decided. Markets and hierarchies are two of the main alternatives.

Some legal background to the study of transactions is briefly reviewed in Section I. Of the three dimensions for describing transactions that I propose, investment attributes are the least well understood and probably the most important. The special relevance of investments is developed in the context of the economics of idiosyncrasy in Section II. A general contracting schema is developed and applied to commercial contracting in Section III. Applications to labor, regulation, family transactions, and capital markets are sketched in Section IV. Major implications are summarized in Section V. Concluding remarks follow.

I. Some Contracting Background

Although there is widespread agreement that the discrete-transaction paradigm—"sharp in by clear agreement; sharp out by clear performance"[8]—has served both law and economics well, there is increasing awareness that many contractual relations are not of this well-defined kind.[9] A deeper understanding of the nature of contract has emerged as the legal-rule emphasis associated with the study of discrete contracting has given way to a more general concern with the contractual purposes to be served.[10]

[8] I. R. Macneil, The Many Futures of Contract, 47 S. Cal. L. Rev. 691, 738 (1974) [hereinafter cited without cross-reference as Macneil, Many Futures of Contract].

[9] With respect to commercial contracts, see Karl N. Llewellyn, What Price Contract?—An Essay in Perspective, 40 Yale L. J. 704 (1931); Harold C. Havighurst, The Nature of Private Contract (1961); Lon L. Fuller, Collective Bargaining and the Arbitrator, 1963 Wis. L. Rev. 3; *id.*, The Morality of Law (1964); Stewart Macaulay, Non-Contractual Relations in Business, 28 Am. Soc. Rev. 55 (1963); Lawrence M. Friedman, Contract Law in America (1965); Arthur Allen Leff, Contract as a Thing, 19 Am. U. L. Rev. 131 (1970); I. R. Macneil, Many Futures of Contracts; *id.*, Contracts: Adjustment of Long-Term Economic Relations under Classical, Neoclassical, and Relational Contract Law, 72 Nw. U. L. Rev. 854 (1978) [hereinafter cited without cross-reference as Macneil, Contracts]; and Victor P. Goldberg, Toward an Expanded Economic Theory of Contract, 10 J. Econ. Issues 45 (1976). Labor lawyers have made similar observations regarding contracts governing the employment relationship. See Archibald Cox, The Legal Nature of Collective Bargaining Agreements, 57 Mich. L. Rev. 1 (1958); Clyde W. Summers, Collective Agreements and the Law of Contracts, 78 Yale L. J. 525 (1969); and David E. Feller, A General Theory of the Collective Bargaining Agreement, 61 Cal. L. Rev. 663 (1973).

[10] The technical versus purposive distinction is made by Clyde Summers, *supra* note 9. He distinguishes between "black letter law," on the one hand (539, 543, 548, 566) and a more circumstantial approach to law, on the other (549-51, 561, 566). "The epitome of abstraction is the *Restatement*, which illustrates its black letter rules by transactions suspended in mid-air, creating the illusion that contract rules can be stated without reference to surrounding circumstances and are therefore generally applicable to all contractual transactions" (566). He observes that such a conception does not and cannot provide a "framework for integrating rules and principles applicable to all contractual transactions" (566) but that this must be sought in a more

Ian Macneil, in a series of thoughtful and wide-ranging essays on contract, usefully distinguishes between discrete and relational transactions.[11] He further supplies twelve different "concepts" with respect to which these differ.[12] Serious problems of recognition and application are posed by such a rich classificatory apparatus. More useful for my purposes is the three-way classification of contracts that Macneil offers in his most recent article, where classical, neoclassical, and relational categories of contract law are recognized.

A. *Classical Contract Law*

As Macneil observes, any system of contract law has the purpose of facilitating exchange. What is distinctive about classical contract law is that it attempts to do this by enhancing discreteness and intensifying "presentiation,"[13] where presentiation has reference to efforts to "make or render present in place or time; to cause to be perceived or realized at present."[14] The economic counterpart to complete presentiation is contingent-claims contracting—which entails comprehensive contracting whereby all relevant future contingencies pertaining to the supply of a good or service are described and discounted with respect to both likelihood and futurity.[15]

Classical contract law endeavors to implement discreteness and presentiation in several ways. For one thing, the identity of the parties to a transaction is treated as irrelevant. In this respect it corresponds exactly with the "ideal" market transaction in economics.[16] Second, the nature of the agreement is carefully delimited, and the more formal features govern when formal (for example, written) and informal (for example, oral) terms are contested. Third, remedies are narrowly prescribed such that, "should the initial presentiation fail to materialize because of nonperformance, the consequences are relatively predictable from the beginning and are not open-

affirmative view of the law in which effective governance relations are emphasized. Contract interpretation and completing contracts are among these affirmative functions.

[11] See especially Macneil, Many Futures of Contract; Macneil, Contracts; and references to related work of his cited therein.

[12] Macneil, Many Futures of Contracts 738-40; Macneil, Contracts 902-05.

[13] Macneil, Contracts 862.

[14] *Id.* at 863 n. 25.

[15] For a discussion of complex contingent-claims contracting and its mechanics, see Kenneth J. Arrow, Essays in the Theory of Risk Bearing 121-34 (1971); J. E. Meade, The Controlled Economy 147-88 (1971); and Oliver E. Williamson, *supra* note 1, at 20-40.

[16] As Lester G. Telser & Harlow N. Higinbotham put it: "In an organized market the participants trade a standardized contract such that each unit of the contract is a perfect substitute for any other unit. The identities of the parties in any mutually agreeable transaction do not affect the terms of exchange. The organized market itself or some other institution deliberately creates a homogeneous good that can be traded anonymously by the participants or their agents." Organized Futures Markets: Costs and Benefits 85 J. Pol. Econ. 969, 997 (1977).

ended."[17] Additionally, third-party participation is discouraged.[18] The emphasis, thus, is on legal rules, formal documents, and self-liquidating transactions.

B. *Neoclassical Contract Law*

Not every transaction fits comfortably into the classical-contracting scheme. In particular, long-term contracts executed under conditions of uncertainty are ones for which complete presentiation is apt to be prohibitively costly if not impossible. Problems of several kinds arise. First, not all future contingencies for which adaptations are required can be anticipated at the outset. Second, the appropriate adaptations will not be evident for many contingencies until the circumstances materialize. Third, except as changes in states of the world are unambiguous, hard contracting between autonomous parties may well give rise to veridical disputes when state-contingent claims are made. In a world where (at least some) parties are inclined to be opportunistic. whose representations are to be believed?

Faced with the prospective breakdown of classical contracting in these circumstances, three alternatives are available. One would be to forgo such transactions altogether. A second would be to remove these transactions from the market and organize them internally instead. Adaptive, sequential decision making would then be implemented under common ownership and with the assistance of hierarchical incentive and control systems. Third, a different contracting relation which preserves trading but provides for additional governance structure might be devised. This last brings us to what Macneil refers to as neoclassical contracting.

As Macneil observes, "Two common characteristics of long-term contracts are the existence of gaps in their planning and the presence of a range of processes and techniques used by contract planners to create flexibility in lieu of either leaving gaps or trying to plan rigidly."[19] Third-party assistance in resolving disputes and evaluating performance often has advantages over litigation in serving these functions of flexibility and gap filling. Lon Fuller's remarks on procedural differences between arbitration and litigation are instructive:

> . . . there are open to the arbitrator . . . quick methods of education not open to the courts. An arbitrator will frequently interrupt the examination of witnesses with a request that the parties educate him to the point where he can understand the testimony being received. This education can proceed informally, with frequent interruptions by the arbitrator, and by informed persons on either side, when a point

[17] Macneil, Contracts 864.

[18] *Id.*

[19] *Id.* at 865.

needs clarification. Sometimes there will be arguments across the table, occasionally even within each of the separate camps. The end result will usually be a clarification that will enable everyone to proceed more intelligently with the case. There is in this informal procedure no infringement whatever of arbitrational due process.[20]

A recognition that the world is complex, that agreements are incomplete, and that some contracts will never be reached unless both parties have confidence in the settlement machinery thus characterizes neoclassical contract law. One important purposive difference in arbitration and litigation that contributes to the procedural differences described by Fuller is that, whereas continuity (at least completion of the contract) is presumed under the arbitration machinery, this presumption is much weaker when litigation is employed.[21]

C. *Relational Contracting*

The pressures to sustain ongoing relations "have led to the spin-off of many subject areas from the classical, and later the neoclassical, contract law system, e.g., much of corporate law and collective bargaining."[22] Thus, progressively increasing the "duration and complexity" of contract has resulted in the displacement of even neoclassical adjustment processes by adjustment processes of a more thoroughly transaction-specific, ongoing-administrative kind.[23] The fiction of discreteness is fully displaced as the relation takes on the properties of "a minisociety with a vast array of norms beyond those centered on the exchange and its immediate processes."[24] By contrast with the neoclassical system, where the reference point for effecting adaptations remains the original agreement, the reference point under a truly relational approach is the "entire relation as it has developed . . . [through] time. This may or may not include an 'original agreement'; and if it does, may or may not result in great deference being given it."[25]

II. The Economics of Idiosyncrasy

Macneil's three-way discussion of contracts discloses that contracts are a good deal more varied and complex than is commonly realized.[26] It further-

[20] Lon L. Fuller, *supra* note 9, at 11-12.

[21] As Lawrence Friedman observes, relationships are effectively fractured if a dispute reaches litigation. *Supra* note 9, at 205.

[22] Macneil, Contracts 885.

[23] *Id.* at 901.

[24] *Id.*

[25] *Id.* at 890.

[26] To be sure, some legal specialists insist that all of this was known all along. There is a difference, however, between awareness of a condition and an understanding. Macneil's treatment heightens awareness and deepens the understanding.

more suggests that governance structures—the institutional matrix within which transactions are negotiated and executed—vary with the nature of the transaction. But the critical dimensions of contract are not expressly identified, and the purposes of governance are not stated. Harmonizing interests that would otherwise give way to antagonistic subgoal pursuits appears to be an important governance function, but this is not explicit in his discussion.

That simple governance structures should be used in conjunction with simple contractual relations and complex governance structures reserved for complex relations seems generally sensible. Use of a complex structure to govern a simple relation is apt to incur unneeded costs, and use of a simple structure for a complex transaction invites strain. But what is simple and complex in contractual respects? Specific attention to the defining attributes of transactions is evidently needed.

As developed in Section III, the three critical dimensions for characterizing transactions are (1) uncertainty, (2) the frequency with which transactions recur, and (3) the degree to which durable transaction-specific investments are incurred. Of these three, uncertainty is widely conceded to be a critical attribute;[27] and that frequency matters is at least plausible.[28] The governance ramifications of neither, however, have been fully developed—nor can they be until joined with the third critical dimension: transaction-specific investments. Inasmuch as a considerable amount of the "action" in the study of governance is attributable to investment differences, some explication is needed.

A. *General*

The crucial investment distinction is this: to what degree are transaction-specific (nonmarketable) expenses incurred. Items that are unspecialized among users pose few hazards, since buyers in these circumstances can easily turn to alternative sources, and suppliers can sell output intended for one order to other buyers without difficulty.[29] Nonmarketability problems arise

[27] For a recent study of contractual relations in which uncertainty is featured, see Peter Temin, Modes of Economic Behavior: Variations on Themes of J. R. Hicks and Herbert Simon (March 1979) (Working Paper No. 235, MIT Dep't of Econ.).

[28] Gordon Whinston emphasizes frequency in his "A Note on Perspective Time: Goldberg's Relational Exchange, Repetitiveness, and Free Riders in Time and Space" (October 1978) (unpublished paper).

[29] See Lester A. Telser & Harold N. Higinbotham, *supra* note 16; also Yoram Ben-Porath, The F-Connection: Families, Friends, and Firms and the Organization of Exchange (December 1978) (Report No. 29/78, The Hebrew University of Jerusalem) and Yoram Barzel, Measurement Cost and the Organization of Markets (April 1979) (unpublished paper). Note that Barzel's concern with standardization is mainly in connection with final-product markets, whereas I am more interested in nonstandard investments. The two are not unrelated, but identical quality can often be realized with a variety of inputs. I am concerned with specialized (transaction-specific) inputs.

when the *specific identity* of the parties has important cost-bearing consequences. Transactions of this kind will be referred to as idiosyncratic.

Occasionally the identity of the parties is important from the outset, as when a buyer induces a supplier to invest in specialized physical capital of a transaction-specific kind. Inasmuch as the value of this capital in other uses is, by definition, much smaller than the specialized use for which it has been intended, the supplier is effectively "locked into" the transaction to a significant degree. This is symmetrical, moreover, in that the buyer cannot turn to alternative sources of supply and obtain the item on favorable terms, since the cost of supply from unspecialized capital is presumably great.[30] The buyer is thus committed to the transaction as well.

Ordinarily, however, there is more to idiosyncratic exchange than specialized physical capital. Human-capital investments that are transaction-specific commonly occur as well. Specialized training and learning-by-doing economies in production operations are illustrations. Except when these investments are transferable to alternative suppliers at low cost, which is rare, the benefits of the set-up costs can be realized only so long as the relationship between the buyer and seller of the intermediate product is maintained.

Additional transaction-specific savings can accrue at the interface between supplier and buyer as contracts are successively adapted to unfolding events, and as periodic contract-renewal agreements are reached. Familiarity here permits communication economies to be realized: specialized language develops as experience accumulates and nuances are signaled and received in a sensitive way. Both institutional and personal trust relations evolve. Thus the individuals who are responsible for adapting the interfaces have a personal as well as an organizational stake in what transpires. Where personal integrity is believed to be operative, individuals located at the interfaces may refuse to be a part of opportunistic efforts to take advantage of (rely on) the letter of the contract when the spirit of the exchange is emasculated. Such refusals can serve as a check upon organizational proclivities to behave opportunistically.[31] Other things being equal, idiosyncratic exchange rela-

[30] This assumes that it is costly for the incumbent supplier to transfer specialized physical assets to new suppliers. On this, see Oliver E. Williamson, Franchise Bidding for Natural Monopolies—in General and with Respect to CATV, 7 Bell J. Econ. 73 (1976). Klein, Crawford, & Alchian use the term "appropriable quasi rent" to refer to this condition. Use versus user distinctions are relevant in this connection: "The quasi-rent value of the asset is the excess of its value over its salvage value, that is, its value in its next best *use* to another renter. The potentially appropriable specialized portion of the quasi rent is the portion, if any, in excess of its value to the second highest-valuing *user*." Benjamin Klein, Robert G. Crawford, & Armen A. Alchian, *supra* note 1, at 298.

[31] Thorstein Veblen's remarks on the distant relation of the head of a large enterprise to transactions are apposite. He observes that under these impersonal circumstances "The mitigating effect which personal conduct may have in dealings between man and man is . . . in great

tions which feature personal trust will survive greater stress and display greater adaptability.

Idiosyncratic goods and services are thus ones where investments of transaction-specific human and physical capital are made and, contingent upon successful execution, benefits are realized. Such investments can and do occur in conjunction with occasional trades where delivery for a specialized design is stretched out over a long period (for example, certain construction contracts). The transactions that I wish to emphasize here, however, are exchanges of the recurring kind. Although large-numbers competition is frequently feasible at the initial award stage for recurring contracts of all kinds, idiosyncratic transactions are ones for which the relationship between buyer and supplier is quickly thereafter *transformed* into one of bilateral monopoly—on account of the transaction-specific costs referred to above. This transformation has profound contracting consequences.

Thus, whereas recurrent spot contracting is feasible for standardized transactions (because large-numbers competition is continuously self-policing in these circumstances), such contracting has seriously defective investment incentives where idiosyncratic activities are involved. By assumption, cost economies in production will be realized for idiosyncratic activities only if the supplier invests in a special-purpose plant and equipment or if his labor force develops transaction-specific skills in the course of contract execution (or both). The assurance of a continuing relation is needed to encourage investments of both kinds. Although the requisite incentives might be provided if long-term contracts were negotiated, such contracts are necessarily incomplete (by reason of bounded rationality). Appropriate state-contingent adaptations thus go unspecified. Intertemporal efficiency nevertheless requires that adaptations to changing market circumstances be made.

How to effect these adaptations poses a serious contracting dilemma, though it bears repeating that, absent the hazards of opportunism, the difficulties would vanish—since then the gaps in long-term, incomplete contracts could be faultlessly filled in an adaptive, sequential way. A general clause, to which both parties would agree, to the effect that "I will behave responsibly rather than seek individual advantage when an occasion to adapt arises," would, in the absence of opportunism, suffice. Given, however, the unenforceability of general clauses and the proclivity of human agents to make false and misleading (self-disbelieved) statements, the follow-

measured eliminated. . . . Business management [then] has a chance to proceed . . . untroubled by sentimental considerations of human kindness or irritation or of honesty." The Theory of Business Enterprise 53 (1927). Veblen evidently assigns slight weight to the possibility that those to whom negotiating responsibilities are assigned will themselves invest the transactions with integrity.

ing hazard must be confronted: joined as they are in an idiosyncratic condition of bilateral monopoly, both buyer and seller are strategically situated to bargain over the disposition of any incremental gain whenever a proposal to adapt is made by the other party. Although both have a long-term interest in effecting adaptations of a joint profit-maximizing kind, each also has an interest in appropriating as much of the gain as he can on each occasion to adapt. Efficient adaptations which would otherwise be made thus result in costly haggling or even go unmentioned, lest the gains be dissipated by costly subgoal pursuit. Governance structures which attenuate opportunism and otherwise infuse confidence are evidently needed.

B. *Examples*

Some illustrations may help to motivate what is involved in idiosyncratic transactions. Specialized physical capital is relatively straightforward. Examples are (1) the purchase of a specialized component from an outside supplier or (2) the location of a specialized plant in a unique, proximate relation to a downstream processing stage to which it supplies vital input.

Thus assume (*a*) that special-purpose equipment is needed to produce the component in question (which is to say that the value of the equipment in its next-best alternative use is much lower), (*b*) that scale economies require that a significant, discrete investment be made, and (*c*) that alternative buyers for such components are few (possibly because of the organization of the industry, possibly because of special-design features). The interests of buyer and seller in a continuing exchange relation are plainly strong under these circumstances.

Plant-proximity benefits are attributable to transportation and related flow-process (inventory, thermal economy, and so on) economies. A specialized plant need not be implied, but long life and a unique location are. Once made, the investment preempts the unique location and is not thereafter moveable (except at prohibitive cost). Buyer and supplier again need to satisfy themselves that they have a workable, adaptable exchange agreement.[32]

Idiosyncratic investments in human capital are in many ways more interesting and less obvious than are those in physical capital. Polanyi's discussion of "personal knowledge" is illuminating:

> The attempt to analyze scientifically the established industrial arts has everywhere led to similar results. Indeed even in the modern industries the indefinable knowledge is still an essential part of technology. I have myself watched in Hungary a new, imported machine for blowing electric lamp bulbs, the exact counterpart of which

[32] The *Great Lakes Carbon* case is an example of the latter, 1970-1973 Trade Reg. Rep. Transfer Binder ¶ 19,848 (FTC Dkt No. 8805).

was operating successfully in Germany, failing for a whole year to produce a single flawless bulb.[33]

And he goes on to observe with respect to craftsmanship that:

> . . . an art which has fallen into disuse for the period of a generation is altogether lost. . . . It is pathetic to watch the endless efforts—equipped with microscopy and chemistry, with mathematics and electronics—to reproduce a single violin of the kind the half-literate Stradivarius turned out as a matter of routine more than 200 years ago.[34]

Polanyi's discussion of language also has a bearing on the argument advanced above that specialized code words or expressions can and do arise in the context of recurring transactions and that these yield economies. As he puts it, "Different vocabularies for the interpretation of things divide men into groups which cannot understand each other's way of seeing things and acting upon them."[35] And subsequently he remarks that:

> To know a language is an art, carried on by tacit judgments and the practice of unspecifiable skills. . . . Spoken communication is the successful application by two persons of the linguistic knowledge and skill acquired by such apprenticeship, one person wishing to transmit, the other to receive, information. Relying on what each has learnt, the speaker confidently utters words and the listener confidently interprets them, while they mutually rely on each other's correct use and understanding of these words. A true communication will take place if, and only if, these combined assumptions of authority and trust are in fact justified.[36]

Babbage reports a remarkable example of transaction-specific value in exchange that occurred in the early 1800s. Although he attributes the continuing exchange in the face of adversity to values of "established character" (trust), I believe there were other specialized human and physical investments involved as well. In any event, the circumstance which he describes is the following:

> The influence of established character in producing confidence operated in a very remarkable manner at the time of the exclusion of British manufactures from the Continent during the last war. One of our largest establishments had been in the habit of doing extensive business with a house in the centre of Germany; but, on the closing of the continental ports against our manufacturers, heavy penalties were inflicted on all those who contravened the Berlin and Milan decrees. The English manufacturer continued, nevertheless, to receive orders, with directions how to con-

[33] Michael Polanyi, Personal Knowledge: Towards a Post-Critical Philosophy 52 (2d ed. 1962).

[34] *Id.* at 53.

[35] *Id.* at 112.

[36] *Id.* at 206.

sign them, and appointments for the time and mode of payment, in letters, the handwriting of which was known to him, but which were never signed, except by the Christian name of one of the firm, and even in some instances they were without any signature at all. These orders were executed; and in no instance was there the least irregularity in the payments.[37]

While most of these illustrations refer to technical and commercial transactions, other types of transactions also have an idiosyncratic quality. Justice Rehnquist refers to some of these when speaking of the general class of cases where "the litigation of an individual's claim of deprivation of a right would bring parties *who must remain in a continuing relationship* into the adversarial atmosphere of a courtroom"[38]—which atmosphere he plainly regards as detrimental to the quality of the relationship. Examples that he offers include reluctance to have the courts mediate collective bargaining disputes[39] and to allow children to bring suit against parents.[40]

But surely we must ask what is distinctive about these transactions. I submit that transaction-specific human capital is central to each. Why else would it take the Hungarians so long to operate the German light-bulb machine? And what else explains the loss of Stradivarius's craftsmanship? Likewise the understanding and trust which evolve between Babbage's transmitter and receiver are valued human assets which, once developed, will be sacrificed with reluctance. And the disruption of continuing relationships to which Justice Rehnquist refers occasions concern precisely because there are no adequate substitutes for these idiosyncratic relations.[41]

The general argument of this paper is that special governance structures supplant standard market-cum-classical contract exchange when transac-

[37] Charles Babbage, On the Economy of Machinery and Manufacturers 220-21 (1832). More recent examples of contracts wherein private parties can and evidently do "ignore" the law, even at some peril, when the law and the interests of the parties are at variance are offered by Stewart Macaulay, The Use and Nonuse of Contracts in the Manufacturing Industry, 9 Practical Lawyer 13, 16 (1963): "Requirements contracts probably are not legally enforceable in Wisconsin and a few other States. Yet, chemicals, containers, and a number of other things are still bought and sold there on the basis of requirements contracts.

"Decisions of the United States Court of Appeals for the Seventh Circuit indicate that a clause calling for a 'seller's price in effect at time and place of delivery' makes a contract unenforceable. The Wisconsin cases are not clear. Yet steel and steel products usually are sold in this way."

[38] Remarks of Mr. Justice Rehnquist, The Adversary Society, Baron di Hirsch Meyer Lecture, University of Miami School of Law, February 2, 1978, at 19 (emphasis added).

[39] *Id.* at 11-13.

[40] *Id.* at 16-19.

[41] As Ben-Porath puts it, "The most important characteristic of the family contract is that it is embedded in the identity of the partners without which it loses its meaning. It is thus specific and non-negotiable or nontransferable." Yoram Ben-Porath, *supra* note 29, at 6.

tion-specific values are great. Idiosyncratic commercial, labor, and family relationships are specific examples.

III. Commercial Contracting

The discussion of commercial contracting begins with a brief statement on economizing. The proposed schema for characterizing transactions and their governance is then developed, including the relation of the schema with Macneil's three-way classification of contract.

A. *Economizing*

The criterion for organizing commercial transactions is assumed to be the strictly instrumental one of cost economizing. Essentially this takes two parts: economizing on production expense and economizing on transaction costs.[42] To the degree that transaction costs are negligible, buying rather than making will normally be the most cost-effective means of procurement.[43] Not only can static scale economies be more fully exhausted by buying rather than making, but the supplier who aggregates uncorrelated demands can realize collective pooling benefits as well. Since external procurement avoids many of the bureaucratic hazards of internal procurement (which hazards, however, are themselves of a transaction-cost kind),[44] external procurement is evidently warranted.[45]

As indicated, however, the object is to economize on the *sum* of production and transaction costs. To the degree production-cost economies of external procurement are small and/or the transaction costs associated with external procurement are great, alternative supply arrangements deserve serious consideration. Economizing on transaction costs essentially reduces

[42] More generally, the economizing problem includes choice between a special-purpose and a general-purpose good or service. A general-purpose item affords all of the advantages of market procurement, but possibly at the sacrifice of valued design or performance characteristics. A special-purpose item has the opposite features: valued differences are realized but market procurement here may pose hazards. For the purposes of this paper, intermediate-product characteristics are mainly taken as given and I focus principally on production and transaction-cost economies. A more general formulation would include product characteristics in the optimization.

[43] This ignores transient conditions, such as temporary excess capacity. (In a zero-transaction-cost world, such excesses vanish as assets can be deployed as effectively by others as they can by the owner.)

[44] On these hazards and their transaction-cost origins, see Oliver E. Williamson, *supra* note 1, at 117-31.

[45] Dennis Carlton shows that economies of "vertical integration" can frequently be realized in a market where, absent integration, buyers and suppliers are randomly paired. As he defines vertical integration, however, this can be accomplished as effectively by long-term contract as it can by in-house production. Dennis W. Carlton, Vertical Integration in Competitive Markets under Uncertainty, 27 J. Indus. Econ. 189 (1979).

to economizing on bounded rationality while simultaneously safeguarding the transactions in question against the hazards of opportunism. Holding the governance structure constant, these two objectives are in tension, since a reduction in one commonly results in an increase in the other.[46]

Governance structures, however, are properly regarded as part of the optimization problem. For some transactions, a shift from one structure to another may permit a simultaneous reduction in both the expense of writing a complex contract (which economizes on bounded rationality) and the expense of executing it effectively in an adaptive, sequential way (by attenuating opportunism). Indeed, this is precisely the attraction of internal procurement for transactions of a recurrent, idiosyncratic kind. Not only are market-aggregation economies negligible for such transactions—since the requisite investments are transaction-specific—but market trading in these circumstances is shot through with appropriable quasi-rent hazards. The issues here have been developed elsewhere.[47] The object of this paper is to integrate them into a larger contractual framework.

Note in this connection that the prospect of recovering the set-up costs associated with specialized governance structures varies with the frequency with which transactions recur. Specialized governance structures are much easier to justify for recurrent transactions than for identical transactions that occur only occasionally.

B. *Characterizing Transactions*

I asserted earlier that the critical dimensions for describing contractual relations are uncertainty, the frequency with which transactions recur, and the degree to which investments are idiosyncratic. To simplify the exposition, I will assume uncertainty exists in some intermediate degree and focus initially on frequency and the degree to which the expenses incurred are transaction-specific. The separate importance of uncertainty will then be developed in Section III.D. Three frequency and three investment categories will be recognized. Frequency can be characterized as one-time, occasional, and recurrent; and investments are classed as nonspecific, mixed, and idiosyncratic. To further simplify the argument, the following assumptions are made: (1) Suppliers intend to be in business on a continuing basis; thus the special hazards posed by fly-by-night firms can be disregarded. (2) Potential suppliers for any given requirement are numerous—which is to say that *ex ante* monopoly in ownership of specialized resources is assumed away. (3)

[46] Thus a reduction in monitoring commonly gives rise to an increase in opportunism. Monitoring the employment relation, however, needs to be done with special care. Progressively increasing the intensity of surveillance can elicit resentment and have counterproductive (for example, work-to-rule) results. Such perversities are less likely for interfirm trading.

[47] See note 30 *supra*.

The frequency dimension refers strictly to buyer activity in the market.[48] (4) The investment dimension refers to the characteristics of investments made by suppliers.[49]

Although discrete transactions are intriguing—for example, purchasing local spirits from a shopkeeper in a remote area of a foreign country to which one never again expects to visit nor to refer his friends—few transactions have this totally isolated character. For those that do not, the difference between one-time and occasional transactions is not apparent. Accordingly, only occasional and recurrent frequency distinctions will be maintained. The two-by-three matrix shown in Figure I thus describes the six types of transactions to which governance structures need to be matched. Illustrative transactions appear in the cells.

		Investment Characteristics		
		Nonspecific	Mixed	Idiosyncratic
Frequency	Occasional	Purchasing Standard Equipment	Purchasing Customized Equipment	Constructing a Plant
	Recurrent	Purchasing Standard Material	Purchasing Customized Material	Site-Specific Transfer of Intermediate Product Across Successive Stages

FIGURE I
ILLUSTRATIVE COMMERCIAL TRANSACTIONS

C. *Governance Structures*

Three broad types of governance structures will be considered: non-transaction-specific, semi-specific, and highly specific. The market is the classic nonspecific governance structure within which "faceless buyers and sellers . . . meet . . . for an instant to exchange standardized goods at

[48] This seems reasonable for most intermediate-product market transactions.

[49] Production aspects are thus emphasized. Investments in governance structure are treated separately.

equilibrium prices."[50] By contrast, highly specific structures are tailored to the special needs of the transaction. Identity here clearly matters. Semi-specific structures, naturally, fall in between. Several propositions are suggested immediately. (1) Highly standardized transactions are not apt to require specialized governance structure. (2) Only recurrent transactions will support a highly specialized governance structure.[51] (3) Although occasional transactions of a nonstandardized kind will not support a transaction-specific governance structure, they require special attention nonetheless. In terms of Macneil's three-way classification of contract, classical contracting presumably applies to all standardized transactions (whatever the frequency), relational contracting develops for transactions of a recurring and nonstandardized kind, and neoclassical contracting is needed for occasional, nonstandardized transactions.

1. *Market Governance: Classical Contracting.* Market governance is the main governance structure for nonspecific transactions of both occasional and recurrent contracting. Markets are especially efficacious when recurrent transactions are contemplated, since both parties need only consult their own experience in deciding to continue a trading relationship or, at little transitional expense, turn elsewhere. Being standardized, alternative purchase and supply arrangements are presumably easy to work out.

Nonspecific but occasional transactions are ones for which buyers (and sellers) are less able to rely on direct experience to safeguard transactions against opportunism. Often, however, rating services or the experience of other buyers of the same good can be consulted. Given that the good or service is of a standardized kind, such experience rating, by formal and informal means, will provide incentives for parties to behave responsibly.

To be sure, such transactions take place within and benefit from a legal framework. But such dependence is not great. As S. Todd Lowry puts it, "the traditional economic analysis of exchange in a market setting properly corresponds to the legal concept of *sale* (rather than contract), since sale presumes arrangements in a market context and requires legal support primarily in enforcing transfers of title."[52] He would thus reserve the concept of contract for exchanges where, in the absence of standardized market

[50] Yoram Ben-Porath, *supra* note 29, at 7.

[51] Defense contracting may appear to be a counterexample, since an elaborate governance structure is devised for many of these. This reflects in part, however, the special disabilities of the government as a production instrument. But for this, many of these contracts would be organized in-house. Also, contracts that are very large and of long duration, as many defense contracts are, do have a recurring character.

[52] S. Todd Lowry, Bargain and Contract Theory in Law and Economics, 10 J. Econ. Issues 1, 12 (1976).

alternatives, the parties have designed "patterns of future relations on which they could rely."[53]

The assumptions of the discrete-contracting paradigm are rather well satisfied for transactions where markets serve as a main governance mode. Thus the specific identity of the parties is of negligible importance; substantive content is determined by reference to formal terms of the contract; and legal rules apply. Market alternatives are mainly what protect each party against opportunism by his opposite.[54] Litigation is strictly for settling claims; concentrated efforts to sustain the relation are not made because the relation is not independently valued.[55]

2. *Trilateral Governance: Neoclassical Contracting.* The two types of transactions for which trilateral governance is needed are occasional transactions of the mixed and highly idiosyncratic kinds. Once the principals to such transactions have entered into a contract, there are strong incentives to see the contract through to completion. Not only have specialized investments been put in place, the opportunity cost of which is much lower in alternative uses, but the transfer of these assets to a successor supplier would pose inordinate difficulties in asset valuation.[56] The interests of the principals in sustaining the relation are especially great for highly idiosyncratic transactions.

Market relief is thus unsatisfactory. Often the setup costs of a transaction-specific governance structure cannot be recovered for occasional transactions. Given the limits of classical contract law for sustaining these transactions, on the one hand, and the prohibitive cost of transaction-specific (bilateral) governance, on the other, an intermediate institutional form is evidently needed.

Neoclassical contract law has many of the sought-after qualities. Thus rather than resorting immediately to strict reliance on litigation—with its

[53] *Id.* at 13.

[54] Although recurrent, standard transactions are ones for which an active spot market commonly exists, term contracting may also be employed—especially as planning economies are thereby realized by the parties. See Dennis W. Carlton, Price Rigidity, Forward Contracts, and Market Equilibrium, J. Pol. Econ. (forthcoming). The duration of these contracts will not be long, however, since the assets in question can be employed in other uses and/or in the service of other customers. The result is that changing market circumstances will be reflected relatively quickly in both price and quantity and relatively stringent contracting attitudes may be said to prevail.

[55] "Generally speaking, a serious conflict, even quite a minor one such as an objection to a harmlessly late tender of the delivery of goods, terminates the discrete contract as a live one and leaves nothing but a conflict over money damages to be settled by a lawsuit. Such a result fits neatly the norms of enhancing discreteness and intensifying . . . presentiation." Macneil, Contracts 877.

[56] See the articles cited in note 30 *supra*.

transaction-rupturing features—*third-party assistance* (arbitration) in resolving disputes and evaluating peformance is employed instead. (The use of the architect as a relatively independent expert to determine the content of form construction contracts is an example.)[57] Also, the expansion of the specific-performance remedy in past decades is consistent with continuity purposes—though Macneil declines to characterize specific performance as the "primary neoclassical contract remedy."[58] The section of the Uniform Commercial Code which permits the "seller aggrieved by a buyer's breach . . . unilaterally to maintain the relation"[59] is yet another example.

3. *Transaction-specific Governance: Relational Contracting.* The two types of transactions for which specialized governance structures are commonly devised are recurring transactions of the mixed and highly idiosyncratic kinds. The nonstandardized nature of these transactions makes primary reliance on market governance hazardous, while their recurrent nature permits the cost of the specialized governance structure to be recovered.

Two types of transaction-specific governance structures for intermediate-production market transactions can be distinguished: bilateral structures, where the autonomy of the parties is maintained, and unified structures, where the transaction is removed from the market and organized within the firm subject to an authority relation (vertical integration). Bilateral structures have only recently received the attention they deserve and their operation is least well understood.

(*a*) *Bilateral Governance: Obligational Contracting.* Highly idiosyncratic transactions are ones where the human and physical assets required for production are extensively specialized, so there are no obvious scale economies to be realized through interfirm trading that the buyer (or seller) is unable to realize himself (through vertical integration). In the case, however, of mixed transactions, the degree of asset specialization is less complete. Accordingly, outside procurement for these components may be favored by scale-economy considerations.

As compared with vertical integration, outside procurement also is good in eliciting cost control for steady-state supply. Problems, however, arise when adaptability and contractual expense are considered. Whereas internal adaptations can be effected by fiat, outside procurement involves effecting adaptations across a market interface. Unless the need for adaptations has been contemplated from the outset and expressly provided for by the contract,

[57] Macneil, Contracts 866.

[58] *Id.* at 879.

[59] *Id.* at 880. The rationale for this section of the Code is that "identification of the goods to the contract will, within limits, permit the seller to recover the price of the goods rather than merely damages for the breach. . . , ([where the] latter may be far less in amount and more difficult to prove)." *Id.*

which often is impossible or prohibitively expensive, adaptations across a market interface can be accomplished only by mutual, follow-on agreements. Inasmuch as the interests of the parties will commonly be at variance when adaptation proposals (originated by either party) are made, a dilemma is evidently posed.

On the one hand, both parties have an incentive to sustain the relationship rather than to permit it to unravel, the object being to avoid the sacrifice of valued transaction-specific economies. On the other hand, each party appropriates a separate profit stream and cannot be expected to accede readily to any proposal to adapt the contract. What is needed, evidently, is some way for declaring admissible dimensions for adjustment such that flexibility is provided under terms in which both parties have confidence. This can be accomplished partly by (1) recognizing that the hazards of opportunism vary with the type of adaptation proposed and (2) restricting adjustments to those where the hazards are least. But the spirit within which adaptations are effected is equally important.[60]

Quantity adjustments have much better incentive-compatibility properties than do price adjustments. For one thing, price adjustments have an unfortunate zero-sum quality, whereas proposals to increase, decrease, or delay delivery do not. Also, except as discussed below, price-adjustment proposals involve the risk that one's opposite is contriving to alter the terms within the bilateral monopoly trading gap to his advantage. By contrast, a presumption that exogenous events, rather than strategic purposes, are responsible for quantity adjustments is ordinarily warranted. Given the mixed nature of the exchange, a seller (or buyer) simply has little reason to doubt the representations of his opposite when a quantity change is proposed.

Thus buyers will neither seek supply from other sources nor divert products obtained (at favorable prices) to other uses (or users)—because other sources will incur high setup costs and an idiosyncratic product is nonfungible across uses and users. Likewise, sellers will not withhold supply because better opportunities have arisen, since the assets in question have a specialized character. The result is that quantity representations for idiosyncratic products can ordinarily be taken at face value. Since inability to adapt both quantity and price would render most idiosyncratic exchanges nonviable, quantity adjustments occur routinely.

[60] As Stewart Macaulay observes, "Disputes are frequently settled without reference to the contract or to potential or actual legal sanctions. There is a hesitancy to speak of legal right or to threaten to sue in . . . negotiations" where continuing business is valued. Stewart Macaulay, *supra* note 9, at 61.

The material which follows in this subsection was originally developed in connection with the study of inflation. See Michael L. Wachter & Oliver E. Williamson, Obligational Markets and the Mechanics of Inflation, 9 Bell J. Econ. 549 (1978).

Of course, not all price adjustments pose the same degree of hazard. Those which pose few hazards will predictably be implemented. Crude escalator clauses which reflect changes in general economic conditions are one possibility. But since such escalators are not transaction-specific, imperfect adjustments often result when these escalators are applied to local conditions. We should therefore consider whether price adjustments that are more closely related to local circumstances are feasible. The issue here is whether interim price adjustments can be devised for some subset of conditions such that the strategic hazards described above do not arise. What are the preconditions?

Crises facing either of the parties to an idiosyncratic exchange constitute one class of exceptions. Faced with a viability crisis which jeopardizes the relationship, ad hoc price relief may be permitted. More relevant and interesting, however, is whether there are circumstances whereby interim price adjustments are made routinely. The preconditions here are two: first, proposals to adjust prices must relate to exogenous, germane, and easily verifiable events; and second, quantifiable cost consequences must be confidently related thereto. An example may help to illustrate. Consider a component for which a significant share of the cost is accounted for by a basic material (copper, steel). Assume, moreover, that the fractional cost of the component in terms of this basic material is well specified. An exogenous change in prices of materials would under these circumstances pose few hazards if partial but interim price relief were permitted by allowing pass-through according to formula. A more refined adjustment than aggregate escalators would afford thereby obtains.

It bears emphasis, however, that not all costs so qualify. Changes in overhead or other expenses for which validation is difficult and which, even if verified, bear an uncertain relation to the cost of the component will not be passed through in a similar way. Recognizing the hazards, the parties will simply forgo relief of this kind.

(*b*) *Unified Governance: Internal Organization.* Incentives for trading weaken as transactions become progressively more idiosyncratic. The reason is that, as the specialized human and physical assets become more specialized to a single use, and hence less transferable to other uses, economies of scale can be as fully realized by the buyer as by an outside supplier.[61] The choice of organizing mode then turns on which mode has superior adaptive

[61] This assumes that factor prices paid by buyer and outside supplier are identical. Where this is not true, as in some unionized firms, buyers may choose to procure outside because of a differential wage rate. This is a common problem in the automobile industry, which has a very flat and relatively high wage scale.

properties. As discussed elsewhere, vertical integration will invariably appear in these circumstances.[62]

The advantage of vertical integration is that adaptations can be made in a sequential way without the need to consult, complete, or revise interfirm agreements. Where a single ownership entity spans both sides of the transactions, a presumption of joint profit maximization is warranted. Thus price adjustments in vertically integrated enterprises will be more complete than in interfirm trading. And quantity adjustments, of course, will be implemented at whatever frequency serves to maximize the joint gain to the transaction.

Unchanging identity at the interface coupled with extensive adaptability in both price and quantity is thus characteristic of highly idiosyncratic transactions which are vertically integrated. Obligational contracting is supplanted by the more comprehensive adaptive capability afforded by administration.

The match of governance structures with transactions that results from these economizing efforts is shown in Figure II.

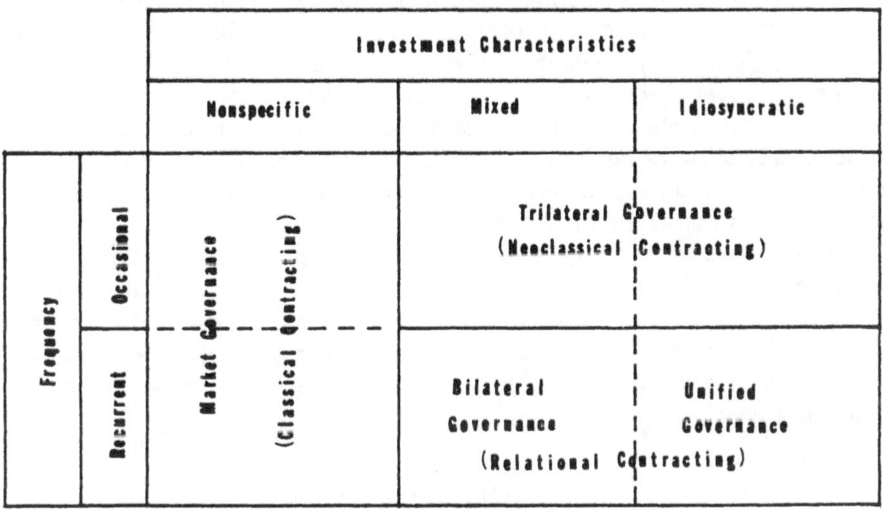

FIGURE II
MATCHING GOVERNANCE STRUCTURES WITH COMMERCIAL TRANSACTIONS

D. *Uncertainty*

Transactions conducted under certainty are relatively uninteresting. Except as they differ in the time required to reach an equilibrium-exchange

[62] See the references cited in note 4 *supra*.

configuration, any governance structure will do. More relevant are transactions where uncertainty is present to an intermediate or high degree. The foregoing has dealt with the first of these. The question here is how the governance of transactions is affected by increasing the degree of uncertainty.

Recall that nonspecific transactions are ones for which continuity has little value, since new trading relations are easily arranged. Increasing the degree of uncertainty does not alter this. Accordingly, market exchange continues and the discrete-contracting paradigm (classical contract law) holds across standardized transactions of all kinds, whatever the degree of uncertainty.

Matters are different with transaction-specific investments. Whenever investments are idiosyncratic in nontrivial degree, increasing the degree of uncertainty makes it more imperative that the parties devise a machinery to "work things out"—since contractual gaps will be larger and the occasions for sequential adaptations will increase in number and importance as the degree of uncertainty increases. This has special relevance for the organization of transactions with mixed investment attributes. Two possibilities exist. One would be to sacrifice valued design features in favor of a more standardized good or service. Market governance would then apply. The second would be to preserve the design but surround the transaction with an elaborated governance apparatus, thereby facilitating more effective adaptive, sequential decision making. Specifically, a more elaborate arbitration apparatus is apt to be devised for occasional, nonstandard transactions. And bilateral governance structures will often give way to unified ones as uncertainty is increased for recurrent transactions.

Reductions in uncertainty, of course, warrant shifting transactions in the opposite direction. To the extent that uncertainty decreases as an industry matures, which is the usual case, the benefits that accrue to integration presumably decline. Accordingly, greater reliance on obligational market contracting is commonly feasible for transactions of recurrent trading in mature industries.

IV. Other Applications

The three dimensions for describing transactions—frequency, investment idiosyncrasy, and uncertainty—apply to transactions of all kinds. The same general considerations that apply to governance structures for commercial transactions carry over as well. The specific governance structures for organizing commercial transactions do not, however, apply without modification to the governance of other types of transactions. Applications of the framework to the study of labor markets, regulation, family law, and capital markets are briefly sketched here.

A. *Labor*

Occasional labor-market transactions typically take the form of repair or replacement services—the plumber, electrician, and so forth. Especially in older homes or structures, these transactions can take on an idiosyncratic quality. Although such transactions can be interesting, the transactions on which I want to focus are recurrent labor-market transactions of the nonspecific, mixed, and idiosyncratic kinds.

Clyde Summers's examination of collective agreements in relation to the law of contracts disclosed that, while the collective bargain differed greatly from the ordinary bargain of commerce, collective agreements are nonetheless a part of the "mainstream of contract."[63] He suggested that the study of contract proceed on two levels: the search for an underlying framework and, within that framework, an examination of the distinctive institutional attributes that distinguish each type of transaction. With respect to the first of these he conjectured that "the principles common to the whole range of contractual transactions are relatively few and of such generality and competing character that they should not be stated as legal rules at all."[64]

I am persuaded that Summers's two-part strategy for studying contract leads to a deeper understanding of the issues. And I believe that the framework set out in the preceding sections of this paper provides much of the underlying unity called for by Summers. What differs as one moves across various contracting activities is the institutional infrastructure.

(1) *Nonspecific Transactions*. Nonspecific labor-market transactions are ones where employer and employee are largely indifferent to the identity of each. Migrant farm labor is an example. Although an unchanging employment association between firm and worker may be observed to continue over long intervals for some of these employees, each party is essentially meeting bids in the spot market. A valuable ongoing relationship, in which specific training and on-the-job learning yield idiosyncratic benefits, is thus not implied. Both wages and employment are variable and market governance applies to transactions of this kind. Consider, therefore, mixed and idiosyncratic labor-market transactions.

(2) *Mixed Transactions*. Probably the most interesting labor-market transactions are those where large numbers of workers acquire an intermediate degree of firm-specific skill. Note that, inasmuch as the degree of idiosyncrasy is a design variable, firms would presumably redesign jobs to favor more standardized operations if it were impossible to devise governance structures which prevented antagonistic bargaining relations from developing between firms and idiosyncratically skilled employees. Although

[63] Clyde W. Summers, *supra* note 9, at 527.

[64] *Id.* at 568.

least-cost production technologies would be sacrificed in the process, net gains might nevertheless be realized since incumbent workers would realize little strategic advantage over otherwise qualified but inexperienced outsiders.

Justice Rehnquist has observed that "Adjudicatory review of the decisions of certain institutions, while perhaps insuring a 'better' decision in some objective sense, can only disrupt on-going relationships within the institution and thereby hamper the institution's ability to serve its designated societal function."[65] Examples of adjudicatory review with respect to which he counsels caution include collective bargaining agreements.

The reasons for this are that adjudicatory review is not easily apprised of the special needs of the transaction and the prospect of such review impairs the incentive of the parties to devise bilateral governance structure. The *Vaca v. Stipes* holding, which Justice Rehnquist cites, is fully consistent with this interpretation. There the Court held that an individual could not compel his union to take his grievance to arbitration, since if the law were otherwise "the settlement machinery provided by the contract would be substantially undermined, thus . . . [introducing] the vagaries of independent and unsystematic negotiations."[66] Archibald Cox elaborates as follows:[67]

> . . . giving the union control over all claims arising under the collective agreement comports so much better with the functional nature of a collective bargaining agreement. . . . Allowing an individual to carry a claim to arbitration whenever he is dissatisfied with the adjustment worked out by the company and the union . . . discourages the kind of day-to-day cooperation between company and union which is normally the mark of sound industrial relations—a relationship in which grievances are treated as problems to be solved and contracts are only guideposts in a dynamic human relationship. When . . . the individual's claim endangers group interests, the union's function is to resolve the competition by reaching an accommodation or striking a balance.

The practice described by Cox of giving the union control over arbitration claims plainly permits group interests—whence the concern for system viability—to supersede individual interests, thereby curbing small-numbers opportunism.

General escalator or predetermined wage adjustments aside, wages are unchanging under collective bargaining agreements.[68] Interim adaptations are nonetheless essential. These take three forms: (1) quantity adjustments,

[65] Remarks of Mr. Justice Rehnquist, *supra* note 38, at 4.

[66] 386 U.S. 171, 191 (1967).

[67] Archibald Cox, *supra* note 9, at 24.

[68] The reason, of course, is that it is very costly and apt to be unproductive to reopen wage bargaining during the period covered by a contract. Since to reopen negotiations for one type of job is to invite it for all, and as objective differences among jobs may be difficult to demonstrate, wage bargaining is foreclosed except at contract-renewal intervals.

(2) assignment changes, and (3) refinement of working rules as a result of grievances.

Quantity adjustments are made in response to changing market opportunities. Either the level or the mix of employment is adjusted as economic events unfold. Given that valuable firm-specific training and learning reside in the workers, layoffs with a presumption of reemployment when conditions improve are common. Conformably, the degree to which the machinery governing access to jobs is elaborated ought to vary directly with the degree to which jobs in a firm are idiosyncratic. Thus promotion ladders in firms where a succession of interdependent jobs are highly idiosyncratic should be long and thin, with access mainly restricted to the bottom, whereas promotion ladders in nonidiosyncratic activities should be broadly structured.[69] Likewise, promotion on merit ought to be favored over promotion strictly by seniority in firms where jobs are more idiosyncratic.[70]

(3) *Highly Idiosyncratic Transactions*. Recall that idiosyncratic transactions involve not merely uniqueness but uniqueness of a transaction-specific kind. Also recall that our concern in this section is with recurring transactions. Thus, although there are many uniquely skilled individuals (artists, athletes, researchers, administrators), unique skills are rarely of a transaction-specific kind. On the contrary, most of these individuals could move to another organization without significant productivity losses.

The exceptions are those where the benefits which accrue to experience (inside knowledge) and/or team interaction effects are great. Whereas commercial transactions of a highly idiosyncratic nature are unified under a common ownership, limits on indenture foreclose this option for labor-market transactions. Instead of "merger," complex contracts designed to tie the interests of the individual to the organization on a long-term basis are negotiated. Severe penalties are provided should either party seek unilateral termination. Nonvested, long-term, contingent reward schemes are devised. More generally, transaction-specific infrastructure will be highly individuated for such transactions.

B. *Regulation of Natural Monopoly*

Again the argument is that specialized governance structure is needed to the degree efficient supply necessarily joins buyers and sellers in a bilateral

[69] Michael L. Wachter & Oliver E. Williamson, *supra* note 60, at 567.

[70] Thus although both nonidiosyncratic and idiosyncratic jobs may be organized collectively, the way in which the internal labor markets associated with each are organized should reflect objective differences between them. Additionally, the incentive to provide an orderly governance structure varies directly with the degree to which efficiencies are attributable thereto. *Ceteris paribus*, nonidiosyncratic jobs ought to be organized later and the governance structure less fully elaborated than for idiosyncratic jobs. Both propositions are borne out by the evidence.

trading relation of a continuing nature. And again, the object of governance is to (1) protect the interests of the respective parties and (2) adapt the relationship to changing circumstances.

Although differing in details, both Victor Goldberg[71] and I[72] have argued that specialized governance structure is needed for services for which natural monopoly features are great. Such structure presumably has the purpose of providing sellers (investors) and buyers with security of expectations, which is a protective function, while at the same time facilitating adaptive, sequential decision making. Rate-of-return regulation with periodic review has these features. To the extent, however, that such regulation is observed in conjunction with activities where transaction-specific investments are insubstantial (as, for example, in the trucking industry), the case for regulation is not at all apparent—or, if it is to be made, must appeal to arguments very different from those set out here.

C. *Family Law*

The issue here is whether the role of adjudication should be *expanded* to help govern family relationships. Granting that adjudication as ultimate relief can and often does serve a useful role for sustaining family relations, such relations are plainly idiosyncratic to an unusual degree and a specialized governance structure is surely the main mode of governance. As the role of adjudication is expanded, reliance upon internal structure is apt to be reduced. Therefore, except when individual rights are seriously threatened, withholding access to adjudication may be indicated.

Justice Rehnquist's remarks concerning the corrosive effects of adversary hearings on the family are apposite: "Any sort of adversary hearing which pits parent against child is bound to be disruptive, placing stresses and tensions on the intra-familial relationships which in turn weaken the family as an institution."[73] Whether, as this suggests, parent-child family relations are optimized where adjudication is zero or negligible is beyond the scope of this paper. It suffices for my purposes merely to note that valued family relations are recurrent and idiosyncratic and that a specialized, transaction-specific governance structure must be encouraged lest the parties withhold investing heavily in the institution.[74]

[71] Victor P. Goldberg, *supra* note 1.

[72] Oliver E. Williamson, *supra* note 30.

[73] Remarks of Mr. Justice Rehnquist, *supra* note 38, at 19.

[74] For a more extensive discussion of family transactions, see Yoram Ben-Porath, *supra* note 29, at 4-7.

D. *Capital Market Transactions*

The ease of verification is critical to the operation of capital markets.[75] Where verification is easy, markets work well and additional governance is unnecessary. Where verification is difficult or very difficult, however, additional governance may be indicated. Occasional transactions are apt to benefit from third-party assistance, while recurring transactions are ones for which bilateral or unified governance will presumably be observed. Assessing capital-market transactions within the proposed framework is thus accomplished by substituting "ease of verification" for "degree of transaction-specific investment." Once this is done, the governance structures appropriate to capital markets are broadly similar to those within which commercial transactions are organized.

V. Implications

Dimensionalizing transactions and examining the costs of executing different transactions in different ways generate a large number of institutional implications. Some of these are summarized here.

A. *General*

1. Nonspecific transactions, either occasional or recurrent, are efficiently organized by markets.

2. Occasional transactions that are nonstandardized stand most to benefit from adjudication.

3. A transaction-specific governance structure is more fully developed where transactions are (1) recurrent, (2) entail idiosyncratic investment, and (3) are executed under greater uncertainty.

B. *Commercial Transactions*

1. Optimization of commercial transactions requires simultaneous attention to (1) production economies, (2) transaction-cost economics, and (3) component design.

2. The reason why Macaulay observes so few litigated cases in business[76] is because markets work well for nonspecific transactions, while recurrent, nonstandard transactions are governed by bilateral or unified structures.

3. As uncertainty increases, the obligational market-contracting mode will not be used for recurrent transactions with mixed investment features. Such transactions will either be standardized, and shifted to the market, or organized internally.

[75] This feature was called to my attention by Sanford Grossman.

[76] Stewart Macaulay, *supra* note 9.

4. As generic demand grows and the number of supply sources increases, exchange that was once transaction-specific loses this characteristic and greater reliance on market-mediated governance is feasible. Thus vertical integration may give way to obligational market contracting, which in turn may give way to markets.

5. Where inventory and related flow-process economies are great, site-specific supply and transaction-specific governance (commonly vertical integration) will be observed. Generic demand here has little bearing.

6. The organization of the interface between manufacturing and distribution reflects similar investment considerations: goods and services that can be sold without incurring transaction-specific investment will be distributed through conventional marketing channels while those where such investments are great will be supported by specialized—mainly bilateral (for example, franchising) or unified (forward integration)—governance structures.

7. The governance of technical change poses special difficulties. The frequently noted limits of markets[77] often give way to more complex governance relations, again for the same general reasons and along the same general lines as are set out here.[78]

C. *Other Transactions*

1. The efficiency benefits of collective organization are negligible for nonspecific labor. Accordingly, such labor will be organized late, often only with the assistance of the political process.

2. Internal labor markets become more highly individuated as jobs become more varied and idiosyncratic.

3. Regulation can be interpreted in part as a response to the transactional dilemma posed by natural monopoly.

4. A transaction-cost justification for regulating activities for which transaction-specific investments are lacking (for example, trucking) is not apparent. The possibility that politics is the driving consideration in such industries warrants consideration.

5. Adjudication should proceed with caution in the area of family law lest valued transaction-specific investments be discouraged.

6. Ease of verification is the capital-market counterpart of transaction-specific investments. Upon making this substitution, the organization of capital markets and intermediate-product markets is broadly similar.

[77] Kenneth J. Arrow, Economic Welfare and the Allocation of Resources for Invention, in The Rate and Direction of Economic Activity 609 (1962).

[78] Aspects are discussed in Oliver E. Williamson, *supra* note 1, at 203-05.

VI. Concluding Remarks

Transaction-cost economics is an interdisciplinary undertaking that joins economics with aspects of organization theory and overlaps extensively with contract law. It is the modern counterpart of institutional economics and relies heavily on comparative analysis.[79] Frictionless ideals are useful mainly for reference purposes.

Although mathematical economics captures only a fraction of the transaction-cost phenomena of interest,[80] this has not been the only obstacle. Headway with the study of transaction-cost issues has been impeded by lack of verbal definitions. Identifying the critical dimensions with respect to which transactions differ has been a significant omission.

This paper attempts to rectify this deficiency and identifies uncertainty, frequency of exchange, and the degree to which investments are transaction-specific as the principal dimensions for describing transactions. The efficient organization of economic activity entails matching governance structures with these transactional attributes in a discriminating way.

Although the main applications in this paper are to commercial contracting, the proposed approach generalizes easily to the study of labor contracts. It also has ramifications for understanding both public utility regulation and family relations. A unified approach to contract thus emerges.

The fact that the broad features of so many varied transactions fit within the framework is encouraging. The importance of transaction costs to the organization of economic activity is thus confirmed. But the world of contract is enormously complex,[81] and the simple economizing framework proposed here cannot be expected to capture more than main features. Elaborating the framework to deal with microanalytic phenomena, however, should be feasible. And extending it to include additional or substitute dimensions (of which the ease of verification, in the case of capital-market transactions, is an example) may sometimes be necessary.

[79] Reliance on comparative analysis has been repeatedly emphasized by R. H. Coase, *supra* note 1.

[80] See Carl J. Dahlman, *supra* note 1, at 144-47.

[81] Benjamin Klein, Robert C. Crawford, & Armen A. Alchian, *supra* note 1, at 325.

Part IV
Economic Analysis of Property Law

[10]

TOWARD A THEORY OF PROPERTY RIGHTS

By Harold Demsetz
University of Chicago

When a transaction is concluded in the marketplace, two bundles of property rights are exchanged. A bundle of rights often attaches to a physical commodity or service, but it is the value of the rights that determines the value of what is exchanged. Questions addressed to the emergence and mix of the components of the bundle of rights are prior to those commonly asked by economists. Economists usually take the bundle of property rights as a datum and ask for an explanation of the forces determining the price and the number of units of a good to which these rights attach.

In this paper, I seek to fashion some of the elements of an economic theory of property rights. The paper is organized into three parts. The first part discusses briefly the concept and role of property rights in social systems. The second part offers some guidance for investigating the emergence of property rights. The third part sets forth some principles relevant to the coalescing of property rights into particular bundles and to the determination of the ownership structure that will be associated with these bundles.

The Concept and Role of Property Rights

In the world of Robinson Crusoe property rights play no role. Property rights are an instrument of society and derive their significance from the fact that they help a man form those expectations which he can reasonably hold in his dealings with others. These expectations find expression in the laws, customs, and mores of a society. An owner of property rights possesses the consent of fellowmen to allow him to act in particular ways. An owner expects the community to prevent others from interfering with his actions, provided that these actions are not prohibited in the specifications of his rights.

It is important to note that property rights convey the right to benefit or harm oneself or others. Harming a competitor by producing superior products may be permitted, while shooting him may not. A man may be permitted to benefit himself by shooting an intruder but be prohibited from selling below a price floor. It is clear, then, that property rights specify how persons may be benefited and harmed, and, therefore, who must pay whom to modify the actions taken by persons. The recognition of this leads easily to the close relationship between property rights and externalities.

Externality is an ambiguous concept. For the purposes of this paper, the concept includes external costs, external benefits, and pecuniary as well as nonpecuniary externalities. No harmful or beneficial effect is external to the world. Some person or persons always suffer or enjoy these effects. What converts a harmful or beneficial effect into an externality is that the cost of bringing the effect to bear on the decisions of one or more of the interacting persons is too high to make it worthwhile, and this is what the term shall mean here. "Internalizing" such effects refers to a process, usually a change in property rights, that enables these effects to bear (in greater degree) on all interacting persons.

A primary function of property rights is that of guiding incentives to achieve a greater internalization of externalities. Every cost and benefit associated with social interdependencies is a potential externality. One condition is necessary to make costs and benefits externalities. The cost of a transaction in the rights between the parties (internalization) must exceed the gains from internalization. In general, transacting cost can be large relative to gains because of "natural" difficulties in trading or they can be large because of legal reasons. In a lawful society the prohibition of voluntary negotiations makes the cost of transacting infinite. Some costs and benefits are not taken into account by users of resources whenever externalities exist, but allowing transactions increases the degree to which internalization takes place. For example, it might be thought that a firm which uses slave labor will not recognize all the costs of its activities, since it can have its slave labor by paying subsistence wages only. This will not be true if negotiations are permitted, for the slaves can offer to the firm a payment for their freedom based on the expected return to them of being free men. The cost of slavery can thus be internalized in the calculations of the firm. The transition from serf to free man in feudal Europe is an example of this process.

Perhaps one of the most significant cases of externalities is the extensive use of the military draft. The taxpayer benefits by not paying the full cost of staffing the armed services. The costs which he escapes are the additional sums that would be needed to acquire men voluntarily for the services or those sums that would be offered as payment by draftees to taxpayers in order to be exempted. With either voluntary recruitment, the "buy-him-in" system, or with a "let-him-buy-his-way-out" system, the full cost of recruitment would be brought to bear on taxpayers. It has always seemed incredible to me that so many economists can recognize an externality when they see smoke but not when they see the draft. The familiar smoke example is one in which negotiation costs may be too high (because of the large number of interacting parties) to make it worthwhile to internalize all the effects of smoke. The draft is an externality caused by forbidding negotiation.

The role of property rights in the internalization of externalities can be made clear within the context of the above examples. A law which establishes the right of a person to his freedom would necessitate a payment on the part of a firm or of the taxpayer sufficient to cover the cost of using that person's labor if his services are to be obtained. The costs of labor thus become internalized in the firm's or taxpayer's decisions. Alternatively, a law which gives the firm or the taxpayer clear title to slave labor would necessitate that the slaveowners take into account the sums that slaves are willing to pay for their freedom. These costs thus become internalized in decisions although wealth is distributed differently in the two cases. All that is needed for internalization in either case is ownership which includes the right of sale. It is the prohibition of a property right adjustment, the prohibition of the establishment of an ownership title that can thenceforth be exchanged, that precludes the internalization of external costs and benefits.

There are two striking implications of this process that are true in a world of zero transaction costs. The output mix that results when the exchange of property rights is allowed is efficient and the mix is independent of who is assigned ownership (except that different wealth distributions may result in different demands).[1] For example, the efficient mix of civilians and military will result from transferable ownership no matter whether taxpayers must hire military volunteers or whether draftees must pay taxpayers to be excused from service. For taxpayers will hire only those military (under the "buy-him-in" property right system) who would not pay to be exempted (under the "let-him-buy-his-way-out" system). The highest bidder under the "let-him-buy-his-way-out" property right system would be precisely the last to volunteer under a "buy-him-in" system.[2]

We will refer back to some of these points later. But for now,

[1] These implications are derived by R. H. Coase, "The Problem of Social Cost," *J. of Law and Econ.*, Oct., 1960, pp. 1-44.

[2] If the demand for civilian life is unaffected by wealth redistribution, the assertion made is correct as it stands. However, when a change is made from a "buy-him-in" system to a "let-him-buy-his-way-out" system, the resulting redistribution of wealth away from draftees may significantly affect their demand for civilian life; the validity of the assertion then requires a compensating wealth change. A compensating wealth change will not be required in the ordinary case of profit maximizing firms. Consider the farmer-rancher example mentioned by Coase. Society may give the farmer the right to grow corn unmolested by cattle or it may give the rancher the right to allow his cattle to stray. Contrary to the Coase example, let us suppose that if the farmer is given the right, he just breaks even; i.e., with the right to be compensated for corn damage, the farmer's land is marginal. If the right is transferred to the rancher, the farmer, not enjoying any economic rent, will not have the wherewithal to pay the rancher to reduce the number of head of cattle raised. In this case, however, it will be profitable for the rancher to buy the farm, thus merging cattle raising with farming. His self-interest will then lead him to take account of the effect of cattle on corn.

enough groundwork has been laid to facilitate the discussion of the next two parts of this paper.

The Emergence of Property Rights

If the main allocative function of property rights is the internalization of beneficial and harmful effects, then the emergence of property rights can be understood best by their association with the emergence of new or different beneficial and harmful effects.

Changes in knowledge result in changes in production functions, market values, and aspirations. New techniques, new ways of doing the same things, and doing new things—all invoke harmful and beneficial effects to which society has not been accustomed. It is my thesis in this part of the paper that the emergence of new property rights takes place in response to the desires of the interacting persons for adjustment to new benefit-cost possibilities.

The thesis can be restated in a slightly different fashion: property rights develop to internalize externalities when the gains of internalization become larger than the cost of internalization. Increased internalization, in the main, results from changes in economic values, changes which stem from the development of new technology and the opening of new markets, changes to which old property rights are poorly attuned. A proper interpretation of this assertion requires that account be taken of a community's preferences for private ownership. Some communities will have less well-developed private ownership systems and more highly developed state ownership systems. But, given a community's tastes in this regard, the emergence of new private or state-owned property rights will be in response to changes in technology and relative prices.

I do not mean to assert or to deny that the adjustments in property rights which take place need be the result of a conscious endeavor to cope with new externality problems. These adjustments have arisen in Western societies largely as a result of gradual changes in social mores and in common law precedents. At each step of this adjustment process, it is unlikely that externalities per se were consciously related to the issue being resolved. These legal and moral experiments may be hit-and-miss procedures to some extent but in a society that weights the achievement of efficiency heavily, their viability in the long run will depend on how well they modify behavior to accommodate to the externalities associated with important changes in technology or market values.

A rigorous test of this assertion will require extensive and detailed empirical work. A broad range of examples can be cited that are consistent with it: the development of air rights, renters' rights, rules for liability in automobile accidents, etc. In this part of the discussion, I shall present one group of such examples in some detail. They deal with the development of private property rights in land among American Indians. These examples are broad ranging and come fairly close to what can be called convincing evidence in the field of anthropology.

The question of private ownership of land among aboriginals has held a fascination for anthropologists. It has been one of the intellectual battlegrounds in the attempt to assess the "true nature" of man unconstrained by the "artificialities" of civilization. In the process of carrying on this debate, information has been uncovered that bears directly on the thesis with which we are now concerned. What appears to be accepted as a classic treatment and a high point of this debate is Eleanor Leacock's memoir on *The Montagnes "Hunting Territory" and the Fur Trade.*[3] Leacock's research followed that of Frank G. Speck[4] who had discovered that the Indians of the Labrador Peninsula had a long-established tradition of property in land. This finding was at odds with what was known about the Indians of the American Southwest and it prompted Leacock's study of the Montagnes who inhabited large regions around Quebec.

Leacock clearly established the fact that a close relationship existed, both historically and geographically, between the development of private rights in land and the development of the commercial fur trade. The factual basis of this correlation has gone unchallenged. However, to my knowledge, no theory relating privacy of land to the fur trade has yet been articulated. The factual material uncovered by Speck and Leacock fits the thesis of this paper well, and in doing so, it reveals clearly the role played by property right adjustments in taking account of what economists have often cited as an example of an externality—the overhunting of game.

Because of the lack of control over hunting by others, it is in no person's interest to invest in increasing or maintaing the stock of game. Overly intensive hunting takes place. Thus a successful hunt is viewed as imposing external costs on subsequent hunters—costs that are not taken into account fully in the determination of the extent of hunting and of animal husbandry.

Before the fur trade became established, hunting was carried on primarily for purposes of food and the relatively few furs that were required for the hunter's family. The externality was clearly present. Hunting could be practiced freely and was carried on without assessing its impact on other hunters. But these external effects were of such

[3] Eleanor Leacock, *American Anthropologist* (American Anthropological Asso.), Vol. 56, No. 5, Part 2, Memoir No. 78.

[4] Cf., Frank G. Speck, "The Basis of American Indian Ownership of Land," *Old Penn Weekly Rev.* (Univ. of Pennsylvania), Jan. 16, 1915, pp. 491-95.

small significance that it did not pay for anyone to take them into account. There did not exist anything resembling private ownership in land. And in the *Jesuit Relations,* particularly Le Jeune's record of the winter he spent with the Montagnes in 1633-34 and in the brief account given by Father Druilletes in 1647-48, Leacock finds no evidence of private land holdings. Both accounts indicate a socioeconomic organization in which private rights to land are not well developed.

We may safely surmise that the advent of the fur trade had two immediate consequences. First, the value of furs to the Indians was increased considerably. Second, and as a result, the scale of hunting activity rose sharply. Both consequences must have increased considerably the importance of the externalities associated with free hunting. The property right system began to change, and it changed specifically in the direction required to take account of the economic effects made important by the fur trade. The geographical or distributional evidence collected by Leacock indicates an unmistakable correlation between early centers of fur trade and the oldest and most complete development of the private hunting territory.

> By the beginning of the eighteenth century, we begin to have clear evidence that territorial hunting and trapping arrangements by individual families were developing in the area around Quebec. . . . The earliest references to such arrangements in this region indicates a purely temporary allotment of hunting territories. They [Algonkians and Iroquois] divide themselves into several bands in order to hunt more efficiently. It was their custom . . . to appropriate pieces of land about two leagues square for each group to hunt exclusively. Ownership of beaver houses, however, had already become established, and when discovered, they were marked. A starving Indian could kill and eat another's beaver if he left the fur and the tail.[5]

The next step toward the hunting territory was probably a seasonal allotment system. An anonymous account written in 1723 states that the "principle of the Indians is to mark off the hunting ground selected by them by blazing the trees with their crests so that they may never encroach on each other. . . . By the middle of the century these allotted territories were relatively stabilized."[6]

The principle that associates property right changes with the emergence of new and reevaluation of old harmful and beneficial effects suggests in this instance that the fur trade made it economic to encourage the husbanding of fur-bearing animals. Husbanding requires the ability to prevent poaching and this, in turn, suggests that socioeconomic changes in property in hunting land will take place. The chain of reasoning is consistent with the evidence cited above. Is it inconsistent with the absence of similar rights in property among the southwestern Indians?

Two factors suggest that the thesis is consistent with the absence of

[5] Eleanor Leacock, *op. cit.*, p. 15.
[6] Eleanor Leacock, *op. cit.*, p. 15.

similar rights among the Indians of the southwestern plains. The first of these is that there were no plains animals of commercial importance comparable to the fur-bearing animals of the forest, at least not until cattle arrived with Europeans. The second factor is that animals of the plains are primarily grazing species whose habit is to wander over wide tracts of land. The value of establishing boundaries to private hunting territories is thus reduced by the relatively high cost of preventing the animals from moving to adjacent parcels. Hence both the value and cost of establishing private hunting lands in the Southwest are such that we would expect little development along these lines. The externality was just not worth taking into account.

The lands of the Labrador Peninsula shelter forest animals whose habits are considerably different from those of the plains. Forest animals confine their territories to relatively small areas, so that the cost of internalizing the effects of husbanding these animals is considerably reduced. This reduced cost, together with the higher commercial value of fur-bearing forest animals, made it productive to establish private hunting lands. Frank G. Speck finds that family proprietorship among the Indians of the Peninsula included retaliation against trespass. Animal resources were husbanded. Sometimes conservation practices were carried on extensively. Family hunting territories were divided into quarters. Each year the family hunted in a different quarter in rotation, leaving a tract in the center as a sort of bank, not to be hunted over unless forced to do so by a shortage in the regular tract.

To conclude our excursion into the phenomenon of private rights in land among the American Indians, we note one further piece of corroborating evidence. Among the Indians of the Northwest, highly developed private family rights to hunting lands had also emerged—rights which went so far as to include inheritance. Here again we find that forest animals predominate and that the West Coast was frequently visited by sailing schooners whose primary purpose was trading in furs.[7]

[7] The thesis is consistent with the development of other types of private rights. Among wandering primitive peoples the cost of policing property is relatively low for highly portable objects. The owning family can protect such objects while carrying on its daily activities. If these objects are also very useful, property rights should appear frequently, so as to internalize the benefits and costs of their use. It is generally true among most primitive communities that weapons and household utensils, such as pottery, are regarded as private property. Both types of articles are portable and both require an investment of time to produce. Among agriculturally-oriented peoples, because of the relative fixity of their location, portability has a smaller role to play in the determination of property. The distinction is most clearly seen by comparing property in land among the most primitive of these societies, where crop rotation and simple fertilization techniques are unknown, or where land fertility is extremely poor, with property in land among primitive peoples who are more knowledgeable in these matters or who possess very superior land. Once a crop is grown by the more primitive agricultural societies, it is necessary for them to abandon the land for several years to restore productivity. Property rights in land among such people would require policing cost for several years during which no sizable output is obtained. Since to provide for

The Coalescence and Ownership of Property Rights

I have argued that property rights arise when it becomes economic for those affected by externalities to internalize benefits and costs. But I have not yet examined the forces which will govern the particular form of right ownership. Several idealized forms of ownership must be distinguished at the outset. These are communal ownership, private ownership, and state ownership.

By communal ownership, I shall mean a right which can be exercised by all members of the community. Frequently the rights to till and to hunt the land have been communally owned. The right to walk a city sidewalk is communally owned. Communal ownership means that the community denies to the state or to individual citizens the right to interfere with any person's exercise of communally-owned rights. Private ownership implies that the community recognizes the right of the owner to exclude others from exercising the owner's private rights. State ownership implies that the state may exclude anyone from the use of a right as long as the state follows accepted political procedures for determining who may not use state-owned property. I shall not examine in detail the alternative of state ownership. The object of the analysis which follows is to discern some broad principles governing the development of property rights in communities oriented to private property.

It will be best to begin by considering a particularly useful example that focuses our attention on the problem of land ownership. Suppose that land is communally owned. Every person has the right to hunt, till, or mine the land. This form of ownership fails to concentrate the cost associated with any person's exercise of his communal right on that person. If a person seeks to maximize the value of his communal rights, he will tend to overhunt and overwork the land because some of the costs of his doing so are borne by others. The stock of game and the richness of the soil will be diminished too quickly. It is conceivable that those who own these rights, i.e., every member of the community, can agree to curtail the rate at which they work the lands if negotiating and policing costs are zero. Each can agree to abridge his rights. It is obvious that the costs of reaching such an agreement will not be zero. What is not obvious is just how large these costs may be.

Negotiating costs will be large because it is difficult for many per-

sustenance these people must move to new land, a property right to be of value to them must be associated with a portable object. Among these people it is common to find property rights to the crops, which, after harvest, are portable, but not to the land. The more advanced agriculturally based primitive societies are able to remain with particular land for longer periods, and here we generally observe property rights to the land as well as to the crops.

sons to reach a mutually satisfactory agreement, especially when each hold-out has the right to work the land as fast as he pleases. But, even if an agreement among all can be reached, we must yet take account of the costs of policing the agreement, and these may be large, also. After such an agreement is reached, no one will privately own the right to work the land; all can work the land but at an agreed upon shorter workweek. Negotiating costs are increased even further because it is not possible under this system to bring the full expected benefits and expected costs of future generations to bear on current users.

If a single person owns land, he will attempt to maximize its present value by taking into account alternative future time streams of benefits and costs and selecting that one which he believes will maximize the present value of his privately-owned land rights. We all know that this means that he will attempt to take into account the supply and demand conditions that he thinks will exist after his death. It is very difficult to see how the existing communal owners can reach an agreement that takes account of these costs.

In effect, an owner of a private right to use land acts as a broker whose wealth depends on how well he takes into account the competing claims of the present and the future. But with communal rights there is no broker, and the claims of the present generation will be given an uneconomically large weight in determining the intensity with which the land is worked. Future generations might desire to pay present generations enough to change the present intensity of land usage. But they have no living agent to place their claims on the market. Under a communal property system, should a living person pay others to reduce the rate at which they work the land, he would not gain anything of value for his efforts. Communal property means that future generations must speak for themselves. No one has yet estimated the costs of carrying on such a conversation.

The land ownership example confronts us immediately with a great disadvantage of communal property. The effects of a person's activities on his neighbors and on subsequent generations will not be taken into account fully. Communal property results in great externalities. The full costs of the activities of an owner of a communal property right are not borne directly by him, nor can they be called to his attention easily by the willingness of others to pay him an appropriate sum. Communal property rules out a "pay-to-use-the-property" system and high negotiation and policing costs make ineffective a "pay-him-not-to-use-the-property" system.

The state, the courts, or the leaders of the community could attempt to internalize the external costs resulting from communal property by allowing private parcels owned by small groups of person with similar interests. The logical groups in terms of similar interests, are, of course, the family and the individual. Continuing with our use of the land ownership example, let us initially distribute private titles to land randomly among existing individuals and, further, let the extent of land included in each title be randomly determined.

The resulting private ownership of land will internalize many of the external costs associated with communal ownership, for now an owner, by virtue of his power to exclude others, can generally count on realizing the rewards associated with husbanding the game and increasing the fertility of his land. This concentration of benefits and costs on owners creates incentives to utilize resources more efficiently.

But we have yet to contend with externalities. Under the communal property system the maximization of the value of communal property rights will take place without regard to many costs, because the owner of a communal right cannot exclude others from enjoying the fruits of his efforts and because negotiation costs are too high for all to agree jointly on optimal behavior. The development of private rights permits the owner to economize on the use of those resources from which he has the right to exclude others. Much internalization is accomplished in this way. But the owner of private rights to one parcel does not himself own the rights to the parcel of another private sector. Since he cannot exclude others from their private rights to land, he has no direct incentive (in the absence of negotiations) to economize in the use of his land in a way that takes into account the effects he produces on the land rights of others. If he constructs a dam on his land, he has no direct incentive to take into account the lower water levels produced on his neighbor's land.

This is exactly the same kind of externality that we encountered with communal property rights, but it is present to a lesser degree. Whereas no one had an incentive to store water on any land under the communal system, private owners now can take into account directly those benefits and costs to their land that accompany water storage. But the effects on the land of others will not be taken into account directly.

The partial concentration of benefits and costs that accompany private ownership is only part of the advantage this system offers. The other part, and perhaps the most important, has escaped our notice. The cost of negotiating over the remaining externalities will be reduced greatly. Communal property rights allow anyone to use the land. Under this system it becomes necessary for all to reach an agreement on land use. But the externalities that accompany private ownership of property do not affect all owners, and, generally speaking, it will be necessary for only a few to reach an agreement that takes these effects into account. The cost of negotiating an internalization of these effects is thereby reduced considerably. The point is important enough to elucidate.

Suppose an owner of a communal land right, in the process of plowing a parcel of land, observes a second communal owner constructing a dam on adjacent land. The farmer prefers to have the stream as it is, and so he asks the engineer to stop his construction. The engineer says, "Pay me to stop." The farmer replies, "I will be happy to pay you, but what can you guarantee in return?" The engineer answers, "I can guarantee you that I will not continue constructing the dam, but I cannot guarantee that another engineer will not take up the task because this is communal property; I have no right to exclude him." What would be a simple negotiation between two persons under a private property arrangement turns out to be a rather complex negotiation between the farmer and everyone else. This is the basic explanation, I believe, for the preponderance of single rather than multiple owners of property. Indeed, an increase in the number of owners is an increase in the communality of property and leads, generally, to an increase in the cost of internalizing.

The reduction in negotiating cost that accompanies the private right to exclude others allows most externalities to be internalized at rather low cost. Those that are not are associated with activities that generate external effects impinging upon many people. The soot from smoke affects many homeowners, none of whom is willing to pay enough to the factory to get its owner to reduce smoke output. All homeowners together might be willing to pay enough, but the cost of their getting together may be enough to discourage effective market bargaining. The negotiating problem is compounded even more if the smoke comes not from a single smoke stack but from an industrial district. In such cases, it may be too costly to internalize effects through the marketplace.

Returning to our land ownership paradigm, we recall that land was distributed in randomly sized parcels to randomly selected owners. These owners now negotiate among themselves to internalize any remaining externalities. Two market options are open to the negotiators. The first is simply to try to reach a contractual agreement among owners that directly deals with the external effects at issue. The second option is for some owners to buy out others, thus changing the parcel size owned. Which option is selected will depend on which is cheaper. We have here a standard economic problem of optimal scale. If there exist constant returns to scale in the ownership of different sized parcels, it will be largely a matter of indifference between outright purchase and contractual agreement if only a single, easy-to-police, contractual agreement will internalize the externality. But, if there are several externalities, so that several such contracts will need to be negotiated, or if the contractual agreements should be difficult to police, then outright purchase will be the preferred course of action.

The greater are diseconomies of scale to land ownership the more will contractual arrangement be used by the interacting neighbors to settle these differences. Negotiating and policing costs will be compared to costs that depend on the scale of ownership, and parcels of land will tend to be owned in sizes which minimize the sum of these costs.[8]

The interplay of scale economies, negotiating cost, externalities, and the modification of property rights can be seen in the most notable "exception" to the assertion that ownership tends to be an individual affair: the publicly-held corporation. I assume that significant economies of scale in the operation of large corporations is a fact and, also, that large requirements for equity capital can be satisfied more cheaply by acquiring the capital from many purchasers of equity shares. While economies of scale in operating these enterprises exist, economies of scale in the provision of capital do not. Hence, it becomes desirable for many "owners" to form a joint-stock company.

But if all owners participate in each decision that needs to be made by such a company, the scale economies of operating the company will be overcome quickly by high negotiating cost. Hence a delegation of authority for most decisions takes place and, for most of these, a small management group becomes the *de facto* owners. Effective ownership, i.e., effective control of property, is thus legally concentrated in management's hands. This is the first legal modification, and it takes place in recognition of the high negotiating costs that would otherwise obtain.

The structure of ownership, however, creates some externality difficulties under the law of partnership. If the corporation should fail, partnership law commits each shareholder to meet the debts of the corporation up to the limits of his financial ability. Thus, managerial *de facto* ownership can have considerable external effects on shareholders. Should property rights remain unmodified, this externality would make it exceedingly difficult for entrepreneurs to acquire equity capital from wealthy individuals. (Although these individuals have recourse to reimbursements from other shareholders, litigation costs will be high.) A second legal modification, limited liability, has taken place to reduce the effect of this externality.[9] *De facto* management ownership and limited liability combine to minimize the overall cost of operating large enterprises. Shareholders are essentially lenders of equity capital and not owners, although they do participate in such infrequent decisions as

[8] Compare this with the similar rationale given by R. H. Coase to explain the firm in "The Nature of the Firm," *Economica*, New Series, 1937, pp. 386–405.

[9] Henry G. Manne discusses this point in a forthcoming book about the American corporate system.

those involving mergers. What shareholders really own are their shares and not the corporation. Ownership in the sense of control again becomes a largely individual affair. The shareholders own their shares, and the president of the corporation and possibly a few other top executives control the corporation.

To further ease the impact of management decisions on shareholders, that is, to minimize the impact of externalities under this ownership form, a further legal modification of rights is required. Unlike partnership law, a shareholder may sell his interest without first obtaining the permission of fellow shareholders or without dissolving the corporation. It thus becomes easy for him to get out if his preferences and those of the management are no longer in harmony. This "escape hatch" is extremely important and has given rise to the organized trading of securities. The increase in harmony between managers and shareholders brought about by exchange and by competing managerial groups helps to minimize the external effects associated with the corporate ownership structure. Finally, limited liability considerably reduces the cost of exchanging shares by making it unnecessary for a purchaser of shares to examine in great detail the liabilities of the corporation and the assets of other shareholders; these liabilities can adversely affect a purchaser only up to the extent of the price per share.

The dual tendencies for ownership to rest with individuals and for the extent of an individual's ownership to accord with the minimization of all costs is clear in the land ownership paradigm. The applicability of this paradigm has been extended to the corporation. But it may not be clear yet how widely applicable this paradigm is. Consider the problems of copyright and patents. If a new idea is freely appropriable by all, if there exist communal rights to new ideas, incentives for developing such ideas will be lacking. The benefits derivable from these ideas will not be concentrated on their originators. If we extend some degree of private rights to the originators, these ideas will come forth at a more rapid pace. But the existence of the private rights does not mean that their effects on the property of others will be directly taken into account. A new idea makes an old one obsolete and another old one more valuable. These effects will not be directly taken into account, but they can be called to the attention of the originator of the new idea through market negotiations. All problems of externalities are closely analogous to those which arise in the land ownership example. The relevant variables are identical.

What I have suggested in this paper is an approach to problems in property rights. But it is more than that. It is also a different way of viewing traditional problems. An elaboration of this approach will, I hope, illuminate a great number of social-economic problems.

[11]

Of Coase and Cattle: Dispute Resolution Among Neighbors in Shasta County

Robert C. Ellickson*

TABLE OF CONTENTS

---

* Robert E. Paradise Professor of Natural Resources Law, Stanford Law School.

My debts are many. Jerry Anderson, Thomas Hagler, and Keith Kelly were able research assistants. Participants in workshops at the Boston University, Harvard, Stanford, and Yale Law Schools provided helpful suggestions. Financial support was received from the Stanford Legal Research Fund, made possible by a bequest from the Estate of Ira S. Lillick, and by gifts from Roderick E. and Carla A. Hills and other friends of the Stanford Law School.

Dozens of people in Shasta County were of immeasurable assistance. I especially thank Bob Bosworth, the President of the Shasta County Cattlemen's Association, and Walt Johnson, the county Farm Advisor, for easing my immersion into Shasta County life.

A few stylistic notes are in order. Except for public figures, the names used are pseudonyms. To reduce clutter, and sometimes to protect privacy, I have generally refrained from footnoting references to individual interviews. The present tense usually denotes the situation in Shasta County in 1982, the year in which I conducted most of my interviews.

This article is part of a forthcoming book to be published by the Harvard University Press. The contents of the book are briefly described in text following note 161 *infra*.

> "I think the whole thing is good neighbors. If you don't have good neighbors, you can forget the whole thing."
>
> —Chuck Searle, Shasta County cattleman

> "My family believes in 'live and let live.' Have you heard of that?"
>
> —Phil Ritchie, Shasta County farmer

This article reports the results of an investigation into how rural landowners in Shasta County, California, resolve disputes arising from trespass by livestock. The results provide an empirical perspective on one of the most celebrated hypothetical cases in the law-and-economics literature. In his landmark article, "The Problem of Social Cost,"[1] economist Ronald Coase invoked as his fundamental example a conflict between two neighbors—a rancher running cattle and a farmer raising crops. Coase used the Parable of the Farmer and the Rancher to illustrate what has come to be known as the Coase Theorem. This unintuitive proposition asserts, in its strongest form, that when transaction costs are zero, a change in the rule of liability will have no effect on the allocation of resources. For example, the Theorem

1. Coase, *The Problem of Social Cost*, 3 J.L. & ECON. 1 (1960).

predicts that as long as its admittedly heroic assumptions are met, the imposition of liability for cattle trespass would not cause ranchers to reduce the size of their herds, erect more fencing, or keep closer watch on their livestock. The Theorem has become the most fruitful, yet most controversial, proposition in law-and-economics.[2]

Coase himself was fully aware that obtaining information, negotiating agreements, and litigating disputes are all potentially costly, and that thus his Parable might not portray accurately how rural landowners would respond to a change in trespass law.[3] Some law-and-economics scholars, however, assume that transaction costs are indeed often trivial when only two parties are in conflict.[4] Therefore, these scholars might assume that Coase's

2. Some recent landmarks in the Coase Theorem literature are Cooter, *The Cost of Coase*, 11 J. LEGAL STUD. 1 (1982); Hoffman & Spitzer, *The Coase Theorem: Some Experimental Tests*, 25 J.L. & ECON. 73 (1982); Regan, *The Problem of Social Cost Revisited*, 15 J.L. & ECON. 427 (1972). A central theme of these articles is that Coase should have explicitly recognized the possibility that disputants may act strategically and thereby fail to carry out mutually advantageous exchanges. An unusually complete review of the literature is provided by Zerbe, *The Problem of Social Cost in Retrospect*, 2 RESEARCH IN L. & ECON. 83 (1980).

3. *See* Coase, *supra* note 1, at 15–19 (entitled "The Cost of Market Transactions Taken into Account").

Ronald Coase has in fact been a militant for the cause of empiricism. In recent years, he seems to have become increasingly frustrated with the sterility of the abstract debates over his Theorem:

> [W]hile considerations of what would happen in a world of zero transaction costs can give us valuable insights, these insights are, in my view, without value except as steps on the way to the analysis of the real world of positive transaction costs. We do not do well to devote ourselves to a detailed study of the world of zero transaction costs, like augurs divining the future by the minute inspection of the entrails of a goose.

Coase, *The Coase Theorem and the Empty Core: A Comment*, 24 J.L. & ECON. 183, 187 (1981).

The central finding of the present work is that the residents of Shasta County often succeed, without the involvement of the state, in coordinating with one another in a mutually advantageous way. Coase's Parable of the Farmer and the Rancher sounds this same general theme of cooperative interaction. This finding is generally consistent with what Coase found in his own microscopic investigation of the supply of lighthouses in England. *See* Coase, *The Lighthouse in Economics*, 17 J.L. & ECON. 357 (1974).

4. Several of Coase's colleagues at the University of Chicago wedded themselves to this assumption in the 1960s. *See, e.g.*, W. BLUM & H. KALVEN, PUBLIC LAW PERSPECTIVES ON A PRIVATE LAW PROBLEM: AUTO COMPENSATION PLANS 58–59 (1965); Demsetz, *When Does the Rule of Liability Matter*, 1 J. LEGAL STUD. 13, 16 (1972) (transaction costs "would seem to be negligible" when a baseball player negotiates with his club).

The current consensus, even among Chicagoans, is that negotiations in bilateral monopoly situations can be costly because the parties may act strategically. *See, e.g.*, R. POSNER, ECONOMIC ANALYSIS OF LAW 45 (2d ed. 1977); Cooter, Marks & Mnookin, *Bargaining in the Shadow of the Law: A Testable Model of Strategic Behavior*, 11 J. LEGAL STUD. 225, 242–44 (1982) ("The obstacle to agreement is the strategic nature of bargaining, not the cost of communicating"); Landes & Posner, *Salvors, Finders, Good Samaritans, and Other Rescuers: An Economic Study of Altru-*

Parable faithfully depicts how rural landowners resolve cattle-trespass disputes.

To explore the realism of the assumptions underlying the Farmer-Rancher Parable, I searched for a jurisdiction that had imposed varying rules of liability in cattle trespass situations and had changed those rules with some frequency. After briefly surveying a half-dozen candidates in California, I settled on Shasta County. Since 1945, a specific California statute has authorized the Shasta County Board of Supervisors, the county's elected governing body, to determine where in the county an owner of cattle is liable for damages stemming from unintentional cattle trespass on unfenced land.[5] Although most of Shasta County is "open range"—territory where a cattleman is not liable for trespass damages of that sort—the Board has the authority to "close the range" in subareas of the county. A closed-range ordinance makes a cattleman strictly liable for any damage his livestock might cause while trespassing within the area affected by the ordinance.[6] The Shasta County Board of Supervisors has exercised this power to close the range on dozens of occasions since 1945, thus changing the exact rule of liability that Coase used in his famous example.[7] I traveled to Shasta County to determine whether these legal changes had had any impact.[8]

---

ism, 7 J. LEGAL STUD. 83, 91 (1978) ("transaction costs under bilateral monopoly are high"). *See also* sources cited at note 2 *supra*.

5. *See* notes 99–103 *infra* and accompanying text.

6. The terms "closed-range" and "open-range" can be a source of confusion. I use the terms throughout this article as they are ordinarily used in Shasta County, to denote the *legal regime* applicable to a particular territory. The potential confusion arises because the terms might be construed as indicating a *method of husbandry*—that is, whether in a particular area it is the custom of cattlemen to run their animals at large or to keep them behind fences. In Shasta County, the correlation between legal regime and method of husbandry is rather weak. For example, most ranchers in the open-range areas of the county keep their herds behind fences.

7. To invoke Calabresi & Melamed's fruitful typology, a closed-range ordinance essentially shifts the legal regime from property-rule protection of the rancher to liability-rule protection of the trespass victim. *See* Calabresi & Melamed, *Property Rules, Liability Rules, and Inalienability: One View of the Cathedral*, 85 HARV. L. REV. 1089, 1105–1115 (1972). Hoffman & Spitzer, *supra* note 2, at 84, deserve credit for noting that Coase had contrasted asymmetrical legal positions. *But cf.* note 112 *infra* and accompanying text (noting the availability of injunctive relief to trespass victims in closed range).

8. A number of other law and economics scholars have investigated empirically the impact of transaction costs on interneighbor coordination. *See, e.g.*, Cheung, *The Fable of the Bees: An Economic Investigation*, 16 J.L. & ECON. 11 (1973); Crocker, *Externalities, Property Rights, and Transactions Costs: An Empirical Study*, 14 J.L. & ECON. 451 (1971). The study closest to mine in its substantive focus, although not its methodology, is Vogel, *The Effect of Changes in Property Rights Entitlements on Production: The Coase Theorem and California Animal Trespass Law*, 15 J. LEGAL

This study presents findings that cast doubt on many of the assumptions undergirding the Coasean Parable. It also strives to help bridge the chasm lying between the law and economics and law and society movements,[9] perhaps the two most significant social-scientific schools of legal research. On the whole, the law and society scholars have gathered the better field data on dispute resolution practices, and the law and economics scholars have developed the more explicit, rigorous, and testable theories of human behavior. Although one might think that members of these two schools would perceive irresistible benefits from collaboration, these two groups have worked largely in isolation from one another. They have separate journals.[10] They gather at separate conferences. They rarely read, much less cite, work by scholars in the other camp. This absence of cross-fertilization stems not only from lack of familiarity with the working language of the other group, but also from a mutual lack of respect, even a contempt, for the kind of work that the other group does. To exaggerate only a little, the law and economics scholars believe that the law and society group is deficient in both sophistication and rigor, and the law and society scholars believe that the law and economics group is not only out of touch with reality but also short on humanity.

In conducting this study, I placed a foot squarely within each of the two camps. Law and economics, the tradition within which I have mainly labored, provided the Parable that inspired the study. By undertaking "microscopic"[11] field research into the

---

STUD. — (1986) (forthcoming) (regression analysis of effects of various closed-range ordinances on agricultural production in California counties between 1850 and 1877).

In recent years Elizabeth Hoffman and Matthew Spitzer have been the most persistent and creative transaction cost empiricists. *See, e.g.*, Hoffman & Spitzer, *supra* note 2 (report on a series of laboratory experiments in which subjects could achieve gains by cooperating); Spitzer & Hoffman, *A Reply to Kelman's "Consumption Theory, Production Theory, and Ideology in the Coase Theorem,"* 53 S. CAL. L. REV. 1187 (1980) (study of the effect of the elimination of the Reserve Clause on the movement of baseball players between clubs).

9. Any discussion of a chasm between academic subcultures brings to mind C.P. Snow's classic 1959 lecture on "The Two Cultures." Snow used as his polar opposites literary intellectuals and physical scientists, and speculated on whether social scientists represented yet a third culture. C.P. SNOW, THE TWO CULTURES: AND A SECOND LOOK 70–71 (1964). The chasm that I identify is a division *between* groups of social scientists. It suggests that Snow was understandably in a quandary about how to classify members of the social scientific disciplines.

10. The core journals are the JOURNAL OF LAW AND ECONOMICS and the LAW & SOCIETY REVIEW.

11. I borrow the term "microscopic" from Clifford Geertz, an anthropologist noted for his devotion to "thick descriptions" of human interaction. *See, e.g.*, C. GEERTZ, THE INTERPRETATION OF CULTURES 3–30 (1973).

resolution of a narrow class of disputes, however, I followed the methods of pioneering law and society scholars such as Stuart Macaulay and H. Laurence Ross.[12] After reading in both literatures, I confess my disloyal suspicion that law and society scholars would generally be more successful than law and economics scholars in predicting the essentials of the story to come.

The Shasta County evidence indicates that Coase's Farmer-Rancher Parable correctly anticipates that a change in the rule of liability for cattle trespass does not affect, for example, the quality of fences that separate ranches from farms. The Parable's explanation for the allocative toothlessness of law is, however, exactly backward. The Parable's explanation is that transaction costs are low and that parties respond to a new rule by agreeing to an exchange of property rights that perpetuates the prior (efficient) allocation of resources. The field evidence I gathered suggests that a change in animal trespass law indeed fails to affect resource allocation, *not because transaction costs are low, but because transaction costs are high.* Legal rules are costly to learn and enforce. Trespass incidents are minor irritations between parties who typically have complex continuing relationships that enable them readily to enforce informal norms. The Shasta County evidence indicates that under these conditions, potential disputants ignore the formal law. As Coase probably suspected,[13] the Para-

12. In preparing his classic article, *Non-Contractual Relations in Business: A Preliminary Study*, 28 AM. SOC. REV. 55 (1963), Macaulay interviewed business executives and lawyers to find out how Wisconsin manufacturing firms resolve contractual disputes. Ross' best known work is H. ROSS, SETTLED OUT OF COURT (rev. ed. 1980), which describes how insurance adjusters process claims covered under automobile liability policies. Notable also is Ross & Littlefield, *Complaint as a Problem Solving Mechanism*, 12 LAW & SOC'Y REV. 199 (1978), a study of how a large appliance retailer in Denver handles consumer complaints.

Law and society scholars have done relatively little field work on dispute resolution between adjoining landowners. *But see, e.g.*, Baumgartner, *Social Control in Suburbia*, in 2 TOWARD A GENERAL THEORY OF SOCIAL CONTROL 79 (D. Black ed. 1984); Ruffini, *Disputing over Livestock in Sardinia*, in THE DISPUTING PROCESS: LAW IN TEN SOCIETIES 209 (L. Nader & H. Todd eds. 1978) (finding that shepherds in Sardinia rely on self-help, not formal legal processes, to resolve rustling disputes). Economists have also done little field work on relations among neighbors. *But see* sources in the first paragraph of note 8 *supra*.

There is a broad interdisciplinary perception that progress in understanding conflict resolution depends upon more low-level empirical work. *See, e.g.*, R. HARDIN, COLLECTIVE ACTION 229–30 (1982) (comments of a philosopher-game theorist). *See also* Felstiner, *Influences of Social Organization on Dispute Processing*, 9 LAW & SOC'Y REV. 63, 86 n.28 (1974) ("Ironically, we have better data about dispute processing in Indian villages, Mexican towns, and East African tribes than we have about that process in American communities." (comments of a law-and-society scholar)).

13. *See* note 3 *supra* and accompanying text.

ble of the Farmer and the Rancher therefore ill-describes how rural landowners actually interact with one another.

Part I of this article introduces the relevant residents of Shasta County and their techniques of cattle ranching and boundary fencing. Part II narrates the political history of the two closed-range battles that occurred in the area where the study was conducted. Part III explains why I chose this area to study and my field research methods. Part IV, the heart of the article, describes how the rural residents of Shasta County resolve their cattle-trespass disputes. Finally, Part V summarizes the article's principal findings and implications.

I. Shasta County and Its Cattle Industry

A. *Physical Environment*

Shasta County lies at the northern end of the 400 mile-long Central Valley of California. The Sacramento River, which drains the northern half of the Central Valley, bisects the county. Redding, Shasta County's county seat and largest city, is situated at an elevation of 500 feet at the spot where the Sacramento River emerges from the mountains north of the Valley to begin its trip south toward San Francisco Bay. High mountain peaks lie within sight of Redding in all directions except south. The Trinity Mountains lie to the west; the towering cone of Mount Shasta stands fifty miles due north, in Siskiyou County; and to the east lie other peaks of the volcanic Cascade Range— notably Mount Lassen, which sits in Shasta County's southeastern corner. To the east, north, and west of Redding, foothills rise irregularly toward these distant mountain peaks.

Weather dictates Shasta County's ranching practices. Like the rest of California, the county has a wet season and a dry season. Redding receives an average annual rainfall of 38.74 inches, most of it concentrated in the winter months.[14] Little rain falls between mid-May and November. During the summer months intense sunlight bakes Redding, and the surrounding mountains block cooling winds.[15] In the spring, the grasslands near Redding are green from the heavy winter rains; by summer, the extreme heat has turned the groundcover brown.

Most of Shasta County's terrain is too mountainous and its

14. Record Searchlight (Redding, Cal.), Aug. 11, 1982, at 15, col. 1.

15. In July, the city's average daily high temperature is 98 degrees. *Id.* at 14, col. 3.

soils too poor to support significant agricultural activity. The majority of the land area in the county is commercial-quality forest, most of which the United States Forest Service and a handful of private timber companies own.[16] Census data describe sixteen percent of the county as "land in farms."[17] The bulk of this agricultural land is unirrigated and used only as seasonal pasture for livestock—principally cattle, the county's major agricultural product. Only one percent of the county's land is used for raising harvested crops,[18] and a majority of this field-crop acreage is devoted to alfalfa or other hay grown as livestock feed.[19]

In 1973, the Shasta County Board of Supervisors voted to "close the range" in a fifty-six square-mile rectangle of territory around Round Mountain, a rural hamlet situated thirty miles northeast of Redding. This ordinance, which county cattlemen now call "Caton's Folly" to embarrass a supervisor who helped pass it, provided the best opportunity in Shasta County to test the effects of an *actual* change in the rule of liability for cattle trespass. Nine years later, in 1982, the Board of Supervisors considered, but rejected, a petition to close the range in the Oak Run area immediately southwest of Caton's Folly.[20] The Oak Run controversy promised to reveal the effects of a *threatened* change in liability rules. Residents of the Oak Run and Round Mountain areas were interviewed to shed more light on these effects. The general area northeast of Redding—what I call the Northeastern Sector—thus warrants closer description.

The Northeastern Sector consists of three ecological zones: grassy plains, foothills, and mountain forest. The elevation of the land largely determines the boundaries of these zones; the higher the terrain, the more rain it receives, and the cooler its summer weather.

The zone between 500 and 1500 feet in elevation, the zone

16. Of the 2.4 million acres of land in Shasta County, 1.3 million have been identified as "commercial forest." CAL. DEP'T OF FINANCE, CAL. STATISTICAL ABSTRACT 2, 129 (1983). The United States Forest Service owns 35% of this commercial forest, and forest industry companies own 46%. *Id.* at 129.

17. *Id.* at 111 (citing data from the 1978 U.S. Census of Agriculture).

18. *Id.* at 2, 111.

19. E. PETERSON, IN THE SHADOW OF THE MOUNTAIN: A SHORT HISTORY OF SHASTA COUNTY, CALIFORNIA 110 (1965).

Coase's Parable involves a pasture adjoining a field of annually harvested crops. These land uses are rarely contiguous in Shasta County. The lessons of the Parable, however, in no way depend on how the Rancher's neighbor uses his land.

20. *See* notes 70–76 *infra* and accompanying text.

FIGURE 1
MAP OF NORTHWESTERN CALIFORNIA

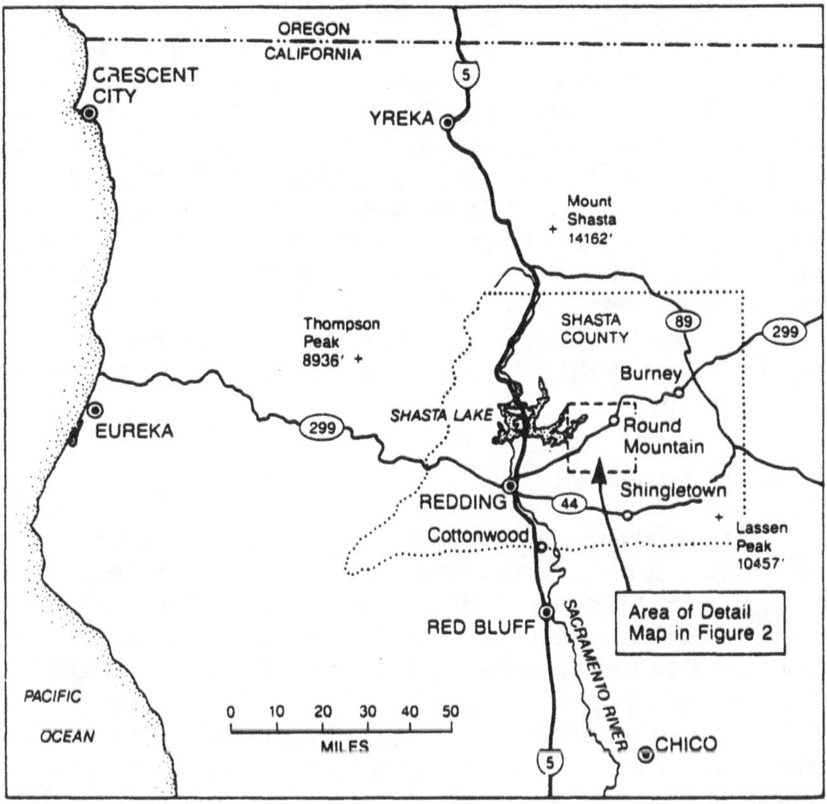

closest to Redding, consists of grassy plains. This idyllic, oak-dotted country provides natural pasture during the spring and, if irrigated, can support a herd year-round. A water supply adequate for irrigation is available, however, only near the streams that flow through the area. Moreover, the soil in much of the grassy plains is infertile hardpan. Because of these natural constraints, the full-time ranchers who operate in this zone typically need at least several square miles of pasture.

The foothills lie between 1500 and 3500 feet in elevation. Both Caton's Folly and the Oak Run area fall within this transition zone. Much of the foothill area has a mixed natural treecover of pine and oak. In open areas the natural ground cover is less likely to be grass than an unpalatable chaparral of manzanita, buckbrush, and like shrubs. To foothill ranchers this brush is almost as repulsive a thought as the importation of Australian beef; the more enterprising foothill ranchers spend much of their energies grappling with this foe.[21]

Mountain forest, the third zone, starts at about 3500 feet. Ponderosa pine, douglas fir, and other conifers that have supplanted the deciduous oaks cover the mountainsides at this elevation. The mountain forests remain green year-round, but most are too cold in winter and too hard to clear to be suitable sites for cattlemen's base ranches. The Roseburg Lumber Company owns much of the mountain forest in the Northeastern Sector.[22] Like other private timber companies in the county, Roseberg has not shown any interest in subdividing its lands for development. For many decades, however, Roseberg and its predecessors in ownership have leased their forests to Shasta County cattlemen for summer range.

B. *Social Environment*

The volatility of population change may affect how people resolve their disputes. Shasta County has experienced rapid population growth. Between 1930 and 1980, the number of county residents increased ninefold,[23] and in the decade from 1970 to 1980, total County population rose from 78,000 to 116,000.[24] The County's population growth rate of 49.0 percent in the 1970's was substantially higher than the overall state rate (18.5 percent), and was somewhat higher than the aggregate rate for California's nonmetropolitan counties (36.4 percent).[25] Redding's location at the northern end of the Central Valley makes it a natural transportation hub. It serves as the gateway to moun-

21. *See* text accompanying note 46 *infra.*

22. The Roseburg Lumber Company is a closely held corporation based in Roseburg, Oregon. It is controlled by Kenneth Ford, a self-made man whom Forbes Magazine has listed as one of the forty wealthiest persons in the United States. San Francisco Chron., Aug. 28, 1982, at 14, col. 4. When Roseburg purchased its forests in the Northeastern sector in 1979 from the Kimberly-Clark Corporation, it became the fourth timber company to own these lands since the early 1940s.

23. In 1930, the County's population was 13,927. U.S. DEPT. OF COMMERCE, BUREAU OF THE CENSUS, 15TH CENSUS OF THE UNITED STATES, vol. 3, pt. 1, at 284 (1932).

24. U.S. DEPT. OF COMMERCE, BUREAU OF THE CENSUS, 1980 CENSUS OF POPULATION, vol. I, pt. 6, ch. A, table 4 (1982). In 1980, 42,000 people lived in the city of Redding. *Id.* By 1984, the city's estimated population exceeded 50,000, and Shasta County achieved the status of a Standard Metropolitan Statistical Area.

25. Calculated from data in the 1980 Census of Population.

FIGURE 2
MAP OF THE OAK RUN/ROUND MOUNTAIN AREA

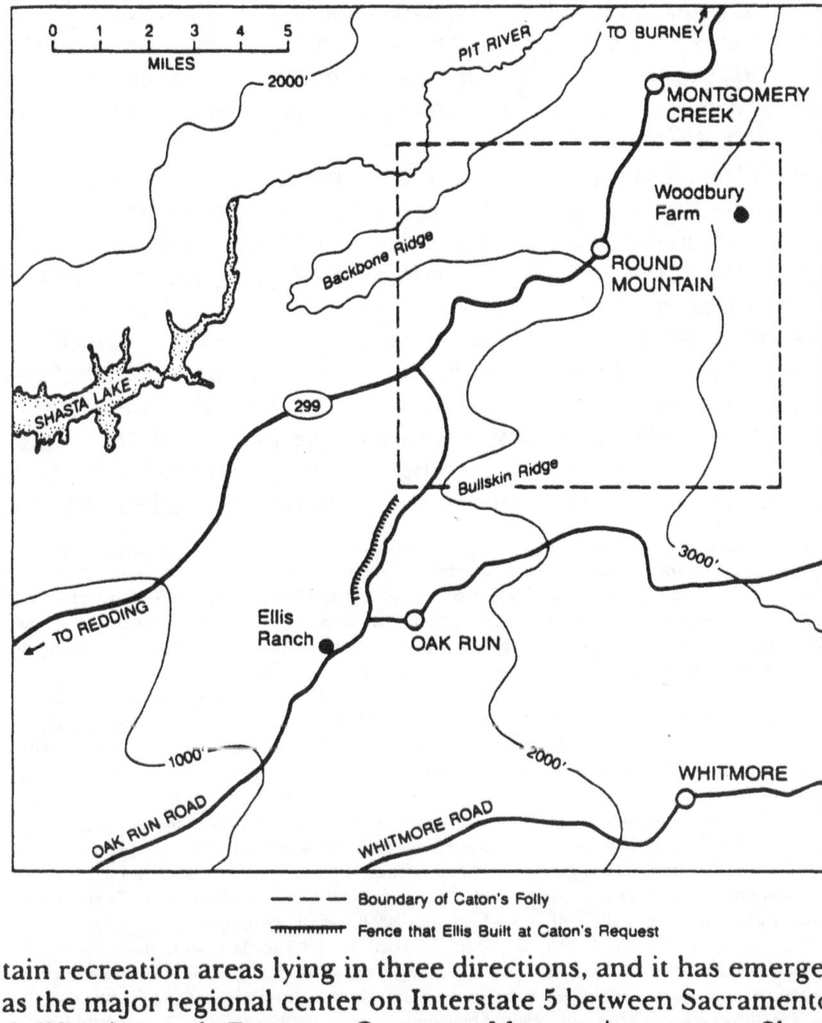

tain recreation areas lying in three directions, and it has emerged as the major regional center on Interstate 5 between Sacramento, California, and Eugene, Oregon. Many migrants to Shasta County have come from the San Francisco and Los Angeles areas. Indications of social instability have accompanied the influx of migrants. In 1981, Shasta had the highest divorce rate of any county in California,[26] and in 1980, the county's unemployment

26. In 1981, Shasta County had 8.7 dissolutions and nullities of marriage per 1,000 estimated persons, compared to a statewide figure of 5.8 per thousand. State of Cal., Dep't of Health Servs., Vital Statistics of California—1981, at 128 (1983).

rate was twice that of the state as a whole.[27]

Precise figures on population trends within the Northeastern Sector are not available. It appears, however, that during the 1970s, the Sector's population grew by an even larger percentage than did the county's.[28] Not surprisingly, the recent demographic histories of the three ecological zones within the Sector are rather different.

Residential patterns in the grassy plains have not changed much in recent years. Beyond the suburbs of Redding most of the acreage in the grasslands and lower foothills remains divided into ranches at least several square miles in size. Approximately half of these ranches are owned by descendants of families that have been in the county for several generations.[29] Although many of these ranches have a current market value of $1,000,000 or more, the ranchers typically have modest annual incomes. For decades, ranchlands in Shasta County have generated an annual cash return of only one or two percent of market value.[30] The cattlemen who own and operate the large family ranches tend to

27. Census data put the County's unemployment rate at 13.8%, compared to the state's 6.5%. U.S. Dep't of Commerce, Bureau of the Census, 1980 Census of Population and Housing, Advance Estimates of Social, Economic, and Housing Characteristics. The timber industry, an important factor in the Shasta County economy, was in a deep slump in 1980, a factor that no doubt contributed to this disparity.

28. The population of what the Census Bureau calls the Central Shasta division increased from 3,049 in 1970 to 6,784 in 1980, or by 122%. U.S. Dep't of Commerce, Bureau of the Census, 1980 Census of Population, vol. 1, pt. 6, ch. A, table 4, n.41 (1982). This division includes both the Northeastern Sector and larger rural territories to the north, south, and southeast.

29. The first pioneers to settle east and northeast of Redding used the grasslands and lower foothills to raise livestock. The descendants of the nineteenth century pioneer families—Coombs, Donaldson, Wagoner—still hold a special place in rural Shasta County society. Oldtimers are quick to identify their roots in the county, and sometimes refer to families who arrived a generation ago as "people who haven't been here very long."

Prior to the 1920s, the Southern Pacific Railroad owned alternate sections in the grassy plains—a reward from the United States for laying track to Redding. The government grant consisted of alternate sections for a distance of 20 miles on both side of the track. S. Daggett, Chapters on the History of the Southern Pacific 50, 122 (1922). During the 1920s, the Southern Pacific sold off most of its grassland sections at the then market price of $2.50 to $5.00 per acre, thereby enabling the pioneer ranching families to consolidate their holdings. Abandoning their prior practice of running their herds at large, these families erected fences around their multi-thousand-acre spreads, cleared patches of brush, and began to irrigate their better pastures.

30. Interview with Robert Shaw, Redding-based appraiser (July 19, 1982). Mr. Shaw attributed the low returns to tax benefits and psychic income that ranching confers.

Cattle ranching is noted for skimpy financial returns. *See* Arthur D. Little, Inc., Final Environmental Statement, Proposed Livestock Grazing Program, BLM Cerbat/Black Mountain Planning Units II-139 to -142 (1978) (returns to cattle ranching in Arizona range

follow self-imposed seven-day-a-week work schedules and live in houses less imposing than those one would find in an average American suburb. When estate taxes or property taxes have squeezed them financially, ranching families have either conveyed their entire holdings to other ranchers or to investors seeking tax shelters or, more commonly, they have sold tree-covered pieces of their ranches to developers for subdivision into ranchettes.

The foothills have seen more subdivision activity and absolute population growth than have the grassy plains. Both supply and demand conditions explain this pattern. Because the foothills are somewhat less suited than the grasslands for agriculture, foothill landowners are more likely to consider subdividing their holdings. Most homebuyers would also prefer the foothills to the grasslands as a residential location because the higher elevations are cooler in summer and offer more tree cover. As a result, the foothills within commuting distance of Redding have experienced a multifold increase in population over the past twenty years.[31]

Many of the recent settlers in the foothills are either retirees or younger migrants from California's major urban areas. These newcomers tend to live on minimally improved lots of from five to forty acres, either in owner-built houses or mobile homes. Many of these ranchettes have sprung up near hamlets, such as Oak Run and Round Mountain, that contain a general store, a post office, an elementary school, and other basic community facilities. Despite these clusters of growth, development in the foothills has been rather diffuse. Especially since the mid-1960s, small-scale real estate operatives have subdivided forested areas in every sector of the foothills.[32] Thus virtually all foothill ranch-

---

from negative to a positive one to two percent; ranchers do it for love); Charlier, *Home on the Range is a Part-Time Deal for Many Cowboys*, Wall St. J., Jan. 8, 1985, at 1, col. 4.

31. Some of the new development has been for second homes. Celebrities such as baseball pitcher Vida Blue, actor Clint Eastwood, country singer Merle Haggard, and ex-Congressman Pete McCloskey are among those who have purchased properties in the rural areas east of Redding.

32. John Williams of the Redding office of the Title Insurance & Trust Co. generously permitted me to use the firm's tract indexes. These indexes showed that in 24 sections near the southern border of Caton's Folly, the number of land parcels increased from 61 in 1930, to 145 in 1972, to 295 in 1982.

Countywide, the number of land parcels quadrupled between 1967 and 1982. Interview with Tony Estacio, Chief, Administrative Services, Assessor's Office of Shasta County (July 8, 1982). These recent rates of parcelization appear atypically high for rural land markets. *See*

ers have some ranchette owners as neighbors. Ranchette owners may keep a farm animal or two as a hobby, but few of them make significant income from agriculture. The ranchette owners nevertheless admire both the cattlemen and the folkways traditionally associated with rural Shasta County.

C. *Work Environment: Modes of Cattle Ranching*

Despite their long hours of work, few ranchers in Shasta County find raising beef cattle a road to prosperity. The typical rancher runs a cow and calf operation. When his calves are seven to twelve months old, he[33] trucks them a dozen miles south of Redding to the Shasta County Auctionyard at Cottonwood, where each Friday some 3,000 head change hands. Agents for feedlot operators and pasture owners buy the calves, take them to feedlots and pastures outside the county, and feed and fatten them for a few months to prepare them for slaughter. In 1982, a six-hundred pound yearling sold at auction in Cottonwood for about $375, compared to the $500 it would have brought in 1979, the year that nominal beef prices peaked.[34] Not only have beef prices recently failed to match the rate of inflation, but in the 1970s per capita consumption of beef in the United States began to fall.[35] Shasta County is at best marginal cattle country, and some cattlemen there understandably fear that they may be among the casualties in their beleaguered industry's continuing shakeout.

Shasta County cattlemen may be loosely grouped into two categories: the traditionalists and the modernists.[36] Traditional-

---

R. Healy & J. Short, The Market for Rural Land 22 (1976) (in only one of five counties studied did the number of rural land parcels double between 1954 and 1976).

33. Although women own, manage, and provide most of the physical labor on a number of the ranches in Shasta County, rural culture generally supports the differentiation of sex roles. Thus a woman rancher who wishes to be active in the county Cattlemen's Association is likely to participate only in the CowBelles, the women's auxillary. The National Cattlemen's Association did recently elect its first woman president, JoAnn Smith, but she had come to prominence by serving as president of the Florida CowBelles. N.Y. Times, Apr. 24, 1985, at C1, col. 1.

34. *See* San Francisco Chron., Aug. 26, 1982, at 38, col. 2.

35. Per capita beef consumption peaked at 95.7 lbs. in 1976, and by 1981 had fallen to 78.3 lbs., as consumers shifted toward poultry and pork. N.Y. Times, Aug. 9, 1981, § IV, at 22, col. 3.

36. These categories inevitably oversimplify. For example, Dick Coombs and Chuck Searle employ modernist land-management and husbandry practices, yet continue the traditionalist practice of leasing mountain forest for summer range.

ists tend to be more marginal economically, and have a greater stake in fighting "closed range" ordinances.

1. *The traditionalists.*

Traditional Shasta County cattlemen continue to follow the husbandry practices that were nearly universal in the county as late as the 1920s. A traditionalist's trademark is that he lets his cattle roam, essentially untended, in unfenced mountain areas during the summer.[37] This customary practice evolved in response to the severity of Shasta County's dry season. In the area northeast of Redding, a rancher lacking irrigated pasture needs about ten to twenty acres per animal unit[38] for winter and spring pasture. Thus, to support 200 cattle—a substantial herd by Shasta County standards—a rancher without irrigated pasture needs at least 2,000 acres, or just over three square miles of land. During the dry season the brutal heat makes unirrigated grasslands almost worthless. To feed his animals during the summer, a lowland cattleman must therefore either have access to irrigated pasture or be able to move his animals to the high foothills and mountains where cooler dry season temperatures enable natural forage to survive. The traditionalist solution is a summer grazing lease on a large tract of mountain forest.

The United States Forest Service, the Bureau of Land Management,[39] and major private timber companies, have regularly entered into grazing leases with county cattlemen. Although the timber company grazing leases typically have only a one-year term, the companies have allowed cattlemen to renew them as a matter of course.[40] Federal leases may run for any period up to

37. The classic study of cattlemen operating on unfenced range is E. OSGOOD, THE DAY OF THE CATTLEMAN (1929) (emphasizing practices in Wyoming and Montana during the latter part of the Nineteenth Century). On the history of traditionalist practices in California, see R. CLELAND, THE CATTLE ON A THOUSAND HILLS (2d ed. 1951); D. DARY, COWBOY CULTURE 44–66 (1981).

38. An "animal unit" is a mature cow plus calf, or the equivalent in terms of forage consumption. A horse converts to 1.25 animal units, a sheep to 0.2 animal units, and so on. An "animal unit month" (AUM) is the amount of forage an animal unit consumes in one month of grazing. H. HEADY, RANGELAND MANAGEMENT 117 (1975).

39. These two agencies manage most of the vast federal holdings in the county. Altogether, federal agencies own 42% of the County's acreage. Walter H. Johnson, *Agriculture as a Competitor for Land*, in ECONOMIC COMPETITION FOR LAND: SHASTA COUNTY 48 (Univ. of Cal., Agric. Extension Serv. 1966).

40. A specialist in brokering private grazing leases stated that most of his landowner-lessee relationships had endured for decades. Interview with Jim Cochran, Wm. Beatty & Assocs., in Redding, Ca. (July 21, 1982).

ten years,[41] and they also tend to be automatically renewable.[42] A cattleman who has been leasing a tract of forest for summer range thus tends to regard the leased tract as a normal part of his operations. Although the forest areas remain green in summer, they contain too few open meadows to support many cattle. Traditionalists may have to lease 300 acres of forest per animal unit: Thus, a traditionalist with a herd of only 100 animals may lease during the summer a forest equal in area to the city of San Francisco.

The fencing of these far flung forest leaseholds has never been cost-justified in the eyes of either the timber owners or their traditionalist lessees. To reduce the risk of livestock trespassing on contiguous lands, forest leasehold boundaries are often drawn to follow natural barriers such as ridges and gulches. But adroit boundary drawing is hardly a foolproof method for controlling strays. Mountain cattle tend to drift down the drainage areas to lower elevations, especially when the weather turns cold or a drought dries the upland creeks. Lessees occasionally erect drift fences across mountain valleys to block the most obvious migration routes. Because drift fences are easily destroyed by winter snows, however, traditionalists often let their animals roam at will in the mountains. Even a forest lessee who has ridden his leasehold periodically during the summer risks being unable to find part of his herd when he gathers his livestock in mid-October. After the October gathering, a traditionalist returns his animals to a base ranch at a lower elevation, and feeds them hay or other stored feed for a few months until the winter rains revive the natural grasses on the base ranch pastures.[43]

2. *The modernists.*

Modernists among the Shasta County cattlemen keep their livestock behind fences at all times in order to increase their control over their herds.[44] To satisfy the need for summer forage that originally caused traditionalist cattlemen to enter into forest leases, modernists install ditches and sprinklers to irrigate base

41. *See* 43 U.S.C.A. §§ 315b, 1752 (Supp. 1983).

42. Interviews with Terry Brumley of the U.S.F.S., in Redding, Ca. (Aug. 9, 1982), and Paul McClain of the B.L.M., in Redding, Ca. (July 9, 1982).

43. Untimely grazing may damage rangeland. If grazing occurs too early, it may kill immature grass; if it occurs too late, the livestock may eat seeds needed for the following year's forage. Grazing leases therefore regulate entry and exit dates.

44. *See* notes 47–50 *infra* and accompanying text.

ranch pastures. One acre of irrigated pasture can support a cow and calf for an entire summer. A modernist who can irrigate about ten percent of his lands is usually able to run a year-round, fenced operation.[45]

Modernists are more active than traditionalists in managing ranchland vegetation. If not controlled, the native brush that thrives in the foothill zone would consume much of the scarce ground water and soil nutrients that competing grasses need. Modernist foothill ranchers fight the brush by setting controlled burns, spreading herbicides, and dragging chains from tractors to uproot the larger plants.[46] Using these clearing techniques, leading modernist cattlemen have transformed unproductive foothill areas into valuable pasturelands.

Modernists tend to be younger than traditionalists, have more formal education, and be more active in the Cattlemen's Association. Some modernists view the traditionalists as old-fashioned and primitive. Traditionalists, however, see themselves as the "real" cattlemen—the ones who can recognize a cow at half a mile and sleep out under the stars in the tradition of the nineteenth century cowboy.

Despite their stylistic differences, modernists and traditionalists have much in common. Members of both groups believe that the life of the cattleman is the best possible in western America. They enjoy riding horses and regularly wearing blue jeans, cowboy hats, and cowboy boots. They regard the late John Wayne as their kind of guy. Although traditionalists have a much greater stake than modernists do in keeping the Board of Supervisors from closing the range, modernist cattlemen typically join the traditionalists in opposing proposed legal changes that would increase the liabilities of owners of stray cattle.

45. A cattleman needs at least ten acres of unirrigated land per AUM for winter range. If he were to irrigate ten percent of this acreage, he would have enough irrigated pasture for summer range. Instead of irrigating, a modernist who prefers operating behind fences may move his herds to fenced summer grasslands located in the high mountain valleys of Superior California. ("Superior California" is a regionally popular geographical designation that, unlike "Northern California," distinguishes the northmost counties from the Bay Area.)

46. *See generally* H. Heady, *supra* note 38, at 253–55, 258, 280–329. On controlled burns, see also Cal. Pub. Res. Code §§ 4475–94 (West Supp. 1981) (delineating the role of the State Department of Forestry); L. Stoddart & A. Smith, Range Management 383–94 (1943) (describing the effects of burning upon various types of rangeland).

D. *The Benefits and Costs of Boundary Fences*

The study of cattle trespass incidents is inevitably a study of fencing. A fence demarcates boundaries, keeps out human and animal trespassers, and keeps in the fencebuilder's own animals. In the Farmer-Rancher Parable, Coase perceived the sole benefit of a fence to be the reduction of trespass damages to crops.[47] In fact, cattlemen enclose their lands largely to prevent damage to their own livestock. Predators, rustlers, winter snows, and poisonous plants such as larkspur all pose potentially lethal threats to cattle roaming unfenced countryside.[48] Cattlemen also worry that a wandering cow will be impregnated by a bull of worthless pedigree. Furthermore, fencing makes it easier for a rancher to provide salt and other useful diet supplements, and to prevent the weight loss likely to occur when cattle walk long distances.

The prices of grazing leases reflect the value that ranchers place on fences. In 1982, fenced land in the Northeastern Sector rented for about $10 per animal unit month, whereas unfenced land rented for about $3.[49] Because both arrangements yield the same quantity of forage, the rent differential provides a rough measure of how much ranchers value the protection and control that boundary fences provide.[50]

Since 1874, the year J.F. Glidden took out the first patent on barbed wire, the barbed wire fence has been the standard American technology for enclosing livestock.[51] California's statutory

47. *See* Coase, *supra* note 1, at 3, 5.

48. Rancher Dick Coombs, the epitome of honor in rural Shasta County, counseled that "[I]f you don't fence, your neighbors get your cattle, and their cattle get your feed."

During the nineteenth century, when cattlemen let their stock loose on the Great Plains during the winter, even the best managers were likely to lose five percent of their mature animals each grazing season. D. Boorstin, The Americans: The Democratic Experience 10 (1973). In the Northwest during the same time period, losses ran about 10%. J. Oliphant, On the Cattle Ranges of the Oregon Country 240–41 (1968). In Wyoming and Montana, during the disastrous winter of 1885–1886, blizzards killed 85% or more of the livestock in some herds. E. Osgood, *supra* note 37, at 216–18.

49. These are rough averages of figures that ranchers and grazing-lease specialists offered in interviews. For the definition of "animal unit month," see note 38 *supra*.

50. The quality of forage of course varies from pasture to pasture, and is apt to be better where a landowner has deliberately tried to cultivate his grasses.

51. D. Dary, *supra* note 37, at 308–31, recounts the impact of the advent of barbed wire on ranching practices nationally. Before barbed wire, the fencing-in of cattle was generally not economical in California. R. Cleland, *supra* note 37, at 62.

A standard barbed wire fence will not contain sheep or hogs. To fence in those animals, Shasta County landowners use woven wire (which they variously refer to as "netting," "hogwire," or "field fence") for the bottom 39 or 47 inches of fence, and top it off with one to

standard for a "lawful fence" was set at the turn of the century. It calls for three tightly stretched strands of barbed wire stapled to posts situated 16–1/2 feet (one rod) apart.[52] Today, Shasta County ranchers tend to use at least four strands of barbed wire[53] and they employ steel posts instead of the cedar posts customarily used earlier in the century.[54]

In 1982, the materials for a new four-strand, barbed wire fence in Shasta County cost about $2000 per mile. Fence contractors charge at least as much for labor and overhead.[55] Both

---

three strands of barbed wire. Because many ranchers in Shasta County owned sheep and swine a half century ago, many boundary fences there still contain woven wire.

Other types of boundary fences, such as electrified fence, are uncommon. However, an owner of horses may use board fencing, rather than barbed wire, to eliminate the risk that barbs pose to the coats of show animals. A natural barrier such as a gulch or a dense growth of brush may obviate the need for any type of boundary fencing. On fence technology, see generally U.S. DEP'T OF AGRIC., FARMERS' BULL. NO. 2247: FENCES FOR THE FARM AND RURAL HOME (1971).

52. CAL. AGRIC. CODE § 17121 (West 1968). *See also* note 109 *infra*.

53. Because he believed his existing three-strand fence to be inadequate, rancher Dick Coombs persuaded his neighbor Ed Donaldson to join him in adding a fourth strand to their common boundary fence. Walt Johnson, the County Farm Advisor, recommends that barbed wire fences have five strands, and this is what Al Levy installed on the long stretch of new fence on the southern boundary of his mammoth ranch.

A rancher often erects "cross" or "division" fences to subdivide his own pastureland into separate fields. These fences enable a rancher to rest a pasture that would be damaged by further grazing, to control breeding, and to keep livestock away from a controlled burn.

Ranchers tend to invest less time and money in their cross fences than in their boundary fences, in part because a breach in a cross fence is less likely to result in the loss of an animal. Al Levy admitted to using only four strands for his cross fences and to not maintaining them quite as well as his five-strand boundary fences.

54. A half century ago, most Shasta County ranchers made their own fence posts by splitting logs. Should his own ranchland lack an adequate supply of logs, a rancher would contract with a private timber company to obtain the right to split downed cedar trees in the mountain forests.

Today farm supply stores offer ready made steel and wooden posts. Ranchers typically prefer the steel posts because they are less expensive, easier to drive into rocky soil, and more likely to survive a controlled burn. Wooden posts are still essential at corners, gates, stretch panels, and other places where extra strength is needed.

55. Interview with Carl Yokum of Northwest Fence, in Palo Cedro, Cal. (Aug. 11, 1982).

Technological advances—particularly the invention of barbed wire—have made fencing much less expensive relative to land and labor than it was in Abraham Lincoln's log-splitting days. Today, a newcomer to rural Shasta County would spend in the neighborhood of $40,000 to purchase a 40-acre ranchette, but for one-tenth of that sum he could hire a contractor to fence it with barbed wire. In the 1850s, "[i]t was certainly a rare farm-maker who had not to invest more capital—or its equivalent in labor in the case of forested areas—in his fence than in land." Danhof, *Farm-Making Costs and the "Safety Valve": 1850–60*, 49 J. POL. ECON. 317, 345 (1941). Fencing costs in California during the 1850s are estimated to have been $300 to $600 per mile in the currency of the time. *Id.* at 345 n.78. *See also* Meade v. Watson, 67 Cal. 591, 595, 8 P. 311, 313 (1885) (complaint asserted "value" of a stone boundary fence to be $1.75 per rod or $560 per mile). In the latter part of the nineteenth century,

ranchers and ranchette owners customarily build their own fences and thereby drastically reduce out-of-pocket labor expenditures.[56]

Barbed wire fences require periodic maintenance, especially in Shasta County, where many natural forces conspire against fence wire. The extreme summer heat loosens the wire while the winter cold pulls it taut. The deer that migrate through the foothills during the wet season are generally able to jump cattle fences; but when a jumping deer fails to clear a fence cleanly, its hoof may break a tightly stretched top wire.[57] Heavy winter rains, rotting posts, downed trees, unruly bulls, or wayward automobiles may also create a breach. A rancher or his hand therefore must spend a few days each spring, either on horseback or in a pickup truck, riding fence. A conscientious rancher also inspects his fences in the fall after the deer season, in part to see what damage trespassing hunters may have inflicted.[58] With emergency repairs needed frequently, fence maintenance chores weigh constantly on a rancher's mind.[59]

Ranchers believe that the many benefits of perimeter barriers outweigh fence construction and maintenance costs. Cattlemen with permanent ranches in either the grasslands or foothills almost invariably have perimeter fences, as well as cross fences to divide their spreads into separate pastures. A ranchette owner, however, is unlikely to fence the boundary of his land unless he

---

mean family income in the United States was on the order of $600–$800 per year. *See* BUREAU OF THE CENSUS, U.S. DEP'T OF COMMERCE, 1 HISTORICAL STATISTICS OF THE UNITED STATES: COLONIAL TIMES TO 1970 322 (1975). Before the arrival of barbed wire, a mile of fence thus cost about as much as an average family's annual income. In 1981, the mean family income in the United States was $24,000. *See* BUREAU OF THE CENSUS, U.S. DEP'T OF COMMERCE, STATISTICAL ABSTRACT OF THE UNITED STATES 1982–1983, at 435 (1982). That income would have then been sufficient to purchase the installation of at least five miles of barbed wire fence in Shasta County.

56. I found only one rancher, and no ranchette owner, who admitted having contracted out fencing work. The fence contractors of Shasta County agreed that the vast majority of rural fencing is done on a do-it-yourself basis. Walt Johnson, the astute Farm Advisor for Shasta County, could not identify the name of a single fence contractor.

57. To qualify as "lawful," a barbed wire fence in California must have its top strand at least 48 inches above the ground. CAL. AGRIC. CODE § 17121 (West 1968). Farm experts recommend that the top wire of a five-strand fence be elevated 52 inches. *See* FENCES FOR THE FARM AND RURAL HOME, *supra* note 51, at 17. The risk of damage from jumping deer has induced some fence contractors to warn against placing the top strand too high.

58. Veteran rancher and ex-Supervisor Norman Wagoner estimated that a cattleman working alone can inspect and repair a fence at a rate of about two miles per day.

59. Rancher Owen Shellworth estimated that he spent 25% of his work hours on fences, including corral fences.

has livestock. In forest pastures, one observes either no fencing or only an occasional drift fence.[60]

Traditionalists running herds in unfenced mountain forests have provoked most of the closed-range political movements in Shasta County.[61] During the summer months mountain cattle sometimes wander onto rural highways and ravage hay fields and gardens in the settled parts of the foothills. The recent proliferation of ranchettes in the foothills has aggravated these two risks and heightened opposition to the practice of running cattle at large.

II. The Politics of Cattle Trespass in the Northeastern Foothills

Loose cattle often cause political flaps in Shasta County. Many rural residents know that the Board of Supervisors has the power to adopt closed-range ordinances. They believe that these ordinances increase the civil liabilities of owners of stray livestock not only for trespass damages, but also, and more significantly, for damages stemming from highway collisions between vehicles and domestic animals. When residents and motorists in a particular area of the county suffer a rash of cattle-related incidents, they are likely to report their grievances to their local supervisor, whom they ask to mediate the conflict or to support a closed-range ordinance designed to cure the problem. A closure reduces the number of loose cattle because fear of liability to motorists makes traditionalists reluctant to run cattle at large in closed range.[62]

At least since 1970, the Board of Supervisors has required constituents who propose adoption of a closed-range ordinance to follow a special procedure. The complainants must draw up a petition that identifies a specific territory for closure, gather signatures on copies of the petition, and forward the signed petition to the Board. Although the Board does not insist upon the sub-

60. I did not learn of a single instance in which a forest owner, or a traditionalist cattleman who leased a forest for summer range, had fenced a forest boundary.

61. But they have not provoked all of them. Farm Advisor Walt Johnson could recall several instances in which the trigger had been a rancher, ostensibly operating behind fence, who had deliberately turned out his animals onto neighboring lands.

62. Rural residents in fact exaggerate the impact of a closed-range ordinance on the legal allocation of losses arising out of vehicle-livestock collisions. I do not discuss the highway collision chapter of the Shasta County story in this article, but will treat it at length in my forthcoming book.

mission of a particular minimum number of signatures, closure proponents gather as many as possible. Upon receiving a petition, the Board's staff drafts an ordinance that will implement the closure and publicizes a hearing on the proposed measure.[63] In practice, opponents usually receive sufficient notice of an upcoming hearing to gather signatures on a counterpetition.[64] At the public hearing, the Board hears statements from proponents and opponents and then votes on the measure. The cattlemen have been quite successful in defeating proposed closures. Between 1946 and 1972, the Board approved sixteen closures in various parts of Shasta County, but most of those ordinances only involved lands on Redding's urban fringe.[65]

Prior to the 1973 Caton's Folly ordinance that closed an area near Round Mountain, the Board of Supervisors approved only one closure that affected a significant amount of rural territory east of the Sacramento River. In the early 1960s, mountain cattle began to appear in number along a stretch of State Highway 44 in the Shingletown-Viola area, thirty miles east of Redding. Highway 44 is the major route between Redding and Mount Lassen National Park. In 1965, the Board voted to close the range in a three-mile-wide strip of land straddling the highway for a distance of 12½ miles.[66] This closure affected an area topographically similar to, but south of, the Northeastern Foothills. The Northeastern Foothills remained open range until the Caton's Folly ordinance. The history of that ordinance and of the Board's rejection of the Oak Run closure petition in 1982 helps reveal the role of elected local officials in cattle trespass disputes.

A. *Caton's Folly: The Closing of the Range at Round Mountain*

The hamlet of Round Mountain lies thirty miles northeast of Redding. Scattered along State Highway 299, the hamlet's main thoroughfare, are a general store, an elementary school, and a substation in Pacific Gas & Electric's hydroelectric power grid.[67]

63. In the early 1980s, the Board held hearings on closed-range petitions no more often than twice a year, on dates in February and July.

64. In 1982, it was the Board's standard practice, upon receiving a closed-range petition, to notify the Shasta County Cattlemen's Association by mail.

65. The county's Department of Public Works periodically prepares and sells to the public a map listing all closed-range ordinances and showing the territories they affect. The statement in the text is based on this map.

66. Shasta County, Cal., Ordinance 459 (Aug. 8, 1966).

67. In March 1984, Round Mountain enjoyed a rare moment of national media attention

The hamlet is 2000 feet in elevation, and is surrounded by higher foothills, the most prominent of which has given the hamlet its name. During the 1960s, the area around Round Mountain, like the rest of the Northeastern Foothills, became increasingly dotted with ranchettes. The frustration of these ranchette owners over the perceived misdeeds of three traditionalists, Paul Totten, Bob Moquet, and Ward Kearney, helped spawn the Caton's Folly ordinance of 1973. The particular activities of these three deserve brief description.

In the early 1970s, Totten, a small-scale traditionalist with a base ranch west of Redding, leased some thirty square miles of Roseburg Lumber Company forest lands for summer range.[68] The western boundary of Totten's leasehold was three miles east of the hamlet of Round Mountain and at a higher elevation. Just west of the boundary was an aging foothill farm with a sixty-acre irrigated field. John Woodbury had acquired this farm in 1966 and over a period of years had converted the irrigated field from natural grass to alfalfa. During the early 1970s, Totten's mountain cattle found and repeatedly used a path that led from the meager offerings of the Roseburg forest to the banquet of Woodbury's unfenced alfalfa field. On occasions when Woodbury would telephone him to complain, Totten would eventually drive the cattle back up into the forest, but neither as promptly nor as irreversibly as Woodbury would have liked.

Bob Moquet's cattle were a more pervasive and longstanding nuisance. A tough and independent leader of a pioneer clan long settled in the Round Mountain area, Moquet aroused particular hostility because he was blatantly unresponsive to his neighbors' complaints. He believed that a cattleman had a divine right to let his cattle loose in the mountains during the summer. Steve Mattingly, a Modernist cattleman who raised registered Galloway cattle on a fenced ranch on Buzzard Roost Road, became particularly concerned that Moquet's hybrid bulls might impregnate his cows.

In the early 1970s, Dr. Arthur Cooley, a Redding physician, obtained a summer grazing lease on a large tract of National For-

---

when a circuit breaker malfunction in the PG&E substation blacked out parts of six Western states. *See* San Francisco Chron., Mar. 1, 1984, at 1, col. 4.

68. The lessor in the early 1970s was actually the Kimberly-Clark Corporation. Kimberly-Clark sold its forest lands in the northeastern sector to the Roseburg Lumber Company in 1979. *See* note 22 *supra*. For simplicity, the text treats Roseburg as the continuous owner of these lands.

est Service land situated a few miles west of Round Mountain, on Backbone Ridge. To manage his mountain herd of several hundred animals, Cooley hired Ward Kearney, a traditionalist cowboy of exceptional ability. Kearney shared Moquet's view that people who object to stray cattle should fence them out. Consequently, after driving Cooley's cattle to Backbone Ridge, Kearney would allow them to drift down into the ranchette areas and heavily traveled stretches of Highway 299 near Round Mountain.

Cooley, Moquet, and Totten's mountain cattle tipped the political balance in Round Mountain in favor of closure. In early 1973, Mattingly, Woodbury, and a few longtime area residents began meeting to discuss the problem of mountain cattle. These anti-traditionalists eventually drew up and gathered signatures on a petition that asked the Board of Supervisors to convert from open to closed range a seven by eight mile rectangle of territory centered on Round Mountain. It is not clear who drew the exact boundaries of this rectangle. Not surprisingly, all of the activists' lands fell within its perimeter. In the end, 72 persons, mostly Round Mountain residents, signed the closed-range petition.

On March 10, 1973, Mattingly mailed the signed petition to John Caton, the newly elected Board member for the supervisoral district that included the Northeastern Foothills. Caton lived on a ranchette in Montgomery Creek, a hamlet situated three miles northeast of Round Mountain on Highway 299. Caton shared many of the cattlemen's values, yet was aware that mountain cattle had been endangering both residents and motorists. The deepening conflict between traditionalist cattlemen and the residents of the Round Mountain area placed Caton in a delicate political position. He offered to help mediate and asked Mattingly and the other petitioners to wait a few months to see whether the problem would abate. It did not. During the summer of 1973, mountain cattle entered Woodbury's alfalfa field on over a dozen occasions. Woodbury said he telephoned Caton to complain on each occasion.

On December 3, 1973, the Board of Supervisors finally held its hearing on the anti-traditionalists' petition to close the fifty-six square-mile rectangle. The hearing was lightly attended. John Woodbury, pasture owner Phil Ritchie, and ranchette owner Ted Plomeson spoke in favor of the closure. The only significant speaker in opposition was Dr. Cooley, whose protestations of economic hardship elicited little sympathy. The official minutes of the Board's meeting contain no indication that a representative of the Shasta County Cattlemen's Association was present. At the end of the session, the Board voted by a margin of 4 to 1, with Caton in the majority, to declare that the fifty-six square-mile rectangle outlined in the March petition had "ceased to be devoted chiefly to grazing"—the legal language necessary to convert the area from open range to closed range.[69]

With the exception of a few modernists such as Mattingly, Shasta County cattlemen soon came to rue their failure to fight the Round Mountain closure. To chide Caton for supporting what they regarded as a lamentable precedent, they referred to the affected area as "Caton's Folly" or "Caton's Acres." Caton got the point. During the next decade, he successfully persuaded the Board to reject all petitions that would have closed additional territories in the Northeastern Foothills.

B. *Caton's Repentance: The Defeat of the Oak Run Closure Petition*

Caton's change of heart is best illustrated by his handling of a 1981 petition that asked the Board to close 96 square miles of range in the Oak Run area just southwest of Caton's Folly. The hamlet of Oak Run sits only three miles south of the southwestern corner of Caton's Folly. The hamlet's elevation is 1600 feet, a level where the grassy plains blend with the tangle of brush and trees that typify the foothills. During 1981-1982, only a few months before I conducted most of my interviews, the Oak Run area had been the site of perhaps the most heated closed-range battle in the history of Shasta County. Frank Ellis, a recent entrant into the bigtime cattle business, had singlehandedly provoked the circulation of a petition that sought to triple the area of closed range in the Northeastern Foothills.

1. *Frank Ellis.*

Ellis, accompanied by his wife and school-age children, first moved to Shasta County in about 1973. A rancher and real estate broker by profession, Ellis was then 58 years old. He immediately acquired a functioning 2500-acre ranch astride the Oak Run Road two miles west of Oak Run and just south of an area sprouting ranchettes. The size and prominent location of Ellis' base ranch helped to make him a conspicuous personality in the

69. Shasta County, Cal., Ordinance 498 (Dec. 3, 1973).

Northeastern Foothills. Ellis (who declined my request for an interview) was by all reports a man capable of great charm. But, according to his neighbors, beneath this appealing surface lay a ruthless ambition for wealth and power. Many who dealt with Ellis came to regard him as capricious, spiteful, and not always good for his word. He became the target of numerous lawsuits, and for a time even had an attorney on retainer. One may think of him as the "J.R. Ewing of Shasta County" (although he lived in a style much less luxurious than that of his television counterpart). Although Ellis' aggressive and colorful personality won him a few admirers, his more honorable neighbors and rural acquaintances came to view Ellis as an untrustworthy bully.

During the late 1970s, Ellis built up the largest ranching empire in the Northeastern Foothills. First, he obtained a grazing lease on a section of BLM land to the west of his base ranch. Then in 1978, he persuaded the absentee owners of the largest ranching estate in the area to hire him to manage their scattered grasslands and foothills. By this one stroke, Ellis won control over another 20 square miles of pasture. Ellis eventually purchased hundreds of cattle on credit and hired a band of Mexican *braceros* to tend them.

The various components of Ellis' ranching empire were not physically connected. Ellis knew that all his holdings were within open range, but he erroneously interpreted this to mean that he could legally herd his livestock onto any land that was not fenced. When moving his livestock about, Ellis' cowboys not only deliberately crossed the unfenced private lands of others, but also used those lands as free pasture.[70] By 1981, Ellis' drovers were aggressively running a herd of two to three thousand cattle at large in the grasslands and lower foothills northeast of Redding, an area where virtually all other cattlemen were Modernists who kept their animals behind fences.

2. *Ellis' antagonists.*

Most of the lands that Ellis' livestock invaded were uncultivated and uninhabited tracts held by speculators, who, if anything, appreciated a herd coming through to beat back the brush. Yet in some areas, particularly those near Oak Run itself, Ellis' trespass victims were ranchette owners who had recently moved

70. Although they occurred in open range, these entries were intentional and therefore tortious. *See* text accompanying notes 109–110 *infra*.

to the Northeastern Foothills in search of a pastoral life. Ellis' marauding herds quickly became the bane of these ranchette owners. At least eight built fences at their own expense specifically to keep Ellis' animals off their lands. Although at least two of these ranchette owners saw Ellis as acting within his rights, most of them—in particular, Doug Heinz— did not.

Heinz, a skilled craftsman from southern California, moved to the Northeastern Foothills in 1978 with his wife and small children. The Heinzes acquired a house on a twenty-acre ranchette situated in open range west of Oak Run and about one mile from Ellis' base ranch. As a hobby, Heinz started to raise a few horses and cows on a twelve-acre portion of his ranchette that was enclosed by a five-strand barbed wire fence. The frequent passage of Ellis' herds punctured Heinz's dreams of small-scale squiredom.

According to Heinz, he and Ellis started off on polite terms. On three or four occasions in 1979, several of Ellis' cattle jumped over or broke through Heinz's fence. Heinz reacted to these early trespasses by telephoning Ellis. Ellis' response was to send his drovers to chase the cows within Heinz's field to tire them so they could then be coaxed through the fence. This method of retrieval battered Heinz's fences and Ellis' drovers never repaired the damage. Heinz's patience ran out one snowy day when he discovered that Ellis' hands had dropped hay for 200 cattle in the narrow snowplowed driveway leading to his ranchette. The milling herd that flocked to the hay included cows that had just calved, and these skittish new mothers frightened Heinz's small children.

Although most of Heinz's ranchette-owning neighbors had passively endured indignities from Ellis' livestock, Heinz was relatively short-tempered. He purchased a shotgun and called the county sheriff to protest Ellis' activities. According to what Ellis later told acquaintances, Heinz also began to threaten that Ellis might find "dead cattle." On the next occasion that Ellis' cattle broke through the fence, Heinz seized three animals and held them for three months without notifying Ellis. This incident eventually led to a lawsuit by Heinz to recover boarding costs and to a countersuit by Ellis for mistreatment of Ellis' animals.[71]

71. *See* Heinz v. Ellis, No. 81 SC 7 (Cent. Valley Just. Ct. filed Jan. 8, 1981); Ellis v. Heinz, No. 81 CV 6 (Cent. Valley Just. Ct. filed Jan. 16, 1981). (The names in these citations are pseudonyms). *See also* text accompanying notes 155–158 *infra*.

In early 1981, while his lawsuit against Ellis was still pending, Heinz began a political crusade to stop Ellis' at-large grazing practices.

Heinz anticipated recruiting a host of allies, and not just among his fellow ranchette owners. During 1978-1981, virtually every foothill motorist had reason to be annoyed at Ellis' failure to keep his livestock off the foothill roads. When Ellis' stock were being moved along the highways, motorists were often delayed for up to an hour. On a half dozen occasions, vehicles collided with Ellis' stock on the Oak Run Road. Heinz succeeded in rallying to the anti-Ellis cause dozens of ranchette-owning newcomers, as well as members of at least one respected and long-established ranching family in the Oak Run area.

3. *Caton's mediation and the battle of petitions.*

During 1981, Heinz and his allies peppered their local supervisor, John Caton, with complaints about Ellis' herds. Since his christening at Round Mountain eight years earlier, Caton had become a veteran of political disputes over trespassing cattle. Caton knew that if he supported a closed-range ordinance for the Oak Run area, he would further alienate the powerful cattlemen's lobby, a group had never forgiven him for supporting the Caton's Folly ordinance. On the other hand, if Caton opposed the closure, he would offend a potentially more numerous, if less organized, group comprised of the ranchette owners and motorists that Ellis' herds endangered. Caton sought to defuse the controversy before a formal closure petition surfaced. Working in the spring of 1981 with County Animal Control Officer Brad Bogue, Caton threatened to support a closed-range ordinance for the Oak Run area if Ellis failed to build a fence along a three-mile stretch of the Oak Run Road that Ellis' herds made particularly dangerous. In response, Ellis promised Caton that he would build the fence. But as the summer of 1981 dragged on without any sign that Ellis would perform, Caton began to regard circulation of a closed-range petition as inevitable.

Caton's political instincts proved to be accurate. Some members of the anti-Ellis group preferred to postpone circulating a petition until they had exhausted other types of mediation; this faction, for example, wanted to ask the Shasta County Cattlemen's Association to request Ellis to manage his herds more responsibly. But Heinz decided to force the issue. In the fall of

1981, without consulting some of his leading allies, he drafted and began to circulate a petition designed to close the range in a 96 square-mile area southwest of, and abutting, Caton's Folly. Heinz drew the boundaries broadly in an effort to cast the entire Ellis empire into closed range. The petition did not mention Ellis by name, but it did state that "Our reasons for this stem mostly from the inconsideration and abuse of the open range law of one rancher."[72] Heinz and his allies gathered 42 signatures—an unimpressive total—and delivered their petition to John Caton in late November 1981.

The Board of Supervisors was scheduled to hold its next hearing on closure petitions three months later, in February 1982. The interval enabled Caton to minimize the political risks posed by the Heinz petition. He immediately publicized receipt of the petition, thereby helping the opposition to organize a counter-campaign. Caton showed the Heinz petition to Wayne Thompson, a small-scale sheep rancher who lived on the Oak Run Road. Thompson enlisted his neighbor Larry Brennan, a college graduate who raised a few horses as a hobby on a large ranchette nearby, to draft a counterpetition urging the Board to keep the area open.[73] Thompson tirelessly circulated the counterpetition in the Oak Run area. Prior to the February hearing, Thompson and his associates submitted to the Board the names of 146 persons, mostly residents of the Oak Run area, who had signed their counterpetition. Heinz's temperamental personality and lack of roots in the area limited his own success and aided Thompson's, who outsolicited him by a margin of more than three to one.

---

72. The petition continued:

Our reasons to list a few are:

1. Unsafe roadways due to poorly maintained fences, cows are continually on the roads and jepardizing [sic] the safety of school children.

2. Property destruction of the trespassing cows on private property.

3. Cutting of fences on private property to herd the cows with more ease to other areas of private property.

4. Interference of range cows with private herds.

73. The counterpetition began:

We feel that the "open range" system serves many purposes for the large and small rancher.

1. Limits of liability.

2. Fire protection—through grazing, keeping the grass down.

3. Biological control—through natural fertilization of soil of rangeland, timber production, fuel-wood production.

4. Natural predator control.

5. Prevention of soil erosion due to stronger root system with annual grasses.

The Board also received a second counterpetition. Following standard procedures adopted after the Round Mountain controversy, the Board's staff had automatically informed the Shasta County Cattlemen's Association that the Board had received Heinz's closed-range petition. The Association's leaders then circulated a petition on their own. Their petition to keep the range open attracted only 24 signers, but many were members of well-known ranching families operating northeast of Redding.

Caton's last major step after the Heinz petition surfaced was to remind Ellis that Caton's decision on the closure petition would rest largely on whether Ellis kept his promise to build the three miles of fence along Oak Run Road. Ellis finally responded—grudgingly. By the time of the Board's hearing on February 2, 1982, Ellis' employees had erected three miles of five-strand barbed wire fence, a project that may have cost Ellis as much as $10,000. The fence was positioned on private lands (mostly owned by speculators) on which Ellis had grazed his herds without fee. The new fence helped to reassure motorists; it thus became a conspicuous monument to Caton's effectiveness. The fence offered no relief, however, to ranchette owners such as Heinz whose lands lay between Ellis' ranch and the new fence.

4. *The hearing and its aftermath.*

At the Board's hearing on February 2, 1982, Caton kept his part of his bargain with Ellis. Caton's decision to oppose the closure had become an easy one. Not only had Thompson's counterpetition attracted far more signatories than the Heinz petition had, but Thompson and the cattlemen were also more successful than the Heinz group in turning out supporters at the Board meeting. As ranchette owner and Heinz ally Jeff Marotta stated, "When I saw all those cowboy hats [in the hearing room] I knew we were going to lose." At the hearing, six speakers, including Doug Heinz, spoke in favor of the closure, but thirteen, including Bob Bosworth, president of the Shasta County Cattlemen's Association, spoke against it. Although the hall was packed, Ellis himself was not present. As someone said that night, "He wouldn't dare to be."[74]

Caton was also the beneficiary of a startling stroke of good

74. Just one speaker at the meeting, cattleman Marty Fancher, referred to Ellis by name. Even the members of the anti-Ellis group discreetly spoke only of "one rancher" whose misdeeds had provoked the petition.

fortune: The Ellis ranching empire had just begun to crumble. Ellis had bought hundreds of cattle on credit in anticipation that beef prices would rise. Instead, prices had fallen. This setback, arriving on top of a variety of other financial reverses left Ellis without funds to pay creditors. A week or two before the Board's hearing, Ellis' banks had begun repossessing his cattle and the news immediately circulated within the gossip mills of the Northeastern Foothills.

When the testimony at the hearing came to a close, the other supervisors stated that they would defer to John Caton, the supervisor in whose district the proposed closure lay. Caton recommended that the area remain as open range but added that, if the problem were to continue, the Board should consider closing four sections of land where Heinz and most of the other complaining ranchette owners lived. The Board promptly voted unanimously to deny the Heinz petition. To smooth the waters, Dan Gover, the Board's chairman and a rancher himself, asked Bob Bosworth, president of the county Cattlemen's Association, to meet with Ellis, Heinz, and county animal control officials to see what could be done to control Ellis' herds.[75] Caton had repented for Caton's Folly.

Within a few months of the hearing, both Heinz and Ellis were gone from the Northeastern Foothills. In 1980, Heinz had begun planning the construction of a house in Redding for his family. Only a few days after the Board rejected his petition, he moved out of the ranchette in Oak Run and into his newly completed Redding house. Ellis' stay in Oak Run lasted only three months longer than Heinz's. The banks seized Ellis' cattle, and his creditors were lining up with claims on his ranch. In May 1982, Ellis moved his family 100 miles south to a farm in another California county in the Central Valley. As his parting shot to Shasta County, Ellis ordered his hands to destroy the three miles of fence along the Oak Run Road that he had ordered built just six months before. On the day the Board held its hearing, the two leading players in the drama both knew that they were about to depart from the stage.[76]

75. The proposed meeting was never held, in part because the cattlemen were willing to use only informal sanctions, and, as Bosworth said at the hearing in response to a supervisor's question, this sort of pressure wouldn't work with Ellis because, "He hasn't been in [the County] all that long."

76. This datum is consistent with the widely accepted theoretical proposition that the lack of a prospective long-term future relationship makes disputants less likely to resolve their

III. RESEARCH METHODS

I chose the Round Mountain-Oak Run area as the focus for the microscopic study because it had witnessed both an actual and a threatened closure of the range. The area presented opportunities for both longitudinal and cross-sectional analyses. A longitudinal analysis would track the behavior of specific cattlemen and farmers over a span of years in the midst of which an applicable closed-range ordinance had been adopted. A cross-sectional analysis would examine varied locations, rather than time periods, to determine whether on a particular date cattlemen and farmers behaved differently in open-range areas than in closed-range areas. I designed the field study to allow both types of inquiries.[77]

The 56 square-miles in Caton's Folly almost equals the size of Washington, D.C. I decided to concentrate the landowner interviews within the subarea that straddled Caton's Folly's southern boundary. This subarea provided opportunities for cross-sectional analysis because it contained both open-range and closed-range, including some open-range that had recently been subjected to an unsuccessful closure petition.[78]

My research techniques were more similar to those used in anthropology or in-depth journalism than to those used in econometrics or sociometrics. I relied primarily on interviews with two groups of people: (1) landowners in the study area, and

differences without the help of third parties, and hence more likely to resort to legal and political action. *See* text accompanying notes 139–141 *infra*.

77. An ideal research design makes use of time-series data for both experimental and control areas. *See* Lempert, *Strategies of Research Design in the Legal Impact Study: The Control of Rival Hypotheses*, 1 LAW & SOC'Y REV. 111, 130–32 (1966).

78. The area around the southern border of Caton's Folly offered several advantages. First, whereas the other three boundaries of Caton's Folly traversed lightly settled private forest, the southern border area was well-settled and thus more likely to be conflict-ridden. Second, only the southern area included some territory that had been threatened with a closure. Third, an investigator conducting a cross-sectional study into the impact of law should pick a situation where the legal boundaries are essentially random with regard to the social and topographic variables that may affect human conduct. Were the boundary not randomly drawn, any differences in landowner behavior that the investigator discovered between the areas might be the result of preexisting conditions (which perhaps caused the line to be drawn where it was), and not the result of differences in legal regimes. The southern boundary of Caton's Folly appeared to be a random line. None of the drafters of the Caton's Folly petition (the persons who selected this boundary) lived near it, and neither did any appreciable number of the petition's signatories. Moreover, the terrain the southern boundary crosses is highly varied, rising from foothills at an elevation of 2100 feet at the western end, to mountain forest at an elevation of 4400 feet at the eastern end. An eight-mile east-west line drawn straight across diverse terrain seems unlikely to have been the product of a gerrymander.

(2) a larger number of "specialists" who were knowledgeable about how rural residents resolve stray cattle disputes. Instead of interviewing many persons who saw the problem from the same perspective, I sought out lesser numbers representing many different perspectives.

Of seventy-three total interviews (most of which were conducted during the summer of 1982), twenty-eight were with persons owning land in the rural area northeast of Redding. Eleven of these twenty-eight owned land inside Caton's Folly; ten owned land outside but within three miles of its southern border, mostly in areas that the Heinz closure petition would have affected; and three more—Hailey, McCall, and Shellworth—owned land both inside and outside Caton's Folly. Of the twenty-eight landowners, eleven could be described as cattle ranchers, four as farmers (whose chief agricultural activity was producing feed for livestock), and thirteen as ranchette owners (some of whom owned farm animals as a hobby). Twenty of the twenty-eight landowners were interviewed face-to-face. Seventeen of these interviews were in-depth sessions lasting one-and-a-half to two hours. The other eight landowner interviews were conducted by telephone; these telephone conversations averaged fifteen minutes in length.

The landowner interviews suffer from several shortcomings as a data source. First, 28 is a small sample. Second, I did not randomly select the people I interviewed; rather, I tended to seek out residents who had either owned cattle, been victims of trespass incidents, or been active in the political battles over closed-range petitions. I also made a particular effort to interview the owners of the largest farms and ranches in the study area. Compared to average foothill landowners, my informants were probably older, wealthier (although still of modest means), longer in residence in northeastern Shasta County, and more active in community affairs. Although most respondents talked without hesitation—indeed, usually with enthusiasm—cooperative people were undoubtedly somewhat overrepresented in the sample. Third, I decided not to use a standardized survey instrument, in part because a formal list of questions might have made respondents ill-at-ease.[79] Fourth, some memories were undoubtedly

79. The authors of many leading microscopic law and society studies have used similar research methods. In his memorable study of contract law, Macaulay interviewed 68 businessmen and lawyers in Wisconsin, apparently without the aid of a standardized questionnaire.

imperfect, and I had reason to suspect that a few landowners had deliberately recast history to place themselves in a better light.[80]

Rather than budget more time to landowner interviews, I chose to mitigate these shortcomings by using government records and interviews with certain specialists to cross-check what the landowners reported. Two types of government records—aerial photographs and court files—contained information relevant to cattle-trespass disputes. Federal agencies had taken aerial photographs of the western portion of Caton's Folly's southern border area in October 1973 and August 1980—that is, two months before, and seven years after, the ordinance had been approved.[81] Although these photos were taken at too high an altitude to indicate the presence of fences or individual animals, they reveal buildings and areas under cultivation. I obtained copies of these photographs in order to have evidence of actual changes in gross land use patterns in and near the study area during the relevant time period.[82] I also searched the records of the state courts that serve the northeastern sector of Shasta County and noted lawsuits arising out of stray livestock incidents.[83]

The other important cross-checks on the landowner interviews were the 50 interviews that I conducted with "specialists,"

See Macaulay, *supra* note 12, at 55–56. Ross's interviews with his 67 insurance adjusters were also unstructured. H. Ross, *supra* note 12, at 10. Llewellyn & Hoebel's study of the Cheyenne was based on what sociologists call "memory cases"—tribal legends and tales related by interpreters. K. Llewellyn & E. Hoebel, The Cheyenne Way viii–ix (1941). *See also* Palay, *Comparative Institutional Economics: The Governance of Rail Freight Contracting*, 13 J. Legal Stud. 265, 271 (1984) (study based on 35 field interviews was conducted without the use of a formal questionnaire, in order to encourage the interviewees to be open in their responses).

On methods of what I call "microscopic" field research, see generally Blanck & Turner, *Gestalt Research: Clinical-Field-Research Approaches to Studying Organizations*, in Handbook of Organizational Behavior 109-25 (J. Lorsch ed. 1986).

80. Because I had concentrated my landowner interviews in a subarea, I often heard several interpretations of the same event; I was therefore better able to make an assessment of the credibility of different sources.

81. In October 1973, the Caton's Folly ordinance was pending and landowners might have anticipated its adoption. Thus, aerial photographs taken on an earlier date, had they been available, would have provided better evidence of the *ex ante* situation.

82. I hired a geobotanist skilled in remote sensing to analyze the two sets of aerial photographs. He detected no cross-sectional or longitudinal variations in land use patterns that would cast doubt on the findings presented in Part IV.

83. None of the relevant state courts index their cases by subject matter. To overcome this obstacle, I asked the judges and court clerks if they could recall stray cattle cases, looked for names of likely litigants in the plaintiff and defendant name indexes, and, in the Justice Courts, reviewed all complaints that had been filed during recent eleven-month periods. *See also* note 152 *infra*.

namely, industry and government officials likely to interact with the subjects of the study.[84] Eighty percent of the specialist interviews were conducted in person and the balance were conducted by telephone. The face-to-face sessions averaged 40 minutes in length. As in the landowner interviews, I took detailed handwritten notes during the sessions.[85]

IV. The Resolution of Animal Trespass Disputes in Shasta County

This Part reports the frequency of cattle trespass incidents in Shasta County, presents relevant California trespass law, and recounts how Shasta County neighbors actually resolve their trespass disputes. In the Coasean Parable of the Farmer and the Rancher, the two neighbors both know and honor applicable legal rules. Much of law and economic scholarship has similarly assumed that law is efficacious in this way.[86] This Part suggests that the assumption of efficacious law is more heroic than certain scholars have realized.

A. *Animal Trespass Incidents*

Every landowner interviewed, including all thirteen ranchette owners, reported at least one instance in which his lands had been invaded by someone else's livestock. Hay farmers grow what cattle especially like to eat, and thus expect frequent trespasses.[87] Owners of large ranches are also common victims be-

84. The specialists interviewed were: the four state court judges most likely to have been involved in livestock-related cases arising in Shasta County's northeastern sector; six Redding attorneys who had rural landowners as clients; five members of the Board of Directors of the Shasta County Cattlemen's Association; eight adjusters and salesmen employed by the insurance companies that underwrite most of the livestock risks in eastern Shasta County; three real estate appraisers and assessors; eleven county officials (including the Brand Inspector, the Animal Control Officer, the Farm Advisor, a former District Attorney, and several supervisors, including John Caton); four fence contractors and fence material suppliers; six agents of forest owners that lease their lands for grazing; and three grazing lessees. Because several interviewees qualified both as specialists and as landowners, the total number of interviews was 73, not 78.

85. To avoid developing a reputation for undue nosiness, I never asked the landowners about either their religious convictions or their financial situations. Those variables might conceivably affect one's method of resolving low-level disputes; however, the interviewees never volunteered that religion or financial plight affected people's behavior.

86. *See, e.g.*, Calabresi & Melamed, *supra* note 7, at 1090–91 (assuming that the "state" is the sole source of entitlements).

87. John Woodbury suffered almost weekly incursions into his alfalfa field in 1973. *See* text following note 68 *supra*. Although the situation improved when many of the mountain

cause they cannot keep their many miles of aging perimeter fence cattle-tight. Thus, when a rancher gathers his animals on his fenced pastures each spring, he is not startled to find a few head carrying a neighbor's brand.

Because cattle eat almost incessantly, a trespass victim's vegetation is always at risk.[88] Nevertheless, a victim usually regards the loss of grass as trivial so long as the owner removes the animals with reasonable promptness—that is, within a day or two if the animals are easy to corral. Trespassing livestock occasionally do cause more than nominal damage. Several ranchette owners reported incidents in which wayward cattle had damaged their fences and vegetable gardens; one farmer told of the ravaging of some of his ornamental trees.

The most serious trespasses reported were ones involving either at-large cattle or bulls. A ranchette owner narrated how mountain cattle had once invaded his house construction site, broken the windows, and contaminated the creek. A part-time horsebreeder told of buying seven tons of hay and stacking it on an unfenced portion of his fifty-acre ranchette, where it was then eaten by cattle that Frank Ellis had let roam free.

Rural residents especially fear trespasses by bulls. In a modern beef cattle herd, roughly one animal in twenty-five is a bull, whose principal function is to impregnate cows during their brief periods in heat.[89] Bulls are twice as heavy as the other herd animals,[90] and tend to be much more ornery. Several respondents had vivid memories of bull trespasses. A farmer who owned irrigated pasture was amazed at the depth of the hoof marks that an entering bull had made. A ranchette owner and a rancher told of barely escaping goring while attempting to corral invading

lessees subsequently declined to renew their leases, Woodbury was still experiencing a couple of cattle trespasses a year in the early 1980s. Another hay farmer, Phil Ritchie, identified six neighbors whose cattle had trespassed on his lands in recent years.

88. Beef cattle eat feed equal to about 2-1/2% of their body weight each day. DIVISION OF AGRIC. SCI., UNIV. OF CAL., LEAFLET NO. 21184, BEEF PRODUCTION IN CALIFORNIA 12–13 (Nov. 1980).

89. *Cf.* CAL. AGRIC. CODE § 16803 (West 1968) (cattlemen grazing herds on open-range must include at least one bull for every 30 cows). The refinement of artificial insemination techniques has enabled some ranchers to reduce the fraction of bulls in herds kept behind fences.

90. A Hereford bull has a mature weight of 2000 pounds, compared to 1100–1200 pounds for a mature Hereford cow. Steers (castrated male cattle) are typically slaughtered when they weigh between 1000 and 1150 pounds. BEEF PRODUCTION IN CALIFORNIA, *supra* note 88, at 3, 5.

bulls.[91] Because an alien bull often enters in pursuit of cows in heat, owners of female animals fear illicit couplings that might produce offspring of an undesired pedigree. Although no cow owner reported actual damages from misbreeding, several mentioned that this risk especially worried them.

B. *Animal Trespass Law*

One of the most venerable English common law rules of strict liability in tort is the rule that an owner of domestic livestock is liable, even in the absence of negligence, for property damage that his animals cause while trespassing.[92] This traditional English rule also applies in the closed-range areas of Shasta County.[93]

---

91. I learned of no cattle trespasses that had resulted in personal injury. Two insurance adjusters who frequently had been called upon to settle dog-bite claims could remember, between them, only one personal-injury claim arising from cattle—an instance in which a cow had stepped on someone's foot.

92. The case that has most commonly occurred, and which is most frequently to be found in the books, is as to the obligation of the owner of cattle which he has brought on his land, to prevent their escaping and doing mischief. The law as to them seems to be perfectly settled from early times; the owner must keep them in at his peril, or he will be answerable for the natural consequences of their escape; that is with regard to tame beasts, for the grass they eat and trample upon, though not for any injury to the person of others, for our ancestors have settled that it is not the general nature of horses to kick, or bulls to gore; but if the owner knows that the beast has a vicious propensity to attack man, he will be answerable for that too.

Fletcher v. Rylands, 1 L.R.-Ex. 265, 280 (1866) (Blackburn, J.). *See also* 3 W. Blackstone, Commentaries *211 ("A man is answerable for not only his own trespass, but that of his cattle also").

The operation of this rule in Great Britain is discussed in G. Williams, Liability for Animals 127–99 (1939). *See also* Wigmore, *Responsibility for Tortious Acts: Its History*, 7 Harv. L. Rev. 441, 450–52 (1894) (asserting, at 451 n.1, that thirteenth century cases applied a strict liability rule to cattle trespass incidents).

93. *See, e.g.*, Montezuma Improvement Co. v. Simmerly, 181 Cal. 722, 724, 189 P. 100, 101 (1919).

Hornbook law provides a few defenses to, and other limitations on, an animal owner's strict liability for trespass damages. When a cattleman has driven cattle along a highway from which they have strayed and damaged plaintiff's adjoining fields, the plaintiff must prove that the cattleman had been negligent in the management of the herd. *See* Restatement (Second) of Torts § 505 (1977). There is authority that trespasses caused by an act of God—for example, an unprecedented windstorm causing a breach in a fence—are not actionable. *See id.* at § 504(3)(c). The Restatement also declines to impose liability for unforeseeable damage. *Id.* at § 504(3)(a); *see also* Williams v. Goodwin, 41 Cal. App. 3d 496, 507, 116 Cal. Rptr. 200, 208 (1974) (recovery granted because personal injury caused by trespassing bull was within the scope of foreseeable harm).

A trespass victim's own misconduct, such as failing to close a cattle gate or breaching a contractual duty to build a fence, may also diminish or bar his recovery. *See* G. Williams, *supra* note 92, at 178–81; *see also* Restatement (Second) of Torts § 504(4) (1977) (trespass

In the open-range areas of the county—that is, in the great bulk of its rural territory—the English rule has been rejected in favor of the pro-cattleman "fencing out" rule that many grazing states adopted during the nineteenth century.[94] In 1850, just after California attained statehood, an open-range rule was adopted for the entire state. In that year, the legislature enacted a statute that entitled a victim of animal trespass to recover damages only when the victim had protected his lands with a "lawful fence."[95] This pro-cattleman policy grew increasingly controver-

victim who fails to erect and maintain a fence required by common law or statute is barred from recovery). In California, misconduct by a plaintiff does not typically operate as a complete defense in a strict liability action. *See* Daly v. General Motors Corp., 20 Cal. 3d 725, 575 P.2d 1162, 144 Cal. Rptr. 380 (1978).

94. Many authorities assert that the Western states have been the chief followers of "fencing-out" rules. *See, e.g.*, 2 F. HARPER & F. JAMES, THE LAW OF TORTS § 14.10 (1956); W. PROSSER, J. WADE, & V. SCHWARTZ, CASES AND MATERIALS ON TORTS 706–07 (7th ed. 1982). Nineteenth century treatises on fence law reveal, however, that in that era, "fencing out" was the dominant rule in the United States, particularly in the *Northern* states. *See* W. THORNTON, THE LAW OF RAILROAD FENCES AND PRIVATE CROSSINGS §§ 8–10 (1892) (identifying 13 states as following the English rule and 21 states as having fencing-out regimes); R. TYLER, THE LAW OF BOUNDARIES, FENCES, AND WINDOW LIGHTS 361–512 (1874) (state-by-state review of fence law, indicating, at 451, that Michigan, for example, enacted a fencing-out statute in 1847); *see also* W. CRONON, CHANGES IN THE LAND: INDIANS, COLONISTS, AND THE ECOLOGY OF NEW ENGLAND 134–35 (1983) (the Plymouth and Massachusetts Bay colonies in Massachusetts required planters of corn to fence out livestock).

95. 1850 Cal. Stat., ch. 49, 131. *See* Comerford v. Dupuy, 17 Cal. 308 (1861) (judgment for defendant cattle owners where plaintiff's fence failed to meet lawful fence requirements of 1855 statute); Waters v. Moss, 12 Cal. 535 (1859) (dictum).

In California during that era, the open-range rule was probably more efficient than the English rule. Where there are many cultivated lands, as in England, a livestock owner is typically the cheapest cost avoider in animal-crop interactions because he can best control the whereabouts of his beasts. *See* Calabresi & Hirschoff, *Toward a Test for Strict Liability in Torts*, 81 YALE L.J. 1055, 1060 (1972) (risks should be assigned to the party best able to perform a cost-benefit analysis of accident costs and accident prevention costs and to act on that analysis once it is made). There was little farming in California in the mid-nineteenth century, however, and the grazing of cattle was widespread. *See generally* R. CLELAND, THE CATTLE ON A THOUSAND HILLS (2d ed. 1951) (despite the impact of the Gold Rush in northern California, southern California remained a typical cattle frontier for nearly 20 years thereafter). Consequently, it was cheaper to install fencing around the rare field crops than around the ubiquitous grazing areas. Cattlemen running animals at large would have incurred high transaction costs in organizing to erect fences that would reduce their common risk of tort liability; in contrast, because a single farmer could decide on his own whether or not to fence, he would incur lower transaction costs. If efficiency-minded frontier lawmakers assumed that actors knew and honored the legal rules, they therefore would have imposed the risk of trespass across an unfenced boundary on the farmer, the cheaper avoider of trespass damages to isolated fields of crops.

Lawful-fence statutes, still found in many western states, adopt an even more sophisticated approach to the allocation of animal trespass risks. The statutes identify specific fence technologies that farmers can employ to revive their rights to recover for trespass damages. *See* note 109 *infra*. When a trespass has occurred despite the presence of a lawful fence, the

sial as California became more settled and field crops became more common. During the latter part of the nineteenth century, the California legislature enacted a series of statutes effectively closing the range in designated counties and thereby granting more protection to farmers who had not built fences.[96]

The closed-range exceptions began to swamp California's traditional open-range rule and eventually triggered a comprehensive legislative response. In the Estray Act of 1915,[97] the legislature adopted for most of California the traditional English rule that the owner of livestock is strictly liable for trespass damage.[98] This statute, however, retained the open-range rule for six counties in the lightly populated northern part of the state where the tradition of running cattle at large remained strong. The Estray Act of 1915 thus specifically excepted all of Shasta, Del Norte, Lassen, Modoc, Siskiyou, and Trinity Counties from the closed-range regime.[99]

---

statutes place the loss on the cattleman, the person who is usually the cheaper avoider of this sort of trespass, because he can best discover whether any of his animals are prone to break through or jump over fences and can best act on that knowledge.

Because lawful-fence rules provide rather bright-line standards, compared to negligence rules, they are relatively easy to communicate and apply. Lawful-fence statutes are thus suited to enforcement by lay "fence viewers"—private individuals whom some states have authorized to judge the quality of fencing and to assess trespass damages or fence construction costs. *See* note 111 *infra.*

96. *See* 3 CAL. JUR. 3D *Animals* § 55, at 676 n.42 (1973) (citing 14 county-specific fencing statutes that the California legislature enacted between 1863 and 1878 and repealed in the 1930s); Note, *Torts: Trespass by Animals upon Unenclosed Lands in California*, 7 CALIF. L. REV. 365 (1919).

97. 1915 Cal. Stat. 636 (current version at CAL. AGRIC. CODE §§ 17,001–17,128 (West 1968)).

98. Although the 1915 statute nominally dealt only with a trespass victim's rights to take up estrays, California case law has consistently held that a statutory right to seize estrays in the absence of a lawful fence carries with it the right to recover trespass damages under the traditional common law rule of strict liability. *See* Montezuma Improvement Co. v. Simmerly, 181 Cal. 722, 189 P. 100 (1919); Hahn v. Garratt, 69 Cal. 146, 10 P. 329 (1886); Williams v. Goodwin, 41 Cal. App. 3d 496, 116 Cal. Rptr. 200 (1974) (dictum).

99. 1915 Cal. Stat. 636 (current version at CAL. AGRIC. CODE §§ 17,123–17,126 (West 1968)). Subsequent amendments deleted the exemptions applicable to all of Del Norte County, and parts of Shasta and Trinity Counties. *See* CAL. AGRIC. CODE §§ 17,123–17,126 (West 1968).

The California code authorizes the board of supervisors of *any* county to declare by ordinance that part or all of the county is "devoted chiefly to grazing." *See* CAL. AGRIC. CODE § 17,124 (West 1968). A declaration of this sort converts the designated area to an open-range regime—that is, it takes from trespass victims who lack lawful fences their preexisting entitlement to seize estrays and to recover trespass damages. *See* Williams v. Goodwin, 41 Cal. App. 3d 496, 503 n.8, 116 Cal. Rptr. 200, 205 n.8 (1974) (dictum); 39 Op. Cal. Att'y Gen. 75 (1962).

Responding in part to lobbying efforts by local cattlemen's associations, an increasing

In 1945, the Legislature enacted two amendments that dealt exclusively with Shasta County, the least rural of the six exempt counties. The first stated that a prime agricultural area just south of Redding was "not . . . devoted chiefly to grazing"—a declaration that the legislature had decided to close the range in that small area of the county.[100] The second amendment empowered the Board of Supervisors of Shasta County to adopt ordinances designating additional areas of the county as places no longer devoted chiefly to grazing. This legal designation would make cattlemen strictly liable for trespass damage occurring in those locations.[101] For the next 29 years, Shasta was the only California county to possess this special authority.[102] Today, Shasta County has a crazy-quilt of open- and closed-range areas unmatched by any other California county.[103]

The distinction between open-range and closed-range has formal legal significance in Shasta County trespass disputes. In closed-range, the English rule governs and an animal owner, with rare exceptions,[104] is strictly liable for trespass damage to prop-

---

number of California's foothill counties have converted parts of their mountain forest to open range. *See, e.g.*, Amador County, Cal., Ordinance 590 (Apr. 26, 1977); Calavaras County, Cal., Ordinance 179 (June 3, 1940) (opening range in entire county), *repealed by* Ordinance 411 (Nov. 7, 1967) (referendum measure); Calavaras County, Cal., Ordinance 779 (Dec. 29, 1975) (townsite of Sheep Ranch); El Dorado County, Cal., Code §§ 16,501–16,505 (adopted Feb. 3, 1976); Mariposa County, Cal., Ordinance 128 (May 7, 1945) (the first of several ordinances opening the range in the National Forest areas of the county); Placer County, Cal., Ordinance 2017–B (June 29, 1976).

100. 1945 Cal. Stat. 1538–39 (current version at CAL. AGRIC. CODE § 17126 (West 1968)).

101. 1945 Cal. Stat. 1539 (current version at CAL. AGRIC. CODE § 17,127 (West 1968)).

102. The state legislature granted the board of supervisors of Trinity County, Shasta's neighbor to the west, similar authority in 1974. 1974 Cal. Stat. 409 (current version at CAL. AGRIC. CODE § 17,127 (West Supp. 1985)). Any closed-range county that exercises its statutory power to open the range in a particular area undoubtedly also has the power to switch that same area back to a closed regime. At least one California county has flip-flopped in this way. See note 99 *supra* (describing legal events in Calaveras County).

A number of western states that generally adhere to an open-range regime also authorize substate entities to selectively "close" parts of their range. *See, e.g.*, Ricca v. Bojorquez, 13 Ariz. App. 10, 473 P.2d 812 (1970) (Arizona procedure entitling landowners to close range by petition to the county board of supervisors unconstitutionally delegates power to private parties); Maguire v. Yanke, 99 Idaho 829, 590 P.2d 85 (1978) (describing Idaho procedure whereby landowners can petition to close range on a district by district basis); WASH. REV. CODE ANN. § 16.24.010 (1962) (option to close range granted to counties without townships).

103. A map issued by the Shasta County Department of Public Works in 1981 showed 28 separate areas the Board of Supervisors had closed by ordinance since 1945. Although most of the closed areas were located near Redding, there were areas of closed-range in the hinterland in every direction from the city.

104. See note 93 *supra*.

erty. In open-range areas, by contrast, even a livestock owner[105] who has negligently managed his animals is generally not liable[106] for trespass damage to the lands[107] of a neighbor.

Even in open range, however, there remain three important pockets of trespass liability. First, owners of goats, swine, and vicious dogs are subjected to the English rule throughout Shasta County.[108] Second, when a cattleman's livestock have trespassed

105. Persons other than the animal's owner could conceivably be held liable for an animal's damage. Livestock owned by one person often permissively graze on the lands of another. For example, both grazing leases and agistment arrangements—contracts to feed and care for the livestock of another—are common in cattle country. The California courts, as expansive as any state's in imposing tort liability, would likely hold a grazing landlord liable were he negligently to abet trespasses by a lessee's livestock. *Cf.* Uccello v. Laudenslayer, 44 Cal. App. 3d 504, 118 Cal. Rptr. 741 (1975) (residential landlord who knew of tenant's vicious dog and had the power to have it removed owed a duty of care to tenants' invitees and could be liable for negligence to dog-bite victim). *But cf.* Blake v. Dunn Farms, Inc., 274 Ind. 560, 413 N.E.2d 560 (1980) (landlord not liable for damages stemming from escape of tenant's horse that he knew little about). *See also* RESTATEMENT (SECOND) OF TORTS § 504 comment d (1977) (only a "possessor" of livestock, not the owner of the land from whence the animals escaped, is strictly liable for trespass damages); Annot., 21 A.L.R.4th 123 (1983) (liability of nonowner of livestock in highway collision cases). Because of this risk, the agent for many timberland owners in Shasta County includes a "hold harmless" clause in his standard grazing lease to entitle the lessor to indemnification from the lessee.

106. Prosser asserts that a trespass victim who lacks a lawful fence required by statute can still prevail against a cattle owner who was "at fault." *See* W. PROSSER, HANDBOOK OF THE LAW OF TORTS 498 n.58 (4th ed. 1971); *see also* W. PROSSER, J. WADE & V. SCHWARTZ, *supra* note 94, at 707. This implies that a fencing-out statute only deprives trespass victims of the right to proceed on a theory of strict liability; it lets them proceed on a theory of negligence.

In California, the weight of legal authority does not support the Prosser view. Except when the defendant intended that his cattle trespass, a plaintiff's proof of the presence of a lawful fence has been regarded as a prerequisite for recovery in open range. *See, e.g.*, Logan v. Gedney, 38 Cal. 579 (1869); Comerford v. Dupuy, 17 Cal. 308 (1861). *See also* RESTATEMENT (SECOND) OF TORTS § 504 comment k (1977); 2 F. HARPER & F. JAMES, *supra* note 94, § 14.10, at 829. To use a phrase that seems almost quaint in the current era of comparative negligence, in open range a California landowner without a lawful fence essentially "assumes the risk" that neighbors will negligently handle their cattle.

107. Other rules may apply when the injury has been to person or chattels. In closed-range, a cattle owner is strictly liable for foreseeable personal injuries that his livestock cause. *See* Williams v. Goodwin, 41 Cal. App. 3d 496, 116 Cal. Rptr. 200 (1974) (owner of trespassing bull strictly liable for trampling of night watchman in closed-range); Annot., 88 A.L.R.2d 709 (1963). *But cf.* RESTATEMENT (SECOND) OF TORTS § 504 (1977) (denying possessor of unfenced land in open-range recovery for personal injuries on a strict liability theory).

In both open- and closed-range, the owner of a trespassing animal would be strictly liable if that animal were to kill animals belonging to the owner of the premises invaded. *See* CAL. CIV. CODE § 3341 (West 1970); *cf.* CAL. AGRIC. CODE § 31501 (West 1968) (owner of trespassing dog is liable for twice the value of damages to livestock and poultry).

108. *See* CAL. AGRIC. CODE. § 17128 (West 1968) (excepting owners of "goats, swine, or hogs" from benefits of open-range rule); Shasta County Ordinance Code § 3306 (declaring it "unlawful" to permit "any vicious dog or other dangerous animal" to run at large).

The California Agricultural Code provides that "[a] person in charge of any stallion, bull,

through, or over, a "lawful fence" that entirely encloses the victim's premises, the cattleman remains strictly liable for trespass damages. (A California statute, unamended since 1915, defines the technological standard that a fence must meet to be "lawful."[109]) Third, common law decisions make a livestock owner in open range liable for trespass when he *intentionally* causes his animals to enter the unfenced lands of another. Thus when Frank Ellis actively herded his cattle across the lands of his neighbors, he was liable for trespass. According to some precedents, he would have been liable for trespass had he merely placed his cat-

---

boar, ram, or male goat shall not turn out or permit such animal to be turned out or to run at large." CAL. AGRIC. CODE § 16702 (West 1968). This provision is not compatible with CAL. AGRIC. CODE § 16803 (West 1968) (*requiring* the presence of one purebred bull for every 30 cows run at large). Brad Bogue, Shasta County's Animal Control Officer, interprets the latter section as controlling the former.

109. Section 17122 of the Agricultural Code reads:

> In any county or part of a county devoted chiefly to grazing and so declared pursuant to this article, a person shall not have the right to take up any estray animal found upon his premises, or upon premises to which he has the right of possession, nor shall he have a lien thereon, *unless the premises are entirely enclosed with a good and substantial fence.*

CAL. AGRIC. CODE § 17122 (West 1968) (emphasis added). Judicial decisions construe this sort of provision as also denying a person without such a fence the right to recover damages for cattle trespass. *See* note 98 *supra*. *See also* CAL. AGRIC. CODE § 17128 (West 1968).

Section 17121 describes the quality of fencing necessary to meet this standard:

> A lawful fence is any fence which is good, strong, substantial, and sufficient to prevent the ingress and egress of livestock. No wire fence is a good and substantial fence within the meaning of this article unless it has three tightly stretched barbed wires securely fastened to posts of reasonable strength, firmly set in the ground not more than one rod [16–1/2 feet] apart, one of which wires shall be at least four feet above the surface of the ground. Any kind of wire or other fence of height, strength and capacity equal to or greater than the wire fence herein described is a good and substantial fence within the meaning of this article . . . .

CAL. AGRIC. CODE § 17121 (West 1968).

This statutory definition of a lawful fence remains essentially unchanged since 1919. *Compare with* 1919 Cal. Stat. 1150. The definition is technologically obsolete because, at least in Shasta County, cattlemen customarily use at least four strands of barbed wire in their boundary fences. *See* note 53 *supra*. A fence that fails the statutory standard for "lawfulness" may be deemed to have been negligently built, thereby exposing the fencebuilder to liability for damage caused by the fence. *See* Loveland v. Gardner, 79 Cal. 317, 21 P. 766 (1889) (plaintiff can recover for damage his horses suffered when they encountered defendant's negligently stretched barbed wire fence).

California's statutory definitions of lawful fences before the invention of barbed wire are described in R. TYLER, *supra* note 94, at 482–84 (some samples: stone walls 4-1/2 feet high; rail fences 5-1/2 feet high; a five-foot high hedge). W. THORTON, *supra* note 94, at 201–23, provides a state-by-state review of statutory standards for the adequacy of fences in the late nineteenth century.

Other states' current statutory definitions of lawful fences vary from California's. *See, e.g.*, ARIZ. REV. STAT. ANN. § 24–501 (1971); NEV. REV. STAT. § 569.450(1) (1979); WASH. REV. CODE ANN. § 16.60.010 (1962). Many of their provisions seem equally antiquated.

tle on his own lands in a way that would make it substantially certain that they would venture onto his neighbors' pastures.[110]

When the law of either open- or closed-range entitles a trespass victim to relief, the remedy is usually an award of compensatory damages.[111] A plaintiff who has suffered from continuing wrongful trespasses may also be entitled to an injunction against future incursions.[112] Moreover, California's Estray Act entitles a landowner whose premises have been wrongly invaded by cattle to seize them as security for a claim to recover boarding costs and other damages. A trespass victim who invokes this procedure must provide proper notice to the Director of Agriculture; if certain statutory requirements are met, the animals can be sold

110. State courts have rather uniformly imposed tort liability on any cattleman who has actively herded his livestock onto the lands of another, even when the victim's land was situated in open-range. In some states, a cattleman has been held liable only when he has deliberately transported animals across the boundary line. *See, e.g.*, Garcia v. Sumrall, 58 Ariz. 526, 121 P.2d 640 (1942); Richards v. Sanderson, 39 Colo. 270, 89 P. 769 (1907). In other states, the entry of a cattleman's livestock has also been regarded as intentionally tortious when he has left them on a range from which it was substantially certain that they would enter the plaintiff's lands. *See, e.g.*, Lazarus v. Phelps, 152 U.S. 81 (1894); Mower v. Olsen, 49 Utah 373, 164 P. 482 (1917). *See generally* Annot., 158 A.L.R. 375 (1945).

Two reported California decisions deal with the issue of intentional trespass by livestock owners; in both, applicable statutes prohibited the "herding" of livestock on the lands of others. The more recent decision, Cramer v. Jenkins, 82 Cal. App. 269, 255 P. 877 (1927), supports the proposition that leaving animals in a range from which they are substantially certain to trespass constitutes tortious misconduct. *But cf.* Logan v. Gedney, 38 Cal. 579 (1869) (implying that active herding may be required). The California Supreme Court's current pro-plaintiff predilections would incline it to follow the *Cramer* approach.

111. Because evidence of damage to forage is fleeting, some states (although currently not California) authorize the appointment of disinterested residents of the area to serve as "fence viewers" to assess the amount of the damages. *See, e.g.*, WASH. REV. CODE ANN. § 16.60.015 (Supp. 1986) ("damages [shall be] assessed by three reliable, disinterested parties and practical farmers, within five days next after the trespass has been committed . . . ."). *See generally* 35 AM. JUR. 2d *Fences* §§ 24–32 (1967). The practice of delegating the valuation of damages to fence viewers was widespread in the nineteenth century and before. *See* R. TYLER, *supra* note 94, at 395, 399, 459 & 476 (describing statutes in New York, Maine, Wisconsin, and Kansas); W. CRONON, *supra* note 94, at 135 (colonial Massachusetts). At least one of the early California fence statutes provided for the appointment of fence viewers. *See* 1860 Cal. Stat. 142 (viewers' role is to assess the contributions that would be needed from the landowners on each side to build a sufficient partition fence).

Some early California statutes authorized cattle-trespass victims to recover double damages in certain situations. *See, e.g.*, 1850 Cal. Stat. 131 (victim enclosed by lawful fence can recover double damages for defendant's second offense). The Estray Act of 1915 contained no double damages provisions, and no reported California decision has granted this remedy in a cattle-trespass case. *But see* NEV. REV. STAT. § 569.440(1) (1979) (entitling trespass victim situated behind a lawful fence to recover double damages for second offense if the animal owner had been negligent).

112. *See* Montezuma Improvement Co. v. Simmerly, 181 Cal. 722, 189 P. 100 (1919); Blevins v. Mullally, 22 Cal. App. 519, 135 P. 307 (1913).

to satisfy the claim.[113]

The formal law provides trespass victims with only limited self-help remedies. A victim can use reasonable force to drive the animals off his land.[114] In addition, a trespass victim willing to give the animals proper care can seize estrays and bill the costs of their care to their owner. But a victim is generally not entitled to kill or wound the offending animals.[115] For example, a fruit-grower in Mendocino County (a closed-range county) was recently convicted for malicious maiming of animals when, without prior warning to the livestock owner, he shot and killed livestock trespassing in his unfenced orchard.[116] We shall see that in this respect the formal law diverges from Shasta County mores.[117]

The distinction between open-range and closed-range has

113. *See* CAL. AGRIC. CODE §§ 17041, 17042, 17091-95, 17122 (West 1968 & Supp. 1985). The animal owner may contest the propriety of the victim's invocation of this self-help remedy. *See* Wigmore v. Buell, 122 Cal. 144, 54 P. 600 (1898) (construing Estray Act of 1878); Yraceburn v. Cape, 60 Cal. App. 374, 212 P. 938 (1923) (victim wrongly invoked power to seize animals). The distraint procedure also poses potentially thorny state action and due process issues. *Cf.* Flagg Brothers, Inc. v. Brooks, 436 U.S. 149 (1978) (warehouseman's sale of entrusted goods).

The "right to distrain animals damage feasant" has deep roots in the English common law. *See* 3 W. BLACKSTONE, COMMENTARIES *211; G. WILLIAMS, *supra* note 92, at 7-123.

114. People v. Dunn, 39 Cal. App. 3d 418, 114 Cal. Rptr. 164 (1974) (dictum).

Shasta County trespass victims sometimes follow the time-honored self-help strategy of herding the intruding stock to a distant and inconvenient location. *See* text accompanying note 145 *infra*. On the issue of whether this represents a reasonable exercise of self-help, compare Gilson v. Fisk, 8 N.H. 404 (1836) (trespass victim who drove herd three miles away held liable in damages for death of eight sheep), with Wells v. State, 13 S.W. 889 (Tex. Ct. App. 1890) (victim of intentional trespass did not violate criminal statute when he drove cattle 3-4 miles afield).

115. *See* Crawford v. Crawford, 88 Ga. 234, 14 S.E. 609 (1891) (statute entitled owner of slain cattle to treble damages); Bruister v. Haney, 233 Miss. 527, 102 So. 2d 806 (1958) (trespass victim held liable in damages for intentionally poisoning entering cattle); Ford v. Taggart, 4 Tex. 492 (1849) (killer of trespassing mules civilly liable to their owner). *But see* Hummel v. State, 69 Okla. Crim. 38, 99 P.2d 913 (1940) (rancher was privileged to castrate a bull that threatened to impregnate pure-bred cows that were grazing on open-range). *See generally* J. INGHAM, THE LAW OF ANIMALS § 45 (1900); Annot., 12 A.L.R.3d 1103 (1967) (liability for accidentally or intentionally poisoning trespassing stock).

116. People v. Dunn, 39 Cal. App. 3d 418, 114 Cal. Rptr. 164 (1974).

117. *See* text accompanying notes 145-146 *infra*.

Self-help justice—occasionally organized on a group basis as vigilante justice—was a tradition in the nineteenth century American West. "The laws [in Wyoming] appeared to require that a farmer fence his land to keep cattle out, but many a farmer preferred to save the cost of a fence, then wait until cattle came in his land, and with a shot or two secure a winter's supply of beef." D. BOORSTIN, THE AMERICANS: THE DEMOCRATIC EXPERIENCE 30 (1973). *See also* E. OSGOOD, *supra* note 37, at 157-60 (lynching of horse thieves), at 242 (killing of trespassing cattle) & at 252-53 (describing how large cattle companies mobilized an army to invade Johnson County, Wyoming, to prevent small ranchers from using violent self-help against the companies' cattle).

formal relevance in public as well as private trespass law. Shasta County's law enforcement officials are entitled to impound cattle found running at large in closed range, but not those found in open range.[118] Brad Bogue, the county Animal Control Officer, relies primarily on mediation and warnings when responding to reports of loose animals. Regardless of whether the trespass has occurred in open or closed range, Bogue's first priority is to locate the owner of the offending animals, and to ask him to retrieve the livestock promptly. For example, if the owner of a ranchette situated in open range were to complain of trespassing mountain cattle, Bogue would inform the complainant of the cattleman's rights in open range, but he would also find the owner of the animals and explain why it would be in the owner's interest to take better care of the livestock. Bogue asserts that little else is required in the usual case. In most years, Bogue's office does not impound a single head of cattle[119] or issue a single criminal citation for failure to prevent cattle trespass.[120]

C. *Knowledge of Animal Trespass Law*

Before examining how Shasta County landowners actually resolve their cattle trespass disputes, I describe their working knowledge of the formal rules of trespass law. The extent of their knowledge is relevant for at least two reasons. First, Coase's Parable is set in a world of zero transaction costs, where everyone has perfect knowledge of legal rules. In reality, legal knowledge is imperfect because legal research is costly and

118. *See* Shasta County Ordinance Code § 3306 (habitual animal trespasses declared to be a public nuisance, "provided that this section shall not apply to livestock upon the open range").

119. The Shasta County Animal Control Office's Monthly Reports for 1980–1982 indicate that the office impounded one "bovine" during that period—a stray animal that Bogue said was found within one block of the office's animal shelter. This figure understates the number of public impoundments, because the Brand Inspector on occasion may ship stray cattle to the Cottonwood Auction Yard, which is better equipped than the animal shelter to board livestock.

120. Robert Baker, the County District Attorney from 1965 to 1979, could not recall a single criminal prosecution for cattle trespass on private lands. Gary Glendenning, the livestock specialist in the Detective's Division of the County Sheriff's Office, affirmed that criminal trespass actions were "never" brought, and that law enforcement officials mainly endeavored to identify and return the trespassing stock.

Criminal proceedings have been initiated against owners of stray livestock, however, when the stray animals have repeatedly posed serious risks to motorists. *See, e.g.*, State v. Whitlach, No. 82 CR 324 (Central Valley Just. Ct., Cal.) (misdemeanor action prompted by 26 telephone calls about cattle on roadways).

human cognitive capacities are limited. The following overview of the working legal knowledge of Shasta County residents provides a glimpse at how people behave in the face of these constraints. Analysts interested in designing legal rules to achieve specific instrumental goals must heed data of this sort, because rules cannot have instrumental effects unless they are communicated to the relevant actors. Second, most residents resolve trespass disputes by applying lower-level norms that are consistent with an overarching norm of cooperation among neighbors. To the extent that residents understand that their lower-level norms are inconsistent with formal legal rules, the more notable it is that the norms prevail.

1. *Laymen's knowledge of trespass law.*

To apply formal legal rules to a specific trespass incident, a Shasta County resident would first have to know whether it had occurred in an open-range or closed-range area of the county. Ideally, the resident would either have or know how to readily locate the map of closed-range areas published by the county's Department of Public Works. Second, a legally sophisticated person would have a working command of the rules of trespass law that were presented in the prior subpart, and know how they vary from open to closed range.

I found no one in Shasta County—layman or professional—with a complete working knowledge of the formal trespass rules just described. The persons best informed are, interestingly enough, two public officials without legal training: Brad Bogue, the Animal Control Officer, and Bruce Jordan, the Brand Inspector.[121] Their jobs require them to deal with stray livestock on almost a daily basis. Both have striven to learn applicable legal rules, and both sometimes invoke formal law when mediating disputes between county residents. Both Bogue and Jordan possess copies of the closed-range map and relevant provisions of the California Code. What they do *not* know is the case law; for example, neither is aware of the rule that an intentional trespass is always tortious, even in open-range. Nevertheless, Bogue and Jordan, both familiar figures to the cattlemen and (to a lesser extent) the ranchette owners of rural Shasta County, have done

121. Bogue is a Shasta County employee; Jordan is an employee of the California Bureau of Livestock Identification.

more than anyone else to educate the populace about formal trespass law.

What do ordinary rural residents know of that law? To a remarkable degree the landowners I interviewed did know whether their own lands were within open- or closed-range. Of the 25 I asked to identify whether they lived in open or closed range, 21 provided the correct answer, including two who were fully aware that they owned land in both.[122] This level of knowledge is probably atypically high.[123] Most of the landowner interviews were conducted in the Round Mountain and Oak Run areas. The former was the site in 1973 of the Caton's Folly closed-range battle. More importantly, Frank Ellis' aggressive herding had provoked a furious closed-range battle in the Oak Run area just six months before I conducted the interviews. Two well-placed sources—the Oak Run postmaster and the proprietress of the Oak Run general store—estimated that this political storm had caught the attention of perhaps eighty percent of the area's adult residents. In the summer of 1982, probably no populace in the United States was more alert to the legal distinction between open- and closed-range than the inhabitants of Oak Run.[124]

What do laymen know of the substance of trespass law? In particular, what do they know of how the rules vary from open- to closed-range? Laymen tend to conceive of these legal rules in black-and-white terms: Either the livestock owners or the trespass victims "have the rights." We have seen that the law of animal trespass in open-range is quite esoteric. Even there, an animal owner is liable, for example, for intentional trespass, trespass through a lawful fence, or trespass by a goat.[125] Only a few rural residents of Shasta County know anything of these subtleties. "Estray" and "lawful fence," central terms in the law of animal trespass, are not words in the cattlemen's everyday vocabulary. Neither of the two most sophisticated open-range ranchers that I interviewed were aware that enclosure by a lawful fence

122. Eleven correctly stated they lived in open-range; eight correctly stated they lived in closed-range; one gave a flatly wrong answer; one, a partially wrong answer; and two "didn't know."

123. My interviewees were disproportionately active in local politics; two had obtained copies of the Department of Public Works closed-range map in conjunction with their political endeavors.

124. Of 11 respondents asked, only three stated that they had known when they bought their land what kind of "legal range" it lay in.

125. *See* text accompanying notes 108–110 *supra*.

elevates a farmer's rights to recover for trespass. A traditionalist, whose cattle had often caused mischief in the Northeastern Foothills, thought estrays could never be seized in open-range, although a lawful fence gives a trespass victim exactly that entitlement. No interviewee believed that Ellis' intentional herding on his neighbors' lands in open-range might have been in excess of his rights.

As most laymen in rural Shasta County see it, trespass law is clear and simple. In closed-range, an animal owner is strictly liable for trespass damages. (They of course never used, and would not recognize, the phrase "strict liability.") In open-range, their basic premise is that an animal owner is never liable. When I posed hypothetical fact situations designed to put their simple rules under stress, the lay respondents sometimes backpedaled a bit, but they ultimately stuck to the notion that cattlemen have the rights in open-range and trespass victims the rights in closed-range.

2. *Legal specialists' knowledge of trespass law.*

The laymen's penchant for simplicity enabled them to identify correctly the substance of the English rule on cattle trespass that formally applies in closed-range. In that regard, the laymen outperformed the "legal specialists"—the judges, attorneys, and insurance adjusters. Although I sought out specialists who I had reason to believe would be knowledgeable about rural legal problems, I found that in two important respects the legal specialists had a worse working knowledge of trespass and estray rules than did the lay landowners.[126] First, in contrast to the landowners, the legal specialists immediately invoked *negligence* rules when asked to analyze rights in trespass cases. In general, they thought that a cattleman would not be liable for trespass in open-range (although about half seemed aware that this result would be affected by the presence of a lawful fence), and that he would be liable *only when negligent* in closed-range. The negligence approach has so dominated American tort law during this century that legal specialists—insurance adjusters in particular—may fail to identify narrow pockets where strict liability rules,

126. This startling finding can be attributed to the fact that trespass and estray claims are virtually never processed through the formal legal institutions of Shasta County. *See* text accompanying notes 151–160 *infra*.

such as the English rule on cattle trespass, formally apply.[127]

Second, unlike the lay rural residents, the legal specialists knew almost nothing about the location of the closed-range districts in the county.[128] For example, two lawyers who lived in rural Shasta County and raised livestock as a sideline, were ignorant of these boundaries; one incorrectly identified the kind of range in which he lived, and the other admitted he did not know what areas were open or closed. The latter added that this did not concern him because he would fence his lands under either legal regime.

I interviewed four insurance adjusters who settle trespass-damage claims in Shasta County. These adjusters had little working knowledge of the location of closed-range and open-range areas or of the legal significance of those designations. One incorrectly identified Shasta County as an entirely closed-range jurisdiction. Another stated that he did not keep up with the closed-range situation because "closed-range" just signifies places where there are fences, and the fence situation changes too rapidly to be worth following. The other two adjusters knew a bit more about the legal situation. Although neither possessed a closed-range map, they were able to guess how to locate one. On the other hand, both implied that they would not bother to find out whether a trespass incident had occurred in open- or closed-range before settling a claim. The liability rules that these adjusters apply to routine trespass claims seemed largely independent of formal law.[129]

D. *The Settlement of Trespass Disputes*[130]

If Shasta County residents were to act like the farmer and the

127. Some legal specialists conceivably may also believe that the negligence principle is in every application normatively superior to the principle of strict liability.

128. Additionally, neither of the two fence contractors interviewed had any notion of these boundaries. The county tax assessor assigned to the Oak Run-Round Mountain area was equally unfamiliar with the closed-range map.

129. In his study of the settlement of automobile-liability claims, Ross found the law-in-action to be simpler and more mechanical than the formal law, but he did not find it to be quite as disconnected as I found it in trespass cases. *See* H. Ross, *supra* note 12, at 134–35, 237–40. One might expect formal liability law to be particularly toothless when it applies to situations—such as animal trespass incidents—that generate few insurance claims, and for which the claims are almost always for paltry monetary amounts.

130. The scholars involved in the Civil Liability Research Project have attempted to standardize the vocabulary of dispute resolution. They use "grievance" to describe a perceived entitlement to pursue a claim against another, "claim" to describe a demand for

rancher in Coase's Parable, they would settle their trespass problems in the following way.[131] First, they would look to the formal law to determine who had what entitlements. They would then regard those substantive rules as beyond their influence ("exogenous" to use the economists' adjective). When they faced a potentially costly interaction, such as a trespass risk to crops, they would resolve it "in the shadow of"[132] the formal legal rules. Because transactions would be costless, enforcement would be complete: No violation of an entitlement would be ignored. For the same reason, two neighbors who interacted on a number of fronts would resolve their disputes front-by-front, rather than globally. My findings cast doubt on the realism of each of these implications of the Parable. Because Coase himself was fully aware that transactions are costly and thus that the Parable was no more than an abstraction, my findings in no way diminish his monumental contribution.[133] The findings may, however, serve as a valuable caution to other law-and-economics scholars who may have underestimated the impact of transaction costs on how the world works.[134]

1. *Norms, not legal rules, are the basic sources of entitlements.*

In rural Shasta County, trespass conflicts are generally resolved not "*in* the shadow of the law" but, rather, *beyond* that shadow. Most rural residents are consciously committed to an overarching norm of cooperation among neighbors.[135] In tres-

redress, and "dispute" to describe a rejected claim. *See, e.g.*, Miller & Sarat, *Grievances, Claims, and Disputes: Assessing the Adversary Culture*, 15 LAW & SOC'Y REV. 525, 527 (1980–1981). I am less precise and employ these terms loosely, as they tend to be employed in ordinary speech.

131. *See* Coase, *supra* note 1, at 15.

132. This now-familiar phrase originated in Mnookin & Kornhauser, *Bargaining in the Shadow of the Law: The Case of Divorce*, 88 YALE L.J. 950 (1979).

133. *See* notes 3, 13 *supra* and accompanying texts.

134. Law-and-economics scholars often employ models that explicitly assume that actors have perfect knowledge of legal rules. *See, e.g.*, A. POLINSKY, AN INTRODUCTION TO LAW AND ECONOMICS 37–49 (1983) (assuming drivers and pedestrians know personal injury law); Shavell, *An Analysis of Causation and the Scope of Liability in the Law of Torts*, 9 J. LEGAL STUD. 463, 471 (1980).

135. Although the rural landowners were emphatic about the importance of neighborliness and could offer many specific examples of neighborly behavior, they never articulated a general formula for how a rural resident should behave. In my forthcoming book on Shasta County I hypothesize that the specific norms they honored were wealth-maximizing, and explore how wealth-maximizing norms might evolve. *See also* text following note 161 *infra*.

For other discussions of the role of nonlegal norms in dispute settlement, see Eisenberg, *Private Ordering Through Negotiation: Dispute-Settlement and Rulemaking*, 89 HARV. L. REV. 637, 638–65 (1976); Macaulay, *supra* note 12, at 61–62.

pass situations, their salient lower-level norm, adhered to by all but a few deviants, is that an owner of livestock is responsible for the acts of his animals. Allegiance to this norm seems wholly independent of formal legal entitlements. Most cattlemen believe that a rancher should keep his animals from eating a neighbor's grass, regardless of whether the range is open or closed. Cattlemen typically couch their justifications for the norm in moral terms:

> Marty Fancher: "Suppose I sat down [uninvited] to a dinner your wife had cooked." Dick Coombs: It "isn't right" to get free pasturage at the expense of one's neighbors. Owen Shellworth: "[My cattle] don't belong [in my neighbor's field]." Attorney-rancher Pete Schultz: A cattleman is "morally obligated to fence" to protect his neighbor's crops, even in open range.

The next several pages describe in greater detail how the norms of neighborliness operate and how deviants who violate these norms are informally controlled. These pages also identify another set of deviants: trespass victims who actually invoke their formal legal rights.

2. *Incomplete enforcement: the live-and-let-live philosophy.*

The norm that an animal owner should control his stock is modified by another norm that holds that a rural resident should "lump" minor damage stemming from isolated trespass incidents. The neighborly response to an isolated infraction is an exchange of civilities. A trespass victim should notify the animal owner that the trespass has occurred and assist the owner in retrieving the stray stock. Virtually all residents have telephones, the standard means of communication. A telephone report is regarded not as a form of complaint, but rather as a service to the animal owner, who, after all, has a valuable asset on the loose. Upon receiving a telephone report, a cattleman who is a good neighbor will quickly retrieve the animals (by truck if necessary), apologize for the occurrence, and thank the caller. The Mortons and the Shellworths, two ranching families in the Oak Run area particularly esteemed for their neighborliness, are known for promptly and apologetically responding to their neighbors' notifications of trespass.[136]

136. A trespass victim who cannot recognize the brand of the intruding animal—a quandary more common for ranchette owners than for ranchers—may telephone county authorities. Calls of this sort are eventually referred to the Brand Inspector or Animal Control

Several realities of rural life in Shasta County help explain why residents are expected to lump trespass losses. First, it is commonplace for a country landowner to lose a bit of forage or to suffer minor fence damage. The area northeast of Redding lies on a deer migration route. During the late winter and early spring thousands of deer and elk move through the area, easily jumping the barbed wire fences.[137] Because wild animals trespass so often, most rural residents come to regard minor damage from alien animals not as an injurious event, but as an inevitable part of life.

Second, most residents expect to be on both the giving and receiving ends of trespass incidents. Even the ranchette owners have, if not a few hobby livestock, at least several dogs, which they keep for companionship, security, and pest control. Unlike cattle, dogs that trespass may harass, or even kill, other farm animals. If trespass risks are symmetrical, and if residents lump all trespass losses, accounts balance in the long run. Under these conditions, the advantage of reciprocal lumping is that each person is made whole without having to expend time or money to settle disputes.

The norm of reciprocal restraint that underlies "live-and-let-live" also calls for ranchers to lump the costs of boarding another person's animal, even for months at a time. A cattleman often finds in his herd an animal wearing someone else's brand. If he recognizes the brand he will customarily inform its owner, but the two will often agree that the simplest solution is for the animal to stay put until the trespass victim next gathers his animals, an event that may be weeks or months away. The cost of "cutting" a single animal from a larger herd seems to underlie this custom. Thus, ranchers often consciously provide other people's cattle with feed worth perhaps as much as $10 to $100 per animal. Although Shasta County ranchers tend to regard themselves as financially pinched, even ranchers who know that they are legally entitled to recover feeding costs virtually never seek monetary compensation for boarding estrays. The largest

Officer, who, as mentioned, then regard their main priority to be return of the animal to its owner.

137. One rancher reported that during the winter he expects to find 30–40 deer grazing in his hayfield each night. The owner of a particularly large ranch estimated that about 500 deer winter there—a condition he likes, because deer are "part of nature." John Woodbury, a key lobbyist for the passage of the Caton's Folly ordinance, stated that elk and deer had eaten more of the grass in his alfalfa field than mountain cattle ever had.

ranchers northeast of Redding who were interviewed reported that they had never charged anyone, or been charged by anyone, for costs of that sort. Even when they do not know to whom a stray animal belongs, they put the animal in their truck the next time they take a load of animals to the auctionyard at Cottonwood, and drop it off without charge so that the Brand Inspector can locate the owner.[138]

3. *The complexity of interneighbor relations: comprehensive mental accounts of who owes whom.*

Residents with few animals may of course not perceive any average reciprocity of advantage in a live-and-let-live approach to animal trespass incidents. What if, for example, a particular rancher's livestock repeatedly caused minor mischief in a particular farmer's fields? In that situation, Shasta County norms call for the farmer to keep track of those minor losses in a mental account. Eventually, the norms entitle him to act to remedy any imbalance.

A fundamental feature of rural society makes this enforcement system feasible: *Rural residents deal with one another on a large number of fronts, and most residents expect those interactions to continue far into the future.* In sociological terms, their relationships are "multiplex," not "simplex."[139] They interact on water supply, controlled burns, fence repairs, social events, staffing the volunteer fire department, and so on. Where population densities are low, each neighbor looms larger. Thus any trespass dispute with a neighbor is almost certain to be but one thread in the rich fabric of a continuing relationship.

A person in a multiplex relationship can keep a rough mental

---

138. Brand Inspector Bruce Jordan estimated that ranchers drop off approximately 300 head of stray livestock at the auctionyard each year, and that these ranchers typically decline to seek compensation from the owners of the strays.

139. *See* R. Kidder, Connecting Law and Society 70–72 (1983). The law and society literature has long emphasized that law is not likely to be important to parties enmeshed in a continuing relationship. For example, Marc Galanter has observed:

> In the American setting, litigation tends to be between parties who are strangers. Either they never had a mutually beneficial continuing relationship, as in the typical automobile case, or their relationship—marital, commercial, or organizational—is ruptured. In either case, there is no anticipated future relationship. In the American setting, unlike some others, resort to litigation is [usually] viewed as an irreparable breach of the relationship.

Galanter, *Reading the Landscape of Disputes: What We Know and Don't Know (and Think We Know) About Our Allegedly Contentious and Litigious Society*, 31 U.C.L.A. L. Rev. 4, 24–25 (1983) (brackets in original).

account of the outstanding credits and debits in each aspect of that relationship.[140] Should the aggregate account fall out of balance, tension may mount because the net creditor may begin to perceive the net debtor as an overreacher. On the other hand, so long as the aggregate account is in balance, neither party need be concerned that particular subaccounts are not. For example, if a rancher were to owe a farmer in the trespass subaccount, the farmer can be expected to remain content if that imbalance were to be offset by a debt he owed the rancher in, say, the water-supply subaccount.[141]

The live-and-let-live norm also suggests that neighbors should put up with minor imbalances in their aggregate accounts, especially when they perceive that their future interactions will provide adequate opportunities for settling old scores. Creditors may prefer having others in their debt. For example, when Larry Brennan lost six to seven tons of baled hay to Frank Ellis' cattle in open range, Brennan (although he did not know it) had a strong legal claim against Ellis for intentional trespass. Brennan estimated his loss at between $300 and $500, hardly a trivial amount. When Ellis learned of Brennan's loss he told Brennan to "come down and take some hay" from Ellis' barn. Brennan declined this offer of compensation, partly because he thought he should not have piled the bales in an unfenced area, but also because, to paraphrase his words, he would rather have Ellis in debt to him than be in debt to Ellis. Brennan was willing to let Ellis run up a deficit in their aggregate interpersonal accounts because he thought that as a creditor he would have more leverage over Ellis' future behavior.

4. *The control of deviants: the key role of self-help.*

The rural Shasta County population includes deviants who do not adequately control their livestock and do not adequately bal-

140. *Cf.* A. Vidich & J. Bensman, Small Town in Mass Society 34 (rev. ed. 1968):

> To a great extent these arrangements between friends and neighbors have a reciprocal character: a man who helps others may himself expect to be helped later on. In a way the whole system takes on the character of insurance. Of course some people are more conscious of their premium payments than others and keep a kind of mental bookkeeping on "what they owe and who owes them what," which is a perfectly permissible practice so long as one does not openly confront others with unbalanced accounts.

141. *See* O. Williamson, Markets and Hierarchies 256–57 (1975) (a party to a continuing relationship seeks to achieve a favorable balance in the overall set of interactions, not in each separate interaction).

ance their informal accounts with their neighbors. Frank Ellis, for example, seemed to care little about his reputation among his neighbors. In general, the traditionalists who let their animals loose in the mountains during the summer are less scrupulous than the modernists are in honoring the norms of neighborliness, perhaps because the traditionalists have less complex, and shorter-lived, interrelationships with the persons who encounter their range cattle.

To discipline deviants, the residents of rural Shasta County use the following four types of countermeasures, listed in escalating order of seriousness: (1) self-help retaliation; (2) reports to county authorities; (3) claims for compensation informally submitted without the help of attorneys; and (4) formal legal claims to recover damages. The law starts to gain bite as one moves down this list.

Self-help. Because most trespass disputes in Shasta County are resolved according to extralegal rules, the fundamental enforcement device is also extralegal. A measured amount of self-help—just enough to "get even," to invoke a marvelously apt phrase—is the predominant and ethically preferred response to someone who has not taken adequate steps to prevent his animals from trespassing.[142]

The mildest form of self-help is negative gossip.[143] This usually works because only the extreme deviants are immune from the general obsession with neighborliness. Although the Oak Run-Round Mountain area is undergoing a rapid increase in population, it remains distinctly rural in atmosphere. People tend to know one another, and they value their reputations in the community. Some ranching families have lived in the area for several generations and plan to stay indefinitely. Members of these families seem particularly intent on maintaining their reputations as good neighbors. Should one of them not promptly and courteously retrieve an estray, he might fear that any resulting gossip would permanently besmirch the family name.

Residents of the Northeastern Foothills seem quite conscious of the role of gossip in their system of social control. One longtime resident, who had also lived for many years in a suburb of a

142. *See generally* Black, *Crime as Social Control*, 48 AM. SOC. REV. 34 (1983) (a trenchant assessment of the phenomenon of self-help).

143. *See* Merry, *Rethinking Gossip and Scandal*, in 1 TOWARD A GENERAL THEORY OF SOCIAL CONTROL 271 (D. Black ed. 1984).

major California urban area, observed that people in the Oak Run area "gossip all the time," much more than in the urban area. Another reported intentionally using gossip to sanction a traditionalist who had been "impolite" when coming to pick up some stray mountain cattle; he reported that application of this self-help device produced an apology, an outcome itself presumably circulated through the gossip system.

The furor over Frank Ellis' loose cattle in the Oak Run area induced area residents to try a sophisticated variation of the gossip sanction. The ranchette residents who were particularly bothered by Ellis' cattle could see that he was utterly indifferent to his reputation among them. On the other hand, they thought that a large rancher such as Ellis would worry about his reputation among the large cattle operators in the county. They therefore reported Ellis' activities to the Board of Directors of the Shasta County Cattlemen's Association. This move proved unrewarding, for Ellis was also surprisingly indifferent to his reputation among the cattlemen. As the Association President later explained in a hearing before the county Board of Supervisors, the problem was that Ellis, a county resident for a decade, "hasn't been [in the County] all that long."[144]

When milder measures such as gossip fail, a person is regarded as being justified in threatening to use, and perhaps even actually using, tougher self-help sanctions. Particularly in unfenced country, a victim may respond to repeated cattle trespasses by herding the offending animals to a location extremely inconvenient for their owner.[145] Another common response to repeated trespasses is to threaten to kill a responsible animal should it ever enter again. Although the killing of trespassing livestock is a crime in California,[146] six landowners—not noticeably less civilized than the others—unhesitatingly volunteered that they had issued death threats of this sort. These threats are credible in Shasta County, because victims of recurring trespasses, particularly if they have first issued a warning, feel justified in killing or injuring the mischievous animals. Despite the criminality of the conduct (a fact not necessarily known to the

144. *See* note 75 *supra*.

145. Two respondents admitted that they had done this. For some scattered precedents on the legality of this practice, see note 114 *supra*.

146. CAL. PENAL CODE § 597(a) (West Supp. 1985); People v. Dunn, 39 Cal. App. 3d 418, 114 Cal. Rptr. 164 (1974).

respondents), I learned the identity of two persons who had shot trespassing cattle. Another landowner told of running the steer of an uncooperative neighbor into a fence. The most intriguing report came from a rancher who had had recurrent problems with a trespassing bull many years ago. This rancher told a key law enforcement official that he wanted to castrate the bull—"to turn it into a steer." The official replied that he "would have deaf ears" if that were to occur. The rancher asserted that he then carried out his threat.

It is difficult to estimate how frequently rural residents actually resort to violent self-help. Nevertheless, fear of physical retaliation is undoubtedly one of the major incentives for order in rural Shasta County. Ranchers who run herds at large freely admit that they worry that their trespassing cattle might meet with violence. One traditionalist reported that he is responsive to complaints from ranchette owners because he fears they will poison or shoot his stock. A judge for a rural district of the county asserted that a vicious animal is likely to "disappear" if its owner does not control it. A resident of the Oak Run area stated that some area residents responded to Frank Ellis' practice of running herds at large by rustling Ellis' cattle. He suggested that Ellis prepare a teeshirt with the following inscription: "Eat Ellis Beef. Everyone in Oak Run Does!"

Complaints to public officials.[147] The long-time ranchers of Shasta County pride themselves on being able to resolve their problems on their own. Except when they lose animals to rustlers, they do not seek help from public officials. Although ranchette owners also use the self-help remedies of gossip and violence, they, unlike the cattlemen, sometimes respond to a trespass incident by contacting a county official who they think will remedy the problem. These calls are usually funneled to the Animal Control Officer or Brand Inspector, who report that most of their callers are ranchette owners with limited rural experience. As already discussed, these calls do produce results. The county officials typically contact the owner of the animal, who then arranges for its removal. Brad Bogue, the Animal Control Officer, reported that in half the cases the caller knows whose animal it is. This suggests that callers often think that requests

147. *Cf.* Engel, *Cases, Conflict, and Accommodation: Patterns of Legal Interaction in an American Community*, 1983 Am. B. Found. Research J. 803, 821 (role of complaints to public officials in a rural Illinois county).

for removal have more effect when issued by someone in authority.

Mere removal of an animal may provide only temporary relief if its owner is a mountain lessee whose cattle repeatedly descend upon the ranchettes. County officials therefore use mild threats to caution repeat offenders. In closed-range, they may mention both their power to impound the estrays and the risk of criminal prosecution. These threats appear to be bluffs; the County never impounds stray cattle when it can locate an owner, and it rarely prosecutes cattlemen (and then only when their animals have posed risks to motorists).[148] In open-range, county officials may deliver a more subtle threat: not that they will initiate a prosecution, but that, if the owner does not mend his ways, the Board of Supervisors may face insuperable pressure to close the range in the relevant area. Because cattlemen perceive that a closure significantly diminishes their legal entitlements in situations where motorists have collided with their livestock, this threat can catch their attention.

A trespass victim's most effective official protest is one delivered directly to his elected county supervisor—the person best situated to change stray-cattle liability rules. Many Shasta County residents are aware that traditionalist cattlemen fear the supervisors more than they fear law enforcement authorities. Thus in 1973, alfalfa farmer John Woodbury made his repeated phone calls about mountain cattle not to Brad Bogue but to Supervisor John Caton.[149] When a supervisor receives many calls from trespass victims, his first instinct is to mediate the crisis. Former supervisor Norman Wagoner's standard procedure was to assemble the ranchers in the area and advise them to put pressure on the offender or else risk the closure of the range. Wagoner's successor, Supervisor John Caton, similarly told Frank Ellis that he would support a closure at Oak Run unless Ellis built three miles of fence along the Oak Run Road. If a supervisor is not responsive to a constituent's complaint, the constituent may respond by circulating a closure petition.[150]

The rarity of claims for monetary relief. Because Shasta County residents tend to settle their trespass disputes beyond the

148. *See* notes 119–120 *supra* and accompanying text.

149. *See* text following note 68 *supra*.

150. This was how Doug Heinz goaded Supervisor John Caton into action at Oak Run. *See* text accompanying note 72 *supra*.

shadow of the law, one might expect that the norms of neighborliness would include a norm against the invocation of formal legal rights. And this norm is indeed strongly established.[151] Owen Shellworth: "I don't believe in lawyers [because there are] always hard feelings [when you litigate]." Tony Morton: "[I never press a monetary claim because] I try to be a good neighbor." Norman Wagoner: "Being good neighbors means no lawsuits." Although trespasses are frequent, *Shasta County's rural residents virtually never file formal trespass actions against one another.* John Woodbury, for example, made dozens of phone calls to Supervisor John Caton, but never sought monetary compensation from the traditionalists whose cattle had repeatedly marauded his alfalfa field. Court records and conversations with court clerks indicate that in most years not a single private lawsuit is filed in the county's courts seeking damages for either trespass by livestock or the expense of boarding estrays.[152] The residents of the Northeastern Foothills not only refrain from filing formal lawsuits, but they are also strongly disinclined to submit informal monetary claims to an owner of trespassing animals or that owner's insurance company.[153]

The landowners who were interviewed clearly regard their restraint in seeking monetary relief as a mark of virtue. When asked why they did not pursue meritorious legal claims arising from trespass or fence-finance disputes, various landowners replied: "I'm not that kind of guy;" "I don't believe in it;" "I don't like to create a stink;" "I try to get along." The landowners who attempted to provide a rationale for this forbearance all implied the same one, a long-term reciprocity of advantage. Ann Kershaw: "The only one that makes money [when you litigate] is the lawyer." Al Levy: "I figure it will balance out in the long run."

151. Investigators have found norms against litigation in other social environments. *See* Engel, *supra* note 147, at 816–22, 851–56 (rural Illinois county); Macaulay, *supra* note 12, at 64 (Wisconsin businessmen).

152. In the Burney Justice Court, the 1980 small claims files showed no animal trespass cases, and the clerks could recall no such cases in their four years on the job.

In the Central Valley Justice Court, no small claims for the 8/81 to 6/82 period involved animal trespass, and the civil clerk who had worked there for 11 years could not remember any. The index of defendants for the 1975–82 period indicated that Frank Ellis was the only large rancher to become the target of any kind of legal action. *See* text accompanying notes 155–160 *infra*.

153. I did hear several secondhand reports of informally settled claims for the costs of boarding estrays. Only one rancher told of paying such a claim; he regarded the claimant's pursuit of the money as a "cheap move."

Pete Schultz: "I hope they'll do the same for me." Phil Ritchie: "My family believes in 'live and let live.'"

Mutual restraint saves parties with long-term relationships the costs of going through the formal claims process. Adjoining landowners who practice live-and-let-live are both better off whenever the negative externalities from their activities are roughly in equipoise. Equipoise is as likely in closed-range as in open. Landowners with property in closed-range—the ones with the greatest formal legal rights—were the source of half of the quotations in the prior two paragraphs.

Shasta County landowners regard a monetary settlement as an arms-length transaction that symbolizes an unneighborly relationship. Should your goat happen to eat your neighbor's tomatoes, the neighborly thing for you to do would be to help replant the tomatoes; a transfer of money would be too cold and too impersonal.[154] When Kevin O'Hara's cattle went through a break in a fence and destroyed his neighbor's corn crop (a loss of less than $100), O'Hara had to work hard to persuade his neighbor to accept O'Hara's offer of money damages. O'Hara insisted on making this payment because he "felt responsible" for his neighbor's loss, a feeling that would not have been in the least affected had the event occurred in open- instead of closed-range. There can also be social pressure against offering money settlements. Bob Bosworth's father agreed many decades ago to pay damages to a trespass victim in a closed-range area just south of Shasta County; other cattlemen then rebuked him for setting an unfortunate precedent. The junior Bosworth, currently President of the Shasta County Cattlemen's Association, could recall no other out-of-pocket settlement in a trespass case.

Trespass victims who sustain an unusually large loss are more likely to take the potentially deviant step of making a claim for monetary relief. I interviewed adjusters for the two insurance companies whose liability policies would be most likely to cover losses from animal trespass. The adjusters' responses suggest that in a typical year these companies receive fewer than ten trespass damage claims originating in Shasta County. In the paradig-

154. A donor who wishes to symbolize an intimate relationship typically gives, not currency, but a gift that apparently required special effort to prepare. *See* Landa, *The Enigma of the Kula Ring: Gift-Exchanges and Primitive Law and Order*, 3 INT'L REV. L. & ECON. 137, 152 (1983) (Melanesians return armshells for necklaces because to return a necklace for a necklace would be interpreted as a rejection of friendship). *See generally* M. MAUSS, THE GIFT (1967).

matic case, the insured is not a rancher, but rather a ranchette owner whose family's horse escaped and trampled a neighboring homeowner's shrubbery. The claimant is typically not represented by an attorney—a type of professional these adjusters rarely encounter. The adjusters also settle each year two or three trespass claims that homeowners or ranchette owners have brought against ranchers. Ranchers who suffer trespasses virtually never file claims against others' insurance companies. An adjuster for the company that insures most Shasta County ranchers stated that he could not recall, in his twenty years of adjusting, a single rancher's claim for compensation for trespass damage.

The landowners, particularly the ranchers, express a strong aversion to hiring an attorney to fight one's battles. To hire an attorney is to escalate a conflict. A good neighbor does not do such a thing because the "natural working order" calls for two neighbors to work out their problems between themselves. The files in the Shasta County courthouses reveal that the ranchers who honor norms of neighborliness—the vast majority—are simply not involved in cattle-related litigation of any kind.

My field research uncovered two instances in which animal trespass victims in the Oak Run-Round Mountain area had turned to attorneys. In one of these cases the victim actually filed a formal complaint. Because attorney-backed claims are so unusual, these two disputes deserve elaboration.

The first dispute involved Tom Hailey and Curtis McCall. For three generations, Hailey's family has owned a large tract of foothill forest in an open-range area near Oak Run. In about 1978, Hailey discovered McCall's cattle grazing on some of Hailey's partially fenced land. Hailey suspected that McCall had brought the animals in through a gate in Hailey's fence. When Hailey confronted him, McCall, who lived about a mile away, acted as if the incursion had been accidental. Hailey subsequently found a salt block on the tract—an object he could fairly assume that McCall had put there to service his herd. Hailey thus concluded that McCall had not only deliberately trespassed, but had also aggravated the offense by untruthfully denying the charge. Hailey seized the salt block and consulted an attorney, who advised him to seek compensation from McCall. The two principals eventually agreed to a small monetary settlement.

Hailey is a semi-retired government employee who spends much of his time outside of Shasta County; he is regarded as reclusive and eccentric—certainly someone outside the mainstream of Oak Run society. McCall, a retired engineer with a hard-driving style, moved to Shasta County in the late 1970s to run a small livestock ranch. The Haileys refer to him as a "Texan"—a term that connotes someone who is both an outsider and lacks neighborly instincts.

The second dispute involved Doug Heinz and Frank Ellis. As already noted, Heinz had the misfortune of owning a ranchette near Ellis' ranch.[155] After experiencing repeated problems with Ellis' cattle, Heinz unilaterally seized three of the animals that had broken through his fence. Heinz boarded these animals for three months without notifying Ellis. Heinz later asserted he intended to return them when Ellis next held a roundup. According to Heinz, Ellis eventually found out that Heinz had the animals and asked for their return. Heinz agreed to return them if Ellis would pay pasturage. When Ellis replied, "You know I'm good for it," Heinz released the animals and sent Ellis a bill. Ellis refused to pay the bill, and he further infuriated Heinz by calling him "boy" whenever Heinz brought up the debt.

On January 8, 1981, Heinz filed a small-claims action against Ellis to recover $750 "for property damage, hay and grain ate [sic] by defendant's cattle, boarding of animals."[156] Acting through the attorney he kept on retainer, Ellis responded eight days later with a separate civil suit against Heinz.[157] Ellis's complaint sought $1,500 compensatory and $10,000 punitive damages from Heinz for the shooting deaths of two Black Brangus cows that Ellis had pastured on BLM lands; it also sought compensation for the weight loss Ellis' three live animals had sustained during the months Heinz had been feeding them. The two legal actions were later consolidated. Heinz, who called Ellis' allegation that Heinz had killed two cows "100 percent lies" and "scare tactics," hired a bright young Redding attorney to represent him. This attorney threatened to pursue a malicious prosecution action against Ellis if Ellis persisted in asserting that Heinz had slain the Black Brangus cows. In December 1981, the parties agreed to a settlement under the terms of which Ellis paid Heinz $300 in damages and $100 for attorney fees. Ellis' insurance company picked up the tab. By that time Heinz was

155. *See* text following note 70 *supra*.
156. Heinz v. Ellis, No. 81 SC 7 (Cent. Valley Just. Ct. filed Jan. 8, 1981).
157. Ellis v. Heinz, No. 81 CV 6 (Cent. Valley Just. Ct. filed Jan. 16, 1981).

spearheading a political campaign to close the range Ellis had been using.[158]

The Heinz-Ellis and Hailey-McCall disputes share several characteristics. Although both arose in open range, in each instance legal authority favored the trespass victim: Hailey, because McCall's trespass had been intentional; and Heinz, because Ellis' animals had broken through an apparently lawful fence.[159] In both instances, the victim, before consulting an attorney, had attempted to obtain informal satisfaction but had been rebuffed. Each victim perceived that the animal owner had not been honest. Each dispute was ultimately settled in the victim's favor. In both instances, neither the trespass victim nor the cattle owner was well-socialized in rural Shasta County norms. Thus other respondents tended to refer to the four individuals involved in these two claims as "bad apples," "odd ducks," or otherwise as people not aware of the natural working order. Ordinary people, it seems, do not often turn to attorneys to help resolve disputes.[160]

V. Summary and Implications

Coase's Parable of the Farmer and the Rancher, like most writing in law and economics, implies that disputants look solely to formal legal rules to determine their entitlements. In rural Shasta County, California, residents instead typically look to informal norms to determine their entitlements in animal trespass situations. In open-range areas, the norm that a livestock owner should supervise his animals dominates the legal rule that a cattleman is not legally liable for unintentional trespasses on unfenced land. Trespass victims mainly employ negative gossip and physical reprisals against trespassing stock to discipline cattlemen who violate this norm.

In Shasta County, the law of trespass had no apparent feed-

158. *See* text accompanying notes 71–76 *supra.*

159. Heinz had technically imperiled his statutory claim for damages under the Estray Act when he failed to notify the proper public authorities promptly that he had taken up Ellis' animals. *See* Cal. Agric. Code §§ 17042, 17095 (West 1967).

160. *See also* W. Nelson, Dispute and Conflict Resolution in Plymouth Colony, Massachusetts 1725–1825 (1981) (Plymouth's particularly litigious individuals during the 1725–1774 period tended to be people who were poorly socialized); Todd, *Litigious Marginals: Character and Disputing in a Bavarian Village*, in The Disputing Process: Law in Ten Societies, *supra* note 12, at 86, 118 (socially marginal people were disproportionately represented in civil and criminal litigation).

back effects on trespass norms. In no instance did the legal designation of an area as open (or closed) range affect how residents resolved a trespass or estray dispute. Thus Rancher Kevin O'Hara paid a neighbor for the loss of a corn crop because he "felt responsible," a feeling he said would not have been influenced by formal trespass law. Being located in closed range did not appear to make a trespass victim more likely to perceive a grievance or to exercise self-help. Insurance adjusters paid virtually no attention to the distinction between open-range and closed-range when settling trespass claims.

Other findings suggest the unreality of other literal features of the Coasean Parable. Victims of stray cattle did not treat the formal legal rules as exogenous; they were aware that one way to use limited resources is to lobby for legal change. Victims' enforcement of their norm-based entitlements was far from complete; they ignored some trespasses altogether and used others to offset outstanding informal debts. Victims tended to shun monetary settlements and instead preferred in-kind transfers, including ones effected through self-help. Although these findings are at odds with the literal features of the Coasean Parable, they are fully consistent with Coase's central idea that, regardless of the specific content of law, people tend to structure their affairs to their mutual advantage.

The Shasta County evidence suggests that law and economics scholars need to pay more heed to how transaction costs influence the resolution of disputes. Because it is costly to carry out legal research and to engage in legal proceedings, a rational actor often has good reason to apply informal norms, not law, to evaluate the propriety of human behavior. Contracts scholars have long known that norms are likely to be especially influential when disputants share a continuing relationship.[161] A farmer and a rancher who own adjoining lands are enduringly intertwined, and therefore readily able to employ nonlegal methods of dispute resolution. Law-and-economics scholars misdirect their readers and students when they invoke examples—such as the Parable of the Farmer and the Rancher—that greatly exaggerate the domain of human activity upon which the law casts a shadow.

This article will be incorporated into a forthcoming book on

161. *See, e.g.*, Macaulay, *supra* note 12; Macneil, *The Many Futures of Contracts*, 47 S. Cal. L. Rev. 691, 715 (1974).

dispute resolution among neighbors. Other parts of the book will describe how Shasta County residents resolve disputes over both the financing of boundary fences and the allocation of losses stemming from vehicle-livestock collisions on highways. The book will explain why proposed closed-range ordinances generate so much political heat in Shasta County even though trespass law is itself practically irrelevant. Finally and more ambitiously, in the book I will use the Shasta County data as a springboard to develop a theory of the content and role of norms. Building on recent work in game theory, I hypothesize that, in the absence of identified "social imperfections," the norms that govern the relations among members of a group tend to maximize the aggregate wealth of group members. The book will explore the normative and positive implications of this theory for the interplay between the legal system and more informal systems of social control.

[12]

INALIENABILITY AND THE THEORY OF PROPERTY RIGHTS

*Susan Rose-Ackerman**

Inalienability is the stepchild of law and economics. Too often, economists note the existence of restrictions on transferability, ownership, and use, only to dismiss them as obviously inefficient constraints on market trades. Even Guido Calabresi and Douglas Melamed, who give inalienability explicit status in their theory of entitlements, treat it as an analytic stepchild to be justified by appeals to paternalism and moralism.[1]

On inspection, however, inalienability turns out to be a very complex concept, and one whose legitimate uses can be clarified through economic analysis combined with a sensitivity to noneconomic ideas—most notably ideals of citizenship and distributive justice. Inalienability can be defined as any restriction on the transferability, ownership, or use of an entitlement. So defined, inalienability is pervasive in modern, developed societies, in developing nations, and in the historical past. The variety and ubiquity of these restrictions suggest that a fuller analysis would help us better understand the role of private property in economic and social life. This Article begins such an analysis by first categorizing the possible types of restrictions, and then developing rationales that may justify some of these constraints on private ownership.

To do this, we must take a broader view of the role of legal entitlements than is expressed in most work on property rights in law and economics. Much of the existing literature emphasizes the way that efficient entitlement rules are affected by the technical characteristics of products and the costs of externality control.[2] Fish, pasture land, for-

---

* Professor of Law and Political Economy, Columbia University. B.A. 1964, Wellesley College; Ph.D. 1970, Yale University. Research for this paper was partially supported by Columbia University's Center for Law and Economic Studies, the International Institute for Applied Systems Analysis, and Yale Unversity's Program on Nonprofit Organizations. Helpful comments were received from Bruce Ackerman, Guido Calabresi, Merritt Fox, Alvin Klevorick, Jerry Mashaw, Daniel Rubinfeld, Matthew Spitzer, Christopher Stone, and seminar participants at Stanford, University of Southern California, Yale, the 1983 annual meeting of the American Economic Association, and at Columbia Law School's Conference on New Directions in Law and Economics. Walter de la Cruz, Katherine Gorove and Tracey Thompson provided helpful research assistance.

1. Calabresi & Melamed, Property Rules, Liability Rules, and Inalienability: One View of the Cathedral, 85 Harv. L. Rev. 1089 (1972).

2. For many of the basic articles, see Economic Foundations of Property Law (B. Ackerman ed. 1975); The Economics of Legal Relationships: Readings in the Theory of Property Rights (H. Manne ed. 1975); see also Demsetz, Toward a Theory of Property Rights, 57 Am. Econ. Rev. (Papers and Proceedings) 347 (1967) (reviewing literature); Furubotn & Pejovich, Property Rights and Economic Theory: A Survey of Recent Liter-

ests, oil pools, and minerals on the ocean bottom are only a few of the resources that have been subject to a property rights analysis.[3] The research focuses rather narrowly on the efficiencies of private ownership systems that require people to take account of all the costs of resource use. Most of this work, moreover, has been excessively confident in the workings of the private market once property rights are firmly established and therefore views restraints on alienation with a great deal of skepticism.[4]

In contrast, Calabresi and Melamed believe that inalienability rules can sometimes be justified, but they do not attempt a full analysis of the rationales for restrictions on transferability, ownership, and use.[5] Their work emphasizes instead the distinction between property rules and liability rules. Under a property rule, property can be sold, donated, or discarded, but only if the owner is willing to give up the entitlement and the recipient is willing to accept it. Under a liability rule, others may take your entitlement by, for example, destroying it in an accident, but they must then compensate you at a rate determined by a governmental body. Because Calabresi and Melamed's treatment of inalienability is colored by this emphasis on quid pro quo transfers, they discuss only one kind of inalienability—where ownership is legal but sales are not permitted—and they fail to discuss the economic rationales for even this form of restriction.

In the present paper I propose a broader based approach that seeks both to identify the range of possible restrictions and to develop normative rationales for some of these restrictions. Because my basic point of view is informed by economic theory, I start with the supposition that unencumbered market trades are desirable unless we can locate a valid reason for their restriction. I reject the idea that market trades are inherently coercive. Nevertheless, some forms of inalienability do have valid public policy justifications in a democratic market society. Three broad rationales are central to my argument. First, economic efficiency itself may require restrictions on property. This rationale goes beyond the familiar problems of externality control to include imperfect information, "prisoner's dilemmas," free rider problems, and the cost of administering alternative policies. Second,

---

ature, 10 J. Econ. Literature 1137 (1972) (reviewing literature); North, Structure and Performance: The Task of Economic History, 16 J. Econ. Literature 963 (1978) (reviewing literature).

3. See, e.g., Anderson & Hill, The Evolution of Property Rights: A Study of the American West, 18 J. L. & Econ. 163 (1975); Gordon, The Economic Theory of a Common-Property Resource: The Fishery, 62 J. Pol. Econ. 124 (1954); Hardin, The Tragedy of the Commons, 162 Sci. 1243 (1968); Sweeney, Tollison & Willett, Market Failure, The Common-Pool Problem, and Ocean Resource Exploitation, 17 J.L. & Econ. 179 (1974).

4. See, e.g., Bureaucracy vs. Environment: The Environmental Costs of Bureaucratic Governance (J. Baden & R. Stroup eds. 1981).

5. See Calabresi & Melamed, supra note 1, at 1111–15.

certain specialized distributive goals can only be achieved through some kind of inalienability rule. A general program of taxes and transfers may be inadequate. Third, unfettered market processes may be incompatible with the responsible functioning of a democratic state.

I begin in Part I by classifying entitlement rules by ownership, use, and transferability. My framework is less complex than the heterogeneity of the legal world, but more complex than previous attempts, such as Calabresi and Melamed's. I draw examples both from current controversies—including the sale of blood, military conscription, the preservation of historic buildings, and the protection of endangered species—and from such historical examples as the Homesteading Acts and the Civil War draft. My hope is that the taxonomy I propose will help scholars recognize similarities and salient differences between the broad diversity of entitlement restrictions currently in force. My framework should not be read, however, as an attempt to justify the entire range of existing constraints on property rights. Many of these have their roots in paternalistic attempts to impose moral values on others or in efforts by interest groups to obtain monopoly power.

In Part II, I develop efficiency and equity rationales for some existing restrictions and point out the analytic similarities between such disparate things as blood and used cars, or babies and lake trout. I demonstrate that inalienability rules can be second-best responses to various kinds of market failures and point out both how some restrictions on property rights serve redistributive goals and how other restrictions may impose unfair costs. Finally, I show in Part III how each of four distinct concepts of citizenship resolves the tension between efficiency and egalitarian values.

I. A Taxonomy of Entitlements

In examining the rationales for legal restrictions on entitlements, one must avoid being overwhelmed by the multitude of individual cases. To keep the analysis manageable, therefore, I will concentrate, in turn, on each of three dimensions of the problem: (1) *who* may hold the entitlement; (2) what *actions* the entitlement holder is required to perform to maintain title, and what actions are forbidden; and (3) what kinds of *transfers* are permitted. After outlining the important possibilities, I select a few of the most representative and interesting cases to discuss in more detail in the body of the paper.

A. *Restrictions on Ownership, Use and Transferability*

I begin first with the question of who may hold the entitlement. Legal rules may permit: (a) anyone, (b) only some specified groups, (c) everyone simultaneously, or (d) no one, to hold title. Cases (c) and (d) cover goods that cannot be privately owned, either because the state has declared them common property, so that exclusion of others is forbidden (navigable waters), or because they are illegal (heroin, liquor under Prohibition). In case (b), the state determines who may hold the entitlement. The class of qualified owners may include only those with some demographic characteristic such as old age or female sex, or it may be limited on the basis of some selection procedure such as an examination or a lottery.

Second, entitlement holders may face restrictions on the use of their property that are designed to produce some benefit or prevent some undesirable activity. We must distinguish between activities that are permitted, required, or forbidden. Since required activities are a subset of all permitted activities, the possible legal relationships between these distinctions are as follows:

TABLE 1
RESTRICTIONS ON USE

	Nothing is Required	All Permitted Activities are Also Required	Some Permitted Activities are Also Required
Nothing is Permitted	1	—	—
Nothing is Forbidden	2	—	3
Some Activities are Permitted and Others are Forbidden	4	5	6

Case (1) is one extreme: nothing can be done with the entitlement. In fact, in such a situation it seems odd to speak of entitlements at all. Case (2) is the opposite extreme: everything is permitted and nothing is required.[6] Case (3) is somewhat more restrictive: everything is permitted so long as some required activities are carried out (e.g., a historic building preservation law). Under (4), some activities are forbidden but nothing is required (e.g., a zoning law). In (5), those who wish to retain title are required to perform certain activities, which are also the only activities permitted (e.g., a homestead law). In (6), a proper subset of the permitted activities is also required while other activities are forbidden (e.g., a zoning law in a community that also regulates historic buildings).

Third, consider the transferability and disposal of entitlements. Since regulation of the external costs imposed by the free disposal of

6. It would be logically possible to consider the middle box in Table 1 but not very realistic. Under such a rule, everything that can possibly be done with an entitlement is legally required.

waste has been relatively well analyzed by others,[7] I shall not emphasize it here. Instead, I concentrate on the difference between sales and gifts. Table 2 summarizes the four possibilities:

TABLE 2
RESTRICTIONS ON TRANSFERABILITY

	Gifts Permitted	Gifts Forbidden
Sales Permitted	pure property A	modified property B
Sales Forbidden	modified inalienability C	pure inalienability D

Under case (A), a pure property rule, all voluntary transfers are permitted. Under case (B), a modified property rule, only sales, generally at market prices, are permitted. Case (C) is called modified inalienability because sales are outlawed while gifts are permitted. Case (D) represents pure inalienability.

B. *A Synthesis*

Putting together the three dimensions along which entitlements can vary yields almost one hundred cases. Since this Article deals with the control of private property, however, I will consider neither goods that cannot be used or legally possessed nor pure public goods. Of the forty cases that remain, the nine I examine can be divided into two general categories: those that affect the allocation and use of market goods and services and those that reflect alternative concepts of citizenship.

Within the market goods and services category, I begin by considering two cases that restrict transferability. Under the concept of *modified inalienability*, sales are forbidden, but gifts are permitted and may even be encouraged by state policy. Modified inalienability rules appear in such diverse contexts as the transplantation of body parts, the adoption of babies, and the preservation of endangered species. The converse of a modified inalienability rule is *modified property*. Under this rule, gifts are forbidden but sales at "fair" market prices are permitted. This rule generally does not apply to particular kinds of property but rather to particular situations. For example, an insolvent person or firm cannot give away valuable assets.

Three other cases involve limits on ownership and use. Thus, *pure property with ownership restrictions* limits the entitlement holders to individuals with particular attributes. They must be, for example, licensed physicians, persons who are over eighteen or over sixty-five, residents of Guilford, Connecticut, or persons approved by the board of directors. Transferability and use, however, are not restricted: the entitle-

7. See, e.g., Calabresi & Melamed, supra note 1.

ment can be sold or given to anyone else who also qualifies for ownership, and can be used without coercive conditions. Two simple cases involve restrictions on use: under *required use*, nothing is forbidden, but some uses are required, while under *limited use*, nothing is required, but some things are forbidden. Thus historical preservation laws require the preservation of certain buildings while zoning laws may forbid apartment buildings or commercial development on some pieces of land.

Finally, under systems of coerced use, all permitted activities are required and all other uses are forbidden. When such requirements are imposed on property owners, it is important to know whether the right is transferable or whether severe restrictions are imposed on an owner's right to dispose of his property. Under the former, called *pure property with coercive use*, a mineral lease, for example, may be sold or given away but will be lost if no mining is carried out. Under the latter rule, which I label *conditional coercion*, requirements are imposed on qualified entitlement holders, but people may waive these reponsibilities if they are willing to waive the entitlement as well. This kind of rule is more complex and restrictive than one that permits sales. The American homesteading laws, for example, gave land to families on the condition that they farm it for a fixed number of years. In a quite different context, many of today's government transfer programs for the needy are conditionally coercive.

Restraints on alienation are also imposed when people perform their responsibilities as citizens. Thus, the final group of categories embodies alternative concepts of citizenship. The categories are alienable rights—analogous to pure property rules with limits on ownership—inalienable rights, alienable duties—equivalent to coerced use—and inalienable duties. These concepts can be understood by considering their different implications for voting rights, military service, and jury duty. *Alienable rights* can be sold or transferred to others and need not be exercised to be retained. Under this concept, the state has a volunteer army and permits the sale or donation of votes. *Inalienable rights* also need not be exercised, but the right cannot be sold or given away and some uses may be forbidden. Once a person is found qualified, however, there are no actions that must be taken in order to maintain the right. In the United States voting is an inalienable right, and some government social benefits also fall in this category. *Alienable duties* are activities required of a subset of the population that can be transferred to other persons willing to perform them. For example, during the Civil War, persons drafted into the army were permitted to buy substitutes. Finally, *inalienable duties* cannot legally be transferred through sales, gifts, or disposal. A military draft with no buy-out possibilities and jury duty are familiar examples.

To help keep these categories in mind as I proceed, Table 3 lists each type to be considered along with some important examples. The numbers and upper case letters in parentheses refer to the labels in Tables 1 and 2, respectively, and the lower case letters refer to alternative restrictions on ownership.

TABLE 3

Entitlement Categories	Examples
1) Inalienable Duties (5.D.b.)	Army draft notices; jury duty; votes in Australia
2) Inalienable Rights (4.D.b.)	Votes in political contests in the United States
3) Conditional Coercion (5.C.b.)	Homesteads; benefits under some government transfer programs
4) Modified Inalienability (2.C.a.)	Kidneys; hearts; wild game; babies
5) Modified Property (2.B.a.)	Prohibitions against gifts prior to declaration of bankruptcy
6) Pure property with ownership restrictions (alienable rights) (2.A.b.)	Liquor; taxis in New York City; volunteer army
7) Pure property with required use (3.A.a.)	Historical preservation laws
8) Pure property with limited use (4.A.a.)	Automobiles; land use zoning
9) Pure property with coercive use (alienable duties) (5.A.a.)	Natural resource rights that must be used or lost; army draft in the United States Civil War

II. EFFICIENCY AND EQUITY RATIONALES

A. *Overview of the Argument*

The objectives of this Article are primarily normative. I do not attempt to explain why any particular legal restriction was enacted into law. Instead, I ask whether plausible justifications can be given for some frequently observed legal patterns. This Part concentrates on three broad normative claims. First, the existence of transaction costs will frequently make a simple system of property-liability rules inefficient,[8] so that more restrictive regulations such as inalienability rules may have merit. Second, distributive goals cannot always be achieved by simple lump sum transfers but may require more intrusive policies. Third, even when inalienability rules are justified on efficiency grounds,

8. See Coase, The Problem of Social Cost, 3 J.L. & Econ. 1 (1960) (arguing that in the absence of transaction costs any clear cut allocation of property rights will be efficient); see also Cooter, The Cost of Coase, 11 J. Legal Stud. 1 (1982) (exploring the implications of the proposition).

compensation may be required to avoid imposing concentrated costs on particular individuals or groups.

The efficiency rationales for inalienability rules are second-best responses to market failures that arise because of externalities, imperfections in information, or difficulties of coordination. The straightforward responses of internalizing the externality through fees or taxes, of subsidizing the provision of information, and of facilitating joint action may, for one reason or another, be costly. In such cases, the alternative of restricting market trades becomes a realistic possibility. Instead of correcting the market failure through policies that rely on price incentives and market processes, inalienability rules address the difficulty with a set of prohibited or required actions that make market incentives less, rather than more, important. I consider each of the three types of market failure in turn.

Externalities figure prominently in discussions of market failure and provide the most commonly recognized rationale for inalienability rules. Production and consumption externalities occur when the profits of firms or the satisfaction levels of individuals are affected by transactions in which they are not directly involved. These third parties would be willing to pay to obtain the benefits or to avoid the harms imposed on them, but because they are not part of the transaction, benefits are too low and costs are too high. For example, in the absence of regulation, a factory may create water pollution as part of its production process because it need not account for the harm caused by pollution. Economists generally seek to control externalities by creating market-like incentives through tax and subsidy schemes that encourage firms and individuals to respond to marginal shifts in costs and benefits.[9] Economic analysts have also recognized that other alternatives that involve the definition or rearrangement of property rights may be equally satisfactory. Thus, externality problems may be solved by "internalizing" them or by providing "separate facilities" solutions. Under the former, a single individual is given title to both the property causing the externality and the property affected by it. So long as this does not create monopoly power, the new owner will have an incentive to behave efficiently.[10] Under the latter, property relations are rearranged so that externality producers are separated from those who would suffer from the externality.[11]

Unfortunately, optimality may be difficult to achieve in a world

9. Any standard text in microeconomics or public finance discusses the public pricing of externalities. See, e.g., R. Musgrave & P. Musgrave, Public Finance in Theory and Practice 692–715 (2d ed. 1976). For applications to environmental pollution, see Economics of the Environment (R. Dorfman & N. Dorfman 2d ed. 1977); A. Freeman, R. Haveman & A. Kneese, The Economics of Environmental Policy (1973).

10. See, e.g., Sweeney, Tollison & Willett, supra note 3, at 186–88 (analyzing oil pools).

11. See E. Mishan, The Costs of Economic Growth 80–99 (1967).

with high transaction costs. Even a tort law system that places liability on the person who can most efficiently reduce the harm[12] may not be effective in all situations, and taxes and subsidies may be difficult to implement because of political opposition or inadequate information.[13] In the second-best world faced by regulators, there will be room for direct regulation of behavior. For example, suppose there is a strong statistical relationship between some characteristic of the user of a product and an external cost. Ex post, however, causation may be difficult to establish in particular cases. Moreover, even if causation can be established, the individuals may not be wealthy enough to pay the claims against them. If a large portion of the class of individuals is involved, then the most effective way of reducing external costs may be to prevent the entire group (e.g., blind people and children) from using the product (e.g., driving an automobile). Similarly, other types of externalities can be prevented by regulating the use of a product. Speed limits and traffic signals control driving over and above tort law rules that penalize negligent behavior.

Markets also frequently work poorly because information is imperfect and asymmetrical. This kind of market failure provides a second, and less widely recognized, rationale for inalienability rules in particular contexts. First, consider information asymmetries. If buyers are unaware of product defects, then high quality sellers cannot command higher prices than low quality sellers, and there may be a general deterioration in quality. A second information problem arises when two products look alike but one can be legally possessed while the other cannot. For example, laws protecting rare birds prohibit the taking of specimens after a set date but permit possession of those killed in the past. We can then expect suppliers fraudulently to claim that their illegal products actually fall into the legal category. Buyers are not harmed by this misrepresentation but some other policy is undermined. A modified inalienability rule—permitting gifts but not sales—may resolve both of these problems.[14]

Finally, difficulties of coordination may cause resources to be allocated inefficiently. This problem is closely related to the more pervasive problem of externalities, but because it has several distinctive features. I consider it as a separate category. The coordination problem arises most clearly in the case of pure public goods—urban parkland, for example—consumed in common by a large group. No one has an incentive to provide the efficient amount of this good because

12. See G. Calabresi, The Costs of Accidents (1970) (recommending that liability be placed on the cheapest cost avoider).

13. For a discussion of some of the problems with pricing policies, see Rose-Ackerman, Effluent Charges: A Critique, 6 Can. J. Econ. 512 (1973); Rose-Ackerman, Market Models for Water Pollution Control: Their Strengths and Weaknesses, 25 Pub. Pol. 383 (1977).

14. See infra notes 25–29 and accompanying text.

the supplier bears all the costs and receives only a fraction of the benefits. Outlawing sales but permitting gifts is one way to achieve conservation while retaining considerable freedom for private action.[15] Closely analogous to this case is the "prisoner's dilemma": all would benefit from coordinated action, but in the absence of coercion, independent action is inefficient. Consider, for example, the problem of coordinating the development of a new geographical region. Everyone is better off if other people have settled first, but no one has an incentive to be the first settler. To alleviate this problem, policymakers may attach coercive conditions such as a requirement that owners actually live on and develop the land in order to perfect their title.[16]

More narrowly focused coordination problems arise in controlling the opportunistic behavior of a person who purports to act on behalf of another. An inalienability rule may mitigate these problems when the law that directly controls the parties' relationship is inadequate. The law protects creditors, for instance, by preventing a person close to bankruptcy from giving away assets. Similarly, mineral leases that require payment of royalties equal to a percentage of the mining profits may include diligence requirements to induce leaseholders to search for resources.

The imposition of restrictions on alienability will, of course, generally have distributive as well as efficiency consequences. While analysts primarily concerned with efficiency may view a policy's redistributive impact as an unwelcome side effect, sometimes the distributive effects of a rule will be its primary justification. Because restrictions on transferability, ownership, and use single out a particular type of good or service for special treatment, these restrictions usually cannot be justified on broad redistributive grounds. Rather, the distributive case for inalienability is more narrowly focused. If policymakers wish to benefit a particular sort of person but cannot easily identify these people ex ante, they may be able to impose restrictions on the entitlement that are less onerous for the worthy group than for others who are nominally eligible. For example, the coercive conditions imposed on the use of land under the Homesteading Acts can be justified as a means of ensuring that the resource was transferred only to worthy recipients—in this case, formerly landless people willing to live on and farm the property for several years.[17]

Restraints on alienation also may have redistributive effects incidental to the primary justification for the policy. Restrictions justified on efficiency grounds frequently impose costs on a small or concentrated group, such as owners of land that has been down-zoned or owners of distilling equipment under Prohibition. Therefore, policymakers

15. See infra notes 21–24 and accompanying text.

16. See infra notes 73–77 and accompanying text.

17. See infra notes 81–82 and accompanying text.

must decide whether to compensate these losers. In some cases, the appropriate response to redistributive effects will be straightforward. Where policymakers believe that the affected group deserves to bear the costs of the policy, there should be no compensation. The group might, for example, be composed of people earning monopoly profits. Although economic discussions of monopoly power commonly stress the inefficiencies of markets with a single seller, a basic distributive principle generally seems to lurk behind these analyses. The principle is this: except as a reward for risk-taking, no one is entitled to profits that exceed the competitive rate of return because of market imperfections. Economic rents or earnings above this level can be confiscated by the state for redistribution to others.[18] Compensation is also not justified if the owners accepted the risk of the restriction at the time of purchase. This expectation will have been reflected in the original purchase price, and it would be redundant to compensate the owners further.[19] Conversely, compensation will be appropriate where there is no principled reason for the group to bear the costs of the policy and where doing so would not undermine the effectiveness of the restriction. For example, compensating owners of historic buildings for the costs of maintaining the structure's historical value would spread these costs among taxpayers without defeating the purpose of the restriction on use.[20]

Fundamental policy conflicts arise, however, when a group does not deserve to bear the costs of the restraint but where compensation would undermine the purpose of the restriction. For example, compensating blood donors for the fact that they cannot sell their blood would convert the process into something similar to a market trade and would undermine the use of a modified inalienability rule to assure high quality blood supplies. If the distributive costs are believed to be high in such situations, policymakers should consider alternatives to inalienability rules.

These issues are addressed first in the context of rules that restrict the transferability of entitlements (i.e., modified inalienability and modified property rules). I then examine rules that limit ownership and use and that may require certain actions as a condition for retaining a property right. Throughout the analysis I point first to market failures that may justify the use of inalienability rules and then discuss the most important distributive consequences.

18. Without this principle, antitrust laws and statutes that regulate public utilities would require the state to compensate monopolists for their loss of monopoly power. See Rose-Ackerman, Unfair Competition and Corporate Income Taxation, 34 Stan. L. Rev. 1017 (1982) (applying this argument in the context of competition between non-profit and for-profit firms).

19. See Blume & Rubinfeld, Compensation for Takings: An Economic Analysis, 72 Calif. L. Rev. 569 (1984); Wittman, Liability for Harm or Restitution for Benefit?, 13 J. Legal Stud. 57, 65–66 (1984).

20. See infra notes 63–64 and accompanying text.

B. *Modified Inalienability Rule*

Modified inalienability provides a useful starting point because of the range of possible rationales for permitting gifts while outlawing sales. The most important efficiency justifications are: (1) conservation and supply management; (2) the regulation of close substitutes; and (3) the assurance of high quality output. I argue that each of the efficiency claims has merit in a restrictive range of circumstances but that using modified inalienability to achieve distributive goals is unjustified except to prevent monopoly gains.

1. *Conservation and Supply Management.* — The law may sometimes prohibit payment of suppliers because of the very responsiveness of supply to price that is the hallmark of a properly functioning market. The problem is an inefficiency caused by the market itself. If market trades are permitted, supply will be larger than under a modified inalienability rule. Suppose, however, that high levels of supply impose external costs on society, which are not reflected in market price. Outlawing sales is then a possible way to improve the allocation of resources. Two examples will illustrate this point: population control and the conservation of wild animals and primitive cultures.

Those concerned with the social costs of overpopulation may wish to restrict the freedom of individuals to decide how many children to bring into the world. They may not only support family planning, subsidized abortions, and birth control but also oppose a legalized market in adoptions. They may want to prohibit the sale of babies for fear that women will produce children for profit, thus exacerbating the problem of overpopulation. As Robert Pritchard notes, however, the prohibition has resulted in shortages of newborn children available for adoption, thereby "leaving many couples deprived of the privileges and joys of child rearing."[21] Thus he raises the issue of concentrated costs to justify using the market even in this context. The difficulty with this argument is that even with a legal adoption market some people will be unable to adopt children because the price will be too high. All adoption policies have distributive consequences for both parents and children. It is not at all obvious, for example, that children themselves would generally be worse off if the sale of newborn infants were permitted. So long as an adoption market is not ruled out ex ante on moral

21. Pritchard, A Market for Babies?, 34 U. Toronto L.J. 341, 342 (1984). But cf. Landes & Posner, The Economics of the Baby Shortage, 7 J. Legal Stud. 323 (1978) (defending a market for adopted children). The "sale" of children is not entirely illegal. Although outright sales are forbidden, "family compacts" in which a mother gives up her child in return for promises of monetary support either for herself or for herself and her child have been upheld in some jurisdictions so long as the arrangement promotes the child's welfare. See, e.g., Clark v. Clark, 122 Md. 114, 89 A. 405 (1913) (mother permitted to give up her child to her wealthy father-in-law in return for his agreement to support the mother for life); Enders v. Enders, 164 Pa. 266, 30 A. 129 (1894) (upholding a grandfather's promise to raise his grandson in return for payments to his son's wife and to the child).

grounds, the issues are largely empirical: How responsive is supply to price? What would be the impact on children and on prospective parents? How would the costs and benefits be distributed?

Consider next the conservation of wild animals. Conservation objectives may be furthered by preventing the commercial exploitation of endangered species through laws that permit the use of the resource for fun (or survival), but not for profit. The best American example is the regulation of wild fish and game resources. It would not violate public policy with respect to fish and game if a hunter, while on a vacation trip, happened to be lucky, shot more pheasants than he could use, and sold a few to friends. If sales were permitted, however, other people might decide to take up hunting because of the profitable opportunities available. Thus, a number of states have rules against sales.[22] These laws facilitate conservation by discouraging the entry of profit seeking hunters or fishermen.

A similar problem arises when the state wishes to preserve a group's way of life. Once again, a modified inalienability rule can help accomplish this aim. Recent federal laws and treaties preserve the right of Eskimos and other Alaskan natives to hunt certain kinds of game in spite of more stringent controls on the general public.[23] These native groups are, however, sometimes prohibited from selling their catch.[24] Without such a prohibition, outsiders and profit-motivated tribal leaders might invest in the tribe's activities and in the process both destroy tribal life and undermine the conservationist aims of the general prohibitions.

22. See, e.g., Me. Rev. Stat. Ann. tit. 12, §§ 7452(9)(A), 7456(5), 7457(3), 7615 (1964 & Supp. 1984–85); N.Y. Envtl. Conserv. Law §§ 11-0536, -1319(2), -1705(10), -1729 (McKinney 1984 & Supp. 1984–85); Tex. Parks & Wild. Code Ann. §§ 65.102, 66.111, 76.039 (Vernon 1976 & Supp. 1985); Wis. Stat. Ann. §§ 29.415(4), 29.48 (West 1976 & Supp. 1984–85); cf. Mass. Ann. Laws ch. 131, §§ 22, 25, 26A (Michie/Law. Co-op. 1972 & Supp. 1985) (excepting a few fur-bearing animals); Va. Code §§ 29-154, -161.1, -164 (1979 & Supp. 1984) (same).

23. Eskimos are explicitly exempted from some provisions of both the Endangered Species Act of 1973, 16 U.S.C. § 1539(e) (1982), and the Marine Mammal Protection Act of 1972, 16 U.S.C. § 1371(b) (1982). Certain treaties permit American Indians to take migratory bird species for food and clothing but not for sale. See Convention Between the United States and Great Britain for the Protection of Migratory Birds, Aug. 16, 1916, art. II, § (1), (3), 39 Stat. 1702, T.S. No. 628; Convention for the Protection of Migratory Birds and Birds in Danger of Extinction and Their Environment, Mar. 4, 1972, art. III, § 1(e), 25 U.S.T. 3329, T.I.A.S. No. 7990. Only one federal law gives Indians an explicit exemption. See Bald Eagle Act of 1940, ch. 278, § 4, 54 Stat. 251 (codified as amended at 16 U.S.C. § 668a (1982)) (allowing Indians to obtain permits to kill eagles for religious purposes). See generally Coggins & Modroin, Native American Indians and Federal Wildlife Law, 31 Stan. L. Rev. 375 (1979) (exploring the conflict between Indian rights and federal wildlife law).

24. Under both the Endangered Species Act and the Marine Mammal Protection Act, Alaskan natives may hunt endangered or threatened species if these are used "primarily" for subsistence or are made into "authentic native articles of handicrafts and clothing." 16 U.S.C. §§ 1317(b), 1539(e) (1982).

2. *Regulating Close Substitutes.* — Sometimes a free market has no adverse effects on the production and distribution of a good but instead complicates some other public policy. For example, if it is difficult for buyers and law enforcement officials to distinguish between a forbidden good and a close substitute, preventing sale of the substitute can aid enforcement of a law against possession or transfer of the forbidden good. To illustrate, consider the use of modified inalienability rules in the Endangered Species Act and the Migratory Bird Treaties. Since there is apparently no reliable way to date stuffed animals, fur, feathers,[25] and most other animal products, enforcement is simplified if the law prohibits all sales of a species, not just the sale of animals killed after the law's effective date.[26]

When a modified inalienability rule makes the administration of a law inexpensive and convenient, there is a strong argument for compensating those who find that their possessions have unexpectedly fallen in value. Otherwise the state would not need to take into account

---

25. See Andrus v. Allard, 444 U.S. 51, 58 (1979). Plaintiffs, however, claimed that even if feathers could not be dated, "feathered artifacts" (e.g., Indian headdresses) could be dated. Id.

26. In United States v. Richards, 583 F.2d 491 (10th Cir. 1978), both the majority and the dissent recognized that an Interior Department rule defining migratory birds to include those raised in captivity is administratively convenient "since it is impossible in most cases to determine whether the bird in the hunter's bag is one raised in captivity or taken from the wild." Id. at 497 (Logan, J., dissenting). The court upheld the regulation and rejected the argument that prohibiting sales of captive birds would reduce the supply. Id. at 496.

In Delbay Pharmaceuticals v. Department of Commerce, 409 F. Supp. 637 (D.D.C. 1976), brought under the Endangered Species Act, the Commerce Department seized Delbay's inventory of imported spermaceti. Delbay argued that it should be able to sell its spermaceti because it was imported before the law went into effect. In rejecting Delbay's claim, the court emphasized administrative difficulties: "If plaintiff's spermaceti were allowed to enter interstate commerce, it could greatly increase the enforcement difficulties. A total ban is easier to enforce than a partial ban. If there were a continued market in this country for spermaceti, it might encourage the illegal taking of sperm whales to supply this market." Id. at 642.

Similarly, in Andrus v. Allard, 444 U.S. 51 (1979), the Supreme Court upheld a prohibition on the sale of eagles and products made of eagle feathers even though the eagles were killed before the law went into effect. Gift giving, however, was expressly permitted by the Court. See id. at 66; see also United States v. Hamel, 534 F.2d 1354, 1356 (9th Cir. 1976) (requiring government to prove that a bird was killed after the Migratory Bird Treaty Act took effect would undermine the purpose of the Act).

An early district court decision, in contrast, rejected administrative convenience as a rationale for the Migratory Bird Treaty Act. See United States v. Fuld Store Co., 262 F. 836 (D. Mont. 1920). In upholding a person's right to hold and sell items made from heron feathers, the court argued that "[a]n intent on the part of Congress to virtually outlaw and destroy such property ought not to be assumed, unless very clear and the only reasonable construction of the act; for it is very doubtful if Congress has any such power . . . . [S]ome incidental advantage in administration of the law . . . avails nothing." Id. at 837-38; see also In re Informations Under Migratory Bird Treaty Act, 281 F. 546 (D. Mont. 1922) (construing Act not to apply to transactions involving birds taken before effective date).

the full costs of its policy, and a group that is unlucky enough to own a close substitute for the regulated product bears a disproportionate share of the cost. The case of *Andrus v. Allard*[27] provides an example. The statutes at issue prohibited the killing of eagles after a certain date. To ease the administration of the statutes, the Secretary of the Interior issued regulations prohibiting the sale of eagles killed before that date. The effect of the prohibition was to reduce the value of Indian artifacts made of "old" eagles by changing the owners' legal entitlement from a pure property rule to a modified inalienability rule. The owners challenged the statutes on the grounds that they constituted an unconstitutional "taking" of property requiring payment of compensation.[28]

The Supreme Court accepted the administrative convenience rationale behind the Interior Department regulations and rejected the owners' compensation claims on the ground that no "taking" had occurred. The government had not "physical[ly] inva[ded]" the owners' property, and had prevented only "one means of disposing of the artifacts."[29] The Court, however, never directly faced the important issue of whether the payment of compensation would undermine the reasons for promulgating the rule in the first place. In particular, in setting up a compensation scheme, the Interior Department would have faced the problem of distinguishing between legitimate holders of "old" eagle feathers and those making dishonest claims. In fact, however, a number of alternatives were open to the Interior Department that would have provided some form of compensation without undermining the legislative purpose. Before the protective law took effect, for example, holders of eagles and eagle feathers could have been required to obtain licenses certifying the legality of their holdings. Sales would then have been legal only if owners had licenses. Alternatively, the government might have stood ready to purchase all specimens presented to it by a certain date, or licensed holders could have retained possession but been paid compensation.

3. *Quality Control.* — In an influential book on human blood, Richard Titmuss[30] argues for modified inalienability on quality control

27. 444 U.S. 51 (1979).

28. Id.

29. Id. at 65. In addition to possession and transportation of their property, the owners could also "donate or devise the protected birds" and could "exhibit the artifacts for an admissions charge." Id. at 66.

In a related case involving a man who raised falcons, a court determined that because the defendant raised hawks under permits—first from Wisconsin and then from Utah—"[h]is permissive possession of the birds did not carry with it the traditional incidences of property rights. . . . At the most the states granted a partial property interest which did not encompass all usual property rights." United States v. Richards, 583 F.2d 491, 498 (10th Cir. 1978). Accordingly, the claim of unconstitutional deprivation of property was denied.

30. R. Titmuss, The Gift Relationship: From Human Blood to Social Policy (1971).

grounds. The argument, developed further by Kenneth Arrow,[31] views modified inalienability as a response to the general problems created by markets with imperfect information. If it is difficult for hospitals to judge whether blood contains the damaging hepatitis virus, while individuals know their own health history, then ideally one would design a collection system that gives contributors an incentive to reveal any past cases of hepatitis.[32] On the one hand, if people are paid for their blood, they may try to hide damaging information. On the other hand, if they are induced to donate their blood for altruistic reasons, those who have had hepatitis presumably will not make contributions. Of course, there may well be other systems of property rights—such as sale followed by liability for damages,[33] labelling by source,[34] or more careful selection of donors[35]—that respond to the quality control problem. But a purely voluntary system is, at the very least, a method worthy of serious consideration.[36]

---

31. Arrow, Gifts and Exchanges, 1 Phil. & Pub. Aff. 343 (1972).

32. New tests do permit better screening for hepatitis A and B, but existing procedures are still not effective for Non-A, Non-B hepatitis. See Non-A, Non-B Hepatitis, 2 The Lancet 1077 (1984). Recent concern about the transmission of AIDS through blood transfusion has raised similar issues even in the context of donated blood. See Chase, "Gift of Life" May Be Also an Agent of Death in Some AIDS Cases, Wall St. J., Mar. 12, 1984, at 1, col. 1; Results of AIDS Tests, N.Y. Times, Mar. 26, 1985, at C2, col. 5 (describing a new test that is still not completely reliable).

33. See Kessel, Transfused Blood, Serum Hepatitis, and the Coase Theorem, 17 J.L. & Econ. 265 (1974).

34. Food and Drug Administration regulations require blood to be labeled "paid donor" or "volunteer donor." R. Scott, The Body as Property 194 (1981).

35. See M. Cooper & A. Culyer, The Price of Blood (1968); Sapolsky & Finkelstein, Blood Policy Revisited—A New Look at "The Gift Relationship," 46 Pub. Interest 15 (1977).

36. The law on this subject varies. The Uniform Anatomical Gift Act (UAGA), 8A U.L.A. 15 (1983), which has been adopted by all fifty states and the District of Columbia, treats only gifts from dead bodies; it does not resolve the legal status of sales from either the living or the dead. A commissioner's note to § 3 states: "The statutes in a few states specify that no donor shall ask compensation and no donee shall receive it. Several statutes provide that storage banks shall be non-profit organizations. On the other hand, most of the states have chosen not to deal with this question. The Uniform Act follows the latter course in this regard." Id. at 41; see also Stason, The Uniform Anatomical Gift Act, 23 Bus. Law. 919, 927–28 (1968) (noting that the UAGA does not address the issue of payment for gifts of body parts); cf. Note, Retailing Human Organs Under the Uniform Commercial Code, 16 J. Mar. L. Rev. 393 (1983) (advocating amendments to the UAGA to permit the sale of organs).

Russell Scott reports that in the late 1960s, Nevada, Delaware, Hawaii, New York, and Oklahoma passed laws banning payment to a person while alive for his or her body parts after death, but these laws did not prohibit the sale of the organs by next of kin. R. Scott, supra note 34, at 190. In 1969, Mississippi "authorized its citizens to sell their body parts to hospitals, which were given the right to take possession upon death. Breach of the contract necessitated repayment of the money plus interest at six percent." Id. In 1969, Massachusetts "prohibited payment to any person for any cadaver organ." Id. Scott goes on to note that most of these restrictions were abolished when the UAGA was passed "since the act was believed to exclude all sales," id., an interpreta-

The argument for modified inalienability, however, is not without weaknesses. First of all, the quality control benefits of gift giving operate only on the *supply* side of the market. Thus, once the blood has been collected, there is no quality control argument against selling the blood to patients.[37] One cannot contend that paying customers are generally less likely to make effective use of blood transfusions than are other users. Such a dual system may not be feasible, however. Quite simply, gifts may not be forthcoming if donors know that the collection agency is selling their gifts[38] and do not consider the collection agency to be a worthwhile charity.[39] Second, even if the blood is of high quality, the supply of donations may be insufficient to meet the demand. This problem can be mitigated by paying donors' expenses,[40] insuring them against future medical complications,[41] or providing other forms of compensation that lower the cost of donating without permitting individuals to profit financially from their blood.[42] Since such expedients may not always be effective, however, undersupply may continue to be a serious potential problem.

Moreover, even if a system of voluntary blood donations proves workable, the Titmuss proposal should not be unthinkingly generalized. Blood is a very special commodity. Once a person gives or sells some blood, more is produced "automatically" so long as the person has not sold or given away so much as to injure his health. The quality of the blood produced is not affected by the price at which it can be

---

tion at odds with that of the commissioners. The Delaware UAGA explicitly prohibits sales. See Del. Code Ann. tit. 24, § 1783(f) (1981).

37. See M. Cooper & A. Culyer, supra note 35; cf. G. Calabresi & P. Bobbitt, Tragic Choices 19–22 (1978) (distinguishing between first- and second-order determinations, i.e., between how much will be produced and who will get it).

38. See R. Titmuss, supra note 30, at 151 ("Altruistic donors can hardly be expected to give their blood to profit-making hospitals.").

39. This problem is not unsolvable. One could, for example, imagine churchs or day care centers raising money by selling donated blood just as they now sell donated food, clothing, and household goods. Blood banks could merge with charities or give their proceeds to the United Way.

40. See Council of Europe, Committee of Ministers, Harmonisation of Legislations of Member States Relating to Removal Grafting and Transplantation of Human Substances, Resolution (78)28, adopted 11 May 1978 & explanatory memorandum 29. Article 9 states that "[n]o substance may be offered for profit. However, loss of earnings and any expenses caused by the removal or preceding examination may be refunded." Council of Europe, Committee of Ministers, International Exchange and Transportation of Human Substances, Recommendation R(79)5, adopted 14 Mar. 1979 & explanatory memorandum, favors outlawing sales of human tissue but authorizes payment for shipping expenses.

41. See, e.g., Comment, California's Response to the Problem of Procuring Human Remains for Transplantation, 57 Calif. L. Rev. 671, 692 (1969) (recommending that both donors and patients be insured).

42. Compensation may take the form of promises to supply blood in the future if donors or their families need it, or to make gifts in the donors' names to charities of their choice. R. Titmuss, supra note 30, at 78–88.

sold, and the quantity inside people's veins is always sufficient to meet the demand. Thus, the only quality control problem is the proper *selection* of suppliers. Furthermore, with the exception of a few people with rare blood types, there is no monopoly power problem.[43] Suppose, in contrast, that the market for used cars were outlawed and the Salvation Army encouraged people to donate cars for distribution to the needy. Since cars do not spontaneously regenerate themselves in the garages of the altruistic, it appears unlikely that many high quality cars will be given away. Yet automobiles are like blood in that individual owners know more about the quality of their cars than the buyers or donees can easily find out.[44] Even if a purely voluntary system would induce people with "lemons" to throw them away rather than donate them, the overall quantity and quality of used cars would be low.[45] As another example, suppose that the military only wanted patriotic fighters to join the armed forces but had no good way to test for patriotism. It might try accordingly to establish a volunteer army that paid only subsistence wages. This plan would be unlikely, however, to attract more than a few super-patriots, and most volunteers might instead be unemployed people with very low skill levels.

4. *Blood, Body Parts, and Fairness.* — Many people oppose the sale of blood to patients on the ground that it is unfair to allocate a basic necessity of life on the basis of ability to pay. In a competitive market, this argument seems difficult to sustain for two reasons. First, the distributive arguments against sales may not be strong enough to overcome the inefficiency of nonmarket transactions. Making free a good that actually has an opportunity cost will produce excess demand, since the value of the good to marginal consumers will exceed its marginal cost. If, in addition, suppliers are not reimbursed, quantity will be inefficiently low. Second, there may not be any distributive reason for treating the good in question differently from close substitutes. Artificial limbs are for sale, but not real kidneys. On purely distributive grounds it seems unfair to treat people whose problem requires a mechanical or chemical solution differently from those who need living tissue. In the field of health, such distinctions seem particularly problematic, since most people are covered by public or private health

43. Cf. United States v. Garber, 607 F.2d 92 (5th Cir. 1979) (tax treatment of the earnings of a woman whose blood plasma contained a rare antigen useful to drug manufacturers).

44. The problem of low quality used cars forcing good ones out of the marketplace is analyzed in Akerlof, The Market for "Lemons": Quality Uncertainty and the Market Mechanism, 84 Q.J. Econ. 488 (1970).

45. Cf. Rottenberg, The Production and Exchange of Used Body Parts, *in* 2 Toward Liberty: Essays in Honor of Ludwig von Mises 322 (1971). Rottenberg criticizes doctors who refuse to transplant purchased organs or use purchased blood. "It is as though a coalition of plumbers had agreed that none of them would install bathroom fixtures that a household had secured in exchange for money but only those altruistically given away by appliance manufacturers." Id. at 327.

insurance.[46]

If the market is not competitive, however, the distributive arguments against sales may have more merit. The monopoly power issue arises most clearly in the provision of human tissue. Because overall supply is not affected by market structure, monopoly power only affects the distribution of benefits between donor and donee. Thus, if tissue typing shows that your kidney is the best one to transplant into your cousin, a bilateral monopoly situation is created,[47] and if sales are permitted, you might hold out for a large payment in return for saving your cousin's life. Similarly, some types of rare antibodies are only available from a few people and are extremely valuable in the production of certain drugs.[48] In such contexts, an entirely unregulated market could have undesirable distributive consequences if people exercise their monopoly over scarce bodily tissues and antibodies at the expense of the sick. Prohibiting sales is not, however, the only response to the problem. One could instead imitate the policy followed in more conventional cases of monopoly power by permitting sales but regulating prices so that they reflect the marginal costs and risks borne by the donor.[49]

C. *Modified Property Rule*

In contrast to modified inalienablity rules, modified property rules are relatively uncommon and apply to particular situations rather than types of goods and services. Under such rules, property may be sold at market prices but cannot be given away. Most commonly, modified

46. Even if a persuasive argument can be made against selling the entitlement to users, it may still be possible to obtain some of the benefits of market transactions by having the state purchase the good or service from suppliers for free distribution to the public based on nonmarket criteria. Thus, if there is an inadequate supply of organs from cadavers for transplant under an entirely voluntary system, people could be paid by the state for promising to donate their organs with the allocation based on medical judgment. Of course, if this change in practice substantially increases supply, then the need for difficult distributive choices by hospitals and doctors will be reduced since supply will more nearly equal demand. For proposals along these lines, see Brams, Transplantable Human Organs: Should Their Sale Be Authorized by State Statutes?, 3 Am. J.L. & Med. 183 (1977); Dukeminier, Supplying Organs for Transplantation, 68 Mich. L. Rev. 811 (1970); Sanders & Dukeminier, Medical Advance and Legal Lag: Hemodialysis and Kidney Transplantation, 15 UCLA L. Rev. 357 (1968); Note, Compulsory Removal of Cadaver Organs, 69 Colum. L. Rev. 693 (1969); Note, The Sale of Human Body Parts, 72 Mich. L. Rev. 1182 (1974).

47. See, e.g., Strunk v. Strunk, 445 S.W.2d 145 (Ky. 1969); McFall v. Shimp, 10 Pa. D. & C.3d 90 (1978).

48. See, e.g., United States v. Garber, 607 F.2d 92 (5th Cir. 1979).

49. Of course, other personal attributes that give people monopoly rents are not so regulated: great beauties, highly skilled athletes, and geniuses frequently earn monopoly profits. One problem with taxing the returns to beauty, strength, and intelligence, however, is that individuals should be given an incentive to develop their natural gifts. In contrast, although people can be compensated for the time, trouble, and risk of organ removal, they cannot affect their tissue type.

property rules have been imposed on people who are either insolvent or about to die. In both cases, these rules solve problems that arise because someone with an interest in the property has no formal legal claim until some event, i.e., bankruptcy or death, occurs. These difficulties are examples of the agency-principal problems familiar to economic analysts in contexts as different as shareholder control of corporate managers and the relationship between insurance companies and their customers.[50] The restriction on gifts substitutes for laws that directly control the relationship between the parties. The modified property rule is a second-best way of recognizing the property interests of creditors, heirs, and tax collectors in situations where the nominal owner may choose to overlook their claims.

Consider bankruptcy law first. Gifts made before a declaration of bankruptcy are condemned as "fraudulent conveyances," but sales of assets are legal so long as "reasonably equivalent value" is received.[51] Without this restriction on gifts, a person who became insolvent could simply give away all his assets to family and friends, go bankrupt, and then accept reciprocal gifts from them afterwards. This practice would introduce an element of risk into the making of loans that would serve no productive purpose. Ex ante the volume of loans would be inefficiently low and interest rates inefficiently high to take account of this possibility of hiding assets from creditors.

In contrast, prohibitions on gifts made close to the time of death can be justified mainly on distributive grounds. Originally, such rules protected heirs against pressure applied by clerics and doctors to dying relatives.[52] At present, the laws of most states and the federal government do not prevent gifts made close to the time of death. However, a weak form of modified property rule remains the legal standard for death related transactions: certain gifts made within three years of death are treated as part of one's estate for tax purposes. The purpose of this rule is to protect the state against the tax avoidance activities of

50. See, e.g., Ross, The Economic Theory of Agency: The Principal's Problem, 63 Am. Econ. Rev. (Papers & Proceedings) 134 (1973); Shavell, Risk Sharing and Incentives in the Principal and Agent Relationship, 10 Bell J. of Econ. 55 (1979).

51. 11 U.S.C. § 548(a) (1982). See generally J. Hanna & J. MacLachlan, Cases & Materials on Creditors' Rights and Corporate Reorganization 204–22, 233–55 (1957) (discussing the Uniform Fraudulent Conveyance Act and providing excerpts from the leading cases).

52. In Louisiana, for example, gifts to either doctors or "ministers of religious worship" cannot be made by a sick person who dies of his illness. The person may, however, pay for services rendered. La. Civ. Code Ann. art. 1489 (West 1952). In Georgia, no one with a spouse or child may devise more than one-third of her estate to charitable or religious institutions if the will is executed within 90 days of the person's death. Ga. Code Ann. § 53-2-10 (1982). Similarly, old treatises on gifts note that a gift to one's "spiritual adviser" will be regarded with suspicion by courts especially if made *mortis causa*. See, e.g., W. Thornton, A Treatise on the Law Relating to Gifts and Advancements 456 (1893).

dying individuals and their heirs.[53]

D. *Limits on Ownership and Use*

Restrictions on ownership and use will sometimes be effective second-best substitutes for more flexible, incentive-based systems of externality control. In this section, I consider a wide range of such restrictions, from limits on who may drive automobiles to controls on the use of historic buildings and undeveloped land. In practice, of course, externality control is not a central reason for many existing limitations. Instead, they are based on paternalistic motives or are blatantly designed to create monopoly rents. My purpose is not to justify such restrictions but rather to indicate the narrow range of cases where economic efficiency may be furthered by limiting who may use or own a product and what may be done with it.

1. *Restrictions on Ownership*. — Ownership restrictions work in conjunction with the tort law system to prevent conduct dangerous to third parties.[54] They prevent groups of people, e.g., people under sixteen or those with diabetes, from owning certain goods or engaging in certain activities, e.g., purchasing liquor, driving a car, or obtaining a pilot's license. Inalienability rules of this kind are second-best methods of control because they treat all members of a group alike. These restrictions thus are likely to be both over- and underinclusive. In contrast, a tort law system, requiring compensation ex post, can be sensitive to individual differences in behavior but may be costly and time-consuming to implement. In practice, we have a mixed system which combines ex ante restrictions with ex post liability. Tort law emphasizes those practices that are inherently most difficult to measure ex ante. For example, while tests of driving ability, knowledge of traffic laws, and color blindness determine who will obtain a driver's license, the possibility of a tort suit after an accident is likely to deter people from driving carelessly.

The use of statistical evidence to sort out applicants is efficacious if the measuring rod is directly related to behavior. Proxies are often used, however, because of measurement difficulties. Simple criteria such as age can often be understood as substitutes for more complex criteria such as health status or ability where problems of measurement

53. In recent years the consolidation of the gift and estate tax systems has mooted the problem of determining intent. Yet, since the federal government taxes gifts differently from sales, it becomes important to define a sale. Within three years of death, the IRS will scrutinize sales to be sure that "adequate consideration" in money or money's worth has been received. If the IRS is not satisfied, the balance will be taxed as if it were a gift. See T. Englebrecht, M. Moore & A. Fowler, Federal Taxation of Estates, Gifts and Trusts 61–66 (1981).

54. See generally Calabresi, Torts—The Law of the Mixed Society, 56 Tex. L. Rev. 519 (1978) (examining the roles of the tort system and direct regulation of behavior in controlling risk).

ex ante and of attributing causation ex post are likely to be serious. Thus, if there is a strong statistical relationship between the age of an automobile driver and the probability of being in an accident, the state can forbid people below a certain age from driving cars instead of designing a costly individualized test to sort out the careful children. Costs are imposed on careful children by this method of accident prevention, but they must be balanced against the costs of more discriminating tests.[55]

There are limits to this method, however. We seem to be reluctant to use statistical patterns to distinguish between people on the basis of demographic criteria beyond their control. Thus, we do not allow white women to drive at an earlier age than males and blacks, even though the statistical evidence shows that white women are safer drivers.[56] Age, however, is less suspect than race or gender since all people age at the same rate and is, therefore, frequently used as a basis for distributing benefits and burdens. Furthermore, even though a demographic characteristic is something over which an individual has no control, it may still be used to distinguish between people if the causal link is well established and close to being deterministic. Thus, diabetics may be prevented from obtaining commercial pilots' licenses or driving trucks with hazardous cargoes, and color-blind people may be unable to obtain drivers' licenses.[57]

Ideally, people should be compensated for unfair burdens resulting from the use of statistical regularities instead of individual behavior. Compensation is impossible, however, for just the reason that statistical

55. Another factor is whether the tests will in fact screen effectively. Some states attempt to screen out more careful younger drivers by requiring that 16 and 17 year-olds complete driver education courses before obtaining licenses. See, e.g., Cal. Veh. Code § 12057 (West 1971). At 18, anyone who passes the state test can obtain a license. See, e.g., id. § 12512. Two commentators have argued, however, that such statutes achieve precisely the opposite result: increasing the number of 16 and 17 year-old drivers increases the automobile accident death rate. See Robertson & Zador, Driver Education and Fatal Crash Involvement of Teenaged Drivers, 68 Am. J. Pub. Health 959 (1978).

56. See Underwood, Law and the Crystal Ball: Predicting Behavior with Statistical Inference and Individualized Judgment, 88 Yale L.J. 1408, 1434–42 (1979) (distinguishing between measures beyond the control of people and those that can be affected by their behavior). The most prominent suspect criteria are race, sex, and national origin. See U.S. Const. amend. XIV, § 1; Civil Rights Act of 1964, 42 U.S.C. § 2000a (1982); Equal Employment Opportunity Act, 42 U.S.C. § 2000e (1982). Other criteria include age, see Age Discrimination in Employment Act of 1967, 29 U.S.C. § 621 (1982), Age Discrimination Act of 1975, 42 U.S.C. § 6101 (1982), and physical handicap, see Rehabilitation Act of 1973, 29 U.S.C. § 701 (1982), Developmental Disabilities Assistance and Bill of Rights Act, 42 U.S.C. § 6000 (1982).

57. Because of a concern for accident risks, the Federal Highway Administration prohibits diabetics on insulin from driving trucks in intercity or interstate commerce. See Hricko, Drivers of Hazardous Cargoes—Legal Aspects of a Maximum Age and Increased Physical Requirements, 31 Fed'n Ins. Couns. 126, 130 (1981). New York City taxi drivers are similarly restricted. N.Y. City Admin. Code, ch. 65, § 2305 (1975).

evidence is used initially to limit ownership and use: individual distinctions are costly or impossible to make.

Even though I have treated ownership restrictions as a second-best response to controlling externalities, I have idealized their role. In practice, such restrictions frequently are designed to give some profession or occupation monopoly power. It is, for example, very difficult to argue that most professional licensure laws are primarily concerned with quality control.[58] Simple restrictions on the number of market participants also are generally explicit grants of monopoly power to a limited group. While limits on the number of taxicabs in a city may reduce traffic congestion, they also benefit license holders;[59] restrictions on the number of bank offices in a state[60] do not even have a limited market failure rationale. Thus, while a combination of externality control and administrative convenience may justify some restrictions, the possibility of such a justification should not create a presumption in favor of these regulations.

2. *Required Use.* — Some entitlement regulations require a small set of actions while permitting a wide range of other uses. As a condition for retaining ownership, the law may mandate actions that produce positive externalities. These regulations substitute for market-oriented systems that pay a subsidy set equal to the external benefits such actions produce.

58. Cf. Stigler, The Theory of Economic Regulation, 2 Bell J. Econ. & Mgmt. Sci. 3, 13–17 (1971) (occupational licensing uses the political process to improve a group's economic circumstances); Brill, Protection for the Hard of Hearing: State and Federal Regulation of Hearing Aid Dealers, 27 DePaul L. Rev. 45, 86–87 (1977) (boards "dominated by members of the industry" help thwart statutory purpose of protecting hard of hearing).

59. Given the casual, short-term nature of individual taxi rides, state regulation of some aspects of quality appears justified. Thus both Chicago and New York require that vehicles be safe to operate. In New York inspections are required every four months, and vehicles must be equipped with emission control devices. Similarly, in both cities, drivers must have a special taxi driver's license that requires them to be in sound physical condition and of good moral character. In New York the law states that applicants will be examined on their knowledge of the city. See N.Y. City Admin. Code, ch. 65, §§ 2301–2319 (1975). Although these restrictions on the ownership and use of taxicabs appear justified on efficiency grounds, limitations on entry, which are less easy to justify, accompany them. See Kitch, Isaacson & Kasper, The Regulation of Taxicabs in Chicago, 14 J.L. & Econ. 285 (1971).

60. See generally Note, Bank Charters, Branching, Holding Company and Merger Laws: Competition Frustrated, 71 Yale L.J. 502 (1962) (summarizing laws governing entry into banking). Some statutes and court decisions, however, seek to foster competition. See, e.g., Moran v. State Banking Comm'r, 322 Mich. 230, 243, 33 N.W.2d 772, 778 (1948) (charter statute should be used "not to deter competition or foster monopoly, but to guard the public and public interest against imprudent banking") (quoting State ex rel. Dybdal v. State Sec. Comm'n, 145 Minn. 221, 224–25, 176 N.W. 759, 760 (1920)); Central Bank v. State Banking Bd., 509 S.W.2d 175, 184 (Mo. Ct. App. 1974) (convenience and needs standard does not contemplate preventing new banks "from entering a market because existing banks are rendering adequate service"); Bank Holding Company Act of 1957, § 1, Ill. Ann. Stat. ch. 17, § 2501 (Smith-Hurd 1981).

Two examples are especially interesting: historical preservation and preservation of the habitats of endangered species. Historical preservation statutes typically require that owners preserve at least the facades of certain buildings. Permission is required for any alterations to the affected portions of the building and demolition is permitted only under very restricted conditions. For example, the New York City Landmarks Preservation Law emphasizes the protection and preservation of external architectural features and internal features, such as building lobbies or auditoriums, that are open to the public, and it only rarely allows demolition.[61] Similarly, the Endangered Species Act may require landowners to avoid destroying the habitat of an endangered species.[62] Both of these policies can be justified by the external benefits of maintaining the affected property in its original form.

Two problems militate against regulatory statutes that require preservation. First, they may lead to too much or too little preservation because the government's criterion of value will not always equal the opportunity costs of foregone development. Second, in the absence of countervailing subsidies, the cost of preservation is borne by those who own the property at the time the law is promulgated, unless, of course, the law actually increases property values.[63] But both the problem of inefficient preservation and the problem of concentrated costs can be avoided by a law that pays owners a bounty to preserve their land or buildings. This system could be more efficient than outright prohibitions if the bounty were set equal to the external benefits of preservation. Historical buildings would be torn down and habitats destroyed only if their external benefits were too low to justify their preservation given the land's alternative uses.[64] Although in practice quantifying these benefits is very difficult, attempts to do so will frequently be preferable to required use regulations when the effect of the latter is to impose all the costs on the producer of the social benefits.

3. *Limits on Use.* — Conversely, other laws forbid certain activities in an attempt to limit negative externalities. For example, land use

61. N.Y. City Admin. Code, ch. 8-A, §§ 207-1.0(g), (m), (n), -5.0(a), -6.0, -10.0 (1976). The law's basic purpose is outlined at § 205-1.0(b).

62. A recent court of appeals decision can be read to support this view even though it dealt with the State of Hawaii rather than private landowners. See Palila v. Hawaii Dep't of Land & Natural Resources, 639 F.2d 495 (9th Cir. 1981); Note, *Palila v. Hawaii Department of Land & Natural Resources*: A New Interpretation of "Taking" Under the Endangered Species Act of 1973, 19 Idaho L. Rev. 157 (1983) (arguing for a broad reading of the *Palila* case).

63. D. Listokin, Landmarks Preservation and the Property Tax (1982), summarizes recent research, including evidence on both increases and decreases in property values under historical preservation statutes. Rose, Landmarks Preservation in New York, Pub. Interest, Winter 1984, at 132, 142, argues in favor of compensation. Rough approximations of this policy are property tax reductions, rapid depreciation of rehabilitation expenses and, in urban areas, markets in air rights. See Pennsylvania Cent. Transp. Co. v. New York City, 438 U.S. 104 (1978).

64. See Wittman, supra note 19, at 75.

zoning laws may prevent owners from using their land for certain things such as a store or a factory but may permit apartment buildings so long as maximum density requirements are met and sewer and water lines are provided.[65] Zoning laws do not require development as a condition of ownership; rather, their economic function is to control the externalities of development *if* it occurs.

Here too, the regulations are second-best substitutes for a policy that balances the benefits and costs of development in individual cases.[66] They also have some of the same undesirable distributive costs as laws requiring certain actions. Once again, those who own the land at the time the zoning law is passed bear the cost along with those who would have benefited if the property had been put to its most profitable use. The purchase of development rights by government is a noncoercive alternative to zoning that forces the state to take into account the costs of restricting land use. In a few jurisdictions this policy has been applied to farmland.[67]

E. *Coerced Use*

I use the term "coerced use" to apply to situations in which all permitted activities are also required. When the government sells, leases, or gives property to private individuals, the state may impose restrictions in an attempt to control the use of the property. If the property is sold to the highest bidder, the regulations will adversely affect government revenues if they require owners to restrict their pursuit of profitable opportunities. How, then, can it be in the public interest to impose such controls? While some such restrictions have little to recommend them on normative grounds, others can be justified by appeals to efficiency and distributive justice. I discuss four rationales in turn: agency-principal problems that arise from the nature of the contractual situation, avoidance of a "prisoner's dilemma," the entitlement holders' poor information and inability to fend for themselves, and the

65. See generally E. Roberts, The Law and the Preservation of Agricultural Land (1982) (summarizing the development of zoning laws in the United States).

66. Because zoning is a local government function, however, it can itself produce external costs. Large lot zoning in the suburbs combined with selective zoning for industry contributes to the clustering of dirty industry and poor, minority families in central cities or old industrial towns while some suburbs maintain themselves as wealthy enclaves. The wealthy are preserving themselves from the negative externalities of living near the poor, but as a consequence they impose costs on the poor by limiting their locational choices. Neither efficiency nor fairness supports this kind of narrowly focused residential zoning. See Mills, Economic Analysis of Urban Land-Use Controls, *in* Current Issues in Urban Economics 511 (P. Mieszkowski & M. Straszheim eds. 1979).

67. For example, the Suffolk County government on Long Island will purchase farmers' "development rights" up to the limit of its budget. The value of these rights is the difference between the value of the property for its highest and best use and its value for agricultural purposes. See E. Roberts, supra note 65, at 76. Less ambitious programs are in effect in Connecticut, Massachusetts, New Hampshire, and New Jersey. Id. at 83–87.

distribution of scarce benefits to the worthy. Three applications are stressed: federal leasing programs for natural resources, the Homesteading Acts of the nineteenth century, and government transfers to the needy.

1. *Contracting Problems: Mineral Leases.* — The federal government sells (or gives away) leases that permit private individuals and firms to exploit natural resources on federal lands and on the continental shelf. Most of these leases—e.g., for coal and oil—provide that holders forfeit their claims if they do not actually extract the resource.[68] A leaseholder who does not wish to exploit the resource, however, can assign or sublease to someone else.[69] These leases thus are pure property entitlements with coercive use.

Coercive conditions will further efficiency only if they help correct agency-principal problems in the basic lease. Under most federal leases, leaseholders must pay a royalty of x percent on sales proceeds.[70] Agency-principal problems arise because one hundred dollars' worth of sales is only worth $(1-x)$ dollars to the lessee. Shifting to the lessee the costs, but not all of the marginal gains, leaves the lessee too little incentive to prospect and exploit the resource. The royalty is inefficient ex

68. See Federal Land Policy and Management Act of 1976, § 302, 43 U.S.C. § 1732 (1982); Outer Continental Shelf Lands Act, ch. 345, 67 Stat. 462, § 6(10), 43 U.S.C. § 1337(b)(2)(B) (1982); Mineral Leasing Act of 1920, ch. 85, 41 Stat. 437, § 7, 30 U.S.C. § 207 (1982); Kalter & Tyner, Disposal Policy for Energy Resources in the Public Domain, *in* Energy Supply and Government Policy 51 (R. Kalter & W. Vogely eds. 1976); Nelson, Undue Diligence: The Mine-It-Or-Lose-It Rule for Federal Coal, 7 Reg. 34 (Jan.-Feb. 1983). Judicial doctrines governing underground coal gasification contain similar holdings. Note, Implied Covenants and the Duty to Develop in Underground Coal Gasification, 59 Tex. L. Rev. 1303 (1981). The Federal Coal Leasing Amendments Act of 1975, Pub. L. No. 94-377, 90 Stat. 1083 (1976) (codified in scattered sections of 30 U.S.C. (1982)), requires development of future coal leases within 10 years, id. § 6, at 1087 (codified at 30 U.S.C. § 207 (1982)), but does not cover leases issued before 1976 unless the lessees consent. Id. § 5(b)(5), at 1086 (codified at 30 U.S.C. § 202a(5) (1982)).

Oil and gas leases are subject to automatic termination for nonpayment of rent unless there is a well on the property capable of producing oil or gas in paying quantities. 30 U.S.C. § 188(b) (1982). However, the rent is generally set at a minimal fee per acre so that this requirement is not onerous. In practice, leases are seldom terminated for failure to exploit the resource. Council on Economic Priorities, Leased and Lost: A Study of Public and Indian Coal Leasing in the West, 5 Econ. Priorities Rep., No. 2 (1974) [hereinafter cited as Council on Economic Priorities]. Even if one observes no active enforcement, however, the law may still affect both leaseholder behavior and the bid prices for contracts so long as bidders think the provision has some chance of being binding.

69. The sublease must be approved by the Secretary of the Interior. 30 U.S.C. § 187 (1982). At least for oil and gas leases, assignments or subleases can be disapproved "only for lack of qualification of the assignee or sublessee or for lack of sufficient bond." 30 U.S.C. § 187a (1982).

70. Low royalties of 8% to 12.5% are common. The royalty can be reduced if the lessee demonstrates that lease stipulations make development of a tract uneconomical. Kalter & Tyner, supra note 68, at 56–57.

post but may be desirable ex ante as a way of sharing the risks of exploitation between the government and the private firm. If such risk sharing is deemed desirable, then a "due diligence" requirement will help correct the inefficiency created by the royalty scheme.[71]

Arguments in favor of restrictive clauses are more difficult to make, however, where the lease is granted in return for a fixed payment. Such provisions are justifiable where market imperfections such as monopoly power or systematically biased information discourage current production.[72] Absent market imperfections, however, due diligence requirements in such leases encourage excess exploration in the present, controlled only by the government's decision on the quantity of leases to make available each year.

2. "*Prisoner's Dilemmas.*" — It is difficult to be a pioneer in an empty land. Life is easier with neighbors who can help in emergencies, share farm equipment, and assist in capital projects such as construction. Furthermore, as more people settle in a given area, more specialized tradesmen, such as blacksmiths and carpenters, will move in, and villages will be built. Since it is easier to develop one's land once others are nearby, everyone has an incentive to wait for everyone else. Speculators with no interest in farming may purchase some land and hold it for resale. In some markets, speculators can serve a useful economic function, but here they can exacerbate the "prisoner's dilemma."[73]

---

71. Private oil and gas leases also frequently contain profit-sharing provisions combined with clauses requiring the lessee to explore for resources and to exploit them if found. For summaries of the current state of the law in this area, see Comment, The Implied Covenant to Reasonably Develop: Should Hard-Mineral Applications Follow Oil and Gas Precedent?, 20 Hous. L. Rev. 883 (1983); Note, Oil and Gas: Preservation of Leaseholds Following Well Failure, 36 Okla. L. Rev. 151 (1983). For an historical overview, see Swenson, Legal Aspects of Mineral Resources Exploitation, *in* P. Gates, History of Public Land Law Development 699 (1968).

72. Nelson, supra note 68, at 36–38. The Department of Interior, however, apparently has not enforced these provisions vigorously. Council on Economic Priorities, supra note 68, at 28.

73. The prisoner's dilemma game between individuals *A* and *B* has the following form where *B*'s net returns are listed first in each box.

		A: Develop Now	A: Develop Later
B	Develop Now	10, 10	6, 12
B	Develop Later	12, 6	7, 7

If both develop now, they share the social overhead costs and maximize total benefits. If both wait, they also share costs and lose the profits of early developments. If *A* develops later while *B* develops now, *B* must bear all the startup costs and cannot prevent some of the benefits of this investment from accruing to *A*. Total benefits are less with sequential development either because the early entrant underinvests in social overhead capital or because of scale economies from joint production.

Substituting (0,0) for (7,7) in the above matrix would create a game called "leader."

Everyone is better off if all settle than if no one settles, but if others settle, then it is best for each person to wait until others have overcome the initial hardships.

One way around the dilemma is to impose a conditionally coercive entitlement rule designed to encourage settlement. The original Homesteading Acts in nineteenth century America, for example, gave people land for a nominal fee after they certified that they had worked the land for five years.[74] The land could not be sold or given away to private individuals during that period. If a homesteader did not complete his term of resident farming, the land was forfeited to the state. The people attracted to the territory by this program both made future economic development easier and aided the political ambitions of the original residents who sought to move their territories toward statehood. Thus, in my terms, the entitlement rule was conditionally coercive, and hence more restrictive than the transferable mineral leases discussed above.[75]

At present, the prisoner's dilemma may well provide an important justification for subsidized housing programs with coercive conditions. Poorly maintained housing affects the value of neighboring property with the net result that no one may find it worthwhile to incur maintenance expenses. If all could be induced to upgrade their property, all would benefit. Subsidies could be provided to landlords and homeowners on the condition that they fix up their property. However, if property owners can sell their upgraded assets to the highest bidder, a subsidy program of this kind is not conditionally coercive. Conditional coercion arises when the government wishes not merely to improve neighborhood quality but also to make it possible for the former residents to remain in the newly upgraded housing. Thus, landlords may be forbidden to evict tenants and tenants may be eligible for subsidy only if they live in apartments that fulfill housing code standards.[76] Similarly, urban homesteading programs, which are quite self-consciously modeled after the homesteading programs for nineteenth cen-

In this game, each participant would try to be the first to announce that he would develop later in order to induce the other player to develop now.

74. See Act of May 20, 1862, ch. 75, 12 Stat. 392; P. Gates, supra note 71, at 393–99.

75. See P. Gates, supra note 71, at 393–99. Eventually, the conditionally coercive features of the Homesteading Acts were weakened by the addition of a commutation clause. Homesteaders could purchase their claim outright after a residence of fourteen months. Act of Mar. 3, 1891, ch. 561, § 6, 26 Stat. 1095, 1098; F. Shannon, The Farmers' Last Frontier, Agriculture, 1860–97, at 51–75, 5 The Economic History of the United States (1945). As a contemporary author pointed out, this clause converted the law into little more than a way of redistributing income to people willing to make a minimal investment in the land. See Hughes, The Abuse of the Homestead Law, 14 Am. Law. 350 (1906). This consequence followed because real estate companies and railroads frequently stood ready to advance the commutation price to the homesteaders in return for a promise to sell the land to the company. Id. at 351.

76. See, e.g., U.S. Housing Act of 1937, § 8, 42 U.S.C. § 1437f(a) (1976).

tury farmers, encourage low and moderate income people to fix up old housing and impose resale restrictions to ensure that the rehabilitated building continues to provide housing for families with low and moderate incomes.[77]

The prisoner's dilemma rationale is less clearly applicable to natural resource leases, but it may be valid in particular cases. Latecomers may have lower costs than early entrants because those who first develop the resource bear costs that must be shared with later developers. Roads must be built to extract timber from inaccessible areas, and oil exploration by one firm in one area may provide information to owners or leaseholders of neighboring areas. In such situations, due diligence clauses can overcome the incentive to hold back and let others move first.

3. *Poor Information and Paternalism.* — Following Charles Reich, many commentators view government transfer programs as creating a kind of "new property."[78] If so, the new property rights are often conditionally coercive. In general, people cannot sell or give away their benefits to others, and for some benefits, such as public housing, people forfeit their claim to a service by not using it. Even the right to receive straight cash grants through a welfare program with no restrictions on use is not a pure property right. An eligible person can give the payments she receives to anyone but cannot transfer the right to receive these payments. In-kind programs providing such benefits as housing, food, or day care also frequently restrict both the use and transferability of the benefit itself. Such coercion is justified as a way of overcoming the market failure caused by poor information and shopping opportunities,[79] or from a paternalistic concern for poor children and their families.[80] Social benefit programs can induce people to consume food, housing, health care, or education by making these services relatively inexpensive and prohibiting transfers.

A similar argument can be used to justify the Homesteading Acts. Those who wished to encourage the development of western lands could well have believed that homesteaders, if left to themselves, would

77. See Department of Housing Preservation and Development, The City of New York, Urban Homesteading, Request for Proposals, Dec. 9, 1983, at 4 (unpublished) (copy on file at the offices of the Columbia Law Review).

78. See Reich, Individual Rights and Social Welfare: The Emerging Legal Issues, 74 Yale L.J. 1245 (1965); Reich, The New Property, 73 Yale L.J. 733 (1964).

79. Barlow v. Collins, 397 U.S. 159 (1970), illustrates a situation in which program beneficiaries themselves argued for restrictions on the transferability of their entitlements. Petitioners were tenant farmers eligible for payments under the upland cotton programs. The law permitted them to assign their payments only "to finance making a crop." Id. at 160. In 1966 the definition of this phrase was changed to permit tenants to use advances to pay land rent. Tenants argued that this apparent increase in flexibility actually reduced their benefits under the program because landlords were now able to insist on assignments as a condition for obtaining a lease to work the land. Id. at 163.

80. See generally Rose-Ackerman, Social Services and the Market, 83 Colum. L. Rev. 1405 (1983) (discussing the rationales for in-kind programs).

have had an inefficiently short time horizon. Conditional coercion encouraged homesteaders to endure the hard initial years by subsidizing fixed costs in a way that gave them an incentive to remain on the land. Eventually, their skills improved, and the risks of farming fell. Here, too, the efficiency rationale based on imperfect information merges into a kind of paternalism.

4. *Distribution to the "Worthy."* — Suppose that for some reason the free market allocation of a scarce public benefit is unacceptable. Assume further that the number of qualified individuals using some clear standard such as income, employment status, or family composition exceeds the supply available. Thus, program administrators face a distributive problem that may be solved in a number of ways, including first-come-first-serve queues, the approval of applications, under-the-table payoffs, or a lottery. Alternatively, restrictions may be imposed that are less onerous for those who most deserve to receive the benefit. If determining worthiness through tests and application approval is costly and unreliable, the restrictions are a substitute sorting device. Such requirements may be particularly desirable if they also serve a productive purpose, as did the rural and urban homesteading laws.

Consider first the Homesteading Acts. Central to the homesteading program was the idea that a newly available resource (e.g., western land suitable for farming) should not go to those who already had capital but to those without other wealth.[81] This, however, was only an argument for giving the land to the poor in the first instance, not for requiring them to work on the property. To justify coercive conditions and restrictions on transfer we must add a second factor: in practice, the number of valuable sites was less than the number of landless people so long as the state took into account both the scale economies of production and the transaction costs of assembling a farm from a multitude of small entitlements. Thus, there needed to be some method to assign sites other than willingness to pay since market sales could defeat the redistributive purpose. In this context, homesteading emerges as a plausible choice. It is a more efficient allocation mechanism than a first-come-first-served queue since the time expended is not wasted waiting in line but is used in productive activities. Seen in this light, a conditionally coercive rule can use willingness to work to determine

81. See, e.g., Seymour v. Sanders, 21 F. Cas. 1133, 1135 (C.C.D. Minn. 1874) (No. 12,690) ("A leading object of the enactment was to benefit the poor man who was unable to buy the lands at government prices and receive his title at once and without conditions."), reprinted in J. Lewis, Leading Cases on the Public Land Laws of the United States 219 (1879). Nonetheless, homesteading accounted for, at most, "less than a sixth of the new homes and a little over a sixth of the acreage' in the United States between 1860 and 1900. F. Shannon, supra note 74, at 51. Gates refers to the mixture of sales and homesteading in the western states as an "incongruous land system." P. Gates, supra note 71, at 435. Although Shannon argues that the Acts had little redistributive impact, Gates points out the Act's role in limiting absentee ownership of large tracts.

who among the poor can best develop the resource. Of course, this policy also means that the very poor with no farming skills do not benefit from the program. It represents a compromise between accomplishing redistributive goals and assuring the efficient development of resources.

A similar rationale underlies many social welfare programs. When the number of needy people exceeds the supply of subsidized goods, it seems prudent to ration the scarce supply only to those people who will actually use the in-kind benefit themselves. Selling subsidized apartments to the highest bidders would undermine the redistributive purposes of the program. Since the price is not set to clear the market, demand will exceed supply even when transferability is restricted. Therefore, costly conditions may be added, such as willingness to perform maintenance chores in the building or to spend time fixing up the premises. The analogy to the Homesteading Acts is particularly close for redistributive programs that also have economic development or growth as a secondary goal. The restrictions on use and transferability in these programs can both accomplish redistributive objectives when demand exceeds supply at the subsidized price and encourage neighborhood preservation in much the same way as the Homesteading Acts induced people to endure the hardships of farming on the frontier.

Once again, however, this mix of efficiency and distributive rationales cannot be extended indefinitely. For example, it cannot be used to justify the coercive conditions in federal mineral leasing programs. Most leases are sold to high bidders, not given to those deemed especially worthy independent of their willingness to pay. Noncompetitive leases that are given to the "first" qualified applicant have distributive consequences, but not ones that make sense on normative grounds.[82] Furthermore, given the specialized skills needed to exploit mineral resources, it seems unlikely that these programs should be designed to serve a redistributive purpose.

III. Inalienability and Citizenship

The analysis of inalienability helps to illuminate a theme that has preoccupied students of capitalist democracy: How insulated should the state be from market pressures?[83] This Part discusses one aspect of the broader problem: When should rights be transferable and when

82. 26 U.S.C. § 226(c) (1982); 43 C.F.R. §§ 3111.1–.7 (1984). Council on Economic Priorities, supra note 68, at 22–23, describes the allocation of coal leases prior to the 1976 law. Of 242 lease offerings during the period 1921–1973, 10% drew no formal bidders and so were awarded at low rates to the original applicant for the sale. In 59% of the competitive sales only two bidders participated. The average bid was $3.31 per acre. The Council on Economic Priorities claimed that the prices paid, even when rent and royalty payments are considered, were far below the discounted present value of the mineral resources. Id. at 27–28.

83. See, e.g., G. Brennan & J. Buchanan, The Power to Tax: Analytical Founda-

must they be exercised by all who possess them? Should people be able to contract out of duties, and should duties be imposed even if the required services could be purchased in a market? My aim here is not to provide a comprehensive answer to these questions. Instead, it is to show how any answer requires us to confront the complexity of the idea of citizenship. To make the analysis concrete, I will show how alternative conceptions of citizenship have different implications for voting, military service, and jury selection. The analysis concentrates on the difference between rights and duties and between alienability and inalienablity.

A. *Alienable and Inalienable Rights*

Under the weakest conception of citizen responsibility, citizenship services are obtained under a regime of alienable property rights. Votes can be sold, given away, or left unused. Both soldiers and jurors are obtained in the regular labor market by offering compensation to people willing to participate. Qualifications may be imposed on both soldiers and jurors to assure a supply of good soldiers and qualified fact finders, but within these groups, market forces operate. This system minimizes the difference between the government and the economy. The impact of economic pressures can be attenuated, however, by moving to a system of inalienable rights.

1. *Votes.* — When voting is an alienable right, everyone meeting statutory requirements of age and citizenship would be entitled to one free voting right from the government, but people could then sell or give their votes to others. The affirmative case for alienability is derived from research on voting behavior which reveals that many voters are poorly informed and apathetic.[84] Similar conditions, after all, apply to voting rights in corporations. Although owners may not sell their proxies,[85] they may give their votes to management or to anyone else

---

tions of a Fiscal Constitution (1980); C. Lindblom, Politics and Markets (1977); S. Rose-Ackerman, Corruption: A Study in Political Economy (1978).

84. See W. Miller, A. Miller & E. Schneider, American National Election Studies Data Sourcebook 1952–1978 (1980) [hereinafter cited as Data Sourcebook].

85. Of course proxies *can* be sold if the shares of stock to which they are attached are sold as well. Manne, Some Theoretical Aspects of Share Voting, 64 Colum. L. Rev. 1427 (1964). Robert Clark has argued that sales of votes should be permitted, especially in fights for corporate control. See Clark, Vote Buying and Corporate Law, 29 Case W. Res. L. Rev. 776, 790–801 (1979). Frank Easterbrook and Daniel Fischel contend that this argument neglects the agency costs of separating voting from ownership. Easterbrook & Fischel, Voting in Corporate Law, 26 J.L. & Econ. 395, 410–11 (1983).

While the sale of proxies is illegal under New York law, N.Y. Bus. Corp. Law § 609(e) (McKinney 1963), no federal statute forbids such conduct. See Clark, supra, at 777 n.9. Furthermore, gifts of proxies can generally be revoked at will. 5 W. Fletcher & O. Smith, Fletcher Cyclopedia of the Law of Private Corporations § 2062, at 256 (rev. perm. ed. 1976). Proxies can be irrevocably transferred to others if coupled "with an interest." Id. A creditor, for example, may demand the right to vote some portion of a company's stock in return for extending funds. Id. at 20–21 (Cum. Supp. 1984). Since

who offers to act as the shareholders' proxies.[86] Scholars have justified this delegation of voting power on the ground that stockholders have little incentive to become well informed about firms' policies.[87] What is wrong, then, with extending this analogy to the state?

I do not want to go so far as to advocate vote selling in political life. Vote selling is widely recognized to be inconsistent with egalitarian, democratic principles because it biases political decisions in favor of the wealthy.[88] However, in a direct democracy in which choices are made by unanimous consent, the buying of votes does assure choices that benefit all citizens given the existing distribution of resources.[89] This can only be a desirable outcome, however, if the existing distribution is believed to be fair.[90] And even this limited defense of vote selling does not survive the move to a representative system making choices by majority rule.[91]

The current prohibition against donations cannot, however, be so easily dismissed. Since voters who pull party levers or follow the endorsements of *The New York Times* are de facto donating their votes, why not permit more formal assignments which, like corporate proxies, can be revoked at any time before the election? In spite of a generally held belief that people should use their own independent judgment in deciding how to vote, we do not impose any tests on the electorate to determine their level of knowledge of candidates and issues. We are torn, then, between two alternative views of democracy. Even when alienability through the market is outlawed, this conflict within democractic theory remains. On the one hand, there is the belief that voting is an individual, private act that should not be examined too closely by the state. On the other hand, the value of a representative democracy depends upon citizens making responsible, well-informed choices. This conflict is illuminated, but not resolved, by trying to determine whether voting rights should be governed by a modified inalienablity rule.

---

this scheme approximates the sale of a proxy, it has caused some confusion in the courts, id. § 2052, at 209 n.5, and is apparently a rather uncommon method of creditor control.

86. Because of the possibilities for abuse by management, the SEC regulates proxy solicitations. Regulations promulgated under the Securities and Exchange Act of 1934 prohibit fraud, permit shareholders to solicit proxies and to include certain of their proposals in the proxy statement, and require disclosure from opposition groups in proxy contests. See 17 C.F.R. § 240.14a (1984). State regulation of proxy solicitations, however, is practically nonexistent. See Eisenberg, Access to the Corporate Proxy Machinery, 83 Harv. L. Rev. 1489 (1970).

87. See, e.g., Clark, supra note 85, at 779–84.

88. For example, even staunch defenders of the market accept this argument. See J. Buchanan & G. Tullock, The Calculus of Consent 270–76 (1962).

89. Id. at 276–77.

90. For a recent critique of Buchanan's position in favor of the status quo distribution, see Rose-Ackerman, A New Political Economy?, 80 Mich. L. Rev. 872 (1982).

91. J. Buchanan & G. Tullock, supra note 88, at 270–76.

2. *Soldiers and Jurors*. — Despite the consensus against the sale of votes, there is no widely held belief that government should be isolated from economic forces. Public agencies commonly pay market prices for capital and other inputs. More controversially, the military's entrance into the labor market to obtain soldiers reflects current American practice and has been widely advocated by economic analysts.[92] An all-volunteer military requires the government to take into account the opportunity cost of personnel.[93] The armed services decide what sort of people they wish to recruit, but the people who actually decide to serve are those who believe that military service, given existing pay and benefit levels, is at least as good as their best private sector option. Unlike a draft with a fixed pay scale, the volunteer army makes taxpayers pay the social costs of military personnel,[94] shifting this citizenship responsiblity from the young to the general public.

Some commentators, however, object to this shift of responsibility on citizenship grounds. They claim that choosing soldiers who prefer military service to their opportunities in civilian life is undesirable in a democracy. Two kinds of people can be expected to volunteer: those with relatively low paying, unattractive job prospects in the private sector and those who like fighting and prefer military service over civilian jobs that pay as well or better. The army's personnel budget reflects the opportunity cost of recruits on the margin, but such an army may have long-term consequences for the stability of the society. The country may be overly likely to engage in militaristic adventures if its soldiers are people who like fighting more than the rest of us.[95] Alternatively, the potential for violent confrontations between rich and poor may be increased if the armed forces are composed of unskilled people who learn little beyond the use of weapons during their years in

92. See, e.g., Amacher, Miller, Pauly, Tollison & Willett, The Economics of the Military Draft, *in* The Military Draft 347 (M. Anderson ed. 1982) [hereinafter cited as Amacher, Military Draft].

93. Id. at 366–75.

94. Of course, so long as wages are set to attract enough recruits and so long as some people would have volunteered at lower pay levels, some soldiers are earning a surplus over their opportunity wages, and payrolls overstate the economic cost of a volunteer army.

95. See Janovitz, The Logic of National Service, *in* The Military Draft 403, 431 (M. Anderson ed. 1982) ("If the armed services—through some sort of nationwide draft—are continuously faced with the task of absorbing recruits to whom the military way of life is basically uncongenial, or even repellent, there is a useful check on the development of a highly differentiated counter-civilian ethos."). Similarly, McNeill criticizes a draft that exempts college students. He argues that "the existing policy of exempting the future leaders of civilian life from military service positively invites divergence of viewpoint and seems almost suicidal in a democracy. . . . [I]t is precisely those who go to college and are headed for the privileged places in our society who should be drafted." McNeill, The Draft in the Light of History, *in* The Military Draft 59, 64–65 (M. Anderson ed. 1982).

uniform.[96]

Analysts have seldom viewed jury duty, unlike military service, as a job like any other that should be made available to qualified applicants. Yet it is difficult to see why a sharp distinction should be made between soldiers and jurors. Using the market to obtain jurors would make the public at large rather than randomly selected individuals bear the cost of jury service[97] and is consistent with an economic analysis that emphasizes the possible trade-off between the opportunity cost of jurors' time and their factfinding ability.[98] The objections, however, parallel those made for the draft. First, jury duty is seen by many as a duty of citizenship that people should not be able to opt out of because of better private opportunities elsewhere. Second, the process itself might be undermined if juries were staffed entirely by volunteers. Within demographic categories, the jury would be unrepresentative because those with high opportunity wages would not serve. This bias might destroy the jury's representative character.[99]

For military and jury service, using the market would imply that these activities are rights rather than duties. However, unlike voting, the distinction between inalienability and alienability is not central. People have a right to serve *if* the government finds them qualified, and no one will serve who does not find the terms of employment desirable. Like most private employment relationships, however, these jobs cannot be sold by the incumbent. As we shall see below, the distinction between alienability and inalienability only becomes salient when these activities are duties assigned by the state.

---

96. See Amacher, Military Draft, supra note 92, at 377–78 (examining the argument that a volunteer army will be disproportionately composed of blacks and members of other disadvantaged minority groups).

97. At present, pay is far below opportunity costs for most people. In New York State, jurors are paid not more than $12 per day plus food and travel expenses and $1.50 for each evening session. Extra compensation is permitted for trials lasting more than 30 days. Furthermore, although employers cannot discharge or penalize employees for serving on juries, they need not pay them for days missed. N.Y. Jud. Law §§ 519, 521 (McKinney Supp. 1984).

98. Klevorick, Jury Composition: An Economic Approach, *in* The Interaction of Economics and the Law 81–99 (B. Siegan ed. 1977).

99. This argument, of course, assumes that representativeness is desirable. The case for this position is made in two very different ways. On one hand, G. Calabresi & P. Bobbitt, supra note 37, at 57–64, argue that juries can be used to make tragic choices that strain the fabric of society. On the other hand, some observers believe that a representative jury will produce more accurate decisions, especially when "reasonableness" or "community standards" are at issue. See, e.g., Weiner, The Civil Jury Trial and the Law-Fact Distinction, 54 Calif. L. Rev. 1867, 1876–94 (1966). For evidence on juror behavior, see H. Kalven, Jr. & H. Zeisel, The American Jury (1966); Severance & Loftus, Improving the Ability of Jurors to Comprehend and Apply Criminal Jury Instructions, 17 L. & Soc'y Rev. 153 (1982).

B. *Inalienable and Alienable Duties*

Under the strong concept of inalienable duties, the state requires certain actions of some or all citizens and forbids the transfer of these duties to others. Every eligible citizen must vote; the military uses a draft or has a universal service requirement; and jury duty is an obligation of those called to serve. The coercive nature of the duties of citizenship can be reduced by making them alienable. Thus, for example, persons drafted into the armed forces could be permitted either to purchase substitutes or locate others willing to take their places.

1. *Votes.* — Consider voting first. In some democratic countries, such as Australia, voting is not only inalienable but also required. The law is enforced by imposing a fine on those who fail to come to the polling place.[100] Thus, in practice, the state has set a price for not voting. People with a very high opportunity cost of time may decide not to go to the polls. A relatively low fine, however, should be sufficient to assure a large turnout.

What can be said for such coercion in the name of citizenship? One argument is based on the free rider problems that arise in politics. Although the cost of voting is usually small, the chance of being decisive, even in a small town, is almost nonexistent.[101] When the law does not require voting, as in the United States, turnout is far less than one hundred percent even in important national elections[102] and may well be under twenty-five percent for relatively unimportant offices or in elections with little at stake. So long as indifference can be recorded, making voting an inalienable duty assures that all eligible citizens' preferences are taken into account and might seem to produce a more legitimate democratic result.[103] However, if many people are lazy or bored by politics, and have only vague preferences, they may not bother to vote without coercion and if coerced might well vote randomly or on the basis of whim and prejudice. Even permitting voters to register their indifference would not solve this problem since the truly apathetic might still vote randomly. They would have no more incentive to record their apathy than to cast a ballot for one of the candidates. The problem for them is not that they realize that one vote is unlikely to affect the outcome, but that they simply do not care which candidate is chosen. Therefore, avoiding coercion may be a better way to preserve democratic values than making voting an inalienable duty. When voting is an inalienable right whose exercise is slightly costly because of the time and trouble of going to the polls, the people who do cast ballots must feel that they have an obligation to do so in spite of their lack

100. See H. Emy, The Politics of Australian Democracy: Fundamentals in Dispute 596–97 (2d ed. 1978).

101. See B. Barry, Sociologists, Economists and Democracy 13–23 (1970).

102. See Data Sourcebook, supra note 84, at 303–28.

103. See Miller, A Program for Direct and Proxy Voting in the Legislative Process, 7 Pub. Choice 107 (1969).

of marginal impact.[104] As a consequence, they will be more likely to find out about the candidates than the citizenry as a whole.[105]

The alternative of treating voting as an alienable duty does not have much to recommend it. It would permit the apathetic and the undecided to delegate their choices to someone else by sale or gift. It has all the problems outlined above for alienable rights, exaggerated by the fact that votes either must be used or transferred. Under both inalienable rights and alienable duties, less than one hundred percent of the eligible voters cast ballots, but the former policy limits the influence of the politically aware to their own vote and does not give those who are wealthy an undue advantage. Of course, as any student of politics knows, making voting an inalienable right does not eliminate the impact of wealth on electoral outcomes, but it seems to be a minimal condition.

2. *Soldiers and Jurors.* — The arguments for forced jury duty and military service are somewhat different. Unlike voting, all qualified people are not called upon to serve at a single point in time. Therefore, the state must decide who should serve. If military service and jury duty are seen as duties of citizenship, rather than jobs much like any other, a draft based on a lottery with no buyout possibilities seems to impose that duty most fairly. However, it is clearly more costly for society as a whole since some people with high opportunity wages in the private sector or little aptitude for soldiering or fact finding will be called. This cost will be borne either by the draftee, if wages are not tied to opportunity costs, or by the taxpayers, if they are. The country's labor resources are being used inefficiently, but in a way that treats the risks of military service and the inconvenience of jury duty as duties of citizenship that every qualified person must be willing to accept.

Suppose, however, that these duties are imposed fairly but are made alienable. In other words, people are assigned duties by the state but can induce others to perform them either for a fee or from altruistic motives. Thus, people are drafted or called to jury duty but may purchase substitutes or try to induce their friends or relatives to serve in their place. Such a system of alienable duties appears to have little to recommend it. Instead of striking a balance between competing values, it reduces *both* the fairness and the efficiency of the system.

To see this, consider a situation in which military service was an alienable duty. During the United States Civil War a compromise was sought between the inefficiency of a draft and its appeal as a fair way of imposing a duty of citizenship. In both the North and the South draftees could either buy their way out or buy a substitute.[106] The system

104. Benn, The Problematic Rationality of Political Participation, *in* Philosophy, Politics and Society (P. Laslett & J. Fishkin eds. 1979).

105. See Shubik, On Homo Politicus and the Instant Referendum, 9 Pub. Choice 79 (1970).

106. See E. Murdock, Patriotism Limited: 1862–1865: The Civil War Draft and the

amounted to a volunteer army financed by wealthy draftees instead of taxpayers as a whole. While soldiers may have ended up being paid the opportunity cost of enlistment, the government in planning its military activity was not required to take these opportunity costs into account. Therefore, it had an incentive to use too much manpower. Most criticism, however, attacked the unfairness of the system that (like the volunteer army today) permitted the wealthy to avoid service. In fact, the system quickly broke down in the North as localities and states first passed laws appropriating money to enable everyone to buy his way out and then began to pay bounties to enlistees.[107] In the South the purchase of substitutes was heavily criticized and was abolished soon after it was begun.[108]

If we rule out the option of alienable duties, then we are left with a choice between a market-based system under which military and jury service are rights that are voluntarily accepted, and a system of inalienable duties. Each alternative has something to recommend it, and a mixed strategy may be desirable. Thus, a volunteer army could be advisable in peacetime when military jobs are no more dangerous than many other forms of employment, but might be replaced by a draft based on a lottery in wartime. Jurors in cases requiring expert knowledge and the commitment of substantial time and energy might be chosen by paying qualified volunteers a high enough wage to clear the market. In situations in which a cross section of the population is required, jury service could be made an inalienable duty with pay levels set approximately equal to the average wage.

IV. Conclusions

The classification of entitlements developed here encompasses a broad range of property relations and analyzes rationales that incorporate and go beyond exclusively economic arguments. The economic rationales themselves are wide ranging and include problems of imperfect information and foresight, as well as administrative costs and externalities. Nonetheless, I have also attempted to incorporate distributive arguments and to point out how alternative conceptions of citizenship affect the analysis of entitlement rules. My aim is not to justify all existing restrictions, but to isolate plausible rationales for some.

We have seen how restrictions on the transferability, ownership,

Bounty System (1967); J. Randall, Constitutional Problems Under Lincoln (rev. ed. 1963). For a relatively favorable view of this practice, see Wittman, supra note 19, at 78.

107. E. Murdock, supra note 106; J. Randall, supra note 106.

108. A. Moore, Conscription and Conflict in the Confederacy (1924). According to Moore, substitution was originally supported in the South as a way "to reserve skill and talent for service in essential industries." Id. at 27. Criticism mounted when it was found that many who sought substitutes were not only wealthy but became war profiteers. Id. at 27–29. The market price of a substitute increased from $1500 to $6000 near the end of 1863. Id. at 29–30.

and use of property can be justified under a range of different assumptions about the structure of the world and the cost of alternatives. I have also tried to show the limited applicability of some kinds of inalienability rules. Easy generalizations are frequently invalid. While an argument can be made for relying on blood donations, it cannot be generalized to products like used cars, even though they share similar informational characteristics. Shareholders, but not citizens, can give away their votes. Federal homesteading laws and federal mineral leases may appear similar in form but have very different rationales. The sale of both blood and "old" eagles might be permitted if certain institutional arrangements are not too costly to establish.

Inalienability is frequently justified not as an ideal policy but as a second-best response to the messiness and complexity of the world. It is generally possible to conceive of an alternative policy that would be superior if transaction costs were lower. The major exception involves the ideal of citizenship, where insulation from market forces may be desirable in principle and the main issue is whether to rely on voluntary donations or on coercion to achieve public goals. Thus, even in a first-best world without transaction costs, few people would advocate selling political votes. In contrast, if the argument against the sale of blood rests primarily on quality control grounds, a cheap and effective test for contamination would undermine the argument. This reliance on imperfect information and transaction costs to justify inalienability rules should not be seen as a weakness of the analysis, however. Instead, it is a way to rescue the concept of inalienability from its simplistic rejection by market-oriented economists or its overly enthusiastic embrace by paternalistic moralists.

Part V
Economic Analysis of Crime

[13]

CRIMINAL LAW AND THE OPTIMAL USE OF NONMONETARY SANCTIONS AS A DETERRENT

*Steven Shavell**

Introduction

In this Article, I analyze the theoretically optimal use of nonmonetary sanctions as a deterrent, and I then examine their actual domain of use and the major principles and doctrines of the criminal law.[1]

The plan of the Article is as follows: Part I describes the model on which the analysis is based. Part II considers the determination of the optimal area of nonmonetary sanctions in the model. This determination is based on a list of factors that may make reliance on monetary sanctions as a deterrent problematic, and that therefore may make resort to nonmonetary sanctions appealing despite the higher social costs presumed to be associated with their imposition. Part II then applies this theory about the model to help explain why the actual domain of nonmonetary sanctions—principally the area of crimes punished by imprisonment—and that of monetary sanctions—including much of the area of tort law—are what they are.

Next, Part III studies the specific nature of the optimal system of deterrence assuming that it is desirable to employ nonmonetary sanctions. The theme that is elaborated in the analysis of the model here is that because nonmonetary sanctions are socially costly to impose, it is best for society to threaten to impose the sanctions only where parties can probably successfully be deterred from acting undesirably. However, it will appear inevitable that sanctions will sometimes be imposed; and from this it is concluded that sanctions should not be too high, and the optimal magnitude of sanctions is deduced. The optimal probability of apprehension of parties is also discussed, and it is emphasized that if the probability is too low, it will not be possible to deter certain parties even with the threat of the highest conceivable sanctions.

Part III then investigates the criminal law in view of the theoretical analysis. For example, one section examines the hypothesis that "intent" may serve as a proxy for factors that raise the optimal sanction,

---

* Professor of Law and Economics, Harvard University. I wish to thank Albert Alschuler, Lucian Bebchuk, Michael Faure, John Kaplan, Louis Kaplow, Daniel Meltzer, Geoffrey Miller, A. Mitchell Polinsky, Richard Posner, and David Rosenberg for comments, and the National Science Foundation for financial support.

1. I consider only the goal of deterrence even though other goals of criminal law, notably incapacitation, rehabilitation, and retribution, would have to enter significantly into any normative or descriptive theory claiming to be reasonably complete. I restrict attention to deterrence because I believe its role, being complicated, is best understood in isolation from that of other goals. The reader will have to be careful to keep this in mind, since the focus on deterrence may at times seem unnatural.

and thus that the importance given to intent in criminal law may promote the goal of deterrence. In addition to the subject of intent, the subjects of attempt, causation, responsibility, justification and excuse, and strict liability are considered.[2]

I. The Model

In order to analyze the use of nonmonetary sanctions as a deterrent, it is helpful to set up a simple and concededly stylized model.[3] According to the model,[4] parties may commit acts that can cause harm. An act will be identified with a set of probabilities[5] of possible consequences; shooting at a person, for instance, will be identified with the probabilities describing where, if at all, a bullet will strike that person. Notice that under this definition of an act, what we would usually call a failure to act (for example, failure to prevent a person from shooting another) will be considered an act, for a failure to act will be associated with some distinctive set of probabilities of possible outcomes. Observe as well that the thoughts[6] of a party when committing an act are quite different from the act itself, that is, from the probabilities of the consequences identified with the act.

The probability that an act will cause harm multiplied by the magnitude of harm will be referred to as the "expected" harm.[7] The harm

2. I will describe below, see, e.g., infra note 53, the specific contribution of this Article to previous writing on the theory of deterrence and criminal law, including C. Beccaria, An Essay on Crimes and Punishments (1872); C. Montesquieu, The Spirit of Laws (T. Nugent trans. 1878); Bentham, An Introduction to the Principles of Morals and Legislation, *in* The Utilitarians 173 (1973); Becker, Crime and Punishment: An Economic Approach, 76 J. Pol. Econ. 169 (1968). The main additions, however, may be mentioned now: (a) the argument of Part II relating the domain of nonmonetary sanctions to the factors that reduce the utility of monetary sanctions; (b) the level of detail with which the theory of the optimal use of nonmonetary sanctions is developed in the first section of Part III; and (c) certain points in the subsequent analysis of criminal law (primarily about intent, attempt, and causation). An interesting article by Richard Posner, which appears in the present Review, follows similar lines. See Posner, An Economic Theory of the Criminal Law, 85 Colum. L. Rev. 1193 (1985). His article and this one were written independently of each other, and the reader will probably wish to examine both.

3. The reason that the study of a simple model can be helpful is, of course, that just because it abstracts from so much of the detail of reality, it may allow one to see more clearly than otherwise the importance of particular factors of interest.

4. I present a formal version of the model and sketch its analysis in an appendix, infra.

5. A party's assessment of these probabilities will be assumed to coincide with the courts', except in the discussion of mistake. See infra text accompanying notes 82, 91–96.

6. The importance of a party's thoughts will be considered in the discussion of intent. See infra subsection III.B.1; infra note 41.

7. Thus if there is a 20% probability of causing harm of magnitude 100, the expected harm is 20% × 100 = 20. More generally, if an act can cause different magnitudes of harm, the expected harm equals the sum of the products of the probabilities of the different possible magnitudes of harm with these magnitudes. For instance, if there

itself will ordinarily be interpreted as physical injury or property loss, although it is recognized that the concept of a natural or objective category of harm is not free from difficulty.[8] The theoretical analysis advanced here, however, is not affected by the definition of harm that one adopts. The analysis assumes only the existence of a category of socially undesirable consequences.

A party may derive private benefits from an act. These benefits may or may not be increased by the occurrence of harm. If a person fires a gun at someone whom he wishes to injure, the benefit that he derives will very much depend on whether harm actually results. A person who drives at high speed to reach a destination on time, however, or an individual who throws heavy shingles from a roof to avoid the inconvenience of carrying them down, will derive private benefits that are not increased by the occurrence of harm.

The benefits that society will be considered to derive from a party's act may be less than or equal to the party's private benefits. In fact, society may derive no benefits at all from a party's act. Allowing for a divergence between social and private benefits gives the analyst greater freedom to describe society's values. In particular, since the analyst can assume that the social benefits from an act are zero, he is able to study a society that finds some acts (rape, for example) objectionable no matter how high the private benefits may be. More generally, allowing social benefits to be less than private benefits permits the analyst to take into account society's apparent tendency to impute little value to acts for which the private benefits inhere in a party's enjoyment of the disutility suffered by the victim. Where the private benefits (for example, benefits from reaching a destination in time) are not obtained from the enjoyment of the victim's disutility, society seems more likely to credit them in the social calculus.[9]

The commission of an act will be said to be socially undesirable if the expected social benefits are exceeded by the expected harm. Thus, certainly where the expected social benefits are zero, a potentially

---

is a 20% probability of harm of 100 and a 10% probability of harm of 300, the expected harm is $20\% \times 100 + 10\% \times 300 = 50$. Note that the expected harm may be interpreted as the average amount of harm that would be done if an act were carried out repeatedly under similar circumstances. The definition of the term "expected" is conventional and will be used throughout the Article.

8. One can cite examples of societies in which acts that would be seen today as harmful were not regarded as such (the Aztec practice of human sacrifice) and in which acts that we would view today as relatively innocuous were regarded as very harmful (the killing of a cat in ancient Egypt). One can also point to contemporaneous examples in which the harmful qualities of acts are much disputed (homosexual relations between consenting adults).

9. While the possible divergence between social and private benefits affects which acts are considered socially undesirable, it does not affect the qualitative nature of conclusions about optimal deterrence, since that will depend only on the existence of some category of socially undesirable acts.

harmful act will be socially undesirable. Where the expected social benefits are positive, however, whether an act is undesirable will depend on a comparison with the expected harm. Thus, it might be desirable for a person to speed to reach the hospital in an emergency, since the expected social benefits might be higher than the expected harm, whereas it might not be desirable for a person to throw shingles from the roof, since the benefits might be lower than the expected harm.

Whether or not a party will actually commit an act—as distinct from whether or not it is socially desirable that he do so—depends on his perception of the possibility that he will suffer a sanction, either monetary or nonmonetary.[10] A party will commit an act if, and only if, the expected sanction would be less than the expected private benefits.[11] If he decides not to commit an act, he will be said to be deterred.

The imposition of monetary sanctions will be assumed to involve lower social costs than the imposition of nonmonetary sanctions. The motivation for this assumption is that the disutility to parties who must make payments may be viewed as roughly balanced by the addition to utility of parties who receive the payments or, where fines are paid to the government, who find their tax burdens reduced.[12] By contrast, the disutility experienced by parties punished by nonmonetary sanctions is not balanced in any automatic way by additions to the utility of other parties.[13] Furthermore, the imposition of nonmonetary sanctions often involves direct claims on goods and services, as with the building and operation of prisons.[14]

Finally, to impose sanctions, society must apprehend parties who commit harmful acts. This requires society to maintain an enforcement apparatus, with accompanying expenses, and these expenses will rise

10. The nonmonetary sanction will usually be interpreted as imprisonment. Other nonmonetary sanctions include loss of reputation, social stigma, and the death penalty.

11. That I make this assumption hardly implies that I adopt the easily-caricatured view that in reality individuals are all the time weighing the threat of sanctions against the benefits of contemplated acts. The assumption is meant only to reflect the belief that the threat of sanctions is sometimes an important consideration for most individuals (for example, those deciding whether to report their full income to the tax authorities) and is often an important consideration for some individuals (for example, professional thieves).

12. There still are, of course, social costs associated with the imposition of monetary sanctions. These reside mainly in the expense of reaching parties' assets and in the costs of "risk bearing," that is, the possible dislocative effects on parties who have to pay large amounts.

13. Some individuals, however, may derive pleasure from seeing guilty parties punished.

14. In assuming that the cost of imposing nonmonetary sanctions exceeds that of monetary sanctions, I do not wish to deny that the reverse might occasionally be true. For instance, the costs of reaching parties' assets might be high in certain situations and exceed the expense of carrying out the death penalty. I nevertheless make the assumption because of the need to keep the model simple and because of my presumption that imprisonment usually involves greater costs than does the imposition of monetary sanctions.

with the level of the probability of apprehension.[15]

Social welfare will be defined as the expected social benefits associated with the commission of acts, less the expected harm caused by the acts, the social costs of imposing sanctions, and enforcement expenses. The problem for society will be to devise a system of sanctions and to select a probability of apprehension so as to maximize social welfare.

II. The Domain of Nonmonetary Sanctions

A. *The Theoretically Optimal Domain of Nonmonetary Sanctions*

Since nonmonetary sanctions are socially more costly to impose than monetary sanctions in the above model, it is easy to say where nonmonetary sanctions should be employed. Specifically, nonmonetary sanctions should be employed only where monetary sanctions cannot adequately deter undesirable acts. Social welfare will be greater if only the less costly monetary sanctions are used to deter undesirable acts.[16]

Upon reflection, moreover, one can see that this argument actually implies that nonmonetary sanctions should be employed only after a monetary sanction equal to a party's wealth has already been imposed. Otherwise, there would be an opportunity to lower social costs while continuing to deter the same number of parties by simultaneously reducing the nonmonetary sanction and increasing the monetary sanction.[17]

In any event, to determine whether monetary sanctions can adequately deter undesirable acts, it proves useful to examine five factors. The initial three factors are important because they bear on the possibility that the monetary sanction needed to deter will exceed a party's assets, and thus that he could not be deterred by threat of a monetary sanction. One of these factors plainly is the size of a party's assets.[18] The smaller a party's assets, the smaller the chance that the prospect of

15. I will assume for simplicity that the probability of apprehension is perceived accurately by parties.

16. This general point has been at least suggested by most writers who have considered the issue of the choice of sanctions from a utilitarian perspective, see Becker, supra note 2, at 193; Bentham, supra note 2, at 183; 1 C. Montesquieu, supra note 2, at 91; but the point has not been developed as below.

17. Suppose, for instance, that a person with assets of $100,000 is fined $5000 and is sentenced to four years in prison. The disutility of this combined sanction could be held constant by increasing the fine from $5000 to $100,000 and reducing the prison sentence to some appropriate level, say one year. This would save society the cost of imprisoning the person for three years. Of course, if a fine of $100,000 would involve greater disutility than the original sanction of $5000 and the four year sentence, then a fine of less than $100,000 and no prison sentence could be substituted for the original sentence.

18. Because in reality a person can earn money in the future, and the state can, in principle, take away these future earnings, "assets" might be interpreted to mean present assets plus future earnings.

their forfeiture will be enough to outweigh the private benefits a party expects to derive from committing an undesirable act and thus the smaller the ability to deter him by use of monetary sanctions.[19] In the extreme case, for instance, it is impossible to deter a person with no assets by the threat of monetary sanctions.

A second factor is the probability that a party will escape being sanctioned. The greater this probability, the higher is the monetary sanction required to deter. If the probability that a party will escape sanctions is one-half, the magnitude of the monetary sanction would have to be approximately doubled; if the probability is one-third, it would have to be approximately tripled; and so forth.[20] Such increases in the monetary sanction needed to deter make it more likely that the sanction will exceed the party's assets.

A third factor is the level of the private benefits a party will derive from an undesirable act. The larger these benefits, the higher the monetary sanction necessary to deter, and again the greater the chance that this amount will exceed the party's assets.[21]

The remaining two factors are the probability that an act will cause harm and the magnitude of the harm. They are relevant because they determine the expected harm that will result if undesirable acts are not deterred.[22]

If the combined importance of these five factors is sufficiently high, that is, if the likelihood of failure to deter undesirable acts, together with the expected harm in which the acts would result, is sufficiently high, then resort to nonmonetary sanctions may be desirable despite the greater social costs attending their use. Nonmonetary sanctions

19. This point should not be confused with the point that a monetary sanction of given magnitude that can be paid will probably serve as a greater deterrent to a person with low assets than to a person with high assets. For example, a sanction of $100 will very likely be a greater deterrent to a person with $1000 of assets than to a person with $100,000. My point, by contrast, is that losing his entire wealth will be a greater deterrent to the person with $100,000 than to the one with $1000 simply because the former has more at stake than the latter.

20. The relationship would be exact—the sanction would have to be multiplied by precisely $1/p$, where p is the probability of escaping the sanction—under the simplifying assumption that parties are "risk neutral," i.e., that the marginal utility of a dollar does not depend on the level of wealth. Under the more plausible assumption that parties are "risk averse" and value dollars more the lower their wealth, the sanction would not have to be multiplied by as high a number as $1/p$ for the expected disutility of the uncertain sanction to be maintained.

21. It should be noted that because I am assuming that the act is undesirable, I am implicitly assuming that increases in the level of private benefits do not imply that social benefits become large enough to make the act desirable.

It should also be observed that it could be impossible to deter a party from committing an undesirable act by use of a monetary sanction alone even if his wealth were unlimited. This is because the private benefits he would obtain from the act might be nonmonetary and exceed the disutility of losing any amount of money.

22. Of course, the two factors also help to determine whether an act is undesirable.

may be helpful of course because their threatened use might deter parties who could not be deterred by monetary sanctions alone.

B. *The Actual Domain of Nonmonetary Sanctions*

The simple theory just discussed helps to explain the basic choices that society has made concerning where to employ nonmonetary sanctions. In the core area of crimes—the crimes that we frequently punish by imprisonment[23]—a brief assessment of the five factors indicates that the level of deterrence would often be inadequate were we to rely on monetary sanctions alone.

The first factor, the level of parties' assets, is relevant because criminals as a class seem to have relatively little wealth.[24] And this is not unexpected, since many personal characteristics that are correlated with criminality (for example, poor education and drug and alcohol abuse) are also correlated with inability to earn. Moreover, a primary motivation for some crimes, particularly theft, robbery, and burglary, is presumably that individuals have little money of their own.[25] The second factor, the likelihood of escaping apprehension, is clearly relevant, for criminal acts frequently go unpunished.[26] The third factor, the level of private benefits obtained by wrongdoers, often seems large, at least by comparison to its size outside the area of crime of present con-

23. For ease, I focus here on imprisonment as a nonmonetary sanction even though there are other forms of nonmonetary sanctions.

24. In one Department of Justice report, statistics are presented showing that criminals have little or no legally obtained income. See Bureau of Justice Statistics, U.S. Dep't of Just., Report to the Nation on Crime and Justice 38 (Oct. 1983) [hereinafter cited as Report]. For instance, according to one survey, almost half of all male inmates in prison had annual incomes under $3000 prior to arrest, and the median income for both male and female inmates was at the poverty level (as defined by the United States government) prior to arrest. Also, 40% of all males in prison had been unemployed when arrested, and of those who were working, about one fifth were working part-time. This compares to an employment rate of 84% for the United States male population in the 18–54 age group, with only 3% working part-time.

25. But needless to say, there are many reasons why individuals who are not poor might steal; a well-paid accountant might embezzle from his employer merely because he has a good opportunity to do so and wants to live the high life. I am speaking here only about general tendencies.

26. According to Federal Bureau of Investigation, U.S. Dep't of Just., 1981 Uniform Crime Reports, Crime in the United States 152 (Aug. 1982), the percentage of reported murders that resulted in arrest was 72%; the figure for aggravated assault was 58%; for rape, 48%; for robbery, 24%; for larceny-theft, 19%; for burglary, 14%; and for motor vehicle theft, 14%. Because many crimes are not fully reported and because arrests do not always result in convictions, the above percentages must be taken as upper bounds for the probability of imposition of sanctions. For example, in 1981 only 26% of household larceny thefts and only 67% of motor vehicle thefts were reported, see Report, supra note 24, at 24, and only about 50% of arrests for all serious crimes resulted in convictions, see Report, supra note 24, at 45. Hence, the probability of imposition of a sanction for larceny-theft may have been not 19% but approximately 26% × 19% × 50% = 2.47%, and the probability for motor vehicle theft not 14% but about 67% × 14% × 50% = 4.69%.

cern. Furthermore, plausible calculations indicate that the magnitude of the private benefits can easily outweigh the highest possible expected monetary sanction.[27] The other two factors, the magnitude and probability of harm, seem to figure predominantly in the core area of crime. The harm caused by serious crimes against persons, such as murder and rape, is obviously great, and the harm resulting from other "lesser" crimes in the core area—theft and counterfeiting, for instance—appears, upon reflection, to be also quite large.[28] Likewise, it is evident that parties who set out to commit crimes that fall in the core area will cause harm with high probability. In fact, we ordinarily *define* crime in a way that implies that the probability of harm is high.[29] All this suggests the validity of the claim that as a general matter something more than monetary sanctions must be employed to achieve an adequate degree of deterrence in the core area of crimes.[30]

For purposes of comparison, it is illuminating to consider the importance of the five factors in the area of unintentional torts, where of course only monetary sanctions, namely judgments paid to victims, are used. First, the assets of parties—especially corporate entities—are probably higher on average in the area of unintentional torts than in the core area of crimes. Second, the likelihood of escaping sanctions seems significantly smaller in the area of unintentional torts than in the core area of crime, for usually a party causing tortious harm cannot avoid being identified as the responsible party or does not try to avoid identification. Indeed, if he does try to avoid identification (as when a driver who strikes a pedestrian leaves the scene of the accident), his act may be converted into a crime. Third, the benefits parties derive from

27. Suppose, for example, that a potential thief with reachable assets of $500 contemplates stealing an automobile and knows that he would be convicted with probability 5%. This would be financially attractive so long as he could obtain more than $25 for the automobile, since the expected sanction he would face is 5% × $500 = $25.

28. Theft can be seen to be very harmful on general utilitarian grounds because it leads individuals to invest resources (for example, in burglar alarms), in order to protect property and to use property in constrained ways (for example, not leaving a new car in an unattended lot). Moreover, if theft is a serious enough problem, work effort and production might suffer because individuals would not be able to count on enjoying their purchases. Counterfeiting, at a minimum, induces individuals to check currency to make sure that it is genuine. And if widespread, counterfeiting would destroy confidence in money as a medium of exchange; transactions would be reduced to barter, and productivity would fall greatly.

29. Before labeling a party's act as criminal, we either insist directly that the act made harm highly likely (as when the party behaved with extreme recklessness) or else that the party wished a harmful outcome to occur—meaning that he probably behaved in a way that raised substantially its chance of occurring. For discussion of intent, see infra Subsection III.B.1.

30. A thorough examination of the claim would discuss how its basis and the relative importance of the different factors varies by the circumstances of the case and by the category of crime. Murder, for example, results in greater harm than the theft of radios from automobiles, but the likelihood of apprehension for murder is greater. See supra note 26.

committing unintentional torts, and thus the difficulty of deterring them, often seem to be of a lower order than in the core area of crime. This is because the benefits are comprised only of the costs avoided by not taking safety precautions.[31] Last, although the magnitude of harm may certainly be high in the area of unintentional torts, the probability of potentially tortious acts resulting in harm appears systematically smaller than the probability of criminal acts resulting in harm.[32] In sum, it seems that, in the area of unintentional torts, the use of monetary sanctions should produce a much better level of deterrence than in the core area of crime.

There are, of course, several areas other than that of unintentional torts where monetary sanctions but not imprisonment are employed: intentional torts either that cannot be punished under the criminal law, such as defamation, or that the state often decides not to prosecute criminally, such as assault and battery; and acts punished by fines only, including many violations of tax, business, and driving regulations. While the point will not be pursued here, it seems clear that the chief difference between these areas and the core area of crime is that the magnitude or the probability of harm is lower. Thus, it is not altogether surprising that monetary sanctions are used in these areas.

At the same time, I should emphasize that the consistency I see between theory and reality is very approximate. It is not difficult to adduce examples of disagreement between the actual use of monetary and nonmonetary sanctions and their theoretically optimal use as deterrents. For instance, my impression is that there are many occasions where a person with not insubstantial assets is sentenced to prison but pays no fine or only a modest one.[33] If so, then as explained previously, a savings in social resources could be achieved by reducing prison sentences and making greater use of fines. An example of plausibly insufficient use of imprisonment may also be mentioned. Where firms might cause harms much greater than their worth or where the harms would be difficult to trace, tort liability may not create an adequate level of deterrence. Hence, more frequent imposition of criminal

31. Contrast the small benefits a person obtains from not shoveling ice from the sidewalk, or the savings a firm enjoys *per unit* of its product for not including a safety feature, with the private benefits the typical murderer derives from his act, or the embezzler or the traitor from his.

32. Contrast the usual likelihood of harm from an intentional criminal act such as shooting at someone or entering a home to steal, with the likelihood of harm from failing to clear ice from the sidewalk, or from negligently failing to signal when changing lanes on the highway. Indeed, that the likelihood of harm is ordinarily small in the context of unintentional torts is reflected by our use of the term "accident" to refer to adverse outcomes.

33. For example, a fine of $5000 and an 18-month prison sentence was recently imposed on R. Foster Winans, a former Wall Street Journal reporter, for his part in a scheme to trade securities based on inside information. One supposes that Winans might have been able to pay a higher fine. See N.Y. Times, Aug. 7, 1985, at D1, col 6.

liability on the officers of firms may be necessary to achieve an acceptable level of safety. These examples illustrate the possibilities for the courts and the legislature to achieve social gains through an altered use of monetary and nonmonetary sanctions.

III. The Use of Nonmonetary Sanctions

Having discussed why nonmonetary sanctions, rather than less costly monetary sanctions, may be required to deter undesirable behavior, I will analyze in this Part the theoretically optimal use of nonmonetary sanctions[34] and then examine the doctrines of criminal law.

A. *The Theoretically Optimal Use of Nonmonetary Sanctions*

To determine the optimal use of nonmonetary sanctions, it is useful to consider the hypothetical situation where the courts[35] can obtain perfect information about parties who are apprehended, before studying the case where the courts' information is imperfect.

1. *The Situation Where Courts Can Obtain Perfect Information.* — Assume that the courts can obtain truly complete information about parties and their acts, once the parties have been brought before them. The courts will then be able to determine two things about any act that a party has committed.[36] First, they will be able to say whether the act was or was not socially undesirable. They will know, for instance, whether the death of *X*'s business partner on a hunting trip was the result of *X*'s deliberate act of shooting his partner to take control of their business, or was just an unfortunate accident.

Second, the courts will be able to tell whether a party could possibly have been deterred from committing an undesirable act *given* the probability of apprehension. A party could not possibly be deterred from committing an act if his expected private benefits exceed the disutility of the highest conceivable *expected* sanction — the highest conceivable sanction (perhaps the death penalty) discounted by the probability of its imposition.[37] The courts will be able to determine whether a

34. For simplicity, I will consider the use of nonmonetary sanctions unaccompanied by monetary sanctions. Hereinafter, "sanctions" will mean nonmonetary sanctions.

35. I use "courts" to refer to the legal entities that determine sanctions.

36. Note that since the courts have perfect information, they will not make a mistake as to whether a particular party has truly committed a particular act.

37. Suppose the benefit a party would derive from committing an act is 200, that the disutility of the maximum sanction is 1000, and that the probability of imposition of sanctions is 10%. Then the party could not possibly be deterred, for the maximum expected sanction would be 10% × 1000 or 100, which is less than 200. It should be clear to the reader that as a formal matter, such a possibility of inability to deter rests on the notion that the disutility of sanctions is bounded. That the disutility of sanctions must be bounded is, in fact, a conclusion deducible from the usual postulates of expected utility theory. See K. Arrow, Essays in the Theory of Risk Bearing 63–69 (1971); L. Savage, The Foundations of Statistics 81–82 (2d rev. ed. 1972).

If the reader is troubled by the idea that deterrence may be impossible, it is likely

party could possibly have been deterred because they will be able to ascertain the benefits the party expected to derive from his act, as well as the disutility of the maximum sanction and the probability of its imposition.[38]

Using these observations about the courts' knowledge, it is straightforward to describe the optimal system of sanctions. Under the optimal system, no sanction will be imposed on a party who committed a socially desirable act, for the courts will recognize the act as desirable and thus have no reason to employ a sanction. Also, no sanction will be imposed on a party who committed an undesirable act if he could not possibly have been deterred given the probability of imposition of sanctions, for the court will know that he could not have been deterred. Therefore, it would serve no purpose and yet be socially costly to impose a sanction. The remaining situation is that in which a party committed an undesirable act and could have been deterred. But this situation will never arise—and sanctions will never in fact be imposed—because it will clearly be optimal to set sanctions high enough to deter an undesirable act wherever deterrence is possible.[39]

In this last case, where undesirable acts can be deterred, there is no single optimal level of the sanction. The sanction could as well be extremely high as barely sufficient to deter since an extremely high sanction is no more costly than a low one if neither will be imposed.[40] Moreover, the magnitude of the expected harm does not affect the size of the sanction (presuming that the expected harm is high enough to make the act undesirable). The sanction is dependent on the level of expected private benefits, however, for the expected sanction must be sufficient to offset those benefits.[41] Similarly, the sanction is dependent

---

that he is thinking that most individuals would do almost anything to avoid a *certain* death. While this is doubtlessly true, it is in no way illogical for the same individuals to act in ways that raise the *probability* of death by only a small amount. It is a familiar fact that individuals subject themselves to increased risks of death for even rather trivial benefits (when they jaywalk for instance). They would not do so were the disutility of death infinite.

38. While I have assumed that the party accurately perceives this probability, in a more realistic model he might not. In such a model, the courts would have to determine what was the party's own assessment of the probability of apprehension to know whether he could have been deterred.

39. Suppose, for example, that as in note 37 supra, the maximum possible sanction is 1000 and the probability of its imposition is 10%, but that a party would obtain private benefits of only 50 from committing an undesirable act. This party could and thus would be deterred by the threat of a sanction, and therefore would never suffer a sanction.

40. The party of the previous note, who would obtain private benefits of 50, could be deterred by any sanction higher than 500—for that would result in an expected sanction higher than 50—and the sanction may as well be the maximum of 1000, since the sanction will not actually be imposed.

41. If the party of note 39 supra would obtain private benefits of 60 rather than 50, the sanction would have to be at least 600 to deter him. And notice that such depen-

on the probability of apprehending parties.[42]

To determine the optimal probability of apprehending parties, two opposing effects must be taken into account. As the probability is raised, enforcement expenses increase, but the maximum possible expected sanction, and thus the number of parties who can be deterred from committing undesirable acts, also increases.[43] The optimal probability will reflect an appropriate balancing of these effects, and in general will be higher the greater the harm that would be done by parties. Furthermore, efficiencies that decrease enforcement expenses will tend to raise the optimal probability.

2. *The Situation Where Courts Cannot Obtain Perfect Information.* — Realistically, the courts cannot obtain perfect information about parties and their acts. The courts therefore cannot employ sanctions as just described, and their use of sanctions will differ from that under perfect information in three significant ways. First, the possibility that the courts will not recognize certain acts as socially desirable and will impose sanctions will deter some socially desirable acts. For instance, a person may decide not to break into a cabin when he is in great need of shelter for fear that the courts will not understand the true character of his situation and will punish him. Second, some socially undesirable acts may not be deterred even though a sufficiently high sanction would provide an effective deterrent. Thus a person might decide to commit a robbery knowing that the sanction, if he is caught, will be a year in prison, while he would not act if the sanction were two years. Third, sanctions may actually be imposed: some parties who commit socially desirable acts will be punished (those who do break into cabins when they need shelter and are erroneously punished), some parties who commit undesirable acts and who could have been deterred will be punished, and some parties who commit undesirable acts and who could not have been deterred will be punished (for example, those who kill others in moments of uncontrollable rage).[44]

The magnitude of each of these problems varies with the level of sanctions. As the level of sanctions rises, more undesirable acts will be deterred, but the social cost of imposing sanctions in a given instance becomes greater, as does the problem of discouraging socially desira-

dence of the sanction on the private benefits a party would obtain means that the sanction depends on his thoughts (since they reflect the benefits he anticipates).

42. If the probability of apprehension of the party who would obtain private benefits of 50 were 20% rather than 10%, the size of the sanction necessary for deterrence would be 250 rather than 500, since 20% × 250 = 50.

43. If p is the probability of apprehension and 1000 is the maximum sanction, then the maximum expected sanction equals $p \times 1000$. Thus, the parties who can be deterred are those who would obtain expected private benefits less than $p \times 1000$. The higher the value of p, the greater the number of parties who can be deterred.

44. A fourth reason why sanctions will sometimes be imposed is that some parties who committed no act at all will mistakenly be thought to have committed a punishable act. I will not be discussing this problem here, however.

ble acts. The optimal level of the sanction will be that which makes the best compromise between these competing effects.[45]

The nature of this best compromise and thus the level of the optimal sanction depends on the characteristics of parties and their acts (as they are perceived by the courts). It is clear, first, that the higher the expected private benefits, the higher will be the optimal sanction – unless the benefits are so large that deterrence is probably not possible. This is because the higher the expected private benefits, the higher is the expected sanction needed to accomplish deterrence where deterrence is possible.[46]

It is also true that the greater the expected harmfulness of an act, the higher will be the optimal sanction. This is for three reasons. First, the greater the expected harm, the more society values increased deterrence, and therefore the more willing society should be to bear the costs of imposing higher sanctions.[47] In addition, an increase in ex-

45. To illustrate the process of determining the optimal sanction, suppose again that the maximum possible sanction is 1000, that the likelihood of apprehension is 10%, that there are two parties *X* and *Y* who each might commit an undesirable act causing expected harm of 800, that *X* would obtain a private benefit of 50 from committing the act (so that he can be deterred only by a sanction of at least 500), that *Y* would obtain a private benefit of 200 from the act (so that he cannot be deterred even by the highest sanction), and that courts are unable to distinguish between *X* and *Y*—the respect in which the courts' information is imperfect—and thus must use the same sanction for each.

It follows that if a positive sanction is optimal, it will be a sanction of 500. In particular, a positive sanction less than 500 would deter neither *X* nor *Y*, and thus sometimes would be imposed but to no purpose. A sanction of 500 (or slightly more) would deter *X* but not *Y*. A sanction above 500 would only increase the sanction that would be imposed on *Y*, since he will not be deterred, and therefore would be inferior to a sanction of 500.

To determine whether a positive sanction of 500 rather than a sanction of zero is optimal, a comparison of levels of social welfare must be made. In computing social welfare, assume for simplicity that the private benefits that *X* and *Y* obtain from committing their acts have no social value and that the social costs of imposing sanctions equal the disutility experienced by the punished parties, and for simplicity ignore society's enforcement expenses. Thus, maximization of social welfare will correspond to a minimization of expected harm plus expected sanctions imposed. If the sanction is 500, these expected social costs are 800 + 10% × 500 = 850 (since *Y* alone commits the undesirable act), and if the sanction is zero, the social costs are 800 + 800 = 1600 (since both *X* and *Y* commit the act). Hence a sanction of 500 is optimal.

46. In the example of the previous note, if the expected benefit of *X* were 60 rather than 50, the optimal sanction would be 600 rather than 500.

47. To illustrate this, the example in note 45 supra must be modified and made somewhat more complicated. Suppose that there is a third party, *Z*, who would obtain a private benefit of 70 from committing the act—and thus who could be deterred, but only by a sanction of at least 700. Suppose also that there are 1000 *X*'s, one *Z*, and 100 *Y*'s. Then it is straightforward to verify along the lines of note 45 that the optimal sanction is still 500. At 500, the expected social costs due to the imposition of sanctions would be 101 × 50 = 5050 since *Z* and the 100 *Y*'s would commit the act. At 700, the expected social costs due to the sanctions would be 100 × 70 = 7000 since the 100 *Y*'s but not *Z* would commit the act. The reason a sanction of 500 is socially superior to one of 700 is

pected harm may be associated with an increase in expected private benefits, for, as previously noted, the private benefits often depend on the harm, as when a party robs or intentionally injures another.[48] And since the optimal sanction rises with the expected private benefits – because parties become harder to deter – an increase in expected harm will tend indirectly to increase the optimal sanction. Finally, raising the sanction with the expected harmfulness of acts gives parties who are *not* deterred incentives to do less harm. Specifically, it encourages them to choose initially to commit less harmful acts (to plan to beat up an enemy rather than knife him to death) and, during the commission of acts, to refrain from increasing the level of harm done (to avoid killing a person in the course of a robbery). Such incentives will be said to reflect "marginal deterrence."

Although the optimal sanction rises with the expected harm associated with an undesirable act, that does not imply that the sanction necessarily rises with the *actual* harm done. Of course, this is because in calculating expected harm, one discounts possible levels of actual harm by their probabilities.[49] For example, act *A* may result in higher actual harm than act *B*, yet *A* may have created a much lower probability of harm and consequently be associated with a lower expected harm.[50] Therefore, the optimal sanction for *A* could be lower than the optimal sanction for *B*. Nevertheless, the actual harm done is relevant to the optimal sanction where, as will often be true, the courts' knowledge of the expected harmfulness of an act is poor. Since they do not directly observe the probability of harm or the different levels of harm that might have resulted, courts must infer these from, among other evidence, the occurrence and magnitude of the actual harm. Thus, the sanction can reasonably rise with the actual harm. In addition, marginal deterrence might not be adequate unless the sanction rises with the level of actual harm.

The relationship between the probability of apprehending parties and the optimal sanction is, one would expect, that the lower the probability, the higher the optimal sanction. This would likely be required to maintain the expected sanction needed for proper deterrence.[51]

---

that it would not be worthwhile to incur additional social costs of 1950 just to deter the one *Z* from committing an act whose expected harm is 800. If, however, the expected harm associated with the undesirable act were above 1950, it would be optimal to deter *Z* by raising the sanction to 700.

48. See supra p. 1234.

49. See supra note 7.

50. Suppose act *A* causes harm of 1000 with probability of 10%, and act *B* causes harm of 500 with probability of 50%. Then the expected harm associated with *A* is 100 and is lower than that associated with *B*, namely, 250.

51. It is theoretically conceivable, however, for the optimal sanction to fall if the probability falls. This can happen if, when the probability falls, many parties become undeterrable and the remaining parties can be deterred easily. To illustrate, consider

Finally, with regard to the determination of the optimal probability of apprehending parties, the main point is the one from before, namely, that the probability should not be too low lest too many parties become impossible to deter. There is now, however, a further reason why the probability should not be too low: the sanction for acts would then generally have to be very high to accomplish adequate deterrence, but that would undermine marginal deterrence because the sanctions for acts of differing severity would be similar.[52]

This completes the theoretical discussion of the optimal use of nonmonetary sanctions as a deterrent. In thinking about the subject, the reader should keep in mind that it cannot be equated with the simple problem of deterring a person with known characteristics from committing an undesirable act. The proper view of the subject takes into account the imperfect nature of the courts' information and the errors that result relative to the situation under perfect information.[53]

---

another modification of the example in note 45 supra. There are three parties: not only *X* who would obtain a benefit of 50 and *Y* who would obtain a benefit of 200, but also *W* who would obtain a benefit of 2. If the probability of imposition of sanctions is 10%, then both *X* and *W* can be deterred, and the optimal sanction would be 500. But if the probability of sanctions were 1%, only *W* could be deterred (as the maximum expected sanction would be 10), and the optimal sanction would fall from 500 to 200.

52. For instance, if the probability of apprehension were very low, the sanction for both robbery and murder might have to be near life imprisonment to create adequate deterrence. Then only a small difference in the sanctions for the two crimes would exist, and robbers would have little reason not to murder their victims.

53. This view of the subject has not been developed by other writers on deterrence and criminal law, although, of course, their contribution is great, and it is worthwhile to describe it briefly. The most important writers on the theory of the use of sanctions as a deterrent are probably Charles Montesquieu, Cesare Beccaria, Jeremy Bentham, and Gary Becker. Montesquieu and Beccaria were among the first to adopt a utilitarian style of analysis. While they were often vague and unanalytical, they suggested that, because nonmonetary sanctions are costly to impose (they considered mostly the disutility to punished parties), sanctions should be used sparingly and only when likely to accomplish deterrence. See C. Beccaria, supra note 2, at 17–19, 21; 1 C. Montesquieu, supra note 2, at 84. They occasionally raised points of considerable sophistication about deterrence, as for instance with respect to marginal deterrence. See C. Beccaria, supra note 2, at 32; 1 C. Montesquieu, supra note 2, at 90. Bentham's work built on Montesquieu and Beccaria (whom he frequently cites) and generally stands out as incomparable. He was the first to state carefully and investigate the assumption that potential wrongdoers weigh possible benefits against the probability and magnitude of sanctions. Of particular interest is his analysis of the optimal magnitude of sanctions. See Bentham, supra note 2, at 169–77. Becker was the first to attempt a formal model of sanctions and deterrence, and was also the first to study the probability of apprehension as an instrument of social choice.

The present Article goes beyond these works and explicitly takes into account the imperfect nature of the courts' information. Only by doing so can one explain why, if a particular level of the sanction will deter, just that sanction, and not a higher one, should be used. Without this, one's theory of optimal sanctions is not really logical, or is at least incomplete. Also, this Article stresses the implications of the possible inability to deter parties given the probability of apprehending them. Only by considering these implications can one explain why extremely high sanctions should not often be used,

B. *The Principles of Criminal Law and the Use of Nonmonetary Sanctions*

The major principles and doctrines of criminal law will now be considered in view of the theory of optimal deterrence.

1. *Intent.* — A central feature of the criminal law is the emphasis it places on intent. To analyze intent, it is best to begin by making several definitions. Let us say that a party "desires" a result if it would either directly or indirectly raise his utility.[54] Let us also say that a party "intends" a result if he (a) desires the result and (b) acts in a way that he believes will raise the probability of the result.[55] This definition of intent seems to comport with its ordinary meaning.[56] According to the definition, we would say that *X* intended that *Y* die if he desired *Y*'s death and shot at *Y* and killed him. If, however, *X* shot at *Y* but instead struck *Z* whose death he did not desire, we would not say that he intended that *Z* die. Also, we would not say that *X* intended that *Y* die if *X* played golf with *Q*, and *Y* happened to be killed in an automobile accident (since the round of golf did not increase the probability of *Y*'s death).

In the criminal law, the role of intent, as I have defined the term, may be summarized by several statements.[57] First, intent to do harm is ordinarily a principal factor in determining liability and the severity of punishment. Second, the effect of intent on liability and punishment is generally the same whether an intended harmful result is directly or indirectly desired. Whether *X* shot *Y* because *Y* was his enemy or only because *Y* stood in the way of an inheritance will not ordinarily affect the punishment of *X* under the law. Third, whether a harmful result different from the desired result occurs does not usually influence a party's legal treatment. Where *X* aimed at *Y* but shot *Z* instead, it is murder just as if he aimed at *Z*.

These features describing the role of intent are roughly consistent with the purposes of deterrence, for intent appears to be linked to the factors that, according to theory, call for, or increase the level of, sanc-

---

and why it is not desirable to allow the probability of apprehending parties to be very low in order to save enforcement expenses.

54. In the language of utility theory, a result is desired if it is an argument in the individual's utility function that would raise his utility or, if the result is not such an argument in his utility function, if its occurrence would lead to an increase in his expected utility.

55. The significance of erroneous beliefs is discussed infra notes 80–82, 91–96 and accompanying text. For now, I assume the party's beliefs about the probability are correct.

56. The traditional definition of intent in the criminal law is broader: a party "intends" a result even where he does not desire it if he acts in a way that makes it highly probable (rather than only more probable).

57. See W. LaFave & A. Scott, Handbook on Criminal Law § 28 (1972) (describing the role of intent). See generally H. Hart, Intention and Punishment *in* Punishment and Responsibility 113 (1968) (a philosophically-oriented discussion of intent and criminal law) G. Fletcher, Rethinking Criminal Law § 6.5 (1978) (same).

tions.[58] Intent is, first of all, positively related to the probability of harm, for by definition, where a party intends to do harm, his act raises the probability of harm. This factor is particularly significant when the courts' direct evidence about the probability of harm is limited, since they can often make inferences about the probability from knowledge of a party's intent. For instance, where the courts hear little testimony about *X*'s shooting of *Y* but know that *X* had the purpose of killing *Y*, they might infer that *X* carefully drew a bead on *Y*.[59] Second, intent may be correlated with the likely magnitude of harm because a party who desires a harmful result is prone to do greater harm than one who does not. *X* may more often hit *Y* in a vital spot than in an arm or a leg if *X* desires to harm *Y*. Intent is also closely related to the private benefits parties expect to derive from their acts. By definition, the utility of parties who intend harm is raised by the occurrence of harm, and as just indicated, both the probability and magnitude of such desired harm tend to be higher where there is intent. Thus, parties who intend to do harm should be more difficult to deter.[60] In addition, intent to do harm may be associated with the absence of social benefits, for as pointed out earlier, society often appears reluctant to value private benefits that are based on the enjoyment of harm.[61] Finally, intent may be linked to the probability that a party will escape a sanction, since a party who intends to commit a harmful act is more likely to choose a particular place and time to avoid identification and arrest, or to take steps thereafter to do so.[62]

58. Oliver Wendell Holmes, Jr., was apparently the first to try to establish a connection between intent and factors that ought to increase the sanction appropriate for deterrence. His discussion was largely limited, however, to the relationship between intent and the probability of doing harm. See O. Holmes, The Criminal Law, *in* The Common Law 34 (M. deWolfe ed. 1963).

59. It is worth developing this example in more detail. Suppose that *X* and *Y* were hunting together when *X* shot *Y*. *X* claims that he fired at a deer running between him and *Y* and unfortunately did not see *Y*. A witness who was standing at some distance confirms that there was a deer running between *X* and *Y*, but he is not able to say whether *X* noticed *Y* or aimed at him rather than at the deer. With only this very imperfect knowledge of *X*'s act, the courts could value highly information about *X*'s intent (for example, evidence that he planned to kill *Y* at a good opportunity) or lack thereof (for example, evidence that *X* had nothing to gain from *Y*'s death). Thus, knowledge of his intent may alter the courts' assessment of the probability of harm due to *X*'s act. If, however, the courts' direct knowledge of *X*'s act were complete (for example, suppose they had a close up movie of his behavior), they would not need to know anything about intent to assess the probability of harm. But, as will be seen, they might well find knowledge of intent valuable for other reasons.

60. If *X* intends to kill *Y*, it will be difficult to deter him, because he wants *Y* dead and because shooting at *Y* makes this result likely. By contrast, if *X* is a true friend of *Y*, to deter a negligent or reckless shot will not require a substantial sanction (if it requires any sanction at all).

61. See supra p. 1234.

62. In some cases, however, the factor of intent could increase the probability of sanctions because a person's motives might be discoverable and lead police to investigate him. The importance of this consideration depends on the type of crime and the

These arguments suggest why intent, though mainly a mental factor, ought to influence liability and punishment according to deterrence theory. Moreover, it should be noted that the arguments do not depend on whether the intended harm is directly or indirectly desired. In either case, the probability and magnitude of harm, the expected private benefits, and the likelihood of escaping sanctions are likely to be higher than for unintentional conduct.[63] Moreover, the arguments are largely unaffected by whether the actual result was the desired result. It therefore makes sense that such distinctions usually do not affect a party's punishment.

Consideration of situations in which a party is not liable despite his intent to do harm sheds further light on intent and the theory of deterrence.[64] A party may intend to do harm but escape liability because circumstances make his act socially desirable; for example, a party forced to choose between two harmful acts may invoke the defense of necessity if he chooses the less harmful.[65] In addition, a sanction is not imposed where deterrence may be impossible, as in cases of insanity[66] or duress.[67]

Conversely, parties are sometimes punished despite their lack of intent to do harm. Where a party does not desire a harmful result but acts in such a way that serious harm becomes very likely, he may be punished. Imposition of sanctions here may be justified because the expected harm is high;[68] the fact that the party does not desire the harm does not make his behavior less dangerous. Similarly, where a party does not desire harm but commits a strict liability crime, his punishment may be justified in principle if the courts find it very difficult to differentiate between desirable and undesirable acts.[69]

2. *Attempt.* — The criminal law punishes attempts to do harm.[70] To understand why punishment of attempts may also be desirable

---

particular case. It might be significant in some cases of murder, for instance, but would probably not be in most cases of theft and robbery.

63. The only argument that is affected concerns the discounting of the private benefits. If the intended result is directly desired, the private benefits seem more likely to be discounted than otherwise.

64. That there should be such situations is not surprising a priori, for intent was only said to be linked with factors leading to the optimality of liability.

65. See infra note 102 and accompanying text.

66. See infra notes 89–90 and accompanying text.

67. See infra notes 100–01 and accompanying text.

68. Notice here the consistency with deterrence theory. Where the result is not desired, the private benefits are lower and thus deterrence is easier, other things being equal. Therefore, to warrant liability, the expected harm associated with the act must be unusually high.

69. See infra notes 109–12 and accompanying text.

70. See W. LaFave & A. Scott, supra note 57, § 59. It is interesting to note that this is in contrast to the situation in tort law, where there is no liability unless harm is done. See W. Keeton, D. Dobbs, R. Keeton & D. Owen, Prosser and Keeton on the Law of Torts § 30, at 165 (5th ed. 1984) [hereinafter cited as Prosser & Keeton].

under the theory of deterrence, it is necessary to consider why punishment of parties only when they actually do harm might not create an effective deterrent. One reason is that even if the sanction were set at the maximum level, the probability of its imposition might not be sufficient to make the expected sanction high enough to deter.[71] In addition, even where it would be possible to deter most parties by punishing them only when they do harm, the necessary sanctions would generally be high (because of a low probability of their imposition) and conflict with the goal of marginal deterrence, since marginal deterrence requires a certain degree of gradation in the schedule of sanctions.[72]

The punishment of attempts may serve to solve these problems by raising the expected sanction without increasing the magnitude of sanctions, for the punishment of attempts in effect increases the probability of sanctions.[73] Moreover, the punishment of attempts is a socially inexpensive means of increasing the probability, since opportunities to punish attempts often arise as a byproduct of society's investment in apprehending parties who actually do harm.[74]

The force of this argument for sanctioning attempts clearly increases with the probability that a party will be apprehended for an attempt. Where an act takes a long time to carry out (especially where it requires preparations) or where it has a substantial chance of not succeeding (for example, shooting from a distance), the probability of being caught for an attempt will be higher than otherwise. Therefore, the deterrent value of punishing attempts will also be higher.

The possible desirability of punishment of attempts according to deterrence theory does not imply that there is any advantage in punishing attempts in the way the criminal law does, namely, less severely

71. This reason does not apply in the usual model of torts, because it is assumed that parties do not escape suit and have assets sufficient to pay for harm done. In that model, making parties pay money damages only when they actually do harm creates adequate incentives to reduce risk. See Brown, Toward an Economic Theory of Liability, 2 J. Legal Stud. 323 (1973).

72. See supra note 52 and accompanying text.

73. An illustration may be helpful. Suppose a party who attempts a crime will succeed in doing harm half the time, that he will be apprehended with probability 30% if he does harm and 20% if he does not, that the disutility of the maximum sanction is 1000, and that the expected private benefit from his act is 200. If sanctions are not imposed for unsuccessful attempts, the probability of imposition of sanctions is just $\frac{1}{2} \times 30\% = 15\%$, so the maximum expected sanction is only 150. Thus, since the party's expected benefits are 200, he cannot be deterred. But if the party is punished whether or not his attempt is successful, the probability of imposition of sanctions is $\frac{1}{2} \times 30\% + 1/2 \times 20\% = 25\%$, so the maximum expected sanction is 250; hence the party can be deterred.

74. Given that the police stand ready to apprehend those who do harm (by giving chase, investigating reports, etc.), it may not be that much more expensive for them to apprehend those who commit unsuccessful attempts. At least it would probably be much more expensive for the police to increase the probability of apprehension comparably by making greater efforts to apprehend only those parties who do harm.

than acts that result in harm. In discussing this feature of the criminal law, it is useful to consider separately "interrupted attempts"—acts discovered before they could have succeeded—and "completed attempts"—unsuccessful acts not discovered until later.

With respect to interrupted attempts, the following argument is sometimes made.[75] If the sanction for an attempt is lower than that for doing harm, a party who begins an attempt might be induced to reevaluate and abandon it, since he then will be punished less. If, however, the sanction for the attempt is the same as for doing harm, he may as well continue. As stated, this argument fails to recognize the possibility of treating the abandoned attempt leniently, while imposing a full sanction on attempts interrupted by others. Suppose for instance that no sanctions are imposed for abandoned attempts and the sanction for an interrupted attempt is the same as the sanction for an act that causes harm. Then the party who sets out to commit a harmful act will certainly have reason to abandon it; not only will he escape sanctions, but he will otherwise face a sanction for a later interrupted attempt equal to the sanction for doing harm.[76]

Nevertheless, punishing interrupted attempts less severely than acts that result in harm may be advantageous. Since interrupted attempts may later be abandoned or fail, there is less evidence of the dangerousness of interrupted attempts and less reason for sanctioning them than acts that actually do result in harm.[77] The significance of this argument plainly depends on the character of the attempt and the point at which it is interrupted. If an attempt is nearly complete and is likely to succeed, the argument does not carry much weight. That would be so, for instance, where a person had already dropped a lethal dose of poison into his intended victim's drink. An attempt interrupted

75. This argument is usually attributed to Beccaria. See C. Beccaria, supra note 2, at 138.

76. However, difficulties courts may experience in distinguishing between interrupted and abandoned attempts lead to qualifications in this line of reasoning. Parties may pretend to abandon their attempts if they suspect that they are going to be interrupted (for example, individuals who are about to rob a bank may notice police approaching and leave). To the extent that parties' acts are mistakenly seen by the courts as abandoned attempts, it would be desirable to impose a positive sanction for apparent abandoned attempts. The opposite mistake occurs when parties who truly abandon attempts are thought by the courts to have stopped only because they believed they were about to be interrupted (for example, suppose the individuals in the bank really did not realize the police were approaching but were thought by the courts to have thought so). To the extent that this mistake arises, it would be desirable to impose a lesser sanction for an apparently interrupted attempt. For a description of difficulties in distinguishing abandoned attempts from interrupted attempts, see W. LaFave & A. Scott, supra note 57, § 60; and for a general discussion of the subject, see G. Fletcher, supra note 57, § 3.3.8.

77. This the reader will recognize as a version of the general argument advanced earlier, see supra text following note 50, that the actual harm done might influence the sanction because of the courts' incomplete information about the dangerousness of an act.

further from completion might properly be sanctioned less severely, however. Indeed, an attempt might escape a sanction altogether if it is interrupted so early that there is great doubt whether and in what manner it would have been continued.[78] Thus, if the person was apprehended merely when leaving a drugstore with poison, it might be unclear whether he would have used the poison, and unclear too whether his behavior would satisfy the definition of attempt in criminal law.

Two arguments analogous to those just discussed are often advanced to justify imposition of a lower sanction for unsuccessful completed attempts than for successful attempts. First, it is asserted that if the sanction for an unsuccessful completed attempt is equal to the sanction for a successful attempt, a party whose initial attempt fails will have nothing to lose by trying again. This argument, however, overlooks the fact that the sanction for an initial unsuccessful attempt may equal the sanction for an initial successful attempt, and yet the party *will* have something to lose by trying a second time so long as the sanction for a second successful attempt is higher. For example, if the sanction for an initial attempt is five years whether or not it succeeds, but the sanction for causing harm on a second attempt is ten years, a party who at first fails will clearly have reason not to try a second time.

The other argument for punishing unsuccessful completed attempts less severely than those resulting in harm is that the failure of an attempt may constitute evidence that it was a less dangerous act. As with interrupted attempts, the strength of this evidentiary rationale depends on the nature of the attempt. And while one can think of situations where the rationale would be important, in most situations that come readily to mind, it does not seem so.[79]

Finally, it is interesting to consider attempts that cannot possibly succeed.[80] There are two types of such attempts. The first, for which it is often said liability should not be imposed, is exemplified by the case of a person who sticks pins in a voodoo doll, intending to kill his enemy.[81] Here an objective observer might say that the type of act com-

78. See O. Holmes, supra note 58, at 56.

79. For instance, if a person puts poison in his intended victim's drink but the victim fails to succumb, it is true that this is some evidence that the act was less dangerous than one which produced a death—perhaps because the dosage of poison was too low. But this would not ordinarily seem to constitute enough evidence to lower the sanction significantly. In any event, there is less reason to lower the sanction than if the person had been interrupted before he completed the attempt, for then there would have been doubt about whether the attempt would have been completed, as well as whether it would have been successful.

80. See W. LaFave & A. Scott, supra note 57, § 60; G. Fletcher, supra note 57, § 3.3.3.

81. Note that because this person *believes* he is raising the probability of his enemy's death, we would say he intends his death under my definition.

mitted never causes harm, so that there is no reason to deter the act.[82] The second kind of attempt, for which there would be liability, is illustrated by the case of a person who shoots a bullet into a dummy that he thinks is his enemy. In this instance, an objective observer would certainly say that the type of act committed creates positive expected harm, for shooting into objects that appear to be individuals will usually result in harm. Hence, according to deterrence theory, the act should be punished.

3. *Causation.* — When a party's act is followed by harm, two causal issues may arise.[83] The first concerns the question whether the act was the "necessary" cause (the "but for" cause) of the harm, that is, whether the harm would still have occurred in the absence of the act. Thus, if *X* poisons *Y*'s drink and *Y* then dies, but an autopsy reveals that *Y* died of a heart attack, *X*'s act would not be the necessary cause of *Y*'s death. The criminal law ordinarily treats an act that was not the necessary cause of harm as if it were an attempt: the party is punished for the act, but less so than if the act were the necessary cause of the harm.[84]

This outcome makes sense—though only partial sense—according to deterrence theory. It makes sense that acts which are not the necessary causes of harm are punished, for this enhances deterrence in the same way that punishment of attempts does, namely, by increasing the probability of sanctions.[85] The reason for the imposition of lesser sanctions, however, is not apparent. That acts sufficient to cause harm turn out not to be the necessary causes of harm is happenstance; it does not mean that the expected harmfulness of the acts was any lower. Therefore, the sanctions for such acts ought not to be diminished, according to deterrence theory.[86]

If a party's act was the necessary cause of harm, the issue arises whether his act was the "proximate cause" of harm. Generally, acts said to be the proximate cause of harm can be recognized as acts which

82. This presumes that the person who failed with the voodoo doll would not have tried other ways of killing his enemy, such as shooting at him. If there is evidence that the person would have done this, then his act would appropriately be defined as "trying to kill an enemy by some means" rather than "trying to kill an enemy using a voodoo doll," and there would be a reason to punish him.

83. See W. LaFave & A. Scott, supra note 57, § 35.

84. This situation is different under tort law, where a party usually escapes liability if his act was not the necessary cause of harm. See Prosser & Keeton, supra note 70, § 41, at 265.

85. In the usual model of torts, there is no reason to enhance deterrence by use of sanctions where a party's act is not the necessary cause of harm. Assuming that parties have the assets to pay for harm done, and that they would not escape suit, the threat of liability only when their acts are necessary causes of harm is enough to induce parties to take adequate care. See Shavell, An Analysis of Causation and the Scope of Liability in the Law of Torts, 9 J. Legal Stud. 463 (1980).

86. The fact that *Y* died of a heart attack does not cast doubt on the potency of the poison. Note that this is in contrast to a failed or interrupted attempt to murder *Y* by poisoning.

substantially increased the probability or magnitude of the type of harm that occurred. To illustrate, if *X* severely beats *Y* and *Y* later dies in the hospital from internal injuries, we would probably say that *X*'s actions were the proximate cause of *Y*'s death. If, however, *Y* dies on the way to the hospital in an automobile accident, we would probably not say that *X*'s actions were the proximate cause of *Y*'s death.[87] In determining punishment, the criminal law usually takes into account whether or not the harm was proximately caused. *X* might be held liable for murder when *Y* dies from his internal injuries, but not when *Y* dies in the automobile accident.

Punishing a party for harm that he proximately caused might sometimes be justified in view of the evidentiary value of the actual harm done. *Y*'s death from internal injuries may be indicative of the severity of the beating he received, whereas his death in an automobile accident would not convey such information. In addition, considerations of marginal deterrence may justify greater punishment for proximately caused harms. *X* might decide against beating *Y* very badly if he knows that should *Y* die in the hospital from his injuries, *X*'s punishment would increase. No such incentive would result were *X* to be punished for *Y*'s death in an automobile accident.[88]

4. *Responsibility.* — The criminal law sanctions a party who commits a socially undesirable act only if he is "responsible," in whole or in part, for his behavior. A party may not be responsible due to insanity, automatism, involuntary intoxication, or youth.[89] That defenses based on these conditions eliminate or diminish liability has an obvious potential justification according to deterrence theory, since the conditions make it unlikely that the use of sanctions would accomplish significant deterrence.[90] An insane or involuntarily intoxicated person, for example, presumably cannot be deterred from committing certain acts by the threat of punishment, so that the elimination of punishment might be appropriate. And it might be proper to impose diminished sanctions on young persons where, although there may be some possibility of deterring them, the dangerousness of their acts and their ability to escape sanctions is less than that of adults.

At the same time, deterrence theory suggests two general reasons for restricting such limitation of liability. First, parties might success-

87. The probability of dying in an automobile accident on a single trip (even if by ambulance) is small, and is therefore not much increased by *X*'s beating. In any event, *Y* might have been going somewhere else by automobile if he had not been going to the hospital.

88. That the logic of this paragraph applies generally and is not a feature of my examples can be appreciated from the characterization of proximately caused harms as those of a type whose probability or severity was increased in a substantial way by a party's act. It is exactly where this is true that the occurrence of the outcome may convey useful information about how much the party's act increased the expected harm.

89. See W. LaFave & A. Scott, supra note 57, ch. 4.

90. This is stressed by Bentham, supra note 2, at 164.

fully feign the conditions which limit responsibility. This possibility is more significant with respect to some of the defenses (for example, insanity) than to others (for example, youth). Second, parties might act in ways that make their conditions especially dangerous. An epileptic might drive an automobile, or a person subject to insane rages might decide to purchase a gun. The imposition of liability could induce these parties to act differently and thereby reduce dangers over which they later would have no control.

5. *Justification and Excuse.* — In addition to the defenses that fall under the rubric of responsibility are defenses ordinarily placed under the heading of justification and excuse. They will be considered separately since the issues they present are different.

a. *Ignorance and Mistake.* — If a party claims that he was unaware that his act was unlawful, he will ordinarily be found liable anyway. He may escape liability if he had little opportunity to learn about the law (as with an unpublished or little-known ordinance) or if he was acting in reliance on a mistaken interpretation of the law made by a court or an appropriate government officer.[91]

Such an approach is clearly suggested by the theory of deterrence.[92] If a party is held liable for violating widely-known laws or laws that can be learned through reasonable effort, whether or not he in fact claims to know such laws, he will have an incentive to learn the law and adhere to it. If, however, a reasonable effort is insufficient to learn a law, it is best to permit parties to escape liability, since a party can be deterred by possible sanctions only if he knows to which acts the sanctions will be applied.

A second kind of mistake arises where a party commits an act that he believes to be different in some material respect from what it is in fact. A mistake of this kind is where a party commits an act that he believes to be innocent although it is actually harmful. In the classic case, a person takes an umbrella from a restaurant assuming that it is his, when it really belongs to someone else. As deterrence theory suggests is desirable, there is no criminal liability in instances like this.[93] Assuming that acts believed to be harmless usually are harmless, the expected harm associated with the acts is too low to warrant use of sanctions.

Another category of mistake arises where a party knowingly commits an undesirable act but believes it to be either more or less harmful than it is in fact. For example, an individual might steal a valuable piece of jewelry, thinking it a mere bauble, or he might shoot to kill the "person" who turns out to be a dummy. The legal principles employed in these situations are not uniform; although sanctions are frequently

91. See generally W. LaFave & A. Scott, supra note 57, § 47 (general discussion of mistake of law doctrine).

92. See Bentham, supra note 2, at 164.

93. See W. LaFave & A. Scott, supra note 57, § 47, at 357.

based on what a party did in fact, many times they are affected by what he thought he was doing.[94]

There are two reasons why the harmfulness of the act the party thought he was committing should influence the sanction. First, the benefits a party expects to derive from committing an act and thus the ability to deter him, depend on what he thinks he is doing, not on what he is in fact doing.[95] Second, the expected harm associated with an act may be more closely related to what the party thinks it is than to what it turns out to be in the particular instance. The act of taking what one thinks is a bauble might usually mean that only a bauble is missing; the act of shooting at what one thinks is a person will usually be very harmful.

Nevertheless, one important factor suggests that the actual harm should influence the sanction. Parties may be able to convince the courts that they thought they were doing little harm when in truth they knew they were doing greater harm. If so, and if the sanction is based on the courts' erroneous assessment of parties' beliefs, sanctions will be too low and diminished deterrence will result.[96] Hence, there is some reason to raise the sanction where the actual harm exceeds what the party claims to have thought it would be. But note that there is no corresponding argument for lowering the sanction where the actual harm turns out to be less than what the party thought it would be, since a party will have no incentive to exaggerate the harm he thought he was doing.

b. *Entrapment.* — A party may raise the defense of entrapment if a law enforcement official induces the party to commit a criminal act that he would not ordinarily commit.[97] Where, for instance, a game warden induces a hunter to shoot at bald eagles and the hunter would not otherwise have done this, the hunter can assert the defense of entrapment.

The argument for this defense on grounds of deterrence theory is that if parties would not ordinarily commit criminal acts, there is no behavior that needs to be deterred. Thus, any punishment of the parties and any effort devoted to their entrapment must be considered a social waste;[98] moreover, their entrapment might also result in the ac-

94. See id. § 47, at 360.

95. The individual who thinks he is stealing a bauble will be easy to deter, but not the individual who knows he is stealing valuable jewelry.

96. Individuals may not be properly deterred from stealing valuable jewelry if they know they can convince the courts that they thought the jewelry was only a bauble.

97. See generally W. LaFave & A. Scott, supra note 57, § 48 (general treatment of entrapment).

98. To clarify this point, consider a situation where a person would *never* commit a criminal act if not entrapped. Here, plainly, punishing the person and devoting effort to entrap him is wasteful, since otherwise the person would not cause harm. It is irrelevant under deterrence theory that he might be thought a "bad" person because he could be induced to commit a criminal act in certain contrived circumstances.

tual doing of harm.[99] Hence, it is best not to punish the parties, and to discourage entrapment. The former is directly accomplished by allowing the defense; and the latter is indirectly accomplished, since enforcement officials do not derive the benefit of having been responsible for additional criminal convictions.

On the other hand, the defense of entrapment is not justifiable where parties would ordinarily commit criminal acts. In such a case, it is desirable to deter the parties. Therefore, it may be useful to employ certain law enforcement activity, including deception and subterfuge, to raise adequately the probability of their apprehension.

c. *Duress*. — A party will not be held liable for a harmful act if he committed the act only because of a threat of death or serious injury. To invoke the defense of duress, the threat must have been both imminent and credible, and the party must not have killed another person (although the sanction may still be mitigated in that case). Whether or not the defense is available, the threatening party will be liable for the act he induced.[100]

The defense of duress is obviously desirable if the threatened party truly cannot be deterred from committing the act.[101] Hence, the law's insistence on the imminence and credibility of the threat, and on its being one of serious injury or death seems understandable. But its refusal to allow the defense where the threatened party has killed someone does not seem rational according to deterrence theory, since it is quite possible that the threatened party could not have been deterred from killing; after all, he will often be comparing an immediate threat to a sanction that will not be immediate, if it is imposed at all. In any case, it is desirable that a party who makes a threat be held liable for crimes committed as a result of that threat, for this will be necessary to deter parties from using threats as a device to circumvent the law.

d. *Necessity*. — The defense of necessity may be asserted when a party, forced by circumstances to choose between two harmful acts, chooses the less harmful act.[102] This makes clear sense according to deterrence theory, since it is socially desirable for a party to minimize harm.

e. *Defense of Self, of Another, or of Property*. — The law regarding self-defense and protection of others and of property is, roughly, that one may use the amount of force apparently necessary to ward off an aggressor whose threat one believes is unlawful and immediate, and who cannot be stopped by police intervention.[103] Plainly, allowing the use of force will enhance deterrence of aggression. Limiting the justified

99. For example, the game warden might not be able to take the hunter into custody before he shoots an eagle.

100. See W. LaFave & A. Scott, supra note 57, § 49.

101. This is pointed out by Bentham, supra note 2, at 165.

102. See W. LaFave & A. Scott, supra note 57, § 50.

103. See id. §§ 53–55.

use of force makes sense under the presumption that the courts are better able than threatened parties to decide on sanctions.

f. *Consent.* — A party may sometimes escape criminal liability if the person affected by his act had consented to its commission. The defense of consent, however, is not available where serious bodily injury is done.[104] The justification for the defense, under deterrence theory, centers on the concept of harm: if consent is taken to mean that there is no harm, then there is no reason to deter acts to which someone has consented.[105] According to this reasoning, of course, a person's consent even to serious bodily injury apparently ought to be allowed as a defense. Yet consideration must be given to the counterarguments that the person's family and friends (or society at large) may feel that harm has been done, and also to the possibility that the injuring party could deceive the courts about the person's consent.

g. *Condonation and Settlement.* — The fact that a person who has suffered harm may later condone or settle with the responsible party[106] may not be used as a defense against criminal liability.[107] If a person is robbed, for example, and he then discovers the robber and forgives him, the robber will still be liable. According to deterrence theory, the major reason for not allowing condonation as a defense is that deterrence would be diluted. Were the defense allowed, the "sanctions" imposed by victims—usually some form of apology, the return of property, or a payment, but never imprisonment—would be less than the sanctions the courts would otherwise impose.[108] Moreover, victims might many times wish to condone injuring parties, for there is no reason to believe that a victim's personal interest in punishing an injuring party would correspond to the social interest in deterrence. Finally, were the defense allowed, there might be a real danger that victims would be coerced into "condoning" injuring parties.

6. *Strict Liability.* — As has been emphasized throughout this discussion of criminal law, much more than the mere doing of harm is ordinarily required before punishment is imposed. In other words, strict liability is an unusual form of liability.[109] It is also true that according to the theory of deterrence, strict liability cannot usually be justified, since under strict liability, socially desirable acts are punished if they happen to result in harm.[110] For strict liability to be justified,

104. See id. § 57.

105. See Bentham, supra note 2, at 163.

106. Condonation is distinct from giving the party prior consent.

107. See W. LaFave & A. Scott, supra note 57, § 57.

108. It should be observed that in tort law—where of course settlement is allowed—payments made in settlement would often approximate the expected court-determined monetary sanctions, since otherwise victims might well prefer not to settle.

109. However, liquor and narcotics laws, and pure food laws, often impose liability without fault. See W. LaFave & A. Scott, supra note 57, § 31.

110. This is undesirable of course both because it might result in deterrence of desirable acts and because the use of sanctions is socially costly. Suppose, for instance,

two conditions must hold. First, the courts must find it difficult or impossible to distinguish between desirable and undesirable acts. This means the courts must in effect opt between strict liability or no liability at all. Second, if there is no liability, the resulting level of undesirable acts must be unacceptably high.[111] Whether strict liability is actually used only where these two conditions are approximately met is not clear.[112] But the basic fact that strict liability is not the common form of liability makes sense.

Conclusion

I do not think that any real comment is required concerning the theoretical analysis of optimal deterrence in this Article.[113] However, my discussion of the many ways in which the criminal law furthers the purposes of deterrence may have created a false impression about the nature of my beliefs in optimal deterrence as the basis for a descriptive theory of the criminal law. I realize that examples of inconsistency of the criminal law with optimal deterrence are not difficult to adduce (as I occasionally noted), that there are differences in the criminal law among countries that cannot be conveniently attributed to differences relevant to deterrence,[114] that incapacitation and other goals omitted from the analysis help to explain many features of the criminal law,[115] and that juries and the judiciary hardly think exclusively in terms of deterrence. Nevertheless, it certainly does appear that deterrence plays an important part in explaining the criminal law.

---

that druggists are strictly criminally liable for narcotics sales to unauthorized individuals. Then a druggist might decide against selling narcotics even though it might be socially desirable that he perform that service. And if the druggist does sell narcotics, he might be sanctioned even if through no fault of his own, he makes a sale to an unauthorized person, such as an individual whom he could not have determined was only posing as a physician.

111. It is interesting to note that these two conditions are needed because sanctions are assumed to be nonmonetary and socially costly. The conditions are not required to justify strict liability where sanctions are monetary and socially costless. Indeed, where that is the case, parties are in theory induced to act desirably under strict liability; thus since the use of sanctions is costless, there is no special reason to avoid adopting strict liability. See, e.g., Shavell, Strict Liability Versus Negligence, 9 J. Legal Stud. 1 (1980).

112. At least the first condition may be roughly met. That the courts find it difficult to obtain information about a party's conduct is often stated to be a reason for use of strict liability. See W. LaFave & A. Scott, supra note 57, § 31, at 218.

113. See sections II.A. and III.A.

114. For instance, the United States appears to be the only country that allows the defense of entrapment. See G. Fletcher, supra note 57, § 7.3 , at 541.

115. To give only one illustration, the fact that attempts are punished could be explained in part by saying that the commission of an attempt constitutes evidence that the party is of a type who needs to be incapacitated. And the fact that attempts are punished less than acts resulting in harm could be explained by saying that the evidence of the need for incapacitation is less where harm is not done, or that the retributive motive does not come much into play unless harm is done.

Appendix

1. A simple formal version of the model of deterrence discussed in the text is described here, and the arguments of section III.A. on the optimal use of nonmonetary sanctions are sketched.[116]

2. According to the model, parties choose whether to commit harmful acts from which they would derive private benefits. Let b be the private benefit a party would derive from committing a harmful act, where $0 \leqq b \leqq \bar{b}$,[117] and let $h \geqq 0$ be the harm that the act would cause; thus, a party is identified by the pair (b,h). If a party commits an act, he will be apprehended with probability p and suffer a sanction s, where $0 \leqq s \leqq \bar{s}$;[118] s will be determined by a sanctioning function, that is, a function of the variables that the courts can observe (as discussed below). The utility of a party who commits an act will be b if he is not sanctioned and $b - s$ if he is; if he does not commit an act, his utility will be 0. Therefore, he will commit an act if $b > ps$. Otherwise he will be deterred.[119] Because s is bounded by $\bar{s}$, it will be impossible to deter a party if $b > p\bar{s}$.

3. Social welfare is comprised of the following elements for each party who commits a harmful act: the social value of the private benefits, namely βb, where $\beta \geqq 0$; the harm h; and the expected social cost of imposing sanctions, σps, where $\sigma > 0$. Social welfare then equals $\beta b - h - \sigma ps$ integrated over all individuals who commit acts, less the expense $c(p) > 0$ of maintaining the probability at p, where $c'(p) > 0$. The social problem is to choose a sanctioning function and p to maximize social welfare.

4. The first-best behavior of parties—that which would maximize social welfare if the parties' behavior could be commanded—is for parties to commit acts if and only if $\beta b > h$.

5. Suppose that the courts have perfect information about b and h. In this case the sanctioning function can depend directly on b and h, and the optimal sanctioning function is easy to describe: (i) $s = 0$ if $\beta b > h$, as then parties will commit desirable acts, and imposing sanctions would lower social welfare; (ii) $s = 0$ if $\beta b \leqq h$ but $p\bar{s} < b$, for where parties cannot be deterred from committing undesirable acts, imposing sanctions would lower social welfare but not affect behavior; and (iii) $s \geqq b/p$ if $\beta b \leqq h$ and $p\bar{s} \geqq b$, for where parties can be deterred from

116. The arguments are made in detail in Shavell, The Optimal Use of Nonmonetary Sanctions as a Deterrent (Sept. 1985) (unpublished manuscript) (on file at the offices of the Columbia Law Review).

117. The benefits and other components of a party's utility are assumed to be bounded because, as is well known, this follows from the axioms of expected utility theory. See supra note 37.

118. The probability of apprehension p is the same for all parties.

119. For simplicity, I adopt the convention that when the party is indifferent, he will be deterred, and I will adopt similar conventions below.

committing undesirable acts, this will be optimal to do since it will prevent harm, yet not involve the socially costly imposition of sanctions.

It is apparent from this description that sanctions are never actually imposed, and that the minimum sanction necessary to deter in case (iii) (namely b/p) depends on b but not on h.

The optimal probability of imposition of sanctions is found by maximizing social welfare, taking into account the optimal sanctioning system; and the first-order condition determining p equates $c'(p)$ with the losses due to the commission of harmful acts by parties who are just at the margin of deterrability.[120]

6. Suppose now that although the courts can observe h, they have only imperfect information about b: rather than observing b, they observe $r = r(b, \theta)$, where θ is a random element and where in general there are a variety of b and θ such that $r = r(b, \theta)$. The optimal sanction given r and h is determined by maximizing

(1) $\int(\beta b - h - \sigma ps)f(b|\, r, h)db,$

where f is the probability density of b conditional on r and h, and where the integration is performed over the set of parties of type (b,h) for whom $r = r(b, \theta)$ and who commit the act, that is, for whom $b > ps(r,h)$. The optimal s might be zero if the conditional distribution of βb is much higher than h (that is, if usually the act is desirable) or if the distribution of b is so high that parties are usually undeterrable. If the optimal s is positive and interior to $[0,\bar{s}]$, then it is determined by the first-order condition

(2) $\sigma p\text{Prob}[b \geqq ps|r,h] = (h + \sigma ps - \beta ps)f(ps|r,h).$

The left-hand side is the marginal cost of increasing s—the expected marginal social cost σp of increasing the sanction per party who commits a harmful act times its conditional likelihood—and the right-hand side is the marginal benefit of increasing s—the expected social savings per party just deterred, namely, $(h + \sigma ps - \beta ps)$, times the density of these individuals.

Notice that in contrast to the situation where the courts had perfect information, sanctions are here sometimes imposed at the optimal s (as reflected by the left-hand side of (2)), that the optimal s depends implicitly on the distribution of b conditional on r, and that the optimal s depends on h and increases with it, other things being equal. To see the latter, observe that equation (2) is of the form $g(s,h) = 0$. Implicitly differentiating this with respect to h and solving for $s'(h)$, we obtain $s'(h) = -g_h(s, h)/ g_s(s,h)$. Now $g_s(s,h) < 0$ (the second-order condition for optimality of s), and assuming that the conditional density f does not change with h (to isolate the effect on s of a change in h), we have $g_h(s,h) = f(ps|r,h) > 0$, so that $s'(h) > 0$; the optimal sanction rises with the level of harm.

120. See Shavell, supra note 116, equation (7).

The optimal probability is determined in a way similar to that in the previous case.

7. Of course, a more general version of the model would incorporate the various possibilities mentioned in the text: an act would cause a probability distribution of harm instead of a single level of harm; the courts might not be able to observe this distribution even though they could observe the harm that actually occurs; private benefits might depend on the occurrence of harm; parties might choose among a variety of acts; and so forth.

[14]

11

ON THE ECONOMIC THEORY OF CRIME

ALVIN K. KLEVORICK

1. Introduction

At the end of his interesting and important article, "Crime and Punishment: An Economic Approach," published in 1968, Gary Becker characterized his efforts at developing an "economic" framework for analyzing illegal behavior "as a resurrection, modernization, and thereby I hope improvement" on the pioneering efforts of Cesare Beccaria and Jeremy Bentham during the eighteenth and nineteenth centuries.[1] Becker hoped, at least implicitly, to give new life and direction to cost-benefit analysis of public policy toward crime. In this effort he surely succeeded, as the fifteen years since his seminal article ap-

This chapter is a revised version of a paper prepared for presentation at the January 1983 meeting of the American Society for Political and Legal Philosophy in Cincinnati. I would like to thank Bruce Ackerman, Guido Calabresi, Owen Fiss, Joseph Goldstein, Geoffrey Hazard, Reinier Kraakman, Rick Levin, George Loewenstein, Jerry Mashaw, A. Mitchell Polinsky, Rob Prichard, Peter Schuck, Stan Wheeler, Kenneth Wolpin, and the Legal Studies Seminar at the University of Pennsylvania Law School for helpful discussions and for their comments on an earlier draft of this chapter. I am also grateful for the helpful research assistance of Jon Pedersen. In revising the paper, I benefited greatly from the discussion at the meeting and especially from the extremely thoughtful comments of the commentators Jules Coleman and Stephen Schulhofer. These people, of course, bear no responsibility for any faults that remain.

peared have seen the development of a substantial literature on the economics of crime and punishment.

Nevertheless, there is a perception, among people in law and economics, that except for the highly controversial empirical work on the deterrent effect of the death penalty, the economists' literature on crime has not entered the mainstream of legal scholarship.[2] This work seems to have remained a literature that is principally of interest to economists rather than to legal scholars, lawyers, and criminologists. In this respect, work on the economics of crime stands in contrast to, for example, the work economists have done on tort law, which has genuinely engaged the interest of torts scholars and teachers.[3]

In this chapter, I wish to suggest that the economists' literature on crime manifests an incompleteness and also a lack of connection among its various strands. Both of these features of the body of work identified as "the economic theory of crime" have restricted the impact that economists' contributions have had in this area. Moreover, these problems reflect an inherent limitation of any economic theory of crime: any such theory must depend on, and simultaneously be confined by, a set of political and legal presuppositions. Furthermore, I believe that an understanding of this intrinsic constraint on the economists' approach to crime will make possible a better appreciation of the kinds of contributions and the scope of the contributions economists can make in this area. Strengths sometimes appear more clearly when inherent limitations are recognized.

2. The Structure of the Literature

I shall frame the discussion in a general description of the work that has been done on the economic theory of crime.[4] My intent is to describe the contours of the landscape or the topography of this vast literature rather than to provide a thorough survey or critical review of it. This literature is comprised of three distinguishable strands. I shall discuss each of these strands in turn and draw out the relations among them as I proceed.

A. *The Individual's Decision About Criminal Activity*

The first branch of this literature applies the microeconomic theory of choice under uncertainty to the decision process of the individual criminal. For the most part, this set of papers views the potential criminal as a rational actor who balances the costs and benefits, uncertain as they are, of his possible actions and allocates his time to legal and illegal activities accordingly.[5] These models analyze the choice of whether or not to commit a criminal act with its potential gain and its potential cost in the form of punishment, where the probability of winning or losing the gamble is determined by law-enforcement agencies' success in catching, convicting, and punishing criminal actors. The literature also models the potential criminal's "labor allocation" between legitimate and illegitimate activities. The kinds of results that emerge take the standard form of the economist's comparative static conclusions about how changes in one or more parameters—for example, the probability and severity of punishment—affect the actor's choice. The perspective emphasized by the models is that the potential criminal responds, as others do, in a rational way to the incentives provided by the environment in which he operates.

In some analytical studies of individual criminal behavior the authors are attentive to the (perhaps) problematic nature of the assumptions about rationality and information concerning the risks presented by the criminal justice system. For example, Philip Cook suggests bringing to bear the literature on bounded rationality[6] and rules of thumb or "standing decisions" in analyses of criminal behavior. Cook also treats in greater detail how the threats that the criminal justice system poses for the criminal are communicated to the actor through the media, the visible presence of enforcers (for example, police), and personal experience and observation.[7] Other analyses of the criminal's choice process[8] emphasize the importance of nonpecuniary aspects of the criminal's decision. They show, for example, the problems with postulating that monetary equivalents of some forms of punishment exist and the assumptions that one must make in deriving such equivalents. They also note that because illegal activity is time-consuming, the criminal's decision must take into account effects on things other than wealth. These considerations lead these authors to focus on labor allocation models that take account of both pecuniary and nonpecuniary characteristics of the potential outcomes that the criminal faces. Finally, some students of individual participation in criminal activity are attentive to the organizational or market environment within which individual decisions are made. Particular examples include Susan Rose-Ackerman's work on corruption[9] and Peter Reuter's work on organized crime.[10]

B. Criminal Justice Policy

While some of the literature on the economic theory of crime focuses on cost-benefit calculations of individuals—the potential criminals—a second strand is concerned with cost-benefit analysis at the social level. Research on the latter, with Becker's 1968 article being the first formal treatment and still the most prominent example, views "optimal policies to combat illegal behavior [as] part of an optimal allocation of resources."[11] Here the tools of economic analysis are applied to derive results about the socially optimal ways to enforce the criminal law. The principal focus of such policy analysis has been on the choice of the optimal probability of punishment and the optimal type and severity of punishment.[12] It is assumed, in these models, that the type and severity of punishment can be set directly while the probability of punishment is determined indirectly by society's expenditures on police, courts, and other law enforcement resources.[13]

Of course, characterization of an optimal set of policies presupposes a function to be optimized. In his 1968 article, Becker introduced as the minimand a general social loss function whose arguments were the damages from offenses, the costs of apprehending and convicting offenders, and the social cost of punishments. For the most part, however, his analysis proceeded with a less general formulation of society's objective function. Specifically, Becker took the social goal to be minimization of the total social loss in real income from offenses, convictions, and punishments. At some points in the analysis, though, he did introduce generalizations—for example, an additional term in the loss function to recognize the social loss due to "*ex post* 'price discrimination' between offenses that are not and those that are cleared by punishment."[14] That is, he recognized explicitly that society may incur an additional loss if two individuals who commit the same crime are, in the end, treated differently, with one being punished while the other is not.

Other writers have generalized the social loss function in a variety of ways. John Harris[15] introduced a term for the social loss from wrongful punishment. Then in their 1977 contribution, Roy Carr-Hill and Nicholas Stern[16] suggested incorporating retributive considerations—specifically, departures from the "retributionist target" punishment—in the term measuring the net social cost of punishment in Becker's social loss function. But in his 1978 paper, "On the Economic Theory of Policy Towards Crime," Stern withdrew the suggestion. He continued to argue for the importance of retribution as a determinant of punishment levels but indicated that it would not be "particularly helpful" to "amalgamate different criteria on modes of conduct into a grand social loss function."[17] Mitchell Polinsky and Steven Shavell in specifying the social loss function in their 1979 article took explicit account of the attitudes toward risk of those who engaged in activities for which they might be apprehended and fined.[18] Finally, Isaac Ehrlich[19] examined the implications of introducing three alternative elements into Becker's social loss function. They were terms representing equality under the law, avoidance of legal error, and retribution. These features correspond to suggestions that others had previously made—including Becker himself, Harris, and Carr-Hill and Stern—but Ehrlich's analysis of the consequences of introducing them is more thorough and complete.

All of these variants of the social loss function share one striking feature. The term representing the net cost or damage to society is, in each case, taken to be the difference between the harm to society *and* the social value of the gain to offenders. That is, the utility of the offender is counted in the social welfare function. Indeed, in two of the more elegant and sophisticated analyses in this literature, by Polinsky and Shavell,[20] the social welfare function to be maximized is the sum of the expected utilities of the individual members of the society. This seems plausible in their 1979 article where the analysis focuses on fines—both civil and criminal—and the heuristic example is double parking. The aggregation seems more questionable in their latest contribution, "The Optimal Use of Fines and Imprisonment," where the harms involved are obviously severe enough for imprisonment to be contemplated as a punishment.

To be sure, this apparent anomaly in the social loss function has been noted before. George Stigler, in a paper stimulated by Becker's "Crime and Punishment: An Economic Approach," and following closely in time upon the publication of that work, made the same observation. He wrote that:

> Becker introduces . . . the "social value of the gain to offenders" from the offense. The determination of this social value is not explained, and one is entitled to doubt its usefulness as an explanatory concept: what evidence is there that society sets a positive value upon the utility derived from a murder, rape, or arson? In fact the society has branded the utility derived from such activities as illicit.[21]

The subsequent literature has never taken serious account of this point. It is an issue to which I shall return below, though I will not resolve the question of exactly whose gains and losses or whose preferences should be counted in the social welfare function that is optimized.

The nexus between the first two strands of the economic analysis of crime is a close one. The models of individual behavior yield predictions about the supply of offenses by individuals. These individual supply functions are aggregated to derive a market supply function—also known as a deterrence function—that relates the total number of offenses to the probability and severity of punishment. This deterrence function is at the heart of the policy model that is used to obtain conclusions about optimal strategies to combat illegal behavior.

Moreover, Becker's model and the theoretical work that followed it have emphasized the two-way interaction between criminal activity and the policies adopted by law enforcement authorities. The latter affect the number of offenses at the same time as the level and effects of criminal activity affect the choice of values for the policy instruments—the probability and severity of punishment. In technical terms, criminal activity and criminal justice system activity are simultaneously determined. This has clear implications for empirical efforts to estimate the deterrence function, that is, the responsiveness of offenses to policy variables. Because of the interdependence between crime and punishment, simultaneous-equations estimating techniques ought to be used if one hopes to unravel the deterrence effects.

C. The Existence of the Criminal Category

The close ties and mutual enrichment that exist between the work on economic theories of individual criminal behavior and the research on economic theories of the criminal justice system stand in sharp contrast to the lack of communication between the social cost-benefit analysis and the third strand in the economics literature on crime. This last enterprise, to which little effort has been devoted, draws upon economic analysis to explain the existence of the criminal category. It maintains that economic analysis can help to explain why we distinguish a set of acts that we call crimes—why we have the criminal law at all. The two principal (perhaps only) contributions to this part of the literature on the economic theory of crime are by Guido Calabresi and Douglas Melamed in "Property Rules, Liability Rules, and Inalienability: One View of the Cathedral"[22] and by Richard Posner in *Economic Analysis of Law.*[23]

Calabresi and Melamed use the framework developed in their article to consider the use of criminal sanctions in cases of theft and violations of bodily integrity. They do not believe that problems of detection and apprehension, which render the probability of apprehension less than one, explain fully why we "charge"[24] people who commit these acts more than the value of what they take. They argue instead that even if every such offender were caught, "the penalty we would wish to impose would be greater than the objective damages."[25] The explanation, Calabresi and Melamed suggest, "lies in a consideration of the difference between property entitlements and liability entitlements. For us to charge the thief with a penalty equal to an objectively determined value of the property stolen would be to convert all property rule entitlements into liability rule entitlements."[26] But they demonstrated earlier in their paper that economic efficiency considerations, distributional goals, and "other justice reasons" would lead a collectivity not to employ only liability rules to protect entitlements. Instead, as Calabresi and Melamed persuasively argue, the state will employ a mixture of property rules, liability rules, and inalienability rules.[27] Consequently, from the perspective of their analysis,

> The thief not only harms the victim, he undermines rules and distinctions of significance beyond the specific case. . . . Since in the majority of cases we cannot be sure of the economic efficiency of the transfer by theft, we must add to each case an undefinable kicker which represents society's need to keep all property rules from being changed at will into liability rules.[28]

Of course, the need for the "undefinable kicker" applies as well to each violation of bodily integrity.

The basic distinction that Calabresi and Melamed draw between the criminal who robs or violates another person's bodily integrity *and* the injurer in an automobile accident or a polluter in a nuisance case is that the criminal resorts to nonmarket transactions when the costs of market transactions are low, while the driver and the polluter find themselves engaged in nonmarket rather than market transactions when the latter are too costly. Posner's analysis is similar except for the singularly important fact that, within his scheme, the sole reason for preferring one form of transaction to another—in Calabresi-Melamed terms, one mode of entitlement protection to another—is economic efficiency, as Posner defines it. For Posner, the only desideratum in social policy is value maximization: the distributional goals that form an integral part of the Calabresi-Melamed framework, and the "other justice" reasons they discuss, receive no weight in his analysis.

For Posner, "A 'crime' is simply an act that subjects the perpetrator to a distinctive form of punishment that is meted out in a distinctive kind of proceeding," where the unlawfulness of the act derives from "the policy of some other body of law—the tort law, in the case of 'the common law crimes' . . . and various laws regulating business and personal behavior, in the case of . . . statutory crimes."[29] Under this approach, "the criminal sanction is simply a method of pricing conduct"[30] and "The function of the criminal law—is to impose additional costs on unlawful conduct where the conventional damages remedy alone would be insufficient to limit that conduct to the efficient level."[31]

Posner, like Calabresi and Melamed, shows how a probability of punishment that is less than one should lead to a punishment that exceeds the damages caused by the criminal. But he also makes the stronger point that although a sanction in which the expected punishment cost is equal to the damage to the victim is "adequate where the crime in question is simply the violation of a regulatory statute,"[32] a heavier penalty is required in other situations. Specifically, "if the law's purpose in prohibiting the act in question was to channel activity into the market, i.e. the arena of voluntary transacting,"[33] then an expected punishment in excess of the damage inflicted is needed to induce the perpetrator to substitute a voluntary transaction for a coercive one. When market alternatives are available, the expected punishment for a violation would be set equal to "the sum of (1) the social costs of the violation and (2) the additional costs to the legal system of substituting coercive transactions for market transactions."[34]

Although Posner is not explicit on this point, it is consistent with his argument that the "additional costs" under item 2 would include the Calabresi-Melamed "kicker." Of course, where there is no market alternative—Posner offers the example of "a driver who violates the speed limit because the opportunity costs of his time are very high"[35]—the penalty should be large enough to reflect the hazards the criminal creates, subsumed in his item 1, but there would be no add-on designed to induce substitution of a market for a legal transaction.

3. Implications of Economic Explanations of the Criminal Category for the Economic Theory of Criminal Justice Policy

This third, relatively undeveloped, strand of work on the economic theory of crime has several important implications for research on the economic theory of policy toward crime. First, it suggests that economists' theoretical work on cost-benefit analysis of public policy toward criminal activity is best viewed as a partial equilibrium approach. The insights offered by economic theories of the criminal justice system are conditional, for those theories take as given the set of acts or activities that are designated as crimes. The results in what I have labelled the second strand of the literature on the economic theory of crime tell us how to allocate resources to apprehension and conviction, on the one hand, and to punishment, on the other, *once* the crimes have been identified. A full, unconditional theory of the criminal justice system—a general equilibrium approach, if you will—would take a more global perspective. It might have Posner's wealth measure, or an appropriate amalgam of the Calabresi-Melamed desiderata, or yet another measure as the criterion to be optimized. The full "solution" would then yield the set of actions that are optimally to be designated as crimes *as well as* the optimal probability and severity of punishment for each crime.

For example, suppose one accepted Becker's measure of the total social loss in real income as the relevant quantity of concern (and the economic theory of the criminal category speaks to this issue as well). Then one can imagine solving the problem that Becker posed for each of the possible configurations of the criminal/noncriminal division of activities. What I have referred to as the full or general equilibrium solution would then be the categorization of activities and the associated set of probability of punishment/severity of punishment values that yielded the minimum minimorum of the Beckerian social loss function.

Of course, to observe that Becker and those who followed him in developing economic models of policy toward crime delimited the scope of the problem they analyzed is not to diminish their contribution. Nor is it to say that they claimed more for their analyses than they ought to have. In particular, Becker himself was quite clear about the confines of his model. But the partial character of these models does suggest difficulties for one who would seek to develop a complete economic theory of crime. Suppose that the objective function of the broader problem, in which one determines the optimal partition of acts into criminal and noncriminal categories as well as the optimal severity and probability of punishment for each of the criminal acts, is not confined to economic values—as, for instance, Posner would seemingly restrict it, but Calabresi and Melamed would not. Then the explanation of, or the derivation of results about, the criminal justice system could not be fully economic in character.

A second important point of contact between the Calabresi-Melamed and Posner contributions, which explain the use of the criminal sanction, and the resource allocation problem that Becker and others have addressed, concerns the function that relates the net cost or damage to society to the number of offenses. This function, which is central to the overall objective function in Becker's and others' analyses of public policy toward crime, is intended to measure the damage or net cost that society sustains as the result of the offenses that occur. But it is difficult to see how one can assess the social damages from offenses unless one has a theory of the criminal category. The thrust of the Calabresi-Melamed and Posner analyses is that an act is classified as criminal precisely because the harm it does to society exceeds the conventional measure of damages. To specify the social loss function in a Beckerian analysis, one must assess the costs of these additional harms and be sure that they are appropriately reckoned in the analysis.

In particular, the socially disapproved nature of the criminal's act, as Calabresi-Melamed and Posner explain its disfavored status, raises serious questions about the appropriateness of subtracting the criminal's gain from the harm that his act does to the rest of society. A theory or an explanation of why certain acts are labelled criminal that provides reasons for objecting to the particular action may also provide reasons for discounting the criminal's gain. Alternatively, since Becker was careful, though others have not been, to say that what ought to be subtracted is the "social value of the gain to offenders," the explanation of the criminal category provides a means to—indeed the explanation is required to—assess that "social value."

Once again, I do not wish to suggest that Becker was not clear about the scope of his analysis; on the contrary, he was precise in drawing the lines around what he did. As he wrote,

> Reasonable men will often differ on the amount of damages or benefits caused by different activities. . . . These differences are basic to the development and implementation of public policy but have been excluded from my inquiry. I assume consensus on damages and benefits and simply try to work out rules for an optimal implementation of this consensus.[36]

His analysis is fine, then, as far as it goes.

The difficulty, however, is that by setting aside issues of how social losses are assessed and by not having a theory of the criminal category to inform that reckoning, Becker's analysis is subject to characterizations that make it unattractive and seemingly unhelpful to legal scholars concerned with criminal law. And the characterization is one that Becker himself uses, not one that is provided as a caricature by a critic. Specifically, he writes, "criminal activities are an important subset of the class of activities that cause diseconomies, with the level of criminal activities measured by the number of offenses."[37] In further characterizing his analysis, he says

> Our analysis of crime is a generalization of the economist's analysis of external harm or diseconomies. Analytically, the generalization consists in introducing costs of apprehension and conviction, which make the probability of apprehension and conviction an important decision variable, and in treating punishment by imprisonment and other methods as well as by monetary payments. A crime is apparently not so different analytically from any other activity that produces external harm and when crimes are punishable by fines, the analytical differences virtually vanish.[38]

The criminal's actions surely have "external effects." But it is difficult to see a student of criminal law vigorously pursuing an approach to crime and punishment that self-consciously characterizes itself as a branch of the theory of external diseconomies, albeit one that extends that theory by introducing costs of apprehension and conviction and by taking account of nonmonetary penalties. Legal scholars will find such an approach even less inviting if they recall the fundamental contribution of Ronald Coase in clarifying the *reciprocal* nature of externalities and his criticism of the view that one party *causes* the harm in an externality situation.[39]

The absence of explicit concern for the origin of the criminal category affects other analyses of public policy toward crime as well. For example, in Polinsky and Shavell's 1982 article, implications for the use of fines and imprisonment are drawn from a truly classical model of external diseconomies. The basic activity that "causes" external harm is socially beneficial and the social welfare function, which is at the heart of the analysis, is the sum of the expected utilities of all the members of the community.[40] The results that Polinsky and Shavell derive are interesting and important for policy settings where both monetary and nonmonetary penalties can be used to control an activity that yields social benefits but also results in harm to others. One can think of many such examples—analyses of public policy toward automobile accidents or pollution are two instances—but the economic literature on the existence of the criminal category suggests that policy about criminal activity is not among them.

4. The Inherent Limitation of Any Economic Theory of Crime

The efforts to use economic analysis to explain why some acts are distinguished as crimes have yet another and more fundamental implication about the kinds of insights economists, or the use of economic analysis, can provide about criminal law. The implication might be viewed by some as negative because it points to an inherent limitation of the economist's approach. But it seems, to me at least, that recognizing this boundary is not in any way depreciatory. Rather, it is to recognize that although economics *can* indeed contribute to our understanding of criminal behavior and optimal enforcement policy, it cannot provide a full or complete economic theory of crime. The work of economists in this area must be informed by work in other disciplines.

What, then, is this implication? It is that although an explanation of the criminal category can be *stated* in economic terms, that vocabulary and mode of analysis does not, in fact, provide the substantive understanding we seek. To see this, it is helpful to frame more generally the answers offered by Calabresi and Melamed and by Posner.

Society (or the collectivity or the state) establishes a "transaction structure" that stipulates the terms on which particular transactions or exchanges are to take place under different circumstances. For example, society might determine that if you and I are walking down the street, having no contact with one another, and you desire my watch, then you are permitted to have it if, but only if, we agree to a voluntary exchange of my watch for something you have (or promise to deliver, etc.). Society might also say that if the circumstances are different—for example, as you pedal your motorized bicycle down the sidewalk you knock me over and my watch is destroyed—you are permitted to "have" my watch but you must pay a collectively set value for it. In Calabresi-Melamed terminology, the first situation corresponds to protecting my entitlement to my watch by a property rule, while in the second setting it is protected only by a liability rule. In Posner's terms, the former exchange, if consummated, would be a market transaction while the latter would be a nonmarket transaction.

As to some possible exchanges, society might impose an absolute bar. In many societies (it is at least stated that) you cannot buy my vote in the sense that you cannot pay me a certain amount of money in exchange for the capacity to cast my ballot in my place. In many societies, an individual cannot sell himself into bondage. This last form of regulating transactions corresponds to what Calabresi and Melamed refer to as protecting my entitlement to my vote and my freedom from bondage with an inalienability rule.

The reason I introduce yet another layer of economics vocabulary, with the term "transaction structure," is to help us to move beyond the Calabresi-Melamed and Posner characterizations of crime. For Calabresi and Melamed, the imposition of the criminal sanction and the characterization of particular acts as crimes derives from a need to keep property rules and inalienability rules from being "changed at will" into liability rules; for Posner, it derives from a desire to induce individuals to substitute voluntary transactions with one another for coercive ones when the former are possible at low enough cost.

Note, however, that a society that imposes the criminal sanction on individuals who engage in the selling and buying of votes makes it a crime to change an inalienability rule into a property rule or in Posner's terms, to substitute a market for a nonmarket transaction. One can also imagine a society in which it is determined that all decisions about pollution should be made in a collective setting, that is, in which all entitlements to be free from pollution are protected by liability rules. Such a society might well apply the criminal sanction to parties who engage in a market transaction in which the polluter "buys off" the pollutees. Similarly, a criminal sanction might be applied to an employer who hires workers at a (mutually agreeable) wage below the legislatively mandated minimum or to a seller who sells goods (to willing consumers) for more than or less than a legislatively set price. A society that would make each of these last two actions a crime would do so because a liability-rule protection had been converted into a property-rule protection.

In each instance, the act that is characterized as a crime involves the actor(s) forcing society to deal with a transaction in a way in which society did not want to treat it. What makes the act a crime is that the individual assaults the transaction structure that has been established by society.[41] One could say, alternatively, that the individual coerces *society* into considering and coping with an exchange or transaction in a way that differs from the mode society had chosen. Finally, one might characterize the criminal as arrogating to himself the power or the authority to determine at least a part of the societal transaction structure, that is, appropriating to himself a power or right that society had reserved to itself. The criminal sanction is then a sanction to enforce the transaction structure that society has chosen as well as to compensate for the harms to individuals within the society.[42]

But, then, an explanation of the criminal category—even an explanation stated in economic terms—requires answers to questions and elaboration of concepts that economic analysis is not particularly well-suited to provide.[43] The point is not that the language describing the grounds for invoking the criminal sanction—for calling an act a crime—is not drawn from economics. One can, after all, describe the reasons in terms that are much less evocative and less clearly located in another discipline than are the terms "assault," "coercion," and "arrogation of power." For example, one could simply say that the criminal acts contrary to the transaction structure society has established.[44] But the critical observation is that the explication of why some acts are crimes while other are not requires an inquiry into the legitimation of the transaction structure. It forces one to confront questions like: Why does the collectivity have the right to decide the terms on which particular transactions will take place under different circumstances? Why do some rights reside in the individual while others rest with the state?

To be sure, one can propose a unified, and unitary, economic basis for determining what acts are categorized as crimes and what probability and severity of punishment is associated with each criminal act. If one posits that wealth maximization[45] is the sole criterion by which social arrangements are to be evaluated, the objective function in Becker's partial equilibrium approach to criminal justice policy, which sets only the probabilities of punishment and the penalties, will be consistent with the global problem in which the categorization of acts is determined as well. Indeed, determination of the optimal probability and severity of punishment will be a subordinated part of the larger problem. In the solution to the global problem, it will emerge that inefficient substitutions of nonmarket transactions for market exchanges are subjected to the criminal sanction, and that probabilities and severities of punishment are chosen to minimize the reduction in society's wealth. But even such a theory necessarily invokes certain political presuppositions—to wit, that society has a right to choose a structure that strives to maximize wealth and that individuals do not have the right to resist that choice. Such a theory does not answer the question: Why is the chosen transaction structure legitimate? And an answer to that question is a necessary component of an explanation of why some acts are treated as crimes.

In sum, to give a coherent explanation of the criminal category, as I have couched it in economic terms, one needs at least a political theory of rights. Undertaking a microeconomic analysis of crime requires as a precondition a certain minimum of political and legal structure.

NOTES

1. Gary S. Becker, "Crime and Punishment: An Economic Approach," *J. Pol. Econ.* 76 (1968): 169, 209.
2. See, for example, the survey by Henry Hansmann, "The Current State of Law-and-Economics Scholarship," *J.L.E.* 33 (1983): 217.
3. This is not to say that economists' writings on crime have had no influence on the way criminal law scholars think about their subject. It would have been difficult, after all, for the outpouring of economists' work on the subject to have been ignored. But the insights about crime that lawyers have drawn from the work of economists have been specialized and fragmented. The economic theory of crime has not taken on anything like the salience of the economic approach to torts, which has been accepted as one of the

competing paradigms that torts scholars use in analyzing their subject. In torts, a scholar may reject the economic approach but must reckon with it. This is not the case with the economic theory of crime.

4. In keeping with the focus of this volume on theories of criminal justice, I restrict my discussion to economists' theoretical work on crime. The vast body of empirical work that has been informed by that theory and that has, in turn, influenced theoretical developments lies outside the purview of this chapter. An interesting set of empirical papers on the economics of crime is collected in J.M. Heineke, ed., *Economic Models of Criminal Behavior* (Amsterdam: North-Holland, 1978), and a useful assessment of empirical work on the subject is provided by Philip J. Cook, "Research in Criminal Deterrence: Laying the Groundwork for the Second Decade," in Norval Morris and Michael Tonry, eds., *Crime and Justice: An Annual Review of Research,* vol. 2 (Chicago: The University of Chicago Press, 1980) p. 211.
5. See Becker, "Crime and Punishment," Michael K. Block and John M. Heineke, "A Labor Theoretic Analysis of the Criminal Choice," *Am. Econ. Rev.* 65 (1975): 314; Isaac Ehrlich, "Participation in Illegitimate Activities: A Theoretical and Empirical Investigation," *J. Pol. Econ.* 81 (1973): 68; John M. Heineke, "Economic Models of Criminal Behavior: An Overview," in *Economic Models of Criminal Behavior,* volume 1.
6. See Cook, "Research in Criminal Deterrence," p. 220. For the classic discussion of bounded rationality, see Herbert A. Simon, *Models of Man* (New York: John Wiley, 1957).
7. Philip J. Cook, "A Unified Treatment of Deterrence, Incapacitation, and Rehabilitation: A Simulation Study" (Durham, N.C.: Institute of Policy Sciences and Public Affairs, Duke University, 1979).
8. See Block and Heineke, "Labor Theoretic Analysis of the Criminal Choice;" Michael K. Block and Robert C. Lind, "Crime and Punishment Reconsidered," *J. L. Stud.* 4 (1975): 241; Michael K. Block and Robert C. Lind, "An Economic Analysis of Crimes Punishable by Imprisonment," *J. L. Stud.* 4 (1975): 479; Heineke, "Economic Models of Criminal Behavior."
9. Susan Rose-Ackerman, *Corruption: A Study in Political Economy* (New York: Academic Press, 1978).
10. Peter Reuter, *Disorganized Crime: The Economics of the Visible Hand* (Cambridge: MIT Press, 1983).
11. Becker, "Crime and Punishment," p. 209.
12. A related interesting literature, which can be viewed as an outgrowth of the early social cost-benefit analysis of public policy toward crime, concerns the comparative advantages of private ver-

sus public enforcement of the law. The principal works are Gary S. Becker and George J. Stigler, "Law Enforcement, Malfeasance, and Compensation of Enforcers," *J. L. Stud.* 3 (1974): 1; William M. Landes and Richard A. Posner, "The Private Enforcement of Law," *J. L. Stud.* 4 (1975): 1; and A. Mitchell Polinsky, "Private versus Public Enforcement of Fines," *J. L. Stud.* 9 (1980): 105. Their analyses rely heavily on Becker's seminal article and its progeny, in particular, on the results concerning the optimal probability and optimal severity of punishment. These analyses of the relative efficacy of private and public enforcement apply to legal commands generally and not to criminal law alone.

13. In reality, the type and severity of punishment are also set only indirectly. There may be legislative directives about sentences or fines, for example, but there is usually at least a residual element of judicial discretion in setting punishments.
14. Becker, "Crime and Punishment," p. 184.
15. John R. Harris, "On the Economics of Law and Order," *J. Pol Econ.* 78 (1970): 165.
16. Roy A. Carr-Hill and Nicholas H. Stern, "Theory and Estimation in Models of Crime and Its Social Control and Their Relations to Concepts of Social Output," in Martin S. Feldstein and Robert P. Inman, eds., *The Economics of Public Services* 116 (London: Macmillan, 1977).
17. Nicholas H. Stern, "On the Economic Theory of Policy Towards Crime," in Heineke, ed., *Economic Models of Criminal Behavior* 123, p. 148.
18. A. Mitchell Polinsky and Steven Shavell, "The Optimal Tradeoff Between the Probability and Magnitude of Fines," *Am. Econ. Rev.* 69 (1979): 880.
19. Isaac Ehrlich, "The Optimum Enforcement of Law and the Concept of Justice: A Positive Analysis," *Int. R. L. & Econ.* 2 (1982): 3.
20. Polinsky and Shavell, "The Optimal Tradeoff," and A. Mitchell Polinsky and Steven Shavell, "The Optimal Use of Fines and Imprisonment," *J. Pub. Econ.* (forthcoming).
21. George J. Stigler, "The Optimum Enforcement of Laws," *J. Pol. Econ.* 78 (1970): 526, 527.
22. Guido Calabresi and A. Douglas Melamed, "Property Rules, Liability Rules, and Inalienability: One View of the Cathedral," *Harv. L. Rev.* 88 (1972): 1089, 1124–1127.
23. Richard A. Posner, *Economic Analysis of Law*, 2d ed. (Boston: Little, Brown, 1977), pp. 163–172.
24. The "charge" to which Calabresi and Melamed refer includes whatever monetary and nonmonetary penalties are imposed on the

criminal. There is no assumption that the payment, if it is a fine, is used to make restitution to the victim.

25. Calabresi and Melamed, "Property Rules, Liability Rules, and Inalienability," p. 1125.
26. Ibid.
27. I will discuss the substance of each of these rules in greater detail below.
28. Calabresi and Melamed, "Property Rules, Liability Rules, and Inalienability," p. 1126.
29. Posner, *Economic Analysis of Law,* p. 163.
30. Ibid., p. 172.
31. Ibid., pp. 163–4.
32. Ibid., p. 165.
33. Ibid.
34. Ibid., p. 166.
35. Ibid.
36. Becker, "Crime and Punishment," p. 209.
37. Ibid., p. 173.
38. Ibid., p. 201.
39. In his classic article about externalities, "The Problem of Social Cost," *J. L. & Econ.* 3 (1960): 1, Ronald Coase considers, in particular, "those actions of business firms which have harmful effects on others . . . [as] a factory the smoke from which has harmful effects on those occupying neighbouring properties" (p. 1). He begins the body of his argument as follows:

    THE RECIPROCAL NATURE OF THE PROBLEM

    The traditional approach has tended to obscure the nature of the choice that has to be made. The question is commonly thought of as one in which A inflicts harm on B and what has to be decided is: how should we restrain A? But this is wrong. We are dealing with a problem of a reciprocal nature. To avoid the harm to B would inflict harm on A. The real question that has to be decided is: should A be allowed to harm B or should B be allowed to harm A? The problem is to avoid the more serious harm . . . (p. 2).

40. Polinsky and Shavell, "The Optimal Tradeoff," p. 21. In addition, "it is assumed that each individual is equally likely to be the victim of someone else's harm" (ibid.). This latter assumption, which is made for reasons of analytical tractability, is common in other areas of law and economics, too, for example, the analysis of alternative

liability rules in torts. Whether or not the assumption is plausible in the accident context, it calls for careful scrutiny in a model analyzing law enforcement policy. It is clear that all the results in the Polinsky and Shavell contribution are robust to some relaxation of the assumption as, for example, if different individuals can have different exogenously given probabilities of suffering harm. How the results would be altered if one went further and had the probability of suffering harm depend on whether or not one engaged in the harm-engendering activity is another matter. The conclusions about (1) the optimal punishment—be it a fine or imprisonment—when only one type of punishment is used and when there is only one wealth class and (2) the desirability of using fines to the maximum feasible extent before imposing nonmonetary penalties, do not depend on the exogeneity of the probability of being harmed. But when the likelihood of being harmed is endogenously determined, some of Polinsky and Shavell's statements about underdeterrence and overdeterrence and some of their results for the two-class model may require modification.

41. In the case of theft, the criminal not only challenges the way in which society has chosen to protect an entitlement but also overturns the placement of the entitlement itself.
42. Those harms include the damages due to violation of what Calabresi and Melamed call moralisms. See Calabresi and Melamed, "Property Rules, Liability Rules, and Inalienability," pp. 1111–2. The compensation is "paid" to society. As noted before (see note 24), there is no assumption that monetary payments, if there are any, are used to make restitution to victims.
43. Economists have, for example, never shed much light on the concept of coercion, despite the fact that the term is often invoked. Some speak of the coercion involved in governmental intervention in the market while others speak of the coercion of the market itself.
44. An interesting issue, but one that I do not address here, is whether all crimes can be usefully described as acts that are contrary to the chosen transaction structure. For example, can one, without straining language, describe the act of perjury by saying that the perjuror forces society to deal with a transaction in a way that society did not want to treat it? If all acts that we characterize as criminal cannot be described in this language—or, more generally, using the vocabulary of economics—then it is clear that the scope of an economic theory of crime is necessarily limited. My discussion applies only to those crimes that the economic theory of the criminal category purports to explain.
45. For the purpose of this discussion, I assume *arguendo* that wealth

maximization can be given a clear, substantive, and commonly agreed upon definition. That providing such a definition is not a straightforward task is attested to by the pages of controversy about it in the law-and-economics literature. The point that follows applies if, for example, one takes as the criterion the maximization of the total value of all goods and services the society produces where quantities are valued at the equilibrium prices, or if one substitutes utilitarianism for wealth maximization.

Name Index

www.ingramcontent.com/pod-product-compliance
Lightning Source LLC
LaVergne TN
LVHW102106300926
849161LV00014B/3063